Mahāmudrā and Related Instructions

Core Teachings of the Kagyü Schools

The Library of Tibetan Classics is a special series being developed by the Institute of Tibetan Classics aimed at making key classical Tibetan texts part of the global literary and intellectual heritage. Eventually comprising thirty-two large volumes, the collection will contain over two hundred distinct texts by more than a hundred of the best-known authors. These texts have been selected in consultation with the preeminent lineage holders of all the schools and other senior Tibetan scholars to represent the Tibetan literary tradition as a whole. The works included in the series span more than a millennium and cover the vast expanse of classical Tibetan knowledge—from the core teachings of the specific schools to such diverse fields as ethics, philosophy, linguistics, medicine, astronomy and astrology, folklore, and historiography.

Mahāmudrā and Related Instructions: Core Teachings of the Kagyü Schools
Compiled by Khenchen Thrangu Rinpoche

The Kagyü tradition began in Tibet in the eleventh century and developed into numerous lineages. Their characteristic teachings are the mahāmudrā tradition of stability and insight meditation and the six Dharmas of Nāropa. Khenchen Thrangu Rinpoche, the principal scholar of the Karma Kagyü school, chose the eleven texts for this volume. The selection consists of a twelfth-century compilation of lectures by Gampopa, the founder of the Kagyü monastic tradition; an eleventh-century mahāmudrā text by Lama Shang and a thirteenth-century text on the mahāmudrā and its preliminaries by Shönu Lha, both of the Tsalpa Kagyü; a collection of four thirteenth-century texts, principally by Sherap Jungné, representing the viewpoints of the founder of the Drigung Kagyü; two short fourteenth-century texts on mahāmudrā by the Third Karmapa of the Karma Kagyü; a sixteenth-century overview of the tantric tradition by Tashi Namgyal of the Dakpo Kagyü; a sixteenth-century text on mahāmudrā by Tashi Namgyal's pupil Pema Karpo, who as the Fourth Drukchen was head of the Drukpa Kagyü; a seventeenth-century text on the six Dharmas of Nāropa by Shamar Chökyi Wangchuk of the Karma Kagyü; a seventeenth-century mahāmudrā text by Tselé Natsok Rangdröl of the Karma Kagyü; and an eighteenth-century commentary on one of the Third Karmapa's mahāmudrā texts by Situ Tenpai Nyinjé of the Karma Kagyü.

THE LIBRARY OF TIBETAN CLASSICS ✦ VOLUME 5
Thupten Jinpa, General Editor

Mahāmudrā and Related Instructions

Core Teachings of the Kagyü Schools

Translated by Peter Alan Roberts

Wisdom Publications ✦ Boston
in association with the Institute of Tibetan Classics

Wisdom Publications
199 Elm Street
Somerville MA 02144 USA
www.wisdompubs.org

Library of Congress Cataloging-in-Publication Data
Mahamudra and related instructions : core teachings of the Kagyü schools / translated by Peter Alan Roberts.
p. cm. — (Library of Tibetan classics)
Includes bibliographical references and index.
ISBN 0-86171-444-X (hardcover : alk. paper)
1. Mahamudra (Tantric rite) 2. Bka'-rgyud-pa (Sect)—Rituals. I. Roberts, Peter Alan, 1952–
BQ7699.M34M34 2011
294.3'438—dc22

2011006427

ISBN 978-086171-444-5
eBook ISBN 978-0-86171-929-7
16 15 14 13 12 11
6 5 4 3 2 1

Cover and interior design by Gopa&Ted2, Inc. Set in Adobe Garamond Premier Pro 10.5/13.5.

Wisdom Publications' books are printed on acid-free paper and meet the guidelines for permanence and durability of the Production Guidelines for Book Longevity of the Council on Library Resources.

Printed in the United States of America.

♲ This book was produced with environmental mindfulness. We have elected to print this title on 30% PCW recycled paper. As a result, we have saved the following resources: 41 trees, 13 million BTUs of energy, 3,856 lbs. of greenhouse gases, 18,570 gallons of water, and 1,127 lbs. of solid waste. For more information, please visit our website, www.wisdompubs.org. This paper is also FSC certified. For more information, please visit www.fscus.org.

Message from the Dalai Lama

THE LAST TWO millennia witnessed a tremendous proliferation of cultural and literary development in Tibet, the "Land of Snows." Moreover, due to the inestimable contributions made by Tibet's early spiritual kings, numerous Tibetan translators, and many great Indian paṇḍitas over a period of so many centuries, the teachings of the Buddha and the scholastic tradition of ancient India's Nālandā monastic university became firmly rooted in Tibet. As evidenced from the historical writings, this flowering of Buddhist tradition in the country brought about the fulfillment of the deep spiritual aspirations of countless sentient beings. In particular, it contributed to the inner peace and tranquility of the peoples of Tibet, Outer Mongolia—a country historically suffused with Tibetan Buddhism and its culture—the Tuva and Kalmuk regions in present-day Russia, the outer regions of mainland China, and the entire trans-Himalayan areas on the southern side, including Bhutan, Sikkim, Ladakh, Kinnaur, and Spiti. Today this tradition of Buddhism has the potential to make significant contributions to the welfare of the entire human family. I have no doubt that, when combined with the methods and insights of modern science, the Tibetan Buddhist cultural heritage and knowledge will help foster a more enlightened and compassionate human society, a humanity that is at peace with itself, with fellow sentient beings, and with the natural world at large.

It is for this reason I am delighted that the Institute of Tibetan Classics in Montreal, Canada, is compiling a thirty-two-volume series containing the works of many great Tibetan teachers, philosophers, scholars, and practitioners representing all major Tibetan schools and traditions. These important writings will be critically edited and annotated and will then be published in modern book format in a reference collection called *The Library of Tibetan Classics*, with their translations into other major languages to follow later. While expressing my heartfelt commendation for this noble project, I pray and hope that *The Library of Tibetan Classics* will not only make these important Tibetan treatises accessible to scholars of Tibetan studies, but will create a new opportunity for younger Tibetans to study and take interest in their own rich and profound culture. Through translations into other languages, it is my sincere hope that millions of fellow citizens of the wider human family will also be able to share in the joy of engaging with Tibet's classical literary heritage, textual riches that have been such a great source of joy and inspiration to me personally for so long.

The Dalai Lama
The Buddhist monk Tenzin Gyatso

Special Acknowledgments

THE INSTITUTE OF TIBETAN CLASSICS expresses its deep gratitude to the Tsadra Foundation for most generously providing the entire funding for this translation project. This is first of the ten volumes being sponsored by Tsadra Foundation from *The Library of Tibetan Classics.*

We also acknowledge the Hershey Family Foundation for its generous support of the Institute of Tibetan Classics' projects of compiling, editing, translating, and disseminating key classical Tibetan texts through the creation of *The Library of Tibetan Classics.*

Publisher's Acknowledgments

WISDOM PUBLICATIONS and THE INSTITUTE OF TIBETAN CLASSICS would like to express their deep appreciation to the Ing Foundation and Ms. Nita Ing for their generous grant toward the publication costs of this volume, and to Drs. Mordehai and Hanna Wosk and family for underwriting the printing and distribution of significant copies of the volume to be offered to various Tibetan institutions and community associations across the world, as well as to selected university libraries in Canada and the United States.

The Publisher also wishes to extend a heartfelt thanks to the following people, who by subscribing to *The Library of Tibetan Classics* have become benefactors of this entire translation series: Tenzin Dorjee, Rick Meeker Hayman, Steven D. Hearst, Heidi Kaiter, Arnold Possick, the Randall-Gonzales Family Foundation, Jonathan and Diana Rose, the Tibetisches Zentrum e.V. Hamburg, Claudia Wellnitz, Robert White, and Eva and Jeff Wild.

Contents

Foreword *by Khenchen Thrangu Rinpoche* xi

General Editor's Preface xiii

Translator's Introduction 1

Technical Notes 27

1. A String of Pearls: A Collection of Dharma Lectures
   Gampopa (1079–1153) 31

2. The Unrivaled Instructions of Shang Rinpoché: The Preliminaries and Main Practice of the Great Meditation of Mahāmudrā
   Shönu Lha (late thirteenth century) 65

3. The Ultimate Supreme Path of the Mahāmudrā
   Lama Shang (1123–93) 83

4. A Record of Mahāmudrā Instructions
   Drukchen Pema Karpo (1527–92) 135

5. Instructions for the Mahāmudrā Innate Union
   Karmapa Rangjung Dorjé (1284–1339) 153

6. Prayer for the Definitive Meaning, the Mahāmudrā
   Karmapa Rangjung Dorjé (1284–1339) 169

7. Oral Transmission of the Supreme Siddhas: A Commentary on *Prayer for the Definitive Meaning, the Mahāmudrā*
   Situ Tenpai Nyinjé (1700–1777) 175

8. The Bright Torch: The Perfect Illumination of the True Meaning of the Mahāmudrā, the Essence of All the Dharma
   Tselé Natsok Rangdröl (b. 1608) 289

9. The Quintessence of Nectar: Instructions for the Practice of the Six Dharmas of Nāropa
Shamarpa Chökyi Wangchuk (1584–1630) 333

10. The Single Viewpoint: A Root Text
Sherap Jungné (1187–1241) 373

I. The Hundred and Fifty Vajra Teachings 373

II. The Forty-Seven Supplements to the Hundred and Fifty Vajra Teachings 390

III. The Four Main Points of the Dharma of the Single Viewpoint 395

IV. The Structural Analysis that Classifies the Sequence of the Seven Chapters 398

11. Light Rays from the Jewel of the Excellent Teaching: A General Presentation on the Points of Secret Mantra
Dakpo Tashi Namgyal (1512–87) 401

SELECTED TOPICS: *The way in which the Teacher appeared*, 402. *The Buddha's teaching*, 408. *The tantras in general*, 426. *The lower tantras*, 447. *Highest yoga tantra*, 460. *Empowerment rites*, 467. *Commitments and vows*, 492. *The two stages in general*, 498. *Generation stage*, 507. *Completion stage*, 550. *The yoga of channels, winds, and drops*, 555. *The illusory body*, 565. *The bardo and transference*, 572. *Mahāmudrā*, 576. *Union*, 582. *Conduct that enhances the path*, 586. *Results of practice*, 598.

Table of Tibetan Transliteration 621

Notes 627

Glossary 701

Bibliography 725

Index 749

About the Contributors 765

Foreword

by Khenchen Thrangu Rinpoche

For this volume, I have selected key classical Tibetan texts from the Kagyü tradition to present the tradition's core teachings. Today, I am happy to see this special anthology of Dakpo Kagyü texts published in English translation as part of *The Library of Tibetan Classics*, a series envisioned by Thupten Jinpa, the principal English translator to His Holiness the Fourteenth Dalai Lama. These teachings are intended to create experiences and realizations in the mind. They contain two kinds of instructions: those that engage with the essential points of the body and those that engage with the essential points of the mind.

Engaging with the essential points of the body is accomplished through the stationary channels, the moving winds, and so on. These instructions for attaining buddhahood are the *path of methods*, which is comprised of the six Dharmas of Nāropa, such as caṇḍālī and the illusory body. The teachings of the six Dharmas are based upon the Guhyasamāja, Mahāmāyā, Hevajra, Cakrasaṃvara, and *Four Seats* tantras. These six Dharmas constitute the ultimate completion-stage practice for all highest yoga tantras, especially the nondual tantras.

The instructions for attaining buddhahood in one lifetime and in one body through engaging with the essential points of the mind are the *path of liberation*, which is comprised of the profound mahāmudrā instructions. The teachings on mahāmudrā explain that there is no stain whatsoever to be removed from the luminous nature of the mind and no additional quality that needs to be created in it. There are both sutra and tantra traditions of mahāmudrā. The former is meditation on luminosity free from conceptual elaboration, while the tantra tradition's mahāmudrā is the accomplishment of the unity of bliss and emptiness. The Dakpo Kagyü tradition is an uninterrupted lineage—sustained until the present—of the stainless realization of mahāmudrā.

The compilation in this volume of the instructions for both the path of methods and the path of liberation will definitely be of great benefit to Buddhist practitioners and also to researchers, facilitating the accurate completion of their research. I both pray and am certain that this will be so.

This was written spontaneously in Rishipattana Deer Park by the one who was given the name Thrangu Tulku.

May goodness flourish!

Thrangu Rinpoche
Varanasi

General Editor's Preface

THE PUBLICATION of this volume marks an important milestone in making key classical Tibetan texts available in contemporary languages. This volume, *Mahāmudrā and Related Instructions: Core Teachings of the Kagyü Schools*, which is volume 5 of *The Library of Tibetan Classics*, brings into the world's literary heritage a collection of a very special genre of spiritual writings of the Tibetan Buddhist tradition. Compiled by the Most Venerable Khenchen Thrangu Rinpoché, a senior master of the Kagyü school, the texts featured in this anthology present the heart of the meditative tradition of the Kagyü school. Distilled in these translations are the insights and instructions of the Tibetan spiritual lineage of such great luminaries as Marpa Lotsāwa, Milarepa, and Gampopa, a school that is acclaimed for its profound and rich meditative practices. It is with both joy and honor that the Institute of Tibetan Classics offers the translation of these precious Tibetan texts to the contemporary reader, especially to those who seek to engage deeply with the Tibetan tradition and its wisdom.

Two primary objectives have driven the creation and development of *The Library of Tibetan Classics*. The first aim is to help revitalize the appreciation and the study of the Tibetan classical heritage within Tibetan-speaking communities worldwide. The younger generation in particular struggle with the tension between traditional Tibetan culture and the realities of modern consumerism. To this end, efforts have been made to develop a comprehensive yet manageable body of texts, one that features the works of Tibet's best-known authors and covers the gamut of classical Tibetan knowledge. The second objective of *The Library of Tibetan Classics* is to help make these texts part of global literary and intellectual heritage. In this regard, we have tried to make the English translation reader-friendly and, as much as possible, keep the body of the text free of unnecessary scholarly apparatus, which can intimidate general readers. For specialists who wish to compare the translation with the Tibetan original, page references of the critical edition of the Tibetan text are provided in brackets.

The texts in this thirty-two-volume series span more than a millennium—from the development of the Tibetan script in the seventh century to the first part of the twentieth century, when Tibetan society and culture first encountered industrial modernity. The volumes are thematically organized and cover many of the categories of classical Tibetan knowledge—from the teachings specific to each Tibetan school to the classical works on philosophy, psychology, and phenomenology. The first category includes teachings of the Kadam, Nyingma, Sakya, Kagyü, Geluk, and Jonang schools, of miscellaneous Buddhist lineages, and of the Bön school. Texts in these volumes have been largely selected by senior lineage holders of the individual schools. Texts in the other categories have been selected primarily in recognition of the historical reality of the individual disciplines. For example, in the field of epistemology, works from the Sakya and Geluk schools have been selected, while the volume on buddha nature features the writings of Butön Rinchen Drup and various Kagyü masters. Where fields are of more common interest, such as the three codes or the bodhisattva ideal, efforts have been made to represent the perspectives of all four major Tibetan Buddhist schools. *The Library of Tibetan Classics* can function as a comprehensive library of the Tibetan literary heritage for libraries, educational and cultural institutions, and interested individuals.

It has been a profound honor for me to be part of this important translation project. I wish first of all to express my deep personal gratitude to H. H. the Dalai Lama for always being such a profound source of inspiration. I would also like to offer my sincere thanks to Khenchen Thrangu Rinpoché for his being such an exemplary representative of the Kagyü tradition, for his selection of the texts featured in this volume, and for providing a special foreword to this translation as well as contributing an introductory essay to the original Tibetan edition of the volume. I thank Peter Alan Roberts for his masterful translation of these precious Tibetan texts into English with such care, respect, and scholarly refinement. To the following individuals and organizations, I owe my sincere thanks: to David Kittelstrom at Wisdom for his incisive editing; to Gene Smith at the Tibetan Buddhist Resource Center for providing assistance with obtaining crucial Tibetan texts needed for the editing of the Tibetan texts; to the Central Institute of Higher Tibetan Studies, Sarnath, for proving full access to its library to the Tibetan editors working on the critical editing of these texts; and to my wife Sophie Boyer-

Langri for taking on the numerous administrative chores that are part of a collaborative project such as this.

Finally, I would like to express my heartfelt thanks to Tsadra Foundation, who most generously provided the entire funding for this translation project. Without this support, no amount of dedication on the part of the Institute or the depth of talent and skill on the part of the translator would have resulted in such successful conclusion of the project. In particular, I would like to express my personal admiration of Eric Colombel for the profound vision and the deep dedication to the Tibetan Vajrayana tradition that underlie the mission of Tsadra Foundation. I would also like to thank the Hershey Family Foundation for its longstanding support of the Institute of Tibetan Classics, without which the task of creating *The Library of Tibetan Classics* simply would not have gotten off the ground. It is my sincere hope that the translations offered in this volume will be of benefit to many people. Through the efforts of all those who have been involved in this noble venture, may all beings enjoy peace and happiness.

Thupten Jinpa
Montreal, 2010

Translator's Introduction

THE KAGYÜ SCHOOL of Tibetan Buddhism has its origins in the eleventh century, a time when individuals went to India in search of teachings unavailable in Tibet. Buddhism had been introduced into Tibet four centuries earlier under royal auspices, and the schools that originated later were known as *Sarma*, "new," to distinguish them from the *Nyingma*, or "old," tradition. Among the numerous Tibetan translators and teachers of that time, the Kagyü meditator Milarepa is perhaps the most famous, and his biography and songs remain popular today. Three feature films have even been made about him recently—in India, Bhutan, and Tibet. His life of simplicity and austerity completely dedicated to meditation is a touchstone for a school that emphasizes meditation practice over scholarship. He is the peerless exemplar of reaching buddhahood in a single lifetime through only guru devotion and dedication to meditation, without any formal studies.

Nevertheless, although the Kagyü is based upon the teachings of a nonmonastic meditator, it became a monastic tradition in the twelfth century through the efforts of Milarepa's pupil, Gampopa, the first author represented in this compilation. Since Gampopa's founding of the first Kagyü monastery, the Kagyü tradition has seen a proliferation of subschools, most of which now have a limited or minimal existence. The Karma Kagyü, now the most popular Kagyü tradition in both Eastern countries and in the West, originated with a pupil of Gampopa who became, retrospectively, the First Karmapa, and the Karmapa lineage was the first line of transmission in Tibet based on identifying the reincarnation of its principal lama. Various Kagyü factions competed for secular rule of Tibet via the Phakmodru and Rinpung dynasties beginning in the fourteenth century, and by the sixteenth century the Karma Kagyü school dominated Central Tibet.[1] It was eclipsed by the rise to power of the Fifth Dalai Lama in the middle of the seventeenth century, but it continued to have a strong following in the eastern regions of the Tibetan plateau. Another one of our authors, the eighteenth-century Karma Kagyü hierarch Situ Tenpai Nyinjé, built Palpung Monastery in the eastern kingdom of Dergé with royal patronage, and although Tsurphu Monastery in Central Tibet was the official center for the Karma Kagyü, Palpung became the most important of its monasteries as a result of the teaching and meditation practice that took place there.

Situ Tenpai Nyinjé's successor, the Ninth Tai Situ, established the tradition of the three-year retreats, in which the deities Cakrasaṃvara and Vajravārāhī in particular are practiced and the six Dharmas of Nāropa may be mastered. These practices together with mahāmudrā meditation represent the ancient core of advanced Kagyü practice. In the last few decades hundreds of Westerners have accomplished the Kagyü three-year retreats in centers established in Europe and North America. Every Kagyü monastery of note has a *khenpo*, who is the head of scholastic studies, and a monastic college called a *shedra*, in which there is an intensive program of study for many years. But the heart of the Kagyü monastery is in its retreat centers, where one finds not only shedra graduates but also monks who become lamas without undergoing intensive scholastic training.

Palpung was also the seat of the polymath Jamgön Kongtrül (1813–99), the nonsectarian author and editor of numerous volumes that have had enormous impact in both the study and practice of the Karma Kagyü.[2] Because of the Kagyü emphasis on meditation over scholarship, the Kagyü lineage before Jamgön Kongtrül did not have an extensive literature. The literature that did exist is well represented by the works included in the present volume, teachings in which study is clearly unified with, and at the service of, meditation practice.

Kagyü Origins

The Kagyü tradition inherited the higher yoga tantric tradition that had become widespread in northern India in the closing centuries of the first millennium, particularly those tantras known as the *yoginī tantras* or, more commonly in Tibet, the *mother tantras*. This esoteric Buddhism was quite different from the Buddhism that was preserved in the Pali Canon. Transformed by the Mahayana ideal, Buddhist philosophical scholasticism, and tantra's antinomianism, the Indian Buddhism inherited by the Kagyü school had undergone an astonishing process of evolution and assimilation since the lifetime of Siddhartha Gautama in the fifth century B.C.E.

The Buddha himself did not found his religion in a vacuum; he had assimilated and transformed the religious traditions he was born into, including the very titles *buddha* and *muni*, the *Bṛhadāraṇyaka Upaniṣad*'s championing of the nontraditional practice of abandoning the lay life at a young age in order to overcome ignorance and attain liberation from *samsara* (itself a pre-Buddhist term), and the lifestyle of a shaven-headed renunciate with yellow robes known as a *bhikṣu*, already a venerable tradition.

Nevertheless, the Buddha's teachings were revolutionary in many aspects, and they proved also a fertile ground for later development of views and practices. Buddhist canonical literature enlarged to many times its original size as accomplished masters received, through meditation and vision, sutras and tantras that had not been previously divulged into the human world. This diverse and remarkable evolution and often bewilderingly rich array of teachings culminated in the Indian *siddhas*, practitioners of the mother tantras. Their views, practices, and conduct may seem far removed from those of the founder of their religion, yet they retained the essence of the original liberating message. This combination of both continuity and innovation within this ancient tradition—now almost a thousand years since the first beginnings of the Kagyü tradition in Tibet and two and a half millennia since the Buddha's lifetime—are clearly testified in the teachings compiled in this book.

The Kagyü school is one of seven religious traditions of Tibetan Buddhism that continue today as independent organizations; the other six are the Nyingma, Bön, Sakya, Geluk, Jonang, and Bodong.[3] Of the antecedents to the Tibetan schools in India, there is no precedent in terms of exclusive institutions, for in India the transmissions of Buddhist practices were primarily between individual gurus and their personal pupils and not specifically identified with formal organizations such as the great monasteries.[4] These large sectarian organizations encompassing a variety of transmission lineages became more solidified in Tibet once secular rule became the province of religious institutions headed by reincarnate lamas, and lineages vied with one another not just for adherents but for political influence and the resources of the state.

The term Kagyü as the name of a school is said to have originated as a shortened form of *kabap shiyi gyü*, which means the "lineage of four instruction transmissions."[5] This refers to the teachings compiled by the tenth-century Bengali now generally known as Tilopa (these four transmissions are discussed in the next section). Tilopa's Indian pupil, Nāropa, became the teacher of the Tibetan translator and tantric master Marpa

Chökyi Lodrö, who in the eleventh century introduced many of Nāropa's teachings into Tibet. All Kagyü schools, extant and extinct, trace their origin to Marpa Chökyi Lodrö, and therefore Marpa Kagyü is sometimes used as a generic term for all Kagyü lineages. Marpa in turn became the teacher of Milarepa.

Of the more than fifteen Kagyü lineages that have appeared since the eleventh century, those that currently survive as major independent schools are the Karma Kagyü, Drukpa Kagyü, and Drigung Kagyü. The Barom Kagyü has over a dozen monasteries in Golok, a region in the northeast of the Tibetan plateau, and most of the other lineages have a small but continuing existence. There are also the Surmang Kagyü and Nedo Kagyü, though they in practice function as a subschool within the Karma Kagyü.[6] The Shangpa Kagyü is technically a distinct, separate lineage from the Marpa Kagyü traditions. Nevertheless, while it can be classified as a school in its own right, it is currently primarily preserved as a lineage of practices within the Karma Kagyü tradition. Volume 8 in this series will feature teachings of the Shangpa school.

Khenchen Thrangu Rinpoche, the principal scholar in the Karma Kagyü tradition, chose the eleven texts that comprise this volume. This volume therefore primarily represents a Karma Kagyü perspective and usage, with five texts from authors of importance within that lineage. The Dakpo Kagyü is a general term for all the lineages that derive from Gampopa, also known as Dakpo Lhajé, but also refers to his own specific lineage. This lineage is represented by a compilation of lectures by Gampopa himself and by Dakpo Tashi Namgyal, the abbot of Gampopa's monastery four centuries later. The works of both authors are studied in the Karma Kagyü as well. The Drukpa Kagyü is represented by a short mahāmudrā text by Pema Karpo that is nonetheless used for instruction by Karma Kagyü teachers. The Drigung Kagyü is represented by Sherap Jungné's *Single Viewpoint* and three associated texts, which codify the viewpoints of Jikten Sumgön, the founder of the Drigung lineage. Two texts from the Tsalpa Kagyü, a lineage that no longer exists, are also included. These Drigung and Tsalpa Kagyü texts are included within Jamgön Kongtrül's *Treasury of Instructions*. The other lineages, such as the Barom Kagyü and Taklung Kagyü, are not represented.

A Syncretic Tradition

The four transmissions that Tilopa received and passed on as a single transmission are said to be:

1. Cāryapa's instructions on *caṇḍālī* (see below)
2. Siddha Nāgārjuna's instructions on illusory body (*māyākāya*) and luminosity (*prabhāsvara*)[7]
3. Kambala's instructions on dreams (*svapna*)
4. Sukhasiddhī's instructions on the *bardo* (*antarābhava*)[8] and transference of consciousness into another body (*purapraveśa*)[9]

Tilopa briefly described these six practices in a short verse text entitled *Instructions on the Six Dharmas.*[10] In Tibet these practices became known as the *six Dharmas of Nāropa*. In English they became known as the six *yogas* of Nāropa through their being first translated in 1935 by Evans-Wentz in *Tibetan Yoga and Secret Doctrines*, even though Evans-Wentz only referred to them as "six doctrines," which is the equivalent of six Dharmas.[11] The term *yoga* (*sbyor ba*) is never used for this set of practices in Tibetan, and they should not be confused with the Kālacakra tradition's group of six practices that *are* called *yogas*.

The six Dharmas of Nāropa are intended solely for advanced practitioners and are normally taught within a three-year retreat. In this volume they are the subject of Shamar Chökyi Wangchuk's text, the *Quintessence of Nectar*. They are also described in Dakpo Tashi Namgyal's overview of the tantras, *Light Rays from the Jewel of the Excellent Teaching.*[12]

Many teachings and practices of the Kagyü school, however, originally came from other Tibetan schools. The monastic Kagyü practitioner follows a tradition of ordination derived from the Kadam tradition, which formed in the eleventh century based on the teachings of the Indian paṇḍita Atiśa (982–1054), who spent his final years in Tibet. Kagyü scholastic studies have origins in both the Kadam and other traditions. For example, the distinctive *empty of other* (*gzhan stong*) philosophy[13] that is particularly propounded within the Karma Kagyü is derived from the Jonang school. The Jonang also provided the Kālacakra practices. Mind training (*blo sbyong*) and White Tārā come from the Kadampas, and the *severance* (*gcod*) practices come from the lineage of that name. Practices of deities such as Green Tārā, Avalokiteśvara, Vajrakīlaya, and various guru yogas of Padmasambhava were introduced from the Nyingma school. Some Nyingma *tertöns* (who by various methods reveal or discover *terma*: teachings, ritual objects, and relics), such as Jatsön Nyingpo (1585–1656) and Yongé Mingyur Dorjé (1628/41–1708), were closely affiliated with the Kagyü. The terma of Namchö Mingyur Dorjé (1645–67), which form the basis of the Palyül Nyingma lineage, also supplied the Kagyü with such deity practices as Amitābha and Bhaiṣajya Guru (Medicine Buddha).

There are also terma from within the Kagyü tradition itself. For example, the founder of the Drukpa Kagyü school, Tsangpa Gyaré (1161–1211), revealed a terma concealed by Rechungpa, one of the Kagyü's earliest masters, that became of central importance to the lineage. Of great importance in the Drigung Kagyü school are the termas of Rinchen Phüntsok (1509–57) and Drigung Nüden Dorjé (1801–59).

Thus, although the Kagyü identity is that of a lineage of instructions descended from Marpa Chökyi Lodrö, the majority of common Kagyü practices are derived from other lineages. Much of Marpa's own transmission, such as Mahāmāyā and Buddhakapāla, have fallen into disuse and are only nominally maintained as a ritual transmission of their empowerments. Certain higher tantra practices introduced by Marpa, however, continue to be the central practices for advanced Kagyü practitioners and form the main part of the traditional three-year retreats.

The Quintessential Kagyü Practices

The advanced higher tantra practices that do derive from Marpa—and that could therefore be said to form the core of the Kagyü identity—appeared in India between the eighth and tenth centuries. They were among a small group of tantras that have been variously named *yoginī tantras*, *mother tantras*, *higher yoga* (*yogottara*) *tantras*, and *none-higher* or *unsurpassable yoga* (*yogānuttara*) *tantras*, which in English are usually referred to as the *highest yoga tantras*.[14] For the Kagyü, the most important of these are the Cakrasaṃvara tantras. It is taught that the deity Cakrasaṃvara originates from a Heruka who defeated Śiva and assumed his form, retinues, and sacred sites. He is a blue deity in sexual union with the red goddess Vajravārāhī. The original Indian tantric texts play only a small role in contemporary Kagyü study and practice, as advanced Kagyü practitioners of Cakrasaṃvara or Vajravārāhī focus primarily on meditation texts of Tibetan origin. For the Karma Kagyü, Vajravārāhī is the principal deity, holding Cakrasaṃvara in the form of a *khaṭvāṅga* scepter in the crook of her arm.[15]

According to the Tibetan view, the practices derived from the higher tantras are classified into two groups—the *stage of generation* and the *stage of completion*.[16] The generation stage entails the visualization of oneself as the deity within a divine palace. The deity is called the *yi dam*, or "commitment deity," in Tibetan and *iṣṭadevatā*, or "chosen deity," in Sanskrit. The practice consists primarily of mantra repetition and a variety of chants, offerings, and visualizations. The practitioner's habituation to the "pure perception" of the deity and the environs is intended to eliminate habituation to ordinary perception and reveal the intrinsic purity of all mental and physical phenomena.[17]

The Kagyü school divides the completion stage into two kinds of practice: the path of methods and the path of liberation. The *path of methods* consists especially of the six Dharmas of Nāropa mentioned above, and the *path of liberation* is primarily the practice of mahāmudrā, the main subject of the present volume.

The Six Dharmas of Nāropa

The principal practice among the six Dharmas of Nāropa is *caṇḍālī*. The primary, though not exclusive, Tibetan word for this practice is *tumo* (*gtum mo*), which literally means a "fierce or savage woman." The Sanskrit *caṇḍālī* or *candalīka* also conveys the meaning of "hot"—as in a hot, wild, passionate woman. In particular, it was the name for the female of the most impure of the untouchables: the caṇḍālas. The Chinese pilgrim Xuanzang, during his seventh-century visit to India, recorded how caṇḍālas were obliged to make noises to warn villages that they were passing through so that the inhabitants could hide indoors and avoid being polluted. It is indicative of the antinomian tendency of the highest yoga tantras that these and other female untouchables, deemed the lowest of human beings, were sought out as consorts in sexual yoga and were deified in such practices as Hevajra, where a caṇḍālī appears in that deity's entourage. Heat was that goddess's specialty: She could burn up the universe, incinerating all impurities that prevent the realization of innate buddhahood.

Caṇḍālī has become known in the West as "inner heat" because of the physical heat generation attributed to the practice. However, the goal of the practice is not heat but rather the experience of bliss and emptiness. Caṇḍālī is based upon an esoteric physiology, consisting of a network of channels (*nāḍī*) that pervade the body, through which move wind (*vāyu*) and in which are located "drops" (*bindu*). These drops can have various forms and may be solid or liquid, semen itself being an example. Though details of this morphology vary, generally the three most important channels are the central channel (*avadhūtī*), which runs parallel to the spine, and two secondary channels that run parallel to its left and right: the *rasanā* and the *lalanā*. The breath enters the left and right channels through the two nostrils. As the mind and the winds are interdependent, the mind can be made to reach a nondual state through making the winds of the left and right channels enter the central channel at the abdomen. Therefore, breath-retention practices are employed to cause this to occur and thus give rise to the nondual state.

The caṇḍālī practice also involves the physiology of sexuality, generally described from a male perspective. It corresponds with far more ancient Taoist practices, which have a greater number of pressure points in breath control, called *jade locks*, and a specific female morphology that has the retention of menstruation as the parallel to the male retention of ejaculation. Caṇḍālī and the cakra system appeared in the Buddhist tradition subsequent to a period of Buddhist and Taoist coexistence in Central Asia. The *cakras*, literally "wheels," are the points where subsidiary channels branch off into the body, but they were unknown in India before the latter centuries of the first millennium, when they first appeared in both Śaivism and Buddhism.

In all these traditions, semen, which in Buddhist tantra is euphemistically called *bodhicitta*, is located in the skull at the top of the central channel. In caṇḍālī, as during sexual arousal, a flame at the navel causes the bodhicitta to melt and descend as liquid, creating stages of bliss as it passes through four cakras at the throat, heart, navel, and genitals. In this practice, the bodhicitta is not ejaculated but drawn back up the central channel, creating four more stages of bliss during which the practitioner realizes the essential nature of the mind. Caṇḍālī is termed *liberation through the upper door* in contrast to sexual practice with an imagined or real consort (an "action seal," or *karmamudrā*), which is called *bliss through the lower door*. A more advanced form of this consort practice involves the semen exiting, blending with the female fluid, and then being drawn back into the body and up through the cakras. This sexual practice was sometimes counted as one of the six Dharmas, and it is described in Dakpo Tashi Namgyal's text within this volume.

Briefly, the other five practices are *illusory body*, which develops a perception of all phenomena as an illusion; *dream yoga* to gain an awareness and control of dreams; *luminosity*, or more literally from the Sanskrit "brightness," which involves maintaining awareness on entering dreamless sleep; *transference*, in which one trains in firing one's consciousness out through the crown of the head at the time of death in order to attain enlightenment, or at least a good rebirth; and the *bardo*, which is practiced in order to attain enlightenment, or a good rebirth, in the state between death and rebirth. Although the number six has remained constant since the introduction of the six Dharmas into Tibet, there was considerable variation in the earlier centuries as to what practices made up that number. The practices enumerated were sometimes more than six, with two practices being classed as one.

The present-day list is similar to that given by Tilopa, although *purapraveśa*, the practice of transferring one's consciousness into a dead body and reanimating it, has been replaced by the less-dramatic companion practice of *transference* (*saṃkranti*), known in Tibetan and popularly in the West as *phowa*, in which the consciousness at death is sent into a *yidam* deity and thereby a pure realm. In Tilopa's instructions this was presented as only one form of *purapraveśa*. *Purapraveśa* literally means "entering a town" but is also called, less obscurely, "entering another's body" (*parakāyapraveśa*). In this practice the consciousness is transferred into a dead (yet healthy) young body, which is then reanimated. This enables the practitioner to avoid the process of rebirth and childhood disrupting the continuum of consciousness and memory. Though there is a popular legend that the transmission of this practice ended with the death of Marpa's son Darma Dodé, there are a number of instances in the biographies of medieval Kagyü masters, where they display their mastery of this practice by briefly reanimating a dead animal or bird while in meditation. In any period, however, accounts of permanently abandoning one's body and continuing one's life in another body are rare.

An ancillary to caṇḍālī practice briefly referred to in this volume is the set of distinctive and exacting exercises called *yantra* (*'khrul khor*), which include jumping and landing in the vajra posture, wherein the feet rest on the opposite thighs, so as to eliminate defects in the flow of wind through the channels.

Mahāmudrā in India

Mahāmudrā is a comparatively simple, direct approach to seeing the nature of the mind, though the teaching also includes many stages for an initial stabilization of the mind. Six of the eleven texts in the present volume are dedicated to explicating the practice of mahāmudrā.[18]

It is not easy to determine what historical kernel survives within Tibetan biographies of Indian masters. However, the Tibetan tradition has the mahāmudrā teachings commence with Saraha and his *doha* verses. Saraha is depicted to be the great-grandteacher of Maitripa, and therefore would be active in the early tenth century if taken in normal human terms, though little in their biographies is normal. Saraha's teacher is said to be the bodhisattva Ratnamati, a tenth-level bodhisattva in Akaniṣṭha, the ultimate realm of the dharmakāya buddha Vajradhara. Therefore Saraha is the first human teacher in this lineage.[19]

The doha is the literary medium most closely associated with the mahāmudrā teachings and was used by successive generations of siddhas from the last centuries of the first millennium onward. However, the meaning of the word *doha* was lost in Tibetan translation. A *doha* is in fact a particular form of rhyming couplets. Famous examples of dohas are the Hindi poetry of Kabir (1440–1518), in which each doha could be an independent separate work. Indian poetry employed various kinds of verse and meters based on patterns of long and short syllables, unlike Tibetan, which counts only the number of syllables per line. As there is no Tibetan equivalent for the word *doha*, it has often simply been transcribed rather than translated. However, the general word for a spiritual song in Tibetan is *mgur*, and the dohas and a related type of verse called *caryāpādas* written in the earliest form of Bengali are generally referred to in Tibetan as *mgur*. This has led to an inaccurate back translation of all instances of *mgur* in Tibetan, including native Tibetan songs, as *doha*, glossed as "a song expressing realization."

The language in which these dohas were written was not Sanskrit but usually a late middle-Indic language such as Apabhraṃśa. The very word *doha* is not Sanskrit; *do* means "two" and is related to the Sanskrit *dva*. Saraha's dohas were written in an eastern form of Apabhraṃśa and appear to actually be a collection of couplets by various authors. Their distinctive rhyming sound pattern is lost in both Tibetan and English translation. For example:

> *Brāhmaṇ to nā jāne to bhed*
> *Ebhāve pāḍ ā hoḥ e catur ved*
>
> The brahmans do not know the truth
> but simply recite the four Vedas.

Saraha is said to have transmitted his mahāmudrā lineage to the siddha Nāgārjuna, the tantric master that Tibetan tradition has conflated with the well-known Mādhyamika master of that name, who in the Tibetan version of his life is said to have lived for six hundred years. However, this would still not span the centuries between these two Nāgārjunas. Moreover, the earliest biographies of the Mādhyamika Nāgārjuna, which are preserved in

Chinese, have him living to only eighty, one hundred, or one hundred and twenty years.

Śavaripa, who is described to be a pupil of both Saraha and Nāgārjuna, is said to have been one of the tribal peoples in what is now Orissa. He is said to have lived as a hunter in the forests, and in one description of how Śavaripa first appeared to Maitripa, he is wearing a peacock-feather skirt and is attended by two tribal women, who are picking lice from his hair.

We enter surer historical footing with Maitripa (986–1063),[20] who became the principal master of mahāmudrā in India. He was a pupil of Nāropa for twenty years and is said to have started teaching in his fifties. His hermitage appears to have been in Mithilā (also known as Tirhut), an area that now corresponds to northern Bihar and neighboring parts of southern Nepal.

The Introduction of Mahāmudrā into Tibet

Atiśa received mahāmudrā instruction from Maitripa, which must have been before 1040, the year of both Nāropa's death and Atiśa's departure for Tibet via Nepal. He arrived in Tibet in 1042, where he stayed until his death twelve years later at age seventy-two. He taught mahāmudrā to his pupil Dromtön (1004–63), but Dromtön decided against making mahāmudrā a part of the Kadam tradition, fearing it would have a negative influence on conduct.[21]

The mahāmudrā lineage of Marpa Chökyi Lodrö, even though he was a pupil of Maitripa and the ostensible founder of the Kagyü tradition, is classed as the *subsidiary translation tradition* (*zur 'gyur*), because initially other mahāmudrā transmissions, many of which originated with Vajrapāṇi (b. 1017),[22] were of greater importance.

Dampa Kor Nirūpa (1062–1102) was a Tibetan who held yet another mahāmudrā lineage. After a curious case of the practice of *purapraveśa*, Dampa Kor, as he was originally called, became known as Kor Nirūpa. A practitioner and traveler to Nepal from an early age, Dampa Kor is said to have died there when he was nineteen. Staying in the same house with him was seventy-three-year-old Nirūpa, a pupil of Maitripa's disciple Karopa. Nirūpa performed the practice of *purapraveśa* and entered Dampa Kor's body and revived it. After Nirūpa's old body was cremated, he went to Tibet in the young Tibetan body but wearing Indian clothing and with the conjoined name of Kor Nirūpa. He then changed to wearing Tibetan clothing and taught mahāmudrā there for twenty-one years, dying at age forty, this time in the more conventional manner.

Following these earliest transmissions of mahāmudrā there came what are called the *middle transmissions*, in which Vajrapāṇi plays a crucial role. Vajrapāṇi is known as one of "the four great pupils of Maitripa." The other three were Natekara (also known as Sahajavajra), Devākaracandra (also known as Śūnyatāsamādhi), and Rāmapāla. Vajrapāṇi moved to Lalitpur (nowadays named Patan, in the Kathmandu Valley) in 1066. In 1074, when he would have been fifty-seven, he was known among Tibetans as one of the three great masters in Nepal,[23] the other two being Pamthingpa and Bharo Chakdum.[24] One account describes him as a white-haired paṇḍita who liked to give sugarcane to Tibetans and enjoyed getting them drunk.[25]

Vajrapāṇi went to Tibet with his Kashmiri pupil, Dharmaśrī, and gave many teachings in the Tsang region of Central Tibet. He had numerous Tibetan pupils and assisted in the translation of nearly forty texts. He authored eleven texts that are preserved in the Tibetan canon. He is absent from a list of great masters in the 1080s, so it seems he had passed away by that time. The lineage of his teachings is called the *upper* or *western* mahāmudrā tradition to differentiate it from two other mahāmudrā traditions, the *lower* and *later* mahāmudrā.

The *lower* or *eastern* mahāmudrā began with Vajrapāṇi's pupil, a Nepalese brahman generally known as Asu.[26] Asu is said to have been passing through Tibet on pilgrimage to China when he married a Tibetan woman and settled down in the Phenyül area of Central Tibet. Asu had many pupils and established a family line of mahāmudrā through two of his four sons.

Asu taught mahāmudrā to Milarepa's pupil Rechungpa (1084–1161), who also studied with Rāmapāla, one of Maitripa's four principal pupils, and with Tipupa, one of Maitripa's seven "middle-ranking" pupils.[27] Rechungpa introduced various teachings into Tibet, even transmitting them to his own teacher, Milarepa. Rechungpa's transmission is central to the Drukpa Kagyü school, which originated with Lingrepa, who was at one time a practitioner within Rechungpa's nonmonastic lineage.

The *later* tradition of mahāmudrā comes from Nakpo Sherdé, a pupil of Vajrapāṇi in Nepal during the master's last years. He focused in particular on the dohas of Saraha.

Mahāmudrā instructions were also introduced into Tibet in the twelfth century. Vairocanarakṣita, a paṇḍita originally from South India, studied in northern India under a number of masters, the most famous being Abhayākaragupta (d. 1125), the greatest Indian Buddhist master of his time. Vairocanarakṣita's principal teacher for mahāmudrā was the great scholar and yogin Surapāla at Nālandā, who taught him the *Twenty-Six Teachings of Nonattention* (*amanasi*).[28] Vairocanarakṣita became a master of mahāmudrā as well as other tantras and visited Tibet a number of times, eventually dying there. He translated many mahāmudrā dohas and teachings, including those of Maitripa. His pupils in Tibet are said to have included Lama Shang (1123–93), one of this volume's authors.[29] The *Blue Annals* also state that he taught the eleventh-century Dampa Kor as a child, but that appears to be a conflation with another teacher.[30]

Tilopa

The traditional dates for Tilopa (also written in the Tibetan texts as Telopa, Tailopa, or Tillipa), whose formal name was Prajñābhadra, are earth ox to earth bird, which would have to be 928–1009. In narratives of his life, Tilopa is described as a solitary dark-skinned wanderer with bulging eyes and long, matted hair. He is said to have been a monk who gave up the monastic life to live a tantric lifestyle, during which he chained himself into the meditation posture for twelve years. He subsequently became a sesame seed (*til*) grinder, which is said to be the origin of his name. He is also said to have worked as a procurer for a prostitute. All who knew him were astounded when he levitated "to the height of seven palm trees" and sang one of his spiritual songs.

Tilopa is depicted as having Vajradhara, the symbol of the dharmakāya, as his guru. A song attributed to Tilopa, though it is not included in the canonical works, even claims he had no human guru, contradicting the history of four transmissions mentioned above. This discrepancy is sometimes explained as Vajradhara having given only the blessing, while the instructions came from his human teachers. Another explanation is that Tilopa *was* Vajradhara, and his studying with gurus was an act performed merely to benefit others. The legends of Tilopa also have him receiving certain instructions from ḍākinīs in their realm, named Oḍḍiyāna.

Nāropa

The earliest known surviving biographies of Nāropa are those written by Gampopa and Lama Shang, two of the authors represented in this volume.[31] They describe how Nāropa underwent a series of hardships under Tilopa, such as leaping off a temple roof, lying on a leech-infested mire, receiving savage beatings after stealing food, sexually assaulting a bride during her procession, and attempting to kidnap a queen. Obeying Tilopa's commands brought him each time to the point of death, and he was only revived by Tilopa's miraculous powers. For the Kagyü tradition, with its emphasis on the liberating power of guru devotion itself, Nāropa's obedience and eventual enlightenment serve as an archetypal example, fortunately beyond literal emulation.

Subsequently Nāropa went to Nālandā, India's greatest Buddhist monastery, and became a great scholar there. Then, in the last years of his life, he established a hermitage, named Pullahari, where he eventually gave up all activity and entered silence, ceasing to teach. Later versions of Nāropa's life, perhaps out of an antipathy to scholasticism, reversed this sequence, first depicting Nāropa as a master of Nālandā and then showing him realizing the futility of mere study, abandoning his post, and going in search of Tilopa.

The dates of his lifetime are given as fire dragon to iron dragon, which would be 956–1040. Atiśa's departure for Tibet is reliably dated to 1040, and he brought relics from the cremation of Nāropa with him. The bronze stupa in which they are enshrined still survives near Lhasa next to the shrine in Nyethang Dölma Lhakhang temple, which Atiśa founded.

A once-common dating for Nāropa of 1016–1100 was the result of taking literally Tsangnyön Heruka's version of the life of Marpa, in which Marpa in his old age goes to India to meet Nāropa, who sings a verse of praise of Milarepa. However, this episode and its verse were derived from one of Tsangnyön Heruka's visions and are without historical basis.[32]

Marpa

In contrast to the early years of the Nyingma traditions, when Tibet was united under a central monarchy, the Tibetan plateau of Marpa's time was divided among small kingdoms, oligarchies, and nomadic regions. Tibetans, on their own initiative, were going to Nepal and India to receive teachings not available in Tibet, sometimes bringing masters back with them. Marpa was one of these Tibetan translators of Dharma texts who during this time were given the honorific title of *lotsāwa* (from a middle Indic *locchāva*, said to mean "eyes of the world").

Also at this time, the far-western kingdom of Gugé, which saw itself as the successor to the ancient monarchy, brought Atiśa to Tibet. Atiśa's pupil, Dromtön, established the Kadam tradition, whose teachings would in turn become a key ingredient in the formation by Gampopa of the monastic

Kagyü. The Gugé monarchs did not approve of higher tantra practices, with their sex and sorcery, meat and alcohol. Nevertheless, Tibetan translators such as Marpa continued to introduce higher tantras, such as Cakrasaṃvara, into Tibet. In time, with the fusion of Marpa's lineage with Kadam teachings, the controversial aspects of the tantras were marginalized. Nevertheless, this higher tantra substratum continued to lie below the surface, reappearing in certain practices or biographical episodes of Kagyü masters. We also see these elements in some of our texts, in particular Dakpo Tashi Namgyal's overview of the tantras.

Marpa's dates are uncertain and vary from one source to another,[33] but he most likely was born around 1011 and passed away in the 1090s. Marpa's first teacher was Drokmi Lotsāwa (992/93–1043/72), whose teachings became the foundation for the Sakya school. Marpa collected gold in his midteens and went to Nepal and India for further teachings. He then met Nāropa and spent many years studying with him. The wealth he received for giving these instructions back in Tibet funded further expeditions.

Marpa in his biographies is portrayed as an aggressive, corpulent landowner with nine wives, engaging in disputes with his neighbors; he even has his pupil Tsurtön kill his cousin through sorcery as his fee for instructions.[34] As is clear from the earliest versions of his biography, Marpa did not receive the entirety of Nāropa's teachings. On his second visit, Nāropa had ceased teaching and maintained silence, but Nāropa did at that time give Marpa one of his last remaining possessions: a skull bowl.[35] Marpa subsequently studied with a number of other teachers, Maitripa in particular.[36]

Among Marpa's pupils, Ngoktön (1036–1102) received practices and teachings that were not received by the more famous Milarepa. They were passed on through Ngoktön's lineage, and in the nineteenth century were introduced into the mainstream Kagyü by Jamgön Kongtrül.

Milarepa

Although Milarepa is particularly famous because of the 1488 biography and song compilation by Tsangnyön Heruka, Milarepa's biographies had been the subject of considerable narrative evolution since the earliest versions. His songs also had multiplied and were transformed through centuries of bardic tradition long before Tsangnyön Heruka's collection, which was the first to be printed, all earlier texts being handwritten manuscripts. From reading the succession of earlier versions, one can trace a song's evolution, the enlarging of a narrative sequence, or the subsequent insertions of new songs into these new pieces of narrative. Milarepa's dates and lifespan vary considerably in the different versions of his life, but 1040–1123 appears the most likely, particularly in terms of the year of his death.[37]

Mila was his family name, and *repa* signified a nonmonastic practitioner who wore a cotton robe as a sign of mastering the practice of caṇḍālī. According to Gampopa and Lama Shang, Milarepa's family consisted of only himself and his father. He first became a sorcerer and then went to Marpa to receive teachings, in return for which he performed chores in the household, such as carrying water. When he eventually left Marpa to return home, he learned of his father's death, finding his home in ruins.

In later versions, Milarepa has a mother who plays a strong role in his life by insisting he take up sorcery. Marpa has Milarepa single-handedly build and demolish houses in order to purify him of the bad karma accrued through sorcery. This does not occur in the earliest versions because sorcery was not only intrinsic to the tantras, it was practiced by many well-known masters of the time, including Marpa and his other pupils. The Tibetan *las* or *phrin las*, for the Sanskrit *karman*, is commonly translated in the context of the *four karmas* as "activities," though it more properly translates as "rites." The first two of the four rites, from a Western perspective, would be classed as white magic—the *pacifying* rituals to remove illness and so on, and the *increasing* rituals to bring wealth, long life, and so on—while the latter two would be called black magic—the *controlling* rituals, which bring people, particularly women, under one's control, and the *wrathful* rituals, which cause illness, madness, conflict, or death. However, these practices, within the Buddhist context, are intended to be performed with the compassionate motivation of a bodhisattva. Moreover, the very sorcery practice that Milarepa mastered, a terma from his teacher Lharjé Nupchung, is currently a part of the Kagyü transmission included within Jamgön Kongtrül's *Treasury of Precious Termas*[38] and is also one of the main practices of the Drigung Kagyü.

Until the 1488 version of Milarepa's life, he was consistently described as an emanation, enlightened from birth. In one biography he is even an incarnation of the Buddha himself, where he states, "I am the emanated rebirth of master Nāgārjunagarbha, who was an emanation of the Buddha himself as prophesied by the Buddha," and the author adds, "Therefore he truly was Nāgārjunagarbha, the emanation of the Buddha."[39] However, Tsangnyön portrayed him as an ordinary being with extremely bad karma who has to overcome many obstacles in order to achieve enlightenment. As the biography is also one of Tibet's greatest literary works, this has made Milarepa a figure of inspiration for practitioners in all schools of Tibetan Buddhism.[40]

Milarepa's pupils were predominantly peripatetic repas like himself. Milarepa literally adopted his first pupil, Rechungpa (1084–1161), on meeting him as a boy of about twelve years old. Some early texts present Rechungpa as Milarepa's principal pupil, with Gampopa relegated to the list of "pupils from the latter days." This is because Gampopa stayed with Milarepa for only thirteen months in 1122, just before Milarepa's death. Rechungpa established a nonmonastic tradition and even had a reputation for refusing to teach monks, especially since sexual practices were intrinsic to the repa lineage of that time.

Gampopa

Gampopa Sönam Rinchen (1079–1153), also known as Dakpo Lhajé, the first of our authors, was a monk from the Kadam tradition. Kadam monks at that time were forbidden to receive highest yoga tantra empowerments because of their sexual content. This would make Gampopa seem to be an unlikely pupil of Milarepa, let alone his successor. However, it is Gampopa's union of two apparently antithetical traditions to form the Dakpo Kagyü that would form the foundation for the immense development of the monastic Kagyü traditions.

By establishing a graded path, a majority of pupils could concentrate on monastic discipline, scholarship, and less-advanced meditations, while a minority could progress to the advanced teachings of Milarepa. Gampopa spent many years in solitary meditation before establishing a monastic community in the Dakpo region. His monastery was on the Daklha Gampo mountain range, which became the name of his monastery and the source of his sobriquet Gampopa.

The biographical literature on Gampopa evolved to portray him as predestined to transform the Kagyü lineage into a great monastic movement, while Rechungpa was increasingly portrayed as temperamental and unreliable. For example, in stark contrast with an earlier version of Milarepa interpreting a dream of Rechungpa's as auspicious, Tsangnyön Heruka has Milarepa interpret Rechungpa's dream to mean he will not achieve buddhahood for three lifetimes because of disobedience. It was Tsangnyön who introduced the concept of Gampopa as the "sun-like" disciple and Rechungpa as the secondary "moon-like" disciple, a status often presented as Milarepa's own viewpoint. Most egregiously, the earlier literature contains a passage where Milarepa, on parting with Rechungpa for the last time, states that he has given all the instructions to him alone and to no other, but that one instruction remains. He then shows Rechungpa his calloused bottom as an exhortation to constant sitting in meditation.[41] The more popularly known Tsangnyön version repeats this episode but substitutes Gampopa for Rechungpa, even though as a monk, Gampopa could not have received Milarepa's entire teachings, which would have included consort practices.[42] Tsangnyön's version omits all references to Milarepa's partners in sexual practices (except for mountain goddesses when he was in his seventies), as this aspect of the Kagyü transmission, although described in this volume by Dakpo Tashi Namgyal, was marginalized by the mainstream monastic Kagyü tradition.

Gampopa, with his scholastic background, was the first in the Kagyü school to author a significant number of texts. His substantial text on the graduated path entitled the *Ornament of Precious Liberation* continues to be an essential foundation text for Kagyü study.[43] The text of his that opens this volume, *A String of Pearls*, is primarily focused on general teachings and is greatly informed by his Kadam studies. Yet it also contains seamless references to mahāmudrā and its Nyingma equivalent, *dzokchen*. A number of texts in Gampopa's collected works are not technically composed by him but are transcriptions and notes of lectures that he gave, and the attributions of certain texts are contested. *A String of Pearls* collects together twenty short transcribed lectures that were intended to serve as guides for others to transmit the teachings they gave. The colophon attributes the teachings to Gampopa and states that they were compiled by by Gomtsül, Gampopa's nephew and successor.[44]

The Original Dakpo Kagyü Lineage

Gampopa's successor was his nephew Gomtsül (1116–69),[45] short for Gompa Tsültrim Nyingpo, whom he had adopted as a ten-year-old boy and declared to be the rebirth of an Indian paṇḍita.[46] He succeeded Gampopa at age thirty-four, three years before Gampopa's death, and became directly involved in resolving religio-political conflicts in Lhasa. He restored the ancient Lhasa temple, which a fire had turned into "ruins and smoke," and established law and order in the Lhasa region.

The original Dakpo Kagyü did not, like other Kagyü traditions, expand by establishing branch monasteries throughout the Tibetan plateau. Nevertheless, one of the most significant Kagyü authors, Dakpo Tashi Namgyal, was a later successor of this lineage. Little biographical information on this master exists, but his works remain of great importance in the Karma Kagyü tradition, particularly his scholastic and practical manual, *Mahāmudrā: The Moonlight.*[47]

The Four Senior and Eight Junior Lineages

During the first hundred years after the founding of the Dakpo Kagyü, there was an initial multiplication of lineages into what are traditionally known as the four senior and eight junior lineages (*che bzhi chung brgyad*). Subsequently, newer monasteries became branches of a central monastery; some lineages developed transregional significance while others, such as the Yelpa, Trophu, Yasang, and Taklung, presently consist of a few monasteries or important lamas. As with Gomtsül, some Kagyü lineages played central roles in Tibet's secular history.

The four senior lineages are those that branched off from the original Dakpo Kagyü, while the eight junior lineages branched off from one of these four, the Phakdru.

Dakpo Kagyü

|

Tsalpa Barom Phakdru Karma

|

Drigung Taklung Trophu Drukpa Martsang Yelpa Yasang Shuksep

The senior lineages are the Tsalpa, Barom, Phakdru, and Karma, although this is a simplification, ignoring lineages such as that of Gampopa's pupil Chökyi Yungdrung.[48] The Barom Kagyü, founded by Darma Wangchuk (1127–99),[49] is not as historically significant, and its teachings are not represented in this volume.

Lama Shang and the Tsalpa Kagyü

Lama Shang (1122–93), also known as Tsöndrü Drakpa,[50] was already an advanced practitioner when in 1157—five years after Gampopa's death—he became a pupil of Gomtsül, who was only six years his senior. Lama Shang had already mastered caṇḍālī under Mal Yerwapa in the lineage of Milarepa's pupil Drigom Repa.[51]

Lama Shang founded a monastery at Tsal, near Lhasa, hence the name of his lineage. Continuing Gomtsül's secular responsibilities, he established a militia, which he used to impose his authority. Lama Shang's successors ruled the entire Lhasa region.

Lama Shang produced a significant body of literature. The third text in this volume is his *Ultimate Supreme Path of the Mahāmudrā*, which was written in verse. Jamgön Kongtrül included this in his *Treasury of Instructions*, a compilation of important texts from throughout Tibetan Buddhism. However the quality of his edition is poor, with numerous lines missing and two pages written out of order. Prior to the Tibetan companion volume to the present work, that edition was unfortunately the only one readily available to Tibetans.

The second text in this volume, the *Unrivaled Instructions of Shang Rinpoché*, is also an early text from the Tsalpa Kagyü lineage. The author is Shönu Lha of Pangshong Lhari Monastery. There is no biographical information on this author other than that he was a pupil of Lharipa Namkha Ö, presumably the founder of Lhari Monastery, whose teacher was Lama Shang. Therefore Shönu Lha would have been active in the first half of the thirteenth century.

This text is an early example of the mahāmudrā preliminary practices. Here they consist of the contemplation of the preciousness of a human life capable of practicing the Dharma, its impermanence, the suffering of samsara, and therefore the urgency to practice. This is followed by the meditation and mantra of Vajrasattva for purification, making a mandala offering for accumulation of merit, and prayers for blessing from the guru. The subsequent instructions for meditation are direct and simple advice on resting in the natural state of mind. The text does not mention the successive stages of meditation found in later mahāmudrā texts, such as that of Dakpo Tashi Namgyal.

Phakdru Kagyü and the Eight Junior Schools

Dorjé Gyaltsen, or Phakmo Drupa (1110–70), had studied and practiced in many traditions before he became a pupil of Gampopa at the age of forty-one, just two years before Gampopa died. Although he spent his later years in solitary hermitages, he attracted a great number of pupils and established the Densathil Monastery, where his relics were later enshrined. The Phakdru lineage became historically important, its dynasty ruling Tibet in the fourteenth and fifteenth centuries.

Eight "junior" Kagyü lineages derived from eight of Phakmo Drupa's pupils. The Taklung Kagyü, which had a period of secular power, had a major monastery and lineage in both central and eastern Tibet, though Nyingma and Rechung Kagyü teachings have become their principal practice. The Yelpa, Trophu, and Yasang continue to have a few monasteries and tulkus in Tibet. The Martsang[52] monasteries were forcibly made Geluk in the 1600s, but its Mahāmudrā and incarnation lineage survives. The Shuksep became a Nyingma tradition, with a famous nunnery. The two "junior" lineages that are currently most active and who are represented in this volume are the Drigung and Drukpa, which will be described in more detail.

Drigung Kagyü

Jikten Sumgön, or Drigungpa (1143–1217), was a pupil of Phakmo Drupa during the last three years of the latter's life[53] and founded Drigung Monastery, which gained secular power. The Drigung succession was initially hereditary but became an incarnate line beginning with two brothers, Könchok Rinchen (1590–1654) and Chökyi Drakpa (1595–1654). These were the first Chetsang and Chungtsang tulkus, the principal Drigung lamas—or Khyapgön Rinpochés—through to the present day.

A group of four Drigung Kagyü texts appears in this volume. In 1226, nine years after Drigungpa's death, Sherap Jungné (1187–1241), who was Drigungpa's nephew and successor, compiled two texts of aphorisms, the second a supplement to the first. To this are added two appendixes, which may be by Sherap Jungné or by a pupil of his, and together these four texts, collectively entitled the *Single Viewpoint*, represent Drigungpa's view on an array of subjects. These are unusual and controversial texts, as each aphorism is basically a rejection of someone else's view. Though the holders of these views are not mentioned by name, the views are often those of Sakya authors. Sakya Paṇḍita (1182–1251), who had met Sherap Jungné in the year before the writing of the *Single Viewpoint*, wrote his major work on the three levels of views specifically to refute the views propounded in this text.

However, Drigungpa also rejected one of Lama Shang's views propounded in the text included in this volume. Lama Shang states that some people who receive a formal empowerment do not receive it, while others may receive it without undergoing the ceremony. According to the twenty-sixth viewpoint in Sherap Jungné's supplementary text, Drigungpa took exception to this position. Drigungpa had little tolerance for moral ambivalence; for example, he rejected the possibility that sorcery could be classed as a good action. Drigungpa also held extraordinary views on the universal nature of the monastic vows and held a low opinion of termas. The practices of many present-day Drigung Kagyüpas are primarily derived from termas and also include wrathful rites of sorcery, but nevertheless, and in spite of the cryptic nature of certain passages, the texts are still regarded in the Drigung Kagyü as fundamentally important because of their numerous astute and striking observations. For example, one aphorism states that the most important results of our actions are experienced in this life rather than the next. To those familiar with the teaching on karma, this seems at first a strange remark. What it points to, however, is the commonsense observation that our practice should bring manifest results, such as less anger, increased patience, insight, and so on.

A number of commentaries in the tradition explain these pithy statements. The translation here has been guided in particular by Sherap Jungné's own commentary to his texts. The very title is problematic, as *dgongs* can have various meanings. Generally it is a polite term for "thought" but can mean view, realization, opinion, intention, meaning, or even intended meaning. This ambiguity is also a feature of its Sanskrit equivalent *abhiprāya*, which can mean intention, opinion, purpose, or meaning.[54] The basic meaning of the word is "approach," and in a Buddhist context it is related to the Pali term *adhippāya*, which can mean both intention and meaning. The title is often translated into English as the *One Intention*, and there are Drigung Kagyü lamas who explain that it refers to the Buddha's one intention of benefiting beings, and there are also those who believe it should be translated as "one mind." It has also been translated as "one import" and "one intent." I have followed Lamchen Gyalpo Rinpoche's view that, in this title, the meaning is closer to "view" than to "intention." It is Drigungpa's intention to demonstrate that not only were there no inconsistencies in the Buddha's teaching, but also there were no differing versions or viewpoints intended for different levels of individuals. I had long chosen "viewpoint," but was uncomfortable as it was too close to "opinion" in feel and tried to cover both sides with "intended meaning." However, "viewpoint" seems to concur with the use of *dgongs pa* in the texts themselves, which declare that "the viewpoint of the precious Dharma Lord Drigungpa is the single viewpoint of all conquerors."

Drukpa Kagyü

The Drukpa Kagyü originates with Lingré Pema Dorjé (1128–88), who started out as a Rechung Kagyüpa. Therefore, he initially had a tantric consort, but in 1165 he became a pupil of Phakmo Drupa, who told him to separate from her. He subsequently practiced peripatetically around Central Tibet. He performed rites to ensure victory for Lama Shang in his battles, and in his last years he was the abbot of Naphur Monastery.

His pupil Tsangpa Gyaré (1161–1211)[55] founded Namdruk Monastery, from which the Drukpa lineage derives its name. Though there have been various branches of the Drukpa Kagyü lineage, the hereditary lineage of Tsangpa Gyaré's monastery became the principal succession. After Künga Paljor (1428–76) declared himself the rebirth of Tsangpa Gyaré and became known as the Second Drukchen, there were both hereditary and incarnation successions.

The Fourth Drukchen, Pema Karpo (1527–92), proved to be one of the great authors of Tibetan Buddhism. One of Pema Karpo's short texts on mahāmudrā, still widely used for meditation instruction, is included in this volume.

A dispute over the recognition of the Fifth Drukchen split the Drukpa Kagyü. The two opposed candidates, even into adulthood, were Paksam Wangpo (1593–1641) and Shapdrung Ngawang Namgyal (1594–1691). The latter was also the hereditary holder of the Drukpa lineage, but as a result of the opposition of the king of Tsang, Shapdrung retreated to the borderlands and created both the independent country of Bhutan and the "southern Drukpa school," which is still the official religion of that country.[56] The successive incarnations of Paksam Wangpo are the Drukchen incarnations of the northern, or Tibetan, Drukpa Kagyü.

Karma Kagyü

Düsum Khyenpa (1110–93) was from a hereditary Nyingma family and had mastered Yamāntaka to the degree that, between the ages of ten and fifteen, he could cause death with its sorcery. He met Gampopa and Gomtsül in 1139[57] and subsequently received instructions from Rechungpa. He then practiced meditation with exceptional perseverance and disregard for personal comfort for many years in various locations.

In 1159, six years after Gampopa's death, he returned to his homeland in east Tibet, and twenty-six years later he established there the foundation for a widespread school by founding Karma Monastery. In 1189, at the age of seventy-nine, he returned to Central Tibet and founded Tsurphu Monastery. He said that he had returned to fulfill a request by Gomtsül, who had died twenty years earlier, and to persuade the sixty-seven-year-old Lama Shang to terminate his martial exploits. Both lamas died four years later.

Düsum Khyenpa was the first in a succession of Karmapa rebirths, marking the beginning of the now ubiquitous *tulku* system of incarnate lamas. Gampopa, Lama Shang, and Düsum Khyenpa had recognized lamas and children as rebirths of great masters, but the Second Karmapa, Karma Pakshi (1204–83), was the first to inherit the monasteries and authority of his predecessor. He was born eighteen years after Düsum Khyenpa's death and was not recognized as the rebirth of the First Karmapa until he became a pupil of the holder of the Karma Kagyü lineage.[58]

The Third Karmapa, Rangjung Dorjé (1284–1339), established a Karma Kagyü canon of practice and study, introducing a number of teachings from other lineages. He performed the enthronement ceremony for the thirteen-year-old emperor Togan Temur (r. 1333–70), the last Mongol to rule China, who was ousted by the founder of the Ming dynasty.

Of all the Karmapas, Rangjung Dorjé has produced the most important body of literary works. This volume presents two of his short works. The first, his *Mahāmudrā Prayer*, is a popular text for teaching the meaning of mahāmudrā and has been translated elsewhere numerous times. The translation here has been made to accord with the commentary of the Eighth Situ that closes the present volume. The other text is less well known: *Instructions for the Mahāmudrā Innate Union*. This practical manual for meditating on mahāmudrā guides the practitioner through the stages of *śamatha* (stability) and *vipaśyanā* (insight). The Ninth Karmapa would later create a series of these manuals, including *Mahāmudrā: The Ocean of Definitive Meaning*.[59] That text and Dakpo Tashi Namgyal's *Mahāmudrā: The Moonlight* are the two most extensive mahāmudrā manuals used in the Karma Kagyü.

The Fourth Karmapa, Rölpai Dorjé (1340–83), recognized his principal pupil and successor, Khachö Wangpo (1350–1405), as the rebirth of Rangjung Dorjé's pupil Drakpa Sengé (1283–1349), thus instituting the succession of Shamarpa tulkus, who were often successors and teachers to successive Karmapas.

The Ming emperor Yong Le (1360–1425; r. 1403–25) presented the Fifth Karmapa, Deshin Shekpa (1384–1415), with a bejeweled black hat, which has since played an important role in blessing ceremonies by all the Karmapas. The Karmapa, however, turned down Yong Le's offer to use his armies to give the Karma Kagyü dominion over Tibet. Emperor Yong Le also bestowed the title Khenting Tai Situ on one of the Fifth Karmapa's pupils, Chökyi Gyaltsen (1377–1488), who became the first in the series of Situ incarnations.

During the period of Karma Kagyü engagement with the Ming dynasty, the Ninth Karmapa, Wangchuk Dorjé (1555–1603), identified the Sixth Shamarpa, Chökyi Wangchuk (1584–1630), who would succeed him as the head of the Kagyü lineage. Although his life was not long, Chökyi Wangchuk had a great reputation as a scholar and debater. He is the author of one of the works in this volume, the *Quintessence of Nectar*. That text on the six Dharmas of Nāropa includes recitations as well as instruction. It is the very text that Karma Kagyü practitioners use in the school's traditional three-year retreats.

Tselé Natsok Rangdröl (b. 1608) was a pupil of both the Sixth Shamarpa and the Tenth Karmapa, Chöying Dorjé (1604–74). He composed the eighth text in this volume, *The Bright Torch*. He was recognized as the rebirth of a lama as a child, and he had both Kagyü and Nyingma teachers.

By the end of the seventeenth century, the Karma Kagyü had lost its political hegemony in Central Tibet to the Fifth Dalai Lama, so that their strongholds in the eastern regions of the Tibetan plateau, such as in the kingdom of Dergé, became increasingly important for them. The Eighth Situ, Tenpai Nyinjé (1700–74)—also named Chökyi Jungné—revitalized the Karma Kagyü in many ways. At the age of twenty-seven, under the patronage of the Dergé monarchy, he established Palpung Monastery, which became, in practice, the most important Kagyü monastery in Tibet. Situ Chökyi Jungné had secular authority within the Dergé kingdom, was honored by the Chinese emperor Chi'en Lung (1735–96), and taught at his court. He introduced the transmission of many practices and promoted the philosophical viewpoint prevalent in the Jonang tradition, which the Fifth Dalai Lama had suppressed in Central Tibet.[60] Tai Situ Chökyi Jungné also oversaw the preparation of a new edition of the canon, the Dergé Kangyur and Tengyur. He was one of the most prolific authors in the Kagyü tradition and even made new translations from Sanskrit. The seventh text in our volume, his commentary upon the *Mahāmudrā Prayer* written four hundred years earlier by the Third Karmapa, is one of Tai Situ Chökyi Jungné's earlier works. He wrote it at the age of thirty-three, around the time he was establishing Palpung Monastery, commencing what was to become the modern era of the Kham-based Karma Kagyü.[61]

Acknowledgments

It has been a great privilege to take part in this visionary work of Thupten Jinpa, whose intelligence and motivation is only matched by his patience, which had to be vast to encompass my apparently never-ending twiddling, three computer deaths, prevarication, and delays. Khenchen Thrangu Rinpoche, who it has been an enlightening delight to translate for over two decades, chose these texts, providing me with a challenge on several levels to live up to Samuel Beckett's dictum: "Fail better." Without the beneficence of Eric Colombel's Tsadra Foundation, I would not have been able to even take my first step on this far longer than expected road. I am particularly indebted to Gene Smith and all the workers at the Tibetan Buddhist Resource Center (TBRC), who have made the life of a translator many gigahertz easier. Many have helped me to be able to reach the stage where I could attempt this work, in particular Akong Rinpoche, the late Tenpa Gyaltsen Negi, and Professor Richard Gombrich. I am thankful for the help in understanding various passages that I have received from Alak Zenkar Rinpoche, Khenchen Thrangu Rinpoche, Lamchen Gyalpo Rinpoche, Yongey Mingyur Rinpoche, Karl Brunnhölzl, Sarah Harding, Edward Henning, and Lodro Sangpo. I am also thankful I had the indispensable guide of two previous translations, the *Lamp of Mahamudra* by Erik Pema Kunsang and *Mahāmudrā Teachings of the Supreme Siddhas* by Lama Sherab Dorjé. And I have greatly benefited from the works of such scholars as Alexander Berzin, Karl Brunnhölzl, Hubert Decleer, Elizabeth English, David Gray, Christopher Lindtner, Dan Martin, Kurtis Schaeffer, Jikido Takasaki, and Shiniichi Tsuda. In particular, thanks to David Kittelstrom, the editor, who with assistance from Lea Groth-Wilson and Laura Cunningham has been on the receiving end of this slow-in-coming and wayward work. And thanks to Emily Bower for support and encouragement in bringing it to its conclusion.

Technical Notes

THE TIBETAN TITLE of the volume translated here is *Mnyam med bka' brgyud lugs kyi phyag rgya chen po dang 'brel ba'i chos skor*, which means *Mahāmudrā and Related Teachings of the Peerless Kagyü Tradition*. It is a special anthology of key texts of the Kagyü school developed specifically for *The Library of Tibetan Classics* and its Tibetan equivalent, *Bod kyi gtsug lag gces btus*. Bracketed numbers embedded in the text refer to page numbers in the critical and annotated Tibetan edition published in New Delhi in modern book format by the Institute of Tibetan Classics (2008, ISBN 81-89165-05-4) as volume 5 of the *Bod kyi gtsug lag gces btus* series. In preparing our translation, the Institute of Tibetan Classics edition served as our primary source, with reference also to other editions of the individual texts.

The conventions for phonetic transcription of Tibetan words are those developed by the Institute of Tibetan Classics and Wisdom Publications. These reflect approximately the pronunciation of words by a modern Central Tibetan; Tibetan speakers from Ladakh, Kham, or Amdo, not to mention Mongolians, might pronounce the words quite differently. Transliterations of the phoneticized Tibetan terms and names used in the text can be found in the table that follows the text. Sanskrit diacritics are used throughout except for Sanskrit terms that have been naturalized into English, such as samsara, nirvana, sutra, stupa, Mahayana, and mandala.

Pronunciation of Tibetan phonetics
ph and *th* are aspirated *p* and *t*, as in *pet* and *tip*.
ö is similar to the *eu* in the French *seul*.
ü is similar to the *ü* in the German *füllen*.
ai is similar to the *e* in *bet*.
é is similar to the *e* in *prey*.

Pronunciation of Sanskrit

Palatal *ś* and retroflex *ṣ* are similar to the English unvoiced *sh*.
c is an unaspirated *ch* similar to the *ch* in *chill*.
The vowel *ṛ* is similar to the American *r* in *pretty*.
ñ is somewhat similar to the nasalized *ny* in *canyon*.
ṅ is similar to the *ng* in *sing* or *anger*.

Abbreviated References Used in Notes

In the notes, some works that come up frequently are cited by the short references listed below. See bibliography for the full publication details of these works.

Abhidharmakośa	Vasubandhu, *Treasury of the Abhidharma*. Toh 4089
Abhisamayālaṃkāra	Maitreyanātha, *Ornament of Realization*. Toh 3786
Analysis of Realization	Atiśa, *Abhisamayavibhaṅga*. Toh 1490
Blue Annals	Gö Lotsāwa, *The Blue Annals*, trans. by George N. Roerich
Bodhicaryāvatāra	Śāntideva, *Entering the Conduct of a Bodhisattva*. Toh 3871
Brief Cakrasaṃvara Empowerment	Vajraghaṇṭa, *Cakrasaṃvaraṣekaprakriyopadeśa*. Toh 1431
Compendium of Practices	Āryadeva, *Lamp of the Compendium of Practices* (*Caryāmelāpakapradīpa*). Toh 1803
Ears of Grain	Abhayākaragupta, *Ears of Grain Practice Instructions* (*Saṃpuṭatantraṭīkā*). Toh 1198
Enlightenment of Vairocana	*Enlightenment of Vairocana* (*Mahāvairocanābhisambodhi*). Toh 494
Five Stages	Nāgārjuna, *Pañcakrama*. Toh 1802
Guhyasamāja Tantra	*Guhyasamāja Root Tantra*. Toh 442
[*Guhyasamāja*] *Uttaratantra*	*Latter Guhyasamāja Tantra*. Toh 443

Hevajra Tantra	*Hevajratantra*. Toh 417
Hevajrapiṇḍārthaṭīkā	Vajragarbha, *An Extensive Commentary on the Condensed Meaning of the Hevajra*. Toh 1180
Illuminating Lamp	Candrakīrti, *Pradīpoddyotanaṭīkā*. Toh 1785
Lamp for the Path	Atiśa, *Lamp for the Path to Enlightenment* (*Bodhipathapradīpa*). Toh 3948
Lamp of the Three Ways	Tripiṭakamāla, *Nayatrayapradīpa*. Toh 3707
Mahāmudrā Tilaka	*Mahāmudrā Tilaka Tantra*. Toh 420
Mandala Rites of Guhyasamāja	Nāgārjuna, *Guhyasamājamaṇḍalavidhi*. Toh 1798
Oral Transmission	Buddhajñānapada, *Oral Transmission Entitled "Meditation on the True Nature of the Two Stages"* (*Dvikramatattvabhāvanāmukhāgama*)
Perfect Lamp	Bhavyakīrti, *The Perfectly Illuminating Lamp* (*Pradīpodyotanābhisaṃdhiṭīkā*). Toh 1793
Praise to the Dharmadhātu	Nāgārjuna, *Dharmadhātustava*. Toh 1118
Primordial Buddha	*Primordial Buddha Kālacakra Tantra* (*Paramādibuddhoddhṛtaśrīkālacakratantra*). Toh 362
Root Verses on the Middle Way	Nāgārjuna, *Mūlamadhyamakakārika*. Toh 3824
Saṃpuṭa	*Tantra of True Union* (*Saṃpuṭatantra*). Toh 381
Saṃvarodaya	*Saṃvarodaya Tantra*. Toh 373
Saṃvarodayapañjikā	Ratnarakṣita, *Commentary on the Saṃvarodaya Tantra*. Toh 1420
Sarvamaṇḍala	*Tantra of All Mandalas*. Toh 806
Seven Yogas	Vitapāda, *Seven Yogas: A Treatise on the Four Empowerments* (*Yogasaptacaturabhiṣekhaprakaraṇa*). Toh 1875
Stainless Light	Puṇḍarīka, *Stainless Light: A Commentary on the Kālacakra Tantra* (*Vimalaprabhā*). Toh 1347

Sublime Continuum	Maitreyanātha, *Mahayana Treatise on the Sublime Continuum* (*Mahāyānottaranatra Śāstra*). Toh 4024
Sūtrālaṃkāra	Maitreyanātha, *Ornament of the Mahayana Sutras*. Toh 4020
Tattvasaṃgraha	*Compendium of Truths*. Toh 479
Treasury of Dohas	Saraha, *Dohakoṣagīti*. Toh 2224
Truly Valid Instructions	Nāropa, *Ājñāsaṃyakpramāṇa*. Toh 2331
Vajraḍāka	*Vajraḍāka Tantra* (*Vajraḍākatantra*). Toh 370
Vajra Garland	*Vajra Garland Explanatory Tantra* (*Vajramālābhidhānatantra*). Toh 445
Vajra Mandala	*Vajra Mandala Adornment Tantra* (*Vajramaṇḍalālaṃkāratantra*). Toh 490
Vajra Pinnacle	*Vajra Pinnacle Tantra* (*Vajraśekharatantra*). Toh 480
Vajra Tent	*Vajra Tent Tantra* (*Ḍākinīvajrapañjarātantra*). Toh 419
Vajrāvali	Abhayākaragupta, *The Vajra Garland of Mandala Rituals* (*Vajrāvalimaṇḍalasādhana*). Toh 3140
White Lotus Sutra	*White Lotus of the Holy Dharma Sutra* (*Saddharmapuṇḍarikasūtra*). Toh 113

1. A String of Pearls

A Collection of Dharma Lectures[62]

GAMPOPA (1079–1153)

I pay homage to the sacred gurus.

·1·

THIS DHARMA TEACHING can be given to anyone.

To have genuine Dharma practice, first meditate on impermanence. Otherwise, your Dharma practice might become merely an aid to your ambitions for this life.

Why should we meditate on impermanence? To turn our minds away from this life. Meditating on impermanence makes us realize that all the phenomena of appearance and existence,[63] of samsara and nirvana, are impermanent. As a result, the mind does not get caught up in this life. This is the purpose of meditation on impermanence. If your mind hasn't turned away from this life, then your meditation on impermanence has been without purpose.

First, turn your mind away from this life by meditating on impermanence. Then meditate on the faults of samsara. The purpose of meditation on the faults of samsara is to turn the mind away from the entirety of samsara.

When your mind has turned away from samsara, meditate on bodhicitta. First there is meditation on *relative bodhicitta*—wishing, from the depths of your heart, that all beings will have happiness, freedom from suffering, and complete buddhahood. Then view everything you do as being for the welfare of all beings. Have no concern for your own desires but develop an aspiration with the Mahayana perspective of benefiting others as your goal. That is how you meditate on relative bodhicitta.

Meditation on *ultimate bodhicitta* is simply remaining in the mind as it naturally is, a state in which all thoughts of perceiver and perceived, self and other, are intrinsically devoid of reality. Practicing in that way during each of the four kinds of behavior[64] is what is called *meditation on ultimate bodhicitta.* Practicing in that way brings the realization and attainment of ultimate bodhicitta.

There is no Dharma other than this.

·2·

[2] This Dharma teaching can be given to anyone.

You must engage, right now, in lengthy contemplation. Think! This life is impermanent. Consider how it is fleeting, like lightning in the sky, bubbles in water, or dewdrops on the grass, so that whatever you gain in it will be of no benefit. Keep this thought in the very center of your heart.

With this thought in the center of your heart, practice. You must follow the perfect, unmistaken path until you reach buddhahood. What is this perfect, unmistaken path? It is taught to have three parts: the preliminaries, the main part, and the conclusion.

Begin with the preliminaries. First think, "May all beings have happiness and freedom from suffering, and may they attain complete buddhahood."

Whatever main practice you then do, make that part of the path through the six perfections. For example, if you give just one thing to a beggar, that itself is generosity. Giving it in a gentle manner is correct conduct. Not generating an affliction, even if the beggar is ungrateful, is patience. Giving it quickly is diligence. Offering the gift without being distracted from love, compassion, and bodhicitta is meditation. Knowing that the recipient, the giver, the gift, and the result are all just a dream or an illusion is wisdom. Be certain that your main practice has the six perfections.

In the conclusion, you seal [your practice] with complete objectlessness. In that way everything is taken onto the path, because everything has the same nature, which is clarity and the lack of real existence.

Thus, you practice in this way: begin with the Mahayana perspective, which is to focus your mind upon the welfare of beings. It is important to develop the Mahayana perspective because buddhahood can only be attained through the Mahayana; not even the slightest fraction of buddhahood can be attained through the lower vehicles.

The main practice is the complete and unmistaken path of the perfections.

The concluding practice is the alchemy of objectlessness, through which you understand that everything is like space. That knowledge prevents propensities (*vāsana*) from being established in the *ālaya*. When propensities are not accumulated in the ālaya, there will be no basis for karma. Free of that basis, you will not be compelled to follow good or bad karma and will therefore not be reborn. That is what is called buddhahood. That knowledge is the perfect, unmistaken path. [3]

Even when on this perfect, unmistaken path, if you don't practice it in order to attain the accomplishment of all benefits, then merely sleeping on the least of beds, consuming minimal food—such as drops of water—and controlling the length of your breaths will not do you any good. Therefore, summon the confidence to practice diligently, starting now.

There is no Dharma other than that.

·3·

This Dharma teaching can be given to anyone.

We need to practice both accumulation and purification. It is important to gather the accumulations and purify the obscurations. This life is like a flash of lightning in the sky, and so on, and thus we don't know when we will depart and vanish. Therefore, it's important that in the depths of your heart you are free from needing anything and that you meditate on relative and ultimate bodhicitta. Meditating on impermanence is vital because that develops relative bodhicitta.

Meditate on love and compassion by [contemplating] the faults of samsara. Then disregard your own benefit and accomplish whatever benefit you can for others.

To attain buddhahood, you must first want to benefit beings. Then, during the intermediate stage, until you attain buddhahood, you must continue to benefit beings. In the end, once you have achieved buddhahood, you will do nothing but benefit beings.

Therefore, first you meditate on death and impermanence; in the middle, you meditate on the faults of samsara; and in the end, with love, compassion, and bodhicitta, you do nothing other than benefit beings.

We need to combine three things in order to meditate on ultimate bodhicitta: (1) training in previous lives, (2) our own efforts, and (3) the blessing of the guru. Had you no training in a previous life, you would not have obtained the freedoms and opportunities of a higher existence perfectly endowed with seven qualities.[65] You must have trained in previous lives, during which you continuously gathered the accumulations.

If you make no effort, you will be left behind on the path of laziness and fail to reach the path of the noble ones.

Without the blessing of the guru, you will develop no qualities; nothing will come to you. Even if something does come, it will fade away. Your merit will be like a dammed river. It is as taught in the scriptures: [4]

> If you have no guru, there will be no end to existence.
> If you do not have oars,
> your boat will never reach the far shore.[66]

Therefore, you first need to have trained [in previous lives]; then you must practice through your own effort; and, as the ultimate commitment on the path of the Mantrayāna, you must rely on a genuine guru; so keep your commitments carefully.

Merely knowing the words of teachings is of no benefit; that is like a parrot reciting. Every guru has gained their accomplishment through their practice, too. Through our devotion to the guru, we too can receive blessing, and through correct practice we can gain various signs of accomplishment.

Nāropa had devotion for his guru Tilopa and was his pupil for twelve years. [Tilopa] did not actually give him any teaching, but because [Nāropa] revered his guru and did whatever his guru told him to do, he attained various signs of accomplishment. Thus, when there is a genuine guru and a worthy pupil, all qualities can be instantaneously accomplished.

First there is peace and stability; in the middle there is clarity and nonthought; and in the end there is complete freedom from all conceptual elaboration. It is taught that you will then rest, like the continuous flow of a river, in the meaning that is like space. The scriptures also say:

> Complete buddhahood in an instant;
> one instant makes the difference.[67]

Therefore, it's important to simply practice and have faith. If you haven't been doing this, keep in mind that when the time comes when you use your hand as a pillow and have no appetite for anything but water,[68] nothing will help you except the Dharma that you've practiced.

Therefore, it's taught that it's important to practice with effort, starting now.

There is no Dharma other than that.

·4·

This Dharma teaching can be given to anyone.

In order to practice the Dharma purely, we must be aware that there is no time for leisure in this life, and we must be totally dedicated to [the Dharma].

It is vital to meditate on love and compassion. You develop them in three ways: (1) through focusing on beings, (2) through focusing on phenomena, and (3) through objectlessness. The first of these, focusing on beings, means developing love, compassion, and bodhicitta. [5] You focus on all beings, on how they suffer from not having realized the true nature, and think that you must somehow free them from suffering and help them meet happiness and attain complete buddhahood. None of your actions should be for your own benefit but should be for the benefit of "the lords"—all beings. It is the lords, all beings, who enable you to attain complete buddhahood; therefore you must focus on beings. If your mind disregards beings, you won't be able to attain liberation and omniscience. It is taught that we should deeply cherish the love, compassion, and bodhicitta that are focused on beings, who are of the greatest importance.

Developing bodhicitta through focusing on phenomena: All phenomena are but dreams and illusions. Therefore, see whatever action you do as a dream or as an illusion. From the scriptures:

> If you have meditated that all phenomena,
> which are like illusions, *are* like illusions,
> you will attain buddhahood, which is like an illusion.[69]

When you know that all phenomena are like dreams and illusions, anger will have no reality, and you will be spontaneously freed from it. Similarly, know that all attachment and aversion are like dreams and illusions, so that your mind will never engage in attachment or aversion.

If you see all actions, such as lying down and sitting, as like dreams and illusions, then your attachment to the reality of appearances will easily cease. This practice will enable you to easily attain the supreme accomplishment during your lifetime. This is called *bodhicitta through focusing on phenomena.*

The bodhicitta with no object is free of all conceptual elaboration. It is the practice that nothing has an existent essence. According to Guru Atiśa:

> All those mistaken in the realization of this meaning are like a deer caught in a trap. Oh pity! If they do not realize that, there is nowhere to go . . .[70]

If you practice the experience of there being neither coming nor going, with no conceptual elaboration of a meditator and meditation, [the bodhicitta] will come.

Those are three ways of developing love, compassion, and bodhicitta. Practice them in this way.

There is no Dharma other than that.

·5·

This Dharma teaching can be given to anyone.

If we sever our ties to this life and always have genuine faith, then every Dharma practice will be profound.

There is a verse taught by the Buddha that appears at the conclusion of the water-torma offering:

> Perform no bad actions,
> perfect the practice of good actions, [6]
> and tame your own mind:
> That is the teaching of the Buddha.[71]

In addition to avoiding all bad actions, we must practice accumulating good actions and tame our minds. When we have tamed our own minds, that will be buddhahood. It is said that all we ever need to practice is that one Dharma teaching. From the *Wisdom upon Passing Away Sutra*:

> All things are impermanent, so meditate on the understanding that is free of attachment to anything. If the mind is realized, that is wisdom. Therefore, meditate on the understanding that buddhahood is not to be sought anywhere else.[72]

Thus, things are impermanent. Your inner cognition is impermanent because it changes. All things that are outer appearances—old people, young people, brothers, sisters, spouse, wealth, material things, and everything else—have no permanence. You have to practice perceiving that nothing has reality. Even your own body is impermanent, because it is only on loan from the four elements—a loan that is easily repaid. Therefore, have no attachment to anything, because all things are impermanent.

It's taught that wisdom means understanding the mind. This is what's known as the realization of the nature of the mind. It is also called knowing the inseparability of self and others, or of appearance and emptiness, or of the ultimate and the relative, or of space and wisdom.

You will not find this meaning if you search for it anywhere else. It is only known and realized by the mind looking at itself. That is what is called buddhahood; you will see the unseen—your own mind, which you have never seen before. [Buddhahood] is the result of realizing your own mind. That is what is meant by not searching for buddhahood elsewhere.

When you practice in this way—leaving behind all concerns for this life—you will accomplish the goal of any Dharma gateway that you enter. This is why it's taught that it's so important for your practice to be free of ambitions for this life.

If you teach the Dharma while having goals in this life, you will just be a wicked person who is able to talk about the Dharma. Therefore, a practice that is unmixed with this life is of the greatest importance.

There is no Dharma other than that.

·6·

[7] This Dharma teaching can be given to anyone.

We individuals who are sincerely practicing the Dharma need to think a little. It's taught:

> Life is short, and there are many things to know.
> We do not even know how long our lives will be.
> Eagerly obtain what you wish for,
> like a goose drawing milk from water.[73]

Life is short, so we don't have much time for leisure. Compared to the heavens of the Four Great Kings and so on up to Akaniṣṭha, and compared to life in the hells, human life is short. The shortest human lifespan is here in Jambudvīpa, where those over sixty are living on borrowed time.

There is such a vast number of ways to know that life is short, we would never reach the end of studying them. The shortest Dharma practice is the water-torma offering to the *mukhajvālas*,[74] but I've heard that a man over in Ü has written a list of all the classes of mukhajvālas that is so long it fills an entire chest. Therefore, there is no end to learning. If there's that much to [know about] the mukhajvālas, the shortest Dharma teaching, it goes without saying that for other teachings there will be even more.

Since there is no end to knowledge, we can't master it all. Therefore, we must obtain what is essential, like a goose drawing milk from water. When cows cross the Ganges River in India, they drip milk into the water. A goose's beak contains yeast, so that when it stirs that water, lumps of milk appear, which the goose can then pick out and eat. We should eagerly obtain what we want in the same way. In other words, we should extract the teaching that we desire from the diversity of knowledge.

We practice this teaching in order to gain control of our own minds and make them capable. Those who are attracted to generation and completion practices must have a mind capable [of practicing] them. This means that the mind must be capable [of practicing] the channels, winds, and drops, the relative and ultimate, the mahāmudrā, and dzokchen.

What is a capable mind? When you have gained the realization that the mind is the true nature, there will be spontaneous compassion, the realization of the sameness of oneself and others, and little attachment to appearances as real. You need to practice rigorously until that realization arises. [8] If you impulsively see things as real, it will be hard for you to obtain a happy rebirth, let alone buddhahood. It is said in the scriptures, within the *Hevajra Tantra*:

> There is no meditation and no meditator;
> there is no deity and there is no mantra;
> the deity and mantra truly reside
> in the nature that is free of elaboration.[75]

There is no Dharma other than that.

·7·

This Dharma teaching can be given to anyone.

Those who are bases [for the Dharma] must turn their minds away from this life and, forsaking their own desires, see whatever they do as being for the sake of beings, with no regard for themselves.

Buddhahood is attained through "the lords"—beings. You must practice developing love and compassion toward beings and think, "I do so wish that beings could become free from suffering and attain happiness."

To summarize and analyze: In the mahāmudrā tradition, your practice must always be free from three faults. Your practice must be free from the fault of appearances, the fault of emptiness, and the fault of birthlessness.

What is such a practice like? Practicing without believing in the reality of appearances is to be without the *fault of appearances*. When you practice, see all appearances as dreams or illusions, and see all appearances as devoid of intrinsic natures. When you know that appearances have no reality, you will understand that suffering has no reality. Suffering will not actually disappear spontaneously, but it will be transformed into Dharma. Simply knowing that the appearances of self and others have no reality is to become free from the fault of appearances.

Freedom from the *fault of emptiness* is said to be freedom from attachment to emptiness. [9] If you think, "This is emptiness," or "I am going to realize emptiness," then there will be a desire for emptiness, which is an error. When you know that the afflictions and thoughts are empty and that the objects that cause suffering are emptiness, they will be birthless. That is freedom from the fault of emptiness.

Freedom from the *fault of birthlessness* is when you do not alternate between appearances and emptiness. It is the knowledge that both appearances and emptiness are birthless. This is freedom from the fault of birthlessness, also known as *freedom from dualistic knowledge*.

In brief, freedom from the fault of appearances is freedom from attachment to the extreme of appearances. Freedom from the fault of emptiness is freedom from attachment to the extreme of emptiness. Freedom from the fault of birthlessness is freedom from attachment to the extreme of dualistic appearances.

According to the mahāmudrā tradition, the qualities of the three *kāyas* are in these three freedoms from faults: freedom from the fault of appearances, freedom from the fault of emptiness, and freedom from the fault of birthlessness.

When there is freedom from the fault of appearances, the extreme of samsara ceases, and there is the union of appearances and emptiness, which is the *nirmāṇakāya* (emanation body).

When there is freedom from the fault of emptiness, you will not be a śrāvaka, nor be in a śrāvaka's state of peace, and so there will be the unceasing *saṃbhogakāya* (enjoyment body).

When there is freedom from the fault of birthlessness, the mind's continued desire for emptiness ceases, which is the birthless *dharmakāya* (Dharma body).

It is taught that the great brahman lord[76] explained this way of practice.

There is no Dharma other than that.

·8·

This Dharma teaching can be given to anyone.

We have no time for leisure in this life. We must continually exhort ourselves with the hook of mindfulness. We must put our trust in the guru and in the [Three] Jewels.

How do we know that this is so? Life is impermanent. Even were we to have the rare opportunity of a long life, we would still have little time for leisure.

No one other than the guru can teach us the path. All the buddhas in the three times rely upon a guru in order to achieve buddhahood, so it's important to depend upon a guru.

It's taught that:

> Before there is a guru,
> there is not even the name "buddha."[77]

Therefore, it's taught that we must depend upon gurus and listen to their teaching.

We must put our hopes in the refuges, the Three Jewels. We Dharma practitioners have no other refuge than the Jewels. We have to truly turn our minds to the Jewels. It's taught that if we do, we will definitely gain everything we need and wish for in this life and in future lives. When we have placed our trust in the guru and the Jewels, we should practice as is concisely described in the tradition of Aro Yeshé Jungné,[78] which teaches that we must practice these three words:

> Appearances, arising, are.[79]

What do these three words mean? If they mean "whatever *appears* and whatever *arises*," then if you look at whatever *appears*, they *are arising* as a variety, and when you look at yourself, it is your own mind that *arises* as a variety [of things] and *appears* as a variety [of things]. Both the *appearing* and *arising are* the thoughts of your own mind. Those very thoughts *are* your own mind, [10] and so as they *arise* from your own mind, they *are* the true nature *arising* as a variety. That *arising* as a variety of *appearances is* [nothing but] the birthless nature of your own mind.

The inseparability of mind and appearances is itself the nature of the mind. It is therefore an appearance of the mind. Meditate knowing that your own mind is birthless. Even though various things occur and are experienced, meditate that they are the birthless, empty dharmakāya. Practice that the mind's nature is birthless. There is no need to fear appearances, for they are your own mind.

Whatever bliss, clarity, or nonthought arises does not transcend the nature of the Mahayana's dharmakāya. Meditate on this without a moment's distraction.

If you believe all appearances are real, even though all appearances are the dharmakāya you will not transcend the three realms of samsara and could become wicked. Appearances are not like that.

Don't develop partial compassion. Even hawks and wolves have partial compassion, which therefore will be of no benefit to you. The compassion that parents have solely for their own children is not true compassion but attachment. Attachment can be mistaken for compassion. The wise should contemplate this carefully; being without [partial compassion] can be mistaken for nonattachment.[80] Therefore, don't develop a compassion that is comprised of partial love and compassion. Meditate on all beings impartially, and do so from the very depths of your heart. Don't let your practice transform into your own aversions and attachments.

As for practice, the dzokchen tradition has two lines of text that contain all practice:

1. The proposition that all the phenomena of appearance and existence[81] are your own mind
2. The attainment of certainty in the meaning of that [proposition]

This means that all the phenomena of appearance and existence are your own cognition. When you are happy, it's your own mind that is happy. When you are sad, it's your own mind that is sad. As it says in the scriptures:

> The higher and lower existences—the outer world and the inhabitants within—are your own mind.[82]

Practice in that way, with the conviction that all the phenomena of appearance and existence in samsara and nirvana are your own mind, [a conviction that] cannot be attained by just practicing this once a year. This is the nature of the practice:

1. Gain certainty that the nature of the mind is birthless. None of the phenomena of appearance and existence in samsara and nirvana have any independent existence whatsoever; they are by nature empty. Therefore, there is certainty that the nature of the mind is birthless.
2. When there isn't even attachment to [phenomena] as being dreams and illusions, [11] and knowing arises without partiality, then you will attain certainty in the unceasing play of the mind.
3. There is no birth or cessation in the essence of the mind and so it is not dual; it is like the ocean and its waves. This is certainty in the nonduality of these characteristics of the mind.
4. The intellect is liberated in the [mind's] essence because this nonduality isn't an object of the intellect and cannot be analyzed by logic. This is certainty in the nonduality of the essence.

What is the purpose of teaching those four reasons?

1. The birthless nature is taught because there is the danger of seeing appearances as independent.
2. The unceasing play is taught because of the danger of the extreme of emptiness.
3. The characteristics are taught to be nondual because of the danger of falling into the extreme of dualistic appearances.
4. Their essence is taught to be nondual because the thought "They are nondual" is the intellectual view.

Therefore, the four reasons negate those four extremes, and you must practice until the intellect's beliefs cease.

There is no Dharma other than that.

·9·

This Dharma teaching can be given to anyone.

To genuinely practice the Dharma, first abandon every single thought about this life. Those who wish to free themselves and all beings from the ocean of samsara must first meditate on impermanence and turn their minds away from this life. Meditation on the faults of samsara will turn the mind away from all phenomena of samsara. Then meditate on love, compassion, and bodhicitta.

If you do not train yourself and meditate, people will scorn you, and you will fail to develop experiences and realizations. Therefore, tame your mind as much as you can. Absorb every teaching you hear. If you can internally tame your own being, the inner signs will manifest externally.

To summarize, the practice of the three words "appearances, arising, are" will accomplish all experiences, realizations, and results.

Know that the diversity of appearances has no reality. Meditate on knowing that the unborn mind is the dharmakāya. Know that the diversity of sensations is also the birthless, empty dharmakāya.

Practicing without distraction will accomplish all experiences, realizations, and results. [12]

There is no Dharma other than that.

·10·

This Dharma teaching can be given to anyone.

To have genuine Dharma practice, you must turn the mind away from this world and meditate on love, compassion, and bodhicitta. Never neglect to think, "I will free all beings from suffering, give them happiness, and lead them to complete buddhahood."

It's important that you focus sincerely on the welfare of beings without any self-interest. Never forsake beings in your mind. If you do, you will abandon the Mahayana and your spiritual teacher, which will bring you great harm.

To follow your own desires and see others as enemies is not the right thing to do. The Mantrayāna teaches that all beings are male and female deities, so how could generating the afflictions toward deities ever be the right thing to do? In mahāmudrā and dzokchen, the appearances of your own mind are called the "light," "adornments," or "great display" of the dharmakāya, so how could generating afflictions toward the light or adornments of the dharmakāya mind ever be the right thing to do?

Dedicate all your positive actions of body, speech, and mind to the welfare of all beings, to the purification of their bodies, speech, and minds from obscurations. [Your good actions] should not be for the sake of your own mind alone.

To sum up, you have been accompanied by these [negative] propensities for a long time, and so you must practice resolutely until you know that anything that appears is an illusion. Because the five poisons are spontaneously present, it is important to practice resolutely until the afflictions are transformed into the path.

The end of time is a long way away, and you have to continue practicing until samsara is emptied. You have become habituated to propensities over a long period of time, and so you must practice until you know that everything that appears is an illusion. Karma from propensities is coming to meet you, karma from propensities is following you, and karma from propensities is presently going [with you].[83] The propensities are active in this way in the three times. If you can see that everything that appears has the nature of a dream or an illusion, then your belief in the reality of appearances will disappear like mist.

The five poisons are naturally present. That is why you need to practice until the afflictions are transformed into the path. Although anger is naturally present, [13] birthlessness is also naturally present. Therefore, you need to habituate yourself to developing birthlessness the moment that anger is arising so that it will not arise. As soon as you know that anger is a dream, it will be transformed into the path. Know all five poisons in that same way. Through simply knowing that the five poisons don't stain, they will be transformed into the path. The five poisons have been present for a long time, so you must be resolute until samsara is emptied.

In general, it is the characteristic of the three realms[84] that samsara is beginningless. One can, however, say that a specific individual has a beginning, for that beginning and end occurs when buddhahood is attained.[85]

You must meditate that you are practicing for the benefit of all the beings in the three realms. Meditate until you reach independent freedom. Until then, there will still be good and bad, and so there will be the danger of the bad distracting you and leading you backward. That would be like an elephant getting its tail stuck [in the doorway] as you lead it outside. Therefore, keep meditating until you cut through the bondage of samsara.

There is no Dharma other than that.

·11·

This Dharma teaching can be given to anyone.

A genuine Dharma practitioner is always ready to give away anything, because life is impermanent and there's no time to waste.

You can train in generosity by giving away just fire or water. If you can't even give away fire or water, you will be reborn as a thin-throated preta. If you can habituate yourself to [giving away] water, you will eventually be able to easily give away your head, legs, arms, and eyes, and this will release you from samsara.

Therefore, train first in giving away fire and water. Then train in giving away minor things. Then give away things to which you're attached or feel you really need. This is how one practices on the path of the perfections.

To summarize, samsara and nirvana are nothing but two words. It is said in the scriptures:

> It was taught that afflictions arise to the extent that there is fixation.
> It was taught that complete purification is when the focus on "me" and "mine" ceases.[86]

As long as there is fixation, there will be afflictions. [14] For example, fixation on the self creates attachment, and fixation on other[87] creates aversion. Fixation on children creates attachment; fixation on enemies creates aversion. Fixation on the pleasant creates attachment; fixation on the unpleasant creates aversion. Fixation on praise creates attachment, and on and on. Fixation on these various dualistic perceptions prevents liberation from samsara and will send you to a place of constant suffering. Therefore, it's taught that you must do the opposite of fixating on "me" and "mine."

This means that you practice by looking at the self to see whether it is real or not, whether it is permanent or impermanent, and whether the self has its own nature or not. Looking at the self in that way makes you see that it is impermanent, which frees you from attachment to the self. With no attachment to the self, you are freed from all attachment.

Until now, because of your perception of "me," there was also "mine." When there is "me" and "mine" you wander in samsara. Because of "me" there is a variety of "mine," such as "my child," "my enemy," "my wealth," and so on. This is why you wander in samsara.

You must know that ["me" and "mine"] are just your own dreams and illusions. When you know that "me" is impermanent, you do not focus on "me." When you do not focus on "me," you will not focus on any "mine." It's taught that complete purification is when there is no focusing on "me" and "mine." That is what is taught in the scriptures.

As that is the case, abandon all fixations on the self and that will tear samsara into shreds. Therefore, practice with no fixation on a self.

Complete purification is a quality of nirvana. Therefore, train in generosity, starting with fire and water and continuing up to your own body, eliminating all attachment. Eliminate all clinging. Recognize and eliminate all faults. Delve into where all your faults are hidden and expose them.

We do not know when the next life will come. Sickness, distress, death, bolts of lightning, and regrets are all the results of bad karma. I beseech you to practice diligently from now on.

There is no Dharma other than that.

·12·

This Dharma teaching can be given to anyone.

During this time, think a little about how we don't know when death will come. Once we are caught in the noose of the Lord of Death, there will be no freedom. [15] So now, while you are still free, make plans to obtain an everlasting harvest.

First, put your trust in the guru, the *yidam* deity, and the Jewels. Pray intensely to them with faith, aspiration, appreciation, and reverence. Fame and praise in this life will not help your mind practice the Dharma, therefore leave it all behind you. Offer your body and possessions to the guru and the Jewels. You must be single-minded about practicing.

Think, "I will practice generosity, maintain correct conduct, meditate on patience, generate diligence, rest in meditation, and develop wisdom so that all beings may attain complete buddhahood," and practice accordingly. The thought, "I must practice the six perfections," should be in the depths of your heart.

To summarize Dharma practice: you must understand the ultimate and the relative. It is taught in the Perfection Vehicle that, on a relative level, there is karma, the ripening of karma, all the phenomena of complete affliction, such as birth, old age, happiness, and suffering, and there is the complete purification of nirvana and the qualities of the kāyas and wisdoms.

Relatively, while there are still thoughts of self and other, all good and bad actions will be real, so you must be extremely careful when it comes to good and bad actions. All the good actions you perform from now on will ripen as good results in a future life. All the bad actions you perform from now on will ripen as bad results, as suffering in lower existences. There is no result without a cause, and buddhahood cannot come from wrong or inferior causes.

It is said in the Perfection Vehicle, within the *Sutra of the Complete Gathering of Qualities*:

> Until you have perfected good karma,
> you will not attain sacred emptiness.[88]

If you don't practice the ten good actions, the ten Dharma conducts,[89] or the six perfections as your causes, you will not attain buddhahood and will be in great danger of having a meaningless view and be left with an ordinary mind. All you listening here, for as long as you see yourself as real, then everyone else in the six classes of existence will also be real. As soon as you no longer fixate on the reality of yourself, you will naturally be liberated [from belief in the reality of] all beings in the six classes of existence.[90]

Until there is that natural liberation from fixation upon reality, there will be relative truth, so there will also be causal actions, and the ripening of the results of actions. [16] Therefore, it's very important to have conviction in karmic cause and effect. It's taught that when there is natural liberation from the relative and you have abandoned "I" and "me," then there will be no ripening of karma in the ultimate.

To whatever extent there is ultimate truth, that is realization. It is freedom from thoughts of attachment and desire, from the pride of arrogance, and from language's terminology. All thoughts of self and others naturally cease so that there are no appearances of self and others. That is the realization of the ultimate, in which there is no karma or ripening of karma. When you have that realization, you are free from self-interest and will do whatever you can to benefit others, to benefit beings.

As this realization improves, your compassion for beings will increase. Ācārya Vairocana has taught:

> Although there is realization that there is no birth or death,
> the continuum of composite good actions does not cease.[91]

Therefore, whether the ultimate has been realized or whether relative appearances persist, you must look into yourself. Even if you have realized the ultimate, you must nonetheless still meditate on compassion for beings and greatly benefit them. According to Ācārya Nāgārjuna:

> The teaching of Dharma by the buddhas
> relies upon the two truths:
> the world's relative truth
> and truth from the ultimate meaning.[92]

Practice the inseparability of these two truths. There is no Dharma other than that.

·13·

This Dharma teaching can be given to anyone.

We have no time to waste in our present lives. Eliminate all that has to be eliminated, leaving no remainder.

Rely upon an excellent remedy that will prevent rebirth into another life. It is important to have shame and faith. Faith may vanish from time to time, but if you still have a sense of shame, it will be a great help in preventing you from becoming separated from the Dharma. A sense of shame can also induce faith, so it is vital.

If you have no shame, then as your faith grows old, you may commit many non-Dharma actions. You may perform easily deeds that should never be done in this world, such as killing your parents. If you commit those kinds of bad actions even just once, you will have no conscience and your ambitions will be uncontrolled. [17] Faith cannot sustain itself on its own, so it's important to also have a sense of shame. It's what prevents someone from becoming a murderous despot.

If faith and shame come together, whatever you do will be Dharma. It will be like glazing gold. Gold is excellent in itself but applying a glaze improves it.

Apart from making you focus solely on practicing Dharma with faith, how can a sense of shame, of feeling shame before others, also bring benefit to yourself and others? A man benefits himself and others if, from the present onward, he is careful concerning his actions through fear of a bad conscience.

While practicing this union of faith and a sense of shame, you must look to see what good qualities have arisen in yourself.

If you see all appearances as real, then happiness, suffering, self, others, and all your wealth, belongings, retinue, and servants will also be independently real. Then you will be no different from a bad or ordinary person. Therefore, you must diminish the contaminating belief in a self.

If you do not have the perspective of seeing whatever you do as being for the benefit of others, you are following the Hīnayāna, and you will attain the result solely of being a realized śrāvaka.

If you know that whatever appears is like a dream or an illusion, then everything you do will be like a dream or illusion. If you accomplish the benefit of beings, you are training your mind in the path of the Mahayana. If you primarily practice benefiting others, and do so as if in a dream or an illusion, without any selfish desires, then that is the activity of a bodhisattva. If you do whatever you can to benefit others, without any thought of cherishing yourself, and you accomplish the welfare of beings without difficulty, then you are called a bodhisattva. If there is an effortless, naturally accomplished, uninterrupted benefit of beings without any thought of "others," then that is complete buddhahood.

Therefore, if your experience is that appearances are what they seem to be, then you are making the error of an ordinary being. If you don't focus on benefiting beings, then you are making the error of a śrāvaka or a pratyekabuddha. If that is the case, then you have not benefited from the general teachings:

> Developing bodhicitta is the wish for
> true complete buddhahood in order to benefit others.[93]

If you do not dedicate the good actions you do for the benefit of others, it will be difficult for your Dharma [practice] to even follow the path. A Dharma that does not follow the path will never bring you to buddhahood. If you do not attain buddhahood, you will be bereft of happiness in samsara. [18]

Therefore, always develop bodhicitta and dedicate [merit] for the welfare of beings. It's very important to know and practice this teaching.

It's important to first have faith and a sense of shame to aid you in the Dharma. You must have genuine love, compassion, and bodhicitta for beings, and you must cherish others more than yourself. You must also have simultaneous emptiness and compassion. It is said in the *Mahāmudrā Tantra*:

> Resting in emptiness without compassion
> is not the attainment of the supreme path.
> If, however, you meditate on compassion alone...[94]

This quotation is saying that you cannot accomplish the path through an emptiness that is devoid of compassion, and you cannot accomplish the path through a compassion that is devoid of emptiness. Therefore, you must have emptiness that has compassion as its essence. You must practice simultaneous emptiness and compassion, which is called *emptiness that has compassion as its essence.*

There is no Dharma other than that.

· 14 ·

This Dharma teaching can be given to anyone.

Those who have turned their minds away from this life and are dedicated to the welfare of the next life should ask their guru for the teaching on blending self and others. As for practices, the Nyingma Mantrayāna explains them to be the nine vehicles, the Sarma Mantrayāna explains them to be four levels of tantra, the Characteristics Vehicle explains them to be the three precious scriptural baskets (*piṭakas*), and the essence teachings explain them to be three vehicles, the four states,[95] and the nine yogas,[96] and they can all be explained to be the two truths or the four truths. To be succinct, all Dharma activity is included within the following: (1) the four methods of digestion, (2) the three methods of remaining in an area, and (3) the two kinds of conducts.

There are many who eat "food"—the sangha, the guru, the faithful, and so on—but there are four methods for digesting it:

a. *Supreme digestion through realization.* The supreme yogin with full realization has the confidence of the view. He has destroyed the reality of appearances and realized they have no nature of their own. In that way he digests naturally, free from concepts of good or bad food. Below that is:

b. *Digestion through meditation.* Generally, we need to correct dullness and agitation, but a meditation such as caṇḍālī naturally eliminates all external faults through meditation on the channels and winds. [19] Meditation on the channels and winds causes all good qualities to appear without center or limit, like space. That is the digestion of the intermediate yogi. Below that is:

c. *Digestion through meditation on love and compassion, in meditation and post-meditation.* This is familiarization with meditation over a period of time, and it's like the moon of the first lunar day.[97] Following the preliminary of love, compassion, and bodhicitta, the meditation develops just the beginning of samādhi, which is simply seeing the essence of the mind. Then in post-meditation, belief in reality diminishes. That is the digestion of the lesser intermediate yogi. Below that is:

d. *Digestion through a practitioner's powerful good actions of body and speech.* The continuous practice of dzokchen or mahāmudrā, circumambulation, making offerings, dedicating tormas, repeating mantras, and recitations throughout the four periods of the day is [the digestion of] the lesser [yogin].

Thus there are four methods for digestion—the best, the two intermediate, and the lesser.

There are three methods for remaining within the area of a Dharma practitioner: (a) The supreme method is to continuously remain within that area by staying in the mountains. (b) The medium method is to remain within that area by staying in a closed retreat. (c) The lowest method is to remain within that area by receiving teachings and keeping the three vows.[98]

There are two kinds of conduct: (a) The supreme conduct is that in addition to staying within the Dharma, you accomplish whatever benefits beings. (b) The lesser conduct is the peaceful and subdued deportment that inspires others to have faith in you.

The four methods of digestion and the three methods for remaining within an area are very important, but the two kinds of conduct are essential.

Therefore, lords, if you do things haphazardly, you will not "digest the food" and you will not enter the ranks of Dharma practitioners. So master those [methods] to whatever extent you can.

Staying in a place where there are villagers that keep your mind occupied, or staying in a place where vows and commitments are not kept, will lead you and others to the lower existences. If you don't have the Dharma, you will malign others. Therefore those three methods for remaining within the area of a Dharma practitioner are important.

Without the two kinds of conduct, you will benefit neither yourself nor others. You must benefit others while keeping the vows and controlling your mind, speech, and body.

A Dharma practitioner must have one of the methods for digesting food, one of the methods for remaining within the area, and both kinds of conduct. It is the combination of these that benefits beings. You must practice to benefit yourself and others. [20] As is said in the scriptures:

> May there be perfect happiness through the sublime good fortune
> of entering the path that accomplishes great benefit for oneself and
> others.[99]

If you benefit others, you are greatly benefiting yourself. That is why it is called the "sublime good fortune." That is how you must practice.

There is no Dharma other than that.

· 15 ·

This Dharma teaching can be given to anyone.

If your Dharma practice is pure, you will inevitably become aware of death and impermanence. This life is impermanent. Death is utterly certain because, having been born, death is inevitable.

We do not know whether we will die now or at some other time. There is no guaranteed lifespan, so death may come at any time. The body has no essence, so death may come at any time.

Many factors cause death: We nurture our bodies with food, but if we choke on food, it causes us to die. We put clothes on our body, but if they suffocate us, they are the cause of our death; and so on. Every favorable factor can also be a cause of death.

Death has numerous causes, such as enemies, water, and illness, so death may come at any time. We don't know when death will come, but can anything prevent it when it does? No, nothing prevents death. Even the wealth accumulated during your lifetime can't prevent it. A rich man can't buy his way out of death; he must leave his wealth behind and go on completely alone.

Your family and friends may be all around you, but they can't prevent your death; instead they can only do you more harm. You may think that your body, which holds your life, can prevent your death, but neither your body nor anything else can prevent your death. Only arrogance blinds us to this.

Death is certain, but the time of death is uncertain. We do not know when death will come, and nothing can prevent death.

You must practice now whatever good actions you are free to do, leaving laziness behind you. You must have desperation in the depth of your heart, seeing everything as being without essence and thinking, "Oh no! I have no time to take things easy!"

When you practice, cast all ambitions for this life behind you [21] and rely on a genuine guru. If you have no guru, then it's as if you've lost the path to liberation. It is taught in the scriptures:

> Though you may possess every good quality,
> without a guru, existence will have no end.
> If you do not have oars,
> your boat will never reach the far shore.[100]

It is also taught that:

> Every buddha in the three times
> becomes so through relying on a guru.
> Before there was a guru,
> there wasn't even the name "buddha."[101]

Rely upon a genuine guru and offer him your body, possessions, and all the good karma you accumulate in the three times. Develop bodhicitta, dedicating every good action that you do in the three times to "the lords"—all beings—in general. View all your faith in and appreciation of the guru and the Jewels as for the benefit of beings, without any self-interest.

It is important that every good action you do with your body, speech, or mind be seen in terms of the alchemy of objectlessness. *Samādhi* is when you have no focus on any phenomenon whatsoever. The yoga of *one-pointedness* is when you [still] have clinging and focus on something. The yoga of *nonelaboration* is when that becomes transformed into objectlessness. The yoga of *one taste* is when whatever appears is known to be the mind. The yoga of *nonmeditation* is when that experience is uninterrupted.

This practice will accomplish both your own benefit and the benefit of others.

There is no Dharma other than that.

·16·

This is a Dharma teaching for meditators.

In the present times, we have impermanent, short lives and have developed only a little of the Mahayana mind. To summarize, practice what are known as the *three yogas*. These three are:

1. Mantra yoga
2. Substance yoga
3. Phenomena yoga

The *Hevajra Tantra* says:

> If the three yogas of mantra, substance,
> and phenomena are completed,
> there is no point in remaining in samsara.[102]

Mantra yoga is the yoga of entering the door of generation, completion, or any other practice. The generation stage is the yoga of meditating on a deity. The completion stage is when you know the deity is like the moon [reflected] on water, like an illusion, [22] or like a rainbow. Both aspects are completed through meditating on a union of the generation and completion stages. That is what brings buddhahood. Even meditating solely on the generation stage will close the doors to the lower existences. Meditation in that way will create the correct mantra conduct. That is mantra yoga.

Substance yoga is the knowledge that all wealth and substances are like dreams and illusions. Practicing in that way destroys your belief in the reality of appearances. The power of knowing them to be just dreams and illusions brings you to the levels of the pratyekabuddhas and the bodhisattvas. In the canon it is taught that:

> If you have meditated that all phenomena,
> which are like illusions, *are* like illusions,
> you will attain buddhahood, which is like an illusion.[103]

Phenomena yoga is the realization that all phenomena are like the center of pure space. This is called the realization of the equality of self and others, of "is" and "is not," and so on. In the canon it is taught that:

When you have meditated that phenomena,
which are like space, *are* like space,
you will attain buddhahood, which is like space.[104]

That is the practice of the three yogas. If you are attracted to the activity of the Mantrayāna's generation and completion stages, then practice mantra yoga. If you like substance yoga, meditate on the instructions on dream and illusion. If you are attracted to phenomena yoga, meditate that all phenomena are like the center of space.

How can you meditate on all three yogas in one sitting? First meditate on the generation and completion stages. Then meditate upon dream and illusion in between sessions, during the four kinds of activity. At the conclusion of any practice, rest in nonattention like the center of objectless space. It's taught that this practice accomplishes every benefit for yourself and others. Therefore, practice in that way.

There is no Dharma other than that.

·17·

This Dharma teaching can be given to anyone.

To practice Dharma purely, you have to practice now, while your mind is based in a human body, while your five sensory faculties are complete, [23] while you live in a land where the sacred Dharma is taught, and before this basis—which has arisen from merit accumulated in previous lives—is struck by death or illness.

In your practice, it's important to forsake the ten actions that are to be avoided and pursue the ten good actions. The ten actions to be avoided are three of the body, four of the speech, and three of the mind.[105] The ten good actions are:

1. In addition to avoiding killing, one saves lives.
2. In addition to avoiding stealing, one practices giving.
3. In addition to avoiding sexual misconduct, one keeps the vow of celibacy.
4. In addition to avoiding lying, one teaches the Dharma.
5. In addition to avoiding the three kinds of slander, one speaks [conciliatory words]. The three kinds are open slander, indirect slander, and secret slander. Open slander is done among a gathering of people.

Indirect slander is made by devious means. Secret slander is told to one individual in private.

6. In addition to avoiding [harsh speech],[106] one speaks gentle words.
7. In addition to avoiding meaningless speech, one keeps silent.
8. In addition to avoiding covetousness, one rejoices at the wealth of others.
9. In addition to avoiding malice, one does whatever one can to benefit others.
10. In addition to avoiding wrong views, one repents the bad actions one has done and rejoices in the good actions.

In that way, you must avoid the ten bad actions and practice the ten good actions and the six perfections. The six perfections are not distinct from each other; each one is within all the others. They are the union of method and wisdom. Know that the action of giving and its karmic result are like dreams and illusions. Know that all six perfections are like dreams and illusions. When performing the perfection of generosity, for instance, do so without objectifying even the perfection of generosity itself. For it has been stated in the Buddha's teaching that: "The path is to be practiced in an objectless manner."[107] He taught that this is the same for all six.

Avoiding the ten bad actions is the root, or the foundation, of the entire Dharma. The practice of the ten good actions is the practice of the six perfections, and it benefits beings.

There is no Dharma other than that.

· 18 ·

This Dharma teaching can be given to anyone.

To practice genuine Dharma, know that worldly phenomena have never been our friends. It's taught:

> Look at these worldly delusions! [24]
> See that all their actions are meaningless and cause suffering.
> Whatever you wish for will be of no benefit to you.
> Accustom yourself to continually observing your own mind.[108]

In our present mental states, we should always be contemplating our own minds, observing worldly phenomena, and seeing that everything we've done is meaningless. Whatever land and homes we have, we will have to leave them behind, so whatever we've done for their sake is meaningless.

All our worldly activities have been nothing but non-Dharma. We have had no time for the Dharma during the day because we've been busy with work and none in the evening because of seeing to our stomach's wishes. This is the pointless suffering of being busy.

Anxious to maintain our lives, instead of avoiding unpleasant bad actions and negative talk, we are deeply involved in them, which brings only suffering. They cause suffering in this life and in the next life, when we will be reborn in a lower existence.

Let us look at the three poisons: We are deeply involved in internal and external desires, which we shamelessly satisfy. In this life our minds are under the power of business and profit and when we die we are reborn as a preta and suffer. This is meaningless.

Anger makes us aggressive and heedless of death. Our minds burn, causing suffering in this life and rebirth in hell in the next. This is meaningless suffering.

Ignorance causes us not to know the difference between good and bad, so that we act incorrectly. We can't tell good from bad, but we become experts in deceit and deception, which is cleverness without purpose. As a result, we suffer in this life, find no satisfaction or contentment, and don't have a single moment of leisure. Because we don't know the difference between good and bad actions, in the next life we will experience the suffering of being reborn as an animal. This is also meaningless.

All worldly actions are causes of meaningless suffering. Whatever we plan will be of no benefit. Whatever clever ideas we have will be of no benefit on the day we die. We cherish our children, but lose them, become separated from them. When we depart this life without land, retinue, and so on, however important something might be to us, we can't say a single word about it or see one person. Arrogantly we never think of this. The scriptures teach: [25]

> At the time of death whatever you think of, whatever you look at, will be of no benefit, so what can you do? None of your children can be of help. Therefore always familiarize yourself with your own mind.[109]

Looking at our own minds is beneficial and so brings happiness, but how do we go about looking at the mind to bring happiness? If we accumulate causal merit and then look at the resultant accumulation of wisdom, that is "looking at the mind." Or if your interest is in the Mantrayāna's generation and completion stages, then that is "looking at the mind."

During the meditation session, know that everything that appears is the mind. Look at your own mind and see that it has no shape or color. It is beyond any identification. All the conceptual elaboration of extremes of "is" and "isn't" are naturally and spontaneously liberated, and the intellect is not engaged in anything. That is "looking at the mind" in a meditation session, which is the true "looking at the mind."

Meditation on dream and illusion in the post-meditation periods is also "looking at the mind."

Continually accustom yourself to looking at the mind in these ways. If you do this kind of practice, the Dharma will be a remedy for your afflictions. When the Dharma is a remedy for your afflictions, you have attained the ability to look at the mind. The Dharma teaches that:

> The afflictions agitate the mind
> and sink you in the swamp of ignorance.[110]

It's very important that the Dharma be a remedy for the afflictions.

If your practice is perfect, you will realize the meaning of deathlessness. If you have medium practice, you will be on the path. If your practice is minimal, you will not be reborn in the lower existences. It's important to practice with effort, and it's important to meditate.

Without meditation, you can only slightly turn your mind away from desire, so you will not be liberated from death. Hence, meditation is vital. Through meditation, appearances will be overcome, and you will be naturally liberated from all belief in reality. Therefore, meditation is important. But does meditation itself actually exist? It's taught that:

> There is no meditation and no meditator.[111]

Therefore, there is nothing about which you can say, "It is on this that I'm meditating." This is the ultimate practice that is called meditation. Practice in that way.

There is no Dharma other than that.

·19·

[26] This Dharma teaching can be given to anyone.

This present life lasts no longer than an instant. Now you have the freedoms and opportunities [of a human existence] with its complete faculties. Therefore, you need to gain the complete, unmistaken causes of buddhahood so that you don't die before gaining the path to liberation. Buddhahood is not attained without a cause, or by mistake, or from inferior causes. Buddhahood is not attained without gathering the two accumulations. It is not attained through the view, meditation, and conduct of the tīrthikas. It is not attained through the Hīnayāna Dharma of the śrāvakas and pratyekabuddhas.

Why can you not attain buddhahood through the Hīnayāna Dharma of the śrāvakas and pratyekabuddhas? It's because they don't develop the motivation to benefit beings but wish for peace and bliss for themselves alone. Omniscience is not attained without focusing on benefiting others.

How should you practice in order to attain buddhahood? You must practice without falling into the extreme of having no causes. You must practice a path that is neither incorrect nor inferior. In such a practice you must:

a. crush that which you have not dared to crush
b. cut through bondage
c. counter attachment
d. recognize faults
e. expose defects
f. bring all happiness and suffering to the Dharma

a) The first of these, crushing that which you have not dared to crush, means that you apply shame, or whatever [antidote] you wish, to each of your attachments.
b) Cutting through bondage means viewing all children, wealth, and so on, as being like dreams and illusions: impermanent, unreal, and with no nature of their own.
c) Concerning countering attachment, the canon teaches:

> Give away whatever you have attachment for.[112]

Thus, forsake and give away whatever you have attachment for.

d) Recognizing faults means seeing the three poisons as faults so that you abandon the fault of fixating upon a self.

e) Exposing defects means being afraid that the three poisons will cause one to wander through the three lower existences. This will result in the defects becoming completely exposed. Eliminate those [errors] and attain the Mahayana mind.
f) Regard all beings with love, compassion, and bodhicitta. View them in that way only. In the center of your heart, resolve that all beings must find happiness, freedom from suffering, and complete buddhahood. In that way, your body, speech, and mind will perform good actions. [27]

It is important, when you get up each morning, that you develop the motivation of thinking, "Today, for the sake of all beings, I am going to apply my body, speech, and mind to good actions." Then your motivation will transform whatever you do on that day into a good action. Throughout the entire Dharma, the most important thing is transformation through motivation. Good motivation is important to have in general, for then whatever you do will be a good action. If your motivation is bad, your actions will be bad as well.

A good motivation is like having a good servant inside you. It's important that your good actions of body, speech, and mind be of benefit to beings, even when you go to sleep at night. If you do that, then everything you do will be a good action and you will be on the path. Therefore, good motivation is vital. With that kind of motivation, the mind turns away from this life with its suffering and happiness, and your practice will be effortlessly transformed into the dharmakāya.

There is no Dharma other than that.

·20·

This Dharma teaching can be given to anyone.

To summarize how we should now turn our minds away from this life and practice: We should have firmly in our minds the thought that we don't need anything. Then as for our practice, that should be the practice of the four yogas. The four yogas are one-pointedness, nonelaboration, the one taste of the manifold, and nonmeditation.

One-pointedness is being totally fixed upon whatever the mind is focused on, aware of whatever it is; that is your meditation. Without distraction, keep your mind on that single focus.

Maintaining this will cause *nonelaboration* to arise. You will know all phenomena without the elaboration of concepts. Everything you've heard and contemplated in the past will vanish like the shedding of a skin, and your mind will be free from attachment. At that time, pray to your guru, make offerings to the Jewels, read and listen to whatever profound Dharma you can, and so on, so as to make your realization endure.

When this realization comes, [28] you might think, "There's no actual Dharma to be practiced. There are no gurus, Jewels, or *yidam* deities. There are no siddhis that have been attained, there are none to be attained." Then you will be in danger of losing your devotion to the guru, causing obstacle-causing māras to arise. It's taught that it's important at such a time to pray intensely to the guru, make offerings to the Jewels and the *yidam* deities, and meditate without partiality on love and compassion.

If your devotion fluctuates, your Dharma experiences will also fluctuate, and you will encounter obstacles. Your devotion to the guru must be continuous. Experience and realization depend upon devotion. The guru creates the path and realization. In the Mantrayāna tradition, blessings are known as "the path of the guru." If you practice in that way, you will have a continuity of experience and realization.

As a result, the *one taste of the manifold* will arise. When the one taste of the manifold arises, you will know that all appearances are the mind, that the mind is of one taste with emptiness, and that emptiness is of one taste with birthlessness.

If at that time you have no faith when you see your guru or vajra siblings, this will be an obstacle from the māras. It's taught that it's important at that time to offer your body and possessions to the guru and Jewels; make prayers to them; compare your realization with your guru's other pupils or with experienced meditators; read what is known as "the profound Dharma of Candraprabhakumāra";[113] and listen to sutras, tantras, and treatises (*śāstra*).

Can there be obstacles after the one taste of the manifold has arisen? There will continue to be obstacles for as long as thoughts continue.

After the one taste of the manifold has arisen, envy is impossible because pure appearances are arising. It's taught that you'll have visions of the *yidam* deities and experience some clairvoyance, but whatever good qualities arise, you won't see them as real and you will know them to be mind. Realization will develop more and more, until there is the realization of *nonmeditation.*

There are those who say that *meditation* is when the intellect conceives of the object of meditation as being real, while *nonmeditation* is without love and compassion. That, however, is the nonmeditation devoid of compassion and the two accumulations, which is not what is meant here. This nonmeditation is the absence of coming and going and a blending into one so that there's no object of meditation that is realized, there's no meditation and no fixation. It's taught that this is the actual meditation of mahāmudrā: [29] When you are naturally liberated from all fixation, attachment, belief in reality, and the focus of desire, you rest in the uncontrived natural state of the mind.

The way in which these yogas are practiced
First train in one-pointedness, then nonelaboration, then one taste, and then the great yoga of nonmeditation—the realization of mahāmudrā—free from using effort to accomplish the path.

The qualities will appear
When you have gathered the accumulations and done what is necessary in order to traverse the path, you will then realize your own mind. As a result, you will attain the benefit for yourself—the dharmakāya, which is like the center of space.

Your body will transform into the vajra body, and thereby you will attain the saṃbhogakāya, which is adorned with inconceivable primary and secondary signs. It is an appearance with no nature of its own, like rainbows or clouds.

You will accomplish benefit for others through the compassion of the nirmāṇakāya. It's taught that there will be the natural presence of an effortless, unceasing continuum that benefits beings throughout space and benefits pupils impartially, like rain falling from the sky.

All we who explain the Dharma should know how to teach the complete unmistaken path: begin every session with the determination to benefit beings, then in the actual session engage in positive practice, and end by making a dedication. Also, those who listen [to the teachings] should know this.

There is no Dharma other than that.

Colophon

Lama Gomtsül, with constant attention to detail, wrote down clearly and exactly the words spoken by the precious Lama Lhajé,[114] without mixing them with other [methods for] liberation and without adding to, or leaving out, any of the lama's speech.[115]

I request that this not be disseminated to those who are not in the guru's tradition, to those who have no interest, and to those who do not practice.

[Gampopa's] lineage has two aspects: the Mantrayāna and the Kadam. Vajradhara and Jñānadākiṇī gave the Mantrayāna lineage to Tilopa and the Great Brahman. They gave it to Nāropa and Maitripa, who gave it on to Marpa. He gave it to Milarepa, and Milarepa gave it to Lama Lhajé.

Another lineage is a successive transmission from Śākyamuni through Maitreya, Asaṅga, Śāntideva, Suvarṇadvīpa, Atiśa, Dromtön, Chengawa, Gyagom, and Lama Lhajé Rinpoché to Lama Gomtsül.[116]

These great Dharma lectures are concluded.

May there be virtue.

2. The Unrivaled Instructions of Shang Rinpoché

The Preliminaries and Main Practice of the Great Meditation of Mahāmudrā

Shönu Lha (late thirteenth century)

[31] I pay homage to the sublime gurus.

I pay homage to the precious guru.
The activity of your compassion comes to all beings
from the state of great bliss, the elaboration-free dharmadhātu,
and the power of your blessing liberates your pupils.

I shall write these instructions from the guru exactly as he taught them;
they are the essence of the Dharma, the highest of all vehicles,
the inheritance from the great Kagyüpas of the past,
the practice of the lords, the path that guides pupils.

The principal teaching of the Lord of Dharma, glorious Lharipa,[117] is the method for revealing mahāmudrā to be within the grasp of your hand. It is an instruction given to karmically worthy pupils. It is the Dharma of the father of the entire Dakpo Kagyü.[118] It is a sublime secret path; the blessing of the direct introduction that enables you to see nakedly the precious nature of the mind; it reveals to us our inner, innate realization. Here are this tradition's preliminary and main instructions.

My sublime guru established the three levels of vows as the foundation for pupils, ripened them with empowerments, and taught them these instructions. The precious guru gave the following teachings:

We have obtained the precious human body with its freedoms and opportunities. We have no defects in our five senses. While we have this independence, we should accomplish the goal of eternal peace and happiness. In order to accomplish that, we need the Dharma. In order to practice the Dharma, perfect faith is indispensable. In order to develop faith, we must contemplate the defects of samsara and meditate on death and impermanence.

Everyone in the past was born and then died. Everyone who is yet to be born will definitely die. For those of us alive now, it's impossible that only one or two of us will die while the rest of us [32] go on living. We're born and then we die—that's the nature of impermanence. It is said in a sutra:

> It is doubtful that you have ever seen
> or even heard of someone
> on a level or world of higher existence
> who was born but has not died.[119]

The death of every being is terrifying and near. It's impossible that it won't happen. We shouldn't even feel certain that we will still be alive tomorrow morning. Ācārya Śāntideva has said:

> It is not right to comfort myself by thinking
> "I will not die today."
> The time will doubtless come
> when I will cease to exist.[120]

We definitely will die, but we don't know when. The young should not feel certain that they won't die, because in this world there is no definite time for death: a baby dies in one family, a child dies in another. Most people die in adulthood, and only a few don't die until they're old. We have short lives because the lifespan has declined in this degenerate age. Even the few who live a full life only reach sixty. So we can't know whether we will die tomorrow, the day after tomorrow, or next year. Suddenly we are seized by something we have not planned, and, terrified, we die with wildly staring eyes and a hundred goals left unachieved. From the *Sutra of the Excellent Night*:

> Who knows if I will die tomorrow or not?
> Therefore, I must be diligent this very day.
> The great army of the Lord of Death
> is not a friend of mine.[121]

As soon as we are born from our mothers, we draw closer and closer to our deaths with each passing day. Yesterday has gone and today is going. We cannot stop it, and we only draw closer and closer to dying. Yesterday was impermanent, so now it's today, but today is also impermanent. The previous month was impermanent, and so it was followed by this one. Last year was impermanent and before long it was over. Without our being aware of it, this attacks and destroys us. It is taught in a sutra:

> Just as the moving water of
> a rapid river never returns,
> the life of a human goes away
> and will never return.[122] [33]

From another sutra:

> If even the vajra body, adorned with
> the primary and secondary signs, is impermanent,
> then those with bodies that have no essence,
> like plantain trees, are obviously so.[123]

Even the great Śākyamuni, the perfect Buddha, and all the gurus and siddhas of the past died and passed away, so what point is there for us to hope to be permanent? Everyone is heading toward death, and I too will fail to defeat death.

A clever speaker can't prevent passing away. The very wealthy can't avoid it. Even the powerful rulers cannot defeat it. Once the supporting conditions for life have ceased, there is nothing anyone can do. Even if you say that you've got to stay alive for just a little while longer, you will not be able to for even another moment. Even though you've amassed great wealth and property, you will leave it all behind and go on alone and empty-handed. Śāntideva has said:

> You may have acquired many possessions,
> amassing them over a long time,
> but just as if a robber steals them all,
> you will leave naked and empty-handed.[124]

It's terrifying to be naked, empty-handed, bound tightly by a rotting rope, and forcibly dragged away. Can you endure contemplating your certain death? Even if you have many friends, followers, and servants, you can't send anyone else in your place. You can't postpone death, and there will be no one to go with you; you will have to leave immediately and totally alone, like a hair pulled out of butter. When the time comes, the riches you've accumulated will not help; your friends and relations will not help; whatever mark you've made in this world will not help. You will leave behind every support in this life. Each of us will leave carrying the burden of our ripening karma. This is definitely going to happen. It is taught in *Entering the Conduct of a Bodhisattva*:

> Even though, as I lie upon my bed,
> I am surrounded by friends and family,
> when my life comes to an end,
> I will have to experience that alone.
>
> When the emissaries of Death seize me,
> what can my family do? What can my friends do?[125]

We are definitely going to die and we don't know when. We don't have the time to take it easy, and nothing but the Dharma can help us. Contemplate this and dedicate yourself to the Dharma.

Those who don't understand think, "Death is going to come whether I practice the Dharma or not. [34] Everyone dies, sooner or later, so why should I feel bad about it?" Those who think that way become thoughtlessly involved with this life and don't understand.

How could there possibly be eternal life? There can be happy deaths and unhappy deaths, but those who don't practice the Dharma, whether they die young or old, will not have any happiness in the land of death.

We don't cease to exist at death but are reborn. If you don't practice the Dharma, you will be reborn in the three lower existences. Can you possibly conceive of that suffering? The suffering in the hot and cold hells is inconceivable. It's taught that in the hot hells you suffer for many eons the unendurable torture of being chopped up, cut into pieces, burned in fire, cooked, and beaten. It's taught that in the cold hells, the body freezes, blisters, cracks, splits, and so on.

Pretas suffer from hunger and thirst. It's taught that they don't even see food or drink for months or years. Even when they do see or find some, there is only more suffering, because it is stolen by others or transforms into puss and blood, or weapons rain down on them, and so on. It's taught that because their bad karma is not exhausted, they can't die, and so their suffering is inconceivable.

Animals suffer from being stupid and ignorant. They also suffer from eating each other: There is the suffering of the larger animals eating the smaller ones, the smaller animals eating the larger, the many eating the few, and the few eating the many. The happiest animals are those who are cared for by humans. But they also suffer from being loaded as if they're carts and used against their will. They are sheared, have their noses pierced, are milked, and so on. They are continually used until they are eventually killed. If humans are happy, they make the animals happy; if the humans suffer, they make the animals suffer. They are used as servants until they become old, and then they are taken to the slaughterer who returns them with staring, bloody eyes. Then they're eaten. Haven't you seen this suffering?

There is nothing but suffering in the three lower existences, but it's taught that there are countless sufferings in the three higher existences too. The devas have the suffering of falling [35] to a lower existence when their life is over. Their adornments age, their light fades, their deva companions abandon them. They know they are dying. They suffer because they can see with their clairvoyance that their next life is a fall into a bad existence. It's taught that their suffering is unendurable, like fish writhing on hot sand.

The asuras suffer because of fighting or because of being killed, wounded, defeated, and so on. It's taught that they too have countless sufferings.

Humans experience the four great rivers of suffering: birth, aging, sickness, and death. In addition, there's the suffering of taking care of what you have, the suffering of seeking but not finding what you don't have, the suffering of meeting, or being afraid of meeting, aggressive, angry enemies; and the suffering of being separated, or the fear of being separated, from beloved friends. In particular, in this degenerate age, there are such afflictions as Mongolian governors, malevolent leaders, and slavery.

If you don't have good things, that causes unhappiness; if you have good things, that causes suffering; if you have bad things, that causes suffering; having something causes suffering and not having it causes suffering.

Once we are born here in samsara, there is nothing that is beyond suffering, beyond the cycle of suffering, beyond the characteristics of suffering. Maitreyanātha has taught in the *Sublime Continuum*:

The nature of samsara is suffering.
Those in samsara have no happiness.
Its nature is like fire.[126]

If now, during this brief time that we have the precious body of a deva or a human, we don't repel the army of samsara and gain the objective of eternal benefit, who knows where we'll be reborn?

The attainment of this precious human existence is extremely rare. If you hurl peas against a wall as smooth as a mirror, it's unlikely even one will stick to it. Gaining a human existence is even more difficult than that. If you throw peas against a mirror, can even one to stick to its surface? No, they all fall. From *Entering the Conduct of a Bodhisattva*:

[Therefore, the Bhagavān] taught that
obtaining the human existence is as difficult
as it is for a turtle to stick its neck through the hole
of a yoke floating on a great ocean.[127]

A yoke floats upon the surface of a great ocean. [36] Once a century, a turtle rises to break the surface with its head. It's extremely unlikely the turtle's head will come up through the yoke. It's even more difficult than that to attain a human existence. Therefore, Ācārya Śāntideva[128] taught:

These opportunities and freedoms are difficult to obtain,
[but] human beings have gained this success.
If they do not accomplish its benefits,
who knows when they will fully acquire it [again]?[129]

Thus, it's taught that human existence is difficult to obtain. During the short time we have this fragile human body, it is possible to end our wandering in samsara, so that's what you should do. Perform this great act of kindness to yourself. It's crucial that you don't deceive yourself. Whatever you do, you don't have the leisure to not practice the Dharma.

You must first take vows in order to practice the Dharma, and you have taken them. Now, whether you wander in samsara or attain buddhahood depends on your mind. If you don't know its nature, you wander in samsara; if you do know it, that's buddhahood; so you must know it. What prevents you from knowing it? Bad karma and impurity. To purify bad karma, there is first the hundred-syllable mantra instruction, which is very important and really must be practiced.

Enter a strict retreat in a solitary place, such as in a sealed chamber. Sit upon a comfortable cushion and make a sincere oath, thinking, "Oh! I'm so fortunate that I haven't died before today. Time has passed so quickly without my paying attention. Now I only have the last part of my life left, so during this brief time I must accomplish the goal of everlasting benefit. I shall practice nothing but the Dharma. I shall dedicate what little of my life remains to this purpose. Gurus and Jewels! Be my witness for this!"

Meditate a little while on death, impermanence, and the harmfulness of samsara, so that you will not remain idle or neutral. Then develop bodhicitta sincerely, thinking, "I will attain buddhahood for the sake of all beings and bring them to the level of perfect buddhahood. [37] For that purpose I will practice the meditation and mantra of Vajrasattva." Then recite three times the bodhicitta prayer that begins "[In] the Buddha, the Dharma..."[130]

Then clearly meditate that you are the *yidam* deity, with glorious Bhagavān Vajrasattva one cubit[131] above your head. Clearly meditate that he is white in color, with one face and two arms. The right hand holds a golden five-pronged vajra to his heart and the left hand, holding a silver bell, rests upon his hip. He is bejeweled with all precious adornments and is inseparable from the wisdom being (*jñānasattva*). The syllable *hūṃ*, which is on a full-moon disc and lotus in his heart, is the essence of nondual wisdom, the minds of all the buddhas. It is white and shining, the color of mercury. For the sake of all beings, it radiates light in all directions to invoke the essence of nondual wisdom, the minds of all the buddhas in the three times. This essence melts into nectar, which is drawn in from all directions and enters glorious Bhagavān Vajrasattva through the fontanel on the crown of his head, completely filling his body with its whiteness.

The nectar flows out from under the nail of the big toe on his right foot, pouring down to the crown of your head and entering into you. It washes away your bad karma and obscurations, and these come out from your ten toes and your anus in the form of black liquid, like charcoal-stained water. Imagining that, repeat the hundred-syllable mantra about a thousand times.

Oṃ vajrasattva, samayam anupālaya, vajrasattva tvenopatiṣṭha, dṛdho me bhava sutoṣyo me bhava, supoṣyo me bhava, anurakto me bhava, sarva siddhim me prayaccha, sarva karma suca me, cittaṃ

> *śreyaḥ kuru, hūṃ, ha ha ha ha ho, bhagavān, sarva tathāgata, vajra ma me muñca, vajrī bhava mahā samaya sattva, āḥ.*
>
> [Oṃ Vajrasattva! Protect the commitment! Vajrasattva, you be present! Be steadfast for me! Be pleased with me! Take care of me! Bestow all the siddhis upon me! Make all my actions good! Make my mind glorious! *Hūṃ*, ha ha ha ha ho! Bhagavān, all the tathāgatas, Vajra, do not abandon me! Be a vajra holder! Great commitment being! Āḥ.]

When you finish, visualize Vajrasattva merging into you. Then your body and mind become relaxed from within, and you rest unwaveringly in a state of ease. Conclude by sealing it with a dedication.

In general, to practice this meditation and mantra repetition well, the meditator does four practice sessions. [38] At dawn, the third part of the night, think, "Oh! I didn't come to this hermitage so that I could sleep. I didn't come to these mountains so that I could sleep. I did not seal myself into this retreat so that I could sleep. I have slept so much throughout beginningless samsara and I'm still unsatisfied. So sleeping now is not going to give me satisfaction." Get up immediately and start the practice described above. Meditate until it's time for breakfast. When it's breakfast time, seal your practice with a genuine dedication. Then eat breakfast while practicing the yoga of food.[132] After breakfast, diligently sit on your cushion and practice until lunch. When it's time, again end with a dedication. Apply yourself to practice throughout the afternoon until it is time for the daily torma offering. Then practice the complete torma [offering], offerings to the Jewels, and so on. When the torma has been offered, sit diligently on your mattress. Without lying down, dedicate yourself to practice for the first third of the night: the evening. Seal each evening with dedication and prayer. For the sake of your health, sleep in the correct physical posture for the middle part of the night. At dawn, begin practicing as described.

Always keep to this program of four sessions: the evening, the dawn, the morning, and the afternoon. Spend your day in that way. Spend a month in that way. Spend a year practicing in that way. Spend your entire life dedicated to practicing in that way.

That's how it's taught you should dedicate yourself to practicing the meditation and repetition of the hundred syllables in four sessions.

The supplication to the guru is the principal preliminary practice, which should be done in this way:

In the dawn session, wake early and contemplate death and impermanence. Practice one rosary each of the refuge, the bodhicitta, and the hundred syllables, meditating as far as Vajrasattva merging into you, as described above.

In front of you, there should be either a mirror mandala, a clay mandala, a wood mandala, a slate mandala, or whatever kind of mandala you have, with twenty-three heaps [39] of barley arranged on it. Meditate that you are a deity and your root guru is above the crown of your head. Above his head is his own root guru, and above that guru's head is his root guru, and so on, up to the sixth Buddha, Vajradhara.[133]

Meditate that all space, your entire visual field, is filled with gurus, buddhas, bodhisattvas, ḍākas, ḍākinīs, guardians who are Dharma protectors, and so on, gathered like clouds. Confess your bad actions in their presence by thinking, "I confess and regret all bad actions I have done throughout all my lifetimes from beginningless samsara until now. I pray that you cleanse and purify me!" Thinking, "You know whether I should be sent upward or downward," put yourself completely into their care.

The mandala serves simply as the basis for the visualization. There is a great ocean upon a ground of gold. In its center is the supreme mountain surrounded by four continents, eight subcontinents, and the seven precious possessions of the cakravartin king, with the open vase of treasure as the eighth. There are the sun and moon, the oceans, the continents, a variety of jewels, a variety of grains, and various mounts, such as horses and elephants. There are wish-fulfilling cows, bathing tanks for washing, unploughed harvests, and different kinds of precious substances such as jewels, gold, silver, lapis lazuli, and *asmagarbha*,[134] the precious "stone essences." There are countless, unimaginable, specific offerings: varieties of silk adornments, such as parasols, victory banners, flags, and tassels; different kinds of music, such as drums, horns, cymbals, and lutes; myriad sensory pleasures of form, sound, smell, taste, and physical sensations; and possessions that are cherished in the world, such as gold, turquoise, horse harnesses, clothes, woolen cloths, cattle, sheep, meat, and butter. The world is completely filled with these pleasures, and you offer them.

There are also innumerable varieties, or classes, of offerings, each one filling all space. There are many kinds of offering goddesses, each holding a specific offering. There are heaps of every kind of jewel reaching the sky. There is the multicolored beauty of brocade, and so on. There is the melodious sound of cymbals, [40] and so on.

Offer all worlds, imagining them filled with offerings. Offer everything you can think of that could be an offering. Offer, without attachment, your own body, possessions, and things. With great devotion that is not just verbal, not just words, with feeling from the depth of your heart, recite sincerely the following prayer:

> Oh! I pray that while I am on this seat, within this very session, upon this very cushion, in this very instant, you will cleanse and purify me of all bad karma and obscurations in my being.
>
> I pray that while I am on this seat, within this very session, upon this very cushion, in this very instant, an exceptional samādhi will arise in me.
>
> I pray that while I am on this seat, within this very session, upon this very cushion, in this very instant, love, compassion, and bodhicitta will arise in me.

Sincerely repeat this prayer over and over again. All the gurus, buddhas, and bodhisattvas—who are assembled in space—become pleased and immediately, simultaneously, say the following words:

> We do nothing other than benefit beings, but until now, no one has prayed to us, which is sad; but now you, child, have prayed to us, so we will give you our blessing.

From the three places of their body, speech, and mind, and from all their pores, countless light rays of blessing and compassion radiate to your body, speech, and mind. Imagine that they completely purify all bad karma and obscurations from your body, speech, and mind, and then pray to them.

So that they will bless you with the power of overwhelming compassion, the buddhas dissolve into the lineage gurus. The lineage gurus, beginning with Vajradhara at the top, dissolve one into the other until they have all dissolved into the root guru. The root guru, the precious master who is the essence of all the buddhas, is brilliant and majestic on the crown of your head, and looks upon you with love and happiness. [41]

Feel intense devotion with great emotion and intense longing. Place your palms together at the heart and—grimacing, choked with inner emotion, your face covered in tears—recite this prayer with intense feeling:

> If children cannot rely on their father, on whom can they rely?
> If children are not protected by their father, who will protect them?
> Give me your blessing right now!

Imagine that your root guru says to you, "Ah, I am a guru who is worth praying to. Pray to me, my child!" Pray until you shed tears. The main part of the session is spent praying in this way.

When you finish, meditate that the guru completely melts into light and dissolves entirely into your body, so that he blesses you with the power of his overwhelming compassion. You and he blend, and your body and mind rest completely at ease, perfectly relaxed. If no thoughts arise, just rest until they appear. When thoughts do arise, offer a mandala and make the mental offering and supplication described above.

Repeat just this again and again, supplicating with devotion, and when you end, imagine that the guru dissolves into you.

Whether the blessing of the Kagyü lineage enters you or not, whether you develop meditation or not, depends on your devotion. Develop devotion until you shed tears. A dry supplication will bring you only dry blessing, and you will develop only dry meditation. Therefore, pray in such a way that you weep.

This alone is the heart of the practice dedicated to devotion. In Dharma terms, it's called the aspect of method. Here it's given the name "preliminaries." It's taught to be the most important of all practices, so dedicate yourself to devotion for half a month.

The instructions for the main practice

> The Conqueror taught that emptiness
> is the samādhi of all the buddhas.
> It can only be attained through the recognition
> of the mind and not through anything else.[135]

From the *Wisdom upon Passing Away Sutra*:

> If the mind is realized, that is wisdom. Therefore, meditate perfectly on understanding that buddhahood is not to be searched for elsewhere.[136]

It's called "mind." It's called "knowing." [42] It's called "thoughts." It's called "mindfulness." Essentially it's simply this continuous cognition, this flow of thoughts, that you continually call "my mind." When you know its nature, you attain buddhahood. When you don't know it, you wander in samsara. Therefore, you must know the nature of the mind.

This is what the general Dharma teachings call "the aspect of wisdom," but here it's called "the instruction of the main practice." Therefore, I earnestly request you to practice it.

As taught above, develop love, compassion, and supreme bodhicitta; recite the hundred syllables; offer the mandala; supplicate; and so on. It's taught that after completing those:

> Supplicate with intense faith and devotion.
> Clear your mind of its pollution.[137]

And also:

> Without much darkness from examination and analysis,
> rest in a relaxed, free, uncontrived state.[138]

After tears have flowed from genuine devotion to the guru, meditate that the guru, with overwhelming compassion for you, melts into light and dissolves into your body completely. It's taught:

> Merge and deeply, totally relax the body and mind. Relax loosely and rest completely. Do not meditate on anything. Do not pollute the naturally pure mind with the stains of meditation.[139]

Do not meditate on dharmakāya. Do not meditate on transcendence of the intellect. Do not meditate on emptiness. Do not meditate on birthlessness. Do not meditate on luminosity. Do not meditate on mahāmudrā. So, what *do* you do?

Do not move the body. Do not close the eyes. Do not go after past consciousnesses. Do not go to meet future consciousnesses. Completely rest solely in the present, without any calculation, but with vivid appearances, clear knowing, and a completely natural, naked consciousness. Rest in a state of clarity and naturalness. Rest relaxed, without tightness. Do not examine or analyze good and bad. Do not have doubts about what is or isn't. When thoughts appear, do not follow after their numerous appearances. Rest completely, like a sheaf of hay that has had its string cut. Rest, relaxed, in natural consciousness. Past thoughts have ceased, the future ones have not arisen. In this relaxed in-between state of the present, [43] it's taught:

> That mind is no mind; the mind's nature is luminosity.[140]

Just this mind alone, which is completely empty, clear, aware, and lucid, is what is called *the perfection of wisdom*, *luminosity*, *mahāmudrā*, *dzokchen*, and *dharmakāya*.

> Look directly and don't be blind!
> Go where you're going and don't wander!
> See the truth and don't obscure it!
> That is the true nature! Rest naturally![141]

With firm control, rest, relaxed and naturally, solely in empty, stainless knowing. It's taught that *meditation* is simply a term used for when, without meditation, you are naturally at rest in simple equanimity. Therefore, that is the "meditation" that you should do. That's what's meant by "good practice," and that's what's meant by "essence." Rest in that alone, naturally, as it is, relaxed. If thoughts are not appearing in that state, just rest until they appear. Resting in that way is called "mind" and is called "knowing."

When there is movement, with all kinds of thoughts spontaneously arising, it's taught:

> If you relax this tightly bound mind,
> there is no doubt but that it will be liberated.[142]

Therefore, rest, relaxed, on whatever thought arises, whether it is about an external object or the internal mind. When the arising of thoughts ceases, there will be spontaneously the nature of emptiness, without any existence as anything whatsoever. There will be inevitably a perfect clarity, like the center of an autumn's cloudless sky.[143] Don't be glad if it lasts a long time, and don't be upset if it lasts only a short time.

That was a teaching on *mahāmudrā* based on the key point of neither stopping nor creating [thoughts].

When you rest loosely in that way, if the mind is unstable and has strong thoughts, it means you are not free of the wish to meditate. Therefore, free yourself from a sense of purpose. Whether the mind is still or not, do not stop anything or create anything.

> A swift mountain river is made pure through its flowing.
> A silver mirror is made clear through being polished.
> A yogin's meditation is made blissful through being destroyed.[144]

Therefore it's taught:

> Rest, relaxed, without meditation. [44]
> If you rest relaxed, the turbidity of this ocean
> of cognition will become clear.[145]

A relaxed mind is all that is necessary. Perfect meditation will arise in a perfectly relaxed mind. A middling meditation will arise in a semi-relaxed mind. The least kind of meditation will arise in the least relaxed mind.

Therefore, just rest on whatever thought arises. This alone is the root of the instructions, so be firmly fixed upon any spontaneously appearing thought, and relax loosely on it alone. When the next thought appears, rest relaxed in that.

> Meditate in a great number of short sessions.
> When sessions are short, there can be no faults.
> When they are numerous, faults cannot continue.[146]

Therefore, relax before a thought arises, before even wishing to give rise to a thought. If you relax like that, it's impossible that this cognition alone will not arise as the dharmakāya. From the *Tantra of the Ocean of Vows*:

> Without contrivance, without distraction, there is spontaneous liberation.
> The spontaneous liberation of appearances is the expanse of great bliss.
> There is just ordinary, fresh relaxation.
> Practice the meditation that is nonmeditation.[147]

When thoughts clearly arise as the dharmakāya, there is no need to eliminate thoughts, and there is no need to create the dharmakāya. Therefore, all that you need is just the relaxed mind.

When you are resting in the uncontrived mind, in relaxation, if the mind becomes unstable and manifests thoughts, just leave it alone. Clean and offer a mandala, offering countless mental offerings as described earlier, and just pray with very intense devotion until you're exhausted. Then totally abandon yourself into that state of exhaustion, into the uncontrived mind. If thoughts do not appear, rest completely in that state where there are no thoughts.

If, when you relax and observe in that way, you are destabilized by thoughts, it means that you have lost your mindfulness. You cannot stop thoughts; you cannot eliminate thoughts; you cannot control them; you cannot hold them.

> Do not draw back the mind that moves toward objects,
> but let it be, like a raven that flies from a ship.
> The wise are like cattle herders:
> They let the practicing mind roam freely.[148]

It is said in the *Secret Lamp of Wisdom Tantra*:

> Nondependent, self-illuminating, nongrasping,
> resting nakedly in unimpeded knowing.[149]

If you try to stop [45] thoughts, they keep moving. If you try to hold them, they go away. Therefore, let them go to wherever they want without stopping any of them. They won't find anywhere to go. They come naturally, so don't deliberately stop any of them. Don't control any of them. Don't hold on to any of them. Don't deliberately create any of them. Don't contemplate and don't meditate.

When you are simply resting, loose and relaxed, in the uncontrived natural state, thoughts of like or dislike will sometimes arise spontaneously. Look directly at whatever thought arises. Where does it come from? Where is it now? Where does it eventually go? What shape does it have? Is it square? Is it round? Is it triangular? Is it oval? What color is it? Is it white? Is it red? Is it yellow? Is it blue? Is it black? Where is it? Is it on the crown of my head? Is it inside my head? Is it in my upper body? Is it in my limbs? Look to see where it is. Look directly at it to see where it is right now.

It's taught that if you always apply yourself solely to devotion to the guru, resting in an uncontrived state of mind, and looking at the mind, this practice will cause the way things truly are to appear from within. Therefore, gain complete, utter certainty, in which you think "this nature was here all the time, but until now I was deluded. Now, there is no mistake." At that time, this precious mind of yours alone will manifest perfectly as the dharmakāya. Therefore, since you will attain liberation naturally without the need to eliminate thoughts and since emptiness will naturally arise without the need to cultivate it, you need not seek the dharmadhātu elsewhere. So it has been taught. Thus, since this very variety of thoughts—arising perfectly as the dharmakāya—*is* the true nature, there is no need to meditate with eyes closed; there's no need to meditate to stop appearances. What the eyes perceive is the union of appearance and emptiness. What the ears perceive is the union of sound and emptiness. The mind is empty. As it is stated:

> The nature of appearances is primordially empty.
> They're not called "empty" because they're vanquished and destroyed.[150]

Forms appear to the eyes, but they are merely appearances without any truly existing essence; that is why they are called the "inseparability of appearance and emptiness." Sounds are heard by the ears, [46] but they are merely sounds with no truly existing nature; that is why they are called the "inseparability of sound and emptiness." Various things appear in the mind, but they have no truly existing nature whatsoever; that is why they are called the "inseparability of knowing and emptiness."

This is what is called "receiving your father's inheritance." It's also called "receiving the blessing of the sacred oral lineage." It's also called "putting the precious jewel in your pocket." It's also called "repaying the guru's kindness." Dedicate yourself to this until it occurs.

First, there is this kind of extensive introduction to the nature of the mind that is repeated over and over. Afterward, there is the main practice's instruction, which is the meaning lineage called "flowing out as buddhahood." The introduction by the guru is no longer necessary, and it arises perfectly within yourself. Therefore, have devotion to the guru and rest, relaxed, in the uncontrived mind.

Thus, the teaching is simply: "As your own mind is the root of all samsara and nirvana, look to see what it's like."

As a continuation of the teachings of Lord Śākyamuni,
Candraprabhakumāra,[151] the lord of the tenth level,
spread his emanation activity in this land of Tibet.
Thus, Dakpo Lhajé came to Daklha Gampo,[152]
led the faithful along the path of devotion,
and had countless accomplished pupils.
Because of his kindness, Tibet became filled with the Dharma.

He entrusted the tradition of this unsurpassable Dharma
to his lineage's countless practicing sons.
Later, the emanated individual, the birthless Shang Gom,[153]
in the presence of the two Buddha statues of Lhasa,[154] and in Tsal,
and in Gungthang,
taught solely these instructions
to worthy pupils he had gathered through his compassion.
Many became realized, supreme siddhas.

The practice lineage has spread through the kindness of this lord.
He is the lama who spread these teachings.
Subsequently, the Shang emanation, the unequaled Dharma Lord,
that unrivaled lama,[155] came to the monastery of Pangshong Lhari.[156]
He taught nothing but this Dharma
to everyone in his community of pupils,
and every year there was an unceasing appearance of realized beings.
This is how he liberated every single one of his pupils.

This is the essence of that lama's practice; [47]
therefore, it is superior to all other teachings.

It is the principal teaching of the Kagyüpas;
therefore, it is the quintessence of the Dharma, the life essence
of the ḍākinīs.

I received the lama's teaching again and again.
It remained clear and naked in my mind.
Without forgetting anything, I have written it out correctly,
without error.

As it is an oral transmission of direct practice instructions,
writing it down could cause its blessing to diminish,
but when done with a pure motivation of respect and love,
without any self-interest, it can't be wrong to do so.

There are great pupils of that lord, who by ripening qualities in others
have maintained the lineage and cared for the sangha,
but as this is an unmistaken, accurate record of the lama's teaching,
it is good that it be preserved and used to teach pupils.

Though I was perfectly seized by the father's hook of compassion,
I had no karma of previous practice and little diligence,
so I'm still someone who hasn't developed qualities.
Therefore even this beggar should dedicate himself to this.

I ask for forgiveness from those with eyes of wisdom,
especially from the true guru himself,
for whatever errors there are in what I have written,
and for any faults, such as omitting parts of his speech.

Through the merit of writing this, may all beings throughout space,
without exception, practice this Dharma
and manifest within one lifetime
the single quintessence of the equality of the dharmakāya.

I have written, without error, the instructions for the preliminaries and main practice as taught by the precious lama, glorious Lhariwa of the lineage of undiminished blessing.

I, Devakumāra,[157] wrote this at Pangshong Lhari.

Ithi
Maṅgalam

3. The Ultimate Supreme Path of Mahāmudrā

Lama Shang[158] (1123–93)

[49] I pay homage to the venerable glorious gurus.

Reverently, I bow to the feet of the realized gurus
who are the union of infinite, beneficial lassos,[159]
the empowerments that are the ultimate, compassionate activity
of all conquerors throughout the three times.

I will joyfully write, one-pointedly and without error, a representative fragment
of the innermost essence of all supreme vehicles, scriptural baskets, and tantras,
which is the mind of all the sugatas,
transmitted from mind to mind by the lords of yogis.

I, Tsöndrü Drakpa, do not have the power to benefit others,
but I have been urged on by my pupils,
who are wise and devoted followers of the Dharma.
I mustn't ignore the faintest possibility of benefit,
so I will write about the mother who gave birth to all conquerors and their children,
who is realized by all the trained, worthy ones,
who is the mind treasure of the venerable lineage holders,
who is the essence of all vehicles, scripture, logic, and instruction,
who is the essence of the ultimate, definitive meaning, the dharmakāya,
and who is the naturally pure expanse of luminosity.

1. The View

Whether the conquerors of the three times appear or don't appear,
whether the āryas realize it or don't realize it,
whether the buddhas teach it or don't teach it,
whether the commentators explain it or don't explain it,
this pure, elaboration-free luminosity of the true nature
is primordially, naturally present, with neither increase nor decrease.

Worlds are formed within pure space and are destroyed
by burning fire, scattering winds, and so on.
Although this destruction occurs throughout many incalculable eons,
space remains unharmed, never altered, and neither increases nor decreases.

There is darkness when the sun's primordial brightness
is completely obscured by clouds, and there is brightness when the clouds vanish.
Despite this apparent increase and decrease,
it is impossible for the sun's essence to increase or decrease.

The unchanging dharmakāya, which is present in the same way,
is nothing other than your own mind. [50]
The entire variety of samsara and nirvana arise in the mind.
The sufferings of the world and its beings arise from the confusion
caused by the erroneous delusion of not understanding your own mind.

When you have definite understanding of your own mind,
there will be great bliss and the infinite wisdom of nirvana.
Everything manifests from your own mind.
When you recognize the true nature of your mind,
you will know the true nature of all beings.
Knowing that, you will know nirvana and all other phenomena.
Knowing all phenomena, you will transcend all three realms.
By knowing one thing, you become wise in all.
By pulling up the roots, the leaves and petals naturally wither.
Therefore, gain certainty in the mind alone.

This true nature of the mind, the seed of everything,
primordially identical with the minds of all conquerors and their children,
is present as the birthless dharmakāya.

It is immaterial, self-knowing, and self-illuminating.
It is not a thing: It has no color, shape, or size.
It isn't nothing: Through conditions, it appears as everything.
It isn't permanent: It is empty by nature.
It isn't nonexistent: Its nature is unchanging self-illumination.
It is not a self: When examined, it has no essence.
It is not selfless: It is the great selfhood of freedom from elaboration.
It is not the extremes: It has no fixation whatsoever.
It is not the middle way: It is devoid of all dependency.
It cannot be identified by an example's names and symbols.
It has no example: It is like space.
It is not words: It cannot be described by speech.
It is not wordless: It is the cause of all expressions.

It cannot be reached through words such as
existence and nonexistence, truth and falsity,
empty and not empty, peace and no peace,
elaborated and unelaborated,
conceivable and inconceivable,
happiness and suffering, perceivable and unperceivable,
dual and nondual, beyond the intellect and not beyond the intellect,
devoid and not devoid, existent and nonexistent,
pure and impure, naturally present and not naturally present.

However profound the words used are,
and however many synonyms are employed,
it is impossible for them to pinpoint the true nature of the mind.

However wise you are, however profound your analysis,
though you describe it for many incalculable eons,
it will be impossible to realize the true nature of the mind,
for its natural condition is not an object for analysis. [51]

However well you try to sieve for
the planets and stars that appear in a lake,
it is impossible to catch a single planet or star,
because those planets and stars are not existent things.

However long you use words to describe it,
no matter what refined terms you use, they are not the true nature.
For however long you analyze with your mind,
no matter how profound your understanding, that is not the true nature.

As long as there is the duality of seer and seen,
it is impossible to realize the nondual true nature.

In brief, to think that things "are" is the root of attachment to everything.
From the root of attachment all samsara develops.

If you identify by thinking "It's emptiness,"
or thinking "It is signless and aspirationless,"
thinking "It is unidentifiable," thinking "It is completely pure,"
thinking "It is birthless," thinking "It is unperceivable,"
thinking "It has no nature," thinking "It is without elaboration,"
thinking "It is not an object for analysis by speech or mind,"
thinking "It is uncreated and naturally present," and so on,
however profound these thoughts, our recognition of emptiness
will not transcend the conceptualization of an arrogant mind.
Attachment to concepts leads to a fall into inferior states
and a continuous ripening of karma from inferior actions.

If the chronic condition of samsara is not cured, the illness will continue to occur.
Meditators who have views created by their intellect
remain chronically ill from attachment to sectarianism.
You must have the innate knowledge that is free of thought.

It's impossible that even Śākyamuni could see what is described by
"There are embellishments that are provisional in meaning,
while this is the definitive meaning, the true nature."

Even what I'm saying now cannot fathom it.
Understand that it's like a finger pointing at the moon.

If you understand this, words and terminology will not obscure;
you will be unstained by the faults of words.
Therefore, without abandoning words and analysis,
have no arrogant attachment to their meaning.

The true nature of your own mind
pervades all beings, including their afflictions,
thoughts, aggregates, sensory elements and bases,
and all worlds, including their earth, stones, plants, and trees.

In brief, it pervades everything without exception,
including all inner and outer things.
That pervasion is without the duality of pervader and pervaded;
it is the manifestation of one single great identity. [52]

All the planets and stars that appear on a lake
are pervaded by the lake, from which they cannot be separated.
All the waves that move upon the water
are pervaded by water and are inseparable from it.

The movement of mirages in the air
are pervaded by the air and are inseparable from it.

Statues, jewelry, and so on, which are made of gold,
are pervaded by gold and are inseparable from it.

Representations of the six kinds of beings made from molasses
are pervaded by molasses and are inseparable from it.[160]
Space is not separate from a rainbow;
a rainbow is nothing other than space.
The rainbow is space, and space is the rainbow.
They are not separate; they are inseparable and indivisible.

In the same way, the mind and the variety of appearances are inseparable.
The mind and emptiness are inseparable;

emptiness and bliss are a great inseparability, a sameness.
In the same way, existence and nirvana are inseparable.

This pervading mind is the mahāmudrā.
Its nature is empty, so there is nothing to be identified.
Its characteristic is clarity—[the mind's] cognition can manifest anything.
Its essence is their inseparability, the union of the vajra mind.
The precious mind is the source of countless qualities.
It is inexhaustible, imperishable, indestructible,
and no one can steal it, this mind that is the treasury of space,
the mind that is as pure as crystal, untarnished by stains.

The mind is like a lamp's flame: It is self-knowing and self-illuminating.
The mind has the essence of enlightenment: It has a nature of luminosity.
The mind is like a river: It is a constant continuum.
The mind is like space: There is nothing that can be identified.

It is a mind of immaterial wisdom, completely transparent,
like a clean vessel filled with water.

The mind, from which arises all appearances that result from
  propensities,
is like the surface of a polished and unblemished mirror.

2. Separating Samsara from Nirvana

When your own natural mind, present in that way,
is not understood or is misunderstood,
there is the embellishment of conceiving "me" and "mine,"
and these misconceptions cause
afflictions and thoughts to increase.

This accumulates karma, and the ripening of karma causes
the endless suffering of birth, death, and so on,
which are waves on the endless river of samsara,
distracting [53] and disturbing, continuously afflicting.

The myriad propensities for misperceiving
the myriad appearances of the six classes of beings
become established in the mind and multiply thoughts.

Various kinds of bad, errant behavior
cause a continuity of various, unendurable sufferings,
which are experienced over and over again.
These experiences cause stupidity to further increase.
Utterly overcome by ignorance,
the mind is troubled over and over
by anger, pride, desire, miserliness, and the rest.
Oh! Who would put their trust in samsara?

When you realize the true nature of your mind,
the darkness of mistaken views vanishes;
you are liberated from belief in a self, from afflictions and from attachment,
and are therefore truly free from all karma and suffering;
the primordially present dharmakāya is revealed,
and the power of your prayers effortlessly accomplishes benefit for others.

That which nirvana is dependent upon is so blissful—
a blissful cause, a blissful path, and bliss when there is the result!
How frightful are the sufferings of the three realms of samsara:
suffering as its cause, path, and result!
So why would you not escape the swamp of samsara
to reach the solid ground of nirvana?

Those who are attracted to nirvana's Dharma,
even the ugly, let alone the good-looking,
will appear beautiful to everyone
as soon as they enter the Dharma,
because their minds have turned toward faith and virtue.

Though you forsake fame, your fame spreads everywhere.
Though you forsake honors, all honor you.
Though you remain humble, all raise you on high.

Though you take on suffering, your life is happy.
Though you are poor, you have plenty of possessions.
Food and clothes effortlessly, spontaneously appear.
Though you flee alone, you meet a host of pupils and followers.
Though you do not chase them away, misleaders and hinderers flee from you.
Though you do not summon them, deities and Dharma guardians gather around you.

Even when those who are principally charlatans and frauds,
motivated by attachment, anger, pride, and so on,
do various good activities, such as studying,
it is not a waste, for we can directly see that those people
enjoy the full benefit from those good qualities.

As for those who pretend to be high persons but have little learning
and are proud and have the rest of the afflictions,
their miscellany of an outer appearance of good actions [54]
creates an infallible miscellany of good qualities;
so it is obviously so for a genuine Dharma practitioner.

If such qualities are immediately gained on entering the Dharma,
imagine how many qualities come from dedication to its practice!

In empty valleys and ownerless rocky mountains,
a conduct that is free of pretense is so spacious!
The happiness that never loses mindfulness is so sublime!
The companionship of deer, who never complain, is so pleasant!
The clothing and food of pure conduct is warm and beautiful!
The wealth of contentment, free of craving, is inexhaustible!
The armor of patience is so thick and strong!
The powerful, fast steed of diligence is so excellent!
The guru and Jewels, who give blessings, are such an excellent refuge!
The instructions on the essentials of the path of method are such a joyful experience!
The samādhi of bliss, clarity, and nonthought is so delicious!
The empty, stainless self-knowing is so bright!
The baseless arising of everything is so hilarious!

Whatever arises never departs from the essential nature, which is
so blissful!
The satisfaction from the nectar of experience is so fulfilling!
Arising from within nonelaboration, the mind is so pure!
Knowing the nature of thought, there is so much certainty!
Gaining mastery over the treasury of knowledge, there is so much wealth!
Enjoying appearances and beings as the dharmakāya, there is so much
happiness!
Controlling appearances and sounds, there is great power!
Defeating the armies of māras and wrongs views, there is such wrathfulness!
Escaping from the dungeon of samsara, there is such freedom!
Spontaneously accomplishing the benefit of beings, there is great benefit!
Racing across the plain of great bliss, there is such speed!

Even if you spent an eon, you would still not be able
to describe all the qualities that come from diligent practice.
If that is true for the qualities that come from diligent practice,
then it is obviously so for the qualities that come from gaining signs of
heat.[161]
Even if you spent an eon, you would still not be able
to describe all those qualities, such as miraculous powers and clairvoyance.
If that is true for the qualities that come on gaining signs of heat,
then it's obviously so for qualities when the three kāyas manifest.
It's impossible to ever finish describing the qualities of the conquerors,
such as their unsurpassable and inconceivable wisdom.

3. Forsaking Activities

However wise you are in contemplating and analyzing words,
if you do not practice, nothing will arise from within.
It's impossible for intellect's conceptual labeling to realize the true nature.
If you do not realize the true nature, it is impossible to purify your
propensities.
Therefore, do not be attached to the academic wisdom of words,
but practice the instructions from the guru. [55]

Repeating like a parrot becomes a song of aging and death.
Blind to yourself and others, there is the danger of falling into an abyss.

When you are practicing the sacred instructions,
have no attachment to life or body and forsake activities.
Even if you are hungry, cold, sick, or dying from starvation,
forsake everything, for they are just a dream.

Even if everyone reviles you and you acquire a bad reputation,
be humble and dedicate yourself to the essence of practice.

The fear of death from cold and hunger
is a cause for not abandoning worldly activities.
The few qualities that this beggar monk Shang has
are the benefit of using my life and body like targets.

Even if you have abandoned all wealth, right down to a needle and thread,
if you worry about supporting yourself, you are not a renunciate.
If you don't reject the wish to avoid what is bad,
there will never be a time when you abandon worldly activities.

If you do not banish the entire world from your mind,
even though you can be generous, maintain conduct,
make offerings to the guru, remain in solitude,
dedicate yourself to meditation, have good experiences,
have great wisdom, have high realization,
or perform any good action, you will just be meaninglessly tiring yourself.

If you don't understand how to banish the world from your mind
and you don't even wish for the happiness of the devas,
it's obvious that you must be aspiring for happiness in this life.

As long as thoughts have not ceased,
it's impossible to avoid preoccupation with future days.
Therefore, cast everything aside, become a devotee of the sacred.
Devote yourself to the treasury of instructions,
be unaffected by the armies of outer and inner māras,
and maintain a pure conduct whether in public or in private.

If you can do this by yourself, then wander alone in the mountains.
Maintain a pure conduct, free of pretense.

Have a motivation to benefit others, free of bias and attachment.
Develop the aspiration for enlightenment for the sake of all beings.
Apply yourself to genuine practice that is neither too tight nor too loose.

Practice the instructions just as they have been taught,
without focusing the mind on any happiness or unhappiness,
such as danger to life, heat and cold, hunger and thirst,
and without becoming seduced by fame and material wealth.

4. The Different Classes of Individuals and the Gradualist Path

[56] Beings have an inconceivable variety of conducts
and all their individual capabilities are countless.
Because of the different levels of their training,
the teachings of the conquerors are endless.

Summarizing them, the teachings are of three kinds,
which accord with different levels of training:
There are individuals who are gradualist,
those who are immediate, and those who are nonsequential.

The perfect path for a gradualist
would be an inappropriate Dharma for an immediate.
The perfect path for an immediate
would be an inappropriate Dharma for gradualists.

The perfect food for the peacock is aconite,[162]
but if others eat it they will die.
The perfect dwelling place for fish is water,
but humans and others drown in it
while fish die if they are on dry land.

That which heals a hot illness
is harmful for someone with a cold illness.
That which is good for someone with a cold illness
is very harmful for someone with a hot illness.

Thus, different vehicles are taught
to the same individual at different levels.
That which is beneficial at an earlier level
is bondage at a higher level.
That which is beneficial at a higher level
is a cause of downfall at a lower level.

A cooling potion is beneficial
at the onset of a hot illness,
but is very harmful while recovering from it.

Therefore, know that there are different phases
and different levels of capabilities,
so that different paths should not malign each other.

The individuals who are gradualists should first
contemplate the difficulty of obtaining a precious human existence,
become saddened by the terrors of the lower existences,
contemplate the impermanence of the precious human existence,
and quickly go for refuge in the Three Jewels.

They should then take the eight fast-day vows
and then the five lay vows,
And the successive training of the novice monk and fully ordained monk.

They should turn away from the phenomena of samsara,
have their minds fixed on nirvana,
keep the discipline of striving for liberation,
and learn the philosophies of the Vaibhāṣikas and Sautrāntikas.

Then, in order to reject the lesser enlightenment,
they should meditate on repaying the kindness of beings,
become habituated to love and compassion,
and develop the aspiration to supreme enlightenment.

In the three phases of preparation, main part, and conclusion,
they should practice the six perfections
and gather the two accumulations.

Uniting emptiness and compassion,
they should become familiarized with *śamatha* (stability) and *vipaśyanā* (insight),
training well their own beings.

They should dedicate themselves continuously to the benefit of others
with an altruistic motivation free of self-interest.

An individual who has trained in that way
should then enter the Vajrayāna
and train in the four tantras in sequence
in order to accomplish the kāya with seven aspects.[163] [57]

Those in the highest yoga tantras
should receive the vase empowerment,
keep their commitments properly,
and train in the generation stage.

Then they should receive the secret empowerment
and bless themselves with the power of the channels and winds.

Then they should meditate on the bliss and emptiness of the third empowerment
and become familiar with the ultimate fourth empowerment.

I have specifically described the gradualist individual,
but there are countless classes of individuals:
There are those who must progress through the vehicles from the beginning;
there are those for whom a rough training will suffice;
and there are those who have no need to train.

There are those who obtain the empowerment without receiving it;
there are very many who have not obtained the empowerment even though they have received it;
there are those who have both received and obtained the empowerment;
there are those who have neither received nor obtained it;
there are those who have the primordial possession of the empowerment.

Therefore, with the knowledge of what kind of individual the pupil is,
the pupil should practice accordingly.

5. *The Method of Meditation*

I, Tsöndrü Drakpa, on the urging of my pupils,
who are wise and devoted followers of the Dharma,
and not wanting to ignore the slightest chance of being beneficial,
will explain the training that worthy ones should understand.

The immediate kind of individuals
should please the guru of the lineage
with their bodies and every possession.

They should receive empowerment and blessing
and, uplifted by the bodhicitta,
together with the practice of a deity,
should meditate from the very beginning
on the definitive meaning: the mahāmudrā.

A guru who has the quintessence of realization
directly introduces them to the wisdom they already have,
as if it were a treasure in their own hands.
They should remain, without distraction, in a state of nonmeditation,
where there is neither meditator nor anything on which to meditate.

The desire for numerous complexities
obscures the naturally present wisdom.
There is no need for a precise plan of action
in the meditation of mahāmudrā;
it does not have the stages of preliminaries, a main part,
and a conclusion, nor does it have any definitive numbers;
there is no need to calculate times and dates.
Whenever one has mindfulness, rest with relaxation.

Your mind is birthless and continuous,
without a beginning, middle, or end.

The rising and sinking of agitated waves
ceases by itself without interference.
This mind that is obscured by thoughts,
when left as it is, unmodified, will clarify as the dharmakāya.

Do not modify it, but rest in relaxation.
Do not control the mind, but let it go free.
Do not have intentions, but be spacious.
Do not focus on anything, [58] but be expansive.

Do not be overactive, but rest in stillness.
Do not seek out somewhere to rest the mind;
rest without any basis, like space.

Keep the mind fresh, without thinking
of the past, the future, or the present.

Whether thoughts are appearing or not,
do not purposefully meditate, but rest naturally.

In brief, do not meditate on anything,
but let the mind go wherever it wants.

There is no need to be afraid of anything:
You will never depart from the dharmakāya.
Just by allowing the mind to relax
there will be an experience of clarity and nonthought,
and you will rest as if in the center of pure space:
This is the luminosity, the dharmakāya.

When a thought instantly springs from
that resting state,
do not think of it as something that is
other than the luminosity, the dharmakāya.

It is the same as when waves rise
from a clear, still sea

and are nothing other
than that clear sea.

The mind is the basis of thoughts.
Clarity and knowing are the characteristics of the mind.
Emptiness is the nature of that clarity and knowing.
Great bliss is the essence of emptiness.

The darkness of concepts has never existed
within the nature of the mind,
and so it is named *luminosity*.
Its knowing and emptiness are inseparable,
And therefore it is named *union*.

The nature of all phenomena
is the essence of the mind's knowing.
The essence of the mind's knowing
has no body with features;
it is a bodiless body, which is the supreme body.

Bodilessness is the body of the "true nature" (*dharmatā*),
and therefore it is named the "truth body" (*dharmakāya*).

Therefore, the appearance of a thought
is emptiness appearing from emptiness,
the dharmakāya appearing from the dharmakāya,
luminosity appearing from luminosity,
union appearing from union,
the dharmadhātu appearing from the dharmadhātu,
purity appearing from purity,
Vajrasattva appearing from Vajrasattva,
enlightenment appearing from enlightenment.

Ignorant persons, who have no propensities from previous training
and have not obtained the true instructions,
make a distinction between the appearance
and the nonappearance of thoughts,

between thought and nonthought,
and between the mind and the dharmakāya.

They see thoughts as faults and stop them.
They wish for nonthought and deliberately create it,
but the wandering waves keep on moving.

The nonthought created by stopping thought
is thought. It is a delusion.
It is a great darkness that obscures the dharmakāya.

Those who do not wish to give rise to thought [59]
are those who wish to remain in nonthought.
That desire leads to becoming a *gongpo* demon
and exhausts the treasury of natural wealth.
Meditators who stop their thoughts
are like people churning water for butter:
They will not see any benefit, even if they meditate for an eon.

Therefore, it's unnecessary to stop thoughts.
If they've stopped, there is no need to create them.
Though they appear, the dharmakāya is also present,
for they do not depart from the dharmakāya.

If you have the instructions from a sublime guru,
when there is movement, there is liberation; and when there is stillness,
there is liberation.
Without instructions from a sublime guru,
when there is movement, there is bondage; and when there is stillness,
there is bondage.

Therefore, you must receive the instructions.
Be certain that thoughts arise as your friends.
Refrain from preoccupying yourself with much analysis.
Instead, relax freely and be naturally at rest.

Do not follow after externals,
but let the mind go wherever it wants.

Do not look at external objects.
Do not even look at your own mind.

The objects are empty and the mind too is empty.
There is no need to feel afraid.

If you think, "This is it,"
that will plant the seed of attachment to an object.
If the seedling of conceit appears,
it will grow into the tree of samsara.

Do not obscure the mind with the darkness of meditation,
for the mind is primordially pure and luminous,
and meditation will destroy the effortless result.

Do not stir up the turbidity of desire
in the clear sea of the mind,
for that will obscure the jewels of the dharmakāya.

Do not smear the stains of meditation
upon the unblemished mirror of the mind,
for then you will not see the reflection of wisdom.

Do not use the clay of concepts to cover up
the precious jewel of the mind,
for that will prevent the desired and required result.

In brief, rest the mind without thinking, "This is it!"
Rest the mind without thinking, "This isn't it!"
The mind's thoughts of "is" and the mind's thoughts of "isn't"
are two mutually dependent fixations.
If there is absolutely no "is" at all,
then there will be absolutely no "isn't" at all.

Let go completely in a state free from thinking.
Don't think of "resting" or "not resting."
Don't think of "letting go" or "not letting go."
Don't even think "Think!" or "Don't think!"

Whether you are moving, sitting, or standing,
whether you are meditating, sleeping, or eating,
whether you are talking, sleeping, or anything,
it's essential that it be done with the natural mind. [60]

6. Experience

Rest your own mind, this naturally present dharmakāya,
as it is, without modification,
and specific experiences will happen.

There are three kinds: those of the gradualist,
the indeterminate, and the immediate.

The way that experiences happen for gradualists:
At first there is simply resting,
then experiences definitely happen,
and then clear realization arises.

When there is the first state of resting,
thoughts arise uninterruptedly,
like water rushing down a cliff.
So you think, "Am I not able to meditate?"

The experience of this amount of thoughts arising
is the result of the mind being able to rest a little.
Before you rested in this way,
thoughts arose as they wished,
and you were not aware of the procession of thoughts.

Next, the mind slows and thoughts diminish,
becoming like a slowly moving river.

Then the mind will rest, immovable and stable,
like the depths of the ocean.

Then there will come experiences:
experiences of clarity, nonthought, and bliss,

like the center of pure space.
There is undistracted self-illumination,
like a lamp's flame undisturbed by wind.
There is lucidity, vividness, and ease,
like a rainfall of beautiful flowers.
There is brightness, evenness, and insubstantiality,
like the sun shining in a cloudless sky.
There is transparency and purity,
like a bronze vessel filled with water.

There is no end to words such as these.
They have no basis, appearing like dreams.
They are insubstantial, appearing like rainbows.
They are ungraspable, appearing like the moon on water.
It is like enjoying the pleasures of space—
everything is experienced but is experienced as nothing.
This nonexperience is the supreme experience.
All experiences have gone away.
Within nonexperience, there is nothing to be freed from.

7. Nondual Realization

When you have those kinds of experiences,
realization's wisdom clearly arises.
If realization's wisdom doesn't arise,
however excellent those experiences may be,
they're like cutting down a tree but not touching the roots,
so that the agony of the afflictions will still grow.

Therefore, the arising of realization is crucial.
The arising of the wisdom of realization
certainly does not happen through desire,
it does not come through skill in analysis,
it does not come through great learning,
and it is beyond the scope of academics.

The nonthought created by stopping thought,
however deep and strong it may be,
is a great obscuration that prevents the birth of wisdom.

The spontaneous arising of realization's wisdom
certainly does not come
through desire or acquisition, [61]
through being skilled or unskilled in analysis,
through great or little learning,
through wisdom or stupidity,
through good or bad experiences,
through intense or weak efforts, and so on.
It comes through relying upon a guru
and through your own merit.

"Relying upon a guru," means that
you receive it by pleasing a realized guru.
"Through your own merit" means that wisdom
comes to those predisposed through former training.

Therefore, as the wisdom of realization
is acquired on the path of blessing,
it is experienced by those who have faith,
it arises within those who have veneration,
and it is realized by those who are trained.
Diligence is a help in all of these.
It is the worthy ones with the highest capability who see wisdom.
The minds of those only skilled in words can't comprehend it.

The nondual realization that worthy individuals have
comes through the blessing of a sublime guru:
The dharmakāya arises from the middle of realization,
nonduality arises from the middle of the mind,
wisdom arises from the middle of the afflictions,
and realization arises from the middle of experiences.

The delusion of dualism will completely vanish,
as when a sleeping man wakes up.
On meeting nondual wisdom you awake and think,
"Oh! It's been here all along,
but I hadn't realized it before!
Nondual wisdom: what a joy!
My previous conduct: oh, so shameful!

It's realizing and not realizing it
that differentiates samsara from nirvana.
Up until now, before this realization,
I was like a man who was just
asleep and dreaming dreams:
I dreamed that I wandered in the ocean of samsara.
I dreamed that I suffered in the hells and so on.
I dreamed that, troubled, I turned to the guru.
I dreamed that I practiced his instructions.
I dreamed that experiences arose in my mind.
I dreamed that the luminosity arose as the dharmakāya.
I dreamed that the darkness of thought was dispelled.
I dreamed that there was no separation between meditation and post-meditation.
I dreamed that realization arose.
I dreamed that objectless compassion arose
toward beings without realization.
I dreamed that I attained the supreme mahāmudrā
and that my form kāyas spontaneously accomplished the benefit of beings."

When you suddenly wake from that sleep,
there was no suffering of samsara,
there was no turning to the guru because you were troubled,
there was no practicing his instructions,
there was no arising of experiences in the mind,
there was no arising of luminosity as the dharmakāya, [62]
there was no dispelling the darkness of thoughts,
there was no remaining in nonthought,
there was no arising of wisdom's realization,
there was neither beings nor compassion,
there was neither enlightenment nor attainment,
there was neither beings nor benefiting them,
there was neither truth nor falsity.

They were nothing but dream appearances.
Where did the samsara that you dreamed of
come from and where did it go?

Where did nirvana, the elimination of samsara,
come from and where did it go?
They and everything else were dream phenomena.
Where did they come from and where did they go?

It is the same as when a great king,
without leaving his throne for an instant,
in an illusion sits on a horse that runs away,
crossing many mountain passes and valleys.
Many months and years go by,
and he experiences all kinds of happiness and sorrow,
all without ever leaving his throne,
and without even the morning having passed by.

In the instant when realization arises,
when there is that great wisdom,
you comprehend the nature of all phenomena,
without becoming conceited by thinking, "I comprehend."
The nondual wisdom becomes manifest,
yet you don't become conceited by thinking, "It has manifested to me."
You are liberated from the three realms and from the Hīnayāna,
yet you don't become conceited by thinking, "I'm liberated."

In the instant that you realize nonduality,
you have certainty that all appearances and sounds are mind,
so that the Aspectarian[164] doctrine is made manifest.
You have certainty in the clarity of the mind,
so that the Non-Aspectarian[165] doctrine is made manifest.
You know self-knowing to be like an illusion,
so that the Illusion[166] doctrine is perfected.
You know illusion to be empty,
so that the Utterly Nonabiding[167] doctrine is perfected.

Emptiness arises as bliss
so that the view of nondual union is perfected.
That union has nonattention,
so that the mahāmudrā is made manifest
but without any identification through thinking, "It has manifested."

This wisdom through realization
does not come from anywhere,
does not go anywhere,
and does not reside anywhere.

The wisdom of realization and what it realizes
both dissolve into the nonconceptual essence of phenomena
without the arrogance of identifying it as the essence.

Now, remain within the equality that is like space.
Truly look at that which is true
and makes all thought and words meaningless.
When you truly see, you will be liberated.

The children have become tired
of the games that I have played.
If there is anything, offer it to the guru.
If there isn't anything, let the mind relax.

That is the gradualist's process of development.

In the indeterminates' process of development,
they gain stability, experiences, and realization. [63]
An exceptional realization may arise first,
but that realization will be unstable, like waves.
They may sometimes have experiences and
sometimes have stability, in no certain order.
They are able to have both higher and lower experiences.

For the immediate kind of individuals,
experience, realization, and stability
arise simultaneously, without meditation,
as soon as a guru, who has the essence of realization,
teaches the instructions to them
or simply looks at their minds.

Whether their experiences increase or decrease,
their realization remains unchanged,

just as a tree remains unchanged
even though a monkey climbs up and down it;
just as the sky remains unchanged
even though rainbows appear or disappear in it;
just as the depths of the ocean do not change
whether waves rise or cease upon its surface.
It doesn't matter what experiences come or go
in the mind that is the natural presence of the dharmakāya.

If those who have clear experiences
do not blend those experiences with realization,
they will be like lamp flames in the midst of a tempest,
which will be ruinous for beginners.

For meditators who have gained stability,
everything, whether good or bad, will be an aid.
So, beginners, don't be afraid.

When a lamp is tiny,
even a faint breeze will extinguish it.
When a great fire blazes in a forest,
any strong wind will only increase it.

Meditators who don't have stability,
may have occasional realizations,
but they have to feed the torch of realization
with the dry wood of experiences
while too much damp wood will extinguish it.

However high your realizations,
if your stability and experiences are not stable,
if you have no control over your own mind,
the afflictions—your enemies—will capture you.

That is like when an important man,
seized by enemies and held captive by weapons,
is on the road that leads home
but is not free to follow it.

Therefore, it's essential to maintain the torch of realization
through having stable experiences.
If you don't have control over your own mind,
you will lose the confidence of realization.

It's not in the mouth of someone who's all talk.
Be careful all you meditators,
for talking counteracts experiences.

8. Conduct

For the practitioner of mahāmudrā,
the colors of experiences appear
in the wish-fulfilling jewel of realization, [64]
and needs and desires are fulfilled through their conduct.

When individuals who are gradualists
enter onto the Mantrayāna path,
they keep far from negative thoughts
and wish to be free from samsara.

Their minds are fixed upon great enlightenment,
and with motivation devoid of self-interest
they develop the bodhicitta to benefit beings.

They always have the pride of being the deity;
they repeat mantras, recite, and offer mandalas and tormas;
they practice the seven branches, such as offerings;
they make a gift of tormas to pretas;
and they offer water and medicine to the nāgas.

With their possessions, they honor and serve the guru,
provide feasts for the sangha, hold gaṇacakras,
give to beggars without reservation,
perform the outer and inner *homa* fire rituals,
creates tsatsas,[168] stupas, and statues,
save the lives of animals, and chant the canon.

In brief, in between the generation and completion practice sessions,
they do nothing but good actions
with a motivation of great compassion,
never remaining in neutral activity,
let alone engaging in bad conduct.

They behave like venerable monks
or just like new brides:
maintaining careful conduct,
their actions all conforming to goodness.

They purify their outer and inner obscurations
and are dedicated to the accumulation of merit.
They keep their good qualities secret, augmenting them privately.

Those who ignore karma
and malign relative methods
are like birds without wings;
they will certainly fall into the abyss of lower existences.
Therefore, avoid even the smallest bad action
and practice even the smallest good action.

Those who have continuous diligence
in the practice of good actions
gain a small degree of stability
and distinguish between outer and inner conduct.

Their public conduct accords with other beings.
In solitude, they develop the inner conduct of samādhi.
When they increase the experience of inner conduct,
they adopt a conduct that accords with that experience,
which then increases their samādhis and realizations—
something beginners cannot experience.

They practice with the five nectars[169]
and depend upon the five powers.[170]
They do not give up the five sensory pleasures
but give up attachment to them and use them as aids.

Water and compost cause
rice sprouts to grow in the fields.
Reliance on sensory pleasures causes
the sprouts of practice's wisdom to grow.

In their conduct they have no attachment to anything
because they have the continuous experience of birthlessness.
This relaxed natural conduct of the six consciousnesses
is accompanied by the realization of nonduality.

They perform any conduct they wish
without discriminating between what should and should not
be done. [65]

Experiencing the realization of nonduality,
they wear anything, good or bad,
without thinking about which clothes can be worn and which not.

Without thinking about which food can be eaten and which not,
they eat anything, pure or impure,
and nonconceptual wisdom increases.

Without thinking about what can be said and what can't,
they just say whatever comes to mind.

They do not deliberately do anything.
They remain in a natural state of relaxation.
They are never apart from the experience of the dharmakāya.
They have no attachment to anything.

They are not disturbed, even for an instant,
by any good or bad thing
their own followers or others do,
but remain as unresponsive as matter.

They never perform
activities that are harmful to the mind.

They flee from humans,
just like deer flee from humans.

They do not argue about whether others are good or bad
while proudly thinking of themselves as good.
They always conceal their qualities,
just like swindlers keep their faults secret.

They do not talk big like an important man
but always remain humble.
Even if they have realized every level of meaning,
they always make offerings to the gurus and ḍākinīs.

In brief, they abandon all self-interest,
deception, and artifice.

For as long as there is a meditation and post-meditation,
they examine to see if their minds
are stable or unstable in meditation.
If the mind in meditation is unstable,
it's pointless to practice a stupid meditation
within a state of dullness and obscurity;
instead, they dedicate their body and speech
to good actions motivated by love and compassion.

However, when meditation is stable,
even if it means desisting from good conduct by body and speech,
they apply themselves solely to becoming adept in meditation.

Meditation and *post-meditation*
doesn't mean "sitting down" and "standing up."

The beginner's meditation
is unwavering one-pointedness
upon any positive object whatsoever;
whether sitting or moving around, it's meditation.
If they don't remain one-pointed

and become lost in thought,
though they meditate on a cushion, it's post-meditation.

The meditation of realizing your own mind
is known as the successive four yogas.

The one-pointed yoga arises
when you realize the characteristics of your own mind
as unceasing emptiness and clarity, without center or edge,
like the middle of pure space.
That pure and vivid state
is the meditation of the first yoga. [66]

When thoughts arise within that state,
even if you're meditating on a cushion, it's post-meditation.
If you remain in that pure, vivid clarity and emptiness,
whether you're talking, moving, or sitting,
you remain in the state of meditation.

The yoga of nonelaboration arises
when you realize the essence of your own mind
as a continuity of knowing, free from conceptual elaboration,
in which your own mind is the dharmakāya,
without birth or cessation, adoption or rejection.
That is the meditation of the second yoga.

When you remain in that meditation,
whether you're moving, sitting, or talking,
you remain in the state of meditation.
If you become distracted by the elaboration of concepts,
even if you're meditating on a cushion, it's post-meditation.

The yoga of one taste arises
when you realize the character of your own mind,
when you realize that the multiplicity of samsara and nirvana
arises from your mind, which is the dharmakāya free from conceptual elaboration.

The entire array of thought and nonthought,
appearances and no appearance, resting and no resting,
empty and not empty, clarity and no clarity,
are all one taste in the luminosity of the dharmakāya.

You see no appearances that are not the dharmakāya.
You see no thought that is not luminosity.

When the mind has that realization of equal taste,
it is the meditation of the third yoga.

While there is that natural mind,
whether you're running, jumping, or talking,
you remain in the state of meditation.
When you don't have the natural mind,
even if you're meditating on a cushion, it's post-meditation.

The yoga of nonmeditation arises
when the nature of knowing has no basis.
The practitioner has nothing to meditate on;
there is no meditator, only a state of evenness.

You will know what is meant by
"Buddhahood, with its three kāyas
and five wisdoms, is complete in me."
You will have complete certainty that this itself
is the accomplishment of mahāmudrā.
You will not be conceited, thinking,
"I have attained the primordially present accomplishment!"
There will be neither mindfulness nor the absence of mindfulness.
There will be neither attention nor nonattention.
There will be neither one taste nor the absence of one taste.

There are no stages of meditation and post-meditation
in that self-sustaining knowledge of nonduality.
There is no death and there is no birth
in the continuous presence of knowing and emptiness.

A gāruda's powers are already complete within the egg;
as soon as it hatches, it flies into the sky.
The qualities of the three kāyas are already complete within the mind;
as soon as the body's trap is destroyed, they will benefit others.
When this nonmeditation arises,
there are no stages of meditation and post-meditation.

However high your realization, [67]
while you are still familiarizing yourself with it,
there will still be stages of meditation and post-meditation,
there will still be mindfulness and the absence of mindfulness,
and there will still be distraction and the absence of distraction.

When you have completed the process of familiarization,
that is called *nonmeditation*,
where there are no stages of meditation and post-meditation,
there is nothing but a continuous state of meditation.
The mind of natural realization is present,
so whether you are moving about, sitting, or lying down,
whether you are sleeping or dreaming,
whether you are talking or eating,
there is nothing but meditation.

It is the jewel that naturally fulfills all needs and wishes.
It is the sun that naturally has light.
It is the yoga of constant meditation.
It is called *manifest nonduality*.

In the post-meditation of one-pointedness,
things appear to be solid
but are meditated upon as illusions.

In the post-meditation of nonelaboration,
things sometimes appear as illusions
and sometimes they appear to be solid,
but they are meditated upon as the dharmakāya.

In the post-meditation of the one-taste phase,
things arise as the dharmakāya when there is mindfulness,
but there are brief periods of solidity, when there is no mindfulness.

In nonmeditation, both meditation
and post-meditation are nothing but the dharmakāya,
and the two form kāyas appear to others.

It's not in the mouth of someone who's all talk.
It's not in a mouth that boasts empty words.
Don't keep yourself in the dark![171]
When there is nonmeditation,
whether you are asleep or not, there is clarity.
Whether you are analyzing or not,
whether you have mindfulness or not,
there is clearly the dharmakāya, with no self or others.
Without any thought of making an effort,
Objectless compassion arises spontaneously.

Until you reach that level,
You are in grave danger of deceiving yourself
with a nonmeditation that's just clinging to empty talk.

Therefore, worthy meditators,
until you reach the level of nonmeditation,
honor the guru and accumulate merit.
If you are not deceived by clinging to empty talk,
your accumulation of merit will never let you down.
That is the heart advice of the realized ones.

As for being with others or being in solitude,
if you always have the wisdom of the dharmakāya,
are free from attachment to duality,
and are not overcome by the eight worldly concerns,
you will always be in solitude, even though you wander through a crowd.
However, if you have attachment to duality,

have ups and downs, and so on,
you are always in a crowd, even when you're in solitude. [68]

Therefore, whether in solitude or with others,
always have the realization of nonduality,
don't go through ups and downs,
and prize having no attachment to anything.

The distinction between solitude and company,
between meditation and post-meditation, and so on,
are taught with the intention of guiding
those individuals who are beginners.
Ultimately, there are no such dualities
as solitude and company, meditation and post-meditation.

Why is that? Because the mind
is the innate dharmakāya
and appearances are the innate light of the dharmakāya,
just like a lamp's flame and its light.

Dharmakāya is the nature of knowing;
it can't possibly have discontinuity or fluctuation,
so how could there be meditation and post-meditation?
Who can deny the absence of meditation and post-meditation
in a meditator who has this enduring realization?
That is why they cannot be judged like ordinary individuals.

You may have experiences or realizations and think you are special,
but no matter how good the experiences are,
liberation is impossible without realization;
no matter how high the realizations are,
without compassion, they will be the śrāvaka path.

Even if you have experiences and samādhis
within the four dhyānas, and so on,
if you have the great fault of being without realization,
those experiences will cease, and afterward
you will fall into the three lower existences and so on
and experience unendurable suffering; think about that!

All experiences are composite;
everything composite is impermanent and will end.
Therefore, have no attachment to experiences
and realize nondual wisdom.

This nonabiding nirvana
is solely the province of realization.
Mentally fabricated nonduality,
which is what great scholars realize,
is solely the province of thought.

The nonduality that arises within
is nothing but the blessing of the guru.
The faithful who have veneration for the guru
develop the certainty of realization within themselves.
What does someone who just analyzes have?
Even I have understood it as words, too.

When realization arises in your mind,
examine to see whether it can withstand negative factors.
If someone on your right is swinging an axe at you
and saying all kinds of unpleasant things to you,
while someone on your left offers you the aroma of sandalwood
and respectfully says all kinds of pleasant thing to you,
if while you're having this experience,
you have no happiness or suffering, no like or dislike,
without having to make an effort to deal with it,
then you're ready to perform crazy behavior in public.

However, if you have no faith or if it's unstable,
if you haven't gained unimpeded powers,
and you publicly carry out the secretly taught conduct,
you will bring yourself and others to ruin. [69]

When you have gained unimpeded powers,
such as various kinds of clairvoyance,
some of which may possibly be of benefit to others,
don't distinguish between secret and public conduct.

The venerable Mila taught that
the ten virtuous actions are not to be performed,
that the ten bad actions are not be abandoned,
and that you should rest in natural relaxation.

The venerable Loro[172] taught that
the powerful, high, Three Jewels
are completely present in a state of devotionless knowing
in which there is nothing that can be called "going for refuge."

These viewpoints of those venerable ones
are as clear as a butter lamp in a vase
to me, the beggar monk from Shang,
and to all my realized vajra siblings.

But if I explain it, you will find it hard to understand,
for it's experienced only by those in whom it has spontaneously arisen,
by those who have faith, by those who have pleased their gurus
and whose blessing has entered into their hearts.

I am not going to describe the "all-victorious" conduct,
the "great meditation" conduct, or any of the others,[173]
as I think that it would take too long;
since you can read about them within the ocean of supreme tantras,
I don't have to write too much here.

Perform the appropriate conduct at the appropriate time.
Avoid senseless behavior and empty chatter.
Practice without being too tight or too loose.
Maintain a view that is free of partiality.
Have a conduct that is free of artifice.
Have compassion that is without bias.
Meditate free from distraction.
Then there will be unceasing good qualities
and the accomplishment of unending benefit for beings.

If, without the realization of nonduality,
you could be liberated by
deliberately senseless behavior—

regarding enemies and friends, and gold and clods of earth, as the same,
and having no regard for respectability or reputation—
then why don't little children become liberated?

If, without the realization of nonduality,
you could be liberated by disregard for what is proper,
then every lunatic would be liberated.

If, without the realization of nonduality,
you could be liberated by disregard for cleanliness,
then every dog and pig would be liberated.

If, without the realization of nonduality,
you could be liberated by skillful conduct,
then every new bride would be liberated.

If you could be liberated by a natural relaxation
that lacks the realization of nonduality,
then every idiot would be liberated.

If you do have the realization of nonduality,
then however you act, whether wild or precise, you will be
liberated.

If you don't have the realization of nonduality,
whether your conduct is precise or wild, you will be in bondage.

If you are permeated by impartial compassion,
whatever you do will be the supreme path. [70]
If you are not permeated by impartial compassion,
whatever you do will be the inferior path.

9. The Commitments

How do you keep the commitments?

When you are on the level of a beginner,
do not break the pratimokṣa vows
or other commandments of the Sugata and gurus.

When you are at the level of meditating on channels and winds,
avoid anything that is contrary to bliss and heat.

When the experience of nonthought arises,
avoid anything that is contrary to samādhi.

When you have seen the essence of your own mind,
avoid anything that is harmful to the mind.

When the realization of nonduality has arisen,
avoid all goal-oriented action.

Make your own mind the judge of everything.
When the meaning you realize is always the true nature,
then there is no commitment to keep, and that is the supreme commitment.
That is what is called the *white panacea*.[174]

10. The Result

If you have a view that is unmistaken,
receive instructions that are appropriate and correct;
meditate without error, neither too tight nor too loose;
have conduct free of attachment, unstained by faults;
and keep your commitments without feeling shame before the deities.
Then you will without doubt gain the necessary desired results.

It is like the example of a medicinal tree:
When the ground, seed, time, water, compost,
and all the correct factors for the dependent origination of the result are present,
then even the seedling will be able to cure illness.
Therefore, the entire trunk, branches,
leaves, flowers, and fruits,
with their complete qualities
will heal all illness.

If negative factors of dependent origination
have the power to result in suffering,

then good, unmistaken factors
will obviously bring excellent happiness.

If composite dualism's factors of dependent origination
result in happiness and suffering,
then the nondependent, the noncomposite, the inconceivable
will obviously result in infinite wisdom.

If virtuous actions performed with attachment to reality
result in happiness in the higher existences,
then objectless, nonconceptual virtue
will obviously result in buddhahood.

If bliss, clarity, and nonthought accompanied by attachment
result in the bliss of devas within the three realms,
then bliss, clarity, and nonthought that is free from attachment
will obviously result in attaining the three kāyas of the conquerors.

If emptiness without method and wisdom
results in the bliss of the śrāvakas and pratyekabuddhas, [71]
then the inseparability of emptiness and compassion
will obviously result in the location-free great bliss.

Ideally, beginners with the correct practice
of meditation and post-meditation in the generation stage
will cause the perfect union—the saṃbhogakāya—
to manifest within their lifetime
or, otherwise, to manifest in the bardo.
Otherwise, they will definitely attain the perfect good fortune
of a deva's existence in the next life,
where they will then manifest the union, the saṃbhogakāya.
Otherwise, if they are reborn as humans,
they will accomplish it within seven lifetimes.

The medium result is that when experiences arise
in the completion stage with attributes,
they will instantly purify a great mass of bad karma,
and the ḍākiṇīs will bestow their blessings on them.

Familiarization with the experiences
of bliss, clarity, and nonthought will definitely result in realization,
so that the three kāyas will definitely manifest in their lifetime,
or at least will definitely manifest in the bardo.

Even if the realization of nonduality does not arise
in practitioners who have great diligence
and who have received the profound instructions,
they will truly attain transference of consciousness,
either through entering into another's body
or through an upward transference of consciousness.
If they fail to do that, they will appear in the bardo,
where the best will manifest the luminosity,
the medium will accomplish the illusory body of union,
and the least will close the entrance to the city of the womb
or will control where they will be reborn,
after which the three kāyas will doubtless manifest.

When the mahāmudrā yogins
loosely relax their minds,
an experience of clarity without thought—
like the center of pure space—arises.

At the very moment when that arises,
countless bad karmas and obscurations will definitely end.
Even if certainty does not arise,
this is meeting the dharmakāya.

When the nondual, innate
realization perfectly arises,
all the bad karma that has been accumulated
throughout beginningless time will, without exception,
be instantaneously, totally vanquished,
like darkness by a lamp.

The ignorant make the error of analyzing
all-accomplishing mahāmudrā in terms of paths and levels.
So here, too, in order to please the ignorant,

I will give an analysis of its correspondence
with the paths and levels of the Vehicle of Characteristics
(Lakṣanayāna).[175]
The perfect arising of realization
is the path of seeing, the level (*bhūmi*) of Perfect Joy.
Familiarization with the realization
of one taste is the path of meditation.
Nonmeditation is the path of complete accomplishment.

As soon as nonduality is realized,
even though suffering is not yet eliminated
and the power of the qualities are not developed,
who can say that this isn't the path of seeing?

When the sun rises in the morning, [72]
it does not immediately melt the ice
and the ground and stones stay cold,
but who can deny that it's the sun?

The stages of the paths and levels
and all the individual, particular signs of heat
are nonliteral teachings given by Śākyamuni
as provisional truths for pupils who pass through stages.

The ignorant are attached to temporary things
and there are countless higher and lower grades of pupils,
and so the Buddha's teachings are countless too.
If there is a teaching that conflicts with your own tradition,
do not malign it or reject it
but pray that you'll eventually understand it.

The all-accomplishing mahāmudrā
has, like the jackfruit,
a simultaneous cause and result;[176]
it is conceptualization liberating itself.

Monkeys have to climb to get fruit,
but crows just fly down to get them.

It's evident that crows get to the fruit
without even having to see the branches.

In the same way it's evident
that immediate individuals attain the dharmakāya
without even seeing the signs of heat in the paths and levels.

Whatever their individual training and capabilities,
the instant they realize the natural state,
they attain the kingdom of nirvana.
From then on they know the result to be
this pure nature of the mind, which has no attainment.

This knowledge or realization is without conceptual identification;
it is natural liberation, without meditation or post-meditation, without birth or death.
This is liberation as Vajradhara,
which means the natural presence of the five kāyas.

It is taught that omniscience
is attained through completing the two accumulations
and purifying the two obscurations.
In this too, the two accumulations are completed
and the two obscurations spontaneously purified.

When nonduality is realized,
this instantly pleases all gurus and buddhas,
which completes the great accumulation of merit,
and you are permanently purified
of the seeds of miserliness and other obscuring afflictions.

While you are becoming familiarized with this realization,
there remains the subtlest obscuration of knowledge,
but the instant there is nonmeditation,
the great accumulation of wisdom is completed
and you are permanently purified of the seeds of the triple aspects [of conceptualization],
which is the obscuration of knowledge.

This is what is called complete enlightenment.
This is the accomplishment of mahāmudrā.

E ma! This wonderful, marvelous Dharma
brings complete buddhahood in an instant!

11. Impartiality

The true nature in that view,
and all other qualities, such as meditation,
conduct, commitment, and result, [73]
are all manifestations of your own mind.

The mind is a state of clear self-knowing.
That clarity has an empty nature,
like space; it cannot be divided.
There are no directions, center, or limits to be identified.

There is no duality of viewer and viewed
in the nature of the mind.
Therefore, there is no view and no realization.

There is no duality of meditator and object of meditation.
Therefore, there is no meditation and no experience.

There is no duality of familiarizer and familiarized.
Therefore, there is no familiarization and no absence of familiarization.

There is no duality of someone distracted and an object of distraction.
Therefore, there is no nondistraction and no distraction.

There is no duality of performer of conduct and performed conduct.
Therefore, there is no conduct and nothing that is performed.

There is no duality of someone who attains and something attained.
Therefore, there is no accomplishment and no attainment.

There is no duality of cause and result,
just like the center of empty space.
Therefore, there is no generation and no ripening.

There is no obscuration and no purification
in the mind that is primordially empty;
it is the immaterial inseparability of knowing and emptiness.
Therefore, there is no wisdom and no ignorance.

The meditators who thus know,
in the luminous essence of the mind,
the equality of view, meditation,
conduct, commitment, and result
have no attachment to a viewer and a viewed.
Therefore, they are the kings of attachment-free view.

They have no attachment to a meditator and object of meditation.
Therefore, they are the kings of attachment-free meditation.

They have no attachment to a performer of conduct and a performed conduct.
Therefore, they are the kings of attachment-free conduct.

They have no attachment to someone who attains and something attained.
Therefore, they are the kings of attachment-free result.

12. The White Panacea

In the instant that you realize your own mind,
all good qualities, without exception,
are simultaneously completed without having to accomplish them.

The three kāyas are primordially, naturally present
in the nature of the mind, which is like space;
the Jewel of the Buddha is completely within it.

The nature of the mind is free of elaboration, free of desire;
the Jewel of the Dharma is complete within it.

Its nature is birthless and irreversible,
with the variety of thoughts arising as its companions;
the Jewel of the Sangha is complete within it.

Even the Three Jewels
are complete in your own mind's knowing.
Therefore, there is no need to seek refuge elsewhere;
the definitive refuge is complete in it.

In the nature of the mind, which is without elaboration,
there is no basis for desire and selfishness.
Therefore, the aspiration bodhicitta is complete in it. [74]

Everything is understood to be an illusion,
so that objectless compassion arises
and benefiting others is naturally present.
Therefore, the bodhicitta of engagement is complete in that.

In the nature of the mind, which is like space,
there is freedom from all fixation and attachment.
Therefore, the perfection of generosity is complete in that.

It is perfectly pure of the stains of concepts.
Therefore, the perfection of conduct is complete in that.

There is no fear of emptiness and the seeds of anger are vanquished.
Therefore, the perfection of patience is complete in that.

The union of knowing and emptiness is never interrupted.
Therefore, the perfection of diligence is complete in that.

One-pointedness is primordially, naturally present.
Therefore, the perfection of meditation is complete in that.

There is spontaneous liberation from the concepts of wrong views.
Therefore, the perfection of wisdom is complete in that.

Everything that appears arises as companions.
Therefore, the great method, the great accumulation of merit,
is complete in that.

The meaning of nonduality is realized.
Therefore, the great accumulation of wisdom is complete in that.

In the nature of the mind, which is like space,
there are no stains whatsoever from the body.
Therefore, the supreme vase empowerment is complete in that.

There is primordial purity from the stains of speech.
Therefore, the supreme secret empowerment is complete in that.

There is no location for the stains of the mind.
Therefore, the supreme empowerment of the prajñā's wisdom is
complete in that.

There is no location for stains that come equally from body, speech,
and mind.
Therefore, the supreme fourth empowerment is complete in that.

The naturally clear knowing is unceasing
and appears as every kind of body, color, and insignia.
Therefore, every kind of generation stage is complete in that.

The clarity has no conceptual identification.
Therefore, the completion stage is complete in that.

The superior realization of your own mind as
nondual luminosity is the path of seeing,
its unbroken continuity is the path of meditation,
its effortlessness is the path of complete attainment.

Not being limited by anything is the supreme sign of heat.
Therefore the signs of heat on the paths and levels are complete
in that.

Being nothing whatsoever: that is the dharmakāya.
Appearing as anything whatsoever: that is the nirmāṇakāya.
All that appears is enjoyed (*saṃbhoga*) as the dharmakāya.
Therefore, the resultant three kāyas are complete in that.

As there is no partiality in self-knowing,
which is like space, the view is complete in that.
As there is no attachment to objects of perception, meditation is complete in that.
As there is no adoption or rejection, conduct is complete in that.
As there is no loss, commitment is complete in that.
As there is natural presence, the result is complete in that.

There are no three times, there is no before and after,
in the empty luminosity of the mind.

For as long as there is fixation upon a self,
there will be view, meditation, conduct, result, and commitment,
and there will be karma and the ripening of karma.
So it's essential to avoid bad actions and accumulate merit. [75]

13. Prayer

I, the beggar monk from Shang,
on the urging of Chökyi Lodrö, my attendant,
have written these conceptual embellishments
for the purpose of guiding a few pupils
to the true nature of their own minds,
which is primordially devoid of conceptual embellishment.

It was not wrong to write this, for it was written with love
and with the thought that anything is possible.

May this good action and all other good actions,
without exception, become one
and cause the nondual dharmakāya to appear
to all beings throughout space.

May objectless compassion, free of attachment,
effortlessly spread form kāyas to the ends of space
in order to benefit beings,
manifesting whatever is necessary to train them.

From this day onward, throughout all time,
may I obtain a perfect existence of freedoms and opportunities
and, with faith, wisdom, and compassion,
apply myself solely to powerful, good conduct.

May I always be a perfect vessel for the supreme Vajrayāna,
have the instructions of the perfect guru,
gain the supreme realization with his compassionate blessing,
and always please him.

May I continuously see the guru's qualities,
never see a single fault,
and with uninterrupted faith and veneration
always see him as Vajradhara.

With great, objectless compassion,
unstained by negative motivation,
may I attain all the qualities
of every guru and buddha.

May I attain the pure view, free from bias,
which leads to the marginal extremes of eternalism and nihilism.
May I attain bliss, clarity, and nonthought, free from attachment,
and may I attain the supreme conduct of one taste.

May I never shame the ḍākinīs but always apply myself
to keeping and practicing the commitments,
unblemished by the stains of afflictions,
deception, and pretense.

May I always wander in the mountains,
never experiencing fear, sadness, or obstacles.

May I attain powerful miracles and qualities,
such as experiences, realizations, and signs of heat.

May my gurus, Dharma companions,
and all other beings
see whatever conduct I perform
as pleasing.

May seeing, hearing, remembering, and touching
my body, speech, and mind,
my dwelling, clothes, name, family, and so on,
fulfill whatever desires others have.

May I give away all things, without attachment. [76]
May I not have faults such as hope and desire.
May I have a pure conduct, an undisturbed mind,
and realize an ever joyful, undistracted knowledge.

May I attain stability in the generation and completion practices;
may I gain the final goal of union and luminosity
and fulfill the hopes of the six classes of beings
with naturally present blessings.

May I, through objectless compassion,
powers, and miracles beyond measure,
tame all powerful, worldly deities
such as devas, nāgas, yakṣas, and māras.

When the time comes to benefit beings,
may I, without regret, happily and perfectly
give away my head, my legs, my arms,
my flesh, my blood, my breath, and everything else.

May I, without pride, provide the unending
benefit of whatever is needed,
every possession that is desired,
such as food, drink, jewels, and steeds.

May my glorious power give protection from
all dangers from enemies and demons,
from the dangers of suffering,
such as sickness and famine.

From this day on, throughout all time,
may I act only to benefit others.
May I, without being disturbed or saddened,
benefit others, no matter what wrongs they have done.

May I benefit all beings,
without arrogance, pride, or envy,
without self-interest, bias, or partiality,
and unblemished by the stain of bad actions.

May I not delight in such things as praise from others
and not be displeased by such things as criticism,
but have the effortless compassion of equanimity,
unblemished by the stains of attachment and aversion.

May the compassion of Avalokiteśvara,
the wisdom of Mañjughośa,
and the power of Vajrapāṇi
be totally complete within me.

May I attain the entirety of
the knowledge of Nāgārjunagarbha,
the realization of Saraha,
and the power of Virūpa.

May I know the practices of every tantra,
accomplish all activity rites without impediment,
be the master of countless instructions,
and please all of the ḍākinīs.

May there be benefit for others through the eternal,
definitive realization of the meaning of equality:

No phenomenon comes from anywhere,
goes anywhere, or is present anywhere.

May I, for the sake of others, be free from the fault of desire,
become skilled, without bias,
in the arts, commentaries, poetry, and so on,
and never be defeated by opponents in debate.

May I never lack any favorable condition, [77]
such as family, qualities, possessions,
unmistaken words and meanings,
wisdom, power, and confidence.

14. Colophon

Nowadays, in these evil times, it is rare for Dharma practitioners
to tame their beings and speech with study.
Though skilled in words, they don't realize their meaning,
so that arrogance and quarrels increase.

We should follow and accomplish the meaning
taught by the venerable gurus of the practice lineage,
completely eliminating pride, and so on,
and realize the meaning, which fulfills the purpose of scripture and logic.

Tilopa did not speak
a single word to Nāropa,
yet all scripture, logic, and instruction
became complete in Nāropa's mind.

Therefore, this chattering of mine,
though eloquent in its expression of humility and so on,
has the faults of contradiction, connection, calculation, and repetition,
and it is comprised of empty, unexamined words.

Nevertheless, there is the faintest possibility that
when passed on to my pupils it will help them.

That is the reason why I've written this.
If a single word of it contradicts
scripture, logic, or the instructions, may my head split open!

This is the extent of beggar monk Shang's realization.
I wrote it on the urging of Marpa, my attendant,
In front of the Pangbu Thül cliffs.

Do not show this to people, or you will accumulate bad karma.

This has been my description of the words of the Buddha, their commentaries, the viewpoints of the sublime gurus, and my own realization.

Ithiḥ[177]

4. A Record of Mahāmudrā Instructions

DRUKCHEN PEMA KARPO (1527–92)

[79] I pay homage to the precious Kargyü.[178]

THESE ARE THE instructions for the mahāmudrā innate union, which is a direct introduction to the continuum of the ordinary mind as true wisdom. It is in three parts:

I. Preliminaries
II. The main part
III. The conclusion

I. The preliminaries

These are of two kinds:

A. The general preliminaries
B. The special preliminaries

A. The general preliminaries

These are clearly explained elsewhere.

B. The special preliminaries

First one does the practices of taking refuge and so on, up to guru yoga. Then, as taught in the *Enlightenment of Vairocana*:[179]

> Straighten the body, perform the vajra posture.
> The mind is one-pointed mahāmudrā.

Thus there are these seven Dharmas of Vairocana: (1) Sit with the legs in vajra posture. (2) Arrange the hands in the meditation mudrā below the navel. (3) Straighten the spine. (4) Broaden the shoulders. (5) Bend the throat like a hook, with the chin just pressing on the Adam's apple. (6) Place the tongue against the upper palate. (7) In general, your mind is changed by your senses, and in particular by the eyes. Therefore, gaze a yoke's distance in front of you, without closing or moving the eyes.

There is also the presentation, in terms of function, of the five Dharmas of dhyāna: (1) The crossed legs cause the downward-expelling wind to enter the central channel. (2) The meditation mudrā causes the coexisting fire [wind] to enter the central channel. (3) The straightened spine and straightened abdomen cause the pervading wind to enter the central channel. (4) The bent throat causes the upward-moving wind to enter the central channel. (5) The tongue against the upper palate and the gaze cause the prāṇa (the life-force wind) to enter the central channel.

As a result of those five winds entering the central channel, every karmic wind enters the central channel and nonconceptual wisdom arises. This is called the *solitude of the body*, the *unmoving body*, and the *naturally resting body*.

Expelling the stale breath and remaining silent is called the *solitude of the speech*, the *unmoving speech*, and the *naturally resting speech*.

Do not contemplate the past. Do not think of the future. [80] Do not meditate by deliberate application of the intellect. Do not view "emptiness" as nonexistence. Do not examine or analyze whatever appears in the present as the objects of the five senses, using thoughts such as "is" or "isn't," but look inward. Be loose, like a baby, letting the mind rest naturally, without an instant's distraction.

> Cast away all thinking and thoughts
> and be like a relaxed, resting baby.
> If one keeps to the guru's transmission and makes a devoted effort,
> there is no doubt but that the innate will appear.[180]

According to Tilopa:

> Do not contemplate, do not think, do not analyze,
> do not meditate, do not mentate, but rest naturally.[181]

According to the Dharma king Candraprabhakumāra:[182]

> Nondistraction is the path of all buddhas.[183]

This is called the *solitude of the mind*, the *unmoving mind*, and the *naturally resting mind*.

According to Nāgārjuna:

> Lord, mindfulness within the body is taught to be
> the one path that has been traversed by the sugatas.
> Discipline yourself in that and truly protect it.
> If mindfulness is lost, then all Dharma is destroyed.[184]

That is mindfulness without distraction. From the Abhidharma:

> Mindfulness is not forgetting the object with which one has become familiar.[185]

II. The main practice

This is in two parts:

A. The general practices
B. The special practices

A. The general practices

This is in two parts:

1. Seeking the experience of the basis of meditation: the meditation of one-pointed yoga
2. Analyzing the basis of stillness and movement and identifying it through vipaśyanā: the meditation of elaboration-free yoga

1. Seeking the experience of the foundation of meditation: the meditation of one-pointed yoga

This is in two parts:

a. Meditation with a base
b. Meditation without a base

a. [One-pointed yoga meditation] with a base

This is in two parts:

i. Meditation without the breath [as a base]
ii. Meditation with the breath [as a base]

i. [One-pointed yoga meditation] without breath [as a base]

This is in two parts:

A) Arranging an object such as a pebble or little stick as an impure [base]
B) Arranging a [representation of the Tathāgata's body, speech, or mind as a pure [base]

A) [One-pointed yoga meditation without breath] upon an object such as a pebble or little stick as an impure [base]

Meditation 1

Place in front of you a little pebble as the base for your focus. Do not allow your mind to wander externally or be absorbed internally but look one-pointedly on that [object] alone.

Meditate that the guru is on the crown of your head, and think that he is truly a buddha. Recite the "My mothers throughout space" prayer.[186] Request his blessing by reciting, "I pray that you give your blessing for the attainment of the supreme siddhi of mahāmudrā," [81] and think that the guru merges into you so that your minds are blended. Rest in meditation for as long as you are able. Meditate that every state of mind that suddenly appears blends with the guru.

If [the mind] becomes dulled, raise your gaze and meditate in a place that has a wide-open space. If the mind sinks into a stupor, clarify it with mindfulness as just described. If the mind is agitated, sit in a solitary place, gaze downward, and most of all, relax.

B) [One-pointed yoga meditation without breath] upon the arrangement of the Tathāgata's body, speech, and mind as a pure base

This is in three parts:

1) An image of the Buddha's body as a base
2) A letter of the Buddha's speech as a base
3) A quintessence (*bindu*) of the Buddha's mind as a base

1) [One-pointed yoga meditation without breath] upon an image of the Buddha's body as a [pure] base

Meditation 2

Focus the mind continuously upon the Buddha, either a statue, a painting, or a visualization that resembles a golden statue: yellow, adorned by the primary and secondary signs, radiating light, and wearing the three Dharma robes.

2) [One-pointed yoga meditation without breath] upon a syllable of the Buddha's speech as a [pure] base

Meditation 3

Meditate that in front of you, upon a moon disc the size of a pea, stands a *hūṃ* that is written as if with a single hair.

3) [One-pointed yoga meditation without breath] upon a quintessence of the Buddha's mind as a [pure] base

Meditation 4

Focus the mind as previously described upon the special symbol of an egg-shaped spheroid that is the size of a pea and shines with light.

ii. [One-pointed yoga meditation] with breath [as the base]

This is in two parts:

A) Based upon the vajra repetition
B) Based upon the vase breathing

A) [One-pointed yoga meditation upon the breath] based upon the vajra repetition

Meditation 5

Allow the mind and body to rest naturally and focus the mind upon the inhalation and exhalation of the breath. Count the breaths from one, two, and so on, until 21,600. As a result, you will become knowledgeable in the number of the inner and outer movements of the breath.

Meditation 6

During the exhalation and inhalation, think that the breath moves throughout the body, or through just one part of it, and follow the exhalation and inhalation of the breath in that way. As a result, you will become knowledgeable in the characteristics of the breath.

Meditation 7

Blend your consciousness with the breath and observe it moving from the tip of the nose down to the navel, resting, and coming [back up]. As a result, you will see the color and length of the individual winds.

Meditation 8

Examine the five elements individually, [82] without mixing them. As a result, you will know the increase and diminution of the inner and outer movements of the breath.

Meditation 9

The exhalation becomes a white *oṃ* syllable, the inhalation a blue *hūṃ*, and the resting a red *āḥ*. As a result, there will be the cessation of the outer and inner movements of breath.

B) [One-pointed yoga meditation upon the breath] based upon the vase breathing

Meditation 10

Expel the stale breath three times. Slowly inhale the upper air through the nose. Draw up the lower air and apply yourself to holding it as much as you can. That which is called the *mind difficult to completely tame* is focused upon as being nothing other than wind, so that when the movement of wind ceases, thoughts that stray toward objects will also cease.

b. [One-pointed yoga meditation] without a base

This is in three parts:

i. The complete cutting through of suddenly appearing thoughts
ii. Not changing whatever arises
iii. The key point for resting the mind

i. [One-pointed yoga meditation without a base:] the complete cutting through of suddenly appearing thoughts

Meditation 11

If, while meditating as described above on the arising of a thought, the mind becomes involved with an object of thought, clarify the mind with mindfulness, thinking, "I must not have even a single thought that will cause me to continue with this thinking." Meditate on repeatedly cutting through the arising of suddenly appearing thoughts.

Meditation 12

When you extend the above meditation, thoughts will eventually multiply until in the end one thought will come on top of another in an unbroken continuity. Identifying these thoughts is like recognizing an enemy. It is the first stage [of śamatha], which is like a river rushing down a steep mountainside. The mind is aware of the arising and ceasing of thoughts because it is at rest in every instant. The result is that it seems as if thoughts are multiplying, but thoughts have always been rising, so there is no change in their quantity. It's the nature of thoughts to arise one moment and cease the next.

ii. [One-pointed yoga meditation without a base:] not changing whatever arises

Meditation 13

Meditate by allowing thoughts to go wherever they wish, while having your own mind spy on them without stopping them or falling under their power. This will result in a one-pointed śamatha that cannot be disrupted by thoughts.

Meditation 14

Thoughts and so on continue to move rapidly, but by meditating as before, states of stability will last longer. This is the middle stage of stability, which is like a slowly flowing river. This key point of naturally resting the mind [83] will make it become clear.

According to the Dharma lord [Gampopa]:

> If the mind is unaltered, it becomes happy.
> If water is not disturbed, it becomes clear.[187]

According to the great lord of yogins [Lingrepa]:

> If you rest in unaltered freshness, there will be realization.
> If you can maintain this like the flow of a river, realization will be complete.
> Oh yogins! Completely abandon all ideas of focusing the mind
> and rest continuously in equanimity.[188]

Concerning these two kinds of meditation, Saraha has taught the following:

> If it is bound, it will attempt to flee into the ten directions
> If it is set free, it will not move and be still.
> I have understood this paradox, which is just like a camel.[189]

iii. [One-pointed yoga meditation without a base:] the key point for resting the mind

This is in four parts:

A) Resting like weaving a brahman's thread
B) Resting like a sheaf of hay after its cord has been cut
C) Resting like a baby looking at a temple
D) Resting like an elephant being pricked by a thorn

A) Resting like weaving a brahman's thread

Meditation 15

A thread should be [woven] so that it is neither too tight nor too loose. In the same way, if your meditation is too tight, you lose it in thoughts; if it's too loose, you will lose it in idleness. Therefore you must have the right balance between being too tight or too loose. Beginners should be tighter at first, cutting through the sudden arising [of thoughts]. Then when that becomes tiring, they should become looser by not altering whatever [thoughts] arise. By alternating these two approaches, a natural balance between being too tight and too loose will develop. Therefore it's taught that mind should first be tightened and then loosened and relaxed, as when weaving a brahman's thread.

B) Resting like a sheaf of hay after its cord has been cut

Meditation 16

Think that all previous remedies were just the arising of thoughts and that all you need is to be undistracted. Stopping thoughts is merely a remedy, and "mindfulness in pursuit" stains meditation, so abandon that kind of mindfulness and awareness and rest naturally in the continuum of śamatha. This resting, free from any mental effort, is like a sheaf of hay after its cord has been cut.

C) [Resting like] a baby looking at a temple

Meditation 17

When you tie the elephant of the mind firmly to the post of mindfulness and awareness, the breath will become naturally stilled. This will result in seeing empty forms, such as smoke and so on; you will almost faint with bliss; there will be a state of nonthought that is like empty space with no physical or mental sensations and so on. However, whatever kind of experiences you have, neither be pleased with them nor see them as faults. Don't fixate on them or stop them from occurring. Neither stopping nor fixating on appearances, which never cease, is like a baby looking at a temple. [84]

D) [Resting] like an elephant being pricked by a thorn

Meditation 18

When a thought arises in a state of stability, simultaneously there is mindfulness that is aware of it. As the remedy and the fault are in direct contact, the thought cannot lead to a second thought. There is no deliberate application of a remedy; instead there is the "spontaneous maintenance of mindfulness." You experience thoughts arising, while simply remaining at rest, without either stopping or creating them. This is the meaning of resting "like an elephant being pricked by a thorn."[190]

That is the last stage of stability, which is said to be like an ocean without waves. In this state of stability, there is the self-recognition of the mind's movements, and while there are these movements, the stability continues. Therefore this is called *eliminating the distinction between stability and movement*. That is the self-recognition in the one-pointed state.

That which recognizes this stability and movement is called correct attention or discriminating wisdom or self-knowing. From *Ornament of the Mahayana Sutras*:

> Therefore through that, one attains
> great functionality of mind and body,
> as well as attention and analytic knowledge.[191]

2. Analyzing the basis of stillness and movement and identifying it through vipaśyanā: the meditation of yoga without elaboration

This is in three parts:

a. Analysis of the root of stillness and movement
b. Recognition through vipaśyanā
c. Yoga without elaboration

a. Analysis of the root of stillness and movement

Meditation 19

When nonconceptual śamatha has become discriminating wisdom, it analyzes stillness to see what its essence is, how it is still, how movement comes from it, whether stability is lost or persists when there is movement, what the nature of movement is, and how it ceases.

Meditation 20

There is no movement separate from the stability and there is no stability that is separate from movement; so you won't find that stability or movement has an essence.

In that case, is that viewer's knowing different from the stability or movement that it is looking at, or is it itself the stability and the movement?

The analysis with the eyes of self-knowing does not result in finding anything, so that you realize the inseparability of the viewer and the viewed. No essence whatsoever can be located. Therefore, this is called the *view that transcends the intellect* and the *view without an assertion*. According to the lord of conquerors:

> The mentally fabricated view [85] is excellent but destructible.
> That which transcends the intellect does not even have the name
> "view."
> It is through the guru's kindness that you attain
> certainty in the inseparability of the viewer and the viewed.[192]

Ācārya Śāntideva has taught this kind of analysis:

> Be dedicated to concentration
> without losing it for an instant;
> examine your own mind
> to see what it is doing.[193]

There is the example of fire and firewood from the *Sutra Requested by Kāśyapa*:

> Fire comes from two sticks being rubbed together;
> its appearance burns up the two sticks.
> In the same way, when the power of wisdom appears,
> its appearance burns up both those two.[194]

This kind of analysis is the analysis of the inward-looking, self-knowing. It is called *kusali's analytic meditation*. It isn't the paṇḍita's analytic meditation, because that is an outward-looking knowledge.

b. Recognition through vipaśyanā

Meditation 21

Whatever thoughts or afflictions arise, don't reject them. Without falling under their power, let all things that arise be just what they are, without altering them. Recognize them at the very instant they arise so that, without eliminating them, their arising is naturally purified as emptiness. In this way, you can transform all adverse factors into the path. This is called *bringing conditions into the path*.

Thoughts are liberated simply by recognizing them, which means you have realized the inseparability of the remedy and the remedied. This realization is the essence of the practice of the Vajrayāna and is called *paradoxical meditation*.

Exceptional compassion will arise for all beings who have not realized the nature of their own minds. This transcends methods of body, speech, and mind that are practiced for the sake of all beings, such as the generation stage. This wisdom purifies you of all attachment to reality, so that there will be no afflictions. It's like consuming poison that has been blessed by mantras. It's taught that with this view of practice, whatever path you follow will be "without adoption or rejection."

c. The yoga without elaboration

This is in three parts:

i. The analysis of past, present, and future [86]
ii. The analysis of things and nothing
iii. The analysis of singleness and multiplicity

i. The analysis of past, present, and future

Meditation 22

The past mind has ceased, is destroyed; the future mind is not born, has not arisen; the present mind cannot be identified. When you analyze in that way, you will see that all phenomena are like that. Nothing has reality;

everything is just a creation of the mind. Therefore, you will understand that arising, remaining, and ceasing have no reality at all. Analyze as taught by Saraha:

> The arising of things has a nature like space,
> so when things are eliminated, what can arise afterward?
> Their nature is primordial birthlessness.
> Realize today what the lord guru has taught![195]

ii. The analysis of things and nothing

Meditation 23

Examine in this way: Does your mind exist? Is it a real thing? Or does it not exist? Is it nothing? If it exists as a thing, is it the perceiver or the perceived? If it is perceived, what is its shape and color? If it is the perceiver, there would be nothing else. If it is nothing, then what creates all this variety of appearances? Examine in this way.

If there is an existent essence, then that essence can be established, but your cognition's examination does not find anything that exists. There is nothing to be found that can be established as existent, as having the quality of a thing. As this is the province of self-knowing, it is not nonexistence or nothingness.

Therefore, as there is neither a thing nor nothing, you do not fall into the paths of eternalism or nihilism. Therefore, this is called the *path of the middle way*. This does not come from establishing reasons or gaining certainty through negations. It is through the guru's instructions that you see it clearly, like a jewel in the palm of your hand. That is why it's called the *great middle way*.

> When the guru's words enter your heart,
> it's like seeing a treasure in the palm of your hand.[196]

iii. The analysis of singleness and multiplicity

Meditation 24

Is this mind single or multiple? If you say it's single, this word *mind* is used for something that has various manifestations, so how can it be single? If you say it's a multiplicity, how could they all be the same in the mind's empty essence? [87] Thus, [the mind] transcends multiple or not multiple. This is called the *completely unlocated mahāmudrā*.

In the meditation of the practitioners who have this realization, there is only their own self-knowing, and there is nothing else that appears. Therefore, it is called *devoid of appearances*.

In the post-meditation period, everything appears as an illusion, because this path has purified them of attachment to anything as being real. Thus, [according to Saraha]:

> Lord, someone like me has today cut through delusion!
> So it doesn't matter what I see,
> in front, behind, or in the ten directions,
> I no longer have a question for anyone![197]

B. The special practices

This is in two parts:

1. The yoga of one taste: the equal taste of all phenomena as the inseparability of mind and appearances
2. The yoga of nonmeditation: the certainty that all phenomena are the natural, innate dharmakāya

1. The yoga of one taste: the equal taste of all phenomena as the inseparability of mind and appearances

This is in three parts:

a. Recognizing appearances as mind through the example of a dream
b. Recognizing the unity of appearances and emptiness through the example of water and ice
c. Gaining certainty in the equal taste of all phenomena through the example of water and waves

a. Recognizing appearances as mind through the example of a dream

Meditation 25

During sleep, whatever appears is nothing other than the mind. In the same way, all present appearances are also the dreams of ignorant sleep and are nothing other than your own mind. If you rest, relaxed, on whatever apparent objects appear, the externally appearing object and what is called "one's own mind" become blended indivisibly into one taste. According to the lord of yogins:

> The experiences of last night's dreams
> are teachers that show you that appearances
> are the mind. Do you understand that?[198]

And he taught:

> Transform the colors of the entirety of these three realms into the single great desire.[199]

b. Recognizing the unity of appearances and emptiness through the example of water and ice

Meditation 26

All phenomena that appear, at the very time that they appear, have no existent essence. Therefore, they are called "empty." [88] In the same way, though they have no existence whatsoever, they appear as anything whatsoever. Therefore, they are said to be the *union of appearance and emptiness*, or the *one taste*, as in the example of ice and water. Knowing in the same way the union of emptiness and bliss, emptiness and clarity, and emptiness and knowing is called the *realization of the one-taste of the many.*

> When that is realized, everything is that.
> No one can know anything that is other than that.
> That is what is read, memorized, and meditated on.[200]

c. Gaining certainty in the equal taste of all phenomena through the example of water and waves

Meditation 27

Waves arise from water. In the same way, all phenomena are created by the nature of your mind, which is emptiness, arising as every kind of appearance. Saraha has taught that realization:

> While being manifested from the mind,
> have the nature of the lord.[201]

The single true nature pervades the entire expanse of phenomena. This is called the *one taste arising as many*. For the practitioners who realize this, their subsequent knowledge will arise as all-pervading emptiness.

2. The yoga of nonmeditation: the certainty that all phenomena are the natural, innate dharmakāya

Meditation 28

As the afflictions that were to be eliminated have ceased, the eliminating remedies also cease and the path ends. There is nowhere else to go. There is nothing more to enter. You cannot get any higher. You have attained the unlocated nirvana, the supreme siddhi of mahāmudrā. From the "blending" teaching [of Tilopa]:

> *Kyeho*! This is self-knowing wisdom!
> It transcends the path of speech; it cannot be experienced by the mind.
> I, Tilopa,[202] have nothing to teach.
> Know that it is revealed to you by yourself.[203]

It is also the meaning of this teaching [by Tilopa]:

> Do not contemplate, do not think, do not analyze,
> do not meditate, do not mentate, but rest naturally.[204]

III. The conclusion

This is in three parts:

A. The recognition: direct introduction to the mahāmudrā
B. Analysis of obstacles and errors
C. Distinguishing comprehension, experience, and realization

A. The recognition: direct introduction to the mahāmudrā

Meditation 29

The four yogas that manifest the result are:

1) Gaining certainty in the basis [89]
2) Practicing the path
3) Distinguishing the details of experiences
4) Distinguishing the signs of heat on the paths and the stages

B. Analysis of obstacles and errors

Meditation 30

Knowing that appearances are mind eliminates the obstacle of appearances arising as enemies. Knowing that thoughts are the dharmakāya eliminates [the obstacle of] thoughts arising as enemies. Knowing the union of appearance and emptiness eliminates [the obstacle of] emptiness arising as an enemy.

The *three errors*[205] are attachment to the experience of śamatha. Enhancing vipaśyanā eliminates them. The *four mistakes* are mistakes concerning the nature of emptiness. Taking up emptiness as compassion eradicates them.

The correct realization of the way things are eradicates mistakes in "sealing." The inseparability of the "remedy and the remedied" [eradicates] mistakes in remedy. The realization of the simultaneity of arising and liberation brings to an end the mistakes of the path.

C. Distinguishing comprehension, experience, and realization

Meditation 31

Comprehension is the realization gained through hearing about and contemplating the nature of the mind. *Experience* is one-pointed, general realization. *Realization* is direct realization, from the level of "freedom from conceptual elaboration" upward. As the same word is used for them all, there is nothing wrong in calling them all "realization."

• • •

Shenphen Sangpo, the king of Zangskar in Kashmir,[206] offered me over one load of saffron blossoms and asked me to write a record of instructions for both the mahāmudrā and the six Dharmas. As I have never found anything reliable among the many manuscript records of the oral tradition, I, Pema Karpo, while staying in the Bodhgaya of the southern land of Kharchu,[207] compiled this [text] solely in order to benefit future times.

May goodness result from this!

5. Instructions for the Mahāmudrā Innate Union

KARMAPA RANGJUNG DORJÉ (1284–1339)

[91] I pay homage to the sublime gurus.

THE TRULY PERFECT Buddha Vajradhara taught glorious great Tilopa[208] the introduction to the innate self-knowing wisdom. [Tilopa taught this] to glorious Nāropa after his twelve great hardships. This introduction to the meaning of realization given to the followers [of this path] is in three parts:

1. The preliminaries
2. The main practice, which consists of attaining a mental state of śamatha and an introduction to the innate meaning of vipaśyanā
3. The teaching of the conclusion

The preliminaries

THE FIRST MEDITATION

A true guru with the necessary qualities only gives this teaching to pupils who practice properly, have abandoned the activities of this life, and are intent on attaining unsurpassable enlightenment. First of all [the guru] gives [the pupils] the vows of correct conduct (*śīla*) and bodhicitta. Then [the guru] gives them empowerments that completely ripen them. Then they should practice in a pleasant and solitary place.

First, cutting through the body, speech, and mind's bondage to the world, sit in the key physical posture upon a comfortable seat: The legs are crossed, the hands are resting level, the waist is straight, the throat is bent, and the eyes are looking toward the tip of the nose. Sitting naturally in this way is the key point for the body.

Then meditate on compassion, sincerely thinking, "Oh, I feel such pity for these beings who have been wandering in the ocean of samsara, experiencing countless sufferings throughout beginningless time. They are wandering in endless samsara because they have not realized their own minds to be the essence of buddhahood and have developed attachment to an I and a self."

Then develop devotion, thinking, "The sublime refuges are the kind buddhas. This guru who gives the teachings directly to me is performing the activity of a buddha for me and therefore is showing me even greater kindness than they do."

Meditate that Vajradhara, Vajrasattva, [92] or your root guru is upon the crown of your head. He is an appearance without a real nature and is inseparable from all the buddhas and bodhisattvas in the ten directions and inseparable from all the Kagyü gurus. Offer your body and possessions to him, reciting:

> I pay homage to the glorious, sublime guru
> in the palace of Akaniṣṭha Dharmadhātu;
> he is the essence of all the buddhas in the three times
> and is the one who truly shows my own mind to be the dharmakāya.
>
> I praise you and offer to you my body, my possessions,
> and all the offerings manifested by my mind.
> I confess to you every bad action I have done in the past,
> and from now on I will not do any other bad actions.
>
> I rejoice in the good actions of all beings.
> I make a dedication as a cause for supreme enlightenment.
> I pray that you remain and do not pass into nirvana.
> I request that you turn the wheel of the unsurpassable supreme
>   vehicle.
>
> Give me your blessing so that I will develop unbiased love and
>   compassion
> and will directly realize the ultimate, innate wisdom,
> just as all the buddhas and bodhisattvas have realized it.
>
> Give me your blessing so that I will realize my illusory body to be
>   the nirmāṇakāya.

> Give me your blessing so that I will realize my life-force to be the saṃbhogakāya.
> Give me your blessing so that I will realize my own mind to be the dharmakāya.
> Give me your blessing so that the three kāyas will manifest indivisibly.

Then one-pointedly rest in the meditation of the guru yoga. If that becomes unclear or thoughts arise, meditate that the guru yoga melts into light and just relax in the unaltered mind. At the conclusion of the sessions make a dedication, reciting:

> May this be for the benefit of all beings.

In that way, just the essential posture of the body and the guru yoga can develop samādhi. The Vinaya tells the story of how a monkey who had watched a pratyekabuddha in this key physical posture taught it to five hundred non-Buddhist rishis, who then attained the five kinds of clairvoyance, while [the monkey himself] attained enlightenment.

Throughout the sutras and tantras appear scriptural passages telling of how devotion to the guru and the buddhas is the cause of enlightenment; so even though I will not relate them here, believe it.

The main practice

This is in two parts:

1. Śamatha.
2. Vipaśyanā.

The causes of śamatha: The branch of dhyāna that is the meditation of focusing the mind

The second meditation

[93] The key physical posture is as before.

The gaze of the eyes should be directed at [a point] four finger-widths beyond the tip of the nose.

Do not follow the past, do not go forward to meet the future, but rest in present realization, in a state of clarity and nonthought.

If you cannot rest in the one-pointed inseparability of clarity and nonthought, meditate by relying on the six objects:

1. Direct your gaze upon any clear visual object and focus the mind upon it. Sometimes gaze upon something like a statue, sometimes on something like a twig or pebble. Keep your cognition focused on it, without interruption by any other thought.
2. When [meditation on a visual object] has become stable, meditate upon sound, such as the sound of water, the sound of the wind, the sounds of creatures, and so on, directing the mind to any clear [sound] and keeping it there.
3. When [meditation on sound] has become stable, focus the mind on whatever good or bad smell is experienced by the nose and meditate upon that.
4. Similarly, meditate by focusing the mind upon the delicious or unpleasant tastes that are experienced by the tongue.
5. In the same way, focus the mind on any distinct pleasant or unpleasant physical sensation that is experienced.
6. When you are able to focus to some degree upon those [objects of meditation], meditate upon the phenomena that are experienced by the mind, by the sixth [consciousness], which are comprised of:
   a. Composite mental phenomena
   b. Noncomposite mental phenomena

Composite mental phenomena

The third meditation

First, samsaric phenomena—thoughts that should be eliminated—such as desire, anger, pride, the five kinds of [wrong] views, and distraction-inducing thoughts caused by the primary and secondary afflictions: Focus your awareness one-pointedly upon whichever of these appears clearly as an object of thought and meditate. Focus also on remedial thoughts, upon whatever arises in a virtuous mind, keeping the mind one-pointedly on them without interruption from any other thought. If you know this key point of mindfully focusing the mind, then whatever thought appears, there will be stability unaffected by dullness or agitation.

However, some people think they must forcefully stop thoughts, which are things to be eliminated. This is an extra obstacle on top of the instability of their minds and makes it difficult to develop samādhi. In relation to this, from *Ornament of the Mahayana Sutras*:

> Because of engaging correctly
> with that desire and so on, [94]
> there will definitely be liberation from them.
> Therefore, those liberations definitely arise from them.[209]

From the *Hevajra Tantra*:

> Through desire, beings become bound;
> through desire itself, they become liberated.[210]

That is what is meant by being skillful in method. *Distinguishing the Middle Way from the Extremes* also says:

> Objectlessness perfectly arises
> through dependence on an object.
> Objectlessness perfectly arises
> through dependence on objectlessness.
> Therefore an object is proved to be
> the very essence of objectlessness.
> As that is so, know that an object
> is the same as objectlessness.[211]

Therefore, first focus the mind by concentrating on an object such as a visual form. Through a single concentration of the six consciousnesses, the mind's focusing on anything else will cease completely.

Noncomposite mental phenomena

The fourth meditation

When that [meditation] is stable, [meditate] on the noncomposite. Do not even use the six objects as bases for focusing the mind but leave the mind just as it is, without creating any thoughts whatsoever, without any concepts concerning appearances and emptiness, defects and remedies. Gaze into space with both eyes, with the body motionless, without speaking, and with a gentle and natural coming and going of the breath. Tilopa has said:

> Hold the mind as if it is space.[212]

Saraha has said:

> Make it like space and bind the breath evenly.
> When there is complete knowledge of equality, it dissolves completely.
> Saraha says that when you have this ability,
> impermanent wavering will quickly be eliminated.[213]

This is what is to be understood when the *Perfection of Wisdom* also says:

> To make the perfection of wisdom your practice is to make space your practice.[214]

If you meditate in that way, you will have good stability and will establish an excellent cause for [the development] of dhyāna and śamatha. In order to understand these aspects in detail, read my teachings on the nine methods of mental stability and the eleven mental engagements.[215] Śamatha's cause is reliance on correct conduct; its essence is to be devoid of afflictions and thoughts; its conditions are the creation of an exceptional mental stability; its benefits are the subjugation of coarse afflictions and sufferings.

The above was the stage of stabilizing the unstable mind. [95]

The direct introduction that gives rise to vipaśyanā

The fifth meditation

Glorious Tilopa has said:

> *Kyeho*! This is self-knowing wisdom!
> It transcends the path of speech; it cannot be experienced by the mind.
> I, Tilopa, have nothing to teach.
> Know that it is revealed to you by yourself.[216]

This means that having now stabilized the mind, examine the manifestations of six consciousnesses within that state of clarity and nonthought. Do the thoughts created by form, sound, smell, taste, physical sensation, and mental phenomena appear as external objects [of perception], or do they come from the eyes, the ears, the nose, the tongue, or the body? When you examine like this, you will see that the thoughts do not come from any of these. You will gain the certainty that the six objects and the five senses are naturally clear but nonconceptual.

The consciousnesses of the five senses—the visual consciousness that perceives forms, the auditory consciousness that perceives sounds, the olfactory consciousness that perceives smells, the gustatory consciousness that perceives tastes, and the tactile consciousness that perceives physical sensations—appear instantaneously in dependence on the sensory faculties and objects, and they are naturally clear and nonconceptual. Therefore, from among the six consciousnesses, that of the mind alone needs to be thoroughly examined.

When the mind is directed toward phenomena, such as the consciousnesses of the five senses, it is naturally clear and nonconceptual in every instant. Therefore, there is no delusion within the six consciousnesses themselves.

When the previous consciousness has ceased and the subsequent consciousness has yet to appear, that which is in the present instant appears clearly. Therefore, this relative truth is not to be rejected.

Although [the present consciousness] is clear, it does not exist as a shape and it does not exist as a color. Creators such as self, fate, Shiva, Brahma, atoms, unperceivable externals, puruṣa, and so on[217] have not created it. It is devoid of a real nature, and therefore the ultimate truth is not rejected.

Even appearances and emptiness are inseparable; they can appear as anything, can be called anything, and therefore are completely liberated from being itself or other. This is what you should realize.

"This is self-knowing"[218] means that the unmistaken realization of that which is self-knowing is wisdom, because it knows the primordial true nature. Ordinary beings, who are [like] children, [96] don't know how to describe that direct perception. It is not within the experience of the afflicted mind's thoughts. Therefore, there is nothing to teach you until you have experienced it for yourself. This is also said in a doha:

> Don't disturb water or a lamp's flame; they are naturally clear.
> I neither perform going and coming nor reject them.[219]

And also:

> *Kyeho*! This is self-knowing.
> Other than that there is nothing that can be directly taught.
> Do not be deluded about this.[220]

Also, in *Summary of the View*:

> That elaboration-free self-knowing
> appears while empty and is empty while appearing.
> Therefore, it is the inseparability of appearance and emptiness.
> It is like the example of the moon on water.
> In this way gain certainty in nonduality.[221]

All texts have such teachings that can bring certainty through quotation and reasoning, but I shall stop here, so as to keep it simple. That concludes the introduction to the six consciousnesses.

Thus, śamatha and vipaśyanā arise by resting in the clear and nonconceptual mind and becoming familiarized to the nature of self-knowing, to the inseparability of appearance and emptiness. The coarser afflictions will then be overcome, and you will enter the true path. Therefore, the great masters of the past gave direct introductions by saying, "See the mind!" This stage accords with the following teaching:

> A vipaśyanā that has excellent śamatha
> is a knowledge that completely defeats the afflictions.
> Therefore, first seek śamatha
> and accomplish it with true joy free from worldly attachment.[222]

Next I will explain:

1. How the guru introduces you to your own nature and you have experiences
2. How you train with experiences
3. How you maximize the results

How the guru introduces you to your own nature and you have experiences

The sixth meditation

First, know the signs that indicate when [meditation] experiences are accompanied by realization or not. When the mind is controlled, dhyāna develops, from which come three benefits:

1. Bliss
2. Clarity
3. Nonthought

Bliss

There are two kinds of bliss: physical bliss and mental bliss.

Physical bliss

This is at first mixed with the afflictions, but subsequently, bliss free from afflictions pervades the entire body. In the end, even if one feels heat, cold, and so on, the bliss is only intensified.

Mental bliss

The mind becomes happy, joyful, and free from pain. This has the same three stages as in physical bliss.

Clarity

[97] Clarity is also of two kinds:

1. The clarity of the five senses
2. The clarity of the mind

The clarity of the five senses

The sign that the mind has become controlled is the appearance of what seem to be objects of visual perception: mirages, bright sparks that resemble fireflies, lamp flames, moons, suns, firelight, dots of light, rainbows, and a variety of beings and forms.

The clarity of the mind

As all thoughts of faults and their remedies arise, there is the knowledge of [the mind's] cognition, emanations [of thought], and their harmonious interdependence. And there is purity, clarity, freedom from sleepiness, and you think that you know all phenomena.

Nonthought

First, you maintain the mind's focus upon any object. Then thoughts cease and your mind remains resting wherever it has been placed. In the end, you experience the cessation of all thought activity.

When [these experiences] are accompanied by wisdom, you will know that *bliss* has no real nature, so that you will not be savoring its taste. *Clarity* will be free from the fault of becoming scattered and unstable through thoughts about causes and results. In *nonthought*, even though you've attained an unwavering state of mind, self-knowing will directly know the instantaneous arising and ceasing of mental activity. These are the signs that you are following the true path.

You will go astray if you become attached to the taste of the experience of bliss, if you become proud of clarity and believe in its perfection, and if, through experiencing the taste of nonthought blended with neutral emptiness, you start ignoring the law of karma. This may result in rebirth in the form realm, but this isn't the path to enlightenment. Therefore it's important [that your experiences] be accompanied by true wisdom.

There are many ways of going astray during this time, but they are all included in these three:

1. Emptiness becomes your enemy.
2. Compassion becomes your enemy.
3. Thoughts about cause and result become your enemy.

Emptiness becomes your enemy

You think, "All phenomena are my mind. My mind is free of [conceptual] elaboration. Therefore, nothing is real. So why should I make any effort with the body, speech, and mind? What is the point of doing composite good actions?" This is going astray as a result of emptiness becoming your enemy.

Compassion becomes your enemy

You think, "I must benefit beings through my compassion for all who don't have my kind of realization." Then, no [longer] listening [to teachings] or practicing, you abandon meditation and [98] dedicate yourself to composite [actions], exhausting yourself by your attachment to the reality of yourself and beings. This is going astray as a result of compassion becoming your enemy.

Thoughts about cause and result become your enemy

You see that everything is created by thought, and you think, "I shall make myself omniscient," and then practice the minor, ordinary activities of grammar, logic, crafts, and medicine, throwing aside the power of śamatha and vipaśyanā. This is going astray as a result of thoughts about causes and results becoming your enemy.

How you train with experiences

When you have the experience of bliss, seal it with emptiness and unreality. When thoughts manifest as clear appearances in the mind, enter into a clear and nonconceptual knowing. When you experience clairvoyance, the ten signs,[223] or other vivid perceptions of the five senses, be certain that they are nothing but your mind and have no attachment to their reality, fixating on their characteristics; instead, transcend it through your own freedom from [conceptual] elaboration.

When you experience nonthought and emptiness, seal it with the two experiences of clarity[224] and apply the analytic explanation of the causal and resultant interdependence, faults, and their remedies.

If, while you are in solitude, you experience that everything has blended into one taste, without any distinction between day or night, then blend happiness and suffering to see whether they become one taste or not.

If you feel proud of your experiences, know that it is the work of the māras and meditate on pure perception of everyone, developing compassion toward all beings, and developing an equanimity that will never have clinging attachment, or rejecting aversion, toward anything in samsara or nirvana.

Maximizing the results

You realize that the six consciousnesses and their six objects are nothing but your own mind and have no other creator. First, you understand that perceiver and perceptions have no reality; then you experience it; and finally you see it directly.

It is important to identify the immediate mentation[225] of the arising and cessation of all consciousnesses. Whenever any of the six consciousnesses arise, they arise because of the mentation of "immediate activity," which when they cease, cause all good, bad, and meditation karma[226] to blend with the mind's ālaya consciousness. This is a secret that you should know.

Along with [immediate mentation] there arises "the afflicted mentation," which is the thought of "I," belief in a self, attachment to a self, [99] and pride, which, because they obscure you, create ignorance. When the six consciousnesses develop upon that basis, subject and object are not recognized to be your own clarity, which creates thoughts of belief in the reality of the subject and object as "me and mine." This is how all afflictions are created.

It's taught that afflictions from the six consciousnesses, which are created by looking outward, are eliminated by [the path] of seeing,[227] while the afflictions created by looking inward are eliminated through [the path] of meditation.

Śrāvakas on the paths of seeing and meditation gain peace through eliminating the afflictions that come from only one aspect of the view that there is an individual self, but they are ignorant of "mental immediacy" and of its remedy—the selflessness of phenomena—and therefore they remain far from the great enlightenment of buddhahood.

Therefore, a wise ordinary individual who has reached the mental state of dhyāna should meditate in the following way. When you rest in dhyāna without thoughts, the six consciousnesses cease in space. When you arise from that samādhi, you can see the movement of the subtle mental activity of thought. If at this time, you don't have the view taught by a true guru, you will have the following deluded thoughts:

You may have the nihilistic view, thinking, "There is no reality to the mind and no reality to its arising and ceasing, and therefore thoughts have no cause."

You may have the eternalistic view, thinking, "Even though thoughts themselves cease, they are permanent because they will always continue to arise and appear."

You may have thoughts about the self, thinking, "These movements of consciousnesses all occur within a single mind."

You may have the deluded thought that external objects should be stopped, thinking, "If I stopped the appearance of external objects I would be in a state of nonthought, and so I must stop the appearances of objects."

You may go astray by thinking that dhyāna is the ultimate path, thinking, "The ultimate path is the dhyāna in which the activities of thought have ceased, in which joy and bliss have ceased, in which the movement of mindfulness and awareness has ceased, and in which the inhalation and exhalation of the breath have ceased."

You may go astray in a meditative state without identification, thinking, "The ultimate [path] is the nonconceptual clarity in which the identification that recognizes the characteristics of objects ceases." [100]

You may go astray into the formless [realm] if you believe that the ultimate [path] is when all appearances and solidity cease into a consciousness like space, or into an infinite [consciousness], or into nothingness, or into the absence of both identification and nonidentification.[228]

This ignorance of the mind is the root of these and all other negative views in the three realms, such as that of belief in the individual self.[229] It is [also] the source of all afflictions. Therefore it is called the *afflicted mentation*. Its root is invalid conceptualization. When you have seen this, in the state of the clarity and nonthought of the external six consciousnesses, you will enter into wisdom.

The agitation of the mind's grasping at characteristics and engaging in acquiring and rejecting creates all the sufferings of samsara, while remedial knowledge creates all good karma and happiness in samsara. When you have understood this, mind, which thinks of and runs toward faults and remedies, should rest in meditation, in its own clarity and emptiness, and train in each of the four dhyānas, the four formlessnesses, and in cessation.

During post-meditation, understand and be skilled in all the ways in which all faulty and remedial thoughts create causes, conditions, and results. Know that all thoughts of identification through the triple aspects [of conceptualization] are obscurations. Seal all phenomena with impartiality, with their empty and selfless nature. Don't have the arrogance of seeing the mind, the ālaya, as "me and mine," but practice with diligence until all afflictions are purified and you have all thoughts under your power.

This is taught in detail in *Training Thoughts* and the *Four Connections*, so read those [texts].[230]

> By becoming familiar with the direct nonconceptual knowledge
> of the clarity and nonthought of the six sensory consciousnesses,
> you will see the mind's direct perception, its self-cognition,
> and its mental immediacy as being like the moon's [reflections] on
>   water.
>
> Because of this the obscured ālaya
> and the unobscured mirror-like wisdom
> will see, in the manner of an inference, the true nature.
>
> Through remedies, you will eliminate, transform, and realize the
>   nature
> of both the obviously manifest and the latent afflictions.
> Then you will have mastery of pure discriminating wisdom

with its samādhi, which realizes the eliminations of both [manifest and latent afflictions].
At that time, the ālaya will directly appear. [101]

The ālaya will be purified in the very instant that it is freed
from all concepts concerning true nature and results,
and at that time, you will attain the enlightenment of buddhahood.

Alas! Immature beings, who do not understand this nature,
bind themselves to "me and mine."
Those who are śrāvakas are bound
by the bondage of selflessness as a remedy.

Although training in concepts of phenomenal percepts
leads to the attainment of pratyekabuddhahood,
the perceiver aspect is not realized to be the ālaya,
so they remain on the path.

Complete buddhahood is total realization.
That is why [buddhahood] is unsurpassable.

Conclusion

While you are developing śamatha and vipaśyanā, agitating or dulling thoughts may arise.

Recognize the causes of dullness and eliminate them by using methods such as cooling yourself, bloodletting, directing your awareness toward all your objects of perception, contemplating cause and result, reading profound sutras, tantras, and treatises, and then meditating.

If agitation or dispersal occurs, focus and control the breath, because it is the steed of the mind; concentrate directly on an object of meditation; examine yourself and meditate on the true nature; and seal your meditation with the samādhi of bliss.

While practicing in this way and experiencing being free from the two extremes, your behavior should transgress neither the rules of correct conduct nor your commitments. Thus I say:

Have no doubt that the practitioner
who meditates upon this will gain realization.
Do not stop the conduct of realization
but rely on benefiting yourself and others.

Begin every session with taking refuge and developing bodhicitta and conclude them with a dedication for the benefit of all beings throughout space, sealed with prayers of aspiration.

Glorious Tilopa has described the true nature of view, meditation, and action:

The king of views is liberation from the margins and extremes.
The king of meditations is the absence of distraction.
The king of conduct is the absence of effort.
The manifest result is the absence of hope and fear.[231]

Nāropa has also said:

In that way, if meditation and conduct
are in true accord with the unmistaken view,
they will be like a horse and rider,
and enlightenment will be attained.[232]

He also said:

If you do not have the true view, you will gain nothing but meaningless exhaustion.[233] [102]

He also said:

Your meditation and conduct will be erroneous
if they do not accord with the true view.
You will be like a blind person without a guide
and will not gain the true result.[234]

The successive stages of mahāmudrā instructions are: The innate mahāmudrā that resides within you; the direct recognition of the meaning of the inseparability of appearance and emptiness; meditation on the inseparability of emptiness and compassion; the correct experience of śamatha and vipaśyanā; and the absence of mental activity within the nonconceptual meditation free from the five kinds of adverse factors.[235]

Rangjung Dorjé composed this slightly expanded version of a teaching by Daö Shönu[236] according to his own understanding, unmixed with words from academic texts.

> The Conqueror taught the profound path of innate union
> in all his sutras and tantras.
> Tilopa and Nāropa summarized
> it as practice instructions,
> which their followers have taught.
>
> Some have taught in accordance with experience,
> while some have explained through conceptual analysis.
> It is not that all these [teachings] are not good,
> but they are only partial [teachings].
>
> Therefore, here the meaning of innate union
> has been revealed—by words, meaning, and realization—
> as the wisdom that liberates all by knowing one thing.
>
> By the merit of this,
> may all beings realize the innate union.

This should be practiced in combination with the six Dharmas [of Nāropa].

This was composed in Dechen[237] on the first day of the fifth month of the wooden rat year.[238]

6. Prayer for the Definitive Meaning, the Mahāmudrā

Karmapa Rangjung Dorjé (1284–1339)

[103] *Namo guru.*

1. Gurus, deities of the *yidam* mandalas,
conquerors and their children in the three times and ten directions,
regard me with love and give me your blessing
so that my prayer will be perfectly fulfilled.

2. May the rivers of accumulations of virtue, unpolluted by the triple aspects,
that come from the snowy mountains of the pure thoughts and actions
of myself and all endless beings
enter the ocean of the four kāyas.

3. Until the time that we attain that,
may we throughout every lifetime
never even hear the words "bad actions" and "suffering"
and enjoy the glorious ocean of good actions and happiness.

4. May I obtain the supreme freedoms and opportunities; have faith, diligence, and wisdom;
rely on an excellent spiritual friend; obtain the quintessence of the teachings;
practice them correctly and without any obstacle;
and thus practice the sublime Dharma throughout all my lifetimes.

5. Hearing the scriptures and logic brings freedom from the clouds of ignorance.
Contemplating the instructions defeats the darkness of doubt.
The light of meditation illuminates the true nature, just as it is.
May the radiance of the three wisdoms increase.

6. The two truths, free from the two extremes of eternalism and nihilism, are the meaning of the basis.
The two accumulations, free from the extremes of embellishment and denigration, are the supreme path.
The attainment of the two benefits, free from the extremes of existence and peace, is the attainment of the result.
May we meet this Dharma that is free of error.

7. The basis for purification is the mind—the union of clarity and emptiness.
The purifier is the great vajra yoga of mahāmudrā.
The purified are the stains of extrinsic delusion.
May the result of purification, the stainless dharmakāya, become manifest.

8. The confidence of the view cuts through doubts about the basis.
The essential point of meditation is to remain undistracted from that.
The supreme conduct is training in the entire meaning of meditation.
May there be the confidence of view, meditation, and conduct.

9. All phenomena are manifestations of the mind.
The mind is without mind, devoid of an essence of mind,
empty and unceasing, appearing as anything whatsoever.
May it be perfectly examined and be completely understood. [104]

10. The self-appearances that have never existed are mistaken as objects.
Through the power of ignorance, self-knowing is mistaken for a self.
Through the power of dualism, we wander in the vastness of existence.
May the error of ignorance be thoroughly understood.

11. It has no existence: Even the conquerors have not seen it.
It is not nonexistent: It is the basis for all samsara and nirvana.
There is no contradiction: It is the path of the middle way, of union.
May the true nature of the mind, free from extremes, be realized.

12. It cannot be indicated by saying, "It is this."
It cannot be refuted by saying, "It is not this."
The true nature that transcends the intellect is noncomposite.
May there be certainty in the extreme of the true meaning.

13. If this is not realized, there will be circling within samsara.
If this is realized, there is no other buddhahood.
There is no "This is it; this isn't it" anywhere.
May we know the true nature, the hidden secret of the ālaya.

14. Appearances are mind and emptiness is mind.
Thoughts are mind and delusion is mind.
Origination is mind and cessation is mind.
May we cut through all conceptual embellishments in the mind.

15. Unadulterated by mentally fabricated, forced meditation;
unshaken by the winds of ordinary preoccupations;
knowing how to naturally rest in unaltered naturalness—
may we master and maintain the practice of the meaning of the mind.

16. The waves of obvious and subtle thoughts cease by themselves;
the undisturbed river of the mind becomes naturally calm.
May there be an untroubled peaceful sea of śamatha,
free from the polluting impurities of dullness and agitation.

17. When we look again and again at the mind that cannot be seen,
we will perfectly see that which is not seen, just as it is.
May we cut through doubts as to what the meaning is or isn't
and have unmistaken knowledge of one's own nature.

18. Looking at objects, there are no objects: They are seen to be mind.
Looking at the mind, there is no mind: It's devoid of essence.

Looking at both spontaneously extinguishes dualism.
May we realize luminosity, which is the nature of the mind.

19. The freedom from attention is the mahāmudrā (Great Seal).
The freedom from extremes is the mahāmadhyamaka (Great Middle Way).
This is also named the all-inclusive dzokchen (Great Perfection).
May there be the confidence that through knowing one all will be realized.

20. Continuous great bliss, free from attachment;
unveiled luminosity, free from fixation on attributes;
naturally present nonthought, transcending the intellect:
May there be a continuity of these effortless experiences.

21. Attachment to good and fixation on experiences [105] is spontaneously liberated.
Bad thoughts and illusion are naturally purified in the element.
The ordinary mind has no rejection and adoption, no elimination and no attainment.
May we realize the truth of the true nature, free from conceptual elaborations.

22. The nature of beings is always buddhahood,
but not realizing that, they wander in endless samsara.
May I have overwhelming compassion
for beings in limitless, endless suffering.

23. When there is love with the unceasing power of overwhelming compassion,
the meaning of the empty essence appears nakedly.
May I meditate inseparably, day and night,
on the union, the supreme path, which is free from error.

24. Through the power of meditation, there is sight and clairvoyance;
beings are ripened and buddha realms are purified,
and the prayers for accomplishing the qualities of buddhahood are perfected.

May there be buddhahood, where perfection, ripening, and fulfillment are brought to completion.

25. Through the compassion of the conquerors and their children in the ten directions,
and through the power of all the good karma there can be,
may my pure prayers, and those of all beings,
be perfectly fulfilled.

This *Prayer for the Definitive Meaning, the Mahāmudrā,* was composed by the lord Karmapa Rangjung Dorjé.

7. Oral Transmission of the Supreme Siddhas

A Commentary on *Prayer for the Definitive Meaning, the Mahāmudrā*

Situ Tenpai Nyinjé (1700–1777)

> [107] I bow down to the Karmapa, the lord of the world,[239]
> whose activity of saving our mothers in samsara from the ocean of suffering
> and bringing them to the dry land of liberation
> surpasses that of the conquerors in the three times.

The supreme glorious Karmapa Rangjung Gyalwa, the guide of this world, composed the *Prayer for the Definitive Meaning, the Mahāmudrā*, which is brief but contains the entire graduated path for advanced individuals. In my view it is an indispensable Dharma teaching for mahāmudrā practitioners. It is the unsurpassable essence of the practice instructions. Through it we can understand what we haven't understood before and can increase the understanding we already have. Therefore, although we followers can understand its meaning in general, I am going to explain a fraction of the meaning of its words to the extent that I have been able to comprehend them. [The prayer] will be explained in three parts:

1. The preparation for making this prayer
2. The actual prayer
3. The conclusion of the prayer

The preparation for making this prayer

In order that this prayer may be fulfilled, recite it sincerely in the presence of a flawless representation[240] that you have requested to be your witness. It has been taught:

> It will be accomplished through a stupa that contains relics
> and through the mantra of the Sugata.[241]

It is also taught:

> All phenomena are completely based
> upon the factor of aspiration as their root.
> Whoever makes whatever prayer,
> that alone is the result that will ripen.[242]

Therefore, [the first verse] is a call to a representation to act as a witness, and it implies one-pointed aspiration.

[Verse 1]

> ***Namo guru*** **(Homage to the guru!)**
>
> **Gurus, deities of the *yidam* mandalas,**
> **conquerors and their children in the three times and ten directions,**
> **regard me with love and give me your blessing**
> **so that my prayer will be perfectly fulfilled.**

[108] This verse is easy to understand, except that "and their children" implies that śrāvakas and pratyekabuddhas are also included,[243] as is taught in *Entering the Middle Way*:

> Śrāvakas and medium-level buddhas[244] are born from the Lord of Sages.[245]

The actual prayer

This is in two parts:

1. A general dedication of good karma to complete enlightenment
2. The specific prayer

A general dedication of good karma to complete enlightenment

[Verse 2]

> **May the rivers of accumulations of virtue, unpolluted by the triple aspects,**

that come from the snowy mountains of the pure thoughts and actions
of myself and all endless beings
enter the ocean of the four kāyas.

"Myself" is the one who is making the prayer. To speak of "all beings" is the way of pure beings. From the *Abbreviated Perfection of Wisdom in Verse*:

> There is no enlightenment without benefiting beings.[246]

From the *Sutra Requested by [the Nāga King] Anavatapta*:

> If a bodhisattva mahāsattva has one quality, he will be in complete possession of all the qualities of buddhahood, which has all supreme aspects. What is that one quality? It is thus: It is an omniscient mind that does not abandon beings.[247]

The pure thoughts of "pure thoughts and actions" are not negative motivations, such as avarice, malice, and wrong views, but positive motivations, such as love, compassion, and bodhicitta. From *Twenty Vows*:

> A good mind does no wrong.[248]

[For example,] when Captain Mahākaruṇika slew a villainous merchant, he accumulated many eons' worth [of good karma].[249] Also, when Geshé Ben[250] was about to meet some patrons, he carefully dusted [his room] and cleaned his face, images, and offerings, but on examining his motivation, he perceived it to be an insincere wish to create a good impression, and so he scattered a handful of dirt over everything. When Phadampa [Sangyé][251] heard about this, he composed a praise of [Geshé Ben].

Thus, even if an activity is slightly impure, with a powerful good motivation, it is the same as performing a pure action. Pure action means good conduct with body and speech, but all it requires is the development of a good motivation. [109]

"Snowy mountains" is a metaphor for pure thoughts and actions. "Rivers" is a metaphor for the accumulations of virtue that come from [pure thoughts and actions]. This encompasses both stained and unstained good karma, such as the ten good actions of body, speech, and mind; the six perfections, such as generosity; the thirty-seven qualities of the factors for enlightenment; and so on.

These "rivers of accumulations of virtue" are said to be "unpolluted by the triple aspects," which means that they are free of the polluting dirt of focusing on the triple aspects. This is because focusing can never be the path to enlightenment. From *Entering the Middle Way*:

> Even though you dedicate [merit] to buddhahood's complete
> enlightenment,
> that [dedication] will be mundane if made with the threefold focus.
> If there is no focusing, that itself
> was taught by the Buddha to be *supramundane perfection*.[252]

Thus, such texts as the *Mother of the Conquerors*[253] teach that every good action that is accompanied by focusing is the "māra activity of bodhisattvas." According to *Entering the Middle Way*, which uses generosity as an example, the "triple aspects" are focusing on these three: the object [of the action], the action, and the agent.

> Generosity that is devoid of giving, receiver, and giver...[254]

None but āryas have true wisdom free from focusing on the triple aspects, but ordinary beings can have an equivalent understanding gained from scriptures and the guru's instructions.

Generally, wisdom devoid of method is bondage to the aspect of nirvana, while method devoid of wisdom is bondage to samsara. Therefore, you have to practice both [wisdom and method] inseparably. This is why the words "all...beings" teach the method of great compassion, and the words "unpolluted by the triple aspects" teach the wisdom of emptiness. Similarly, from the *Sutra Requested by Akṣayamati*:

> Wisdom devoid of method binds you to nirvana, while method devoid of wisdom binds you to samsara. Therefore, they must be united.[255]

The "accumulations of virtue" are dedicated to "the four kāyas": the dharmakāya, the saṃbhogakāya, the nirmāṇakāya, and the svabhavakāya.

The dharmakāya

[110] This is the wisdom that directly realizes the ultimate nature of the dharmadhātu. It is the primary condition for the sugatas' accomplishment of unsurpassable benefit. Ārya Nāgārjuna has taught:

> I pay homage to that which is neither one nor many; which is the basis for the great, perfect benefit for oneself and for others; which has the nature of not being nothingness and not being a thing; which has an equal taste, like space; which is difficult to realize; which is without stain; which is without change; which is peace; which is equality of the unequal; which is pervasive; which is without any elaboration; which is an individual self-knowing: the dharmakāya of all the conquerors, for which there is no example.[256]

The saṃbhogakāya

This is described in the *Ornament of Realization*:

> It has the nature of the thirty-two primary signs
> and the eighty secondary signs.
> It is taught to be the Sage's *saṃbhogakāya* (enjoyment body)
> because it enjoys the Mahayana.[257]

Although there appear bodies with every single attribute of the sugatas' form kāyas, they have no nature of their own, and thus they have no limitation. This is what the Vajrayāna calls "bodies and faces with every feature." Moreover, the saṃbhogakāya teaches the Mahayana alone, because its pupils and realms are completely pure.

The nirmāṇakāya

When there is true buddhahood in the form of a sugata's saṃbhogakāya, just like the sun radiating light, the embodiments of spontaneous activity immediately appear within a variety of pure and impure realms. Tibetan scholars have taught that there are: *supreme nirmāṇakāyas*, who demonstrate the twelve deeds in Jambudvīpa; *born nirmāṇakāyas*, who appear as beings, such as āryas and ordinary beings, but who can also appear as matter, such as stupas, ships, and bridges; and *created nirmāṇakāyas*, such as the lute player who was emanated to teach King Nanda of the gandharvas.[258] However, Indian scholars have clearly taught in their texts that a *born nirmāṇakāya* is when a supreme nirmāṇakāya takes birth in the kṣatriya or another caste; a *created nirmāṇakāya* demonstrates a mastery of various skills; and a *supreme nirmāṇakāya* demonstrates the attainment of enlightenment. That conforms to the meaning of this passage from *Ornament of the Mahayana Sutras*:

> The nirmāṇakāyas of the Buddha,
> which always demonstrate skills, birth,
> great enlightenment, and nirvana,
> are the great method for liberation.[259] [111]

THE SVABHAVAKĀYA

This is great peace and is the nature of all phenomena. It is attained through the power of the dharmakāya, through realization. The Vajrayāna calls this the *body of great bliss* (*mahāsukhakāya*) because its distinctive quality is supreme, unchanging bliss. Ārya Nāgārjuna has said:

> I pay homage to that which is free from the activity of the three realms; which is the equality of space; which is the nature of all things;
> which is purity, which is peace; which has the nature of supreme peace; which is the yoga of absence; which is realized by the yogin;
> which is difficult to realize; which is difficult to analyze; which is beneficial to oneself and others; which is pervasive; which is featureless;
> which is free of thoughts; which is the one kāya; which is the bliss kāya, the equality of the unequal, of all the conquerors.[260]

Thus, [Rangjung Dorjé] portrays the four kāyas as the ocean, the embodiment of vastness and depth, and [he prays] that the previously described rivers of accumulations of virtue will enter it.

This verse is a prayer that summarizes the qualities of the Sugata's path and its result. You must understand that everything that follows is simply an elaboration of this [verse].

The treatises on poetry teach that this style of writing, in which the symbol and the symbolized are conjoined, is called *decorative metaphor*.

The specific prayer

This has five parts:

1. A prayer for a perfect basis for the path
2. A prayer for wisdom that realizes the path
3. A prayer for an unmistaken path
4. A prayer for an unmistaken practice of that path
5. A prayer for the result that is the path's completion

A prayer for a perfect basis for the path

This has two parts:

a. A general prayer
b. A specific prayer

A general prayer for a perfect basis for the path

[Verse 3]

> **Until the time that we attain that,**
> **may we throughout every lifetime**
> **never even hear the words "bad actions" and "suffering"**
> **and enjoy the glorious ocean of good actions and happiness.**

The first two lines refer to all lifetimes, from this life onward, [112] until the time that we attain that unique level of the four kāyas of the conquerors that has just been explained.

The next two lines are a prayer to enjoy solely the glory of causal good actions and their resultant happiness, which is like the ocean, and to never even hear the words "causal bad actions" and "resultant suffering." From *Precious Garland*:

> Bad actions are those that originate from
> desire, anger, and stupidity.
> Suffering originates from bad actions,
> as do all the lower existences.

Good actions are those that originate
from the absence of desire, anger, and stupidity.
All the higher existences and
the happiness of all lifetimes originate from good actions.[261]

From *Entering the Conduct of a Bodhisattva*:

Also, this is what should always be,
day and night, my constant thought:
"Wickedness means suffering;
how can I get away from it?"[262]

A specific prayer for a perfect basis for the path

[Verse 4]

May I obtain the supreme freedoms and opportunities; have faith, diligence, and wisdom;
rely on an excellent spiritual friend; obtain the quintessence of the teachings;
practice them correctly and without any obstacle;
and thus practice the sublime Dharma throughout all my lifetimes.

The earlier line "Until the time that we attain that" could be applied to this verse as well.

The freedoms and opportunities in "May I obtain the supreme freedoms and opportunities" refer to a human body in which the eight freedoms and ten opportunities are complete. The eight freedoms are called "freedoms" because they are freedoms from eight unfavorable states. From the *Applications of Mindfulness Sutra*:

The eight unfavorable states are:
hells, pretas, animals, savages,
long-living devas, those with wrong views,
[beings in an era] devoid of a buddha, and idiots.[263]

The ten opportunities are comprised of [five of one's own and five from others]. The five opportunities of one's own are:

Being human, being born in the central land, having complete faculties,
not committing the error of extreme acts,[264] and having the correct object for your faith.[265]

The five opportunities from others are:

A buddha has appeared, he has taught the Dharma,
the teachings have remained, it has followers, and
they have love in their hearts for the benefit of others.[266]

A body that possesses these eighteen freedoms and opportunities can become a basis for attaining liberation and omniscience. Therefore it is called "supreme." A "basis" with these perfect freedoms and opportunities, and which has been born in Jambudvīpa, [113] creates good and bad karma that is more powerful than that of beings in other worlds. Therefore, this is supreme among the supreme. From the *Saṃvarodaya Tantra*:

Those born in the three [other] continents have the six elements.
The supreme, excellent births in Jambudvīpa
are renowned as "beings on the level of karma."[267]

You may have attained an excellent foundation with the freedoms and opportunities, but if you do not have the combination of faith, diligence, and wisdom, you will not be able to cross over the ocean of samsara's sufferings. From the *Avataṃsaka Sutra*:

Those who dwell in existence and have little faith
cannot know the enlightenment of the Buddha.[268]

The *Sutra of Ten Dharmas* also teaches the fault that comes from not having faith:

Good qualities will not be born
in humans who have no faith,
just as a green sprout [is not born]
from a seed that has been burned by fire.[269]

The *Sutra Requested by Sāgaramati* teaches the defects that result from lacking diligence in such passages as:

> The lazy do not have [the perfections], from generosity to wisdom. The lazy do not accomplish the benefit of others. For the lazy, enlightenment is very far, completely far.[270]

Without going into lengthy detail, there are teachings on the defect that results from lacking wisdom, such as those in *Abbreviated Perfection of Wisdom in Verse*:

> A trillion blind people who are without sight
> cannot even see the road, so how can they reach the city?
> Those who have no wisdom, whose five [other] perfections are blind,
> cannot, without that vision, reach enlightenment.[271]

According to Vasubandhu:

> The afflicted, lacking discernment of phenomena,
> have no method to bring complete pacification,
> and the afflictions cause them to wander in this ocean of worldly existence.[272]

Thus, it is taught that you must "have faith, diligence, and wisdom." But what is the essence of faith, diligence, and wisdom?

Faith

From [*Treatise on the Five Aggregates*]:[273]

> What is faith? It is having true conviction in, aspiration to, and attraction to [respectively] karma and results, the truth, and the Jewels.[274]

Therefore, faith can be classified into three kinds: (1) faith that is certainty that the phenomena of actions and results are the process of dependent origination, (2) faith that is aspiration toward the enlightenment of buddhahood, and (3) faith that is attraction to the Three Jewels. [114]

Diligence

This is a mental event that remedies laziness, which has no enthusiasm for good actions. From [*Treatise on the Five Aggregates*]:

> What is diligence? It is the remedy for laziness; it is the mind's enthusiasm for good actions.[275]

There are also such classifications [of diligence] as the two categories of perseverance and dedication.

Wisdom

From [*Treatise on the Five Aggregates*]:

> What is wisdom? It is the complete discernment of phenomena.[276]

Wisdom can be categorized into two kinds: mundane and supramundane.

Even with faith, diligence, and wisdom, you will be unable to realize omniscience without the primary condition of reliance on a spiritual friend (*kalyāṇamitra*). From the *Eight-Thousand-Verse Perfection of Wisdom*:

> In this way, the bodhisattva mahāsattva who desires the unsurpassable, truly complete enlightenment of truly complete buddhahood should first serve, rely upon, and venerate the spiritual friend.[277]

There are countless such quotations. In particular, the great, secret Vajrayāna teaches:

> The guru is the Buddha, the guru is the Dharma,
> and likewise, the guru is the Sangha.
> The guru is glorious Vajradhara;
> the guru is the cause of all.[278]

From the *Guhyasamāja*:

> I will emanate in the form of the ācārya.[279]

From the *Kālacakra*:

> These vajra clubs against the māras are renowned as *vajrasattvas*
> in this world.[280]

Therefore, even though the vajra master who gives you the empowerment for the true meaning appears to be an ordinary being, see him as Vajradhara. In fact this is what he is, and therefore without Vajradhara as your guru, you will fail to attain even the smallest siddhi, let alone enlightenment. Therefore, [Aśvaghoṣa] taught:

> [The holder of the vajra has taught]
> that siddhis follow the master.[281]

And [Indrabhūti taught]:

> If there is no one to use the oars,
> a boat will not reach the other shore.
> Even if you perfectly complete all qualities,
> without a guru, there will be no end to existence.[282]

From the *Hevajra Tantra*:

> Nothing else can describe the innate [joy].
> It cannot be found in anything [else].
> It is known by yourself, through [your own] merit,
> and through relying upon your time with the guru.[283] [115]

This is also taught elsewhere, and here too, therefore, it is taught that you must "rely on an excellent spiritual friend."

Pupils should wish to learn from guides who are compatible with their potential, who can give pupils Dharma teachings at the appropriate time. They should know the methods that at specific stages will develop previously undeveloped good qualities and make previously developed qualities increase. They should have the compassion that wishes to liberate beings from the ocean of existence. For example, a guru who is compatible with someone ready to enter the Dharma of the Vinaya should be a preceptor (*upādhyāya*) who has the four necessary aspects: the nobility [of being a monk], scholarship, stability, and benefit. Similarly, those masters who perform the activity of giving secret teachings and so on should be capable of [making pupils] develop perfect qualities and the relative and ultimate bodhicittas for the first time, and [make them] increase those [qualities] they have already developed. According to Śāntideva:

> Even at the cost of your life,
> never abandon the spiritual friend
> who has perfect bodhisattva conduct
> and is learned in the meaning of the Mahayana.[284]

Those are the qualities [the spiritual friend] should have. According to the Kālacakra, when someone is to be guided in the special methods of the Mantrayāna:

> First, correctly depend on gurus who keep the commitments,
> remain correctly in the Vajrayāna,
> meditate, be free of attachment, be completely unstained, follow
> the path of patience,
> bestow the path upon pupils, free them from the fear of the hells,
> and have pure conduct (*brahmacaryā*).
> These vajra clubs against the māras are renowned as *vajrasattvas*
> in this world.[285]

Also, they should be vajra masters with qualities as described in the tantras.

Generally, while pupils are in samsara, within the shell of thick obscurations, they rely upon the guru in the form of an ordinary being. When their obscurations are slightly diminished, [the guru] will be in the form of an ārya bodhisattva. From the great path of accumulation onward, [the guru] will be in the form of the supreme nirmāṇakāya. When [the pupils] have reached the ārya path, they are able to depend upon a guru appearing in a saṃbhogakāya form. [116] Therefore, at this time, do not have a deficient aspiration.

The guru is called a *spiritual friend*. This is the terminology of the Perfection Vehicle, and it means an *unsurpassable* friend, because no father, mother, or friend shows the kindness of liberating you from the ocean of existence. Being free of faults and having all good qualities, the [spiritual friend] is said to be "excellent." To "rely on" [the spiritual friend] means to rely through the five methods of pleasing, the nine kinds of service, and so on.[286] Fulfill the wishes of the sacred spiritual friend, who has the power of compassion, in the same way as the merchant's son Sudhana and the bodhisattva Sadāprarudita relied on their spiritual friends,[287] and in the same way in which the early masters of this practice lineage relied upon their gurus.

"Teachings" in the phrase "obtain the quintessence of the teachings" refers to the Dharma that was taught—both provisional and definitive teachings, general and special teachings, the three vehicles, the three trainings, and so on. These are in accordance with the capabilities of pupils, so that they gain within themselves higher and higher qualities on the path. "The quintessence" is that which enables pupils to grasp the very heart of liberation.

When you obtain these teachings, you shouldn't just receive them, but also "practice them correctly," practicing them only as they were taught in the Sugata's teachings, in the commentarial treatises, and in the guru's instructions. Practicing like that "without any obstacle" means to be free of external obstacles from the four elements, humans, nonhumans, and so on, and free of internal obstacles from afflictions and thoughts. In brief, be free from every obstacle on the path to liberation and omniscience.

The last line summarizes the first three: having attained the freedoms and opportunities; having faith, diligence, and wisdom; relying upon an excellent spiritual friend; receiving the teachings from that spiritual friend; practicing them correctly; and having no obstacles; you are thus someone with the perfect good fortune of "practicing the sublime Dharma." Therefore pray that it be may be like this throughout your entire succession of lifetimes, from this life until you attain enlightenment. [117]

A prayer for the wisdom that realizes the path

[Verse 5]

> **Hearing the scriptures and logic brings freedom from the clouds of ignorance.**
> **Contemplating the instructions defeats the darkness of doubt.**
> **The light of meditation illuminates the true nature, just as it is.**
> **May the radiance of the three wisdoms increase.**

The first line teaches the wisdom that is born from hearing. The second line teaches the wisdom that is born from contemplation. The third line teaches the wisdom that is born from meditation. The fourth line teaches a summary of this prayer.

THE FIRST LINE

> **Hearing the scriptures and logic brings freedom from the clouds of ignorance.**

"Scriptures" means the teachings in both the Buddha's words and their commentaries. From the *Sublime Continuum*:

> That which is meaningful and connected with the Dharma,
> that which teaches the elimination of the three realms' afflictions,
> and that which teaches the benefits of peace—
> that teaching is the Sage's, and that which is contrary is not.[288]

Thus, all the teachings that have come from the Buddha are the primary condition. We can categorize these teachings into three kinds: words spoken by the Buddha himself, teachings that he authorized, and teachings that had his blessing. Alternatively, there are the three categories according to the subject of the teachings: Vinaya, Sutra, and Abhidharma. Is the Mantrayāna included within these scriptural baskets? It is the essence of all three. Therefore, although it is classified separately as the Vidyādhara basket, it is certainly included [within these three]. According to [Karmapa] Rangjung Gyalwa it is:

> [Practicing] the profound Sutras, Vinaya, and Abhidharma...[289]

From Vajragarbha's commentary [on the *Hevajra Tantra*]:

> It is not the Sage's viewpoint that
> there is a fourth or fifth [vehicle] in buddhahood.[290]

As for the treatises, from the *Sublime Continuum*:

> That which is taught by minds free from distraction,
> that which concerns solely the teachings of the Conqueror,
> and that which is in accord with the path that attains liberation
> should be placed on the head as if it were the Sage's.[291]

These are the commentaries to the views contained in the Buddha's words. Ārya bodhisattvas, ārya śrāvakas, and paṇḍitas who were ordinary beings composed them after the Buddha demonstrated passing away from this world. There are many ways of categorizing the commentaries, such as the two categories of "general commentaries" and "specific commentaries."

"Logic" is obtaining complete certainty through propositions, reasons, examples, and so on, in accordance with the textual tradition of *Compendium on Valid Cognition*,[292] the seven texts [of Dharmakīrti], and so on. [118] Logic brings a general understanding of any subject that has to be understood.

Through hearing the scriptures and logic from the guru, there arises the wisdom that is born from hearing. This brings freedom from its contrary: the clouds of ignorance of scriptures and logic. Ācārya Candra[kīrti] has taught that:

> Just as a man with sight can easily lead
> a crowd of blind people to the place they wish to go,
> in the same way the intellect
> leads the sightless qualities to buddhahood.[293]
>
> How does the intellect understand the very profound Dharma?
> It does so through scripture and through logic.[294]

From the *Jātaka*:

> Hearing is a torch that dispels the darkness of ignorance.
> It is a supreme wealth that no thief can steal.
> It is like a weapon that defeats the enemy, who is total stupidity.
> It is a supreme friend who teaches methods and instructions.[295]

The second line

> **Contemplating the instructions defeats the darkness of doubt.**

"Instructions," *upadeśa* in Sanskrit, are what the Sugata taught, as a result of his compassion, to enable people to liberate themselves from the bondage of existence and peace. "Contemplating the instructions" means to apply them to your being, to reflect correctly upon them. In particular, there are various kinds of provisional and definitive teachings because the Sugata taught various vehicles in accord with individual aspirations. Especially, the great secret Vajrayāna tantras are extremely abstruse, because they are "bound by six boundaries."[296] Therefore, when a master with pure Dharma eyes, relying upon the four reliances,[297] correctly explains their essential meaning and you ponder the instructions within these teachings, contemplating the instructions, this causes wisdom born from contemplation to arise, and this defeats its contrary, "the darkness of doubt," which is uncertainty concerning profound subjects.

The third line

> **The light of meditation illuminates the true nature, just as it is.**

Extensive hearing and accurate contemplation of the meaning heard brings certainty free from doubt. Meditation on that, resting in that, causes the wisdom born from meditation to arise. [119] The light of that wisdom illuminates the essence of the true nature, just as it is.

The "true nature" is the nature of all phenomena from form to omniscience, and this nature is also called the *mahāmudrā of the basis phase*, the *natural truth*, the *primordial lord*, the *tathāgata family*, and the *essence*. There are the true nature of the body and the true nature of the mind.

The true nature of the body

From the *Hevajra Tantra*:

> The Teacher with the thirty-two marks,
> the Lord with the eighty signs,
> is present in the form of sperm
> within the great bliss of the Queen's vagina.
>
> In its absence there will be no bliss.
> It cannot exist without bliss,
> for they are [individually] ineffective; they are dependent.
> The bliss comes from the deity yoga.
>
> Therefore, buddhahood is not a thing
> and neither does it have the form of nothing.
> It has the form of faces and arms,
> and because of great bliss, it is also formless.

Therefore, the innateness is all beings.[298]

Here the word "sperm" means: that which is created and appears from the relative bodhicitta; that which is the base for the supremely unchanging bliss; that which is the vital energy of the channels, winds, and drops; that which transcends having a nature of atoms; that which is the essence of wisdom; and that which is the "natural body."

Therefore, glorious Rangjung Gyalwa[299] taught that the channels, winds, and drops are a dependent origination arising as a manifestation of the mind and that they are created by and appear from the relative bodhicitta. They are the base for innate wisdom and therefore are the true nature of the vajra body.[300]

It appears that the seventh lord [Karmapa] has taught that the four kāyas are present in the absence of the stains of the eight aggregations [of consciousnesses] and that this is the same essential meaning as Venerable Rangjung's teaching of "the primordial, increasing family."[301] There are many scriptures and much reasoning that establishes this as valid, but I will not go into them here.

The true nature of the mind

This is the dharmadhātu, which is uncircumscribed, nonaligned, and free from every [conceptual] elaboration. From the *Tilaka of Liberation*:

> It is devoid of every conceptualization
> and is therefore beyond thought or speech.
>
> It is as stainless as space, is the source of everything,
> and is called *profundity beyond examination*.
>
> It has the form of mahāmudrā.
> It is like an illusion or a rainbow.
>
> It is that which purifies your own and other's beings.
> It is called *true clarity*.
>
> It is the supreme nature of nonduality.
> It is the lord that pervades all things. [120]

> It cannot be seized by samsara.
> It is taught to be the dharmadhātu.[302]

Thus, it is taught to be nondual profundity and clarity. It is also the *natural mind* and the *naturally present family*.

Understand that the true nature is taught toward the end of this text. It is being taught at this point simply so as not to have a gap in this explanation [of the prayer].

The body and the mind's true nature of the basis are inseparable, like water and ice, and this is called the *union of the two kāyas at the time of the basis*. This is revealed to the direct perception of self-knowing only through the power of meditation and not through any other method.

> There is nothing whatever to be removed in this;
> there is not the slightest thing to be added.
> Truly look at the truth;
> if you truly see, you will be liberated.[303]

This alone is the sequential relationship of the three wisdoms. It's not definitely so for individuals with instantaneous realization, but generally, for individuals of gradual realization, a later wisdom cannot arise without there first being the earlier wisdom, because of the dependent relationship of one not arising if the other does not exist. Also, it is said [in *Treasury of the Abhidharma*]:

> Those with good conduct, who have heard and contemplated,
> can dedicate themselves to meditation.[304]

The fourth line

> **May the radiance of the three wisdoms increase.**

This describes the "three wisdoms" born from hearing, contemplation, and meditation through the implied metaphor of the sun. So you pray that, freed from the clouds and such of ignorance that obscure them, may the strong increase of the great radiance of their own bright light clearly reveal the true nature.

A prayer for the unmistaken path

[Verse 6]

> **The two truths, free from the two extremes of eternalism and nihilism, are the meaning of the basis.**
> **The two accumulations, free from the extremes of embellishment and denigration, are the supreme path.**
> **The attainment of the two benefits, free from the extremes of existence and peace, is the attainment of the result.**
> **May we meet this Dharma that is free of error.**

The first line teaches that which is to be known: the unmistaken true nature of the basis. The second line teaches that which is to be practiced: the unmistaken practice of the path. The third line teaches that which is to be accomplished: the unmistaken stage of the result. [121] The fourth line teaches that the Dharma that is unmistaken in those three ways is the genuine, error-free path and prays for that.

The first line

> **The two truths, free from the two extremes of eternalism and nihilism, are the meaning of the basis.**

"Eternalism and nihilism" are the terms for an erroneous and ignorant analysis of the basis, the true nature, and the mahāmudrā. This has two aspects: the eternalist view and the nihilist view. Their [respective] characteristics are (1) the conceptualization that believes in the extreme that all phenomena exist, and (2) the conceptualization that believes in the extreme that all phenomena do not exist. It is said [in Nāgārjuna's *Praise to the Inconceivable*]:

> To say "it exists" is the view of eternalism.
> To say "it doesn't exist" is the view of nihilism.[305]

Who holds these views? They are primarily found among the tīrthikas, but they are also found among Buddhists. Within the tīrthikas, Rishi Bṛhaspati, in order that the devas would be victorious over the asuras in battle, wrote a text teaching that there were no past or future lives and no good or bad karma.[306] Those who followed this, such as Rishi Jayarāśibhaṭṭa (a contemporary of Dharmakīrti),[307] spread [this teaching]. It became known as Lokāyata or Cārvāka. This is the nihilistic view.

These are what are known as the four eternalist schools:

1. The Sāṃkhya: followers of the teacher Kapila, who believed in five principles[308] and proclaimed that knowing them brings liberation
2. The believers in Īśvara:[309] followers of Rishi Kaṇāda[310] or Rishi Akṣapāda,[311] who were given the supreme boon by the god Īśvara, and who believed in six categories,[312] and so on, that were to be understood
3. The Vaiṣṇavites: the followers of such teachers as Jayatīrtha,[313] who believe Viṣṇu to be God
4. The Jains (*Nirgranthas*): the followers of Rishi Jina,[314] who believe in six substances,[315] and so on

There are also those who are known as Tajiks (Iranians), or Mlecchas ("barbarians"), who follow the tradition of the texts composed by the teacher Abraham,[316] who was a follower of the asuras. In Tibet, there is the Yungdrung Bön tradition, followers of Miwo Shenrap.[317] In China, there are the followers of the tradition of Taoism.[318] These [three] are not actual tīrthikas.[319] The first of them, the Tajiks, have a conduct that is worse than that of the tīrthikas. The latter two are slightly better than tīrthikas in terms of not believing in a self and so on, but they are still to be included among the eternalists. [122]

Among the Buddhists, Vaibhāṣikas and Sautrāntikas do not, generally speaking, deny the self of phenomena. They say that there are externally existing indivisible atoms and so on.[320] Cittamātrins state that knowledge of the emptiness of dualism has true existence, and therefore they believe in the perceiver as the self of phenomena.

Those are the views of belief in the extremes of existence or nonexistence. Ācārya Sthiramati has written in his *Commentary on the Thirty Verses*:

> Those who say, "The known exists, just as the knower does," believe in the extreme of eternalism. Those who say, "A knower does not exist, just as the known [does not]," believe in the extreme of nihilism.[321]

"The two truths, free from extremes, are the meaning of the basis" means that the unmistaken meaning of the basis, the true nature, is free from the two extremes of incorrect analysis; this meaning is the understanding of the union of the two truths. The two truths are ultimate truth and relative truth.

Ultimate truth is the true nature of all animate and inanimate phenomena. It is devoid of the eight extremes of conceptual elaboration. It is completely pure, like the center of space. It is uncircumscribed, nonpartial, and totally transcends being an object of thought or speech. It is called the "first buddha," the "primordial lord," "truth," and so on.

Relative truth is the apparent nature of all animate and inanimate phenomena. It is the dependent origination of a diversity of conceptual elaborations. It is like an illusion. According to Ācārya Jñānagarbha:

> The apparent nature—that alone
> is relative; the rest is the other.[322]

The two truths are primordially one. All the phenomena that have appeared within samsara and nirvana, animate and inanimate, have never had an individual essence even while they were appearing. They are free from the extreme of eternalism, like reflections in a mirror. They are also free from the extreme of nihilism, because even though they are always devoid of an essence, nevertheless, their diverse appearances arise unceasingly. Concerning this, Ācārya Nāgā[rjuna] has said:

> That which has emptiness,
> that can be anything.
> That which has no emptiness,
> that cannot be anything.[323]

If phenomena had their own real existence, they wouldn't lose their individual characteristics. [123] One thing would prevent there being another, and there would be no origination, destruction, and so on. There is no such difficulty if all phenomena are emptiness, for there can be dependent origination in emptiness. It is extremely important to know this and other [reasonings] in the six Madhyamaka texts of Nāgārjuna.[324] From *Fearing Nothing: A Commentary on the Root Middle Way*:

> The Dharma taught by all the bhagavān buddhas has come about through these two truths:
>
> 1. The worldly relative truth: The [people of this] world fail to understand the empty nature of phenomena and perceive phenomena as having birth. That is relatively true for them; therefore, it is relative truth.

2. The ultimate truth: The āryas' understanding is without error. Therefore, they perceive the birthlessness of phenomena. That is ultimately true for them, and therefore it is the ultimate truth.[325]

And from the same text:

> One cannot teach the ultimate without relying on terminology,
> and one cannot attain nirvana without relying on the ultimate.
> Therefore, one has to state that there are two truths.[326]

You must understand this secret essential point, which has been taught at length.

THE SECOND LINE

> **The two accumulations, free from the extremes of embellishment and denigration, are the supreme path.**

"Embellishment and denigration" are ignorance of the path that leads to the attainment of liberation. These are:

1. The extreme of embellishing nonexistence as existence: This is being without wisdom because of not knowing the process of dependent origination from emptiness. It is thinking, "Only these appearing phenomena, such as karmic causes and results, are real, and nothing else has any reality."
2. The extreme of denigrating existence as nonexistence: This is having no method because of not understanding the essential point that the Jewels, karmic causes and results, and so on appear through dependent origination and can be effective simply as appearances. It is thinking, "Only emptiness is real; nothing else has any reality."

"The two accumulations, free from the extremes... are the supreme path" means that through accumulating merit in order to accomplish the form kāyas of the tathāgatas, we avoid being in the extreme of denigration, [124] and through accumulating wisdom in order to accomplish the dharmakāyas of the tathāgatas, we avoid being in the extreme of embellishment.

The *unmistaken supreme path for the attainment of liberation* is the name for the practice of an inseparable union of [the accumulation of merit and wisdom]. Within the six perfections, generosity and conduct are the accumulation of merit; wisdom is the accumulation of wisdom; while patience, diligence, and meditation are both. From *Ornament of the Mahayana Sutras*:

> Generosity and conduct are the accumulation
> of merit; wisdom is that of wisdom;
> the other three are of both.[327]

The necessity of practicing the union of [merit and wisdom] is described in *Lamp on the Path to Enlightenment*:

> Wisdom that is without method
> and method that is without wisdom
> were taught to be bondage.
> Therefore, do not be without either.[328]

From the *Vimalakīrti Sutra*:

> Wisdom that is not supported by method is bondage.
> Wisdom that is supported by method is liberation.
> Method that is not supported by wisdom is bondage.
> Method that is supported by wisdom is liberation.[329]

The third line

> **The attainment of the two benefits, free from the extremes of existence and peace, is the attainment of the result.**

"Existence and peace" are inferior goals and results. Method by itself, without wisdom, does not result in transcending existence. Wisdom by itself, without method, does not result in transcending partial peace.

"The attainment of the result"—that is, "the two benefits, free from the extremes," which means free from the two extremes of existence and peace—is (through practicing the path described above, the union of the two accumulations) the attainment of the unmistaken result, which is also the union of the two kāyas: the dharmakāya—a perfect benefit for oneself that does not fall into the extreme of existence—and the form kāya—which is a perfect benefit for others and does not fall into the extreme of peace. From the *Sublime Continuum*:

> The kāya of ultimate truth and the relative kāyas based upon it
> are the benefit for oneself and the benefit for others.[330]

THE FOURTH LINE

> **May we meet this Dharma that is free from error.**

We are in error if we fall into any of the two extremes taught in relation to basis, path, and result. [125] Therefore, in order to avoid these errors and extremes, with the view of the basis, we eliminate the extremes of eternalism and nihilism. If they are eliminated, we will be free from the extremes of embellishment and denigration in our practice of the path. If these are eliminated, we will be spontaneously liberated from the two extremes of peace and existence as results. Therefore, the unmistaken path "that is free from error" is that which has the basis, path, and result described here.

A prayer for the unmistaken practice of the path

This is in two parts:

1. A summary
2. A prayer for the practice of meditation

A summary of the unmistaken practice of the path

[Verse 7]

> **The basis for purification is the mind—the union of clarity and**
> **emptiness.**
> **The purifier is the great vajra yoga of mahāmudrā.**
> **The purified are the stains of extrinsic delusion.**
> **May the result of purification, the stainless dharmakāya,**
> **become manifest.**

The most important thing to understand in the practice of the mahāmudrā yoga of the path phase, which has the characteristics of an unmistaken path that have just been described, are these four aspects: (1) the basis for purification, (2) the yoga that purifies, (3) the stain that is purified away, and (4) the result that is attained through purification. Therefore, they are taught sequentially by one line of verse each, ending with an expression of prayer.

The first line

> **The basis for purification is the mind—the union of clarity and emptiness.**

"The basis for the purification" of every stain that prevents the accomplishment of liberation is identified as the mind, which has a pure nature. Its characteristics are established to be "the union of clarity and emptiness." The *Sublime Continuum* teaches the reason why the pure mind is the basis for purification:

> Earth is based on water, water on air,
> and air upon space.
> Space is not based upon
> the elements of air, water, and earth.
>
> In that way, the aggregates, [sensory] elements, and sensory faculties
> are based upon karma and afflictions.
> Karma and afflictions are always
> based upon improper mental engagement.
>
> Improper mental engagement
> is based upon the mind's purity,
> but the mind's nature is not based
> upon any phenomenon at all.[331]

Thus, the basis of all samsara and nirvana is taught to be the purity of the mind, which is the essence, or element, of the tathāgatas. [126] It is the basis for the purification, but it is not that which is purified, as it doesn't have even an atom of a phenomenon that has to be purified away. From *Praise to the Dharmadhātu*:

> That element, which is a seed,
> is said to be the base for all phenomena.
> Through its gradual purification
> the state of buddhahood is attained.[332]

And also:

> Those sutras spoken by the Conqueror
> in which he taught emptiness
> all eliminate the afflictions
> but do not diminish the element (*dhātu*).[333]

It's possible that some who analyze this will not be convinced, believing that the word *mind* designates something that is an accumulation, and as buddha nature is noncomposite, the word *mind* should not be used for it; it is also contraindicated in the Abhidharma and elsewhere, where the mind is taught to be the consciousness that is the abode (*ālaya*) of all [karmic] seeds. However, we are not incorrect, because the mind has both pure and impure aspects, and those teachings are in reference to the impure aspect. There is also no contradiction in designating the mind to be an "accumulation," because it has, in a nondual manner, the sixty-four qualities[334] present in the basis and is therefore the source of all good qualities. From the *Perfection of Wisdom Sutra*:

> As for [that] mind, the mind does not exist; the nature of the mind is luminosity.[335]

There is the *Sublime Continuum* quotation given earlier, but also Ācārya Nāgārjuna has said:

> In that same way, the five obscurations—
> desire, malice, laziness,
> agitation, and doubt—
> obscure the mind of luminosity.[336]

In the sutras, tantras, and commentaries there are very many such instances where the purity of the mind is called *mind.*

Secondly, it is a union of clarity and emptiness, but the *Guhyasamāja* teaches its empty nature:

> It is devoid of all things.
> It has no aggregates, [sensory] elements, or [sensory] bases.
> It has no perceiver nor perceived.
> Phenomena are selfless and equal.
> Therefore your own mind, which is primordially unborn,
> is the nature of emptiness.[337]

The *Sublime Continuum* teaches that it is naturally luminous and cannot be polluted by transitory stains:

> The luminosity that is the mind's nature,
> like the sky, never changes.
> It is undefiled by extrinsic stains, such as desire,
> arising from incorrect thought.[338] [127]

Countless such quotations establish the mind to be clarity and emptiness. The emptiness is never separate from the clarity, and the clarity is never separate from the emptiness. Therefore, they are a union with the characteristic of inseparability. This is what Lord Maitreya[339] taught.[340] There are academic scholars in this land of Tibet who have not understood this secret, essential point and explain this union to be a clarity and emptiness that accompany each other. They have strayed from the teaching of the Sugata.

The second line

> **The purifier is the great vajra yoga of mahāmudrā.**

The meaning of the second line is that on this basis of purification, the "vajra yoga of mahāmudrā" is the path that is "the purifier" of the stains that are to be purified. In the Dakpo Kagyü's graduated instructions, worthy pupils rely upon qualified gurus and, according to the level of their ability, whether they first receive an elaborate empowerment or not, they practice the three preliminaries: (1) The general preliminaries, (2) the special preliminaries, and (3) the particular preliminaries. Then they practice the main practice, which are the two yogas of śamatha and vipaśyanā. This is followed by gaining certainty through direct introduction, in which there is the special realization of the ordinary mind seeing itself. There is also realization through the yogas of the two stages, which has the same essential meaning.

There are some pupils who, because of the level of their capability and their master's power, gain realization solely by being blessed by the transference of wisdom. There are some who continuously familiarize themselves with the direct recognition that they gained during a word empowerment or the experience gained during the third empowerment of a sequence of four empowerments that they have received. There are therefore various ways in which wisdom can manifest.

During the [paths] of accumulation and engagement, wisdom is primarily an experience. On reaching the path of seeing, wisdom manifests within your own being. From that point on, the wisdom is stabilized in meditation sessions and becomes subtler during the illusory appearances of post-meditation. This gradually eliminates what is to be eliminated, just as one arm of a weighing scale rises as the other descends. Finally, there is the vajra samādhi at the end of this continuum, which leaves nothing to be eliminated and which brings the attainment of buddhahood. What is the nature of this wisdom? From the *Mahāmudrā Tilaka Tantra*:

> Listen, Devi Mahāmudrā!
> Mahāmudrā is a great secret.
> It is inexpressible, inexhaustible, unborn.
> It has the form of everything and has no form. [128]
> It is formless and the sublime, supreme form.
> It is not thin or thick and so on.
> Its nature can never be measured.[341]

From Ācārya Nāgārjuna's *Commentary on Bodhicitta*:

> The buddhas have taught that
> bodhicitta is not obscured by
> thoughts that conceive of a self, aggregates, and so on.
> It always has the characteristic of emptiness.[342]

According to Saraha:

It has no color, qualities, words, or symbols.
I have poorly indicated the indescribable.
It is like the bliss that fills a maiden's heart.
To whom can one reveal this sublime lord?[343]

It is beyond speech and thought but can be clearly perceived by self-knowing, which sees the true nature of the basis for purification described earlier.

It's taught that you can attain the wisdom of mahāmudrā without receiving an elaborate empowerment, but in earlier and recent times there have been those in Tibet who, even though they had a reputation for being scholars, were unable to accept this teaching and made many criticisms of it. For example, some have said that no one can accomplish the Mantrayāna's mahāmudrā without an empowerment and the two stages [of generation and completion]. Others have said that it's possible, with good meditation, to gain realization solely through the view of the Madhyamaka, but if they have not [practiced] the logic taught in the Madhyamaka texts, such as the "reasoning that negates the four possibilities of generation,"[344] they will have many defects, such as a lack of certainty.

The Bhagavān, in order to train various kinds of pupils, taught countless such methods. Siddhas and scholars have taught these separately in various ways, disagreeing with each other over their explanations and disparaging [each other] saying, "I am the one who knows. Only this teaching of mine is true and no other teaching."

This supreme Kagyü tradition of instruction cannot be faulted on the above points, because, as will be explained further on, none of the different kinds of instructions teach that it is compulsory for a pupil with exceptionally sharp faculties to receive an elaborate empowerment. Still, they must first receive the blessing of the vajra-wisdom empowerment from a vajra master, and through that they will definitely gain the benefits of the two stages.

There are those who say that empowerment by transmitting a blessing is not a real empowerment and that guru-yoga meditation is not the same as the two stages. [129] However, if [the first of those statements were true], then empowerments given through colored sand mandalas and so on would not be true empowerments, because an "empowerment" must engender the realization of the empowerment's meaning within an individual, and an elaborate empowerment is less effective in engendering that realization than a simple empowerment. [If the second objection were true], meditation on deity yoga could not be the true practice of the two stages, because during that stage of the Mantrayāna you have to see the guru and deity as inseparable. The guru seals the deity. If a deity is not sealed as is required, then it is simply an imaginary deity that cannot bestow the supreme siddhi. Therefore, our tradition's samādhi empowerment, or vajra-wisdom empowerment, is the supreme of all empowerments, and it is obvious that it is a true empowerment. It is a mistake for a realized guru not to give this empowerment to those with exceptionally sharp faculties, who are ready for the mahāmudrā, and instead to bind them with an elaborate empowerment. Know Indrabhūti's extensive teaching on this subject in the *Accomplishment of Wisdom*. For example:

> The empowerment of vajra-wisdom,
> which is the attainment of excellent, supreme wisdom,
> and the elimination of all thoughts
> causes the accomplishment of the supreme siddhi.
>
> If you have the complete possession of true wisdom,
> you will be breaking your commitment
> if you bestow the empowerment
> separately as a drawn mandala.
>
> What suffering accrues from breaking the commitment?
> The benefits of the body
> and likewise the mind will diminish
> and you will quickly die.
>
> When you have died, you will have to experience
> the suffering of hells for hundreds of millions of eons.
> Even after you have left those existences,
> you will be born as an untouchable, or in an inferior caste,
> you will be born as mute or deaf,
> or you will be born blind;
> of that there is no doubt.
>
> The wisdom of all the tathāgatas
> is called the *vajra wisdom*.
> If the wise one gives its empowerment,
> that should be known as an empowerment.[345]

Whether you have truly received an empowerment or not depends on whether the meaning of the empowerment has arisen in your being or not. Therefore, if the realization of the inseparability of appearance and emptiness has arisen in a pupil, that is receiving the vase empowerment, and so on.

In the same way, meditation on the guru suffices as the generation stage. Familiarization with guru yoga [130] causes all appearances and beings to arise as the guru's manifestations, which is a greater cessation of ordinary grasping than even in meditation on a *yidam* deity. Also, many tantric commentaries state that the guru is the union of all the Jewels and that meditation on the guru will accomplish all siddhis.

The [guru yoga] is also taught to be the completion stage, as it is the supreme path—free from all hindrance and error—which through the power of intense devotion, cultivates the experience of an objectless mind.

This kind of secret, essential meaning is the province of those with the highest faculties and will never satisfy academics, and therefore should be recognized as an extraordinary, profound secret.

As for the second criticism, this is also without substance, because the Mantrayāna mahāmudrā's elaboration-free view corresponds with the Madhyamaka view. Therefore the realization of the Madhyamaka view is not a defect in the Mantrayāna. The academic teaching [of the Madhyamaka] was merely intended for debate with tīrthikas, while its meditation through analysis cannot even be classed as belonging to the Madhyamaka.

> The Madhyamaka that is unadorned
> by the guru's speech is merely middling.[346]

The reason why the mahāmudrā's cessation of all conceptual elaboration corresponds with the Madhyamaka view:

> Were anything higher than the Madhyamaka,
> that view would be a conceptual elaboration.[347]

Thus, it is impossible that there is a higher view in the Buddha's teachings than that of the Madhyamaka. Concerning this, Ācārya Jñānakīrti has said in his *Entering the Truth*:

> Another name for Mother Perfection of Wisdom is mahāmudrā,
> because of its being the essence of the nondual wisdom.[348]

He thus teaches that the perfection of wisdom taught in the sutras is a synonym for the Mantrayāna's mahāmudrā.

The third line

> **The purified are the stains of extrinsic delusion.**

What stains are purified by the purifier upon the basis of purification? This line states that the purified are the phenomena of perceiver and perceived, which even though they are not intrinsic, appear as a result of extrinsic delusion. As for the process of delusion and so on, this will be explained further on [in verse 10], which begins "The self-appearances that have never existed are mistaken as objects," and can be understood there. [131]

The fourth line

> **May the result of purification, the stainless dharmakāya, become manifest.**

What is "the result of the purification" of the purified by the purifier? With the eternal elimination of all extrinsic stains, which are all the phenomena of perceiver and perceived, the dharmakāya, which is the true nature of the basis, becomes manifest. From *Praise to the Dharmadhātu*:

> When obscured by the net of afflictions,
> it is that which is called a "being."
> When it is free from the afflictions,
> it is called a "buddha."[349]

If the dharmakāya alone is the result of purification, does that mean that the two form kāyas are not the result of purification? The form kāyas are in essence inseparable from the dharmakāya and therefore *are* the result of purification. This is why it is enough to mention only the dharmakāya. The term dharmakāya can be used to mean all three kāyas.

The dharmadhātu, the great bliss, which is naturally stainless, is known as the dharmakāya, or the svabhavakāya. This has two purities because there is [also] the purification of extrinsic stains.

When there is the purification and transformation of the *ālaya* consciousness, the afflicted consciousness, the mental or sixth consciousness, and the consciousnesses that engage with objects, then they become the dharmakāya, or the wisdom kāya, which is the attainment of the wisdom that knows ultimate nature and the wisdom that knows relative variety.

The svabhavakāya and wisdom kāya are not two different kāyas but are totally complete as the dharmakāya.

When there is this attainment of the dharmakāya, the purified consciousnesses I have listed [become] four categories of wisdom: (1) mirror wisdom, (2) equality wisdom, (3) discriminating wisdom, and (4) accomplishing wisdom. Equality wisdom is the saṃbhogakāya. Accomplishing wisdom is the manifestation of the nirmāṇakāya. Discriminating wisdom is included within both these kāyas. If you wish to know this in more detail, read *Ornament of the Mahayana Sutras* and Lord [Rangjung Dorjé's] own commentary to his [*Profound*] *Inner Meaning.* I will not write more on this subject here, as it would make this text too long.

A prayer for the practice of meditation

This is in two parts:

1. A summary
2. A detailed explanation

A summary of the practice of meditation

[Verse 8]

> **The confidence of the view cuts through doubts about the basis.**
> **The essential point of meditation is to remain undistracted from that.**
> **The supreme conduct is training in the entire meaning of meditation.**
> **May there be the confidence of view, meditation, and conduct.**

[132] Correct meditation on the mahāmudrā path is to first have the true view via cutting through doubts about mahāmudrā—the true nature of the basis. The correct, "essential point of meditation" is to rest in, or to remain

undistracted from, that view. "The supreme conduct" is training in this meaning of meditation, through which there will be swift enhancement. If you have the essential points of the view, meditation, and conduct, you will accomplish them with little difficulty; that is why this prayer is made.

A detailed explanation of the practice of meditation

This is in four parts:

1. The view that cuts through doubts concerning the basis
2. Attaining certainty, which is gained through meditation on that [view]
3. Reaching completion through that conduct and thereby reaching the fulfillment of the path
4. A prayer for the result of reaching the conclusion of the path

The view that cuts through doubts concerning the basis

This is in two parts:

1. A summary of the view
2. A detailed explanation of the view

A summary of the view that cuts through doubts concerning the basis

[Verse 9]

> **All phenomena are manifestations of the mind.**
> **The mind is without mind, devoid of an essence of mind,**
> **empty and unceasing, appearing as anything whatsoever.**
> **May it be perfectly examined and be completely understood.**

The first line teaches the certainty that all appearances "are manifestations of the mind." The second line establishes that the mind is without a nature of its own. The third line teaches that there is no contradiction in a union of emptiness and dependent origination. The fourth line teaches, in the form of a prayer, that we must, by examining with discriminating wisdom, cut through conceptual embellishments concerning the meaning of the basis.

A detailed explanation of the view that cuts through doubts concerning the basis

This is in four parts:

1. An explanation of the first line
2. An explanation of the second line
3. An explanation of the third line
4. An explanation of the fourth line

An explanation of the first line of the verse on the view that cuts through doubts concerning the basis: "All phenomena are manifestations of the mind"

[Verse 10]

> **The self-appearances that have never existed are mistaken as objects.**
> **Through the power of ignorance, self-knowing is mistaken for a self.**
> **Through the power of dualism, we wander in the vastness of existence.**
> **May the error of ignorance be thoroughly understood.**

This describes the certainty that appearances are manifestations of the mind. There is the evident, actual teaching on the certainty that the phenomena of samsara are appearances of the mind. There is also the subtle, implied teaching that the phenomena of enlightenment are the power of the mind. Therefore, this [verse] has two aspects: [133]

1. The actual teaching
2. The implied teaching

The actual teaching on the first line of the verse on the view that cuts through doubts concerning the basis: "All phenomena are manifestations of the mind"

This is the actual teaching of the verse, which is in three parts:

1. The illusion of subject and object
2. Delusion's creation of samsara
3. The prayer to know the hidden fault of delusion

The actual teaching on the illusion of subject and object

> **The self-appearances that have never existed are mistaken as objects.**
> **Through the power of ignorance, self-knowing is mistaken for a self.**

From Lord [Rangjung Dorjé's] *Profound Inner Meaning*:

> The limitations of partiality do not exist
> in the cause, which is the beginningless mind.
> However, it has an unimpeded display,
> an empty essence, and a nature of clarity.
> Its unimpeded manifestation appears as anything whatsoever.
>
> When the [mind] is ignorant of itself,
> the movement of mental activity,
> a movement that is like waves on water,
> appears as the duality of perceiver and perceived.
> [The mind] focuses upon and grasps itself.
>
> That which appears to the externally oriented mind
> creates the consciousness that perceives that object.
> The adoption and rejection of it creates a sensation.
> Thoughts concerning it create identification.
> The composite appearance of the object is conceived of as "other,"
> and attachment to it creates the aggregate of form.[350]

In his own detailed commentary to these [verses, Rangjung Dorjé states that] the luminosity of the naturally pure true nature of the basis, the mind vajra, does not know its own essence because of its generative power. This means that there is mental activity, which is the movement of mentation, from which arises the appearances of causes and conditions. This creates the state of being afflicted, so that there is ignorance.

That mentation has two aspects: (1) *immediate mentation*, which causes the powers of the six consciousnesses, as they arise and cease, to be based upon the ālaya consciousness, and (2) *afflicted mentation*, which fixates upon the thought of the ālaya as being "I." Therefore, immediate mentation creates consciousnesses and afflicted mentation creates states of affliction. The ālaya serves as the base for both these mentations; it is said to contain "all seeds" because it has the propensities for all afflictions.

The ālaya and our mentations act as causes and conditions for each other, like water and waves, and therefore this is the source for all the delusions of samsara. According to Ācārya Vasubandhu:

> [Whatever is conceived of as self or phenomena,
> which form in various ways,
> is the formation of consciousness.
> That formation has three aspects:
>
> *Ripening*, that which is called *thinking*,
> and *consciousness of objects*.]
> As to those, *ripening* is the consciousness
> named *ālaya*, which has all seeds.
>
> It is a nonconscious "acquisition"
> and a [nonconscious] discernment of location.
> It always has *contact*, *attention*,
> *sensation*,[351] *identification*, and *intention*.[352]
>
> Its *sensation* is equanimity,
> which is unobscuring and neutral.
> It is the same for *contact* and the others.
> It continues like the flow of a river.
> It ceases in the state of an arhat.[353] [134]

And [also from that text]:

> Based upon it, there develops the consciousness
> named *mentation* (*manas*) that has [the ālaya] as its object
> and is the nature of *thinking*.
>
> That [consciousness] is constantly accompanied by
> the four obscuring neutral afflictions.[354]

Compendium of the Mahayana[355] and other texts explain this at length, so you can learn the details by reading them.

Thus, the external six sensory objects and the internal six consciousnesses, which in fact are not different from each other, *appear* from the ālaya through the power of mental movement. They appear through the interdependent combination of sensory objects, sensory faculties, and consciousnesses. Then appearances *increase* and become connected with conceptual mind, and that causes them to be seen as sensory objects. This is *appearance, increase*, and *attainment*.

Thus, those appearances arise solely as dependent origination from the power of the continuous presence of the seeds of consciousnesses, faculties, and objects within the ālaya. From the *Vajra Pinnacle*:

> The ālaya, which has all seeds,
> is said to be the identity of the internal and the external.[356]

As for the order in which appearances arise: The activity of mental events creates a mentation that cognizes the six sensory objects; this creates the consciousnesses that perceive those objects; which causes thoughts of acquisition and sensations of happiness, thoughts of rejection and sensations of suffering, and neutral states in which sensations are neither [pleasant nor unpleasant]; this then results in identifications that fixate on concepts concerning those objects; which establishes the propensity to conceive sensory objects as "other"; which solidifies into the creation of aggregates of form.

Thus, phenomena appear through the power of the mind without ever being a part of the actual nature of the mind, so it's impossible that they can exist. However, when the mind doesn't understand this, it is deluded, perceiving itself as a sensory object. This ignorance means that there is no realization of baseless, sourceless, self-knowing, and the perceiver of objects is mistaken for a self. For that reason, any phenomenon that is a perceiver or is perceived is nothing but an illusion. The basis of these illusions is the mind. Therefore, they don't even have an atom that exists apart from the mind. They are empty. They are like the apparitions of horses and elephants conjured up by magic, which have no existence separate from their emptiness.

When did the mind sink into delusion? [135] No such time can be established, because the very appearance of time itself is an illusion, a conceptual embellishment without any existence whatsoever. Nevertheless, it's described that we have been deluded for as long as we have not known ourselves, which has been throughout beginningless time. This being so, because ignorance is causing them to appear incorrectly, the pure mind's essence is called the *ālaya*, [the pure mind's] nature of clarity is called *afflicted mentation*, and [the pure mind's] unimpeded manifestations are called *consciousnesses*. This is taught in detail in the canonical sutras and commentaries of the Dharma wheel's last turning, such as the *Entry into Laṅka Sutra*, and the *Densely Arrayed Adornments Sutra*, so there is no need for me to write any more about it here.

There are some differences in the way the Mantrayāna tantras and commentaries describe the process of delusion, because these texts have a different purpose and perspective, but they have the same basic meaning. From the *Hevajra Tantra*:

> All beings have arisen from me.
> The three realms have arisen from me.
> All of this is pervaded by me.
> Visible beings consist of nothing else.[357]

From the great commentary to the *Kālacakra Tantra*:

> Knowing (*vidyā*) is the great, supremely unchanging desire. Ignorance (*avidyā*) is the beginningless propensity for desire within beings.[358]

Also from the great commentary to the *Kālacakra Tantra*:

> Māras are propensities for samsara and stains in the minds of beings. Buddhas are minds free from the propensities for samsara.[359]

From the *Bodhicitta Commentary*:

> Relative [truth] arises from afflictions and karma.
> Karma originates from the mind.
> The mind is accumulated through propensities.[360]

The actual teaching on delusion's creation of samsara

Through the power of dualism, we wander in the vastness of existence.

This is the way we circle in samsara as a result [of delusion]: Although subject and object are not different from each other, in our state of delusion we fixate upon them as being dual, and until that delusion dissolves back into the ālaya, there is an unceasing continuum of those appearances, during which we wander in the vastness of existence, going round and round like buckets on a water wheel.

The ālaya creates mentation (*manas*). Mentation creates the six engaging consciousnesses. The mentation then stores in the ālaya the propensities accrued from sensory experiences, forming an unceasing continuity of dependent origination in the form of interrelated causes and conditions. [136] Therefore, in the ālaya there is an unceasing latent continuity, like a flowing river, until buddhahood is attained. That is why [Vasubandhu] wrote:

> It continues like the flow of a river.
> It ceases in the state of an arhat.[361]

From the *Entry into Laṅka Sutra:*

> The mind (*citta*) has a nature of clarity.
> Mentation (*manas*) is that which pollutes it.
> Mentation and consciousnesses together
> continuously create propensities.[362]

Also from the *Entry into Laṅka Sutra*:

> Mentation arises from the ālaya.
> Consciousnesses arise from mentation.
> All minds also, like waves,
> arise from the ālaya.[363]

In the same way, the constant continuum of the twelve stages of dependent origination arises from a constant continuum of seeds. There is the ignorance that has been described, the grasping at sensations, and the increase of that grasping until there is acquisition of the yearned-for object of desire. Those three afflictions create the karma for creation and becoming. From them arise the mass of suffering of these seven: [(1) consciousness,] (2) name and form, (3) the six bases, (4) contact, (5) sensation, (6) birth, and (7) death. The three afflictions then arise from them in a sequential cycle. According to Ācārya Nāgārjuna:

> From those three there come two.
> From those two there come seven, and from those seven
> there come the three. That is the wheel of existence...[364]

Also according to Ācārya Nāgārjuna:

> The first, eighth, and ninth are afflictions;
> the second and the tenth are karma;
> the remaining seven are suffering.[365]

The actual teaching of the prayer to know the hidden fault of delusion

> **May the error of ignorance be thoroughly understood.**

The necessity of knowing the hidden fault of delusion: As long as you do not know this essential meaning of delusion, you will not see delusion to be delusion. If you cannot see delusion as delusion, you will be unable to eliminate delusion. Therefore [Rangjung Dorjé] prayed in this way to teach the great importance of knowing this essential meaning.

The implied teaching on the first line of the verse on the view that cuts through doubts concerning the basis: "All phenomena are manifestations of the mind"

The implied meaning

The evident teaching that the phenomena of samsara are mental appearances enables us to understand the subtler teaching that all phenomena of nirvana are also mental appearances. We are so strongly habituated to the propensity to see things as solid, the obvious appearances of existing things seem extremely contrary to the nature of the mind, which makes it difficult to comprehend that they are the mind. If we can comprehend that, then it isn't difficult to understand that the phenomena of enlightenment [are mind], because they correspond to the true nature of mind. [137] Therefore, this verse also teaches the phenomena of enlightenment to be nothing other than the nature of pure mind.

When the mind is stained, it is "mind," "mentation," and "consciousness." When it is stainless, these three are the three kāyas. Therefore, when the bodhisattva is on the path and the stains become increasingly diminished, the qualities that exist within the pure mind become clearer until they appear as the qualities that are the aspects of enlightenment. When purified of all stains, all the qualities of the basis will appear. This can be learned in detail in the *Sublime Continuum*.

However, Ācārya Candrakīrti teaches that the mind ceases on the attainment of enlightenment:

> Through burning all the dry firewood that is phenomena,
> there is the dharmakāya of the conquerors.
> At that time there is neither birth nor cessation.
> Through the cessation of the mind, the [dharma]kāya manifests.[366]

Why does Candrakīrti say this? He is saying that the mind that is mind, mentation, and consciousness is eliminated, but that the pure mind is the great bliss of the dharmadhātu, which is free of cessation and abiding. Omniscient wisdom is also nothing other than the dharmadhātu and therefore completely transcends the phenomena of the impure mind. Because the phenomena of enlightenment are nothing other than the pure mind, pupils will perceive the appearance of the nirmāṇa[kāya] or saṃbhoga[kāya] according to whether their minds are slightly or mostly purified.

Thus, the evident meaning and the implied meaning of this teaching establish that all phenomena of samsara and nirvana are your own mind. This teaching comes from the sutras, the tantras, and the Mahayana commentaries. From the *Vajra Tent Tantra*:

> There are no buddhas and there are no beings
> that exist outside the precious mind.
> The consciousnesses' objects of perception
> have no external existence whatsoever.[367]

Also from the *Vajra Tent Tantra*:

> The mind, because it is as pure as space,
> is a mind of pure, perfect bliss.
> The [mind's] sensory objects and faculties
> have no existence external to the mind. [138]
> Individual appearances such as forms and so on
> are nothing but the appearances of the mind.[368]

According to the *Secret Charnel Ground Tantra*:

> Even the buddhas have never seen
> a buddhahood that is other than the mind
> or any other phenomenon that is other than the mind.
> Therefore, they have never taught and will never teach that there are such.
> This secret in the minds of all the buddhas
> is the supreme secret.[369]

From the *Sutra of the Ten Levels*:

> O bodhisattvas! These three realms are nothing but mind.[370]

From the *Entry into Laṅka Sutra*:

> The mind, agitated by propensities,
> manifests as the appearance of objects.[371]

From Ācārya Nāgā[rjuna]'s *Praise to the Dharmadhātu*:

> The mind is seen as having two aspects—
> the mundane and the supramundane.
> Through fixation on self, there is samsara,
> but with particular knowledge, there is the true nature.
>
> Through the cessation of desire, there is nirvana.
> There is the cessation of ignorance and anger,
> and through their ceasing there is buddhahood,
> which is the refuge of all beings.[372]

According to *Bodhicitta Commentary*:

> Whatever appears to the consciousness
> as having the nature of perceiver and perceived
> is nothing other than consciousness
> and has no external existence whatsoever.[373]

According to Saraha:

> The mind alone is the seed of everything;
> samsara and nirvana manifest from it.
> I pay homage to the mind, which, like a wish-fulfilling jewel,
> grants the results that we desire.[374]

There are countless such quotations.

The implied teaching on the second line of the verse on the view that cuts through doubts concerning the basis: "The mind is without mind, devoid of an essence of mind"

Establishing that the mind has no nature of its own

From *Bodhicitta Commentary*:

> Those with great worthiness also reject
> remaining as a Cittamātrin.
> The Vijñānavāda teaching
> establishes this variety [of phenomena] to be mind.
> What is the nature of consciousness?
> That is what I shall now explain.
>
> When [Śākya]muni taught,
> "All of these are mind alone,"
> it was in order to avoid frightening
> the immature; it is not the truth.
>
> The "imaginary," the "dependent,"
> and the "absolute" are just
> names for the mind, which in essence
> has only emptiness as its nature.
>
> The Buddha taught, in brief,
> to those individuals who were attracted to the Mahayana
> that phenomena are selfless and equal
> and that the mind is primordially unborn.[375]

From *Ornament of the Mahayana Sutras*:

> When the intellect has understood that there is nothing other
> than mind, [139]
> then the mind is also understood to be nonexistent.
> When the wise know that both are nonexistent,
> they dwell in the dharmadhātu, which is devoid of both.[376]

Thus, all the phenomena of samsara and nirvana are known to be mind, but if the mind is not understood to be baseless or rootless and to be emptiness beyond all extremes, the perceiver will be unable to become completely freed from the self of phenomena. This means that you must know the nature of the mind. This [knowledge] has two aspects:

1. Elimination of the extremes of existence and nonexistence
2. Elimination of the extremes of identity and nonidentity

Elimination of the extremes of existence and nonexistence

[Verse 11]

> **It has no existence: Even the conquerors have not seen it.**
> **It is not nonexistent: It is the basis for all samsara and nirvana.**
> **There is no contradiction: It is the path of the middle way,**
> **of union.**
> **May the true nature of the mind, free from extremes, be realized.**

The meaning of the first line

> **It has no existence: Even the conquerors have not seen it.**

Does the pure mind that has been described above have a definitively true reality? No, let alone true reality, it is not even any kind of truth or falsity. This is known because even all the conquerors with their wisdom vision have not seen it. From the *Densely Arrayed Adornments Sutra*:

> Neither is there an ordinary nonexistence of the mind,
> nor is there no limit, no measure, or both.[377]

From the *Kāśyapa Sutra*:

> Kāśyapa! The mind does not exist within. It does not exist without. It is not to be seen in between those two. Kāśyapa! The mind cannot be analyzed. It cannot be shown. It cannot be relied upon. It has no appearance. It cannot be cognized. It has no location. Kāśyapa! Even all the buddhas have not seen the mind, do not see it, and will not see it.[378]

From the *Perfection of Wisdom*:

> As for [that] mind, the mind does not exist; the nature of the mind is luminosity.[379]

From the *Tantra of Vairocana's Enlightenment*:

> Guhyapati! The tathāgatas [the arhants, the completely perfect buddhas] have not seen, do not see, and will not see [that] mind.[380]

There is also an extensive teaching on this in the *Tantra of Vairocana's Enlightenment*, such as:

> How can you completely know your own mind? In this way: if you make a complete investigation, you will not see aspect, color, shape, object, form, sensation, identification, activity, consciousness, self, [140] possession, percept, perceiver, purity, impurity, element, base, or any other aspect. Vajrapāṇi! This is called the doorway to the completely pure bodhicitta of the bodhisattva; it is the doorway to the appearance of Dharma; it is the nature of Dharma's first appearance.[381]

This teaching on how the conquerors see the dharmadhātu and on how the mind is self-knowing and self-illuminating is called the *great vision of wisdom*. This great vision does not see even an atom of characteristic in the dharmadhātu, which is free from all the extremes of conceptual elaboration. When there is no knower or known, no illuminator or illuminated, that is what is called *knowing and clarity*. This is the secret, essential meaning that you must understand. You must not equate this with the seeing and so on of worldly people.

In other [teachings] a knowing that knows itself and so on is not accepted, and its implausibility is pointed out. For example, from the *Entry into Laṅka*:

> Just as a sword cannot cut
> its own edge, just as fingers
> cannot touch their own tips,
> the mind cannot see the mind.[382]

From *Entering the Conduct of a Bodhisattva*:

> You may say that a lamp's flame
> truly illuminates itself,
> but it does not illuminate itself
> for it is not obscured by darkness.[383]

The meaning of the second line

> **It is not nonexistent: It is the basis for all samsara and nirvana.**

Can the nature of the mind be held to be completely nonexistent and unobservable? It cannot be so held. If there were no pure element of the mind, there would be no arising—even on a relative level—of the appearances of samsara and nirvana. This is because whether there is an appearance of samsara or nirvana depends upon whether their basis has been realized or not. Thus, from *Praise to the Dharmadhātu*:

> When there is the element, work
> will make the pure gold visible.
> When there is no element, the work
> will create only distress.[384]

Praise to the Dharmadhātu also uses examples to teach this clearly, such as:

> In that way, from all seeds
> arise results that accord with their causes.

There is no wise person who can prove
that there can be a result without a seed.

That element, which is a seed,
is said to be the base for all phenomena. [141]
Through its gradual purification,
the state of buddhahood is attained.[385]

At this point, we must understand this essential meaning that all the phenomena of samsara and nirvana that appear as characteristics have, in terms of their own nature, never been present and have never existed, and yet this does not prevent their being able to appear. Though it is taught that there is the "mind vajra" and the "naturally pure element" and so on, it's impossible that they exist as the extreme of being real and permanent.

Therefore, what do the sutras of the last Dharma wheel mean when they teach the perfection of purity, permanence, bliss, self, and so on? What do the tantras mean when they teach "invincible, indestructible wisdom"? From *Ornament of the Mahayana Sutras*:

That which is nonexistence
is said to be the "sublime existence."
That which is total nonperception
is said to be the "supreme perception."[386]

Thus, it is taught that the truth that is naturally pure cannot be divided by the conceptual elaboration of characteristics; it transcends being an object of the intellect; it does not undergo change during different phases, and so on.

These teachings were given for the purpose of eliminating the great demon of fixation on emptiness, because that fixation is even worse than the eternalist view. From a sutra:

Fixation on a self the size of Mount Meru is easy,
but fixation on selflessness is not like that.[387]

According to Nāgārjuna:

The wrong view of emptiness
will bring ruin to those with little wisdom.[388]

Therefore, emptiness is taught in order to destroy fixation on reality, but if you take emptiness to be real, your fixation on reality will be greater than that of a worldly person and therefore much worse. For example, a purgative is used to cure an illness, but the purgative itself can be poisonous. Therefore, from the *Sutra of Samādhi for Four Youths*:

> Those who know emptiness as emptiness,
> they do not apprehend emptiness.
> Those who do not see emptiness,
> they are the ones who know emptiness.[389]

From *Root Verses on the Middle Way*:

> If there existed just a tiny amount of nonemptiness,
> then a tiny amount of emptiness could exist.
> But as even a tiny amount of nonemptiness does not exist,
> how could there be any emptiness that could exist? [142]
>
> The conquerors have taught that emptiness
> is the rejection of all views.
> They taught that those who have a view of emptiness
> will be those who accomplish nothing.[390]

That is what you should understand.

The meaning of the third and fourth lines

> **There is no contradiction: It is the path of the middle way, of union.**
> **May the true nature of the mind, free from extremes, be realized.**

Does this have the fault of "contradiction" because it teaches that the mind's true nature both exists and doesn't exist, even though it's impossible for something to both exist and not exist? No, because it refutes both existence and nonexistence without establishing that there are both.

In brief, you cannot describe it with words such as "existent," "nonexistent," "empty," and "not empty." It has no location anywhere. It transcends being an object of the intellect. It is simply a teaching for stopping the extremes of conceptual embellishment so that there will be realization without there being a *process* of realization. Although this teaching denies the extremes, neither does it establish even an atom of anything. According to Venerable Nāgārjuna:

> You taught the nectar of emptiness
> so that conceptualization would be abandoned.
> When anyone became attached to that,
> you strongly rebuked them.[391]

According to the *Sutra Requested by Gaganagañja*:

> Wise people do not hold the view
> that there are things or that there is nothing.
> They use the word *emptiness*,
> but emptiness is not in that word.
> There is no word for it; it is indescribable.
>
> Therefore, although the buddhas have all taught
> something that is called *emptiness*,
> emptiness is indescribable.
> Also, that which is called "empty"
> has an indescribable meaning.[392]

Therefore, the essence of the mind should not be perceived in terms of the two extremes, nor as being located in a "middle way." It is merely given the name "the middle way of the completely objectless union."

Therefore, the prayer instructs us to realize the meaning of the great middle way, the characteristics of the mind that is free from all extremes.

Elimination of the extremes of identity and nonidentity

[Verse 12]

> **It cannot be indicated by saying, "It is this."**
> **It cannot be refuted by saying, "It is not this."**
> **The true nature that transcends the intellect is noncomposite.**
> **May there be certainty in the extreme of the true meaning.**

[143] The earlier passage on the refutation of existence and nonexistence has already explained the meaning of this verse, but I will say a little about it. We can use many good-sounding words about the nature of the mind free from extremes, such as *emptiness*, *birthless*, *union*, *ultimate*, *innate*, *great bliss*, and so on, but nothing can indicate it, for there is no phenomenon whatsoever to be indicated.

In the same way, there is nothing that can be refuted, because the logical refutations of one and many, eternalism and nihilism, coming and going, and so on cannot possibly cause the nature of the mind to diminish or change. Even though you state a refutation, saying, "This is not what the absence of an intrinsic nature is like," it remains unrefuted, because no basis for the refutation exists. From *Ornament of the Middle Way*:

> It is truly free from all the aggregations
> of [conceptual] elaborations.
> It is impossible for it to be birthless and so on
> because there is no birth and so on.[393]

From the *Two Truths*:

> The refutations of birth and so on
> are stated in a correct manner.
> As there is nothing to be refuted,
> it is clear that in fact there is no refutation.[394]

Also from the *Two Truths*:

> That which is truly nondual
> has no conceptual elaboration.
> Mañjuśrī questioned correctly:
> The bodhisattva did not speak.[395]

Therefore, [the nature of the mind] is beyond the intellect. According to Śāntideva:

> The ultimate is not within the range of the intellect.
> The intellect is said to be relative.[396]

For those reasons, it is impossible for the relative to have the ultimate as its object. This that "transcends the intellect" has been primordially present as the true nature of all phenomena and is therefore noncomposite, for no conceptually elaborated factor can alter it. It is also called "the extreme of the true meaning" because it is nothing other than simply the extreme that is the meaning of the true conclusion of all phenomena. From *Distinguishing the Middle Way from the Extremes*:

> To summarize emptiness:
> Its synonyms are the true nature,
> the true extreme, featurelessness,
> the ultimate, and the dharmadhātu.[397]

"May there be certainty!" means that if we are uncertain about the true nature, we will fail to have a one-pointed mind in meditation. Therefore, it is taught that we have to be free from doubt and have certainty in this teaching.

You might ask, "Is this view taught in the Mantrayāna?" It is, for there is no difference between the Mahayana and Mantrayāna views of freedom from conceptual elaboration, [144] which is as described above. There are countless such passages in the profound tantras, such as this one from the *Root Kālacakra Tantra*:

> It completely transcends existence and nonexistence.
> It is nondual, as both things and nothing have ceased.
> It is the inseparability of emptiness and compassion.
> It is the vajra yoga, the great bliss.
>
> It does not possess even the smallest atom.
> It has completely dispelled the phenomenon of emptiness.
> It is completely liberated from eternalism and nihilism.
>
> It is the undifferentiated vajra yoga.[398]

The implied teaching on the third line of the verse on the view that cuts through doubts concerning the basis: "Empty and unceasing, appearing as anything whatsoever"

This is a teaching on the noncontradictory union of emptiness and dependent origination.

[Verse 13]

> **If this is not realized, there will be circling within samsara.**
> **If this is realized, there is no other buddhahood.**
> **There is no "This is it; this isn't it" anywhere.**
> **May we know the true nature, the hidden secret of the ālaya.**

If this true nature, this secret of the mind that has just been described, is not realized, there will be the progression of dependent origination, which is circling within samsara. If this is realized, buddhahood will be attained as the result of the reversal of dependent origination, and that buddhahood is nothing other than this meaning of the true nature. This true nature, emptiness, which has been primordially present as buddhahood, pervades all phenomena. Therefore, you can seek anywhere, but you won't find any phenomenon of which you can say, "This is it, but this isn't it."

We can prove that phenomena are emptiness, because they appear through the process of dependent origination. Were they not emptiness, they could not appear through dependent origination. From a sutra:

> That which is born from conditions is not born.
> That birth has no intrinsic existence.
> It was taught that whatever depends upon conditions is empty.
> Those who know emptiness are observant.[399]

According to Nāgārjuna:

> No phenomena exist
> that have not arisen through dependent origination.
> Therefore, no phenomena exist
> that are not emptiness.[400]

As dependent origination does not exist apart from emptiness, and as emptiness does not exist apart from dependent origination, it is correct to say they are in union. [145]

Thus, the name "ālaya" is used here [in verse 13] for the actual nature because it is the true nature of all phenomena. Therefore, he prays: "May we know the hidden secret." This secret is the entire essential meaning. Thus, here *ālaya* refers to the naturally pure mind. From *Densely Arrayed Adornments*:

> The children of the conquerors see and hear
> the natural goodness of the ālaya.[401]

Also from *Densely Arrayed Adornments*:

> You will become a tathāgata
> through the stainless merit of the ālaya.[402]

Therefore, this should not be confused with the ālaya consciousness, which is the cause of samsara.

The implied teaching on the fourth line of the verse on the view that cuts through doubts concerning the basis: "May it be perfectly examined and be completely understood"

This teaches that we must examine with discriminating wisdom in order to cut through conceptual embellishments concerning the ālaya.

[Verse 14]

> **Appearances are mind and emptiness is mind.**
> **Thoughts are mind and delusion is mind.**
> **Origination is mind and cessation is mind.**
> **May we cut through all conceptual embellishments in the mind.**

This is an instruction—through the medium of prayer—that we should gain certainty, for the reasons previously given, that all appearances and emptiness, thoughts and delusion, and origination and cessation have no nature of their own, and thereby cut through all conceptual embellishments concerning the true nature.

You might ask, "But isn't this teaching on ultimate realization the Vijñaptivāda view that all phenomena are mind?" In this context, this is not an inconsistency, because as earlier, the meaning of the basis, the true nature, is taught as "mind."

Attaining certainty through meditation [which is the second part of the detailed explanation of meditation]

Attaining certainty through meditation on the meaning that is attained through cutting through conceptual embellishments is in two parts:

1. A summary
2. A detailed explanation

A summary of attaining certainty through meditation

[Verse 15]

> **Unadulterated by mentally fabricated, forced meditation;**
> **unshaken by the winds of ordinary preoccupations;**
> **knowing how to naturally rest in unaltered naturalness—**
> **may we master and maintain the practice of the meaning of the mind.**

It will be easier to explain by starting with the second line. This will be in three parts:

1. The beginning: How to engage in meditation
2. The middle: How to rest in meditation
3. The end: How to maintain the meditation [146]

The beginning: How to engage in meditation

When you have been blessed by a perfect guru, your mind will be able to comprehend the profound Dharma. Worthy individuals, who have the four qualities of faith, diligence, wisdom, and patience, will then practice the mahāmudrā yoga. It is important that they first be in solitude, free from the ordinary preoccupations of the body, speech, and mind. "Preoccupations" means that with a continuing attachment to samsara, you employ your body, speech, and mind for gain, honor, the eight worldly concerns, and so on. If you don't abandon them, you will fail even to gain rebirth in the higher existences, let alone attain liberation. From *Entering the Conduct of a Bodhisattva*:

> In the forests, the deer, the birds,
> and the trees don't speak unpleasant words.
> I will live among those
> whom it is pleasant to be with.
>
> I will go without a care
> and, without looking back,
> dwell in an empty temple,
> at the foot of a tree, or in caves.
>
> Once I am living
> in a naturally expansive
> place that I do not see as being mine,
> I will be free and without attachment.[403]

Therefore, dwell in a solitary place, go through the stages [of practice], and train the mind well in the general preliminaries. When you rely on this external solitude and train the mind in the general preliminaries, all your preoccupations will naturally cease. This is described by Ācārya Avadhūtipāda:

> Kapilā, a heron, and a snake,
> a hunter of deer in the forest,
> an arrow maker, and a maiden:
> Those six are my teachers.[404]

[Also from this text]:

> Being without longings, possessions, and home,
> being habituated to the solitude of the forest,
> maintaining a firm focus and remaining in solitude:
> That is what I have learned from my gurus.[405]

Danaśila has explained the meaning of [these verses].[406] Once a woman named Kapilā arranged to meet a man at a certain time. While she waited, she suffered from longing for him to come, but when it became clear that he wasn't coming, she was able to go to sleep happily. When Avadhūtipāda witnessed this, he learned that he should have no longing.

A heron carrying a large fish was being chased by other herons. When he dropped the fish, another heron picked it up. Then the same thing happened again and again. When Avadhūtipāda witnessed this, he learned that he should have no possessions, for they cause conflicts for their owners. [147]

Avadhūtipāda saw a snake that had given birth to many young in its nest, which made it uncomfortable, so she moved to another hole where she could sleep peacefully. Avadhūtipāda learned from this that he should have no home.

A hunter who was always going into the forest to search for deer saw a meditator there. As the hunter was used to being in the forest, eventually he became a meditator, too. When Avadhūtipāda witnessed this, he learned that he should be familiar with solitude.

Avadhūtipāda saw an arrow maker who was so concentrated on making arrows he didn't see the king and his army pass by in front of him. From this, Avadhūtipāda learned that he should have a one-pointed mind.

Avadhūtipāda saw a maiden whose bangles jingled as she ground incense. This continued to annoy her until she took all the bangles off and then she was happy.[407] From this, Avadhūtipāda learned that he should give up companionship and live in solitude.

He did all these things and developed marvelous states of meditation. Therefore, be free of preoccupations. Also, in the beginning, the special preliminaries are an absolutely essential practice for whoever wishes to create the auspicious factors for the effortless arising of mahāmudrā's wisdom.

The middle: How to rest in meditation

This has two parts:

1. The essential points for the body
2. The essential points for the mind

The essential points for the body

Though this prayer does not actually teach them, I include this as a supplement. From the *Vajra Garland Tantra*:

Practitioners should sit on a comfortable seat
and direct their eyes to the tip of the nose,
keeping the nose within their gaze.
The shoulders should be level and the tongue against the palate.
The teeth and lips should rest comfortably.
The inhalation and exhalation of the breath should be relaxed.
Sit in this perfect vajra posture
without making too much effort.[408]

From the *Vajra Pinnacle Tantra*:

Sit cross-legged in a clean place
free from disturbances,
just as the bodhisattva
sat in Bodhimaṇḍa.[409]

Close your eyes and place the teeth together,
creating the mudrā of the straight body
and the mahāmudrā of one-pointed mindfulness.[410]

It is important that you have the correct posture in accordance with these essential points for the body, as found in practice instructions such as the *seven Dharmas of Vairocana* or the *five Dharmas of dhyāna*. [148]

The essential points for the mind

It is important to be free from the adulteration of every kind of mentally fabricated, forced meditation—such as resting in a mentally fabricated clarity, emptiness, or union; intentionally stopping thoughts; intentional concentration, and so on. From the *Guhyasamāja Tantra*:

There are no things and there is no meditation;
to meditate is not meditation.
Thus, as things are nothing,
meditation is objectless.[411]

From the *Hevajra Tantra*:

The entire world is meditated upon
by not meditating with the intellect.[412]

From *Innate Accomplishment*:

The conception of something that is like
the empty interior of a vase
or the intellect that describes emptiness—
these do not describe the innate.[413]

According to Saraha:

Know the single nature of what is apparently self and others.
Without being distracted, perfectly maintain solely that knowledge.

As that is painful to the mind, abandon that too.
Without attachment to anything, obtain happiness.

When you are free from all actions that are harmful to the mind,
there will be no stain from any activity of acquirement and acquisition.

This mudrā of the variety of appearances, free from effort,
with no transitory conditions or phases, is the great vision![414]

From a sutra:

When there is no adoption, keeping, or discarding of any phenomenon, that is meditation on the perfection of wisdom.
When there is no dwelling on anything whatsoever, that is meditation on the perfection of wisdom.
When there is no thinking or cognizing of anything, that is meditation on the perfection of wisdom.[415]

From the *Eight-Thousand-Verse Perfection of Wisdom*:

Meditation on the perfection of wisdom is not meditating on any phenomenon.[416]

From the *King of Meditations Sutra*:

> Any identification that arises,
> such as thinking "I will eliminate identification,"
> is the usage of identification's conceptual elaboration
> and is not freedom from identification.[417]

From the *Sutra Requested by Sāgaramati*:

> Do not create phenomena in your mind,
> completely avoid excessive activity,
> and understand correctly
> the equality of all phenomena.[418]

There are countless such teachings in the Mahayana sutras, tantras, and commentaries. [149]

Therefore, [the meditation] is just to naturally rest in an uncontrived, natural state. The way that this is done, according to those who know the practice instructions of our Kagyü lineage, is as follows:

> Do not investigate the past and do not greet the future, but let your consciousness be what it is, without modification.[419]

According to Lord Gampopa:

> "Do not investigate the past" means that our minds should not follow previous thoughts. "Do not greet the future" means that our minds should not greet subsequent thoughts. "Perfectly resting in the natural, present consciousness" means not focusing on anything in the present. If the mind is not altered, it will become clear, just as undisturbed water becomes clear. Therefore perfectly rest in an unaltered state, just as it is.[420]

As [Gampopa] describes, the meaning of the preceding quotations is that you cannot meditate using any thought created by your conceptual mind. [The meditation] is accomplished through following the wonderful, secret essential point that is the instruction not to engage in conceptual elaborations of the past, present, or future. According to Mahāsiddha Indrabhūti:

> For as long as there are thoughts,
> everything will be completely false.
> When you no longer examine the true nature,
> that validity, in that way, will be the truth.[421]

According to Saraha:

> *Meditation* is the name that is given to maintaining
> that inseparable natural state, free of mental activity,
> in all the three times and in all circumstances.[422]

In this context, "natural" should be understood to mean the true nature of the basis, the genuine state that is unadulterated by conceptualization. According to Prajñākaramati in his *Commentary on Difficult Points in "Entering the Conduct of a Bodhisattva"*:

> Thus, this absence of an own nature is present as the natural ultimate form of all things. For an individual's supreme goal, that itself is considered to be the superior, supreme, special goal. But one should not have attachment even to that.[423]

Someone has claimed, "This mahāmudrā of yours is the meditation of the Chinese Hashang because all mental activity in relation to the three times ceases." However, he said this without examining [mahāmudrā].[424] We Kagyüpas do not say, "Deliberately stop mental activity and rest upon that thought of cessation," but as previously explained, we teach maintaining an unfabricated, present consciousness. [150] However, you may object that this still means [mahāmudrā] is subject to that criticism because thoughts of the three times naturally cease when maintaining the present, unaltered consciousness. If you say that, you must be someone who can't let go of your thoughts because you're too attached to them. There appear to be plenty of other people who hold such pure views as yours, so why not just enjoy your thoughts along with them and stop analyzing *our* view. We aren't following any other path than that taught by the Tathāgata and followed by the siddha lords. From the *Kālacakra Tantra*:

> Thus, the oneness of the vowels and consonants, of the moon and the sun, is not the vajra holder's seat. It is not the transformation

> of the *hūṃ* and of the insignia into other colors and forms. It arises from the changelessnesses[425] and ends change; it possesses the supreme powers, all the quintessences that are the "supreme of all aspects"; it is the lord of all conquerors, with a variety of illusory manifestations.[426]

This teaches that a contrived meditation consisting of thought cannot accomplish the changeless, supreme state. That is also stated in the Hevajra and Guhyasamāja quotations above and also in *Enlightenment of Vairocana*:

> The sublime Conqueror taught that [meditation] with attributes
> brings siddhis with attributes,
> but dwelling in that which has no attributes
> can also accomplish [siddhis] with attributes.[427]

This teaches that the yoga without attributes and concepts can bring not only the supreme siddhi, which is without attributes, but also the attainment of even the general siddhis, which have attributes. According to Nāgārjuna:

> Discard conceptualizing and examining
> all phenomena, the principal of which is mentation,
> and meditate on the dharmadhātu,
> the absence of an intrinsic nature in all phenomena.[428]

From Vīravajra's *Sequence of the Four Mudrās*:

> Maintaining the continuity of direct nonconceptual experience;
> that is what is given the name *meditation*.[429]

From Drokmi Lotsāwa's translation of Ācārya Vajrapāṇi's *Instructions from the Successive Guru Lineage*:

> There is no meditator and no meditation.
> There is no deity and there is no mantra.
> The deity and the mantra are truly present
> in the state free from conceptual elaboration.

> Therefore, mahāmudrā is nonconceptual: It is not the deliberate focusing of a contrived meditation.[430] [151]

And [from the same text]:

> There is no meditator whatsoever.
> There is no meditation whatsoever.
> There is nothing to be meditated upon.
> Meditate upon the truth of that.

> Thus, you should not create a meditator, an object of meditation, or meditation, but just rest in that way without distraction. However, even in a meditation without distraction, other factors will cause every kind of thought to suddenly arise.
>
> The natural essence itself is unborn and does not have the aggregation of factors necessary for those thoughts. Therefore consciousness itself remains, unadulterated by those factors, as the natural state, uncontrived, and free from conceptual embellishment. That is the mahāmudrā.[431]

The text continues in this way at length, giving many quotations. There are also teachings that accord with this in the profound sutras. From the *Sutra of the Excellent Night*:

> Do not follow after the past.
> Do not have hopes for the future.
> Whatever is past has ceased.
> The future has not come.
> Look well upon each and every
> phenomenon that appears in the present.
> Fully comprehend them all,
> without being kidnapped by thoughts.[432]

From the *Sutra Requested by Sāgaramati*:

> Past identifications have ceased; future identifications have yet to come; present identifications do not remain. The one who does not focus on identification in the three times fully understands identification.[433]

I have thus provided many quotations to establish the validity [of this teaching].

Should we practice maintaining an uncontrived natural state right from the beginning? That depends on your own individual level. If you can, that is extremely excellent, but if you can't, then with the rope of mindfulness you must tie the elephant of your mind to the pillar that is the object of your meditation. Everyone who knows the instructions teaches this. Therefore, we have the [two] categories of [meditation] with the mind focused outward and with the mind focused inward. Each of those categories is then divided into evident and subtle practices. Thus, there are practices that are based upon anything the mind can focus on, such as a statue of a deity, a round spot (*bindu*), a syllable, or the breath. There is nothing wrong in practicing on this level in accordance with your guru's instructions. [According to Maitreyanātha]:

> Reliance on focusing on objects
> will cause objectlessness to perfectly arise.[434]

The end: How to maintain the meditation

With these key practice instructions [152] you will master practicing the meaning of the mind. You will also become adept in eliminating such faults as dullness and agitation. You will be able to cut through errors, enhance benefits, and so on, until the true result mahāmudrā is manifest. [According to Advayavajra]:

> Keep following the nature of mantra,
> like the flow of a river,
> like the continuity of a lamp's flame,
> and you will attain uninterrupted dhyāna.[435]

In order to teach how you maintain [meditation] that [Rangjung Dorjé] prayed: ["May we master and maintain the practice of the meaning of the mind!"]

The detailed explanation of attaining certainty through meditation

This is in three parts:

1. The śamatha and vipaśyanā yogas

2. The arising of experiences and realizations in śamatha and vipaśyanā
3. The practice of the union of emptiness and compassion

Śamatha and vipaśyanā

This is in three parts:

1. Śamatha
2. Vipaśyanā
3. Synonyms for the practice of the union of śamatha and vipaśyanā

Śamatha

[Verse 16]

> **The waves of obvious and subtle thoughts cease by themselves;**
> **the undisturbed river of the mind becomes naturally calm.**
> **May there be an untroubled peaceful sea of śamatha,**
> **free from the polluting impurities of dullness and agitation.**

As described earlier, according to the level of one's capabilities, one may practice the stages of concentration, with or without focus, or one might engage in objectless [meditation] from the beginning. Whichever way is practiced, one will first attain the samādhi of śamatha.

The term *śamatha* means that the mind's afflicted thoughts have ceased and you are one-pointedly focused upon virtue. Dīpaṃkara explained the nature of śamatha in this way:

> When you are focused upon worldly activities,
> everything you do will be meaningless and cause suffering,
> and whatever you think cannot be beneficial.
> Therefore, look into your own mind and meditate.[436]

From the *Tantra of True Union*:

> Thoughts, which are great ignorance,
> cause you to fall into the ocean of samsara.
> Nonthought, resting in samādhi,
> is as stainless as space.[437]

Thus, giving up worldly activities precedes nonconceptual samādhi.

We can categorize thoughts into two kinds: obvious and subtle. The obvious are simply the mind's observation of an object. [153] Subtle [thoughts] are the examination of that observation. From *Treasury of the Abhidharma*:

> ... obvious observation and subtle examination.[438]

However, in terms of practice instruction, the obvious thoughts are the thoughts and examination of a subject that we are clearly aware of, while subtle thoughts are those that engage with a subject without our being aware of them.

The "waves" of the mental activity of evident and subtle thoughts are not forcibly stopped but naturally cease, so that they cease by themselves. The ālaya consciousness, which is the flow of "the river of the mind," also becomes undisturbed and naturally calm.

[Rangjung Dorjé] prays for an "untroubled, peaceful sea of śamatha, free from all polluting impurities," such as "dullness and agitation." This is the poetic device called *embodiment*.[439] Here, "dullness and agitation" represent all obstacles to śamatha, which must be eliminated. From [Nāgārjuna's] *Letter to a Friend*:

> Agitation and regret, malice, stupor and
> sleepiness, desire, and doubt:
> The Sage taught that those five are thieves
> who steal the wealth of meditation's virtues.[440]

Therefore, the obstacles [to śamatha] are of five kinds: (1) agitation and regret, (2) malice, (3) sleepiness and stupor, (4) desire, and (5) doubt. *Agitation* is the movement of thoughts toward a variety of subjects, and *regret* concerns inappropriate actions. Both of these prevent the development of śamatha. *Malice* prevents being in a state of happiness. *Dullness* clouds the mind and develops into *stupor and sleepiness*, which prevent states of clarity. *Desire* for people and things prevents the mind from being useful. *Doubt*, such as wondering whether samādhi is even possible, prevents a one-pointed state. All five obstacles can be summarized into the two categories of dullness and agitation: dullness, stupor, and sleepiness form the category of dullness, and all the other obstacles form the category of agitation.

The method for eliminating these obstacles is to rely on the specific remedies taught in the stages of meditation instructions. Alternatively:

> There is nothing whatever to be removed in this;
> there is not the slightest thing to be added.
> Truly look at the truth;
> if you truly see, you will be liberated.[441]

Therefore, primarily look directly at dullness and agitation and rest in their nature without altering them. This is profound. [154] It is crucially necessary as the foundation for vipaśyanā. According to Śāntideva:

> Know that śamatha perfectly conjoined
> with vipaśyanā defeats the afflictions.
> But śamatha should be sought first,
> without attachment to the world, and with delight.[442]

The sutras teach these categories of śamatha: (1) nine different aspects of engaging in śamatha called the *nine methods of stabilizing the mind*;[443] (2) the seven attentions,[444] which are called "preparations" because you have to apply yourself to them in order to attain real dhyāna; (3) the four real dhyānas—that is, the first dhyāna and so on; (4) the four formless samādhis; and (5) the equanimity of cessation.[445]

The dhyānas, the formless [samādhis], and the equanimity of cessation are known collectively as the *nine concentrations*.[446] These nine methods of resting the mind are in the *Perfection of Wisdom*:[447] (1) resting the mind in equanimity, (2) truly resting the mind, (3) completely resting the mind, (4) subjugation, (5) true subjugation, (6) pacification, (7) true pacification, (8) singleness, and (9) samādhi.

The *seven contemplations*, from *Ornament of the Mahayana Sutras*:

> Then first, that devotee,
> in examining the meaning of nonduality,
> the Dharma of the sutras, and so on,
> memorizes the names of the sutras, and so on.
>
> Then, he analyzes the separation
> of words in their proper order

and analyzes the meanings
that are contained within.

Having understood those meanings,
he should also bring them together in the Dharma.
Then, he should make an aspiration
to attain that meaning.

With continuous conceptualization of the mind,
he should individually examine that which is investigated
and also analyze them with mental engagements
that are of one taste and without conceptualization.

The path of śamatha that is to be known:
The Dharma and its inclusive terms.[448]

Thus, there are seven mental engagements: (1) the aspiration toward specific knowledge, (2) solitude, (3) joy, (4) unification, (5) analysis, (6) application to the conclusion, and (7) the result of application to the conclusion. The last of these seven is called the *indispensable preparation*.

The *four dhyānas*, from *Treasury of the Abhidharma*:

The first has five aspects: examination,
analysis, joy, bliss, and samādhi.

The second has four:
joy and so on, and clarity.

The third has five: equanimity,
mindfulness, awareness, [155] bliss, and stability.

The last has four: neither bliss nor suffering,
equanimity, mindfulness, and samādhi.[449]

The *six clairvoyances* also arise because they are based on the fourth dhyāna:

> With the attainment of an extremely pure fourth dhyāna
> and the attainment of nonconceptual wisdom,
> the clairvoyances arise without impediment
> through the contemplation of things just as they are.[450]

The *four formless* [*samādhis*] are (1) infinite space, (2) infinite consciousness, (3) nothingness, and (4) neither existence nor nonexistence. Those are when identification of form has ceased and there is increasingly subtler meditation.

The *equanimity of cessation* is when suffering and sensations cease. No one other than śrāvakas, pratyekabuddhas, arhants, or bodhisattvas can enter this state.

The stability gained through the nine methods of stabilizing the mind is purely śamatha, while the others are conjoined with vipaśyanā. You might object that this is incorrect, because vipaśyanā is taught to be supramundane wisdom while all the concentrations aside from the *equanimity of cessation* are mundane and the general path. But this is not incorrect, because mere mundane wisdom is also called vipaśyanā, even though this [prayer], from the very beginning, is teaching the special [vipaśyanā] that is supramundane.

The teachings on the concentrations and so on are not essential for this practice, but it is nevertheless beneficial to understand them, which is why I have just planted a seed here, so that you may learn the details elsewhere.

In the special, definitive, secret teachings of the Kagyü masters, there is the description of an initial stability that is like a waterfall, a second that is like a slow moving river, and a third that is like a still sea. These are solely descriptions of śamatha.

Vipaśyanā

This is in two parts:

1. Vipaśyanā itself
2. Understanding the fundamentals [of vipaśyanā]

Vipaśyanā itself

[Verse 17]

> **When we look again and again at the mind that cannot be seen,** [156]
> **we will perfectly see that which is not seen, just as it is.**

May we cut through doubts as to what the meaning is or isn't
and have unmistaken knowledge of one's own nature.

As [the mind] transcends being an object that can be looked at, rest in equanimity in "the mind that cannot be seen," which is the true nature of things. When we look again and again, with eyes of wisdom that have come from meditating on the instructions of the guru, we will perfectly see the meaning that cannot be seen, just as it is. Because of that, we will cut through all doubts and conceptual embellishments concerning the meaning of the true nature, such as what it is or isn't, whether it exists or doesn't exist. And we will develop the wisdom of vipaśyanā, which has the clear experience of an unmistaken knowledge of one's own nature, so that the innate mahāmudrā will manifest.

This knowledge of the true nature is free from all attributes such as contemplation, view, knowledge, vision, experience, and so on. It is free from the veiling obscurations of ignorance, such as naming it this or that, or the teaching of material emptiness, which believes that the total cessation of mere vacuity is the true meaning. It is the *attainment of certainty* because of its knowledge of one's own nature and the elimination of conceptual embellishments and doubts. It is *great bliss* because of its elimination of all unpleasant thoughts. From the *Saṃvarodaya* [*Tantra*]:

> Completely liberated from [the duality of] perceiver and perceived,
> the use of mere intellectual understanding has been completely
> discarded.
> The mind and mental events have become stable.
> Such a being has the manner of the [true] nature.
>
> The mind truly remains pure,
> just like a crystal, a jewel, or space.
> Its nature is beginningless and endless.
> It is devoid of faculties and free from elaboration.
>
> It is devoid of appearances and free from change.
> Everything is empty and there are no afflictions.
> It is beyond expression in words.
> It vanquishes the bondage of existence and is a light for beings.

It is not within the range of the intellect.
There are no afflictions and it is liberated from duality.
It bestows the ultimate liberation.
I pay homage to that unchanging truth!

When you reach this truth,
there are no thoughts that can be thought.
When there is mind without thought,
then there is inconceivability.

Can beings be without thought? [157]
Can having no thought bring buddhahood?
Yes, because the Buddha, who was free of thought,
perfectly taught these thoughts.

That mind that is without thought
is free from the process of all thoughts.
It has none of the various conceptual embellishments.
It has no attachment but has great bliss.

It is the supreme of all aspects.
It transcends all senses and has no aspect.
It is the very self of both things and of nothing,
but it has completely eliminated both things and nothing.

It is self-knowing because it is not a thing.
It isn't knowing and it isn't seeing.
It has no location because it has no form.
It is permanent because it does not change.[451]

From the *Mahāmudrā Tilaka Tantra*:

In the ultimate meaning, there is nothing to be seen,
but it isn't not seeing, and neither is it both.

That which is known by itself is the supreme peace,
which ends both things and nothing.

This is the supreme great truth:
the ceasing of the selves of things and nothing.[452]

From the *Hevajra Tantra*:

That which has the nature of self-knowing is purity.
There is no liberation through any other purity.[453]

From the *Kālacakra Tantra*:

It does not have change because of the increase of increase;
neither does it have the diminishing of diminishing.

It does not have the cessation of cessation;
it does not have the arising of arising.

It does not have perfect clarity of perfect clarity;
it does not have the obscuration of obscuration.

It does not have the birth of birth;
it does not have the death of death.

It does not have the liberation of liberation;
it does not have the nonlocation of nonlocation.

It does not have the nothing of nothing;
it does not have the things of things.

It does not have the change of change;
it does not have the changelessness of changelessness.[454]

There are endless such teachings. Also, from among the profound sutras, in the *Abbreviated Perfection of Wisdom*:

Beings say the words, "I see space."
Examine how it is that they see space.

> Those who can see in that way see all phenomena.
> No other visual example can indicate it.[455]

Also from within the commentaries, from *Entering the Two Truths*:

> When you examine without using thought,
> that is what is called *seeing emptiness*.
> The extremely profound sutras
> have taught that this not seeing is seeing.[456]

There are endless such quotations. [158]

Understanding the fundamentals [of vipaśyanā]

[Verse 18]

> **Looking at objects, there are no objects: They are seen to be mind.**
> **Looking at the mind, there is no mind: It's devoid of essence.**
> **Looking at both spontaneously extinguishes dualism.**
> **May we realize luminosity, which is the nature of the mind.**

"Objects" are any appearances that arise—form, sound, smell, taste, physical sensations, and [mental] phenomena. By looking upon them, there will be the wisdom that arises from meditation, which sees that objects have no reality of their own and are therefore just mind. In the same way, simply "looking at the mind" in meditation makes us realize that the mind also is devoid of a basis or root. Meditation on the one taste of appearances and mind spontaneously extinguishes, without leaving a root, the dualism of subject and object. May we, through those methods, become naturally free from obscurations, so that there arises the wisdom of vipaśyanā that perfectly "realizes luminosity, which is the true nature of the mind."

In the sequential practice instructions there is the description of *direct introduction* as: (1) Appearances are mind. (2) The mind is empty. (3) Emptiness is naturally present. (4) Natural presence is spontaneous liberation. You can first realize the true nature through such instructions as the *eleven contemplations*, but if you do not subsequently receive direct introduction through conclusive instructions, you will not gain certainty. These principal instructions for gaining certainty, such as looking for the mind, have been made the subject of ridicule by some Tibetans, but that's the same as all the superficial things I've ever heard. From the *Enlightenment of Vairocana*:

> The omniscience of enlightenment should be sought in your own mind. That is because the mind is naturally completely pure. It cannot be seen on the inside, on the outside, or in between.[457]

And also:

> A noble man or woman who wishes to completely know enlightenment [159] must thoroughly search for his or her own mind.[458]

The *Enlightenment of Vairocana* continues with a detailed teaching on why you should search for your mind and the methods for doing so. It concludes by teaching these and other benefits:

> Guhyapati! This is what is known as the doorway to the completely pure bodhicitta of the bodhisattva. It is the first doorway to the appearance of the Dharma, the first way in which the Dharma appears. Wherever the bodhisattvas dwell, they attain a samādhi that eliminates all obscurations with little difficulty. When the bodhisattvas have that attainment, they will enjoy the constant company of all the buddhas. They will have the five clairvoyances and the power to remember infinite languages, sounds, and melodies. They will know the thoughts of beings and be blessed by all the tathāgatas, so that they will have the quality of never regressing into samsara. They will never weary of benefiting beings. They will continue perfectly in noncomposite conduct. They will eliminate all wrong views and will realize and fully understand the true view.[459]

[Nāgārjuna's] *Commentary on Bodhicitta* and other texts give this same teaching in a brief form. It seems therefore that those [Tibetans who mock the instructions] haven't read these texts. Kamalaśīla explains in detail how to search for the mind in his *Stages of Meditation*, where he provides quotations from the *Heap of Jewels* (*Ratnakūṭa*) *Sutra*. Therefore, it appears that this instruction is important for the Madhyamaka tradition of meditation also.

When it is said that you look with eyes of wisdom at the object, the mind, and both, those are the three wisdoms that were described earlier. The nonconceptual wisdom that arises from meditation is this direct encounter with the true nature, exactly as it is. Therefore, our highest, secret, quintessential point is that our lineage does not practice analytic meditation while in meditation. There are those who claim that even a higher level of meditation should still have examination and analysis, but they are transforming the Buddhist tradition into a non-Buddhist one, for no genuine Buddhist tradition teaches that meditation requires thought. In our tradition, all agree that the vipaśyanā that is analysis through wisdom is that of the post-meditation stage. [160] In the Mahayana, in particular, *Ears of Grain of Practice Instructions* says:

> Only these aspects are practiced: right thought, right speech, right livelihood; effort and mindfulness are not possible in the meditation of the path.[460]

This teaches that right thought and analysis is impossible in higher meditation. All the sutras and tantras concur that you practice meditation with nonconceptual wisdom. Therefore, really think about what purpose is served by openly denying this.

Synonyms for the practice of the union of śamatha and vipaśyanā

This is in two parts:

1. The actual synonyms for the union of śamatha and vipaśyanā
2. A supplement

The actual synonyms for the union of śamatha and vipaśyanā

[Verse 19]

> **The freedom from attention is the mahāmudrā.**
> **The freedom from extremes is the mahā madhyamaka.**
> **This is also named the all-inclusive dzokchen.**
> **May there be the confidence that through knowing one all will be realized.**

[Rangjung Dorjé] composed this prayer in order to teach the following:

The perfect realization of the innate nature is "free from all attention." That is why it is called *mahāmudrā* ("the great seal"). It has other names: It is the *great madhyamaka* ("the great middle way"), because it is free from all extremes. The realization of all Dharma is included, and therefore it is also named *dzokchen* ("the great perfection"). We need to have the confidence that through knowing this one true nature alone, we will realize every secret in all Dharmas.

The word "also" indicates that it includes all names and meanings in the profound and vast Dharma and therefore is also established to be the one thing that liberates all. With this in mind, the sugata Phakmo Drupa wrote:

> It subjugates all thoughts and afflictions,
> and therefore it is the Vinaya.
>
> It is the stage that gives birth to the certain knowledge
> that thoughts are the dharmakāya.
>
> This is the teaching of the guru,
> for it internally cuts through conceptual embellishments.
>
> It is the Madhyamaka because it is free from extremes
> such as eternalism, nihilism, and conceptual embellishment.
>
> It is the teaching of the perfections
> because it is indescribable by word or thought.
>
> It is dzokchen because the phenomena
> of samsara and nirvana are complete in the mind. [161]
>
> It is mahāmudrā because the mind
> does not focus on any good or bad thought.
>
> It is pacification (*shiché*)[461] because it pacifies suffering.
>
> It is the Mantra[yāna] because it adopts
> all afflictions and thoughts as the path.

The mind, thoughts, and the dharmakāya
are connate from the beginning.
They become united through the teachings
and are therefore taught to be the innate union (*sahajayoga*).

It was taught that even obstacles
from demons, māras, and so on should be exalted.[462]

You may ask, "But how can all names and meanings in the profound and vast Dharma be included within mahāmudrā?" The answer is that each separate name doesn't exist within what it is particularly signifying. Therefore, it can be changed to something else, or any kind of definition could be made for that name. Therefore, they can [all] be included within this [mahāmudrā] because they can [all] indicate some aspect [of it]. A few examples of mahāmudrā's inclusion of all names were given in the preceding quotation. As for [the inclusion of all] meanings, there is the profound meaning, which is the actual one taste of emptiness, and there is the vast meaning, which is diverse. These are simply methods for the direct or indirect engagement with mahāmudrā and can therefore be classified as ancillaries to that realization. From the *Sublime Continuum*:

The subtle and profound teaching
is like the single taste of honey.
Know the diverse teaching
to be like [honey] in different containers.[463]

Therefore, this [mahāmudrā] is the ultimate meaning of the Sugata's various teachings, and through realizing this alone you will reach the heart of the entire Dharma, and you will perfect all qualities and eliminate all obscurations. Therefore, [mahāmudrā] is also given the name the *white panacea*. There is nothing wrong in using such a name for a meditation that brings realization. It is correct to do so, as shown in this quote from Dignāga:

The perfection of wisdom is nondual.
This wisdom is the goal
that tathāgatas accomplish,
and therefore the path is taught by that name.[464]

It says [in the root text] that "freedom from attention is the mahāmudrā." Some who call themselves authorities are skeptical, stating that to teach that mahāmudrā is free from attention is absurd, but this is faultless. The Sanskrit term for [nonattention] is *amanasikāra*.[465] The syllable *a* [162] indicates the emptiness that transcends all conceptual elaborations, such as "selfless" and "birthless." The rest of the word teaches that the mind (*manas*) has the attention that is free of attention and that has no attachment even to emptiness. Thus this establishes the mahāmudrā that is a union free from extremes. *Recitation of [Mañjuśrī's] Names* says:

> *A* is the supreme of all syllables,
> It is the sacred syllable that has great meaning.
> It arises from within and is birthless.
> It is beyond being described in words.[466]

From the *Hevajra Tantra*:

> She who has the nature of the first vowel
> is considered by the buddhas to be Dhīti (Intelligence).
> She is the Bhagavatī Prajñā (Wisdom)
> in the practice of the stage of perfection.[467]

Dhārāṇi of Entering Nonthought has passages such as:

> Noble ones, what causes attention to the element of nonthought? It is gained through truly transcending the attributes of all thoughts.[468]

And also:

> Bodhisattvas! Mahāsattvas! Thoughts that are the attributes of method are thoughts concerning appearances. They are completely eliminated through nonattention.[469]

According to Ācārya Maitripa:

> *Amanasikāra* has the *a* syllable (*a-kāra*) as the primary member [of the compound], and like *śāka-pārthiva* ("vegetarian king"), [*amanasikāra*] is a compound that omits the middle word.[470]

And also:

> Alternatively, *a* is the word for luminosity, while attention (*manasikāra*) is the word for self-blessing. Therefore, as there is *a* and as there is attention (*manasikāra*), there is *amanasikāra* ("*a* and attention"). Therefore, this inconceivable state of *amanasikāra*—the nature of luminosity and self-blessing—develops true awareness of the continuum of nondual union, the inseparability of emptiness and compassion.[471]

THE MEANING OF THE WORD MAHĀMUDRĀ

Mudrā is [Sanskrit] for a "seal" (Tib. *rgya*), which prevents deviation, because it eliminates any other foundation for error. The translators added the extra syllable *phyag*[472] translating it as *phyag rgya*. It means that none of the phenomena of samsara and nirvana deviates from it. *Mahā* ("great," Tib. *chen po*) means that there is no Dharma that is higher than it; or it means that it is superior to the action seal, the Dharma seal, and the commitment seal. Therefore because it is both a seal and great, [*mahāmudrā*] is a conjunction of [two] words with the same basis. [163] According to Ācārya Vajrapāṇi:

> The essence of mahāmudrā is "nondeviation," and that is why it is called a "seal." For example, just as ministers, minor kings, and so on cannot deviate from the command with the seal of authority of a great universal sovereign (*cakravartin*), in the same way the entire variation of inner and outer phenomena do not deviate from the essence of the union, do not deviate from naturally present wisdom, do not deviate from the mahāmudrā. That is why it is a seal. *Mahā* means it is great, because it is the essence of the action seal, Dharma seal, and commitment seal.[473]

According to Ācārya Rāmapāla:

> It is both a seal and great because it seals the three mudrās.[474]

From *Lotus Endowed: A Commentary on Difficult Points*:

> Mahāmudrā is the perfection of wisdom that has given birth

> to all the tathāgatas who have ever been, who are yet to come, and who exist in the present. It is a seal (*mudrā*) because it seals the completely unlocated nirvana or unchanging bliss. It is great (*mahā*) because it is superior to the action seal and wisdom seal and because it is free from the latent propensities for samsara.[475]

If you ask, "This mahāmudrā of yours is one of the four mudrās, and the other three mudrās must be its preliminaries, so why don't you teach it in that way?" In answer, we are not at fault, because the tantras teach practicing mahāmudrā from the very beginning to those with the sharpest of sharp faculties—those who are not concerned with gaining the siddhis of the desire and form realms. For example, from the *Kālacakra Tantra*:

> Completely casting aside the action seal,
> abandoning the imagined wisdom seal,
> meditate on the mahāmudrā
> with perfectly unchanging union.[476]

And also:

> The action seal accomplishes
> the siddhis of the activity of desire.
>
> Know that the wisdom seal grasps
> all up to the ultimate Akaniṣṭha.
>
> It is meditation on the seal
> called mahāmudrā that accomplishes
> the great yoga of omniscience,
> the unique buddhahood of great bliss.[477]

From the great commentary [on Kālacakra]:

> Completely casting aside the action seal,
> totally abandoning the wisdom seal, [164]
> it truly arises from the mahāmudrā;
> the innate does not accompany anything else.[478]

From Kālacakrapāda's *Instructions on the Six Yogas*:

The best realize through the first,
the medium through prāṇāyāma and so on,
and the least meditate on all six in succession.[479]

Thus it is taught that those with the very highest faculties can realize mahāmudrā solely through *withdrawal* and *dhyāna* from among the six yogas, and the branch of *sevā*. However, it's not wrong even for someone without extremely sharp faculties to start by practicing mahāmudrā. It is said:

As soon as you have truly received empowerment,
abandon worldly activities
and meditate upon nondual wisdom.

It is only from emptiness
that nonthought will come.
Therefore, yogins should always
meditate first of all on emptiness.

Afterward, having seen a variety of forms,
they should rely on the action seal and so on
in order to accomplish perfectly unchanging bliss.[480]

And also:

One who practices the action seal alone
without knowing the mahāmudrā
will fall from the lineage,
and that yogin will be wailing.[481]

Also, to say that the mahāmudrā must be preceded by the other three mudrās is an "over-extensive [syllogistic] pervasion." This is because there are many well-known authentic accounts of siddha masters in India and Tibet who didn't need to give an elaborate empowerment, a reading transmission, or instructions to a worthy pupil but caused them to develop wisdom effortlessly simply by blessing them or showing them a symbol. There is also the teaching that mahāmudrā wisdom arises during the "descent of wisdom [deities]" and so on. Therefore, there is no definitive [sequence]. Moreover, as in the quotation from Kālacakrapāda's oral transmission given above, the Kālacakra instructions teach infinite ways to accomplish mahāmudrā through any of the three mudrās, depending on the level of your abilities.

Therefore, in our tradition, solely within the innate union (*sahajayoga*) instructions taught by Dakpo Lhajé, there are supplementary instructions on the different kinds of teachings to be given according to the teacher's powers and the pupil's level of capability. Among these, there is the approach of teaching the Mantrayāna to pupils who are not vessels for the special Mantrayāna teachings but are of either the definite or uncertain general Mahayana family. [165] In that context, even though the other three mudrās are not taught, on reaching the culmination of this path and developing the Perfection Vehicle's wisdom of union, they are transformed into Mantrayāna pupils with sharp faculties. Then special blessing and a direct introduction [to the mind] will cause them to gain the supreme accomplishment of mahāmudrā.

It is evident that some Indian scholars also taught that mahāmudrā is the Perfection Vehicle's wisdom of union, because both sides of the argument are given in Sahajavajra's *Commentary on "Ten Verses on the True Nature."*

> Some have said that mahāmudrā is the wisdom of the true nature:
>
> > The supreme yoga is meditation
> > on the union of method and wisdom.
> > The Conqueror taught that this meditation
> > on union is mahāmudrā.
>
> Mantrikas have said:
>
> > Meditation on method and wisdom's union alone is not mahāmudrā meditation. If that were so, we would have to conclude that the Perfection Vehicle and Mantrayāna are identical.[482]

He does not explicitly state his own tradition here, but it is evident that there is no difference between these two sides in terms of the view. You can learn the details by reading *Commentary on "Ten Verses on the True Nature."* I could write at length on this subject, giving many reasons with scriptural quotation and logic, but to avoid length, this much will suffice.

A supplement to the synonyms for the union of śamatha and vipaśyanā

How does the union of śamatha and vipaśyanā, which has been described above, come to be? If the wisdom of vipaśyanā is developed on becoming adept in śamatha, then that wisdom will also be in one taste with the samādhi. This is called *union* because in the meditation of the individual with that realization, there is no separate focus on a yoga of either śamatha or vipaśyanā. You develop this genuine vipaśyanā wisdom for the first time on the *supreme Dharma* stage of the path of accumulation, and as you progress higher, it becomes clearer and more stable. From this point on, the true union of śamatha and vipaśyanā has appeared.

According to the Perfection Vehicle, until the meditation and post-meditation phases have blended, the post-accomplishment wisdom will analyze, while meditation will be one-pointed without thoughts about a meaning that is being analyzed. [166] After the meditation and post-meditation phases have blended, the conceptual elaboration of there being an analyzer and an analyzed will cease, and naturally present wisdom will effortlessly know the true nature of phenomena. Therefore, you must understand that an examining and analyzing wisdom is simply an aspect of "analytic vipaśyanā" and not true vipaśyanā, even though it's called *vipaśyanā*. You must know that the union of śamatha and vipaśyanā that occurs before you attain the true yoga of union is merely this "[analytic] vipaśyanā."

Some think that vipaśyanā is the wisdom that perfectly distinguishes phenomena and therefore does not transcend examination and analysis while śamatha is without examination or analysis. The holders of such a view cannot agree with this teaching of their union.

Others say that their union has examination and analysis that is never apart from the elixir of śamatha, like a clear lake, unruffled by wind, through which little fish move. However, they disagree with us because of their basic error of attachment to the idea that vipaśyanā's wisdom must entail examination and analysis, which is completely incorrect. Vipaśyanā is as described in the *Bringing Out the Hidden Meaning Sutra*:

> Matisāra! This is because the bodhisattvas do not see internal, individual acquisition. Neither do they see an acquiring consciousness. They do not see the ālaya, the ālaya consciousness,

> accumulation, mind, eyes, form, visual consciousnesses, and all the rest up to physical consciousness. They do not even see internal, individual minds. And that is how things truly are. Therefore, bodhisattvas are called "wise concerning the ultimate."[483]

From the *King of Meditations Sutra*:

> They appear as they are: They are like space.
> They see this characteristic of phenomena
> in those that arise in the present,
> those throughout the past, and those throughout the future.
>
> It is taught that they are ungraspable, like space.
> The failure to find something graspable
> is itself the nature of phenomena.
> It was taught that phenomena are
> ungraspable, like space.
>
> There is nothing whatsoever to be seen.
> Those who do not see phenomena
> have inconceivable qualities.[484]

From the *Sutra of the Samādhi that Accumulates All Merit*: [167]

> When all phenomena are seen to be naturally at peace, naturally in a state of equality, to be completely unborn, unarisen, and eternally and completely nirvana, that which is seen is not seen, and that seeing through not seeing, through completely not seeing, is called *seeing correctly*.[485]

There are countless such quotations in the profound sutras. Therefore, when you analyze phenomena with an analysis that accords with wisdom, even the knowledge that nothing is seen ceases within that nature. That is the experience of self-knowing, with no duality of subject and object. It is also the perfection of wisdom because it dispels the thick darkness of ignorance, and because it can do that, it is the wisdom that completely distinguishes phenomena. If that were not so, then the wisdom of vipaśyanā would be a succession of thoughts, which would not only be unable to dispel the darkness of ignorance, but also the thoughts themselves would be the nature of ignorance. From the *King of Meditations Sutra*:

> Thoughts are great ignorance:
> They cause you to fall into the ocean of samsara.
> If you rest in a samādhi without thought,
> nonthought will be as clear as space.[486]

Some object to this, saying it contradicts the Mantrayāna teaching of *paradox meditation*, which is the great remedy of using like against like. They also object that it undermines our own tradition's teaching that thoughts are the dharmakāya. However, we are not at fault, because we teach *paradox meditation* as a method for dispelling such things as ordinary desire through using special Mantrayāna methods that employ desire, and so on. For example, when desire is employed by a method, it no longer has the characteristics of desire but of the remedy for desire. You might argue that this is not *paradox meditation*, but it is: In the example of desire, you embrace, kiss, grind against the "lotus root," and so on during the action seal, which is similar to the activity of desire, and all other [examples] are similar in the same way. You must remember what the word "similar" means:

> Because it is similar, it is not identical.[487]

[168] Otherwise, if you still think the afflictions are able to dispel themselves, just try repeated sexual desire as its own remedy, and then you will know!

One might object that examination and analysis during the concentration that is the union of śamatha and vipaśyanā is examination and analysis as a method and therefore cannot be considered faults, but this is incorrect. Analytic meditation is taught in the Madhyamaka stages of meditation so that we can attain the unattained wisdom of vipaśyanā, but it is contradictory and pointless after that meditation has been attained. The Mantrayāna's mahāmudrā meditation doesn't even teach the practice of analytic meditation in the beginning. In general, the Mantrayāna tradition's special methods, the paradox meditations, are methods for gaining the realization of mahāmudrā, but they are not necessary for those who have already truly accomplished the yoga of union, the mahāmudrā.

Our tradition's famous Dharma teaching that "thoughts are the dharmakāya" means that all these phenomena, which appear as just thoughts, are nothing other than the dharmadhātu, nothing other than great bliss, and therefore appearances are the dharmakāya. For example, the moon on the water is nothing other than the water, and therefore that appearance is water. That explanation should be enough, but if you are still unable to understand its meaning, know that if thoughts *were* the dharmakāya, that would mean just a mere continuous succession of thoughts alone would be liberation, and that is never the case.

There are those who say that the terms *śamatha* and *vipaśyanā* don't belong in the Mantrayāna and that they have never seen them used in that context. However, that's only said by people who haven't studied enough, for there are many tantra commentaries that teach śamatha and vipaśyanā. In particular, from Ācārya Vīravajra's commentary on the tantra called *Yoginī's Activity*:

> What is meant by the words "mahāmudrā" and so on? "Mahāmudrā" means the dharmadhātu; "all yogas" are what bring knowledge, and they are śamatha and vipaśyanā.[488]

Also [from that commentary]:

> "The victorious lords of all yogas" are śamatha and vipaśyanā, mentioned above, which are taught to be the supreme creators of the dharmakāya.[489]

Therefore, not only are the names śamatha and vipaśyanā used, [169] they are also taught to be the supreme yoga for the practice of mahāmudrā.

The arising of experiences and realizations in śamatha and vipaśyanā

This is in two parts:

1. Experiences
2. Realization

The arising of experiences in śamatha and vipaśyanā

[Verse 20]

> **Continuous great bliss, free from attachment;**
> **unveiled luminosity, free from fixation on attributes;**
> **naturally present nonthought, transcending the intellect:**
> **May there be a continuity of these effortless experiences.**

Three faultless experiences arise when you are in the meditation of the practice of śamatha and vipaśyanā: (1) an experience of "continuous great bliss, free from attachment"; (2) an experience of self-knowing and "luminosity, free from fixation," on the attributes of objects; and (3) the experience of the "naturally present nonthought," emptiness, transcending the scope of the intellect. These [experiences] are effortlessly accomplished and will naturally continue while you remain in a natural state unadulterated by hope that these three experiences of bliss, clarity, and nonthought will arise, or by fear that they will not arise, and so on.

These are the incorrect experiences: (1) an experience of bliss that has attachment, (2) an experience of luminosity that has fixation on attributes, and (3) an experience of nonthought that is grasped by the intellect. The first of those will mislead you to the desire realm; the second will mislead you to the form realm; the third will mislead you to the formless realm. Therefore, you must eliminate these faults, such as attachment. In particular, the effort to create experiences when there are no experiences and holding on to experiences that have arisen are equally faults. The first stops experiences from arising and the second causes experiences to vanish. This prayer was made to teach that it's essential to eliminate thoughts of effort, thoughts of fixation on attributes, and thoughts of hope and fear.

The experience of "bliss" referred to here is both physical and mental. The experience of "clarity" is knowledge of the nature of phenomena. This knowledge is unobscured by such faults as dullness and agitation and is experienced as self-knowing and as self-illuminating. It is the arising of the ten signs and so on.[490] [170] The experience of "nonthought" is seeing everything as empty because nonthought predominates, and so on.

If you meditate on these [experiences] as being of one taste in the natural state that is free from attachment or fixation on them as separate, you will perfect such yogas as the union of bliss and emptiness and also the inseparability of the three experiences, which will cause all qualities to be naturally present. According to Saraha, this is how the experiences arise:

> Stopping the mind and stopping the breath:
> Those are the guru's instructions.[491]

Therefore, by controlling the mind, you control the breath. As a result, you develop heat and thereby develop bliss, which results in clarity and nonthought. If you know this essential point in the practice instruction tradition, then even if you don't meditate on the path of methods and so on, still the Mantrayāna path's ten signs, the signs of heat, and so on will genuinely appear.

In general, when there is direct realization and not just a general conception of the equal taste of the experiences of bliss, clarity, and nonthought, this is categorized as realization and not experience. This is the appearance of the meaning of the basis as a result of the obscurations weakening.

The bliss referred to here is the *supremely unchanging bliss*, for you have eliminated the changeable bliss of the body and mind, and this bliss doesn't have a nature of being either happiness or suffering. This is what the *Hevajra Tantra* is referring to in the following passage:

> In it there is no center and no edge.
> There is no samsara and no nirvana.
> It is the supreme great bliss.
> There is no over there and no over here.[492]

It is incorrect to distinguish clarity and emptiness as phenomena that are separate from this great bliss. Great bliss is the natural mind, which is the union of clarity and emptiness. From Ācārya Āryadeva's treatise entitled the *Hundred Verses on the Essence of Understanding*:

> Through eliminating conceptualization,
> there will be no intense aspiration.
> This clear appearance
> is self-knowing and great bliss.[493]

The arising of realizations in śamatha and vipaśyanā

[Verse 21]

> **Attachment to good and fixation on experiences is spontaneously liberated.**
> **Bad thoughts and illusion are naturally purified in the element.**
> **The ordinary mind has no rejection and adoption, no elimination and no attainment.**
> **May we realize the truth of the true nature, free from conceptual elaborations.**

[171] The consciousness of pride owing to the arising of good experiences, as described above, is spontaneously liberated.

Thoughts that engage with illusory phenomena prevent you from seeing the meaning of the true nature, and therefore they are classed as bad. Although those thoughts are bad, they are not to be intentionally rejected but rather naturally purified in the element of the true nature through the power of concentration. As a result, the "ordinary mind," the natural mind, becomes evident.

The obscuring phenomena that are to be rejected should be fully understood without rejecting them. The same applies to the elimination that comes from adopting remedial phenomena and rejecting what is to be rejected, and also to the result that is attained as the result of rejection and adoption. This prayer teaches us to understand that they have no existing nature of their own, no presence. As a result, we will realize the truth of the true nature, which is free from all extremes of conceptual elaborations, such as "creation and cessation," "eternalism and nihilism," "coming and going," and "one and many." Thus, every attribute of rejection and adoption, elimination and attainment, spontaneously cease in the ordinary mind. This is the reason why [the "ordinary mind"] means seeing the true nature. From the *Great Drum Sutra*:

> Mind and enlightenment
> are not seen as two aspects.
> The characteristics of enlightenment
> are also the characteristics of the mind.[494]

From the *King of Meditations Sutra*:

> It is not taught that the nature of form
> is one thing while that of emptiness is something else.
> Those who perfectly know form
> perfectly know emptiness...
> Those who perfectly know
> emptiness, know nirvana.
> Those who do not know this,
> who have another perception, will be crushed into dust.[495]

The sutra continues by saying the same thing about the other five aggregates. From *Casket of Jewels*:

> There is no difference whatsoever between afflictions and the qualities of buddhahood.[496]

From the *Kālacakra Tantra*:

> Nirvana, the form of freedom,
> is not beyond samsara.
> Their union is the supreme nonduality,
> truly liberated from eternalism and nihilism.[497]

As is said in countless such teachings, samsara and nirvana, or the two truths, have never had any existence. They are nondual and objectless. This is the ordinary mind, the truth of the true nature. When this is seen, the concepts of adoption and rejection and so on naturally go away. [172] According to Ācārya Nāgārjuna:

> When there is no addition of nirvana
> and no removal of samsara,
> then what samsara is there?
> What nirvana can be differentiated?[498]

Therefore, it is impossible for the attributes of rejection and adoption to spontaneously cease in those who have not seen the true nature.

Those who know the practice instructions of the Dakpo Kagyü use the term *seeing the natural mind* for the full realization of the true nature, which has neither rejection nor adoption. Ācārya Ḍombipa clearly described this [natural mind]:

> Rejecting all particular conceptual elaborations that have come from the teaching, search for the mind that has the extremely brilliant essence of enlightenment: the natural mind. When that is completely embraced, there is a blending like that of space with space. There is none of the previously occurring particular distractions due to pleasure from—and attachment to—objects. You are free of thought, like space, so that all the seals (*mudrās*) will bless you. You have self-knowing's field of experience, which is birthless and beyond the senses. There is primarily great bliss, which is the nature of method and wisdom beyond all terminology, and which has never manifested previously.[499]

This was taught in the profound sutras for the worthy ones who could believe it. For example, in the *Sutra Teaching Bodhisattva Conduct*, when Kumāra Ratnadatta asks Mañjuśrī what Dharma should be taught to beginner bodhisattvas, he answers:

> "Do not reject desire. Do not extinguish anger. Do not eliminate ignorance. Do not transcend the belief in the individual self."[500]

And later on:

> "Do not contemplate the Buddha. Do not think of the Dharma. Do not make offerings to the sangha. Do not correctly adopt the trainings. Do not seek the pacification of existence. Do not cross over the river." Teach in this way; give this instruction to beginner bodhisattvas. Why should you do that? Because that alone is the presence of the true nature of all phenomena. [173] It is the immature that are taught that phenomena arise and that they cease. If you teach, "This nature of phenomena (*dharmadhātu*) is made manifest through nonconceptuality. Those who thus realize the nature of phenomena attain enlightenment" and they do not become afraid, scared, or terrified, then you should think, "Oh! Those bodhisattvas are irreversible. They have the good fortune

> of having reached the state of irreversibility!" And this instruction will bring them joy over and over again.[501]

To see the truth in this way is the birth of the wisdom of mahāmudrā. From the *Hevajra Tantra*:

> This wisdom is self-knowing.
> Its range is beyond the path of speech.
> It is the stage of blessing.
> It is the wisdom of omniscience.
>
> Earth, water, and air,
> fire and space too,
> and the sensation of seeing self and others
> will all instantaneously cease to bind.
>
> Instantaneously the heavens, the land of mortals,
> and the underworld will become one body,
> and the thoughts that divide self and others
> will fail to oppress.[502]

This teaches that while you are on the path, the instant that the wisdom of mahāmudrā arises, all phenomena of perceiver and perceived will be realized to have one nature, so that no conceptual elaboration of attributes will be able to destroy it.

There are those who say that the recognition of thoughts is the full extent of seeing the mind, but that will not be enough for seeing the mind. Both essence and nature have the same meaning, while thoughts, because they are extrinsic illusions, are neither the nature nor the essence of the mind.

The necessity of practicing the union of emptiness and compassion[503]

This is in two parts:

1. Identifying compassion
2. How compassion is united with emptiness

Identifying compassion

[Verse 22]

The nature of beings is always buddhahood,
but not realizing that, they wander in endless samsara.
May I have overwhelming compassion
for beings in limitless, endless suffering.

[174] In general, there are two kinds of compassion—*compassion directed toward beings* and *compassion directed toward phenomena.* There is also a third kind of compassion: *objectless compassion.* The first two compassions are practiced in the preliminaries of these instructions. Objectless compassion comes when you see the meaning of the true nature, when there is "emptiness that has compassion as its essence." The compassion that is taught here is this third compassion.

What is objectless compassion? As taught in the verse, "The nature of beings is always buddhahood," which is present as the essence of the Buddha's dharmakāya. But solely because they do not realize that, beings wander in endless samsara, drowning in a limitless ocean of suffering. When you see the meaning of the true nature, you have the effortless appearance of an uninterrupted continuum of overwhelming compassion for those beings. It's said:

> The bodhisattva who has mastered
> familiarization with meditation
> develops compassion particularly for
> those in the grasp of the demon of belief in reality.[504]

According to Nāgārjuna:

> Thus if the yogin
> meditates on this emptiness,
> there will undoubtedly arise
> a mind devoted to the benefit of others.[505]

Because of this compassion, bodhisattvas are dedicated solely to the benefit of others. Therefore, they take on existences that specifically accord with that of all beings. They do not abandon samsara, and yet they are unstained by its faults. [Also according to Nāgārjuna]:

> When those who have stability in meditation
> are startled by the sufferings of others,
> they will abandon the bliss of the meditative state
> and even enter the Avīci hell.
>
> This is what is wonderful; this is what is praiseworthy;
> this is the supreme way of the sublime ones.
> It's not their giving away their bodies
> and wealth that is marvelous.
>
> To depend on karma and its results
> even though you know phenomena are empty
> is more marvelous than marvelous,
> more wonderful than wonderful.
>
> Those who wish to protect beings
> are born within the swamp of existence
> and yet are unstained by its faults,
> like the petals of a lotus on the water.[506]

The word "may" [in verse 22] makes the prayer that this will be so. [175]

How compassion is united with emptiness

[Verse 23]

> **When there is love with the unceasing power of overwhelming compassion,**
> **the meaning of the empty essence appears nakedly.**
> **May I meditate inseparably, day and night,**
> **on the union, the supreme path, which is free from error.**

The power of objectless compassion arises unceasingly. When there is that love, then the meaning of the empty essence of the true nature free of conceptual elaboration appears nakedly and directly and not just as a vague generality. Therefore, the path of union, which is the blending of emptiness and compassion into one-taste, is "the supreme path, which is free from error." From the *Binding Net of the Ḍākinīs*:

> The Buddha, the Dharma,
> and also the Sangha, were taught
> so that the mind might realize
> the inseparability of emptiness and compassion.[507]

From the *Vajra Pinnacle*:

> Dividing emptiness from compassion
> is like dividing a lamp's flame from its light.
> Emptiness and compassion are one,
> just like a lamp's flame and its light.[508]

This is the meaning of bodhicitta and of the perfection of wisdom teachings, too. According to *Ears of Grain of Practice Instructions*:

> Here, the inseparability of emptiness and compassion, the unlocated mind, means bodhicitta and the perfection of wisdom.[509]

If wisdom and emptiness are not united, then you are practicing only one aspect and will be unable to attain the unsurpassable state. If you are unable to do that, then this will not be the vajra yoga. From the *Guhyasamāja Tantra*:

> Yoga is not the way of method;
> it is also not wisdom alone.
> The union of method and wisdom—
> that is what the Tathāgata named *yoga*.[510]

From the *Hevajra Tantra*:

> Because method is creation,
> and wisdom, which ends existence, is destruction.[511]

From the *Sutra Requested by the Nāga King Anavatapata*:

> Māra has two activities: method devoid of wisdom and wisdom devoid of method. These should be recognized as the activity of Māra and rejected.[512]

From Atiśa's *Lamp for the Path to Enlightenment*:

> Wisdom that is without method [176]
> and method that is without wisdom
> were taught to be bondage.
> Therefore, do not be without either.[513]

From *Ornament of Realization*:

> Through wisdom, you will not remain in existence.
> Through compassion, you will not remain in peace.[514]

This teaches that you must have the union of method and wisdom in order to attain the nirvana that remains neither in existence nor peace. There are countless such teachings. Also, if you have compassion without the realization of emptiness, you may be proud of benefiting others. Then not only will you fail to benefit them, but also your own practice will be swept away by a wind, and you will be prevented from benefiting others for some time. If you meditate on emptiness alone, you will go astray onto the path of the śrāvakas and pratyekabuddhas, which will be a long-term obstacle to benefiting others. It is said:

> Going to hell is not a lasting
> obstacle to enlightenment.
> Becoming a śrāvaka or pratyekabuddha
> is a lasting obstacle to the attainment of enlightenment.[515]

As this is most certainly the case, this would be an error on the path of the Mahayana. Therefore, [Rangjung Dorjé] taught in the form of a prayer that we must meditate inseparably, day and night, which means all the time, on this path of union that is free from error until we have reached the state of union, the state of great Vajradhara. From *Bodhicitta Commentary*:

> The buddhas have taught that
> bodhicitta is not obscured by

thoughts that conceive of a self, aggregates, and so on.
It always has the characteristic of emptiness.

The mind, moistened by compassion,
should diligently meditate upon that.[516]

One should know that the first line, which describes the development of experiences, teaches the paths of accumulation and engagement. The second line, which describes the development of realization, and the last two lines teach the paths of seeing and meditation.

Reaching completion through that conduct and thereby reaching the fulfillment of the path [the third part of the detailed explanation of meditation][517]

You may wonder why has conduct not been taught yet? The teaching of conduct has in fact been given through the teaching of meditation. Generally speaking, there is the elaborate Mantrayāna conduct and the simple Mantrayāna conduct. The first of those is called *external conduct* and the second *internal conduct*. The internal conduct is the higher of the two, and it is nothing other than this practice of mahāmudrā yoga. [177] That includes the *perfectly excellent conduct*, so everything that needed to be taught has been taught. From the *Guhyasamāja Tantra*:

This [mahāmudrā] is the supreme yoga and is therefore
worthy of homage from the tathāgatas.
It is renowned that infinite
ordinations come from it.

Therefore, all infinite
deity meditations truly come from it,
and all mudrās, mandalas, and mantras
are purely from that yoga.

Both peaceful and increasing karmas
and everything else that arises from mantras,
as numerous as the sands of the Ganges,
and even all the smallest siddhis

> and every other mudrā siddhi,
> as many as there are known upon the earth,
> are created from this yoga,
> which is taught to be the *mind vajra*.[518]

You must know that Mantrayāna conduct is meditation on knowing the inseparability of method and wisdom. From the *Latter Guhyasamāja Tantra*:

> The mind (*manas*) that is activity
> dependent on the senses and their objects,
> that mind is taught to be *man*,
> while *tra* means "protection."
>
> The *samaya* vows are any teaching
> that brings definite liberation from worldly conduct.
> All the vajra refuges
> teach that to be the mantra conduct.[519]

Venerable Abhayākara explained the meaning of this passage in his commentary on it:

> "The mind (*manas*)" is that which results from the activities of the senses and so on. The essence of "that mind is taught to be *man*." *Man*, as a verbal root, means "to know," and therefore *man* is the wisdom of emptiness. Dispelling its two obscurations will bring the attainment of the *perfectly excellent*. This has the meaning of "protection," so with *tra* that means never being devoid of it. *Mantra*, which is solely the wisdom of the inseparability of emptiness and compassion, has the meaning of "conduct."[520]

That conduct is the supreme conduct. From *Ears of Grain of Practice Instructions*:

> Even though the body and speech are pure, it is only through complete purity of mind that there is purity, and therefore the mind's conduct is superior to all other conducts. Therefore it is the true [conduct].[521]

The fifth of the main parts of this text: The prayer for the result of completing the path

[Verse 24]

> **Through the power of meditation, there is sight and clairvoyance;**
> **beings are ripened and buddha realms are purified,** [178]
> **and the prayers for accomplishing the qualities of buddhahood are perfected.**
> **May there be buddhahood, where perfection, ripening, and fulfillment are brought to completion.**

This is in two parts:

1. The actual result of completing the path
2. A supplementary brief explanation of the stages of the path

The actual result of completing the path

This is in two parts:

1. Sight and clairvoyance
2. An explanation of fulfillment, ripening, and purification

Sight and clairvoyance

Unsurpassable buddhahood, when all phenomena are true complete enlightenment, is the ultimate result gained through the power of meditation by practicing the unmistaken instructions in that way. Possessing extremely pure qualities, such as sight and clairvoyance, is fulfillment, ripening, and purification being brought to completion.

You first develop the clairvoyances and so on while on the path but then have to gradually bring perfection, ripening, and purification to completion. Therefore, the first results are "sight and clairvoyance." There are five sights and six clairvoyances. The five sights are physical sight, divine sight, wisdom sight, Dharma sight, and buddha sight.

Physical sight

From a sutra:

> The physical vision of a bodhisattva sees for a hundred *yojanas* or more, seeing as far as every world in the universe.[522]

Divine sight

> Bodhisattvas have perfect knowledge of the divine sight of devas, from those in the heavens of the Four Great Kings up to the devas in Akaniṣṭha. However, those devas do not know the divine sight of bodhisattvas.[523]

It is taught that with divine sight one can, in particular, see the deaths and rebirths of all beings in the ten directions.

Wisdom sight
This is the wisdom that realizes selflessness.

Dharma sight
According to Ācārya Vasubandhu, this is comprised of nine strengths, which are the ten strengths with the omission of the knowledge of what is possible and impossible.

Buddha sight
This is the realization of the complete perfection of all phenomena.

The six clairvoyances are (1) miracles, (2) divine hearing, (3) knowing the minds of others, (4) remembering previous lives, [179] (5) divine sight, and (6) knowing that stains have ceased.

Miracles
This is manifesting miracles.

Divine hearing
This is hearing the sounds of infinite realms.

Knowing the minds of others
This is knowing exactly what is occurring in the minds of every individual being.

Remembering previous lives

This is knowing the continuous succession of previous and future lifetimes of each individual being.

Divine sight

This is knowledge of the birth, death, actions, and results of all beings.

Knowing that stains have ceased

This is the knowledge that all obscurations and impediments have no intrinsic presence and they therefore are completely eliminated.

The divine sight in this list of clairvoyances is not the same as that in the list of five sights, because that divine sight comes from the ripening of karma while this [divine sight] comes from meditation.

You might ask, "If it's taught that the sights and clairvoyances arise while we're still on the path, how can they be called special qualities of buddhahood?" This is answered in Abhayākara's *Adornment of* [*Śākyamuni's*] *View*:

> Whichever path one is on, from that of *accumulation* and through higher and higher levels of mind, there is attainment of each successive development of the five sights in such particular forms as *supreme*, *perfectly supreme*, and so on, and there are also the six clairvoyances.[524]

Also [from Abhayākara's *Adornment of Śākyamuni's View*]:

> If you ask, "How can bodhisattvas have a buddha's five sights and six clairvoyances?" the answer is that bodhisattvas acquire both of these separately on the eighth stage, but at the stage of buddhahood they are totally perfected, totally purified, and in their ultimate form.[525]

Therefore, as described, the sights and clairvoyances become completely pure and attain their ultimate form at the level of buddhahood, where one is able to perceive all things without limitation and so on. Therefore we should know that these are exceptional.

Explanation of perfection, ripening, and purification

Thus, the bodhisattvas—with their higher motivation, prayers, and vast conduct; with their great powers, such as sight and clairvoyance; and with infinite methods—ripen all beings, completely purify buddha realms, and attain true perfection by bringing their prayers to completion with the complete perfection of the phenomena that are the qualities of a sugata. [180]

Ripening beings is described in *Ornament of the Mahayana Sutras*. First it's taught that bodhisattvas must ripen themselves through the nine characteristics of ripening. In conclusion it states:

> Just as one declares a wound or food is ripened
> when it has suppurated or is ready to be enjoyed,
> in the same way, it is taught that the [individual as a] basis
> must have ripened the two aspects of pacification and application.
>
> It is taught that beings[526] are ripened through separation [from
> obscurations],
> and similarly, totally ripened, perfectly ripened,
> harmoniously ripened, excellently ripened,
> ripened with realization, constantly ripened, and ripened higher.[527]

The teaching continues in detail. For example, a wound is ripened so that it will heal, and food is ripened so that it will be edible, while pupils are ripened so that they can eliminate faults and create remedies. Ripening is categorized into those eight different kinds beginning with "ripening through separation," but I will not describe them here.

The *Prayer for Excellent Conduct* describes the purification of realms:

> In that way, all enter into the display of buddha realms
> throughout all of the directions.[528]

And also:

> Upon each atom there are as many realms as there are atoms...[529]

And also:

Purifying an ocean of realms . . .[530]

Thus, there is entry into an ocean of realms in order to attain the wisdom of the characteristics of countless, endless world realms, and in order to make them manifest. Those realms are made completely pure through seven aspects of purification. The seven aspects of purification are general purification, the purification of power, the purification of perfect enjoyment, the purification of beings, the purification of causes, the purification of results.[531] I am not going into these in detail; they can be learned from such texts as the *Sutra of the Ten Stages.*

The fulfillment of the prayers for accomplishing the phenomena of buddhahood

The sutras teach ten kinds of prayers. Each of those is made up of countless trillions of prayers. When they are fulfilled, the qualities of buddhahood are completely perfected.

Buddhas perceive the buddha qualities, but even high bodhisattvas can only give a vague indication of what they are. Therefore, [ordinary] beings who have childlike minds can never comprehend them. Nevertheless, the sutras and treatises describe countless classifications, such as: (1) a single dharmakāya that is comprised of all the kāyas, wisdoms, qualities, and activities; [181] (2) two kāyas: the dharmakāya and form kāya; (3) three kāyas, with the form kāya divided into two; (4) four kāyas, with the addition of the svabhavakāya; and (5) five kāyas, which are the embodiment of the five wisdoms.

In terms of wisdom there are, for example, the *two wisdoms*—the knowledge of the true nature and the knowledge of the diverse apparent nature of things—and the *five wisdoms*—mirror-like wisdom and so on. There are countless classifications of kāyas and pupils. The classifications of qualities are similarly countless, including the sixty-four qualities of ripening and liberation. Activity has countless classifications, starting with two: naturally present activity and uninterrupted, continuous activity. Learn these exactly as they appear in the sutras, tantras, and treatises.

The word *buddha* can mean both "awakened" (*sangs pa*) and "blossomed" (*rgyas pa*),[532] hence the [Tibetan] name *sangs rgyas*. It has been taught that:

> The buddhas are like awakened, blossomed lotuses
> because they have awakened from the sleep of ignorance
> and because their minds have blossomed in knowledge.[533]

Thus, when the bodhisattvas "bring purification and ripening to completion," all [the goals] of their original prayers are perfected, and they attain buddhahood. You must know that in the Mantrayāna's manifestation of the state of buddhahood in one lifetime, perfection, ripening, and purification are quickly completed through the inconceivable, special power of skillful methods and samādhis.

Ācārya Jñānākara in his commentary [on his own text] *Entering the Mantra*[*yāna*,][534] responds to Ārya Śāntimati's questions thus:[535]

> For example, a place that a weak man, or a cart pulled by animals, would take a long time to reach, someone with the power of miraculous speed, or the sun and moon, would quickly reach. Similarly, the level that it takes the noble ones who practice the Perfection Vehicle countless eons to reach, a well-trained holder of the Mantrayāna—because of the difference in the power of [those paths]—can attain within one lifetime.[536]

A supplementary brief description of the stages of the path

In Mahāsiddha Nāropa's *Mahāmudrā in Brief*,[537] [182] the special teachings of this lineage are explained in terms of four yogas:

1. The stage known as the yoga of *one-pointedness*: You attain and remain in the one-pointed state of mind of śamatha. Then vipaśyanā arises, accompanied by the experiences of bliss, clarity, and nonthought.
2. [The yoga of] *nonelaboration*: You see that all phenomena of appearances and mind have the nature of the dharmadhātu and great bliss. Therefore, you are spontaneously liberated from all fixations upon conceptual elaborations of dualistic phenomena. You attain genuine vipaśyanā, which is the wisdom that is the union of emptiness and compassion. Therefore, you truly obtain the yoga of śamatha and vipaśyanā.
3. [The yoga of] *one taste*: As you become increasingly adept, all phenomena are realized to be the "manifold that has one taste," and there is unceasing, effortless wisdom.
4. The yoga of *nonmeditation*: The luminosity of meditation and the luminosity of the basis blend into one, so that all obscurations that conceal the true nature are completely purified away. The boundary between meditation and post-meditation is annihilated, and all ultimate qualities are naturally present.

Each of these yogas is subdivided into a lesser, medium, and greater yoga, thus making twelve yogas. You can learn from the teachings of the previous great masters the details of this classification and the manner in which the qualities develop.

In terms of the yogas' equivalence with the paths and stages of the Perfection Vehicle, it is taught—and it is true—that: (1) *One-pointedness* is equivalent to the path of accumulation. (2) The lesser and medium levels of *nonelaboration* are equivalent to the path of engagement. (3) The greater level of *nonelaboration* is equivalent to the path of seeing. (4) The yoga of *one taste* and the lesser and medium levels of the yoga of *nonmeditation* are equivalent to the path of meditation. (5) The great level of *nonmeditation* is taught to be the level of buddhahood. From *Ornament of the Mahayana Sutras*:

> The bodhisattva, having excellently gathered
> an infinite, perfect accumulation of merit and wisdom,
> because of his contemplation's complete certainty in phenomena,
> understands the nature of meaning and the process of speech.
>
> He also knows those meanings to be only speech,
> and as in that way they exist as mind alone,
> he has the direct realization of the dharmadhātu (the nature of phenomena)
> as being free of the characteristics of dualism.[538]

Also from *Ornament of the Mahayana Sutras*:

> The wise, through the power of nonconceptual wisdom,
> are always completely in a state of equanimity,
> so that a thick accumulation of faults present in them
> is eliminated, as is venom by a great poison [as an antidote].
>
> One who dwells perfectly in the Dharmas taught by the Sage [183]
> rests his understanding in its root, the dharmadhātu (the nature of phenomena).
> Then the wise one, understanding the process of thinking to be just thought,
> quickly reaches the farther shore of an ocean of qualities.[539]

The first of those verses describes the path of accumulation. The first half of the second verse describes the path of engagement. The second half [of the second verse] describes the path of seeing. The line of verse[540] that begins "Then the wise one..." describes the path of meditation. The last line describes the path of no more training. This is taught in detail when teaching the instructions for the *Ornament of the Mahayana Sutras*,[541] for all those characteristics are contained within it.

However, [in the four yogas] does one actually obtain the powerful qualities of each individual path, such as receiving instructions directly from nirmāṇakāya buddhas and using miraculous powers to travel to many worlds as one would obtain on the greater path of accumulation? When you have correctly followed the path of realizing the meaning of the true nature, it's impossible for the qualities that are signs of the path, like heat is for fire, to not appear, but they do differ as to whether they appear as a common perception for all beings or not. It is also taught that when the result is attained within one lifetime, the karmic body will obscure [those qualities] to some degree until the karmic body transforms into the wisdom body.

When you meditate on the Mantrayāna's completion stages, such as the six branch yogas, this is essentially the same as going through the paths and stages. Gyalwa Rangjung [Dorjé] has stated in his *Profound Inner Meaning*:

> First, there is receiving empowerment and the generation and
> completion stages;
> perfectly understanding them and practicing with aspiration is the
> path of accumulation.
>
> Knowing the essential meaning of the channels, winds, and drops,
> performing "perfectly excellent activity" and attaining "heat" is to be
> on the path of engagement.
>
> Then to traverse the path of engagement through *vrata* conduct
> so as to unite with [the path of] seeing: that is withdrawal[542]
> and the path with four dhyānas,
> which is also called the *purification of the channels*.
>
> It is taught that perfecting the aspects of dhyāna brings attainment of
> the five clairvoyances.
> That is the entry into the body mandala.[543]

The text continues in this way in detail and is explained in the accompanying commentary. Then there is the correspondence between the four yogas and the four empowerments. According to Saraha:

> One-pointed knowledge is the vase empowerment.
> The bliss of nonelaboration is the secret empowerment.
> The third [empowerment] is union with equality.
> Nonmeditation is the fourth [empowerment].[544]

[184] According to Nāropa:

> The first mahāmudrā realization
> is turning away from
> the ignorance that views
> extrinsic thoughts as true.
> Realizing knowledge to be clarity without fixation
> is called the *knowledge empowerment.*
>
> If the five poisons become the five wisdoms,
> it is said to be the *vase empowerment.*
>
> When its unimpeded power
> arises without limitation,
> bliss will arise from emptiness,
> and this is called the *empowerment of the second clarity.*
>
> The wisdom that is connate
> is the inseparability of bliss and emptiness, the nature of space.
> In the great one-taste of union,
> appearances and mind are experienced as great bliss.
> That is taught to be the prajñā's wisdom empowerment.
>
> When the three empowerments are inseparably united in the mind,
> and the mind is as pure as space,
> in a state of meditation that is not intermittent,
> that union of the two truths is the fourth [empowerment].[545]

How long does it take to attain the mahāmudrā result through practicing these mahāmudrā instructions? There is no definitive answer to that question. Those who have extremely marvelous capability and have the ideal situation of being pupils of an accomplished master will attain it effortlessly within their lifetime. Otherwise, according to an individual's level of potential, it will be accomplished in the bardo, within seven lifetimes or within sixteen lifetimes.

Even the path that is a union of Sūtrayāna and Mantrayāna is far faster than the Perfection Vehicle. Sahajavajra, in his extensive *Commentary on "Ten Verses on the True Nature,"* states that this is superior to the path of other Perfection Vehicle practitioners:

> It is extremely superior because of its definitive realization of emptiness, of the true nature of union, analyzed through the instructions of the sublime guru.[546]

That is what you need to know.

The third main part of this text: The conclusion of the prayer

[Verse 25]

> **Through the compassion of the conquerors and their children**
> **in the ten directions,**
> **and through the power of all the good karma there can be,**
> **may my pure prayers, and those of all beings,**
> **be perfectly fulfilled.**

This verse is easy to understand. The words "all the good karma there can be" means both composite and noncomposite good actions. [185] Although there are those who say that the noncomposite dharmadhātu is not a good action, according to our tradition this is stated clearly many times in the last turning of the Dharma wheel. For example:

> Virtue is the nature of the ālaya.[547]

Therefore, although [the ālaya] isn't a good action from the categories of composite good or bad actions, it has the power to enable the emergence of all the phenomena of enlightenment and virtue. It is called a virtue because of that aspect.

"Pure prayer" here primarily means this actual prayer, but it also includes all the pure prayers made by infinite beings and āryas.

I have now concluded my rudimentary explanation, which was limited by the extent of my intellect's powers, of the stages in *Prayer for the Definitive Meaning, the Mahāmudrā*. Now I will add two brief supplements:

1. Synonyms for the practice of mahāmudrā instructions
2. The succession of gurus in the mahāmudrā lineages

Synonyms for the practice of mahāmudrā instructions

Previously, there was only a brief reference made to these two kinds [of mahāmudrā practice]:

1. The special Mantrayāna tradition
2. A merger of Mantrayāna and Sūtrayāna realization

The special Mantrayāna tradition of mahāmudrā

If the master has the power and the pupil has the ideal capability, there will be no need for preliminary elaborate empowerments but only the vajra-wisdom empowerment. Pupils with less capability must first receive the elaborate empowerments.

The first of these two approaches is for the "immediate" individual, who attains liberation solely through being blessed, shown a symbol, or given a little instruction, as in the accounts of Indian masters who attained siddhi. In particular, there are many accounts of that kind of liberation occurring within our own lineage in Tibet. In these cases, it is not a definite necessity for all the stages of instructions to be taught. This approach is that of the second of Milarepa's two lineages, those of (1) the elaborate path of methods and (2) the unelaborated path of innate union.

As for individuals who progress through stages, according to Rangjung Dorjé in his teaching on preliminaries in *Instructions for the Mahāmudrā Innate Union*: [186]

> A true guru with the necessary qualities only gives this teaching to pupils who practice properly, have abandoned the activities of this life, and are intent on unsurpassable enlightenment. First of all, [the guru] gives [the pupils] the vows of correct conduct (*śīla*)

> and bodhicitta. Then [the guru] gives them empowerments that completely ripen them. Then they should practice in a pleasant and solitary place.[548]

Thus, there is this definite procedure for the practice of the lineage. As for the preliminary ripening [empowerment], although it could be for any deity in the highest yoga tantras, it appears that in practice the empowerment is for the mandala of Cakrasaṃvara and consort. Also, Mahāsiddha Lodrö Rinchen[549] taught that there should be the reading transmission for the *Vajra Verses of the Aural Tantra*,[550] and this is given.

There are two traditions for how these instructions are given:

1. As soon as the empowerment for the instructions is given, [the pupils] practice the generation stage. Once they have mastered that, they practice the yoga without attributes.
2. First, [the pupils] master to some extent the śamatha and vipaśyanā yoga without attributes, and then they practice the generation stage. This makes it easier to attain clear appearances and quickly attain siddhis.

In both approaches, however, the generation stage is followed by the completion stage, either with or without attributes, and they are practiced together as they will enhance each other.

The merger of the Mantrayāna and Sūtrayāna traditions

Lord Maitripa created this tradition by emphasizing certain aspects in the teaching of Saraha's lineage. Advayavajra[551] taught this in his text named *Ten Verses on the True Nature*. Dakpo Rinpoché [i.e., Gampopa] then adorned this tradition with Atiśa's teaching on the graduated path for three kinds of individuals. Dakpo Rinpoché received that teaching from many Kadampa lamas, such as Geshé Chakriwa, Nyukrumpa, Gya Yöndak, and Jayülpa.

[Dakpo Rinpoché's tradition] is known as the merger of the two great rivers of the Kadam and mahāmudrā traditions. However, there is nothing in [Dakpo Rinpoché's tradition] that is different, in terms of either words or meaning, from the "instructions on the innate union of nonmeditation," which therefore brings a swift attainment of the mahāmudrā siddhi. According to Dakpo Rinpoché:

> I have benefited many beings through the Kadam Dharma, in accordance with my dream-omens and with prophecies given by Milarepa.[552] [187]

Dakpo Rinpoché also said:

> I have now been able to benefit beings a little, and that is because of the kindness of the Kadampa lamas.[553]

[Dakpo Rinpoché] dreamed that he beat a drum, many deer came to listen to him, he fed them milk, and so on, all of which referred to these instructions. The view of our tradition is that there are very few who are worthy of the special Vajrayāna in this time of great degeneration, but by teaching the graduated path for the three kinds of individuals to pupils with dull abilities and inferior capability, they will become beings perfectly worthy to be vessels for the special Mantrayāna and will achieve liberation within one lifetime. Even if they don't, many of them will see the meaning of the mahāmudrā and reach the path that is irreversible. Since the time of Venerable [Dakpo Rinpoché] up to the present, there has been this tradition of giving instructions to guide all pupils, without discrimination, whether they are of high or low capacity.

Teaching the Mantrayāna's profound path of methods to worthy pupils is called the *causal-phase teaching* or *foundation instructions*. It is unnecessary to examine the nature of the pupils because even those with doubts will gain great benefit from it, not to mention those who aspire to practice this profound meaning. From the *Four Hundred Verses*:

> Even those with little merit
> will not doubt this Dharma.
> Even if they do have doubts,
> it will still destroy samsara.[554]

When, in the *Sutra Teaching Bodhisattva Conduct*,[555] Kumāra Ratnadatta had Mañjuśrī make the statement about having no rejection or adoption, eight monks with dualistic minds who had no inclination for it vomited hot blood, died, and went to hell. The Bhagavān prophesied that because those skeptical monks had heard that profound Dharma, they would definitely be liberated from hell that very day and be reborn in Tuṣita. There, they would serve a billion buddhas over a span of sixty-eight eons and then attain primordial buddhahood.

In the *Sutra of Mañjuśrī's Dwelling*[556] there is also a prophecy that a hundred monks who had no inclination for the profound Dharma fell into hell but were then immediately [188] reborn in Tuṣita because they had heard that Dharma. There, they were pupils of Maitreya and become arhants. There are many such instances in the sutras, so this is definitely true.

The succession of gurus in the mahāmudrā lineages

According to the special Mantrayāna tradition, one lineage is: (1) Vajradhara, (2) Tilopa, (3) Nāropa, and (4) Marpa Lotsāwa. Another lineage is: (1) Vajradhara, (2) Matiratna, (3) Saraha, [(4) Nāgārjuna], (5) Śavaripa, (6) Maitripa, and (7) Marpa Chökyi Lodrö. Afterward, both lineages merge in Lord Milarepa, Lord Daö Shönu [i.e., Gampopa], and so on. This is the lineage of the Kamtsang [Kagyü].[557] This tradition of blending the understanding of the Sūtrayāna and Mantrayāna is solely the river of the second lineage, which has its origin in Saraha.

The graduated path of the three levels of beings, which is an adornment [for the mahāmudrā], is of three lineages:

1. The lineage of vast conduct
2. The lineage of the profound view
3. The lineage of the blessing of practice

The lineage of vast conduct

(1) The Lord of Sages [the Buddha], (2) Regent Ajita [Maitreya], (3) Asaṅga, (4) Vasubandhu, (5) Ārya Vimuktisena, (6) Bhadanta Vimuktisena, (7) Varasena, (8) Vinayasena, (9) Vairocanabhadra, (10) Siṅghabhadra, (11) Kusali Senior, (12) Kusali Junior, (13) Sauvarṇadvīpa, and (14) Atiśa Dīpaṃkara.

The lineage of the profound view

(1) The perfect Buddha, (2) Mañjuśrī, (3) Nāgārjuna, (4) Āryadeva, (5) Candrakīrti, (6) the first Vidyākokila, (7) the second Vidyākokila, and (8) Atiśa.

The lineage of the blessing of practice

(1) Vajradhara, (2) Tilopa, (3) Nāropa, (4) Ḍombipa, and (5) Atiśa. From Atiśa a union of all three lineages was transmitted successively to (1) Geshé [Drom]tönpa, (2) Chengawa, (3) Jayülpa, and (4) Gampopa. Jayülpa met all three Geshé brothers.[558] Dromtön's pupils included Neusurpa, Nyukrumpa, Gyachak Riwa, and Shawa Lingpa, all of whom were teachers of Gampopa, and the lineage then continued from him.

> The child poisoned by sixty thousand contrived meditations
> was washed clean by innate mahāmudrā, the supreme purifier.
> Then the ascetic pleased Brahmā, who is the scholars
> and siddhas of India and Tibet,[559]
> and became the true fortunate chariot[560] that illuminated the three
> paths.
>
> However, in these latter times, there are those whose objectives
> are to cause confusion through scholasticism.
> They are pretas whose throats have become narrow.
> What can you do with such unworthy vessels?
>
> Nevertheless, using scripture and the guru's instructions, [189]
> I've written this brief text so as to increase my certainty,
> with the belief that it will be of benefit to myself alone.

I have written this brief commentary to *Prayer for the Definitive Meaning, the Mahāmudrā* in order to fulfill the requests that my younger brother, Karma Ngelek Tenzin—a creator of *satsa* images—has been making for a long time.

I, Situpa Tenpai Nyinjé completed this in Thupten Chökor Ling,[561] in the year of the water ox.[562]

May there be excellent goodness!

Maṅgalaṃ śrījaya puṣṭiṃ bhavatu.[563]

8. The Bright Torch

The Perfect Illumination of the True Meaning of the Mahāmudrā, the Essence of All the Dharma

TSELÉ NATSOK RANGDRÖL (B. 1608)

[191] *Namo mahāmudraye* (Homage to mahāmudrā)

> I make an offering through the homage of perfectly realizing
> the luminosity of the true nature, the supreme wisdom,
> the primordial, completely pure, natural state,
> which is devoid of all conceptual elaboration.
>
> I give this teaching so that we may recognize for ourselves
> the natural state of the innate inseparability
> of the apparent aspect, the variety of manifestations,
> and the essential aspect, their lack of any existence.

THE ESSENTIAL MEANING of all the infinite, endless teachings of all the conquerors is that the essence of a tathāgata's wisdom is present in the nature of beings. In order to reveal this, the conquerors teach countless, specific aspects or vehicles of the Dharma, within which there are as many different teachings and instructions as there are different aspirations and capabilities among pupils. This is the special, marvelous power of the compassionate activity of the buddhas.

Supreme among these teachings is mahāmudrā, which is as famous as the sun and moon. It is the fast path of the ultimate meaning, the summit of all the resultant Mantrayānas or Vajrayānas. It is the supreme method that easily and directly reveals the face of the mind's nature, the natural presence of the three kāyas. It is the single great path traveled by all the supreme siddhas and vidyādharas.

I will briefly teach the necessary essentials of its meaning in three parts. What are these three?

I. The basis mahāmudrā, which is the true nature of things: a brief teaching on the two aspects of delusion and liberation [192]

II. The path mahāmudrā, which is self-arisen, natural resting: a detailed explanation of how a practitioner follows the path of śamatha and vipaśyanā

III. The result mahāmudrā, which is stainless true buddhahood: a conclusion that explains how beings are benefited by the manifestations of the three kāyas

I. The basis mahāmudrā

Samsara and nirvana have no real existence whatsoever. Their nature is without aspect or division, unstained by such terms as happiness or suffering, is or isn't, existent or nonexistent, eternalism or nihilism, self or other. Therefore, it is free from all extremes of [conceptual] embellishment and has no existent essence. The key point is that it is the basis for any kind of appearance or characteristic to arise, but that whatever appears has no real existence.

This noncomposite dharmadhātu, the great emptiness free from the three extremes of arising, remaining, and ceasing, has primordially been the naturally present three kāyas. This is the basis, the true nature of things, which is called *mahāmudrā*. It is said in the *Secret Essence* [*Tantra*]:

> This mind, which is without root or basis,
> is the root of all phenomena.[564]

It is not like that in just one individual or in the mind continuum of just one buddha; it is the all-pervading basis for the entirety of all appearances and beings, all of samsara and nirvana.

Those who realize or know this true nature or identity are called *buddhas*. Those who do not realize or know it are deluded and are called *beings*. This is the basis for wandering in samsara. Therefore, it is known as the *basis of samsara and nirvana*. The Great Brahman Saraha has said:

> The mind alone is the seed of all.
> Samsara and nirvana emanate from it.[565]

Thus, there is one essence with different aspects, and these aspects appear simply as a result of it being realized or not. However, the essence of these two aspects is the great primordial inseparability of the three kāyas, which is never polluted by faults such as [the duality of] good and bad, or change. Within the general vehicles this is called the *changeless absolute*.[566] This is the true nature of the primordial basis. [193]

The true nature as a neutral impartiality, neither realized nor unrealized, is called the *ālaya* ("basis of everything") because it is the basis of both samsara and nirvana. The ālaya is not a total emptiness in which there is nothing. Rather, like a mirror and its clarity, there is an unimpeded self-illuminating knowing, which is called the *ālaya consciousness*.

The way in which samsara and nirvana arise separately from this single ālaya

The knowing or wisdom aspect of self-illuminating cognition is the essence of the knowing that is an inseparability of the essence, which is emptiness, and the nature, which is clarity. It is the seed, or cause, of all the qualities of buddhahood and all the Dharmas of the true path. Therefore, all the synonyms for nirvana correspond to it, such as the true ālaya, buddha nature, self-knowing, dharmakāya, perfection of wisdom, the buddhahood of one's own mind, and so on. This is what practitioners of the path have to directly perceive and recognize.

Alternatively, the dullness aspect of the neutral ālaya is not knowing oneself, that is to say, obscuring oneself through not knowing one's true nature. This is called *innate ignorance*, the *great darkness of beginningless time*, and also the *ālaya of diverse propensities*, as all afflictions and deluded thoughts arise because of it. It is the basis for the delusion of all beings. It is said in the *Tantra of the Unimpeded View*:

> When knowing does not arise in the basis
> there is a dull mindlessness.
> This is the cause of ignorance and delusion.[567]

Accompanying this ignorance, as a kind of retinue, are the seven kinds of thought that arise from ignorance, such as medium attachment and forgetfulness.

The conception of an "I" or self arises from that innate ignorance, and that causes the conception of others in relation to the self. Appearances coming from you are not recognized to be coming from you but are conceived of as external objects. That is how delusion begins: by not recognizing the concepts of subject and object for what they are. This is *conceptual ignorance*. It is also called *mental consciousness*. It is the deluded mind that creates the separation between mind and objects. It has a retinue of forty kinds of thoughts, such as craving and grasping, that arise from desire. [194] This mental consciousness has the power to create and multiply a variety of propensities and delusions. It is aided by karmic wind as a pervasive condition and the ālaya's causal ignorance. The developing power of factors of dependent origination such as these—the triad of body, appearances, and mind—are completely created. The arising of separate five sense consciousnesses and the thoughts and perceptions of all six sense consciousnesses is what is called the *dependent*.[568]

The five major root winds, the five minor branch winds, and the rest serve as steeds for thoughts. At the same time habituation to being fixated on delusion causes the appearances that come from yourself to appear to be the world and its inhabitants. Thus this forms both the foundational basis and its object and gives rise to everything. This is what is called the *afflicted mind*. It is also called the *consciousnesses of the five senses*, because it creates attachment and so on through each of the five sensory organs. This is accompanied by thirty-three thoughts that arise from anger, such as medium nonattachment.[569] The ālaya and its diverse propensities are the roots, and the eighty kinds of thoughts have the nature of being branches. This is a sequential development that forms the unbroken continuum of delusion that causes you to wander endlessly in samsara. That is how beings without realization are deluded.

The propensities for every phenomena of samsara and nirvana are present in the form of seeds within the ālaya. They are the cause of the appearance, through a process of dependent origination, of all internal substances (the evident material body and also its various channels, winds, and drops, and its purities and impurities) and all external substances (the worlds and beings of the three realms of samsara and nirvana). These do not truly exist but are relative, illusory appearances, just like whatever appears in a dream. Extremely strong habituation to the belief that they are permanent, and to attachment to solidity and reality, causes the experience of the various states of happiness, suffering, and neutrality within the three realms and the six classes of beings. Thus, the causes and results of samsara cycle continuously and naturally, like a water wheel. That is the general characteristics of beings, but even while they are deluded and wandering in samsara, all these obscurations cannot cause even an atom's worth of degeneration in the element of buddha nature, which is the essence of knowing. It is said in the *Hevajra Tantra*:

All beings are indeed buddhas
but are obscured by extrinsic impurities.[570] [195]

Ultimately, the primordial true nature is brilliant since it is the inseparability of the three kāyas. Even during the intermediate period, when the extrinsic stains of illusory appearances obscure it, its own nature is as radiant as the three kāyas. In the end, too, when the obscurations have been cleared away and the result of developing the two wisdoms has been made manifest, it shines as the three kāyas.

Therefore, the terms *liberation* and *illusion* signify only whether there is freedom from the stains of ignorance and illusory thought or not. It is said in the *Sublime Continuum*:

As it was before, so it is afterward.
It has the quality of changelessness.[571]

Therefore, the mind naturally has a primordially pure essence. The extrinsic illusions or innate ignorance are like discolorations forming on gold, arising from itself and obscuring itself. [The Buddha] taught a variety of distinct methods for its cleansing and purification, but [the mind's] essence is the aspect of wisdom itself, the self-arising wisdom that remains unchanged throughout the three times and is free from conceptual elaboration. Thus, the ultimate viewpoint of the Conqueror is that method and wisdom includes all paths.

You might ask, "But how can samsara and nirvana possibly be divisions of this single ālaya?" The answer is that camphor as a medicine can be either beneficial or harmful according to whether the illness is a hot or a cold illness. A poisonous substance can be transformed into medicine by certain methods, such as mantras, but it will kill you if you take it without those methods. In the same way, you will be liberated if you know and recognize the two essences of the ālaya, but you will be deluded if you do not and, instead, conceive of a self. This difference is simply the result of having or not having realization. Ārya Nāgārjuna has said:

Those who are caught in the net of afflictions,
are those who are called *beings*.
Those who are free from the afflictions
are those who are called *buddhas*.[572]

Therefore, if you follow the instructions on mahāmudrā, which is the definitive meaning and the essence of the entire Dharma, you will attain the true nature itself, which is the basis mahāmudrā. The path mahāmudrā purifies you of the stains of illusory thoughts, and the result mahāmudrā is gaining the kingdom of the three kāyas. As this opens the treasury of the two benefits, worthy and prepared individuals should seek out a guru with the necessary qualities and the quintessential blessing. They should follow him as described in the accounts [196] of Sudhana and Sadāprarudita[573] or in the biographies of Tilopa and Nāropa.

You definitely need to be ripened by the stages of a ripening [empowerment], whatever its degree of nonelaboration or elaboration. That is the principal entranceway into the Vajrayāna path. Until you have obtained the signs [of accomplishment], dedicate yourself, without being perfunctory, idle, or indifferent, to all the general and special preliminaries, which are highly valued as leading to the liberating instructions.

In particular, dedicate yourself to the sincere practice of guru-yoga devotion, which will definitely bring the power of blessing to you. That is the essence of the practice of all Kagyü siddhas and vidyādharas. It is said in the *Tantra of the Great River of Pacification*:

> This innate wisdom, which is beyond description,
> is solely the result of gathering the accumulations, purifying the obscurations,
> and receiving the blessing of a realized guru.
> You must know that those who rely on other methods are foolish.[574]

As for the main practice, there are different traditions with some recognizing meditation through the view and some gaining certainty in view through meditation, and so on. Whichever tradition you follow, the main important thing is receiving the blessing of the guru and lineage.

As for the view, there are countless ways of teaching it in the different philosophical traditions and vehicles, and each of them has established its own view as being true. All these vehicles are countless, infinite doorways established by activity of the Conqueror, and therefore I don't declare one to be correct and another not, or one good and another bad; instead I rejoice in them all.

The view that I will explain here is that the nature of the mind is a primordial, naturally present, great, complete purity. It is free from the elaborations of coming and going, arising, remaining, and ceasing in the three times of the past, future, and present. It is unpolluted by the concepts of samsara, nirvana, and the path. It does not have the conceptual embellishments of existence or nonexistence, being or not being, eternalism or nihilism, good or bad, high or low, and so on. It does not have cessation or creation, rejection or adoption, transformation or establishment of any phenomena within the appearances and existences that are samsara and nirvana.

This primordial state or quality has the nature of the vivid inseparability of appearance and emptiness; [197] the radiant unity of clarity and emptiness; the brilliant, all-pervading, primordial liberation; and bright, noncomposite natural presence. This is the primordial, self-arising nature of the principal view. It is the primordial, all-pervading essence of samsara and nirvana. Any other view is partial, fragmentary, and biased.

Knowing the falsehood of dualism through knowing this primordial nature is called *realizing the view*, *seeing the mind*, and *knowing the meaning of phenomena*. It is said in *Treasury of Dohas*:

> When you have realized it, it is everything.
> There is nothing else for anyone to know.[575]

Ultimately, all the phenomena of appearance and existence, of samsara and nirvana, are the display of the three kāyas. Even your own mind has the nature of the three kāyas. The [three kāyas] too are not outside the essential element that is the ultimate true nature.

All the phenomena of samsara are the characteristics of the mind. All Dharmas of the path are the qualities of the mind, and all the qualities of the result are the power of the mind.

The mind's unborn nature is the dharmakāya. [The mind's] unimpeded clarity is the saṃbhogakāya. [The mind's] power to appear as anything is the nirmāṇakāya. Those three are naturally present as an inseparable essence. Gaining certainty through recognizing this nature is called the *faultless, unmistaken view* and *true realization*.

Any other view with concepts, such as of being liberated or not being liberated from the extremes, of being high or low, or of being good or bad—any view or meditation in which mental fabrication and analysis create concepts—will not be the view of mahāmudrā.

II. The path mahāmudrā, which is self-arisen, natural resting: a detailed explanation of how a practitioner follows the path of śamatha and vipaśyanā

This teaching includes śamatha, vipaśyanā, faults and qualities, meditation and post-meditation, how the practitioner should follow the path, and so on.

[A. Śamatha]

Generally, the word *meditation* can refer to many things. There are countless methods of meditation in the different traditions, but here the word or term *meditation* refers solely to internal familiarization with the natural state, that is, to the view that has just been explained. [198] It does not signify a mentally contrived meditation on things with color and shape, or meditation on an artificial emptiness where all the mind's movements, thoughts, appearances, and perceptions have ceased. Here, meditation is solely maintaining your mind just as it is, without creating anything.

Specifically, there are varying capacities or minds. There are "immediate" individuals who have sharp faculties and evidently have trained in their past lives. They don't need to be guided through sequential stages of śamatha and vipaśyanā because they become liberated immediately on their direct introduction [to the nature of the mind].

However, ordinary people need to be guided in stages. They begin with training in śamatha on an object such as a twig, a pebble, a deity's image, a syllable, a round spot (*bindu*), or the breath. When they have gained stability in those practices, they practice supreme, objectless śamatha. This is true śamatha, and it is taught through three methods:

1. The mind rests in a fresh and undistracted state, in which it is not distracted by any internal or external object.
2. The three doors rest effortlessly, naturally, and loosely, without being very tightly controlled.
3. There is no separation or division, as when applying a remedy, between cognizance and the essence of thoughts. Instead there is just resting in the mind's self-knowing, self-clarity, and self-purity.

These three [methods] are also known as *nondistraction*, *nonmeditation*, and *nonfabrication*.

These also include the three doors of liberation taught within the general vehicles:

1. The door of liberation called *signlessness* is when the mind is not concerned with past activities, with thoughts about what was done or what happened, and so on.
2. The door of liberation called *emptiness* is when the present mind performs no mental modifications, neither creating nor stopping anything because of thinking that something has appeared or something needs to be done.
3. The door of liberation named *no aspiration* is [the mind] not thinking forward to what may happen in the future and having no expectations, such as hoping to be able to meditate or worrying about not being able to meditate.

These can be briefly summarized into just resting the mind naturally, as it is, unpolluted by alteration.

When a thought suddenly appears within that state, [199] it is enough to simply be clearly aware of it, without becoming involved with it. Don't try to stop the thought in any way. Don't try to bring back meditation or apply some other remedy. Anything like that isn't the key point for maintaining an unaltered, unfabricated mind.

There are various [teachings] in other different paths, but this is the path of simply recognizing whatever arises. Any other method you use will not be mahāmudrā meditation. The Great Brahman has said:

> Beings are polluted by seeking meditation.
> There is nothing at all on which to meditate.
> A single instant of being without any yearning.
> That is the meditation of mahāmudrā.[576]

When directly resting in the nature of mind as it is, the experiences of the three states of śamatha will sequentially arise. What are they?

The first [śamatha]

There will be brief periods when the mind appears to be wilder, with more thoughts than ever before. Don't think that producing these thoughts is a fault, for there has never been anything but this production [of thoughts]; it's just that you were not aware of them. When you become aware of the difference between the mind at rest and the mind producing thoughts, [you will have reached] the first śamatha, which is like a waterfall.

[The second śamatha]

As a result of maintaining that [first śamatha], most of your thoughts will be subdued and move gently. Your body and mind will feel comfortable. You will be attracted to meditation and have no longing to engage in other activities. Most of the time, you will have a powerful stability without any movement or production of thoughts. This is the intermediate śamatha, which is said to be like the slow flow of a great river.

[The third śamatha]

If you continue to practice diligently, without distraction, you will reach a state where your body will have intense bliss with no sensation of pain. Your mind will have an unblemished purity and clarity that transcends the afflictions, which are no longer experienced. For as long as you meditate, you will be unwavering, with nothing being able to disturb you. Obvious afflictions will cease. You will have little attachment to food, clothes, and so on. You will have various experiences of the sights and limited clairvoyance. You will gain many such general "qualities." That is the ultimate śamatha, which is like an unmoving ocean.

There have been many meditators with strong dedication but little learning, and without an experienced teacher, who during this stage became proud of these outward qualities. Then people believed them to be siddhas, [200] which proved disastrous for others as well as themselves. So be careful this doesn't happen to you.

It's been taught that the practice of śamatha alone cannot be the true practice of mahāmudrā, but as it is its foundation, it is truly of great importance. Gyalwa Lorepa has said:

> Even if you meditate for a long time in a relaxed śamatha
> that is devoid of clarity, you will not realize the meaning.
> Meditate, with the sharpness of knowing's gaze,
> in a continuity of successive short sessions.[577]

B. The main practice: vipaśyanā

You need to investigate, until doubts are eradicated, whether the nature of the mind has truly existing characteristics, such as shape and color, and whether it has arising, abiding, and going; birth and cessation; or existence or nonexistence; whether it is eternal or nothing; has edges or a center; and so on. If you do not do that, you will not gain the actual view, and therefore you will not know how to maintain natural resting, natural meditation. Then, however dedicated you are to controlling your mind, your śamatha will be stupid and forced, and you will never transcend the karma of samsara's three realms. Therefore, with a genuine teacher, you must eradicate your misconceptions. In particular, as you are a practitioner of the Mantrayāna, the path of blessing, devote yourself to devotional prayers, dedicating yourself to the method for receiving the lineage's blessing for realization.

When you do that, your own knowing will be the natural presence of the primordial dharmakāya, as previously described in the description of the view. It is a nonconceptual, directly experienced wisdom that does not fall into any extreme, such as existence or nonexistence, being or not being, eternalism or nihilism. Although you will know and experience the inseparability of clarity, knowing, and emptiness, you will have no example to give for it and no way to express it in words. This clear, self-arising self-illumination is called *vipaśyanā*.

At first, while you're still an ordinary being, although it's never apart from you for even an instant, you fail to recognize it because you haven't received the instructions and the blessing. In the intermediate period, it is what rests in śamatha, what sees and knows whether you are at rest or not, and so on, but though it is all this, it does not see itself. The continuous production of thoughts in the ordinary state is nothing other than this vipaśyanā itself appearing as thoughts. The experience of śamatha and of bliss, clarity, and nonthought are nothing but the arising of this vipaśyanā's knowing. [201]

If you do not know your own naked nature, free from thought, you will have mental stability only, which cannot be a cause of enlightenment. Once you have seen your own nature, all mental stillness or production will be nothing other than vipaśyanā or mahāmudrā. Lorepa has said:

> Do not engage in mental fixation upon
> anything that appears to the six consciousnesses.
> Everything is self-appearing and self-liberating.
> All you meditators, have you realized this inseparability?[578]

In general, it is said:

> Śamatha is when thoughts cease of themselves and the mind rests in clarity, bliss, and nonthought. Vipaśyanā is clearly seeing the naked nature of the mind as self-illuminating, objectless, and without embellishment.[579]

It is also taught:

> Alternatively, śamatha is freedom from the production and dissolution of thoughts, while vipaśyanā is the recognition of that process itself.[580]

There are many such statements, but their meaning is that whatever appears, whatever arises, is nothing other than the inseparability of śamatha and vipaśyanā. All [mental] stillness and movement is nothing other than the play of the mind itself. Therefore, if you have this recognition during either stillness or movement, that is vipaśyanā.

Śamatha is when there is no attachment to solidity in relation to any external appearance to the six consciousnesses. Vipaśyanā is the unimpeded appearance of whatever arises in the mind. Therefore, appearances possess the complete union of vipaśyanā and śamatha.

Śamatha is the clear awareness of a thought as it vividly arises. Vipaśyanā is when that thought is liberated within the naked, intellect-free mind. Therefore thoughts, too, contain the union of vipaśyanā and śamatha.

Śamatha is when you do not perceive the arising of intense afflictions as solid but see instead their very nature. Vipaśyanā is naked clarity and emptiness in which there is no separation between the seer's knowing and the seen afflictions. Therefore, in afflictions also you find the complete union of vipaśyanā and śamatha.

In brief, there is no stillness or movement, emanation or absorption, or good or bad within the nature of the mind. All those appearances are simply its unimpeded power of display. Śamatha and vipaśyanā, too, are simply that kind of inseparable union. Nevertheless, to make it easier for people to engage in their different aspects, there is the teaching of their having separate names and categories.

The reason why it's said that śamatha alone is not true mahāmudrā meditation is that mental stability alone is only a mundane teaching. It's the same as the dhyānas of the tīrthikas, the Buddhist śrāvakas and pratyekabuddhas, and the samādhis of the deva realms. [202] It is not the genuine path of the Mantrayāna's fourth empowerment, and it especially cannot be mahāmudrā if there is any attachment to the experience of mental stability, because in mahāmudrā, all appearances and existences become the path of the dharmakāya. If the mind's stillness is practiced and its movement is avoided, with one seen as good and the other bad, with one seen as meditation and the other not, then appearances and existences will not be the dharmakāya. Rather, practice where everything that appears, without any alteration, *is* the mahāmudrā.

Having briefly described what śamatha and vipaśyanā means, I now give a brief description of faults, qualities, and possible errors. This has two parts:

1. The general errors of not knowing how to maintain meditation
2. Various specific errors and blunders, and how to eliminate them

1. The general errors of not knowing how to maintain meditation

Resting in the unaltered mind is the essential meaning of all the countless, profound, and vast meditation instructions, such as mahāmudrā, dzokchen, result as the path (*lamdré*), severance (*chö*), and pacification (*shiché*). Nevertheless, these different kinds of instructions exist because individuals differ in their understanding.

Some meditators say that meditation is simply the nonconceptual knowledge that all the obvious and subtle perceptions of the six consciousnesses have ceased, but this is just relaxed śamatha. Some arrogantly assume that their meditation is stable when there is a neutral state of dullness devoid of aware mindfulness. Some state that meditation is a state of mind that has perfect clarity, vivid bliss, and utter emptiness, but this is merely being fixated on meditation experiences. Some say that all meditation is simply the blank consciousness that comes between the cessation of one thought and the arising of the next, but that is fragmentary meditation. Some say that meditation is maintaining such thoughts as "The mind is the dharmakāya. It is empty. It is ungraspable," or "Nothing has any reality. Everything is like an illusion, like space," and so on, but this is falling into the extreme of mental fabrication and mental analysis. Some say that meditation is just whatever you think of, whatever comes up in the mind, but this is to fall under the power of ordinary thoughts, which brings the danger of insanity. Most others say that the mind's movements are faults that must be stopped, that you rest in meditation by restraining the mind's movement, but this is having a mindfulness that is too strict and too tight, [203] which results in an uncomfortable mental bondage.

In brief, whether your mind is still or in movement, whether you have intense thoughts and afflictions or are in a vivid state of bliss, clarity, or nonthought, whatever is happening, there is no need for fabrication, alteration, elimination, or transformation. You only need to maintain a natural, innate process. In these times, when there are very few who know this, we need a faultless practice that accords with the actual view taught in the collected works, practice instructions, and manuals of the siddha lineages and in the sutras and tantras that teach the definitive meaning.

2. Various specific errors and blunders

The past masters in the practice lineage taught extensively and in detail about these errors and mistakes, whereas I will describe them here in just a few token sentences.

Attachment to experiences of clarity, bliss, or nonthought in your meditation will cause rebirth in the desire, form, or formless realms. When that life ends, you will fall into the lower existences, where you will no longer be on the path to buddhahood. We can examine this process in detail through the specifics of the nine dhyānas of concentration:

1. When you can rest in śamatha without any obvious thoughts of subject and object, but are still constrained by belief in there being a meditator and meditation, this is called the *first dhyāna's samādhi*, because this is how the devas in the first dhyāna realms meditate. Therefore, meditating in this way will cause you to be reborn as a first-dhyāna deva.
2. In the second dhyāna you do not analyze or examine with your thoughts, but you nevertheless are experiencing the flavor of blissful samādhi.
3. In the third dhyāna, your mind is unwavering, dependent solely upon the inhalation and exhalation of the breath.
4. The fourth dhyāna is a samādhi that is devoid of all thought and has a space-like unobstructed clarity.

Although those [four dhyānas] are renowned to be the highest among all mundane samādhis and are a basis for vipaśyanā, to meditate on them with attachment will be an error in mahāmudrā that causes rebirth as a dhyāna deva. There are also:

5. [The meditation of] thinking "All phenomena are infinite like space."
6. [The meditation of] thinking "This consciousness is not limited. It is infinite." [204]
7. [The meditation of] thinking "There is neither identification nor the absence of identification, so that the mind has no activity."
8. [The meditation of] thinking "This mind is empty. It is nothing whatsoever."

Resting in those four levels [of dhyāna] has the defect of straying into the four *āyatana* permutations of the formless [realms]: *infinite space, infinite consciousness, neither existence nor nonexistence,* and *nothingness.*

9. The śrāvaka's samādhi of peace: This is the state of mind in which all those thoughts are eliminated, all engagement with objects has ceased, and there is a stability in which both mind and breath's movements have ceased.

That is taught to be the ultimate śamatha, but if it's devoid of vipaśyanā, it's not what is meant here by faultless meditation.

Each of those nine concentration dhyānas have only the qualities of accomplishing such things as the clairvoyance or miraculous powers of their level, but you must also know that according to this teaching, let alone the ultimate goal of complete buddhahood, they don't even accomplish the relative, ostensible qualities. Even if they do incidentally accomplish them, if that causes attachment and pride, they will truly be obstacles to enlightenment.

Having explained those errors and wrong paths, I will now teach "the eight failings."

1. *The primordial failing in relation to the nature of emptiness*: This is not realizing the mind to "have the supreme of all aspects,"[581] a term that means the unity of appearance and emptiness as an unimpeded interdependence of causes and results. Instead, your focus is on emptiness alone. You must know this to be a defect.
2. *The circumstantial failing in relation to the nature [of emptiness]*: This is meditating with a comprehension of the meaning but without the experience of it having arisen within you—or you forget whatever experience you've had—so that though you can explain the meaning to others, you don't have it within yourself.
3. *The primordial failing in relation to the path*: This is thinking that what you need now is the path while the result is something else that will be obtained later.

4. *The circumstantial failing in relation the path*: This is thinking that simply maintaining the "ordinary mind"—your own mind—is not enough. Instead, you seek elsewhere for some longed for, imagined, marvelous meditation.
5. *The primordial failing in relation to remedies*: This is not realizing that when something like an affliction arises, that itself should be brought onto the path. Instead, you meditate by using other methods from the lower vehicles.
6. *The circumstantial failing concerning remedies*: This is not knowing that when something like a thought arises, it should be used as the path. Instead, you think that you must stop or destroy these factors in order to be in meditation.
7. *The primordial failing concerning the seal of emptiness*: This is not understanding that the mind is primordially empty, without any root. [205] Instead, you apply a seal of emptiness, such as a mentally fabricated emptiness or a transitory emptiness, by such thoughts as "This has no existing nature," or "This becomes empty."
8. *The circumstantial failing concerning the seal [of emptiness]*: This is continually thinking such thoughts as, "I used to be involved in thoughts, but now I meditate well." Or it's having no aware mindfulness[582] but thinking that you do have it, and so on.

To sum up, cutting through conceptual embellishment about the nature of things and knowing the flaws concerning the true nature are the key factors without which you will be in danger of falling into these similitudes of meditation; and all kinds of other things can happen too. However much effort you put into these similitudes of meditation, you will just tire yourself out to no purpose. Some even create the cause and conditions for a bad rebirth (such as meditation on a śamatha of "cessation" causing rebirth as a nāga). Therefore, it's very important that your meditation be without error.

Also, there are those who are attached to a dull, dim state of mind without thought, believing it to be śamatha. There are those who are proud of their conceptual examination and analysis, believing it to be vipaśyanā. There are those whose goal is a mindfulness that clings tightly to the solidity of existence. There are those who mistake a neutral equanimity for the unaltered state. There are those who mistake the common ordinary mind, which does not see the actual face of the true nature, for the unaltered, unfabricated, intrinsic "ordinary" mind. There are those who become attached to a good samādhi. There are those who believe that mere stained bliss, which is free of pain, is the natural supreme bliss. There are those who have not reached certainty in the recognition of objectless true nature and instead mistake fixation on a perceived object for the fixation-free, objectless, unceasing, natural clarity. And there are those who mistake mental dullness that is due to the cessation of clarity for nonconceptual wisdom.

C. A summary of the cause of every kind of error, similitude, mistake, and failing

In the beginning, there is the error of not purifying the stains of bad karma because of not properly engaging in the preliminaries, such as gathering the accumulations and purifying the obscurations.

In the intermediate period, there is the fault of having a mind that is coarse and stiff because it has not been moistened by blessing. There is also the error of becoming intractably focused on words and verbal Dharma because the main practice hasn't cut through conceptual embellishments in your mind.

In the end, you become unable to assimilate practice and are just a yellow-clad person belonging to neither this world nor the Dharma, or you will be just a merchant in the teachings of the practice lineage. There are plenty of people like that in this final stage of the era of degeneration. It is said in the *Ten Wheels of Kṣitigarbha Sutra*: [206]

> Those who are Cārvāka tīrthikas
> do not believe in the ripening of karma.
> As soon as they die, they are reborn in Avīci hell.
> They cause the ruin of others and also destroy themselves.[583]

It's important to make an effort to be in control of yourself so that you don't end up like that. Apply yourself single-mindedly to meditation without falling under the power of the errors and failings in view and meditation. The "subsequent knowledge" [of post-meditation] should also be in the grip of mindfulness and awareness, so that you don't inattentively remain in ordinary illusions. If you can do this, you will have experiences and realization according to your individual mentality and capability.

[D. Meditation and post-meditation]

Generally, scholars and siddhas have given numerous distinct teachings on meditation and post-meditation at this level, so that there are many different ways of identifying them. Some teach that in the four yogas there is no actual teaching on meditation and post-meditation below the level of nonelaboration. Some make a distinction between "realization's meditation and post-meditation" and "experience's meditation and post-meditation." Some teach easily perceived forms of meditation and post-meditation as distinct in each of the four yogas. There are innumerable teachings like this and, similarly, a variety of explanations on the difference between experience and realization. Some teach that all three [levels] of one-pointedness have only experience and no true realization. Some teach that when you have the true meditation [of one-pointedness] you see the essence of the mind. There seem to be innumerable subtle classificatory teachings like this. They manifest from the compassionate wish for methods that will train the countless different dispositions and natures that individuals have. Therefore, I have no doubt that they are all are true, and I take refuge in them all. I don't have the training, insight, and knowledge of that level, so if I were to give reasons why some are right and some are wrong, I'd be no different than a blind person trying to distinguish between good and bad colors.

Nevertheless, to briefly describe what I have been able to understand, *meditation* and *post-meditation* are terms or signifiers used in the practice of both [the generation and completion] stages. *Meditation* is concentration on the actual practice without being mixed with any other kind of activity. The term *post-meditation* is used for when [the practice] is mixed with other [activities] during the period in between sessions and so on. [207] Its knowledge is called *subsequent knowledge* and its "appearances" are called *subsequent appearances*. This use of these terms is agreed upon by all. In this teaching, *meditation* is used for when beginners are engaged in actual meditation, and *post-meditation* is used for when they are doing things, moving around, walking, eating, sleeping, and so on. However, when higher practitioners are completely free of delusion, they are said to have "inseparable meditation and post-meditation" or "ceaseless meditation."

Similarly, to make a distinction between experience and realization, they are, respectively, like a fault and a remedy in a practice that is not blended with the nature of the mind, at whatever level it may be. Experience is when the meditator and the meditation appear to be separate. Realization is gaining complete certainty that they are not separate from the mind but that it is the mind itself that arises as their natures. In brief, these two occur not only in meditation but in most practices of the path, such as guru yoga, compassion, bodhicitta, and the generation stage. For example, *comprehension* is like hearing from others a description of the shape and layout of Bodhgaya[584] so that you get a general impression of it in your mind that you can also relate to others. *Experience* is like seeing Bodhgaya from a distance or looking at a painting of its layout, so that you comprehend most of what there is to be known about it. *Realization* is like arriving at Bodhgaya and having the certainty of seeing it in all its details.

[E. How the practitioner should follow the path]

The way in which meditation and post-meditation are introduced into the mind depends on which of three levels of capability an individual is on. The immediate individuals are great beings who make their previous training evident; they have immediate comprehension, experience, and realization the moment they are shown a symbol, and without difficulty or effort they perfect these qualities. Medium individuals are of the "nonsequential" type. They are those for whom qualities of realization don't arise in a fixed order but are unpredictably high or low and may increase or decrease. Gradualist individuals are ordinary beings who progress, depending on their diligence, through a definite sequence of common, general practices.

[208] The graduated path for gradualist individuals includes the other two [paths], so I will explain that.

The common vehicles teach that you reach buddhahood by traversing the general ten levels and the five paths, but the unequaled Dakpo Kagyü succession of gurus and pupils teaches the particular four stages of yoga, each one divided into greater, lesser, and medium levels, making twelve. Lord Daö Shönu explained this to be the view of the [*Cakrasaṃvara*] *Tantra of the Inconceivable Secret*. That tantra says:

> The samādhi of the awesome lion awakens
> pure, unwavering, one-pointed knowledge
> from within self-knowing wisdom.
> The stable *patience* eradicates the suffering of the lower existences.

Second, through the samādhi that is like an illusion,
inconceivable samādhi arises as power
from the great meditation of nonelaboration.
Heat is attained and there is control over birth.

Third, the samādhi that is heroic
causes the realization of the one taste of multiplicity to arise.
You are a child of the buddhas of the three times and benefit others.
The *summit* is attained and there is continuous development.

Fourth, through application to the practice of nonmeditation,
which is the samādhi that is like a vajra,
there is the knowledge of wisdom and the Buddha realms are seen.
There is the unsought, naturally present state of the great *supreme quality*.[585]

This viewpoint is taught extensively in the *Laṅkāvatāra Sutra*, and it has also been clearly explained by Ācārya Śāntipa, who made classifications such as the five sights and omniscience. Guru Rinpoché also taught this in brief in the Nyingma tradition's mahāmudrā teachings, in the *Record of Key Points*, which combines the four yogas with the four eliminations. One-pointed [yoga is explained by the lines]:

Good and bad actions are purified in the mind
so that bad actions are naturally eliminated.

Nonelaboration:

The elaboration-free nature of the mind
eliminates all subjects and objects.

One taste:

Appearances arise as the dharmakāya
so that thoughts are spontaneously eliminated.

Nonmeditation:

Samsara and nirvana are known to have no real nature,
so that all dualism is eliminated.

It also teaches the view that the four yogas correspond with the *four certainties* of the path of engagement and so on:

Heat is seeing the essence of the mind.
Summit is realizing the birthless dharmakāya.
Patience is having neither samsara nor nirvana, neither adoption nor rejection.
The *supreme quality* is samsara and nirvana dissolving into the mind.[586] [209]

I will now give a seed-like description of:

1. The meaning of the four yogas
2. The way in which the four yogas arise in sequence
3. A supplement that explains how the sutra tradition's paths and stages are completely included within the four yogas

1. The meaning of the four yogas

This has four parts:

a. One-pointed yoga
b. Nonelaboration
c. One taste
d. Nonmeditation

a. One-pointed yoga

Lesser one-pointed yoga

Capable individuals who can cut through attachment to this life, see the guru as truly being a buddha, and truly receive blessing will, when resting in meditation, abide in states of clarity, bliss, and nonthought. They will attain stability and certainty. Their thoughts will be spontaneously liberated as they recognize them. This will be accompanied by the fixation of thinking "This is meditation."

Past practice-lineage masters taught that all three levels of one-pointed yoga were solely śamatha. However, in my understanding, there are some definite differences between individuals on these different levels. There are others who view these levels as being within the province of vipaśyanā because the single knowledge of the true nature always has the inherent quality of being a union of śamatha and vipaśyanā.

At this level, the "subsequent knowledge" predominantly perceives things as real, and the practitioner's sleep is no different from that of an ordinary person. In brief, as this is the initial stage, there will be various degrees of ease and difficulty to maintaining the practice.

Medium one-pointed yoga

During this stage, you are able to remain in meditation for as long as you wish. Samādhi will even arise sometimes when you're not meditating. Your "subsequent knowledge" will have a diminution of belief in reality, and appearances become spacious and clear. You can even at times practice while asleep. In brief, during this stage, whenever you meditate, you *will* be meditating.

Greater one-pointed [yoga]

It's taught that there will be a constant experience, day and night, of bliss, clarity, and nonthought. There will be no distinct "subsequent appearances," "subsequent knowledge," and so on, as they will always be within samādhi. You will have no external or internal parasites. You will have no attachment to sensory pleasures. You will attain clairvoyance, miraculous powers, and so on. However, you will still not be free yet from attachment to good experiences and you will not yet be liberated from the bondage of your mind's fixation on meditation. Therefore, there can be many individual variations because of such factors as someone's diligence or level of capability for engaging in these three stages of one-pointed [yoga]. [210]

Seeing the essence of one-pointed [yoga] is dependent on attaining the confidence that comes from the certainty of self-knowing in the very essence of bliss, clarity, and nonthought. Similarly, attaining mastery depends on your experiences being continuous. "Thoughts arising as meditation" depends on simply training in mindfulness of every thought that arises. The "arising of qualities" depends on your mind becoming tractable. Planting the seed of the form kāyas depends on uncontrived compassion arising during "subsequent knowledge." Fully understanding relative [truth] depends on certainty in the interdependence of causes and results. Past Kagyü masters have taught that we must know these categories.

b. Nonelaboration yoga

Whatever experiences you have in one-pointed [yoga], if you can apply yourself to practice and prayer without falling under the power of the arrogant belief in a self and attachment to good [experiences], then you will progress to [the yoga of] nonelaboration.

Lesser nonelaboration

You truly realize that the mind has no extremes of arising, remaining, and ceasing. When you have mindfulness, your "subsequent knowledge" is liberated as meditation, but when there is no mindfulness it still has the perception of solidity. In your dreams, you are sometimes deluded and sometimes not. At this level, there is fixation on emptiness, with such thoughts as, "All the phenomena of appearance and existence are nothing but emptiness," and so on.

Medium nonelaboration

You are purified of fixation on emptiness, on the reality of thoughts, and so on, though there remains the impurity of a subtle fixation on the reality of external appearances. During subsequent [attainment] and sleep, there may or may not be delusion and perception of solidity. In your practice, too, there can be many different levels and both progress and regress.

Great nonelaboration

You completely cut through all conceptual embellishments concerning samsara and nirvana, outer appearances and the mind. You become liberated from attachment to whether there are appearances or no appearances, emptiness or no emptiness, and so on. During most of your waking hours you have continuous meditation, while in your dreams you are occasionally fixated on delusions. However, at this level there still isn't an uninterrupted, unchanging continuity of mindfulness. Therefore, you still need some control of mindfulness.

In brief, the key point of the stage of nonelaboration is that it is principally the experience of emptiness [211] and the experience of the unreality of everything. Therefore, there is the possibility of a decline in devotion, pure perception, compassion, and so on. So it's important not to become overpowered by the obstacle of emptiness becoming your enemy.

At this level, seeing the essence of nonelaboration depends on becoming purified of the stain of certainty that is fixation on emptiness. Attaining mastery of it depends on becoming free from hope and fear concerning appearances and emptiness, and on cutting through conceptual embellishment of the path. Thoughts arising as meditation depend on training, during both subsequent appearances and sleep, in the realization of meditation that recognizes all movement of thought to be nothing other than emptiness. The arising of qualities depends on being connected with such apparent signs of accomplishment as the twelve hundred qualities from seeing the truth of the realized meaning. The full understanding of relative [truth] and planting the seed of the form kāyas depends on gaining certainty in the radiant power of emptiness manifesting as causes and results, and on then establishing the factors of dependent origination through bodhicitta and prayer. It's been taught that we must know these and other categories.

c. One-taste yoga

When you have fully realized the level of nonelaboration, you realize that all dualistic names and categories, such as samsara and nirvana, appearance and emptiness, generation and completion, relative and ultimate, and so on, are of one taste in the mahāmudrā. You are able to absorb all the path's Dharma teachings into self-knowing.

The lesser level of one taste

This is while there is still some bondage to certainty or to fixation on experience.

Medium one taste

This is when you are purified of fixation on experience and realize the inseparability of appearances and mind. The realizer's knowing and that which is realized are not fixated upon as having either a separate reality or a single one. Therefore, there is liberation from subject and object.

Greater one taste

This is when all phenomena appear as the "one taste of multiplicity" so that there is the increasing power of wisdom, which is the realization of one taste itself arising as multiplicity. The great holders of the practice lineage have taught that at this time meditation and post-meditation become blended.

All appearances and thoughts have the primordial nature of the dharmakāya, or the mahāmudrā, but there is a perception of solidity, a duality of subject and object, and so on, in relation to appearances, to illusion. If you train in self-knowing mindfulness of these things, they will be spontaneously liberated. [212] This occurs in the lower yogas, too, but the training on this stage doesn't require a separate mindfulness or recognition, as any appearance or arising is itself enough. Seeing the essence of one taste depends on that. The mastery of it depends on the one taste arising as multiplicity and there not being any residue of subtle attachment to remedy. Thoughts arising as meditation depend on there being neither bondage nor liberation in the unrestricted appearance of all perceptions to the six consciousnesses. The arising of qualities depends on wisdom controlling all inner and outer phenomena and having the autonomy of performing miraculous emanations and transformations. Understanding the relative depends on the cause and result of power over appearances and existences being adopted as the path, which occurs through blending mind and appearances so that there is realization of the one taste as multiplicity. Planting the seed of the form kāyas depends on the treasury of benefiting others being opened by the power of effortless, all-pervading compassion.

d. Nonmeditation yoga

When you have completed [the yoga] of one taste, you will be purified of all dualistic appearances, such as meditation or no meditation, distraction or no distraction. All appearances will be liberated as the great primordial meditation.

Lesser nonmeditation

This is when, at night or at other times, there is a subtle fixation on the illusion-like nature of the propensities for subsequent appearances.

Medium nonmeditation

This is when you are completely purified of fixation on illusion. Day and night, everything is one great meditation, and the true nature is manifest. However, you are still not free from wisdom's own obscuration, which is a subtle self-illuminating aspect of consciousness that is the "stain of knowledge."

Greater nonmeditation

This is when there is the complete elimination of the subtle obscuration of knowledge, which is like the remainder of the *ālaya* consciousness and is the failure to recognize nonthought. The mother and child luminosity blend together, so that everything ripens as the single quintessence of the dharmakāya, the total expanse of wisdom. This is also called *true, complete buddhahood.* It is the final result.

It's taught that seeing the essence of nonmeditation depends on being purified of the "knowledge of experience," such as habituation to repeated meditation on the full realization of one taste. [213] The mastery of nonmeditation depends on the wisdom of realization being free of all the subtlest stains of ignorance and all the propensities for objects of knowledge.

Thoughts arise as meditation through the *ālaya*'s propensities dissolving into dharmadhātu wisdom. Qualities appear through the material body becoming a rainbow body, through the mind becoming the dharmakāya, through infinite pure realms appearing, or through liberation. The seeds of the form kāyas manifest through the body as a "wheel of inexhaustible adornments," effortlessly benefiting beings throughout space. All relative aspects are purified into the essential nature through all the great qualities of buddhahood being complete. Past Kagyüpas have explained these and all other very subtle categories.

2. A brief summary of the four yogas: [the way in which the four yogas arise in sequence]

One-pointedness is being able to remain in meditation for as long as you wish. Nonelaboration is the ordinary mind recognizing itself and the realization of baselessness and sourcelessness. One taste is when attachment to the dualism of samsara and nirvana is liberated within knowing. Nonmeditation is the purification of all stains, which are certainties and propensities.

In particular, during one-pointed [yoga] the difference between meditation and post-meditation is whether you are in stillness or not. During nonelaboration, the [difference between] meditation and post-meditation is whether you have mindfulness or not. In the one-taste yoga and above, meditation and post-meditation are inseparably blended.

Also, one-pointed yoga is when the nature of thoughts arises as nonthought. Nonelaboration is when they arise as emptiness. One taste is when they arise as equality. Nonmeditation is when they arise transcending the intellect.

Also, during one-pointedness, delusion arises just as it is. Within nonelaboration, it is realized to be baseless and sourceless. During one taste, delusion arises as wisdom. In nonmeditation, there are no longer the terms *delusion* and *no delusion*.

Also, each one has its own consummation: The supreme realization in one-pointedness is the inseparability of stillness and movement; in nonelaboration, it is the inseparability of delusion and liberation; in one taste, it is the inseparability of appearances and mind; in nonmeditation, it is the inseparability of meditation and post-meditation.

Also, in one-pointedness, the mind has the perception of solidity. In nonelaboration the mind has meditation and post-meditation. In one taste the mind has union. In nonmeditation the mind is manifest. [214]

Also, during one-pointedness, thoughts are subjugated. During nonelaboration, thoughts are cut through. During one taste, self-arising wisdom appears from within. During nonmeditation that wisdom becomes stable.

To sum up, it seems the list of divisions and categories is endless and indescribable, but the most important thing we need to know and the only thing that matters is recognizing the true nature, the true meaning of the mind exactly as it is, and to know how to maintain the natural state of the ordinary mind, just as it happens to be, without polluting it with mental fabrication. According to Jñānaḍākinī Niguma:

> If you do not know that whatever appears is meditation,
> how can you attain it through relying on remedies?
> You cannot eliminate objects and conditions by eliminating them,
> but if you know they are illusions, they are spontaneously liberated.[587]

Most Dharma practitioners in these times are proud and bound tightly by this world's bondage. They are interested only in accumulating food, clothes, happiness, desires, objects, and artifacts for this life. Some have no control over their own minds because they're intoxicated by the poison that is their pride and arrogance of knowing many terms and teachings.

There are a few people interested in meditation on the definitive meaning, but lacking a genuine teacher and teachings, they are imprisoned in the discomfort of forced meditation. Not knowing how to practice open spaciousness, they practice a lot of stupid meditation, bought at the cost of their life force.

Most other meditators are bad; they're all talk, they're like an empty bellows or a stew made from lungs, and the mountains and valleys are filled with them. In such times as these, there's little point in teaching the qualities of the four yogas. It's like describing water in a desert.

Foremost worthy ones, who have unalloyed experience and realization, don't rely on external words and letters. Their wisdom is from meditation; it has come from within. So I'm well aware that there's no need for teachings such as mine that resemble someone describing some faraway place they've never seen.

Worthy individuals with diligence who rely on a pure teacher, receive blessing, and dedicate themselves to practice are genuine individuals who gain the realizations and experiences of the four yogas as taught here and elsewhere. They also incidentally pass through the entire five paths [215] and ten levels of the common vehicles. It is said in the *King of Meditations Sutra*:

> Whatever man holds this supreme samādhi,
> wherever that Dharma holder goes,
> [he will completely illuminate all beings]
> and will have a perfectly peaceful conduct and mind.
>
> He will also attain the ten levels:
> Perfect Joy, Stainless, Shining, Blazing,
> Difficult to Master, Manifest, Gone Far,
> Undisturbed, Excellent Intelligence, and Dharma Clouds.[588]

[3. A supplement that explains how the sutra tradition's paths and levels are completely included within the four yogas]

First, on the lesser, medium, and greater stages of the path of accumulation, there appear the four mindfulnesses, the four complete eliminations, and the four bases of miraculous powers. However, the way in which these are completely included within the swift path of mahāmudrā instructions is as follows:

First, there are the general preliminaries, in which there is the contemplation on the suffering of samsara, the difficulty of attaining the freedoms and opportunities, the impermanence of life, and so on. This naturally includes:

a. The mindfulness of the impurity of the body
b. The mindfulness of the sensation of suffering
c. The mindfulness of the impermanence of the mind
d. The mindfulness of the selflessness of phenomena

Therefore, when you have experienced, contemplated, and gained certainty in the key points of [the general preliminaries] you will have traversed the lesser path of accumulation.

In the same way, taking refuge, developing bodhicitta, reciting the hundred syllables, and offering the mandala include the four complete eliminations:

a. Not giving rise to bad actions
b. Rejecting those that have arisen
c. Developing good qualities
d. Increasing those that have been developed

Therefore, this is traversing the medium path of accumulation. Subsequently, the four bases of miraculous powers are in the guru yoga:

a. One-pointed devotion to the guru is aspiration as a basis for miraculous powers.
b. Prayer [to the guru] is diligence as a basis for miraculous powers.
c. Receiving the four empowerments is conduct as a basis for miraculous powers.
d. The final blending of the guru with your own mind is the mind's samādhi as a basis for miraculous powers.

This is traversing the greater path of accumulation.

The Perfection Vehicle teaches that through completing the path of accumulation you develop such qualities as being able to go to pure realms and see the faces of nirmāṇakāya buddhas. The mahāmudrā corresponds with that view, because the supreme guru is the essence of the three kāyas of buddhahood and all his "realms of pupils" are nothing other than nirmāṇakāya realms. [216]

The stages of lesser, medium, and greater one-pointedness correspond to the path of engagement:

a. Seeing the essence of the mind is [the path of engagement's level of] *heat.*
b. Developing certainty in that is [the path of engagement's level of] *summit.*
c. Being unaffected by circumstances is [the path of engagement's level of] *patience.*
d. The continuous experience of one-pointedness is the path of engagement's worldly *supreme quality.*

During this stage, the specific qualities of the *five powers* arise:

a. The arising of limitless certainty is the power of faith.
b. Viewing the meaning without distraction is the power of mindfulness.
c. Not having laziness as an obstacle is the power of diligence.
d. An unbroken continuity of meditation is the power of samādhi.
e. The realization of the definitive meaning is the power of wisdom.

Each of those five develop into consummations of their power, which are called *strengths*. Therefore, when the three levels of one-pointedness are realized, you have completed the path of engagement.

At [the level of] nonelaboration, you enter the path of seeing the realized truth that you have learned about but have never seen before. This level naturally includes the meditations on the aspects of enlightenment taught in the Perfection Vehicle:

a. Remaining in the meaning of the true nature of phenomena, exactly as it is, is the enlightenment aspect of *samādhi*.
b. Being untainted by afflictions is the enlightenment aspect of the *perfect differentiation of phenomena*.
c. Mere mindfulness of samādhi spontaneously purifying stains on the path of seeing is the enlightenment aspect of *mindfulness*.
d. Freedom from the distraction of laziness is the enlightenment aspect of *diligence*.
e. The experience of immaculate joy is the enlightenment aspect of *joy*.
f. The purification of all faults is the enlightenment aspect of *total purification*.
g. The realization of the equality of samsara and nirvana is the enlightenment aspect of *equality*.

Thus, all the seven aspects [of enlightenment] are completed. Moreover, you attain the many qualities and countless samādhis of the path of seeing. Some teach that you attain both the first level [of enlightenment] (*bhūmi*) and the path of meditation on perfecting the three [levels of] nonelaboration and reaching one taste. However, most others teach that you reach the first level [of enlightenment] on seeing the nature of nonelaboration and developing the path of seeing. Clearly there is no definitive conclusion concerning this because beings have different capabilities. There must certainly be varying natures and speeds of progressing through the paths. [217]

When you have developed the true realization of the path of seeing, you will have created the source or foundation for all qualities. That is why it's said that you have attained a level [of enlightenment] (*bhūmi*). From the *Avataṃsaka Sutra*:

> As soon as you reach the levels, you will be free from the five fears:
> You will not have the anxiety of lacking sustenance,
> of dying, of lacking praise, of the lower existences, or of [lacking] a retinue.[589]

Thus the qualities become greater and greater within the ten levels. When you reach the levels, this is called the *path of meditation*, because you are familiarizing yourself with the meaning of the path of seeing. On this level you practice the eight aspects of the noble path. All meditation is nothing but immaculate samādhi, but during post-meditation you are polluted and familiarizing yourself with the noble eightfold path. These eight are: correct view, correct realization, correct speech, correct action, correct livelihood, correct effort, correct mindfulness, and correct samādhi.

In brief, these accomplishments have the quality of being purely unmistaken. Therefore, they truly have the many distinguishing qualities of the superior actions in the lower vehicles.

The first level [of enlightenment]

The first level is called Perfect Joy because there is supreme joy at these special qualities. During this stage, "meditation sessions" are a birthless state without thought and in "subsequent [attainment]," through [seeing phenomena] as being like illusions, you benefit beings primarily by accomplishing the perfection of generosity through giving away, without fear or sadness, your head, limbs, and so on. You continue traversing the path in this way, passing through the sequence of the ten perfections combined with the ten levels. This is what is taught in extensive detail within the general vehicles. In this teaching, however:

a. The first level is called Perfect Joy, because the joy of samādhi greatly increases during the first [level] of nonelaboration.
b. The second level is called Stainless, because of freedom from all the stains of meditation.
c. The third level is called Shining, because of benefiting beings through the power of the realized meaning.

d. The fourth level is called Blazing, because of the increase in revealing buddhahood's qualities of greatness during the medium [level of] nonelaboration. [218]
e. The fifth level is called Difficult to Master, because of realizing the union of emptiness and compassion, which purifies all the stains of propensities, which are so difficult to purify.
f. The sixth level is called Manifest, because it is reached through the great [level] of nonelaboration becoming manifest. This is the realization that samsara and nirvana are birthless.

The śrāvakas and pratyekabuddhas can reach those first six levels also.

g. The seventh level is called Gone Far, because at the beginning [level] of one taste, such dualistic appearances as meditation and post-meditation, samsara and nirvana, and so on are liberated in union.
h. The eighth level is called Undisturbed because at the medium [level of] one taste there is no deviation from the true mindfulness that is the quality of realization.
i. The ninth level is called Excellent Intelligence because at the great [level of] one taste, all stains apart from subtle illusion-like dualistic appearances are purified.
j. The tenth level is generally known as Dharma Clouds, which in this teaching is the lesser and medium [levels of] nonmeditation. This is when even the subtlest dualistic appearances are spontaneously purified and you fully attain the qualities of the paths and levels. Nevertheless, there still remains the very subtlest obscuration of knowledge, which is the propensity for fixation—the remaining stain on the *ālaya* consciousness. At this level, you will have the same qualities as bodhisattvas who are lords of the tenth level.

The true state of buddhahood is when you reach the conclusion of the supreme, ultimate path of the common vehicles. This is when the stain of not recognizing nonthought, which is the subtle propensity of [the obscuration of] knowledge, dissolves into the nature of vajra-like wisdom, which is the great self-arising self-knowing. You are then eternally freed from every obscuration; you have completely perfected the wisdom that knows the ultimate nature and the wisdom that knows relative multiplicity; and you have perfected wisdom, compassion, and power.

In the context of mahāmudrā, this is called *great nonmeditation*. In the general Mantrayāna, this is the eleventh [level], Complete Illumination, and the twelfth [level], Attachment-free Lotus. At these levels there are no obscurations of karma, afflictions, and propensities, and there is no actual traversing of a path of purification, but their names indicate the distinguishing aspects or special characteristics of an increase in qualities. Both these special, internal levels manifest in a single instant.

The final level of buddhahood is called the thirteenth [level], or [the state] of the sixth [buddha], Vajradhara. This has benefit for oneself, which is the complete attainment of the dharmakāya, and benefit for others, which is its power of manifestation as form kāyas that continuously bring great benefit to all beings throughout space until samsara is emptied.

Progressing through the [first four] paths and [the ten] levels [219] is called the *path of training*. When you reach their conclusion and there is nowhere higher to go, that is called the *path of no training*. For the Mantrayāna, the ultimate result is the thirteenth [level], or [the level of] Vajradhara.

What qualities do you gain when you reach the levels?

1. On attaining the first level:
   - You can go simultaneously to a hundred nirmāṇakāya realms in the ten directions.
   - You can see a hundred buddhas and hear their teachings.
   - You can perform simultaneously a hundred different acts of generosity, such as giving away, without regret, your body, life, possessions, kingdom, child, wife, and so on.
   - You can radiate simultaneously a hundred different kinds of light rays, such as radiating a red light and reabsorbing it as white light, radiating a yellow light and reabsorbing it as blue light, radiating many light rays and reabsorbing them as few light rays, and so on.
   - You can teach simultaneously a hundred entranceways into the Dharma to accord with the nature and thoughts of a hundred different individual pupils.
   - You can rest simultaneously in a hundred different kinds of samādhis that have been taught in the *Mother of the Conquerors*,[590] such as the "heroic," "massed forces," "awesome lion," and so on.
   - You can manifest simultaneously a hundred different miracles: You can fly up into the sky, sink down into the earth, pass unimpeded through mountains and rocks, stand on water, blaze with

flames from your upper body while water gushes from your lower half, do those one after the other, transform one thing into many or many things into one, and so on.

You become thus endowed with these seven qualities each in a hundredfold form. In the same way, sequentially:

2. On the second level, there is a thousandfold form of each of these seven.
3. [On the third level, there is a ten-thousandfold form of each of these seven.][591]
4. On the fourth [level], there is a hundred-thousandfold form of each of these seven.
5. On the fifth [level], there is a millionfold form of each of these seven.
6. On the sixth [level], there is a ten-millionfold form of each of these seven.
7. On the seventh [level], there is a hundred-millionfold form of each of these seven.
8. On the eighth [level], there is a billionfold form of each of these seven.
9. On the ninth [level], there is a ten-billionfold form of each of these seven.
10. On the tenth [level], there is a hundred-billionfold form of each of these seven.
11. On the eleventh [level], there is a trillionfold form of each of these seven.
12. On the twelfth [level], there is a ten-trillionfold form of each of these seven.
13. On the thirteenth [level], the manifest nature of the three kāyas of buddhahood, or Vajradhara, has an infinite form of each of these qualities. They are incalculable because their nature is beyond the scope of the intellect. [220]

Thus, all ten levels and five paths taught in the common vehicles are perfectly complete and distinct within the mahāmudrā, the pinnacle of all the vehicles. Naturally, someone who truly manifests the four yogas will gradually—or immediately—complete every quality of the paths and levels. However, it is a special quality of the secret, swift Mantrayāna path that some don't reveal these qualities as actually perceivable characteristics on the apparent level. For example, most beings, such as birds and wild beasts, are born from their mothers' wombs and don't become fully developed for a while. The gradualists are like that. However, the garuda, who is the lord of birds, and the lion, who is the king of wild beasts, already have their complete powers inside the egg or mother's womb. At that time they can't be seen, but as soon as they're born, their three powers[592] are fully developed so that they can accomplish all activities, such as flying in the sky with their mother. In the same way, some yogins do not have actually visible signs while they are still confined within their material bodies, but on being freed from the traps that are their bodies, the result simultaneously ripens as the fully developed power of their qualities. There are also numerous individuals who, having accomplished the path that unites method and wisdom, visibly manifest the signs of that path, such as miraculous powers and clairvoyance, in that very life.

Basically, you attain freedom in the wisdom that knows the equality of space and wisdom, the intellect-transcending true nature, and the intrinsic nature of the mind itself. Otherwise, all you will get is just a few signs of heat through the practice of the generation and completion, the channels, winds, drops, and so on. In these times there are so many siddhas possessed by the *gongpo* demons who rejoice in these [few signs], prize them, fixate on them as wonderful, become conceited, and herd themselves and others into the lower existences. Therefore, I beseech those with critical minds to realize this for themselves.

That was a brief teaching on the view, meditation, and stages of the path. [221] I now give a short teaching on the ancillary subject of how to enhance results through performing the conduct of "bringing into the path."

In general, most Mantrayāna paths have different kinds of conduct, such as the three categories of elaborate, simple, and very simple [conduct]. There are also many different categories such as secret conduct, public conduct, *vidyāvrata*, and victorious conduct. Most of these are primarily for enhancing the results of generation and completion stage practices. Here the only conduct that is highly valued is the "completely excellent conduct," which maintains an intrinsic, intellect-transcending approach.

Even at the beginning, those who practice the preliminaries—gathering accumulations, purifying obscurations, and receiving blessings—should dedicate themselves to the completely excellent conduct: a behavior that is unpolluted by any stain from life's activities or from the eight worldly concerns, and gives no reason to feel ashamed.

In the middle stage, those engaged in the main practices—thoroughly examining view and meditation and gaining certainty in self-knowing—should dedicate themselves to the completely excellent conduct: beating out from within the nails of many thoughts; cutting through the mind's bondage of arrogant conceptual embellishments; mastering everything through knowing one thing; and becoming liberated from all through knowing one thing.[593]

In the end, there is the particular conduct to enhance the results of practice, for which there are different texts and practice instructions, but the essential point is to develop:

1. The conduct of a wounded deer, which means completely cutting through bondage to this world and wandering in uninhabited mountains.
2. The conduct that is like a lion running alongside ravines, which is not fearing negative circumstances.
3. The conduct that is like wind moving through the air, which is having no attachment to sensory pleasures.
4. The conduct like that of a lunatic, which means not involving yourself in either ending or engendering the eight [worldly] concerns.
5. The conduct that is like a spear being whirled in the air, which is allowing the mind to move freely as it wishes, unrestricted by the bondage of dualism.
6. The supreme, completely excellent conduct, which is cutting through the bondage of delusion, distraction, hope, and fear, and focusing solely on maintaining an unfabricated state, because even a hair tip of hidden, internal desire for signs, omens, experiences, realizations, siddhis, and so on, will only obscure the face of the ultimate nature, the dharmakāya.

Even if there are thoughts, afflictions, suffering, fear, pain, death, or anything that seems to be a special circumstance, [222] don't hope for or depend on any remedial method other than knowing this main practice, the mahāmudrā, the ultimate nature. This is the king of all enhancement practices. Yogins who can practice it in this way gain power over all appearances and existences in samsara and nirvana; they are free from all obstacles; they accumulate an ocean of siddhis; the darkness of the two obscurations disappear; the sun of the signs of accomplishment rises; they find buddhahood in their own minds; and they open a treasury of benefit for beings. That is the nature [of this conduct].

But it's sad to now see meditators doing nothing but spending their lives planning, like a child by a pond of lotuses, thinking, "I'm going to choose this—no, that one would be better!" while having thrown away this all-sufficing jewel they had in their hands.

That concludes my brief teaching on the nature of the basis, the path, the view, and the meditation.

III. The result mahāmudrā

I will conclude with a brief teaching on the result mahāmudrā, which is the inseparability of the three kāyas, or the union of the two kāyas.

Yogins who see the face of the true nature, the basis mahāmudrā, have truly accomplished through their practice the mahāmudrā of view, meditation, and path. This is the manifestation of mahāmudrā as the final result, the ultimate truth, and the dharmakāya.

The essence of the dharmakāya is self-knowing. It is the original, unaltered wisdom, which is changeless, neither increases nor diminishes, primordially pervades all beings in the three realms, and manifests through the profound key methods of practice. There is no buddha or dharmakāya other than this. It is not something previously nonexistent that is newly created.

Characteristics [of the result mahāmudrā]

It is called *possession of two wisdoms* because it has the wisdom that knows ultimate nature and [the wisdom] that knows relative multiplicity. It is called *possession of two purities*, because its essence is primordially pure and it has also been purified of connate, nonintrinsic stains. Therefore, it is free from every stain that prevents seeing or knowing all the phenomena that can be known, and it has completely perfected every positive quality.

The dharmakāya's radiance, or wisdom's unimpeded display, is the manifestation of the saṃbhogakāya and nirmāṇakāya. These three kāyas have the qualities of the *seven aspects of union*. What are these seven? The three particular qualities of the saṃbhogakāya (enjoyment body):

1. The aspect of enjoyment, which is the continuous, eternal enjoyment of the profound and vast Mantrayāna Dharma wheel for the bodhisattvas in Akaniṣṭha. [223]
2. The aspect of sexual union, which is union with a consort formed from light as a wisdom body with all the primary and secondary signs.

3. The aspect of great bliss, which is an uninterrupted continuity of great, immaculate bliss.

The three particular qualities of the nirmāṇakāya:

4. The aspect of being completely filled with compassion that is objectless compassion, which, like space, pervades everywhere.
5. The aspect of uninterrupted continuity, which is a vast, nonconceptual, naturally present activity that extends to the limits of samsara.
6. The aspect of noncessation, which is not to rest in the extreme of nirvana's peace.

The particular quality of the dharmakāya:

7. The aspect of having no nature: this is the union of emptiness and compassion, transcending all conceptual elaboration.

[The saṃbhogakāya] also guides with *eight qualities of lordship*:

1. Lordship over body: having any form of any body in order to train particular beings
2. Lordship over speech: the continuous turning of whatever Dharma wheel is necessary to train [particular beings]
3. Lordship over mind: having nonconceptual compassion
4. Lordship over miracles: having unimpeded, miraculous powers
5. Lordship over omnipresence: having the true enlightenment of one taste, which is the equality of the three times, samsara and nirvana
6. Lordship over desire: being unstained by desire, even if as many goddesses as there are atoms in twelve Mount Merus made offerings of sensory pleasures
7. Lordship over the creation of whatever is desired: being able, like a wish-fulfilling jewel, to fulfill the hopes and desires of beings
8. Lordship over residence: eternally dwelling in Akaniṣṭha dharmadhātu as the Dharma king of the three realms

"Guiding with the eight lordships" is primarily a synonym for the qualities of the saṃbhogakāya. The dharmakāya and saṃbhogakāya manifest the nirmāṇakāya as emanation-teachers who are like reflections of the moon in all the countless water bowls that are their pupils. The nirmāṇakāya is the appearance of infinite emanations in whatever form is necessary to teach beings, such as created, born, and great enlightenment [emanations].[594] They are called the "secret body, speech, and mind of the buddhas as a wheel of unceasing adornments." [224]

The cause for the kāyas to arise

The dharmakāya is the result of truly accomplishing the ultimate—emptiness and mahāmudrā—while upon the path. The nirmāṇakāya is an aspect of it, or part of its method, because it arises through having developed pure bodhicitta, aspiration prayers, and so on. The saṃbhogakāya arises from the causes and results of meditation on the profound generation stage. The everlasting domain of the three kāyas' inseparability is the result not of doing those practices separately or alternately but of engaging in the union of method and wisdom, in the great complete purity from the triple aspects of conceptualization.[595]

There are many more categories of these three kāyas, and also of four, five, or more kāyas, which are essentially one but given different names in terms of aspects of qualities and activities. However, they are nothing other than the nature, radiance, and power of the present mind, which we call the three kāyas at the time [of the result].

In the causal vehicles, the lower tantras, and so on, there are various traditions of explanation based on certain scriptures that were intended for particular circumstances, or in which the true meaning is only implied. There appears to be controversy over these grounds for debate involving a lot of proofs and refutations. The disagreement is over whether the dharmakāya has a face and arms or not, whether it truly manifests a realm or not, whether buddhas have wisdom in their own individual beings or not, whether the two form kāyas have individual experiences of sensory perceptions or not, and so on. Each viewpoint may be valid in its own context, but in this quintessential essence of the vehicles, we don't depend on finding proofs for views in the lower vehicles. We have the viewpoint described as "in agreement with all and distinct from all."

What is this viewpoint? It has no attachment to such things as reality or unreality, existence or nonexistence, identity or nonidentity, arising or ceasing, coming or going, eternality or nothingness, to any phenomena within appearance or existence, within samsara or nirvana. Therefore it neither proposes, refutes, nor proves. Why? Because if we say that there is nonexistence, we fall into the extreme of nihilism, but if we say there is existence, we fall into the extreme of eternalism, and if we hold the belief that there is neither existence nor nonexistence, we are failing to transcend a state of mental fabrication.

As for others, if they say their perceptions exist, we can agree with that, because, [225] through the infallibility of dependent origination and causes and results, there is an unceasing, unstoppable manifestation of appearances.

If they say they have no existence, we can agree with that, because having no existing nature of their own whatsoever, appearances are never apart from emptiness. If they say that appearances are neither existent nor nonexistent, we can agree with that, too, because this does not fall into an extreme and is without partiality or bias.

In the deluded perceptions that arise from the propensities of impure beings, everything that appears as an external world and its inhabitants appears to be formed from the solid, material five elements. In the perception of yogins on the path, they are the unimpeded appearances of their own mind. For buddhas and bodhisattvas, it is the realm of self-illuminating wisdom. Thus, ultimately, everything is simply the display of the mind itself.

Similarly, for impure, deluded beings, their minds, and the mental events that are their thoughts, have the nature of karma, afflictions, and propensities. For yogins on the path, they are particular aspects of view, meditation, experience, and realization. For the buddhas, the three kāyas of the sugatas, they are the display of knowledge, compassion, and wisdom. Therefore, in the true nature of the basis, or cause, there isn't even an atom of difference, the only difference being whether one is thickly obscured by "imaginary" extrinsic obscurations, only partially obscured, or entirely free from obscuration.[596] The single key point is to relax in your own unaltered mind, the mahāmudrā, which is the essential meaning of never having been apart from, not being apart from, and never going to be apart from the union of the two kāyas, or the inseparability of the three kāyas, which is the essence of the basis, path, and result.

Those with composite intellects, who embellish or denigrate the noncomposite Dharma and who are attached to the extreme of words and to disputes between different traditions, are like childish people arguing about how far space extends. If you rest in a state of great, all-pervasive equality within unfabricated relaxation, you will no doubt be liberated in a state that transcends concepts of traveler and destination: the expanse of the naturally present result of the four yogas, the ten levels, the five paths, and the three kāyas. [226]

> *Kye ho*!
> All beings, from mites on upward,
> are obscured by ignorance but are never apart from
> the element of buddha nature, primordial innate liberation,
> and the three kāyas of naturally present buddhahood.

[The Buddha] taught as many Dharma entranceways as there are pupils to be taught,
and yet they remain deluded by their own appearances,
in the bondage of wrong, mistaken, or erroneous paths.[597]
Those who travel the true, excellent path are [as rare as] fig tree flowers.[598]

Although the extremes do not exist, [beings] are chained by their belief in the extremes.
They do not know what it is they possess, like a poor woman who has a treasure.
They pollute with contrivance that which is uncontrived and self-arisen.
Without knowing how it is complete within them, what can they ever find?[599]

The merit of those with power and wealth falls under the power of the māras.
All who are arrogant through learning have minds like stiffened leather.[600]
Those who practice stupid, forced meditation strive to squeeze oil out of sand.
Who is there who will sit in the presence of the true nature, of the mahāmudrā?[601]

Alas! This supreme teaching that unites the sutras and tantras, the sun and the moon,
descends to the water goddess, with the vermilion clouds of a session's end.[602]
Why are you not saddened by having only its branches, and why, for the sake of this world's appearances,
do you deliberately throw your freedoms and opportunities into the dust?

Oh, don't you see that the teaching of the practice lineage
is to look at your own natural face, the supreme, eternal goal,
while perfectly living on whatever food
you happen to obtain to sustain you in uninhabited mountains?

In such a time as this, when practitioners do not truly practice,
and actions that destroy the teachings are called the "meaning of the teachings,"
who could need, and who would want to read,
a book like this written by someone like me?

Texts written in black ink that even the author doesn't need
and are not respected by others can fill caves,
but if they're unable to tame even a few minds,
all the paper and ink does is tire out fingers.

For a long time someone has been insistently entreating me to write this,
and so as not to refuse to give him what he has asked for,
out of necessity, I've written whatever came to my mind,
so its words will be neither meaningful nor faultless.

What I have written is completely devoid of such things as
the discernment that is skillful in the medium of writing
or the experience of understanding this great subject matter;
so what else can it be but a cause for hilarity among scholars and siddhas?

Nevertheless, I have written this so as not to prevent the faint possibility
that a beautiful garland of jasmine flowers, blossoming
in the light of good aspiration, undarkened by bad motivation, [227]
might adorn the ears of a few novice meditators like myself.

Through the power of the merit of writing this, united with
all stained and stainless merit in the three paths, within samsara and nirvana,
may the teachings of the practice lineage spread in all directions
and may all beings manifest the result of mahāmudrā.

The vidyādhara of Mengom, Tsültrim Sangpo,[603] asked me repeatedly over a long time to write an extensive and detailed text for practitioners of mahāmudrā to understand the enhancement and the signs on the path's stages. However, I felt there was no need for such a text as there were already countless deep and profound teachings within the collected works of the past Kagyü masters.

In particular, there are the profound mahāmudrā [instructions] that kind refuge lords have bestowed upon me out of their compassion: such renowned Sarma teachings as the *Innate Union* (*Sahajayoga*),[604] the *four letters*,[605] the *Ganges* [*Mahāmudrā*],[606] the *Letterless* [*Mahāmudrā*],[607] the *root symbols*,[608] the *essence of practice* teachings,[609] the *inconceivable secret*,[610] the *illumination of wisdom*,[611] the *fivefold* [*mahāmudrā*],[612] the *wish-fulfilling jewel*,[613] the *six nails of essential meaning*,[614] and many practice instructions.

I also received through their kindness such Nyingma mahāmudrā teachings as: the *Vast Expanse Free from Extremes*; the *Sun's Essence*; *Giving Rise to the Single Knowing*; *Dispelling the Darkness of Ignorance*; *Seeing the Naked Intrinsic Nature*;[615] and also many [mahāmudrā teachings] from the termas.

However, being carried away by waves of karma, afflictions, and distraction, I was unable to develop even the tiniest fraction of experience and realization. Therefore, I didn't have the confidence to write this text. Nevertheless, I have now written this blindly in the dark so as not to leave the request unfulfilled. I pray from my heart that I will not bring shame to the wise scholars and siddhas.

May the merit of this cause all my old mothers—all beings throughout space—to attain the sublime state of unsurpassable enlightenment within their lifetime.

Maṅgalaṃ bhavantu
(May they have good fortune!)

A lazy man, who is not Götsangpa but is known as Götsangpa, wrote this in Palri Götsang cave, which is not Latö Götsang.[616]

May there be goodness! May there be goodness! May there be goodness!

9. The Quintessence of Nectar

Instructions for the Practice of the Six Dharmas of Nāropa

SHAMARPA CHÖKYI WANGCHUK (1584–1630)

[229] I pay homage and go for refuge to the guru and the deity Sahajā.
I pray for the authorization to explain the meaning.

THIS IS A summary of the profound completion stage's six Dharmas of Nāropa, which is a tradition of the precious practice lineage, the Karma Kamtsang. Those who wish to practice this must do so in three parts:

I. The preparation
II. The main practice
III. The conclusion

I. The preparation

First you must properly receive, within the mandala of a highest yoga tantra *yidam* deity, such as Cakrasaṃvara and Hevajra, an empowerment from a genuine guru.

(Practice 1)
Then, in a place that is not disturbing to meditative stability, train the mind in the common preliminaries, such as the difficulty of obtaining the freedoms and opportunities [of a precious human existence]. Inspire yourself by developing an unendurable and overwhelming compassion for beings. Take refuge and develop bodhicitta. Then imagine upon the crown of your head Guru Vajrasattva, who has a body of light and is seated upon a moon disc in the center of a tent of light. He is white with one face and two arms. The right hand holds a five-pronged vajra to his heart. The left hand rests a bell against his hip.

He is majestic. Develop intense devotion for him. From his body, a flow of nectar resembling milk descends, enters through your fontanel, and fills your entire body. This causes your karma-ripened aggregates and their matter to leave you, like when a snake changes its skin. Your body becomes transparent, like a crystal ball. Imagine that all the bad karma and obscurations you have accumulated throughout beginningless time have been purified. Recite:

> White Guru Vajrasattva is upon a moon seat
> in the center of a tent of light upon the crown of my head.
> Because of my devotion to him, nectar descends,
> washes away my karmic body, and purifies me of bad karma and
> obscurations.

Do that recitation and visualization and chant the hundred-syllable mantra many times. Imagine that Vajrasattva merges into you and end the session.

(Practice 2)

[230] Next is the meditation of guru yoga, in order to quickly receive blessing. From baseless space arises the sound of emptiness as *ahaṃ*, causing the world and its beings to melt. They reappear as an inconceivable palace with no nature of its own. You are in its center as Bhagavān Heruka. You are blue in color, with one face and two arms. Your two arms, holding a vajra and bell, embrace your consort, Vajrayoginī. She is red and holds a flaying knife and *kapāla* skullcup. Her left leg is straight, and she bends her right leg around you. Jewels, a vajra cross, and a crescent moon adorn your topknot. You wear a a long garland of fifty freshly severed heads and a crown of five skulls, topped by jewels. You stand on your unbent right leg. On the crown of your head is Guru Vajradhara, who is blue and seated in vajra posture and holds a vajra and bell. He is embraced by his consort, Vajravārāhī, who is red, holds a flaying knife and *kapāla*, and is seated in the lotus posture. You are standing upon a lotus and moon, in the midst of an expanse of brilliant light rays.

Imagine that light rays radiate from your body transforming all beings into offering goddesses that make offerings to you. For that visualization, recite:

> *Ahaṃ*, the sound of emptiness, comes from empty space,
> causing me to appear as the heruka.

The guru and his consort are pleasurably seated on the crown of my head.
All beings become offering goddesses and make offerings to us.

Following that visualization, recite:

In the presence of the guru, who is the union of all buddhas,
with devotion I offer to the sublime ones
Mount Meru with the four continents,
a hundred million four continents,
a hundred billion and a hundred trillion,
all gathered into a single mandala.
I offer the three doors, the possessions,
and the accumulation of good karma of all beings and pray that you accept it.

I offer to the glorious supreme guru
a variety of external offerings,
and urine, feces, blood, semen, and brain,
the tastes of which bring the realization of great emptiness,
and the flesh of humans, horses, dogs, oxen, and elephants,
the tastes of which are brilliant great bliss
with the purity of being wisdom nectar.
I pray that you give your blessing.

The offering goddesses merge into the guru's consort.
Because of the nondual union of the male and female consort,
they are pleased by the secret offering of bliss and emptiness,
and their beauty shines brilliantly.

Following that meditation and recitation, in order to receive empowerment, recite:

E ma ho! *E ma ho*! Dharma!
E ma ho! The meaning of the Dharma appears. [231]
The pure meaning of the Dharma is selflessness.
Vajra king, I bow down in homage to you.
Bestow the vajra of space upon me today.

As a result of that supplication, the sound of the union of the male and female deities invokes all the buddhas of the ten directions. They gather and reside in the guru's heart. They melt into bodhicitta, which flows through the pathway of the vajra and emanates into the lotus of the female consort. It makes an offering to the mandala deities in the female's body, and then the vajra "bee" completely drinks the "honey," which is all of the mandala deities melted into nectar in the female's body. This flows from their point of union, enters through your fontanel, enters the interior of the central channel, and emanates and pervades the seventy-two thousand channels. In this way you receive the vase empowerment, and the purified channels manifest the vajra body.

The overflow of the liquid nectar reaches the guru and his consort's feet so that they become even more brilliantly beautiful than before. Then the guru and consort kiss, embrace, squeeze together their hip channels, and fiercely grind together their vajra and lotus. As a result, white and red bodhicitta is produced as a flow of liquid. It reaches your tongue, which is in the form of a three-pronged vajra. From there it passes through the *ya*, *ra*, *la*, and *va* letters that are in the throat and spreads and pervades the twenty-one thousand winds that make up the ten winds. As a result, you obtain the secret empowerment, and the purified winds manifest the vajra of speech.

Then from the guru's consort, a second Vārāhī is emanated. She merges into the consort that is united with you as the heruka. This union of the heruka and consort causes bodhicitta to descend from the crown of your head to the throat so that "joy" is experienced. The vajra completely entering the lotus causes the bodhicitta to descend to the heart, so that *supreme joy* is experienced. Fastening the lower air and preventing emission causes the bodhicitta to reach the navel, and *special joy* is experienced. Then the vajra slowly sucks the lotus anthers so that it holds the melted vitality element. The bodhicitta spreads, pervading to the very tip of the secret organ, and *innate joy* is experienced. In this way you obtain the wisdom and knowledge empowerment, and the purified drop manifests the vajra of mind.

After that, the experience of the nonconceptual, inexpressible true nature, the wisdom of great bliss, develops within your own being. It becomes blended with the nondual great bliss wisdom of the minds of Guru Vajradhara and his consort in an elaboration-free one taste. The nonconceptual wisdom of the path proceeds to become the nonconceptual wisdom of the result. It emanates, pervading, to become the wisdom of the animate and inanimate. As a result, you obtain the fourth empowerment, [232] and the purified consciousness manifests the great bliss kāya.

Then the vajra of the guru and consort stabilizes the mind *samaya* at the crown of the head and at the heart. The bell stabilizes the speech *samaya* at the throat and secret organ. The mudrā stabilizes the body *samaya* in the completely pure central channel. As a result, you obtain the Vajrācārya great master empowerment and you develop the confidence to remain for as long as samsara lasts in order to practice infinite activity. Visualizing that, recite:

> The nectar from the union of the guru and consort fill the channels.
> The flow of bodhicitta cleanses the winds.
> I experience the four joys of union and realize the true nature.
> My three *samayas* are stabilized; I have received the empowerment
> and have become an ācārya.

Following that recitation and visualization, recite this wishing prayer:

> Throughout all my lifetimes, may I never mistake my family lord.
> May I possess the mandala of the Bhagavān Rudra,
> drink the nectar of the prajñā's lotus,
> and purify existence within the essence of enlightenment.

Those are the instructions for the preparatory or preliminary practices.

II. The main practice

The main practice consists of the six Dharmas—caṇḍālī and so on.

A. The yoga of caṇḍālī

This has three parts:

1. Attaining that which has not been attained
2. Stabilizing the attainment
3. Increasing the benefit of that attainment

1. Attaining that which has not been attained

[Practice 3]

First there is training in the *empty body*. For the physical posture, be seated upon a comfortable seat with your legs crossed like interwoven netting. Press the hands downward in the meditation mudrā. Keep your back as straight as an arrow. Make your elbows face in toward the body with the biceps facing outward,[617] so that the upper arms are uplifted like a vulture's wings. Slightly lower the chin. Your eyes look toward the tip of the nose. Allow your lips and tongue to rest naturally. Wear a meditation belt that goes below the knees and around the shoulders to keep the body straight. Pray to the guru with devotion, reciting:

> *Oṃ āḥ hūṃ kāya vāk citta jñāna vajra svabhāva atmako 'haṃ.*
> [*Oṃ āḥ hūṃ*. I am the identity of the nature of the body, speech, mind, and wisdom vajras.]

This causes all worlds and beings within the three realms to become the "basis and based" of the "wheel of wisdom."

In the center is yourself as Bhagavatī Vajrayoginī, red in color, young, and mature. All her physical prominences are dark red, as if highlighted by lacquer. [233] Your single face bares its fangs slightly. Your right hand brandishes a flaying knife, while the left holds a blood-filled skull bowl. The crook of your arm supports a *khaṭvāṅga* staff, which is the heruka [consort]. A third of your hair is tied up in a knot while the rest hangs freely. You wear a long necklace of human heads. Your breasts and vagina are enlarged and prominent. You enjoy a dancing posture upon a lotus, sun, and yellow corpse. You are within an inferno of wisdom fire. The interior of your body is vivid and clear, free of any impurity, like an empty painting made on the surface of space. Visualizing this as without solidity, recite:

> My body is the body of Vajrayoginī.
> Red, with a dark red luster, holding a flaying knife and *kapāla*.
> Vagina and breasts completely enlarged, in a dancing posture.
> Vivid and clear, free of any affliction.

Do that recitation and meditation.

[Practice 4]

In order to practice with a body that is an insubstantial image, meditate well on the "empty body." Follow that with mastering the "family-endowed basis," which is the training of the channels.[618]

Next, imagine the navel cakra. It is red, has sixty-four channel petals, faces upward, and is triangular, in the shape of the letter *e*.[619] The heart cakra is white, with eight channel petals. It faces downward and is round, in the shape of the letter *vaṃ*.[620] The red throat cakra, with sixteen channel petals, faces upward and is triangular, in the shape of the letter *e*. The crown cakra, with thirty-two channel petals, faces downward, is white and round, in the shape of the letter *vaṃ*. Meditate that these [channel petals] have closed ends, are transparent, have the same thickness as the *lalanā* and *rasanā*, but are not connected to the *lalanā* or the *rasanā*. In order to visualize that, recite:

> Within the body is the straight, vivid central channel
> extending from the secret place to the fontanel.
> The *lalanā* and *rasanā* are the same length, red and white in color. [234]
> There are the four cakras, extremely clear.

Perform that recitation and meditation.

(Practice 5)

Next, in order to train the winds, draw in the breath through the nostrils, naturally and with slightly increased mindfulness and effort. At the moment when it has completely gathered within, expel completely all the residual breath, beginning slowly and eventually with intense force, so that the ocean is pressed against Mount Meru.[621] All the bad karma and obscurations that you have accumulated throughout beginningless lifetimes exit through your nostrils and from all the pores of your body as if they are flowing freely through a sieve, and you become completely purified. Rest your mind upon this utterly purified body, which is like a stainless fire crystal.[622]

Then, inhale slowly and at length. Press down on the navel while simultaneously swallowing saliva. Pull up the lower air by contracting the demon's mouth[623] inward. Both the upper and lower winds fill the inflated lower part of the stomach.

When pressing down becomes uncomfortable, concentrate it into the navel and by naturally and slightly relaxing the interior of the body, crush [the air] and imagine that it leaves through the body's pores, in little spurts.

When you think that you can suppress it no longer, imagine that it exits through the crown of your head in great puffs. This "firing like an arrow through the crown of the head" should be done once at the beginning of each session.

At all other times, imagine that [the air] is completely expelled through the nostrils, like the smoke of an incense stick, disappearing in space about sixteen finger-widths away. When you are gathering air back in, imagine that it appears from space, sixteen finger-widths away, like a cord of light that dissolves into the central channel at the region of your heart. This practice is called *firing like an arrow*.

Alternatively, when crushing the breath as described above, practice the *inner crushing of the breath*, in which the winds of the *lalanā* and *rasanā* are made to enter the central channel, like water directed through irrigation ditches. Imagine that they reach halfway between the navel and the heart and disappear. Then focus your mind on the perfect emptiness of the central channel's interior. That is the supreme method of "crushing the breath." However, for a beginner, the previous approach is more beneficial for holding the breath for a long time, while this latter method is beneficial for gaining the final qualities.

The four practices of inhalation, filling, crushing, and firing like an arrow are called the *four applications*.

Even though it's not easy to practice the meditation and recitation together, you should definitely train in the meaning of the following recitation in order to make the mental image clear:

> Through eliminating dead breath, I am purified of bad karma, obscurations, sickness, and demons.
> Inhale slowly, and the upper and lower meet and fill.
> When holding down becomes uncomfortable, crush.
> When I can no longer suppress it, I fire it like an arrow. [235]

That is called *training in the movement of the three secrets*, or *training in the winds*.

(Practice 6)

Next, "the dance of the moon's reflection on water" is training in the drops. Visualize the empty body, the channels, and so on as previously described. The upper end of the central channel continues from the fontanel to the point between the eyebrows. Meditate that the channel terminates in the triangle of bone between the eyebrows. Within it is the nature of the wind-mind condensed into a concentrated, blissful, oily, shining, white sphere (*bindu*). Practice that visualization combined with the air.

When practicing that visualization combined with *firing like an arrow*, imagine that, with a sighing sound and a sensation of bliss, the sphere ascends via the central channel to the level of the fontanel. Rest your mind on the sphere remaining there.

In combination with the inhalation, [visualize that] the sphere descends within the central channel. In combination with *filling*, meditate that [the sphere] resides at the tip of the secret organ as intense, concentrated bliss. Alternatively, in combination with *firing like an arrow*, [the sphere] goes to the crown of the head, and with the inhalation, it [descends to] rest at the mid-eyebrow point.

Train successively in a repeating cycle of these. End the session by dissolving the sphere at the mid-eyebrow point and resting [in meditation]. In order to visualize that, recite:

> Between the eyebrows is a round, oily, shining, white sphere.
> *Firing like an arrow* causes it to ascend to the crown of the head.
> Inhalation causes it to descend via the central channel to the secret place.
> The practice of this procedure and its reversal creates bliss.

Visualize and practice that.

2. *Stabilizing the Attainment*

Having described the method for controlling the uncontrolled, then there is stabilizing that control.

(Practice 7)

The physical posture is as before. Begin by practicing as far as the training in the wind. Clearly imagine the three channels within your own body, which is the body of the deity as previously visualized. The three channels join to become one single interior at a point four finger-widths below the navel. Between the navel and the secret place, at the level of the abdominal crease, there is a *dharmodaya* of fire within the central channel. In the center of that *dharmodaya* is a wisdom caṇḍālī in the form of a sphere the size of a *canaka*.[624] It has these four qualities: It is red in color; hot to the touch; has a nondual nature; and an outer aspect of bliss. Imagine that it is very small. Apply "vase breathing," which will make the fire stronger and produce bliss. [236]

(Practice 8)
Focus the mind upon [the caṇḍālī]; apply the breath; increase the power of the fire; and [visualize that] the sphere increases to the size of a pea.

Focus the mind on its top [which extends into a flame] like a carnivore's single hair that curves three times. As a result, [this flame tip of the sphere] increases to the size of a needle. It has three undulations and continually wavers, without being still for even an instant. It then increases to two finger-widths [in height], and then to four finger-widths. Train your mind in this [visualization]. These features of the sphere can either be practiced in a separate session or included within the seventh visualization session.

The flame, which has the four characteristics of being red and so on and has a wide, stable base and a wavering, fine tip, rises up through the central channel. Focus your mind upon that.

The practice of the sixfold yantra

> It is has been taught that
> turning the waist to the right and to the left loosens the channel knot of the navel.
> Twisting the upper body to the right and left loosens the channel knot of the heart.
> Turning, raising, and lowering the throat loosens the channel knot of the crown of the head.
> Extending and bending the legs and arms loosens the channel knots of the joints.
> Shaking and rubbing the body tames all the channels.

In order to do the visualizations recite the line appropriate to what you are visualizing:

> In the center of a dharmodaya of fire, at the junction of the three channels,
> there is a wisdom-caṇḍālī sphere that is very small.

or:

> . . . a wisdom-caṇḍālī that is sharp and the size of a pea.

or:

> . . . a wisdom-caṇḍālī that is the size of a fine needle and has three undulations.

or:

> . . . a wisdom-caṇḍālī that is two finger-widths with three undulations.

or:

> . . . a wisdom-caṇḍālī that is four finger-widths with three undulations.

> Its color is red and it is hot to the touch.
> Its nature is empty and its outer form is bliss and clarity.

Meditate by practicing that visualization.

These are the instructions for stabilizing the control.

3. Increasing the benefit of that attainment

This has three sections:

a. Increasing the heat
b. Increasing the bliss
c. Increasing the nonconceptuality

The first of those:

a. Increasing the heat

Even though you've performed the preceding practices, if you don't have a clear visualization of the fire and so on, or in order to make it clearer, first adopt the physical posture as previously described. Alternatively, cross your legs at the ankles with the knees raised up and place the elbows of your crossed arms upon the knees. [237] Place the palms of your hands upon your right and left upper arms. In this "binding clasp of the knees," your legs form two triangles of "opposing hearths." Your arms form another four [triangles], making a total of six. There are also six inner and six secret [triangles], making eighteen "opposing hearth" mudrās.

In the visualization, you are the vivid, clear body of the deity with three channels and four cakras, as described earlier. The crown cakra has nine channel petals. It is located at the crown of your head, at the upper extremities of the three channels. The secret cakra has thirty-two channel petals. The twelve cakras of the major joints have eight channel petals each. The cakras of the minor joints have four channel petals each.

In this meditation, there is a wisdom-caṇḍālī at the junction of the three channels. It is in the form of a bright and shining globule with its top inside the central channel. Imagine that the effective application of wind causes the fire to blaze from the [globule]. Meditate that [the flame] reaches as far as the navel. Turn your stomach six times, turning it to the right and the left. Meditate that as a result, [the flame] reaches the heart. Twist your upper body to the right and left. Meditate that as a result, the flame reaches the throat and then the crown of the head. Turn, raise, and lower your throat. Meditate that as a result, the flame spreads to all the limb cakras. Extend and bend your limbs. Meditate that as a result, the flame spreads through the seventy-two thousand channels until it reaches the pores.

Shake and rub your body. Imagine that the blazing wisdom fire incinerates all the channels that create the basis for samsara, and the channel knots, which cause samsara to be based upon them. Imagine that it incinerates the outer central channel, which acts as the basis for the samsara life force, but not the supreme central channel.

In order to imagine all that, recite:

> The three channels, the six cakras, and the minor cakras are visualized.
> At the point of junction, the caṇḍālī blazes.
> It fills the three principal [channels] and fills the cakras.
> It spreads as far as the pores and is gathered back again to the junction.

> Thus, at the conclusion of the session, the flame is gathered back into the basic caṇḍālī at the channel junction, and you rest in meditation. At this point, practice the thirty-seven physical exercises that intensify the result. It is said:

> Perform the earth-touching mudrā and turn the stomach
> six times—three times to the left and three to the right.
> Grasp the right knee and perform those same six turns
> then another six [while grasping] the left [knee]. [238]

> With the thumbs pressing on the channels of the ring fingers,
> perform the "noose-throwing" movement six times each with the right and left fists.
> Perform six "arrow-drawing" movements with the right and left hands.

Perform six "inward-rubbing" movements with the right and left hands.
With the addition of shaking the whole body, there are thirty-seven [movements].

b. Increasing the bliss

(Practice 9)

To intensify bliss, practice the physical posture, the empty body, and the visualization of channels and cakras as you have done before. In this visualization, within the central channel, in the center of the great-bliss cakra, there is a mandala of nectar, the moon, and bodhicitta in the form of a stainless moon. A white *haṃ* adorns its center.

Within the central channel, in the center of the navel cakra, there is a small caṇḍālī, in the form of a small sphere with the four qualities. While visualizing this, use the wind practice to create the key effect, so that a flame that is over a finger-width [in height] will blaze. Because of its [heat], the *haṃ* and moon at the crown become agitated. The *haṃ* syllable begins to drip bodhicitta in the form of upside-down *haṃ* syllables.

Then be completely filled with winds so that the flame burns to two finger-widths in height. The bodhicitta falling in the form of upside-down *haṃ* syllables transform into spheres of bodhicitta, the size of mustard seeds. They fall through the central channel like drips falling from an icicle, descending as far as the throat.

Imagine that the fire blazes to eight finger-widths above the heart, so that the spheres fall to merge inseparably with the caṇḍālī, instantly transforming into red-hued white spheres that fill the entire body.

Rest continuously with a focused mind, with developed bliss, and without thought. Recite:

As a result of the wind application, the caṇḍālī blazes.
Because of that, the moon and *haṃ* at the crown
drip the white element, in the form of spheres.
The spheres, which are a mixture of red and white, pervade the entire body.
Joy, bliss, and contentment are generated.

Recite that and practice the meditation.

[(Practice 10)][625]

There is also the "escape and chase" visualization. The visualization is the same as before except that when the wind practice causes the caṇḍālī's fire to rise in the central channel, immediately upon touching the *haṃ*, red spheres fill the body, and there is pervasive bliss. Then white spheres descend from the *haṃ*, and when they reach the flame, it becomes redder and [diminishes to] four finger-widths in height. At that time, the entire body is filled with white spheres of bodhicitta, so that bliss increases. [239] Imagining that, recite:

> As a result of the wind practice, the caṇḍālī blazes straight upward.
> As soon as it touches the *haṃ*, [the body] is filled with red spheres.
> Spheres descend from the *haṃ*, so that the flame subsides,
> and the entire body is filled with white spheres.

Practice that meditation.

If that practice does not increase bliss to its full extent, perform the following.

(Practice 11)

THE COW-MILKING VISUALIZATION

Place your knees together and stretch out your feet. With complete bliss, a white *hūṃ*, which is the white element, blissfully descends from the *haṃ* at the crown of your head down through the central channel. It blissfully stays at the tip of the secret organ. Imagining that, pull up and push the lower wind. When you think that you can no longer hold the bliss, the *hūṃ* immediately darts back up to the crown, merges into the *haṃ*, and a white five-pronged vajra cross blocks the fontanel. Imagining that, recite:

> A white essence falls from the *haṃ* at the crown.
> It descends through the central channel and comes to rest at the secret tip.
> Bliss increases and it returns above.
> It merges into the *haṃ*, and a vajra cross blocks the fontanel.

Practice that meditation.

(Practice 12)

c. The increase of nonconceptualization

Your physical posture should be motionless, like an oaken stake stuck into the ground. Stare unwaveringly into space. Briefly hold the gentle breath.

Rest, without deliberation, within the nature of thoughts of bliss, thoughts of heat, or in brief, whatever thoughts arise as objects of the mind. Rest the mind in utter stillness like a dove in her nest. Rest the mind, still and unmoving, like a fly stuck to glue. Rest the mind without effort, like a man who has finished his work. Rest relaxed, like a bundle of straw after its fastening knot has been cut. If a thought arises while you're resting in that way, look nakedly at its nature, as before, and rest. Rest in the stillness that is like pure, unstained water free from the agitation of waves. Recite:

> Rest relaxed in the natural consciousness, just as it is:
> clear, pure, and unsullied, with nothing to be identified,
> nothing to be removed, and nothing to be changed
> in the relaxed mind that is like space.

Meditate in that way.

These ancillary practices for intensifying the result conclude the description of visualizations for caṇḍālī practice.

B. The second [of the six yogas]: the illusory body

[240] The practice of the illusory body has three parts:

1. Training in the impure illusory body
2. Training in the pure illusory body
3. The special training in extremely subtle winds and drops as the illusory body

1. Training in the impure illusory body

This has three parts:

a. Attaining that which has not been attained
b. Stabilizing the attainment
c. Increasing the result

(Practice 1)

a. Training in the impure illusory body: attaining that which has not been attained

The physical posture is that of the seven Dharmas of Vairocana, as described before. The principal object of meditation is the variety of appearances. The principal time is primarily the day.

The meditation is to first contemplate that all composite phenomena are impermanent. In particular, the lives of beings are impermanent. Children, wife, friends, wealth, and so on are all without any essence. In brief, apart from the Dharma, nothing else can bring happiness or benefit.

The conclusion of birth is death. The conclusion of accumulation is complete dispersal. The conclusion of companionship is separation. The conclusion of friendship is enmity. The living body is destroyed. The movement of breath stops. Close relatives are left behind. Others enjoy your wealth and possessions. Your body becomes a corpse. You have no freedom. In brief, nothing has any essence and nothing is necessary. This contemplation, which engenders disillusionment with samsara, is the mind training that constitutes the preliminary practice.

Contemplate how fixation on the reality of all these external appearances, such as form, has caused you to wander in samsara. If you examine and analyze all these appearances, you will see that they are nonexistent, like dreams and illusions. Like echoes and drumbeats, they appear because of conditions. They are impermanent, like lightning and water bubbles. They appear and yet have no reality, like mirages and reflections of the moon on water. Meditate well by contemplating in this way. Recite:

> All these appearances—forms, sounds, smells,
> tastes, horses, oxen, and houses—appear but are nonexistent.
> They appear because of conditions but are impermanent, have no reality,
> and are devoid of real existence, like dreams and illusions.

Practice this recitation and meditation. Contemplate in this way in all meditation and post-meditation periods.

(Practice 2)

b. Training in the impure illusory body: stabilizing the attainment

Look at your reflection in a mirror. Contemplate how it makes no difference whether the reflection is adorned or beaten, praised or maligned. Your own body is the same as your reflection. Your voice is like an echo. Your thoughts are like mirages mistaken for water. Recite:

> This reflection in the mirror has no joy or pain,
> beauty or ugliness, pleasure or displeasure.
> My own body is no different from it.
> My speech and mind are like echoes and mirages.

Practice that meditation and recitation.

(Practice 3)

c. Training in the impure illusory body: increasing the result

When you have gained stability in being unaffected by praise and criticism, pleasure and pain, and so on, [241] then have someone you know, such as your lama or a friend, praise and criticize you in various ways. Then go to a place where there are many people, such as on a market day, and behave in either a respectable or an unrespectable way, so that other people will either praise you or criticize and beat you, like or dislike you. Look to see if this makes any difference to you. If it does, return to solitude, pray to the guru and jewels intensely, and repeat the meditation. Sometimes, to make this clearer, recite:

> All these men and women are like dreams.
> These words of praise and abuse are like echoes.
> Isn't this mind that sees, hears, and experiences
> just like a deer mistaking a mirage for water?

Practice that recitation and meditation.

(Practice 4)

2. Training in the pure illusory body

Look at a representation of your *yidam* deity reflected in a mirror. In the same way, your own body is the empty deity's body, devoid of reality. It appears but has no real existence. All beings are bodies of the deities, and all worlds are the "inconceivable palaces," and both of these are mere appearances without any reality.

Your speech is the sound of the mantra, which is like an echo. The movements of your mind are the spontaneous liberation of great bliss, which is like a mirage. Therefore, there is nothing unpleasant or pleasant in the residence, which is the inconceivable palace. There is no aversion or attachment, praise or abuse, for the residents, who are the images of the deities. There is nothing that brings pleasure or pain in the sounds of the mantra. Thinking that, recite:

> All these forms and appearances, such as my own body,
> are the deity's body, which is the union of appearance and emptiness,
> like a reflection.
> Therefore, how could there be something that would have thoughts
> of attachment and aversion, praise and criticism, pleasure or pain?

Practice that meditation and recitation.

In terms of specifics, when stabilizing the understanding through these illusory body visualizations, there should be one session of meditating on the body as being like a reflection in a mirror; one session of going to a place where there are echoes, and meditating that speech is like an echo; and one session of going to a place where there's a mirage and meditating on the mind being like a mirage. This makes a total of three sessions. With the addition of [three sessions on the pure illusory body], there is a total of six. However, practicing four sessions, as taught here, will suffice.

3. The special training in the extremely subtle winds and drops as the illusory body

This is classified as the hidden meaning [of the illusory body] in [Karmapa Rangjung Dorjé's] root text entitled *Molten Gold*.[626] According to the view of the Eighth Lord [Karmapa Mikyö Dorjé]'s commentary on this text,[627] this practice has two aspects:

a. The actual practice [242]
b. The practice for enhancing the result

(Practice 5)

a. The actual practice of the special training in the illusory body

> Rest the three doors as they naturally are, without alteration,
> in the natural, spontaneously present three solitudes.
> Holding the wind and mind causes the three visions to arise in their generative sequence.
> Through the process of their reversal, the illusory body arises.

Thinking of this, sit with the legs in the vajra posture, the back as straight as an arrow, the eyes staring fixedly without the complication of opening and closing. When there is no exhalation or inhalation of the breath, there is neither speech, nor the absence of speech. The tongue not touching the lips is the natural, spontaneous presence of vajra repetition. The hands are unmoving in the meditation mudrā. In brief, rest in the stable, natural, spontaneously present solitude of the body.

In that state, there is the natural, spontaneously present solitude of the mind, where attention to the past, present, and future has come to rest in equanimity. Rest without any thoughts of existence or nonexistence, emptiness or no emptiness, meditation or meditator, meditation or no meditation, and so on. While in that state, if a thought begins, don't remain in its continuity, but hold all obvious and subtle thoughts in a state without thought and without distraction. If stupor and dullness occur, look upward and sharpen your cognition. If dispersal and agitation occur, look downward and relax your cognition. If there is no dullness or agitation, maintain equanimity.

If the beginning of the session is good and the end of the session bad, or if earlier sessions are good and later sessions are bad, this is because the elements are becoming exhausted, like a pond drying up, so revive your elements, relax your mind, and then meditate.

If the beginnings of sessions are bad and the ends of the sessions are good, or if the earlier sessions [of the day] are bad and the later sessions are good, this is caused by a lack of diligent application, like an irrigation channel that isn't bringing in water from a lake. Therefore, develop enthusiastic dedication and then meditate.

Thinking of the guru as the dharmakāya, relinquish your outer, inner, and secret body and your possessions and wealth, and offer them up to the guru, so that the power of blessing and the strength of your practice will cause the mind to maintain the mahāmudrā. Maintaining that will cause the wind to be controlled. As a result of that the following experiences will arise: The dissolving of earth into water causes an appearance that resembles an unstable mirage comprised of light rays in five colors, alive with little movements like restless water. Water dissolving into fire causes an appearance that resembles the arising and thickening of smoke. Fire dissolving into air causes an appearance that resembles fireflies, sparks, and red flashes. Air dissolving into mind causes an appearance that resembles the flames of lamps.

The mind dissolving into mental events causes an appearance that resembles the radiance of moonlight. When mental events dissolve into ignorance, there is an appearance that resembles the sun. When ignorance dissolves into the "total empty," [243] there is an appearance that resembles an eclipse, or darkness. That is followed by the "all empty," which resembles a cloudless sky (which is taught to be the dharmakāya).[628]

Then, the three visions arise in reverse order: From "all empty" arises ignorance, from which arise mental events, from which arises the mind. From those three and the air arises the illusory body adorned by the primary and secondary signs. It is described by the twelve examples of illusion (which is taught to be the nirmāṇakāya). It is directly perceived by self-knowing. You will also see, without obscuration, as clearly as a myrobalan[629] in your hand, all pure and impure appearances, all the animate and inanimate in the three realms and in the three times.

That is a brief description of the methods of meditation on the illusory body created by resting in the three solitudes. There is also the method of practicing it with the first three mudrās and so on, but I will not describe those here.

(Practice 6)

b. The practice for enhancing the result of the special training in the illusory body

If you practice in that way and yet have no experiences, or if you think that an illusory body could not be created from emptiness, then, in order to develop conviction, perform the enhancing practices: the dark retreat, the lac liquid, the sword, and the mirror. These are clearly described in detail in the practice instructions for the inseparability of wind and mind and so on. Therefore, serve at the lotus feet of the vajra master and request [those instructions] from him.

C. The third yoga: dream yoga

The instructions that spontaneously clear away the delusions of dreaming are in three parts:

1. Recognition of dreams
2. Training in dreams
3. Meditation on the true nature of dreams

1. Recognition of dreams

This has two aspects:

a. Continuous mindfulness during the day
b. Recognition by forceful means: instructions for the nighttime

(Practice 1)

a. Continuous mindfulness during the day

Enter a strict retreat in a solitary place. Consider how samsaric activities have no essence. Develop great compassion, thinking, "All beings, my old mothers, are wandering in samsara because they don't know that all phenomena are like illusions."

In all the four kinds of behavior,[630] continually develop mindfulness and aspiration with such thoughts as, "*E ma*! All these appearances are like illusions, like dreams. I am going to know that this is the way they are. In particular, I shall dream tonight and recognize my dreams to be dreams." [244]

(Practice 2)

b. Recognition by forceful means: instructions for the nighttime

Lie down in the lion posture upon a comfortable mattress, and as you are going to sleep meditate that the guru is upon the crown of your head. Develop intense devotion and make this sincere, heartfelt prayer:

Lord Guru, the embodiment of the Three Jewels,
my king, my realized father, think of me!
Give your blessing that I may merge into the luminosity of sleep.
Give your blessing for my dreams to arise as the illusory body.

Recite that supplication numerous times.

Develop intense mindfulness, thinking, "I will tonight recognize sleep as luminosity. My dreams will arise as the illusory body. I will have many clear dreams that will be the basis for arising as the illusory body. I will dream well. I will definitely recognize my dreams. I will know my dreams to be dreams."

Imagine yourself to be Vajrayoginī as during caṇḍālī. Meditate clearly that in your throat is a multicolored lotus with four petals and the anthers in the center. On the center sits a white *oṃ*. On the front [petal] is a blue *a*. On the right petal is a yellow *nu*. On the rear petal is a red *ta*. On the left petal is a green *ra*. Recite:

I will definitely recognize my dreams.
I will know my dreams to be dreams.
Upon a multicolored four-petal lotus in my throat,
there are five syllables—*oṃ*, *a*, *nu*, *ta*, and *ra*,
which are white, blue, yellow, red, and green in color.

Start with that general visualization. Then focus the mind on the *a*. When you feel like sleeping, focus on the *nu*. When you are drowsy, focus on the *ta*. As the drowsiness deepens, focus upon the *ra*. Then, focus the mind on the *oṃ* and rest in the luminosity of deep sleep. As a result, you will recognize dreams when they come, and be able to use methods in your dream, such as meditation on the deity's body.

If at first you don't recognize the dream, as aspiration is the most important factor for that recognition, intensify your aspiration. Repeating single-minded prayers to the guru and ḍākinī will bring recognition of dreams.

2. Training in dreams

This consists of:

a. Training in increase and transformation
b. Training in illusion
c. Training in liberation from illusion

(Practice 3)

a. Training in increase and transformation

Think, "It isn't enough to just recognize that I'm dreaming. Tonight, when I've recognized that I'm dreaming, I will transform one thing into many and transform the bad things into good, transform my body into the deity, and so on." Go to sleep with that aspiration. Recognize the dream and think, "This dream has no reality, so I can do whatever I like." You can transform yourself from a human into a bird, and so on. If you're having a nightmare, you can transform it into a good dream. [245] You can meditate that your body is the illusory body of the deity, transforming into Cakrasaṃvara, Hevajra, and so on. You can have many different hands and faces and transform one thing into many things and many things into one thing.

In order to train in these manifestations and transformations, develop a strong aspiration as you go to sleep by reciting these words:

> Dreams are unreal, they are illusions.
> Therefore, I will recognize that I am dreaming
> and will perform whatever manifestations and transformations I wish,
> such as changing one into many and becoming various deity bodies.

(Practice 4)

b. Training in illusion

If in a dream you see frightening things, such as a fire, a great river, a precipice, enemies, dangerous animals, and so on, don't be afraid, but train in illusion. Think, "If this dream is a nonexistent appearance, without reality, who can be burned by this fire? Who can be swept away by this river? Who can be harmed by these enemies? Who can be devoured by these wild animals? Who can fall down this precipice? This is unreal, like an illusion, so knowing that all these appearances are illusions, I will not be afraid but will train [in illusion]." Develop that aspiration and recite:

> All the places, appearances, fire, water, poison, weapons, and so on
> that are in a dream do not have any reality as this or that thing;
> they are all illusions, devoid of reality.
> Therefore, I will not be afraid or terrified.

Thinking this, go to sleep and recognize your dreams. If you dream of fire, think, "Who could be burned by this fire?" and stamp your feet upon it. Walk upon water. Think, "Who can fall off this precipice?" and hover and fly like a bird, and so on.

c. Training in liberation of illusion

This has two parts:

i. Training in mundane liberation
ii. Training in supramundane liberation

(Practice 5)

i. Training in mundane liberation

Develop the following motivation as you fall asleep:

> As I can do anything with my dream body,
> I will go to see the details of many places,
> such as the paradises, [the continent of] Kuru,
> and the lower existences, which easily create disillusionment
> with samsara.

Develop that aspiration, go to sleep, recognize you're dreaming, and then take hold of a sunbeam and go to see a deva realm. Train in going to see other continents, the lower existences, India, and so on.

(Practice 6)

ii. Training in supramundane liberation

When training in supramundane liberation, it's important during the day to habituate yourself to aspiring for it. [246] Therefore, in a solitary place, in the same physical posture as for the caṇḍālī, visualize yourself to be the *yidam* deity. Visualize that in your heart there is a wisdom being (*jñānasattva*) an inch in height.

Encourage yourself by thinking, "I will now leave my body and go to the realms of the buddhas." Then your mind, which is the wisdom being, exits your body, which is the commitment being (*samayasattva*), ascends to a great height until you reach the realm of Ghanavyūha. There you see Bhagavān Vairocana teaching while seated upon a lion throne. Prostrate to him, enquire after his health, and receive teachings and prophecies from him. Then think, "Now I've accomplished my goal and will return to my commitment being body." Then you return to it in the way that a wisdom being enters a commitment being. It's very important to do this training at the beginning. Recite:

> Self-knowing, the wisdom being, exits from
> my body, the commitment-being *yidam*.
> I meet a buddha in the pure realms,
> receive his teaching, and return to my body.

Similarly, train in going to the eastern buddha realm and so on.

(Practice 7)
Having trained in that way during the day, when you go to sleep at night, think again and again, "Tonight I will recognize that I'm dreaming, and I will train in seeing the realm of Buddha Vairocana." Recite:

> I will perfectly recognize that I'm dreaming
> and in an illusory body will see
> sugatas in the buddha realms,
> hear their teaching, and receive their prophecies.

Focus your mind on the *oṃ* and train in the realm of Vairocana. Focus your mind on the *a* and train in the realm of Akṣobhya. Focus on *nu* for Ratnasambhava. Focus on *ta* for Amitābha. Focus on *ra* in order to train in and to see the realm of Amoghasiddhi.

In the same way by first developing the wish to go to that particular place and then training in it, go and join the gatherings of ḍākinīs in the twenty-four sacred places, go to Oḍḍiyāna, Shambhala, and so on. When you do this practice, at first [the realm] will be indistinct. Then it will become more vivid, until finally you will be able to see it exactly as it is.

3. Meditation on the true nature of dreams

[247] All phenomena are primordially illusions, like dreams. There is no real difference between the basis for your training, you who are training, and that in which you train. Therefore, rest in a state of clarity and nonconceptuality that is like an illusion. Recite:

All phenomena are primordially like dreams and illusions.
The training, the one who trains, and the basis for training have no reality.
Everything is just an appearance of the mind.
The mind itself is clarity, which cannot be identified, and is an expanse of illusion.

Practice with that recitation and meditation.

That concludes this brief description of the practice of dreams.

D. The fourth yoga: luminosity

In the instructions for the luminosity that dispels the darkness of ignorance, there are two parts:

1. Bringing daytime appearances into luminosity
2. Remaining in the luminosity of nighttime's deep sleep

1. Bringing daytime appearances into luminosity

Seat yourself in the same physical posture as for the caṇḍālī. Keep yourself straight with the meditation staff and the meditation belt. Focus upon the *urna* hair[631] or upon space, and meditate nonconceptually.

If you cannot rest in that state, contemplate a blue *hūṃ* upon a lotus and sun disc in the heart of yourself visualized as Vajrayoginī. Light rays radiate from it so that all worlds merge into the beings that inhabit them. Then the beings merge into you. Then you, as the deity, melt from the crown protrusion (*uṣṇīṣa*)[632] downward and from the soles of the feet upward, dissolving into the *hūṃ*. The *hūṃ*'s *shabkyu*[633] dissolves into the *ha*. The *ha* dissolves into its head, which dissolves into the crescent, which dissolves into the circle, which dissolves into the *nāda*. Imagining that, hold the vase breath and rest in a nonconceptual state.

If there is stupor or instability, meditate on being the *yidam* deity as before and keep repeating over and over the stages of dissolving into the *nāda*. That meditation will cause the winds of the sun, moon, and eclipse to be fixed in the heart, and after the three visions there will be the recognition of luminosity. Therefore, diligently apply yourself to this practice. Recite:

In the heart of myself visualized as the Yoginī,
there is a blue *hūṃ* upon a lotus and sun.

Its light causes the worlds and their beings to merge into me.
I merge into the *hūṃ*, which is absorbed into the *nāda*.

Practice that meditation.

2. Remaining in the luminosity of nighttime's deep sleep

In a solitary place, train well in the daytime training that has previously been described, becoming familiarized with it.

Place the body, speech, and mind at ease. [248] For a little while abandon all other activity. For two or three nights, without sleeping, apply yourself to virtuous activity as much as you can. Eat nutritious food and massage the body. Offer tormas adorned with human flesh to the gurus, *yidams*, and ḍākinīs. Repeat twenty-one times, or as many times as you can, the aspiration of thinking, "I shall definitely recognize the luminosity of sleep."

Lie down in the lion posture with your head pointing to the north and make yourself as comfortable as you can. Visualize yourself as the *yidam* deity. In your heart, inside the central channel, there is a four-petal blue lotus. In its center, upon the anthers, there is a blue *hūṃ*. On the four petals there is a white *a* on the front petal, a yellow *nu* on the right petal, a red *ta* on the rear petal, and a green *ra* on the left petal. Visualize this clearly and recite:

I am visualized as Sahajā,
at the heart, within the central channel, upon a lotus,
there is a very clear *hūṃ*, *a*, *nu*, *ta*, and *ra*,
which are blue, white, yellow, red, and green.

Visualize that and gently hold the vase breath.

First, be aware of the *a* in front. Then be aware of the *nu* as you approach *appearance*. Be aware of the *ta* when you approach *increase*. Be aware of the *ra* as outer appearances dissolve, you merge into emptiness, and there is the vision of *attainment*.[634] Having begun to realize these four empties,[635] when the sign of the *all empty*, which is the fifth enlightenment,[636] begins to appear, focus your mind upon the central *hūṃ* and recognize the supreme, changeless luminosity and rest in that recognition.

That is the unsurpassable teaching of the Kagyü Karma Kamtsang, but if you are having difficulty, as in the case of a beginner, recognizing the arising of the "awakening" and its signs, then when you go to sleep, think again and again, "I am going to recognize the luminosity of sleep tonight!" Then, as in the daytime practice, imagine yourself to be the *yidam* deity and dissolve into the *hūṃ*. The *hūṃ* is then absorbed into a blue sphere (*bindu*) the size of a pea. Focus your mind on that as you go to sleep. As a result, between the time that [daytime] perceptions cease and dreams appear, you will be in a light sleep that is a clear and nonconceptual state.

Have a friend make a signal as a test to see if you have the recognition of luminosity. There will eventually be a blending of that recognition with clarity and emptiness, and with bliss and emptiness. Rest the mind in that. Recite:

> In the heart of myself visualized as Yoginī,
> there is a blue *hūṃ* upon a lotus and sun.
> Its light causes the worlds and their beings to merge into me.
> I merge into the *hūṃ*, which is absorbed into a sphere. [249]

In order to recognize the luminosity of deep sleep, you may also focus your mind upon a blue sphere inside a jewel. If you wish to recognize the luminosity of light sleep, meditate that [the sphere] is at the mid-eyebrow point, where the upper opening of the central channel is. It's easier to recognize [the luminosity] if you focus your mind on a black sphere, the size of a sheep's dropping, at that place.

Those are the methods for recognizing what has not been recognized. Particularly according to Lord Yangchen,[637] that recognition is stabilized when the power of the blazing caṇḍālī in the central channel, as in the earlier caṇḍālī yoga, melts the bodhicitta and there is the realization of bliss and emptiness and the special wind-mind signs of the three visions and luminosity. From that the illusory body arises, which is the manifestation of true luminosity. Two methods cause the very subtle wind-mind to enter the luminosity. The two methods are:

a. Totality
b. Subsequent dissolution

a. Totality

Make your own body, speech, and mind indivisible from that of all beings. Meditate that your physical aspect is Vairocana, the vocal aspect is Amitābha, and the mental aspect is Akṣobhya. These are the commitment beings.

Imagine that in their hearts there are, respectively, *oṃ*, *āḥ*, and *hūṃ*, which are the wisdom beings. Meditate that within the circles of each of these three syllables there is a short *a* with an indestructible sound.

Then the *oṃ*, *āḥ*, and *hūṃ* seed syllables in the hearts radiate light. The commitment beings dissolve from the crowns of their heads downward and from the soles of the feet upward into the wisdom beings in their hearts. The wisdom deities then gradually dissolve into the samādhi beings (*samādhisattvas*), which are the indestructible quintessences: the [three] short *a* with their sound. Then those samādhi beings dissolve into a concentrated point of luminosity, and the mind rests without distraction.

If this visualization is clear, then do just one session. If it isn't clear, do one session each of "totality" for the body, speech, and mind. Recite:

> The body aspect, and the others, of the indivisibility of the three doors
> of all beings and myself is visualized as Vairocana and the others.
> In their hearts are *oṃ* and so on,
> within each of which there is a short *a* with its sound, from which lights radiate,
> causing them to dissolve from the outside inward, merging into a concentrated point.

When you practice these three separately, recite the same verse, but with the appropriate changes in the second and third lines:

> The body aspect of the indivisibility of the three doors
> of all beings and myself is visualized as Vairocana.
> In his heart there is an *oṃ*,
> within which there is a short *a* with its sound, from which lights radiate,
> causing him to dissolve from the outside inward, merging into a concentrated point.

When doing the practice for the speech recite:

> The speech aspect of the indivisibility of the three doors
> of all beings and myself is visualized as Amitābha.
> In his heart there is an *āḥ*,

within which there is a short *a* with its sound, from which lights radiate,
causing him to dissolve from the outside inward, merging into a concentrated point.

When doing the practice for the mind recite:

The mind aspect of the indivisibility of the three doors
of all beings and myself are [250] visualized as Akṣobhyavajra.[638]
In his heart there is a *hūṃ*,
within which there is a short *a* with its sound, from which lights radiate,
causing him to dissolve from the outside inward, merging into a concentrated point.

b. The subsequent dissolution

Lights from the seed syllable in your heart cause the worlds and beings to melt into a mass of light that is absorbed into yourself. After that, the meditation of the three beings is the same as in "totality."

The wind-mind then reappears from that state as the body of the deity. This is what is called the *arising of the illusory body from the luminosity*. In order to visualize that, recite:

Lights from the seed syllable in the heart cause the worlds and beings to melt.
In the form of light, they merge into me.
The commitment deities that are my body, speech, and mind
are gradually merged into a sphere of light.

That was the description of the meditation stages of the luminosity.

E. The fifth yoga: the bardo

The teachings on the spontaneous liberation of the bardo is in three parts:

1. The first bardo: the manifestation of the dharmakāya
2. The second bardo: the illusory body arising as the deity's body
3. The third bardo: closing the doorways to rebirth in the six existences

1. *The first bardo: the manifestation of the dharmakāya*

A practitioner who is about to undergo the experience of dying should think, "If things were truly real, then death would be impossible. However, I can see that there is death and destruction. Therefore, things are not real. This means that death, too, is an appearance that has no reality." Thus the practitioner should think nothing of death.

Donate your possessions to the Three Jewels and avoid sorrowful friends, relatives, and so on who would distract your meditation.

If you can, sit in the same physical posture as in the caṇḍālī practice. If you can't, adopt the lion posture. Focus your mind on the guru and the Three Jewels. Develop faith from the depth of your heart and take refuge in an exceptional manner.

Again and again, develop an intense determination, thinking, "Through death, I will realize the true nature, the luminosity, the ultimate truth. Then, for the sake of all beings, I will manifest the level of the union mahāmudrā in the bardo of becoming."

When you are dying, the perception of the eyes will dissolve, so that forms become unclear. The perception of the ears will dissolve, so that sounds will not be heard. The perception of the nose will dissolve, so that there will be no smell. The perception of the tongue dissolves, so that you will have no sensation of taste. The perceptions of the body will dissolve, so that physical sensations will be dulled.

Earth will dissolve into water, and your body will become powerless. Water will dissolve into fire, and your mouth and nose will become dry. Fire [251] will dissolve into air, so that the warmth of your body will shrink. Air will dissolve into consciousness, so that your external breath will stop, although your internal breath will continue for a little while.

At that first instant, there will be the *appearance*, with an inner sign, which resembles smoke, and an outer sign, which resembles moonlight. In the second [instant], there will be *increase*, with an inner sign, which resembles fireflies, and an outer sign, which resembles sunlight. In the third instant, there will be *attainment*, with an inner sign, which resembles lamp flames, and an outer sign, which resembles darkness. Then, in the fourth instant, attainment will merge into *luminosity*. There will be an outer sign, which is like the appearance of dawn, and an inner sign, which is your consciousness resembling a cloudless sky. There will be nonconceptual luminosity, which transcends the intellect and has no center or edge.

At that time, the luminosity of meditation in this life will encounter the natural luminosity, like the meeting between a mother and her son. Resting in that causes the eighty conceptualizations to cease and the nonconceptual elaboration-free luminosity, the dharmakāya, to manifest. Arising from that as the illusory body, is the *training union*. In order to visualize the first bardo, recite:

> For the sake of all my old mothers, the six classes of beings,
> at the time of death, after the dissolving of appearance, increase, and attainment,
> I will see the mind that is the meeting of the mother and son luminosities,
> the face of the natural, nonconceptual dharmakāya.

Repeat that meditation and recitation with intense aspiration.

2. The second bardo: the illusory body arising as the deity's body

If the first bardo alone does not bring liberation, you will enter the second bardo. The movement of thought mounted on the winds causes *attainment*, with its seven natures, to appear from the state of luminosity.

From that *attainment* comes *increase*. From *increase* comes *appearance*. From *appearance* come air, fire, water, and earth. From these the complete sensory faculties manifest and the bardo body, which can move anywhere unimpeded, is created.

Rest in luminosity for as long as you can. When the reverse process of the three visions begins, develop the intention to arise as the illusory body in the bardo. In order to visualize this in the present, recite:

> If the luminosity of the first bardo is left behind
> and the appearances of the second bardo arise,
> at that time I will arise as the superior deity's body,
> the illusory body in the bardo.

Develop that intention now, so that when the reverse process of the three visions is completed and the second bardo is created, you will appear as the illusory body of Vajrayoginī. [252]

Alternatively, train in ultimate luminosity and so on, so that when you reappear, the reverse process of the three visions and the wisdom wind will appear as the body of nontraining union.

3. The third bardo: closing the doorways to rebirth in the six existences

If those previous practices have not brought you to the supreme state, then the third bardo, such as the appearance of the womb, will appear. Meditate that your future mother is Vajrayoginī and your future father is Heruka. Turning away from desire, close the womb's door. Choose the womb of practitioners who are vidyādharas of the Mantrayāna, a father and mother that you can take to be your own gurus.

When you are being reborn into that womb, pray to the guru as father and mother for the higher empowerments.[639] The bodhicitta of the guru father and mother will blend, and you will experience bliss and wisdom. At this time, recognize the realization of the secret empowerment and know the guru father and mother to be your *yidam* deity.

Maintaining the realization of the five awakenings, become a nirmāṇakāya through birth, which is just a visual illusion: a wisdom illusion with wisdom as its cause. In a state of meditation in which you are thinking in this way, take possession of the womb. In order to develop in this life the intention to attain that, recite:

> If in the second bardo, the body of union
> is not accomplished, then at that time
> I will see my future parents as deities and abandon desire.
> I will choose a womb and knowingly be reborn.

Repeat that recitation and meditation.

This was a brief description of the stages of visualization in the bardo practice. If those three practices are not effective, you must dedicate your good karma and seal it with a prayer of aspiration so that you will have a pure rebirth. In order to create in this life the intention to attain that, recite:

> If in the third bardo, the practice of
> the three kāyas does not lead to a result,

> I will bring together the good karma of the three times
> and with a good dedication and prayer of aspiration, create a pure
> rebirth.

If you are unable to choose a womb, make a prayer of aspiration and dedication in which you say, "I call to mind and collect all the good karma I have accumulated by maintaining correct conduct and so on. Through its power, may I obtain a life in which I will have the good fortune to be able to practice the teachings of the Mantrayāna's Dharma."

This was a description of the bardo practice.

F. The sixth yoga: the transference of consciousness

[253] The instruction of the alchemical transference of consciousness at the time of death has three parts:

1. The superior transference into luminosity
2. The medium transference as an illusory body
3. The lesser transference as a deity's body

The first two of these have already been described.

3. The lesser transference as a deity's body

This has three parts:

a. Training in transference
b. Transference with an arrangement of the body
c. The forceful method of transference

a. Training in transference

This is in two parts:

i. The training
ii. The application to activity

i. The training

Sit with the legs in the vajra posture, the back straight, the two hands placed upon the thighs. Visualize yourself as Vajrayoginī, with the openings of the mouth, urethra, anus, nostrils, ear holes, eyes, and navel each sealed by a red *hrīḥ*.

In the center of the body is the central channel, of the thickness of a stalk of wheat. Its lower end is below the navel. The upper end is wide open at the fontanel. Just above there, create the visualization of Vajradhara and consort, as in the preliminaries, and make offerings and praises to them, confess your downfalls and violations to them, and receive the complete empowerments from them. Recite, with special faith:

> Sacred Guru! Sacred Guru!
> Give your blessing so that my death will arise as the dharmakāya,
> my bardo as the saṃbhogakāya,
> and my birth as the nirmāṇakāya.
> Give your blessing that after I am reborn, I will be able, by myself, to bring all beings throughout space to the Mantrayāna Mahayana.

Recite that supplication intensely.

Visualize your mind as a blue *a* upon the anthers of a four-petal lotus that is inside the central channel and below the navel. Upon each of the four petals there is a *yaṃ*.

Inhaled breath dissolves into the stainless central channel and fills it below the navel, causing the four *yaṃs* to flutter. This causes a draft of air that makes the *a* rise. As you recite *hik kā* seven times, the *a* rises up to the navel. As you recite *hik kā* another seven times, the *a* rises up to the heart. Reciting *hik kā* another seven times causes the *a* to rise directly upward until it touches the guru's feet. Then, release the breath and recite *kā hik* twenty-one times, causing the *a* to descend to the lotus below the navel. In order to visualize that, recite:

> I am visualized as the deity. Within the lower end of the central channel,
> upon a lotus, is my mind as an *a*.
> It is lifted by air so that it touches the guru's feet at the crown of my head.
> The breath is released, and the *a* descends to the lotus below the navel.

Train in this until there is a sign, such as itching, swelling, lymph, [254] or an excrescence at the crown of the head.

ii. The application to activity

Even if the signs of dying have appeared, do whatever you can, using various methods, to prevent death. If nothing succeeds in preventing death, repair any impairment of your vows and commitments, donate the things and implements that you own to the Three Jewels, perform a *gaṇacakra* with companions who have kept the commitments, place an image of your *yidam* deity before you, and set out an arrangement of offerings.

Practice the same visualization as previously described, except that this time, the four *yaṃs* are imagined as bow-shaped mandalas of air that cause the syllable to rise. It ascends as before but then merges into the heart of Vajradhara.

Practice that visualization and repeat the recitation with the first two lines unchanged but the rest modified:

> I am visualized as the deity. Within the lower end of the central channel,
> upon a lotus, is my mind as an *a*.
> It is lifted by air so that it merges into the heart
> of the guru at the crown of my head, becoming indivisible in one taste.

This is called the *nirmāṇakāya transference of consciousness.*

Another visualization is to imagine that there is a wisdom being, visualized as Vajrayoginī about an inch in size, in the heart of the guru. In her heart sits a samādhi being in the form of a red *hrīḥ*. Transferring your consciousness into that is called the *saṃbhogakāya transference of consciousness.*

When the *a* syllable is sent into objectlessness, that is called the *dharmakāya luminosity transference.*

b. The transference with an arrangement of the body

Lie down in lion posture with your head pointing north. Imagine yourself as the *yidam* deity. Meditate that your mind is in the form of an *oṃ* at the throat, a *hūṃ* at the heart, and an *āḥ* at the navel. The *āḥ* merges into the *hūṃ*. The *hūṃ* merges into the *oṃ*. The *oṃ* exits through the left nostril and merges into the *yidam* deity's body.

c. The forceful method of transference

This will not be described in this text.[640]

This concludes the brief description of the practice of the transference of consciousness.

III. The conclusion [of this text on the six yogas]

This is in four parts:

A. Eliminating obstacles
B. Increasing the benefit
C. The way the paths are traversed
D. The way the results are attained

A. Eliminating obstacles

If the breathing practice is too forceful during the breathing exercises, or if the key points of the breathing practices were not understood, the life-force wind may reverse and so on. If these obstacles occur, correct them by speaking with your teacher in person.

A smell comes up while you are washing a bowl, and in the same way, at this time there arise the five mind-poisons and the bad results that we would otherwise experience in other lifetimes in the six existences. Therefore, you will experience a great increase in physical pain, negativity in the mind, [255] and so on. At such a time, meditate on the illusory body and emptiness. Bring these experiences into the path through such practices as the *five nails*.[641]

In particular, there are many into whom the demon of pride enters because of the qualities they have developed through meditating on the path of method. Therefore, a thought such as, "There is nothing like this, even in the Buddha's mind," should be brought to rest in an elaboration-free state and become blended in one taste. Do not be premature in working to benefit others. In brief, there are many obstacles to the teachings of the caṇḍālī short *a* and its ancillaries, such as the illusory body, and it is difficult to know how to avoid them.

When the wind is held in the channel knots or in other places, every kind of experience can occur. If, in response to those experiences, you have suffering, arrogance, hope, or fear, those experiences will become obstacles to you. Therefore, avoid falling under the power of these obstacles by relying on the nectar that comes from the mouth of the sacred guru.

B. Increasing the benefit

Develop a continuity, like that of a river, of faith in the guru, compassion for beings, diligence free of laziness, a perfect knowledge of the methods, a stable meditation in solitude, and so on. Rely on your guru's words until you have attained stability.

Those with inferior and medium capabilities, who practice bliss through the symbolic mudrā, should increase benefit through an *action seal,* a consort who has the necessary qualities, or through a *primordial seal,* which is an imagined consort. They should follow a conduct that accords with [the level of] their [attainment of] heat.

Those with sharp capabilities, who can practice the supreme emptiness mudrā and so on, should follow the conduct of the *bhusuka*[642] and increase results through the mahāmudrā.

In brief, results are increased by practicing in accord with individual's level, the three conducts taught in the father tantras, and the conduct taught in the mother tantras. In general, results are increased by keeping qualities secret. Don't be premature in your wish to be a lama and your claim to benefit beings. You can learn the details of this from your own guru.

C. The way the paths are traversed

On the first path of accumulation, the afflictions and thoughts that cause results in other lifetimes are brought onto the path when the caṇḍālī fire incinerates the five seeds of the mind-poisons, which are located in the impure body's five places. On the second path of accumulation, those results, and also sickness and demons, are brought onto the path. On the third path of accumulation, the continuum of rebirth is brought into the path and cut through. On the fourth path of accumulation, impure bliss, clarity, nonthought, and emptiness are brought into the path.

The first path of engagement is training in the path of absorbing the wind-mind into the five cakras. [256] On the second path of engagement, the retention of wind-mind within countless channels is brought into the path. On the third path of engagement, there is engagement with the first truth as the result of immaculate bliss, clarity, nonthought, and emptiness being brought [onto the path]. The fourth path of engagement is retention of the immaculate winds of the five elements as wisdom winds. The fifth path of engagement is when great bliss and great emptiness arise alternately.

There is the traversal of the path of seeing, which is the first level [of enlightenment] (*bhūmi*), named Perfect Joy, which is when you first see the previously unseen one-taste of bliss and emptiness. There is the traversal of the first and other paths of meditation, which continue up to the twelfth level, named Attachment-Free Lotus, in parallel with the upward traversal of the vital energy and so on, until the [path] of completion is attained.

D. The way the result is attained

This is a conclusive presentation of the results. The general siddhis or results: The cessation of the winds of the five elements within the central channel causes the five, ten, or more signs, such as smoke. Countless qualities appear in the body, speech, and mind. The general siddhis, such as the four activities and the eight siddhis, are also attained. In this way you attain, bring under your power, and increase the mundane siddhis.

When the paths have been fully traversed, you attain the supreme siddhi, the thirteenth stage, or the Vajradhara stage, and attain the state of a Vajradhara. There is the manifestation of the saṃbhogakāya with the seven aspects of union.[643] There will be the dance of the inexpressible, inconceivable, illusory network of emanations. Existence is purified within the heart of enlightenment. In brief, the unique state of Buddha Vajrasattva, the great lord of all the buddha families, will be made manifest.

This concludes a brief description of the visualization sessions of the six yogas of glorious Nāropa.

> I don't have the experience of meditation,
> so it's difficult for me to teach the nature of the path to others,
> but I have conviction in the excellent teaching of my tutors,
> and in the practice lineage: the unsurpassable Karma Kamtsang.
> I have understood and realized a little of this path,
> and so I have presented it in a brief form.

There have been many in this land of Tibet who have described it
with useless words, misunderstanding the completion-stage caṇḍālī
as ultimately being only a method for removing stains
from the basis of purification, which is this body.

My unmistaken tutor, the Karmapa,[644]
using the lamp of the melodious words of Yangchen Shepa,[645]
perfectly separated the meaningful from the meaningless. [257]
Who could begin to compete with him in the realm of knowledge?

If you bow your head to the toes
of Wangchuk Dorjé, the supreme guru,
who has unceasing compassion, and then follow his lineage,
the definitive meaning will not be lost in the general meaning but will directly appear.

If I have made the mistake of giving away secrets in writing this text,
I ask the ḍākinīs for their forgiveness.
May all beings, through this good karma, enter the essential teaching
and gain the supreme changeless accomplishment!

In order to fulfill the request of Karma Wangchuk, the one who teaches the infinite ways of the Mantrayāna, I, Chökyi Wangchuk,[646] a monk of Śākyamuni, prayed to the ḍākinīs for permission, placed the great lord Karmapa upon my head as an adornment, and wrote this text in my twenty-sixth year[647] at Khyung Dzong [Garuda Castle], the palace of the Buddha.[648]

10. The Single Viewpoint: A Root Text

Sherap Jungné (1187–1241)

I. The Hundred and Fifty Vajra Teachings

[259] *Namo ratna gurubhyaḥ* (Homage to the precious gurus).

> I pay homage to you, the precious peerless Drigungpa,[649]
> the omniscient Lord of the Dharma,
> who sees all distinct knowable things, as they are,
> in the mandala of the stainless luminosity of the mind.
>
> Countless teachings have made clear
> the sublime and unique Dharma
> that was taught by the supreme Conqueror,
> but I will write a little so as to guide the ignorant.

The Tathāgata, who is the lord of the Dharma, taught countless scriptural baskets, tantras, sādhanas, and so on. There are different traditions of comprehending and understanding them, but all are profound and marvelous. I will accurately present here some minor differences between our tradition and the others.

The *Single Viewpoint of the Conqueror* has a hundred and fifty specific essential points, which are classified into seven groups.

1. The Thirty Vajra Teachings that Summarize General Key Points of the Wheel of Dharma

1. Some say that, in general, since the Tathāgata is the lord of Dharma, whatever teaching he wishes to give causes [phenomena (*dharmas*)] to become like that. However, this [tradition] states that the entire

Dharma of the Buddha teaches only the nature or true condition [of phenomena].

2. Some say that [the Buddha] taught eighty-four thousand Dharma teachings and one can attain great enlightenment by entering any of these "doorways." However, this [tradition] states that all eighty-four thousand Dharmas [260] are one single method for accomplishing buddhahood.
3. Some say that the three scriptural baskets and the four tantras are various paths that pupils aspire to, but this [tradition] states that the three baskets and the four tantras are stages of development on the [one] path.
4. Some teach that the three turnings of the Dharma wheel are separate, but this [tradition] states that they are the teachings of the single realization that is behind all three turnings of the Dharma wheel.
5. Some say that the three Dharma wheels have distinct, individual subjects, but this [tradition] states that all three Dharma wheels are completely present in each one.
6. Some say that even though the Dharma wheels have such a relationship in terms of meaning, this was not clearly expressed in [their] words. However, this [tradition] states that the preceding Dharma wheel is the seed for the subsequent Dharma wheel.
7. Some say that the three Dharma wheels are so categorized because of their different locations, times, and so on, but this [tradition] states that there are definitively three wheels because of the key points in their sutras and content.
8. Some say that the Abhidharma basket, not the Vinaya basket, is "the Dharma wheel of the four truths," but this [tradition] states that the Vinaya basket is "[the Dharma wheel of] the four truths."
9. Many have taught that "the teaching of many vehicles" is the second Dharma wheel and that the [Dharma wheel] of "the absence of characteristics" is the definitive meaning, but this [tradition] states that the teaching of "[the Dharma wheel] of many vehicles" is the Dharma wheel of the definitive meaning.
10. Some say that the Buddha's words are teachings that have either a provisional or definitive meaning, and so on, so therefore the Tathāgata sometimes used lies as a skillful method, but this [tradition] states that all his teachings, even those that are "the six alternatives," have nothing but a definitive meaning.[650]
11. Some say that the [Buddha's] teachings on the Madhyamaka and

Cittamātra are distinct from each other, [but] the [guru's] vajra speech asserted the Cittamātra teaching to be a Madhyamaka teaching.

12. Some say that the invalid relative cannot accomplish the goal, [but] the vajra speech asserted that even the invalid relative can accomplish the goal.
13. Some say that the path of the Perfection Vehicle or Characteristics Vehicle proceeds through the ten levels while the instantaneous way does not. However, this [tradition] states that all paths must pass through the ten levels.
14. Some say that the gradualist way and the immediate way are different, [261] but this [tradition] states that all paths are gradualist.
15. Some say that [in eliminating] all obscurations, first the obscurations from karma are eliminated, then the obscurations from the afflictions, and finally the obscuration of knowledge, but this [tradition] states that the obscuration of knowledge is [eliminated] first.
16. Some say that the teachings on logic and epistemology (*pramāṇa*) cannot be the Buddha's Dharma because it is also found in the Vedas of the tīrthikas, but this [tradition] states that pramāṇa is the wisdom of the Buddha's knowledge.
17. Some say that pramāṇa is for the refutation of bad philosophies and that pramāṇa can bring no other result, but this [tradition] states that the teaching of true nature and emptiness is the result of pramāṇa.
18. Some say that [pramāṇa] was necessary for use against the tīrthikas of India, and so on, who attacked the various [Dharma] traditions, but this [tradition] states it to be an independent [teaching] for the holders of all traditions.
19. Some say that every tīrthika practice of view and conduct is to be abandoned, but this [tradition] states that there are many practices of natural virtue even among the tīrthikas.
20. Some say that what differentiates Buddhists from the tīrthikas are the four seals that are signs of the Dharma or a variety of other differences, but this [tradition] states that taking refuge is what differentiates Buddhists from non-Buddhists.
21. Some say that the thirty-seven factors for enlightenment, the six perfections, and other such differences in following the path are what differentiates the Mahayana from the Hīnayāna. However, this [tradition] states that it is bodhicitta that differentiates the Mahayana from the Hīnayāna.

22. Some say that the Characteristics Vehicle, or Perfection Vehicle, is differentiated from the Mantrayāna according to whether the paths are formed from cause or from result, and so on. However, this [tradition] states that it is empowerment that differentiates the Mantrayāna from the Characteristics Vehicle.
23. Some say that either the Perfection Vehicle or the Mantrayāna can bring the attainment of enlightenment. However, this [tradition] states that there will be no attainment of enlightenment if either the Characteristics Vehicle or the Mantrayāna is absent.
24. Some say that the three [levels of] vows are the [adoption and avoidance] of specific virtues and bad actions, but this [tradition] states that [all] three [levels of] vows are the [one] essential point of avoiding negative actions, which are to be avoided.
25. Some say that the three [levels of] vows are differentiated because of different vows that are kept, [262] but this [tradition] states that there are three [levels of] vows because of [the vows] having different holders.[651]
26. Some teach that the buddha essence, the element of pure nature, is emptiness. However, this [tradition] states that the natural purity of the element is a superior quality that is the result of freedom [from obscurations].
27. Some teach that the thirty-seven factors for enlightenment are only on the path of the three vehicles, but this [tradition] states that the thirty-seven factors for enlightenment are present within buddha nature.
28. Some say that the four immeasurables are only worldly samādhis, but this [tradition] states that the four immeasurables are the essence of buddha nature, they are the nature of buddhahood.
29. Some say that the three vehicles have different results because of their definitively different causes and paths. However, this [tradition] teaches that all vehicles are one family, one vehicle.
30. Some say that śrāvakas and those with wrong aspiration cannot attain buddhahood and that śrāvakas have an eternal obstacle [to the attainment of buddhahood]. However, this [tradition] states that [Śākya-]muni's viewpoint is that even the śrāvakas and those with wrong aspiration will eventually attain enlightenment.

2. The Fifteen Vajra Teachings on the Interdependence that Benefits All

1. Some teach that there are good, bad, and neutral actions, but this [tradition] states that there are definitely [only] good and bad actions and there are no such things as neutral actions.
2. Some say there can be many thoughts or separate [mental] phenomena simultaneously. However, this [tradition] states that two thoughts cannot be engaged simultaneously, that they do not arise as accompaniments to the mind.
3. Some say that the mind is a basis and particular [mental] phenomena arise from the mind, but this [tradition] states that mental events arise from [preceding] mental events.
4. Some say that it is the mind alone that cycles through samsara, but this [tradition] states that it is the body that cycles through samsara.
5. Some say that ignorance is one of the twelve phases of dependent origination, but this [tradition] states that all twelve [phases of] dependent origination are the movement of ignorance.
6. Some say that the twelve [phases of] dependent origination are completed in three sections or divisions, [263] but this [tradition] states that the twelve [phases of] dependent origination are complete in a single instant.
7. Some say that there is no regularity to the different sizes and origins of worlds and realms, but this [tradition] states that those are different perceptions resulting from different minds.
8. Some say that all happiness and suffering are entirely dependent on the actions of previous lives, but this [tradition] states that you experience right now the results of what you do.
9. Some say that periods of increase and decline[652] occur naturally and there is no method that can affect them, but this [tradition] states that periods of increase and decline can be created right now in the present.
10. Some say that in these times, the results of our actions are experienced in the next life or in later lifetimes but never in this life, but this [tradition] states that the most important [results] are those that we experience ourselves in our lifetime.
11. Some say that the sixteen human Dharmas[653] and so on are a human Dharma that is different from the divine Dharma,[654] but this [tradition]

states that the sixteen human Dharmas and so on are the same as the divine Dharma.

12. Some say that after ten five-hundred[-year periods] of the teaching, the era of results will have passed, but this [tradition] states that the attainment of results will not end; there is only a difference in their extent.
13. Some say the superior training of conduct comes first in the three trainings, but this [tradition] states that the training in exceptional wisdom comes first.
14. Some say that all the stages of the teaching and the path are practiced sequentially, but this [tradition] states that all stages of the path are practiced in one session.
15. Some say there can only be one buddha in each buddha realm, but this [tradition] states there can be a continuous presence of many buddhas in a single realm.

3. The Twenty Vajra Teachings on the Essential Points of the Vinaya Pratimokṣa

1. In some traditions, there are many who state that the Vinaya basket of the sublime Dharma is in the Hīnayāna, [264] but this [tradition] states that the Vinaya is in all the vehicles.
2. Many have stated that the Vinaya is definitely in the Hīnayāna alone and therefore is not Mahayana, but this [tradition] states clearly that the Vinaya, in particular, is Mahayana.
3. Some state that conduct, which is training in doing [good] and not doing [bad], is the Dharma of the śrāvakas, but this [tradition] states that precious conduct is nothing other than the wisdom of omniscience.
4. Some state that they who have "the factors that are obstacles"[655] are unable to receive the vows, but this [tradition] states that these are obstacles to attaining the results of the training in good actions and not obstacles to acquiring the vows.
5. Many have stated well the theory that the essence of vows is the forsaking mind and its seeds, and so on.[656] However, this [tradition] states that the vows are essentially imperceptible forms.[657]
6. Some say that consciousness and matter are the two factors for all vow downfalls, but this [tradition] states that it is the perpetrator's consciousness that is the principal factor in all vow downfalls.

7. Some state that the pratimokṣa vows consist of the seven eliminations and their ancillaries,[658] but this [tradition] states that it is the three [negative] aspects of the mind[659] that must principally be eliminated.
8. Some state that vows are lost at death, on transference [to the next life], and so on, but this [tradition] states that they are not lost through such causes of loss as those.
9. Some say that one "defeat"[660] causes all vows to be lost so that one cannot be a monastic, but this [tradition] states that it's like being a wealthy person who has [to pay] a debt.
10. Some say that the harm caused by just one vow downfall will inevitably result in a fall into the lower existences, with no other possible result, but this [tradition] states that keeping even one [vow] will have nirvana as its result.
11. Many say that there are no rules of permission and prohibition for naturally negative actions but that there are for proscribed actions,[661] but this [tradition] states that naturally negative and proscribed actions are the same.
12. Some say there is a difference as to whether bad actions or downfalls are natural or not, but this [tradition] teaches that there is only one, undifferentiated kind of bad action or downfall.
13. Some state that the proscribed [negative actions] were only proscribed for monks and lay practitioners, who are the foundations for these proscriptions, but this [tradition] states that they are proscribed for all six classes of beings. [265]
14. Some state that if beings other [than monastics] transgress the proscriptions they do not commit an offense, but this [tradition] states that anyone in the six classes of beings who transgresses the proscriptions [commits] an offense.
15. Some say that keeping the proscriptions is beneficial for those who have adopted the training but not for others, but this [tradition] states that there is great benefit to anyone in the six classes of beings who keeps them.
16. Some say that the proscriptions are dependent, and therefore when that which is prohibited by a proscription becomes permissible, it is no longer an offense, but this [tradition] states that it's impossible for that which is prohibited to not be an offense; therefore all that is prohibited is perpetually prohibited and all that is permissible is perpetually permissible.

17. There are famously those who say that one can keep [the vows] without the ritual [of taking them], but this [tradition] states that the rituals are skillful methods within the teachings and extremely important.
18. Some say attachment and especially aversion are the greatest of all evils and assert that ignorance is a lesser [evil], but this [tradition] teaches that ignorance is foremost.
19. Some say that in the lower existences, hell beings are lower than animals, but this [tradition] teaches that animals are inferior, because of their greater ignorance.
20. Some say that if someone who has adopted the training commits an offense, then it is a heavy [offense], but if someone who has never adopted [the training] commits [an offense, there is] no offense. However, this [tradition] states that those who have not adopted [the training] who [commit] an offense of violation, commit a great and heavy offense.

4. The Twenty-Four Vajra Teachings that Are a Compilation of the Essential Points of the Bodhicitta Training

1. Many say that as compassion is the distinctive feature of the Mahayana, then bodhicitta is compassion. However, this [tradition] states that bodhicitta and compassion are different.
2. Some say that as there is no definite development of bodhicitta, it is a vow without a basis. However, this [tradition] states that the vow of the bodhisattva conduct does have a basis, because it is a mental experience.
3. Some say that the [bodhicitta] vow of engagement is generated after reaching the levels [of enlightenment] (*bhūmis*), [266] but this [tradition] states that even an ordinary being can generate the vow of engagement.
4. Some say that there can be no vow of engagement without keeping all three levels of vows, but this [tradition] states that any kind of correct conduct can be the vow [of engagement].
5. Some say that bodhicitta downfalls are of two kinds: those with afflictions and those without afflictions, but this [tradition] states that there is no downfall without affliction.
6. Some say that great bodhisattvas can perform negative actions because they transform them into good actions, but this [tradition] states that there is no bad action that is not an offense.

7. Some say that "skillful methods of the bodhisattva" means doing bad actions, but this [tradition] states that there are no bad actions in the conduct of "skillful means," and if there were, they would bring the results that come from bad actions.
8. Some say that, with great compassion, one can make prayers that will benefit others and take the suffering of others onto oneself, but this [tradition] states that if one is not skilled in method, then taking the [suffering] of others onto oneself is an error.
9. Some say that harming a bodhisattva can be a cause that brings a happy result, but this [tradition] states that this is a harmful cause and therefore it is impossible that harming a bodhisattva can bring a connection with happiness.
10. Some say that when good "propelling karma" propels, and bad "completing karma" completes, the cause and result can differ, but this [tradition] states that there are definitely separate results from good and bad actions as different [sets] of cause and result.
11. Some say that offenses that are similar to "the defeats," such as the four black deeds,[662] cause the loss of bodhicitta, but this [tradition] states that they can only cause one to forget [bodhicitta] but cannot possibly cause its loss.
12. Some say that the three obscurations are distinct from each other, but this [tradition] states that the three obscurations are the single obscuration of afflictions.
13. Some say that the truth of the nature of phenomena is realized by refuting negative philosophies and comprehending good philosophies, but this [tradition] states that all philosophies obscure the truth.
14. Some say that the philosophy of the śrāvakas is false, [267] but this [tradition] states that even the śrāvaka tradition has partial realization of the true nature.
15. Some say that the nature of phenomena cannot be realized through Cittamātra alone, but this [tradition] states that the Cittamātra is the realization of those on the seventh level, called *Gone Far*.
16. Some say the two selflessnesses[663] are realized from the first level onward, but this [tradition] states that it is correct to say that the selflessness of phenomena does not manifest until the eighth level.
17. Some say that true realization, the path of seeing, and the "heroic [samādhi]" are different stages, but this [tradition] states that a single realization proceeds through all levels and paths.

18. Some say that the hundredfold twelve qualities[664] and so on appear as soon as one attains the [first] level, but this [tradition] states that the qualities derived from training appear on the levels as six variations[665] and so on.
19. Some say that the accumulation of wisdom is a result, with gathering the accumulation of merit as its cause, but this [tradition] states that both accumulations are a union of the entire cause, path, and result.
20. Some say that śrāvakas and pratyekabuddhas cannot see even the first level [of enlightement], but this [tradition] states that the realization of the śrāvakas and pratyekabuddhas is the same [as that of the bodhisattvas] up until the sixth level.
21. Some say that because of the difference between the Mahayana and Hīnayāna, they have different fields for gathering accumulations, but this [tradition] states the profound, quintessential point that anything, however high or low, should be a field [for accumulation].
22. Some say you transcend samsara by not fixating on the self and therefore you should eliminate fixation on the self, but this [tradition] states that fixating on the self while gathering the accumulations is a skillful method for gathering the accumulation of merit.
23. Some say you should dedicate only the good karma you have created yourself, but this [tradition] states that you should dedicate all good karma throughout samsara and nirvana.
24. Some say it's unnecessary to dedicate [good karma] to the buddhas and sublime gurus, but this [tradition] states that you should make such dedications to the buddhas and gurus also so that their activities will be completed.

5. The Twenty-Eight Vajra Teachings that Are a Compilation of the Essential Points of the Mantra-Vidyādhara Vows [268]

1. Some say that the Mantrayāna does not appear in other teachings, but this [tradition] states that the Mantrayāna does appear in other teachings, in accordance with the particular [qualities] of the pupils.
2. Some say the ritual gives the understanding that you have received a Mantrayāna empowerment, but this [tradition] asserts that it is attained when a qualified guru gives the meaning of the empowerment and it appears within your being.
3. Some say that if all the different families are not present in the

mandala cakra then there is no empowerment, but this [tradition] states that there is an empowerment even if there is only one group of deities.

4. Many do not properly teach the meaning of the third empowerment's symbols,[666] but this [tradition] states that if the symbols and their meaning are not understood, the [empowerment's] meaning will not be truly realized.
5. Some say the generation stage is "imaginary" because you are imagining something that is not, but this [tradition] states that the generation stage is "absolute."[667]
6. Some say that the ritual of entry [into the mandala] is unnecessary for those in whom samādhi spontaneously arises through the awakening of past karma and that the practice alone will suffice. However, this [tradition] states that the ritual of entry is [also] important for those who have the spontaneous arising [of samādhi].
7. Some say Mantrayāna deities have different faces and arms similar to those of the pupils, but this [tradition] states that all deities have the qualities of the primary and secondary signs.
8. Many say that visions of tathāgatas, bodhisattvas, and so on are most important, but this [tradition] states that it is how the deities and so on are taught in the sutras and tantras that is most important.
9. Some say the meditation in which the deity is completely generated in an instant is intended for those who are most capable while the numerous other practices are not necessary for them but are intended for those who are least capable. However, this [tradition] states that all complex practices are extremely necessary and important for those with higher capabilities also.
10. [Some say that] all complex practices are a provisional teaching taught to those attracted to elaboration, but this [tradition] states that all elaboration arises through natural, dependent [origination].
11. Some say that the channels, winds, drops, and bodhicitta are the true nature of the vajra body, but this [tradition] states that the profound cakras are the true nature of the vajra body. [269]
12. Some say that the true nature of the channels, winds, drops, and bodhicitta are taught in the texts, but this [tradition] states that Vajradhara kept some true natures secret.
13. Some say that the channels and winds, in particular, are taught profoundly in the Mantrayāna only, but this [tradition] states that some

of [their] configurations and activities are taught profoundly in the medical tradition.

14. Some say brief teachings and practice instructions on the channels and winds are more profound than the three [levels of] vows and so on, but this [tradition] states that what they regard as not profound *is* profound.
15. Some say that the complete [vajra] body is the result of practicing the profound channels and winds, but this [tradition] states that without [receiving] the profound teachings, one cannot attain buddhahood through the profound channels and winds.
16. Some say that the experience or realization of something that is not taught in the Buddha's words or in the commentaries is a special Dharma, but this [tradition] states that an experience contradictory to the teaching of the Sugata is an incorrect realization.
17. Some say the provisional meaning and the definitive meaning are realized separately and therefore it's enough to be in agreement with just one or the other, but this [tradition] states that you should never disagree with any of the viewpoints in the Buddha's teachings.
18. Some say the faults and good qualities of practice are those described in the profound practice instructions only, but this [tradition] states that what is not [found] in the instructions will be in the Buddha's words.
19. Some say the [three] faultless samādhis[668] are the cause of the three kāyas, but this [tradition] states that the three faultless samādhis are the cause of the third realm's samsara.[669]
20. Some teach that the three kāyas are separate, with the nirmāṇakāya in the twenty-four sacred sites[670] and so on, and then the saṃbhogakāya and so on, but this [tradition] states that each of the three kāyas has the nature of all three kāyas.
21. Many say that the Mantrayāna is the viewpoint of Vajradhara and therefore you do not need to train in the viewpoint of Śākyamuni, but this [tradition] states that the Mantrayāna is useless without correct conduct.
22. It was taught that the Mantrayāna is accomplishment through the practice of desire, but this [tradition] states that this is identical with the teaching that desire causes obstacles.
23. Some say the Mantrayāna is the path through which one transforms the basis—the three afflictions, or poisons—but this [tradition] states

that in the Mantrayāna, a bad action can never be transformed into a good action.

24. Some say that through the practice of skillful methods in the Mantrayāna, even bad actions can be good actions, [270] but this [tradition] states that what is a good action in the Vinaya is a good action in the Mantrayāna, and what is a bad action in the Vinaya is a bad action in the Mantrayāna.
25. It is asserted that the afflictions are the families and lineages of the buddhas, but this [tradition] states that the sugatas result from the purification of the afflictions.
26. Some say the Mantrayāna's sorcery rites are not bad actions but good actions and therefore permissible, but this [tradition] states that in the Mantrayāna's teaching on sorcery there is no permission for the practice of sorcery.
27. Some say that the Vajra Hell is greater than any other hell, but this [tradition] states that *Vajra Hell* means Avīci and all the other hells.
28. Some say that one does not come out [of that hell] until space is destroyed, but this [tradition] states that a vajra master who is a high being can free beings from it.

6. The Twenty Vajra Teachings that Are a Compilation of the Essential Points Specifically Concerning View, Conduct, and Meditation

1. Some say Dharma teachings that are not from a lineage but are earth Dharmas, space Dharmas, termas, and so on are profound and wonderful. However, this [tradition] states that it is tantra Dharma teachings from a lineage that are profound and marvelous.
2. Some say that the appearance of the variety of [external] appearances is unconnected with the inner mind, but this [tradition] states that all phenomena of samsara and nirvana are one's own mind.
3. Some say that all causes and results in samsara depend on the passage of long periods of time, but this [tradition] states that all phenomena are the embodiment of an instant of thought.
4. Some say that things have no definitive single nature but become whatever they are perceived to be, but this [tradition] states that if something is not in the thing's nature, seeing it is not a cause for it to be there.

5. Some say that even a guru who does not have the necessary characteristics can develop qualities in a pupil, but this [tradition] states that a guru without the necessary characteristics is unable to develop good qualities [in a pupil].
6. Some say there is an indefinite variety of methods for generating realization, but this [tradition] states that devotion is the one certain method for generating realization. [271]
7. Some say the Great Madhyamaka and so on are the ultimate views, but this [tradition] teaches that realization of the view comes when perfect realization is attained.
8. Some say that only the "three greats"[671] are high in the realization of emptiness, of the true nature, but this [tradition] teaches a realization that the three greats do not reach.[672]
9. Some say *realization* means the realization that comes from hearing, contemplation, and meditation, but this [tradition] states that any emptiness [realized through] hearing, contemplation, and meditation is an error and a deviation.
10. Some say *meditation* means the samādhi of śamatha, accompanied by bliss, clarity, nonthought, and so on, but this [tradition] states that meditation is familiarization with the path of realization.
11. Some say *view* means the true nature of phenomena—emptiness, the mahāmudrā—while *conduct* means being free from performing good actions and avoiding bad actions, but this [tradition] states that *conduct* is the precious correct conduct of performance and avoidance.
12. Some say ultimate mahāmudrā and correct conduct are contraries, but this [tradition] states that mahāmudrā and correct conduct are the one lord, the unsurpassable special Dharma.
13. Some say view, meditation, and conduct are separate, but this [tradition] states that view, meditation, and conduct are one.
14. Some say there are neither faults nor good qualities in the mahāmudrā, but this [tradition] states that mahāmudrā is the very nature of good qualities.
15. Some say good qualities do not arise in meditation but in post-meditation, but this [tradition] states that all good qualities arise in meditation.
16. Some say that all good qualities can arise even without their causes being created, but this [tradition] states that nothing will arise without its cause being created first.

17. Some say that on realizing emptiness, the process of cause and result ceases and one reaches the level of cessation, but this [tradition] states that when emptiness is realized, emptiness arises as cause and result.
18. Some say that the paths of methods and so on are no longer necessary after attaining realization, but this [tradition] states that the paths of methods and so on are very necessary even for those who have realization.
19. Some say that in order to enhance realization, one must perform the various *vidyāvrata* conducts, such as living in charnel grounds while wearing a yogin's attire, but this [tradition] states that to deeply cherish and beautify oneself with the training of correct conduct [272] is the especially superior "special conduct of wisdom."
20. Some say the ultimate conduct is that of a *bhusuku*[673] meditator, but this [tradition] states that if a *bhusuku* does not have the three Dharmas,[674] [his conduct] will [only] be the conduct of the peace [of the śrāvakas and pratyekabuddhas].

7. The Fifteen Vajra Teachings that Are a Compilation of the Essential Points of the Result—Buddhahood

1. Some say there are [still] the two truths at the level of buddhahood, but this [tradition] states that the two truths do not exist at the level of buddhahood.
2. Some say that the wisdom of the Buddha exists or doesn't exist, but this [tradition] states that the wisdom [of the Buddha] is nothing but nondual wisdom.
3. Some say that even if there were a phenomenon superior to nirvana, it would [still] be like an illusion, and so therefore nirvana is an illusion, but this [tradition] states that [buddhahood] completely transcends illusion-like phenomena.
4. Some say that the Buddha's mind is not valid for the first two instants [of buddhahood], but this [tradition] states that buddhahood is always valid.
5. Some say that when buddhas eliminate the obscuration of knowledge, their minds cease to engage, but this [tradition] states that their minds have wisdom as the result of being freed.
6. Some say that the dharmakāya has no causes and conditions because it transcends all that is dualistic, but this [tradition] states that the dharmakāya has qualities and activities.

7. Some say that buddhahood is the complete result and therefore there is no longer any engagement with causes, but this [tradition] states that bodhicitta is developed even at the level of buddhahood.
8. It is taught that the ceaseless—the adorned wheel of the Buddha's body, speech, and mind—is a mere manifestation [to others], but this [tradition] states that it is the mind [of the Buddha] alone that arises, transcending the views of nihilism and eternalism.
9. Some say buddhas benefit beings through buddha emanations only and not through any other medium, but this [tradition] states that the buddhas' activities are performed through any knowable [phenomena] that exist.
10. Some say every buddha attains buddhahood in a separate realm, [273] but this [tradition] states that if that buddhahood is not attained throughout the entire expanse of phenomena, then it is not buddhahood.
11. Some say the infinite emanations manifested by the buddhas can even manifest without a cause, but this [tradition] states that it is impossible for manifestations to be without a cause and therefore they are independent.[675]
12. Some say the two kāyas and wisdom are [solely] the perceptions of others, but this [tradition] states that a buddha's kāyas are dependent [originations].[676]
13. Some say that as the result of prayer, one enters the nirmāṇakāya and then the saṃbhogakāya arises from the nirmāṇakāya, but this [tradition] states that as the result of prayer, one enters the saṃbhogakāya and the nirmāṇakāya arises from the saṃbhogakāya.
14. Some say the three kāyas appear with separate locations, separate retinues, and separate Dharmas, but this [tradition] states that the three kāyas have no separation.
15. Some say all buddhas reside in Akaniṣṭha or a similar realm, but this [tradition] states that all buddhas reside within the nature of the continuum of beings.

8. A Compilation of Instructions on These Statements

These are renowned to be great statements. There is no end to the ways of explaining each one of them. Those who receive the seal of these statements, study the analytic commentaries, and know how to apply these statements directly to their own being and comprehend them in accordance with the viewpoint of all of [Śākyamuni's] teachings will become the sons born from the mind of the peerless father, Lord Drigungpa. They will have the marvelous and inconceivable enjoyment of their share of the Dharma.

Even if he possesses ordinary wealth,
a father's son is cursed in this world
if he does not hear of and does not hold
his father's special wealth, which no one else has.

The disciples and sons will become the same as that
if in future times, in this world, they do not hold
these special Dharma teachings, previously unheard,
that the peerless lord of the world, Jikten Gönpo, revealed.

Therefore, it is a great marvel when a representative of the wise father's lineage
holds, with great perseverance,
the viewpoints of that famous one's teaching,
without criticizing other mistaken traditions.

The sublime beings who maintain the teaching and teach the Dharma
are said to be superior beings, just as when among a thousand sons
there is a prince with the qualities of a cakravartin king,
and they are the most beautiful among all who have entered the Dharma.

Not ignorant of the essence of the special teachings
and all the infinite teachings of Śākyamuni,
he is like a snow lion, with no fear
of the foxes who are his tīrthika adversaries.

Excellently teaching the special distinct Dharma
to similar followers and a variety of pupils, [274]
he makes a perfect distinction between the inferior and the supreme,
and the loud thunder of his fame resounds in the ten directions.

These profound, vast, unsurpassable viewpoints
are as vast as a great ocean.

I, Bendom Sherap Jungné, have written this description of them,
which is just a drop of its water or the tip of a hair.

By this virtue, as pure white as a snow mountain,
may the precious teachings spread in the ten directions.
May beings become free of ignorance and stupidity
and ultimately achieve the wisdom of buddhahood.

I composed and completed these hundred and fifty ultimate special wealths, which the father had accumulated, in glorious Drigung Akaniṣṭha.

II. The Forty-Seven Supplements to the Hundred and Fifty Vajra Teachings

I pay homage to the precious peerless Drigungpa,
the omniscient lord of the Dharma
who sees all distinct knowable things, as they are,
in the mandala of the stainless luminosity of his mind.

He is the teacher who stopped the three times, who is superior to the entire display of qualities by the buddhas in the three times and ten directions. All the conquerors throughout the entire expanse of phenomena eternally sing the praise of his qualities. The fame of his great body's qualities has spread throughout all infinite worlds. Each of his miraculous displays reaches to the final limit of knowable phenomena, extends to the ends of space, transcends all examples, and is without equal. He is the guru for all samsara and nirvana, for he is continually present, pervading all worlds in the ten directions to the limit where they finally end. He is lord over all Dharmas and master of the precious training's conduct of avoidance and performance. He is the great universal monarch, the peerless guru, and the protector of the three realms. He is the Dharma Lord Drigung Lingpa. These are his teachings:

1. Some say the teachings of all the conquerors in the three times and ten directions are distinct and various, but this [tradition] states that the nature of the Dharma and teachings of all buddhas is one. [275]
2. Some say the buddhas have different Dharmas and distinct philosophies, but this [tradition] states that the vehicles and philosophies are the buddhas' [teaching of] dependent [origination].
3. Some say that, in general, the collection of Dharma teachings amounts

to a single ox-load and so on, but this [tradition] states that it consists of remedies for the eighty-four thousand afflictions.

4. Some say the Buddha's words consist of twelve individual and distinct branches,[677] but this [tradition] states that all twelve branches are totally present within each one.
5. Some say the five perfect aspects[678] do not pervade teachings that are not the Buddha's, but this [tradition] states that all samsara and nirvana are within these five perfections.
6. Some say the three scriptural baskets are separate and unconnected with each other, but this [tradition] states that they were taught together in combination, in an interrelated manner, with all three completely present within each one.
7. Some say that, in general, the perfect Dharma is not complete within any of the introductions[679] to the Buddha's teachings, but this [tradition] states that the five perfect aspects are totally present throughout all the Buddha's teachings.
8. There are many traditions concerning Vinaya, Sutra, and Abhidharma, but this [tradition] states that the general sutras[680] and the Cittamātra teachings[681] are classed as Abhidharma.
9. Some say tīrthikas or Bönpos can see the truth, but this [tradition] states that there is no way that tīrthikas or Bönpos can see the truth.
10. Some say there isn't anything conducive to liberation among the tīrthikas and Bönpos, but this [tradition] states that they have some elements that are conducive to liberation.
11. Some say that non-Buddhists don't have vows or compassion and that all tīrthika practices should be rejected, but this [tradition] states that even non-Buddhists have vows and compassion.
12. Some say buddhahood is attained after three incalculable eons in the Causal Vehicle or Characteristics Vehicle, but this [tradition] states that even through the Causal Vehicle or Characteristics Vehicle, buddhahood is achieved in one lifetime.
13. Some say that the buddhahood of the Mantrayāna and of the Characteristics Vehicle are different, but this [tradition] states that their Dharma and way of practice lead to a single buddhahood. [276]
14. Some say that in the three [levels of] vows, the higher [levels] are more spacious, but this [tradition] states that in the three [levels of] vows, the higher [levels] are narrower.

15. Some say the thirty-seven factors for enlightenment are qualities of the path and that the level of buddhahood transcends them, but this [tradition] states that the essence of the path of accumulation continues up to buddhahood.
16. Some say the śrāvakas and pratyekabuddhas are outside the Mahayana family and therefore can't achieve buddhahood, but this [tradition] states that even the śrāvakas and pratyekabuddhas have the cause of buddhahood and will therefore ultimately attain the great enlightenment.
17. Some say there is an indefinable variety of vehicles and philosophies, but this [tradition] states that all vehicles and philosophies are the Buddha's [teaching of] dependent origination.[682]
18. Some say samsara has an end and some say it is endless, but this [tradition] states that samsara is endless and beyond [conceptual] elaboration.
19. Some say that the aggregation of eighty-four thousand Dharmas consists of remedies for everything that has to be eliminated, but this [tradition] states that all Dharmas are included within each pratimokṣa [vow].
20. Some say the Vinaya of the Dharma is different in each of the four schools,[683] but this [tradition] states that the canons of all four schools are one in essence.
21. Some say there is no offense in ejaculating during a dream, but this [tradition] states that although one is unable to do anything about it, ejaculation in a dream is an offense.
22. Some say that after attaining the first level [of enlightenment], there is no fear of being reborn in the lower existences, but this [tradition] states that even after reaching the levels one can be reborn in a lower existence.
23. Some say the accumulations of bodhisattvas are a lower accumulation, but this [tradition] states that the [accumulations of the bodhisattvas] are the marvelous practice of the kusāla's[684] gathering of accumulations.
24. Some say that if illness or harm occurs while practicing and so on, external and internal interdependence will be of benefit, but this [tradition] states that generosity and visualization are the supreme methods for their elimination.[685]
25. Many traditions state that the Mantrayāna is the fourth scriptural

basket, and so on, but this [tradition] states that the Mantrayāna is the essence of all three scriptural baskets and of each of the three baskets.

26. Many say that some may not obtain an empowerment even though it is bestowed on them, and some can obtain an empowerment without its being given to them,[686] [277] but this [tradition] states that the profound rituals of the lineage are necessary for all three levels of individuals—those of supreme, medium, [and inferior] abilities.
27. Some say the deeds of the three kāyas are definitely three in number, but this [tradition] states that, even though that is so, a single deity can accomplish all activities.
28. Some say that each deity has its own specific name, but this [tradition] states that all deities can be named Āryadeva ("superior deity").
29. Some say it is permissible [not to keep] the root commitment during the four stages of the Mantrayāna,[687] but this [tradition] states there is never a time during the four stages when it is permissible [not to keep] the root commitments.
30. Some say that one cannot practice the deity at first but must approach the practice through stages, but this [tradition] states that the immediate practice of the deity is a profound key point.
31. Some say the number [of mantras] in sevā practice is the principal factor in creating a stable generation stage, but this [tradition] states that you should know the deity to be an aggregation of interdependences.[688]
32. Some say that asceticism and so on is a mistreatment of the deity, but this [tradition] states that [the deity] is abused through conceiving the body to be ordinary.
33. Some say that the first three of the four tantras teach provisional meaning and are therefore not profound and that the highest yoga tantra alone is profound and teaches the definitive meaning. However, this [tradition] states that extensive rites are necessary in all provisional and definitive teachings.
34. Some say that at the beginning of an empowerment it is necessary to engage in an extensive rite, but this [tradition] states that a simple [rite] can also train a being.
35. Some say that the wrathful deities, the vajra wall, and so on, form the profound wheel of protection, but this [tradition] states that the armor of enlightenment[689] is the most wonderful wheel of protection.

36. Some say the instructions on the channels and winds are the wonderful, special practice of the Mantrayāna, but this [tradition] states that a greatly trained [body, speech, and mind] is the superior key point for the channels and winds.
37. Some say that one must purify the channels, winds, and drops that have been made impure through the activity of the three poisons. In agreement with that, this [tradition] states that the degenerate, poisoned channels, winds, and drops are especially profound.[690]
38. Some say that while the commitments are extremely critical for the pupil, the commitments are not critical for the master. However, this [tradition] states that the master and pupil [278] have equal commitments toward each other.
39. Some say even tenth-level bodhisattvas can see only one part or aspect of the ālaya consciousness, but this [tradition] teaches that those who have received the blessing can see the ālaya during all the other levels [below the tenth level].
40. Some say "the excellent white path" commences on seeing the truth of the true nature, but this [tradition] states that even someone on the tenth level will fall into lower existences if they perform a bad action.
41. Some say that the three trainings are the higher graduated path of the Mantrayāna and Vajrayāna, and that the Vinaya, the perfections, and the Mantrayāna are not the same path, but this [tradition] states that the six perfections are the path of all three vehicles.
42. Some say that both good and bad actions obscure the mahāmudrā, but this [tradition] states that it's impossible for the nature of good actions to obscure the dharmakāya.
43. Some say there is no cause for the result that is elimination, but this [tradition] states that a result without a cause is impossible.
44. Some say the nonduality of meditator and meditation that is like the merger of two spaces is the ultimate result, but this [tradition] states that this freedom from all conceptual elaboration is the realization of the śrāvakas.
45. Some say the four yogas of the power of breath[691] and so on are profound, but this [tradition] states that the profound key point is not to hold the breath but to leave it relaxed.
46. Some say the transference of consciousness is transference into the

heart of the guru or *yidam* deity through reciting *hūṃ* or syllables, but this [tradition] states that the supreme transference is when the consciousness becomes the guru's luminosity.

47. Some say that when a buddha enters nirvana, it is similar to when there is neither fire nor wood after the firewood has completely burned, but this [tradition] states that a buddha is the embodiment of bodhicitta, which is free from all extremes.

By this virtue, as pure white as a snow mountain,
may the precious teachings spread in the ten directions,
and may beings become free of ignorance and stupidity
and ultimately achieve the wisdom of buddhahood.

These are known as great teachings, and there are countless specific ways of teaching each one. Having received the seal of those explanations and made a thorough analysis of them, I knew how to apply them to my being in accord with the viewpoint of the entire teaching and so have understood them. [279] They are the inconceivable and wonderful inheritance enjoyed by the son of the peerless father Lord Drigungpa's mind. This collection of advice from the teachings forms the eighth chapter.

III. The Four Main Points of the Dharma of the Single Viewpoint

I pay homage to you, the precious peerless Drigungpa,
the omniscient lord of the Dharma,
who sees all distinct knowable things, as they are,
in the mandala of the stainless luminosity of the mind.

Countless teachings have made clear
the sublime and unique Dharma
that was taught by the supreme Conqueror,
but I will write a little so as to guide the ignorant.

It's taught that the viewpoint of the precious Dharma Lord Drigungpa is the single viewpoint of all conquerors in a hundred and fifty vajra teachings and its supplement, and that this is taught through four main points:

1. The teaching on the single viewpoint of all the conquerors
2. The teaching on the nature of vajra teachings
3. The teaching on the nature of the Dharma
4. The teaching on how to practice

The teaching on the single viewpoint of all the conquerors

This consists of four points:

a. There is one mother,[692] as she gives birth to all the conquerors of the three times.
b. There is one route, as all conquerors attain buddhahood through this [mother].
c. They have one viewpoint, like people in one boat or like a mother and child.
d. All conquerors have the one attainment of wisdom in this perfection of wisdom.

The teaching on the nature of vajra teaching

This consists of four points:

a. They are like vajras because it is difficult for academics and those skilled in terminology to understand them.
b. They are like vajras because, like the material substance of a diamond, they cannot be defeated by anything else.
c. They are like vajras because, like indestructible vajras, they cannot be destroyed by anything else.
d. They are like vajras because they are a rare marvel within the general various traditions from the Tibetans of the past. [280]

The teaching on the nature of the Dharma

This consists of four points:

a. Like space, there is nothing within the entirety of nirvana and samsara that its nature does not pervade.
b. There is nothing, from form to omniscience, that is not empty.
c. Like a wish-fulfilling jewel, it does not lack any of the good qualities of samsara and nirvana.
d. No fault from affliction stains it.

THE TEACHING ON HOW TO PRACTICE

This consists of four points:

a. Whatever guru and Dharma you practice, the guru is Jikten Gönpo.
b. The Dharma teaching is the mahāmudrā.
c. The individual must be one who has forsaken the world.
d. The locations for practice are the mountains and forests.

Those are the four root meanings of the Dharma. Each one is divided into four. Those are the main points of the *Single Viewpoint*. This is the teaching of glorious Damchö Lingpa.[693]

Thus, the peerless Drigungpa's entire Dharma teaching and his unique *Single Viewpoint* is in the *Hundred and Fifty Vajra Teachings*.

It has seven great chapters.

It has a structure that is the Kagyü gurus' [method of] liberation.

It has a lineage and a source.

It has the texts of the five aspects.[694]

It has the practice of the three vows as one essential point.

It has the profound path of devotion to the guru.

It has the direct introduction to innate wisdom.

It has the ultimate certainty of the single viewpoint of the conquerors of the three times.

It has the principal teaching of cause and result.

It has the basis of appearances being one's own mind.

All phenomena are included within samsara and nirvana. All samsara and nirvana are one's own mind. The mind is empty. There is the ultimate certainty that the empty mind is the dharmakāya.

Therefore, it is like a parasol covering all phenomena equally and without differentiation. Like the fringe around the edge of a parasol, when there has been a particular cause there will be a particular result. Like a parasol's spokes, there is a distinct differentiation. Like a parasol's handle, all three vows are practiced through being combined into one. Like the crest jewel of a parasol, devotion to the guru enhances the result.

A genuine treatise (*śāstra*) must be free of six faults and possess three good qualities. From *Commentary on the Compendium of the Mahayana*: [281]

> Meaningless, incorrect, or meaningful;
> dedicated to learning, to debate, or to practice;
> deceitful, cruel, or compassionate.[695]

It should be free of those six faults and possess those three good qualities.

May there be the splendor of sacred goodness!
May there be the spontaneous accomplishment of benefit for beings!
May there be good fortune!

IV. The Structural Analysis that Classifies the Sequence of the Seven Chapters

In the third of the eight parts of the outline [of the *Single Viewpoint*] is a section on the seven chapters in which they are said to be similar to the two wheels in the *Mahayana's Sublime Continuum*. Therefore, there is no error in teaching the seven chapters here in accordance with that sequence. However, it's taught that the chapters on the three vows are definitive, so some of its teaching will be combined here.

The *Mahayana's Sublime Continuum Treatise* is definitively divided into two "wheels":

1. The wheel of the resultant Jewels
2. The wheel of unlocated nirvana

The Buddha, Dharma, and Sangha, which are the first three of [that treatise's] "seven vajra points," are the *wheel of the resultant Jewels*. The Dharmas of the path are the conditions necessary for awakening the stained "element" (*dhātu*)[696] so that enlightenment, qualities, and activities are manifested. These are the *wheel of unlocated nirvana*. From Nāgārjuna's *A Praise to the Dharmadhātu*:

> Through eliminating that
> which is the cause of samsara,
> there is the purity, nirvana,
> which is also the dharmakāya.[697]

The cause of samsara is the ālaya consciousness, which has all seeds and is completely stained by propensities for aggregates, [sensory] elements, and [sensory] bases. When that is purified by the Dharma of the Buddha, which accords with being the cause of nonconceptual wisdom, this purification through stages is called the *unlocated nirvana*. This is also the dharmakāya of all buddhas. This is the explanation that has been taught by paṇḍitas.

THE RELATIONSHIP BETWEEN THE TWO WHEELS

First, one begins with the Three Jewels [282] for many reasons, such as that they engender joy in the result and give refuge on entering into the path. Therefore [*Mahayana Sublime Continuum Treatise*] begins with the three resultant Jewels as the first of the seven vajra points. Also, there is the analysis of the subsequent result: Through purifying the causal "element," the factors of enlightenment, qualities, and activity become manifest, and these are the wheel of unlocated nirvana.

If one considers stainless enlightenment and the resultant Jewels as inseparable, then the qualities and activity are those of the Three Jewels. As in that example, if one teaches the seven chapters starting with the one on view, conduct, [and meditation],[698] the order will be the three trainings,[699] the Dharma wheel,[700] interdependence,[701] and the level of buddhahood,[702] and then [all seven] would be the same as the wheel of the unlocated nirvana.

Alternatively, there is the relationship between the groups of three and four that accord with their being the wheel of the resultant Jewels, such as:

1. The Buddha came to the world.
2. He taught the Dharma.

3–5. What did he teach? The three precious trainings

6. Their interdependence of cause and result
7. The correct practice of that view, meditation, and conduct [as interdependent cause and result]

These characteristics become clear when explaining the two wheels. There is an alternative relationship and sequence in terms of the wheel of the resultant Three Jewels:

> From the Buddha comes the Dharma; from the Dharma comes the Ārya Sangha...[703]

Also, the activity of benefiting beings causes buddhahood and so on, as described above, to arise from the beings of others, so that samsara too can be called the wheel of nirvana.

Alternatively, through the Buddha teaching the Dharma, he obtains a practicing sangha. Then there is, in order, the "element" that is the cause of purification, enlightenment, qualities, and activity, which are the purifying conditions.

Also, some teach enlightenment, qualities, and activity to be the result: So there can also be "four definite continuums":

1. That which is to be purified, which is "the element"
2. The condition that purifies, which is the path
3. The Three Jewels, which teach [the path]
4. The three results

By this virtue, as pure white as a snow mountain,
may the precious teachings spread in the ten directions,
and may beings become free of ignorance and stupidity
and ultimately achieve the wisdom of buddhahood.

Good fortune!

11. Light Rays from the Jewel of the Excellent Teaching

A General Presentation on the Points of Secret Mantra

Dakpo Tashi Namgyal (1512–87)

[283] I pay homage with veneration to the gurus and the supreme deities.

I bow down to Guru Vajradhara, the universal lord over all the phenomena of samsara and nirvana.
Your illusory dancer's body of empty appearance is beautiful, adorned in garlands of the primary and secondary signs of a supreme being.
Your melodious vajra speech of empty sound beautifully sings profound, vast mantras.
Your indestructible, all-pervading mind of empty knowing is the play of activity that brings benefit and happiness.

I bow down to the supreme deity, who is a display of ferocity.
Your powerful nine theatrical expressions[704] destroy the armies of obstacles;
your sharp sword of excellent wisdom slices through afflictions;
and your noose of loving compassion binds the three realms.

I respectfully bow to the learned and accomplished gurus,
known as "the unequaled Gampopa and his lineage,"
who taught the true nature of all secret teachings
and illuminated the excellent path of the profound mantra.

Wishing to become a vajra holder
through reciting mantra rituals
is like a hoofprint filled with water
pretending to be an ocean.

There are beginners who have cast aside such conduct,
who have analytic minds,
and who yearn to see the treasury of the mantra texts.
Today, I will give them the key that opens that door.

It is meaningless to listen with attachment
to teachings that are not genuine.
How could that bring satisfaction to any devotee?
You who have discriminating minds, listen to this.

THIS TEACHING of a general summary of the Vajrayāna, the ultimate vehicle, is in three parts:

I. The way in which the Teacher appeared
II. A presentation of his teaching
III. The special general summary [of the Vajrayāna]

I. The way in which the Teacher appeared

This is in two parts:

A. The way in which buddhas in general appear in the world
B. The way in which our Buddha in particular appeared [284]

A. The way in which buddhas in general appear in the world

There are two kinds of eons: bright and dark. Bright eons are those in which buddhas appear; dark eons are those in which buddhas do not appear.

A thousand buddhas will appear in this bright eon, which is named the Good Eon. After sixty-five dark eons have then passed, ten thousand buddhas will appear in a bright eon named the Greatly Renowned Eon. After another eighty thousand dark eons have passed, eighty thousand buddhas will appear in a bright eon named the Starry Eon. After another three hundred dark eons have passed, eighty-four thousand buddhas will appear in a bright eon named Arrayed Qualities Eon. That is taught in the *Sutra of the Good Eon*.[705]

There are also countless eons and appearances of buddhas throughout the three times. As for the appearance of buddhas within this eon, in this world that is named *Saha*, after the destruction of the preceding world by water, a thousand golden lotuses appeared upon the ocean. When the devas examined this, they understood it to be an omen of the appearance of a thousand buddhas and said, "Oh, this eon will be good!" and so it became known as the Good Eon.

According to the Hīnayāna, buddhas appear only during a period when the lifespan is diminishing from eighty thousand years down to a hundred. They do not appear before that period because the beings of that time have little sorrow and are uninterested in the Dharma. The buddhas do not appear after that period because then the five degenerations have become too strong. The buddhas do not need to appear during the period when the lifespan is increasing, because during that time there is a natural avoidance of bad actions and increase in the power of good actions. However, this Hīnayāna teaching is not certain.

According to the *Sutra of the Good Eon*, Krakucchanda appeared within this eon when beings had a forty-thousand-year lifespan; Kanakamuni appeared when they had a thirty-thousand-year lifespan; Kāśyapa appeared when they had a twenty-thousand-year lifespan; and Śākyamuni appeared when beings had a hundred-year lifespan.

B. The way in which our Buddha in particular appeared

This is in three parts:

1. The Hīnayāna tradition
2. The general Mahayana tradition
3. The Vajrayāna tradition

1. The Hīnayāna tradition of how the Buddha appeared

In a past life, the Buddha was King Prabhāvan. [285] He heard of the great qualities of buddhahood and its causes, and so performed acts of generosity, prayed, and developed bodhicitta. Then during one incalculable eon, he served seventy-five thousand buddhas, beginning with a Buddha Śākyamuni and ending with Rantaśikhin. During a second incalculable eon, he served seventy-six thousand buddhas ending with Dīpaṃkara. During a third incalculable eon, he served seventy-seven thousand buddhas, ending with Vipaśyin. Thus, he accumulated merit for three incalculable eons.

Then he praised Buddha Puṣya with a verse that he repeated continuously for seven days. This [created the merit] equivalent to nine eons of merit accumulation. He then accumulated merit for another ninety-one eons, until the time of the Buddha Kāśyapa of our eon. He therefore created a hundred great eons' worth of causes for the [appearance of the] major signs. He was then born as the deity Śvetaketu, after which he accomplished the [twelve] renowned deeds [of the Buddha], beginning with his departure from Tuṣita. From *Treasury of the Abhidharma*:

> Vipaśyin, Dīpaṃkara, and Ratnaśikhin
> were at the ends of three incalculable eons.
> First of them all was Śākyamuni.[706]

From the Vinaya:

> He made offerings to 75,000 buddhas,
> beginning with Buddha Śākyamuni
> and ending with Lord Dhṛtarāṣtra.
>
> He made offerings to 76,000 buddhas,
> beginning with Sukṛta
> and ending with Indradhvaja.
>
> He made offerings to 77,000 buddhas,
> beginning with Dīpaṃkara
> and ending with Kāśyapa.[707]

2. The general Mahayana tradition of how the Buddha appeared

How the Buddha first developed bodhicitta

The Buddha taught in the *Sutra of Repaying the Kindness*[708] that he had been reborn as a strong man in hell, where he pulled a cart across red-hot iron ground. A hell guardian was continually beating his weak companion. The Buddha had affection for his companion and said to the hell guardian, "Have some pity on him!" This made the guardian furious, and he stabbed the Buddha with a trident, ending his life. This purified the Buddha of hundreds[709] of eons' worth of bad karma.

In a later life, the Buddha was Bhāskara, the son of a potter. He offered a bowl of milk broth to great Śākyamuni and developed bodhicitta. [286] From the *Sutra of the Good Eon*:

In a past life, when I was a poor man,
I offered a bowl of milk broth to Tathāgata Śākyamuni
and for the first time developed bodhicitta.[710]

How the Buddha accumulated merit

The Buddha taught that he was reborn as a king's son, Prince Vīryakārin, who served Buddha Mahākuṭa. From that life onward, he accumulated merit throughout one incalculable eon and reached the first [bodhisattva] level.

He was then born as the merchant leader Prajñābhadra and served Buddha Ratnāṅga. From that life onward, he accumulated merit for another incalculable eon and reached the seventh level.

He was then born as a brahman's son, Dharmamegha, and served Buddha Dīpaṃkara. From that life onward, he accumulated merit for yet another incalculable eon and reached the tenth level.

There are also descriptions of [his accumulating merit] for [more] incalculable eons, such as seven, ten, or thirty-three.

How the Buddha achieved buddhahood

The Buddha taught that he achieved buddhahood countless eons ago as Buddha Indraketu in a realm named Kusumagarbhalaṃkāra.[711] He manifested during the lifetime of Buddha Kāśyapa as a brahman's son who passed away and was reborn as Śvetaketu in Tuṣita. Therefore, his twelve deeds were only in the perception of his pupils.

From the *White Lotus Sutra*:

For countless thousands of millions of eons
I have attained supreme enlightenment
and have always been present,
continually teaching the Dharma.[712]

From the *Sutra of Entry into Laṅka*:

The truly complete Buddha attained buddhahood
in the blissful, supreme realm of Akaniṣṭha,
which has eliminated the [im]pure realms,
and one emanation will achieve buddhahood in this world.[713]

The Buddha's deeds as they appeared to occur are taught in the *Sublime Continuum*:

> The knower of the world looked
> with great compassion at the entire world,
> and without parting from the Dharmakāya,
> with various forms of emanations:
> he took on lifetimes,
> he abandoned pleasant realms,
> entered a womb, was born,
> became skilled in the arts,
> enjoyed the pleasures of queens,
> renounced, and practiced asceticism.
>
> He proceeded to Bodhimaṇḍa,[714]
> vanquished Māra's army,
> accomplished enlightenment, the Dharma wheel,
> and the passing into nirvana.
>
> [287] He manifests this in the impure realms
> for as long as there will be existence.[715]

Those are renowned to be the twelve deeds.

3. *The Vajrayāna tradition of how our Buddha appeared*

According to the action (kriyā) tantras

The Buddha developed the aspiration to enlightenment and then he received the Mantrayāna teachings from Tathāgata Kusumasaṃdarśana.[716] He then practiced the Mantrayāna, accumulating merit, for three incalculable eons. When he was Śvetaketu, he passed away to become the son of King Śuddhodana and achieved buddhahood.

According to the performance (caryā) tantras

It is taught that, in terms of appearances, the Buddha developed bodhicitta, practiced the Mantrayāna, manifested the tenth [bodhisattva] level, and attained saṃbhogakāya buddhahood in Akaniṣṭha.

According to the Yoga Tantra Tradition

The *Compendium of Truths*[717] teaches that all the buddhas invoked the bodhisattva Siddhārtha when he was sitting on the Bodhimaṇḍa. He arose from his unwavering samādhi, developed bodhicitta, was empowered by all the buddhas, and achieved true buddhahood.

According to Śākyamitra[718] and others, when Siddhārtha, the son of Śuddhodana, was practicing asceticism on the banks of the Nairañjana River, he was invoked by the buddhas and went to Akaniṣṭha in a wisdom body. There he was empowered by all the buddhas and achieved buddhahood.

Both those versions are in accordance with the way that things appear to be.

Ānandagarbha gives an excellent explanation,[719] teaching that the Buddha developed the aspiration to enlightenment, gathered accumulations of merit for three incalculable eons, developed all the samādhis of the dhyānas, such as the formless states, and then in his final life received empowerment from all the buddhas. He therefore achieved buddhahood many eons ago and manifested being born in the Śākya family. From the [*Vajra*] *Pinnacle* [*Tantra*]:

> The Bhagavān, who achieved enlightenment
> uncountable eons ago...[720]

From the *Vajra Mandala Adornment Tantra*:

> When they supplicated Bhagavān Śākyamuni, he listened to their words and came from the realm of Akaniṣṭha to reside in the realm of Tuṣita, where he taught the Dharma to the Tuṣita devas. Then, on seeing the family of King Śuddhodana...[721]

According to the Highest Yoga Tradition

Although such teachings as Śākyamitra's accord with the way things appear to be, [288] in terms of how things truly are, the bodhisattva, in his final life, followed the exceptional path of the Mantrayāna in the great realm of Akaniṣṭha. He attained saṃbhogakāya buddhahood through such procedures as "the five awakenings" and subsequently manifested the attainment of enlightenment once again. From the *Abbreviated Tantra of Kālacakra*:

> In order to liberate these, the Lord of Conquerors and his children entered the level of karma and took possession of wombs. They who have the supreme compassion developed enlightenment and defeated the afflictions and the māras. In the realm upon the earth they turned the wheel of the Dharma and created emanations and illusions. Then again the Bhagavān became solely a pure body.[722]

From the *Great Commentary*:

> The Bhagavān Buddha in his previous life was a lord of the twelfth (level), a wise master of illusory manifestations (*mahāmāyā*), endowed with the illusions of illusory manifestations (*mahāmāyā*). In the land of the āryas he was born in Lumbinī from the womb of Mahāmāyā, the queen of Śuddhodana, the lord of the Śākya people, and became Prince Siddhārtha.[723]

From *Illuminating Lamp*:

> Mañjuśrī became King Śuddhodana.
> Lokeśvara[724] manifested as Queen Mahāmāyā.
> Great Vairocana became the truly complete Buddha, Śākyamuni.[725]

From the *Rigi Ārali Tantra*:

> Great King Śuddhodana
> is correctly taught to be Ārali.
> There, Rigi was Mahāmāyā.
> Also, Siddhārtha, the being who is the embodiment
> of wisdom and method, was Vajrasattva.[726]

II. A presentation of the Buddha's teaching and in particular the general meaning of the Vajrayāna

This is in three parts:

A. An explanation of the way in which the Buddha taught, and so on
B. A teaching on the arrangement of the vehicles
C. An explanation of the categories of the teachings

A. An explanation of the way in which the Buddha taught, and so on

This is in three parts:

1. The Hīnayāna tradition
2. The general Mahayana tradition
3. The Vajrayāna tradition

1. The way in which the Buddha taught according to the Hīnayāna tradition

The Buddha, seven weeks after his buddhahood, taught the Dharma of the four truths to the "five excellent disciples" in Vārāṇasī. The Buddha taught nothing but the Hīnayāna scriptural baskets from that time until his nirvana in Kuśinārā.[727] [289]

The first compilation of the canon

In order to quell criticism from the devas, and so that the teachings would endure for a long time, Ānanda compiled the Sutras, Upāli compiled the Vinaya, and Kāśyapa compiled the Abhidharma in the Nyagrodha cave, one year after the Buddha's passing.

The second compilation of the canon

In order to eliminate forty infractions, seven hundred arhats such as Yaśas compiled [the canon] in the Vaiśālī monastery, one hundred and ten years after the Buddha's passing.

The third compilation of the canon

In order to remove what was noncanonical within the eighteen schools, five hundred arhants such as Purtika, five hundred bodhisattvas such as Vasumitra, and sixteen thousand paṇḍitas who were ordinary beings gathered in the land of Kashmir and compiled the canon three hundred years after the Buddha's passing.

The duration of the teaching

The Buddha's teaching will remain for a thousand years and will finally cease to exist as a result of [internal] conflict.

2. The way in which the Buddha taught according to the general Mahayana tradition

The Buddha remained in a state of equanimity for seven weeks after buddhahood, appearing to be in a state of little mental activity. After Brahma and Indra made an invocation to him, the Buddha turned the Dharma wheel of the four truths, which is the first canon, in Vārāṇasī and other places to pupils who were of the Hīnayāna family. He turned the Dharma wheel of the nonexistence of characteristics, which is the second canon, on Vulture Peak and other places to pupils who belonged to the Mahayana family. He turned the Dharma wheel of perfect examination, which is the last canon, on Malaya Mountain[728] and other places to pupils who were of the definitive family, the special Mahayana family.

The compilation of the canon

It is famed that a million bodhisattvas gathered on Vimasvabha Mountain, south of Rājagṛha,[729] and Maitreya compiled the Vinaya, Vajrapāṇi compiled the Sutras, and Mañjuśrī compiled the Abhidharma, although there are other differing accounts.

The duration of the teaching

The Buddha taught in the *Sutra Requested by Candragarbha*[730] that the teaching would remain for two thousand years until a son of the king of Kauśambi, with arms as if drenched with blood, will become the king of Jambudvīpa. In order to purify his bad karma, he will summon all the arhats and monks in Jambudvīpa, but a conversation will lead to a fight breaking out among them in which everyone will kill each other and no one will be left alive. [290] Devas will take away their symbolic robes, and the entire Dharma will cease to exist in Jambudvīpa.

The Buddha taught in the *Lotus of Compassion Sutra*[731] that the Dharma would remain for one and a half thousand years.

Differing teachings say the Dharma will remain for a thousand years, for two and a half thousand years, for five thousand years, and so on. These appear to imply the different periods of [the Dharma], such as those of the pure teaching, the similitude of the teaching, the mere symbols of the teaching, and so on.

3. The way in which the Buddha taught according to the Vajrayāna tradition

The action (kriyā) tantras

The Buddha, the supreme nirmāṇakāya, taught the action tantras in such places as Akaniṣṭha and on the summit of Mount Meru to followers who had been established in the mandalas and to countless buddhas and bodhisattvas.

The performance (caryā) tantras

The Buddha, the supreme nirmāṇakāya, taught the performance tantras in such places as Kusumagarbhalaṃkāra,[732] which is Buddha Vairocana's realm, in his intermediate realm, and in Alakāvatī to followers who had been established in the mandalas and to countless buddhas and bodhisattvas.

The yoga tantras

The saṃbhogakāya Vairocana, without departing from Akaniṣṭha, taught the [yoga tantra's] root tantra, the *Compendium of Truths*, and the explanatory tantra, *Vajra Pinnacle*. The nirmāṇakāya Buddha Vairocana emanated a divine palace on the summit of Mount Meru and there taught those tantras to followers established in the mandalas and also to countless buddhas and bodhisattvas.

The nirmāṇakāya Vairocana, in that divine palace in the pleasure grove of the Trāyastriṃśa paradise, taught all the performance tantras, such as Vairocana's *Purification of the Lower Existences*, to pupils comprised of worldly beings, such as Indra and a hundred billion bodhisattvas.

The highest yoga nondual tantra of Kālacakra

The Buddha manifested the appearance of attaining buddhahood. On the full moon of the [next] third month,[733] he emanated the area of great bliss, the great mandala, at the Dhānyakaṭaka stupa.[734] While the Buddha rested in the samādhi of Kālacakra, he taught the root tantra in twelve thousand verses to followers established in the mandala, to King Sucandra, who had requested the teaching, and to all worthy pupils such as the ninety-six satraps.[735]

The highest yoga father tantra of Guhyasamāja

Paṇḍita Alaṃkakalaśa taught that the Buddha attained buddhahood at midnight, defeated the māras at dawn, and then went to Tuṣita.[736] There he manifested a divine palace from the great elements of his body [291] and emanated the deities of the mandala from his aggregates, sensory elements, and so on. After his followers, who pervaded all space, supplicated the Bhagavān, he taught the glorious Guhyasamāja in order to teach those who have desire. *Perfectly Illuminating Lamp*[737] also says that the Buddha taught the Guhyasamāja in Tuṣita.

Ācārya Ānandagarbha[738] says that the Buddha taught the Guhyasamāja in Paranirmitavaśavarta[739] for the sake of beings who have desire and are attracted to such tantras as those by Viṣṇu.

The Tibetan lamas teach that the Buddha was residing in Śrāvastī when Indrabodhi, the king of Oḍḍiyāna, heard of the Bhagavān's great qualities and recited a supplication of invitation. The Buddha and his pupils came to him. Indrabodhi made offerings to them and prayed for liberation from existence. The Buddha instructed him to take ordination, but he requested [a method that would bring] buddhahood while still enjoying sensory pleasures. The Buddha dissolved his nirmāṇakāya appearance and manifested the mandala of glorious Guhyasamāja. He bestowed the empowerment and teaching of the tantra on Indrabodhi and other worthy disciples and entrusted the tantra to Vajradharma.

The highest yoga father tantra of Yamāntaka

When the Buddha was attaining enlightenment and the māras were trying to prevent him, he entered the samādhi known as *supreme victory over the great māras*, manifested the wrathful Yamāntaka from the vajras of his body, speech, and mind, and emanated Yamāntaka's mandala, subjugating the māras. He then taught the long Yamāntaka tantra. The Buddha taught the short Yamāntaka tantra when he was among a great number of disciples that included the thirteen Yamāntaka deities.

When the Teacher was residing with Mohavajra[740] and others in "the *bhaga* [vagina] of the vajra queen," which means in the divine palace within the *dharmodaya*, he instructed Vajrapāṇi to listen and, on Vajrapāṇi's request, taught Red Yamāntaka.

The highest yoga mother tantra of Cakrasaṃvara

It is taught that all beginningless buddhas have taught the Cakrasaṃvara, and it is taught that this beginningless teaching is taught on the attainment of buddhahood.

It is said that during the third age in this world, at the place where Rudra

Bhairava[741] was subjugated, the nirmāṇakāya Buddha, as the "resultant heruka," gave the Cakrasaṃvara empowerment and taught the tantra to a following of buddhas, bodhisattvas, the five classes of ḍākas and ḍākinīs, Guhyapati,[742] who was the compiler, [292] and to Rudra Bhairava and his followers.

It is said that in the degenerate age, Rudra Bhairava Maheśvara took on the form of four bodies—peaceful, increasing, controlling, and wrathful—that dwelled with their wives on the northeast and the center of Mount Meru, in Paranirmitavaśavarta, and in Magadha.[743] Their followers owned the twenty-four sacred sites and the eight charnel grounds. The twenty-four [sites were owned by] four devas, four gandharvas, four yakṣas, four rākṣasas, four nāgas, and four nonhumans. [The charnel grounds] were in the possession of these eight: four kiṃnaras and four piśācas. In that way, they controlled the whole world, engaged in wrong actions themselves and made others perpetrate wrong deeds.

At this time, Buddha Vajradhara attained true, perfect buddhahood through the process of the five enlightenments and from within the dharmadhātu taught the Dharma of innate luminosity to countless buddhas and bodhisattvas in Akaniṣṭha.

Vajradhara knew that the time had come to subjugate Rudra Bhairava and his followers. He manifested as the nirmāṇakāya resultant heruka and came to the summit of Mount Meru. The five family-buddhas emanated a divine palace with deities such as ḍākas and ḍākinīs, which they offered to him. He resided in the saṃbhogakāya samādhi, regarded those to be trained, and emanated the mandala cakra into a billion [worlds] with four continents. In this world of Jambudvīpa he emanated the four-faced, twelve-armed Cakrasaṃvara, who stood upon Bhairava and Kālaratri, subjugating them. His emanated retinue subjugated the malevolent ones who had taken possession of the twenty-four sites and the eight charnel grounds.

The Bhagavān and his retinue resided in the divine palace on the summit of Mount Meru. Upon the request of Vajrayoginī, he taught the *Root Tantra of Cakrasaṃvara*,[744] and upon the request of Vajrapāṇi, the explanatory tantra.[745] He taught them to his followers established in the mandala, to buddhas and bodhisattvas as numerous as the atoms in Mount Meru, to Rudra Bhairava and his followers, and to worthy devas and humans.

Some say that after giving this, the Buddha was born as Śvetaketu and then became the nirmāṇakāya Śākyamuni. He then rested in the samādhi of Cakrasaṃvara upon the glorious Dhānyakaṭaka Mountain[746] and emanated the mandala, manifesting the appearance of again subjugating Rudra Bhairava and his followers. He then taught the Cakrasaṃvara mantra to eighty million ḍākas and yoginīs. [293] However, some say that when he became the nirmāṇakāya Śākyamuni, he did not teach it again, so there appear to be a variety of explanations.

The highest yoga mother tantra of Śrī Hevajra

According to the commentary to the *Vajra Garland* [*Tantra*], the nirmāṇakāya Buddha taught the Hevajra tantra when he subjugated the four māras in Magadha in this world of Jambudvīpa.[747]

[When the tantra says that the Buddha was] in "the *bhaga* (vagina) of the vajra queen," this means in the *dharmodaya* ("source of phenomena"). The Bhagavān Buddha, encircled by a great following of mundane and supramundane beings, was residing within a divine palace within the *dharmodaya*. Upon the request of Vajragarbha, Nairātmyā, and others, the Buddha taught the long root tantra, and on the request of Vajragarbha, he taught the short tantra, [thus teaching] the *Two Books* [*of the Hevajra Tantra*].[748] In the center of the divine palace, the Buddha taught the explanatory tantra, the *Vajra Tent*,[749] to the deities who maintain the five cakras and to his supramundane and mundane followers.

The way in which the Vajrayāna canon was compiled

Some commentaries state that the compilers of the tantras were those who requested the tantras and those to whom the tantras were finally entrusted. For example, Vajrapāṇi compiled the *Saṃvarabhuta Tantra*, Vajragarbha and Vajraḍākinī Vārāhī compiled the *Two Books of the Hevajra Tantra*, and Sucandra compiled the Kālacakra. There are other teachings also, for example that the Buddha taught summarized tantras, which are summaries of the long root tantras, in which case the Buddha himself is their compiler.

However, the teaching that Vajrapāṇi compiled all the Mantrayāna tantras is good. Vajrapāṇi compiled the Mantrayāna tantras in the land of Oḍḍiyāna while the Buddha was still living in this world and gave them to King Indrabodhi and his followers. They attained siddhi and transformed into naturally existing ḍākas and yoginīs so that the land of Oḍḍiyāna became empty and transformed into a great lake filled with nāgas. Vajrapāṇi then ripened those nāgas [through empowerments] and wrote out all the tantras as texts that he entrusted to them. The nāgas gradually transformed into humans and built a city upon the shore of the lake where they practiced the Mantrayāna. Most of them attained siddhi, the males becoming ḍākas and the females becoming ḍākinīs. Those who did not attain siddhi became humans. The land became renowned as the residence of ḍākinīs. [294] Eventually the Mantrayāna spread from there into Madhyadeśa.[750]

It is also said that [the Buddha] gave the empowerments to King Indrabodhi in Alakāvatī, and then, because of a supplication by a gathering of 96 million bodhisattvas, Vajrapāṇi compiled and wrote out every single Mantrayāna tantra. Vajrapāṇi then gave the empowerments and entrusted the tantras to the ḍākinīs in Oḍḍiyāna, who previously had been nāgas, instructing them to give the tantras to worthy ones in future generations.

Also, in the commentary to the root tantra of Cakrasaṃvara, which was written by King Indrabodhi, it says:

> He orally and secretly turned the Dharma wheel
> of the supreme Vajrayāna
> for King Indrabodhi and his retinue,
> giving them the empowerments, blessings, and Dharma of the highest great secret teaching.
>
> Eventually, at a later time, the compiler of the scriptures,
> in an assembly of 96 million great bodhisattvas and others,
> within the great palace of Alakāvatī,
> the supreme paradise on the northeast of Mount Meru,
> compiled every single tantra.
>
> Thus did I hear, when they supplicated Lord Guhyapati:
> "Write down the supreme teaching
> using lapis lazuli pigment
> upon pages of gold."
>
> Then, considering the times yet to come,
> [Vajrapāṇi] blessed the community of ḍākinīs
> in the land of Oḍḍiyāna, who had previously been nāgas.
>
> In the glorious self-originated gandhola palace
> named Dharmaghājha, which was the treasury of the secret Dharma,
> [Vajrapāṇi] gave to the [ḍākinīs], such as Abhiratī, the mistress of the ḍākinīs,

> the authorizations, the instructions, and the prophecies
> about giving blessings and empowerments to worthy ones of the future.[751]

It is also said that ḍākinīs, such as Vajravārāhī, compiled the mother tantras in Oḍḍiyāna, through a process of questioning each other. From the *Ocean of Ḍākas*:

> The compilers and the rest
> came to me and received them.
> All the matrikas gathered together
> and compiled all the vajra points.
> They explained them to each other,
> prayed, and composed prayers.[752]

Therefore, in general, though Guhyapati was the compiler [of the tantras], there were other compilers. For example, King Sucandra compiled the Kālacakra [teaching] as the root tantra of twelve thousand verses. However, subsequently, after the passing of the seven Dharmarājas,[753] [295] Mañjuśrīkīrti Kalki compiled the summarized *Kālacakra Tantra*.

The Duration of the Vajrayāna

It is said that the Vajrayāna will continue for as long as the Buddha's teachings last. From the *Mañjuśrī Root Tantra*:

> After the supreme Sage is no longer present,
> if you always have faith in the recitation of mantra,
> the benefit of the teachings will be accomplished.[754]

From the *Great Power* [*Sutra*]:

> When these sutras are completely extinct, the entire teachings of the Tathāgata will be extinct.[755]

From *Oral Transmission*:

> It is perfectly explained that
> for as long as those who pass on [the tantras]

remain in this [world], that is how long
the precious teaching of the Buddha will remain.
Everyone should perfectly understand
that when this succession of the tantras ends,
the Buddha's teachings will cease to be.[756]

It is said that the mother tantras will never cease to exist, for they will continue to be practiced by the ḍākas and yoginīs in the twenty-four sites, even after the destruction of [the world] by fire at the eon's end. From the *Ocean of Ḍākas*:

The wisdom tantras are self-originated;
their own natures will exist forever.
They are the Dharma of "the factors for enlightenment."
They follow the state of indestructibility.
When the [world] burns at the eon's [end],
they will go elsewhere and continue to exist.[757]

That is the duration [of the Vajrayāna] according to the perception of ordinary beings in Jambudvīpa, but in the perception of the buddhas and bodhisattvas who teach the tantras, all the tantras of the Vajrayāna will exist forever.

B. A teaching on the arrangement of the vehicles

This is in two parts:

1. A presentation of the vehicles in general
2. A presentation of the Vajrayāna in particular

1. A presentation of the vehicles in general

All the eighty-four thousand entrances to the Dharma and so on, which the Buddha taught to the three kinds of pupils—superior, middling, and inferior—can be summarized as three vehicles: the Śrāvaka Vehicle, the Pratyekabuddha Vehicle, and the Mahayana. From the *White Lotus Sutra*:

The Great Rishi taught three vehicles.
Skilled in the methods of guiding,
he taught the three vehicles for the benefit of beings.[758]

The Śrāvaka Vehicle and the Pratyekabuddha Vehicle, which are collectively called the Hināyāna, were taught to beings with inferior understanding who were weary of samsara but unable to train in the highest training. [296] This way they could still rest temporarily on the level of the lesser nirvana. From the *White Lotus Sutra*:

> Thus, although all the śrāvakas
> consider that they attain nirvana,
> the Buddha has taught that they
> are not in nirvana but are just resting.[759]

Therefore, the only vehicle that leads to perfect buddhahood is the Mahayana. It is the ultimate vehicle and greatly superior to the other vehicles. From the *Entry into Laṅka Sutra*:

> I have said that there is only one single vehicle
> and that there is no arrangement of vehicles,
> but I have taught that there are different vehicles
> in order to guide the immature.[760]

From the *White Lotus Sutra*:

> There is only one vehicle in this world.
> There are not two and there are never three,
> except that supreme beings teach
> a variety of vehicles as a method.[761]

From *Compendium of the Mahayana*:

> It is superior because of its knowledge,
> the qualities that are gained, the causes and results,
> the categories, the three trainings, the resulting elimination,
> and because it is the supreme vehicle of wisdom.[762]

The Mahayana has also been taught to have two vehicles: (1) the general Mahayana, or Perfection Vehicle, and (2) the Mantrayāna, or Vajrayāna. These were taught for two kinds of pupils: (1) those who had inferior minds and aspired to use causes as the path, and (2) those with supreme minds and aspired to use the result as the path. From the *Sutra of the King of the Teaching of Instructions*:

> I have perfectly turned the Dharma wheel of causes
> for those who have aspiration to causes.
> In a future time, the swift path
> of the Vajrayāna will appear.[763]

From *Elimination of the Two Extremes*:

> He perfectly turned the Dharma wheel
> of causes, which is applied to causes,
> and after that taught the result vehicle's swift path.[764]

2. A presentation of the Vajrayāna in particular

Both the vehicles of cause and of result will attain the same result, but the Mantrayāna is superior because of the four ways of traveling the path. From the *Lamp of the Three Ways*:

> There is no ignorance of even a single meaning;
> it has many methods; it is not difficult;
> and it is intended for those with sharp faculties.
> That is why the Mantrayāna is superior.[765]

There is no ignorance in the Mantrayāna

In the Perfection Vehicle there is the practice of external perfections, such as giving away your head, legs, and arms. It takes you a long time to fulfill the desires of all beings, because you cannot fulfill them instantaneously. Therefore, there is some ignorance in the Perfection Vehicle. [297]

The mantrikas reject such methods and use skillful methods. They develop compassion for endless beings and quickly complete the six perfections through the internal samādhi that is the inseparability of method and wisdom. Therefore, there is no ignorance in the Mantrayāna. From *Lamp of the Three Ways*:

> The wisdom that has great compassion
> discriminates and adopts the supreme method.

It rejects ordinary methods
and attains the changeless state.[766]

The Mantrayāna has many methods

Perfection Vehicle practitioners use only hardships, vows, and so on as methods for attaining buddhahood, but everyone cannot be nurtured through these alone because not everyone is able to practice these alone. Therefore, the Perfection Vehicle has few methods.

Mantrayāna practitioners, in order to accomplish the benefit of all beings, first identify their buddha families through examining dreams, casting a flower, and so on and then engage in the corresponding practices. The Mantrayāna has many methods, including the subtleties of meditating on mind and mental events as having the nature of the deity and so on. There is mantra repetition and so on for those unable to practice the subtleties and have attachment to vocal elaboration. There is meditation on the mandala's residence and residents and so on for those who have attachment to evident objects of perception and cannot engage in subtleties. There is also liberation through realizing that there are no afflictions to eliminate, nor wisdom to attain, because all phenomena are completely pure by nature. From *Lamp of the Three Ways*:

The teacher of beings taught
the supreme path in four categories,
which contains all methods, to those with great intelligence
in order to accomplish excellent benefit for all beings.[767]

The Mantrayāna is free of difficulty

Methods for attaining the result that also accord with the individual desires of pupils are rare in the Perfection Vehicle, and so enlightenment is attained with difficulty over a long period of time. Therefore, the Perfection Vehicle has great hardships.

Mantrikas correctly apply [the teaching] to any being in any place at any time, and for whatever length of time is desired. They manifest the result by using easy methods, so that bondage is transformed into liberation. They attain enlightenment easily through the methods, such as the four mudrās, that agree with a person's level of capability. Therefore, the Mantrayāna has no hardship. From *Lamp of the Three Ways*:

[The teaching] is precisely applied
to that which people desire.

The Sage thus taught the sacred meaning
that brings the attainment of the desired goal.[768]

The Mantrayāna is for those with sharp faculties

Hīnayāna [practitioners] do not know the method, and therefore they have blunt faculties. [298] Perfection Vehicle practitioners are mistaken concerning the method, and therefore they have medium faculties. Through special methods, the mantrika is able to transform into causes of enlightenment those actions that would send anyone else into the lower realms. Therefore, the Mantrayāna is for those with sharp faculties. According to Āryadeva:

> The inferior ones have attachment to three things;
> the medium ones become free from attachment;
> the wise ones, who have knowledge
> of the nature of form, become liberated.[769]

Elimination of the Two Extremes[770] states that the Mantrayāna is superior because of these four [qualities]: swift methods, easy methods, many methods, and skill in methods.

The Mantrayāna is superior because of its "swift methods"

In the Perfection Vehicle you have to practice the path for three incalculable eons and so on in order to attain the result, so its methods are slow. The mantrikas attain the result in one, seven, or sixteen lifetimes. Therefore, the Mantrayāna has swift methods. Those with the best faculties and diligence achieve buddhahood within their lifetimes. From the *Kālacakra Root Tantra*:

> If illiterate untouchables and so on
> and those who have perpetrated the five worst actions
> practice the Mantrayāna,
> they will become buddhas within their lifetimes.[771]

From the *Guhyasamāja Tantra*:

> The great nature of this Dharma
> comes from the indivisible three kāyas.

It is an adornment of the ocean of wisdom.
It will be accomplished within this lifetime.[772]

Even those with medium faculties and no diligence, as long as they are without downfalls, will become buddhas within three or seven lifetimes. From *Entering the Mantrayāna*:

[You will be] like a great medicinal tree,
benefiting everyone who sees,
hears, touches, or thinks of you.

When will there be accomplishment?
If there are perfect causes and conditions,
with continuous mantra repetition and meditation
and faith in the conquerors and their children,
the ascetic will become accomplished.

If one has the causes, but some conditions
are incomplete, then in three lifetimes
you will see emptiness perfectly and there will be timeless liberation.[773]

From *Treasury of Secrets*:

If you have truly received the empowerment,
you will be empowered for life after life,
and within seven lifetimes, even though you don't meditate,
you will attain buddhahood.[774]

Even those with the least faculties and extremely inferior minds will, after entering the Mantrayāna, attain buddhahood in sixteen lifetimes as long as they don't commit a downfall, even though they never meditate. From the [*Vajra*] *Pinnacle Tantra*:

Alternatively, just through seeing,
there will be nirvana in sixteen lifetimes.[775]

From the *Five Commitments*:

> As long as there is no downfall,
> it will be accomplished in sixteen lifetimes.[776]

The [Mantrayāna's] superiority because of easy methods, many methods, and skillful methods has already been explained above.

C. An explanation of the categories of the teachings

[299] This is in two parts:

1. The general, simple classification of scripture and realization
2. The presentation of the tantras

1. The general, simple classification of scripture and realization

In general, the Dharma is comprised of the Dharma of scripture and the Dharma of realization. From *Treasury of the Abhidharma*:

> The Teacher's Dharma is twofold:
> It consists of scripture and realization.[777]

a. The Dharma of scripture

The Dharma of scripture is the excellent speech that communicates the teachings that describe the Dharma of realization. One can categorize it into word (*vacana*) and treatise (*śāstra*). From the *Sutra Requested by Devaputra*:

> All Dharmas can be categorized as either *vacana* or *śāstra*—
> the [Buddha's] excellent words and their commentaries.[778]

The *vacana*'s subject is whatever is related to the meaningful Dharma. Its function is that it can eliminate the afflictions of the three realms. Its means of expression is teaching the state of peace and nirvana. Its principal, primary condition is that it appears as the result of buddhahood. From the *Sublime Continuum*:

> That which is meaningful and connected with the Dharma,
> that which teaches the elimination of the three realms' afflictions,

> and that which teaches the benefits from peace,
> that teaching is the Rishi's, and that which is contrary is not.[779]

Vacana

There are three kinds of *vacana*: that spoken from the Buddha's mouth, that spoken through his blessing, and that spoken through his authorization. Most of the *vacana* are words spoken from the Buddha's mouth. The *blessed vacana* are teachings by śrāvakas or bodhisattvas among his followers, or [words] that arose from a divine tree or great drum, and so on, through the power of a blessing from his body, speech, or mind. The *authorized vacana* are the prologues, introductions, supplements, and so on, [which are the words of] the compilers or the requesters of the teachings.

There are the *vacana* of the Hīnayāna, the general Mahayana, and the Mantrayāna. The first two are known as the sutras and the latter as the tantras.

Treatises

The general, ordinary treatises are whatever was composed with the intent to write a treatise to teach a desired teaching. Therefore, *śāstras* are all treatises from both Buddhist and non-Buddhist traditions and paths.

There are two kinds [300] of treatises: the spurious and the genuine. *Invalid treatises* are those that are meaningless, incorrect, negative distractions, devoid of compassion, dedicated to learning, or dedicated to debate. *Valid treatises* are stated to be those that are meaningful, eliminate suffering, or are dedicated to practice. According to Vasubandhu:

> [They can be] meaningless, incorrect, or meaningful;
> deceitful, cruel, or able to eliminate suffering;
> devoted to study, to debate, or to practice;
> six of these are not [genuine] treatises and three are.[780]

The genuine treatises are solely those that explain the meaning of the Buddha's words and have been written by an author with an undistracted mind, teaching in accordance with the path for the purpose of the attainment of liberation. From the *Sublime Continuum*:

> That which is taught by minds free from distraction,
> that which concerns solely the teaching of the Conqueror,

> that which is in accord with the path that attains liberation
> should be placed on the head, as if it were the Rishi's.[781]

b. The Dharma of realization

The Dharma of realization consists of the qualities of realization and elimination within āryas and ordinary beings. It is stated to have two truths: the truth of cessation, which is freedom from desire, and the truth of the path, which brings liberation from desire. From the *Sublime Continuum*:

> That which is, and through which there is, freedom from desire,
> that is the Dharma, which has the characteristics of the two truths.
> Freedom from desire is comprised of
> the truth of cessation and the truth of the path.[782]

Therefore the entire Dharma can be summarized into these two: the *Dharma of realization*, which is the three trainings that are the three [taught] subjects: the superior training in mind, the superior training in conduct, and the superior training in wisdom; and the *Dharma of scripture*, which is the three scriptural baskets that are the three mediums [of teachings]: the Vinaya basket, the Sutra basket, and the Abhidharma basket. The three baskets can be categorized as two: the *lesser basket*, which was taught to those with dull faculties and lesser aspiration; and the *vast basket*, which was taught to those with sharp faculties and vast aspiration. From *Ornament of the Mahayana Sutras*:

> The scriptural baskets, whether three or two...[783]

Ācārya Abhayākara taught that the Mantrayāna is classified within all three baskets, but most say that it is classified as sutras. From [the *Tantra Requested by*] *Subāhu*:

> I shall teach the Mantrayāna in the manner of the sutras.[784]

[301] From the *Compendium of Truths*:

> I shall teach this sutra well.[785]

Śāntipa has said:

> The purpose of the sutras is to teach summaries of the profound meaning.[786]

When there is a classification of four scriptural baskets, the Mantrayāna forms the separate category of the Vidyādhara basket. From [the *Tantra Requested by*] *Subāhu*:

> The many kinds of mantras and vidyās
> are in order to benefit the devas and asuras.
> Therefore, in the Vidyādhara basket,
> the Conqueror taught 3,500,000 [mantras and vidyās].[787]

2. The presentation of the tantras

This is in two parts:

a. A presentation of the tantras in general
b. The categories of the highest yoga [tantras]

a. A presentation of the tantras in general

This is in four parts:

i. A summary of the general categories of the tantras
ii. The way in which the four tantras were taught
iii. The differences among the four tantras
iv. The etymology of the four tantras

i. A summary of the general categories of the tantras

There are many presentations of tantra categories. According to Buddhaguhya:

> There are said to be three tantras
> because of the categories of yoga, performance, and action.[788]

Buddhaguhya also said:

> From looking at the meaning of the mantra,
> there are the yoga, performance, and action tantras
> and similarly the way of the perfections.[789]

Therefore, Buddhaguhya said that there were three tantras: action tantra, performance tantra, and yoga tantra. There are also statements of there being four tantras. From the *Two Books* [*of Hevajra*]:

> Even a tantra of the four [kinds] . . .[790]

From *Entry into the Meaning of the Highest Yoga Tantras*:

> In the Mantrayāna, the result vehicle, the Vajrayāna, there are four doors of entry: the generally renowned action tantra, the performance tantra, the yoga tantra, and the highest yoga tantra.[791]

The statement that there are five tantras has been taught by many great siddhas as well. From *Perfectly Illuminating Lamp*:

> Great Vajradhara, because of the categories of motivation, potentials, natures, and propensities, taught five kinds of Mantrayāna treatises: the categories of action tantras, performance tantras, yoga tantras, highest yoga tantras, and yoginī tantras.[792]

From *Compendium of All Vajra Wisdom* [*Tantra*]:

> It is taught that there are five tantras: the tantra of conception, the tantra of action, the tantra of both, the tantra of purification, and the tantra of great yoga.[793]

From the *Root Tantra of Cakrasaṃvara*:

> The categories of sutra, of action, and of performance,
> of yoga, guhya, and anta.[794]

There is also the teaching that there are six [tantras]: the conceptual tantra of the sutras, the action (*kriyā*) tantra, the performance (*caryā*) tantra, the yoga tantra, the secret (*guhya*) yoga tantra, [302] and the final (*anta*) secret yoga tantra. From the [*Vajra*] *Tent*:

> The yoginī tantra is renowned to be the sixth [tantra].[795]

Atiśa states in his commentary to his *Lamp for the Path to Enlightenment* that there are seven [tantras]: action tantra, performance tantra, conceptual tantra, the tantra of both, yoga tantra, mahāyoga tantra, and highest yoga tantra.[796] All of those can be summarized into two categories: the outer tantras and the inner tantras. From the *Adornment of the Vajra Mandala Tantra*:

> If you know the categories of outer and inner,
> you will know the categories of the tantras.[797]

According to Abhayākara:

> Hold in your heart Vajradhara's lineages,
> which are like outer and inner vajras.
>
> The Teacher divided the rituals of mandalas
> and so on into two tantras.[798]

It is said that the lower three of the four tantras are the outer tantras, while the highest is the inner tantra. *Perfectly Illuminating Lamp* says that the teaching of both generation and completion stages is the inner tantra and the teachings of the generation stage alone are the outer tantras.

ii. The way in which the four tantras were taught

The four tantras were taught in accord with the minds of Vajrayāna pupils

Action tantra was taught to those with inferior minds; the performance tantra was taught to those with middling minds; the yoga tantra was taught to those with superior minds; and the highest yoga tantra was taught to those with exceptionally superior minds. From the *Vajra Tent*:

> Action tantra was for those who were inferior,
> the nonaction [tantra] was for those who were superior.

> The supreme yoga [tantra] was for supreme beings,
> and the highest yoga [tantra] for those who were higher than that.[799]

THE FOUR TANTRAS WERE TAUGHT IN ACCORD WITH FOUR DESIRES THAT HAD TO BE PURIFIED

Action tantra was taught as a remedy for desiring orgasm through looking at each other, for beings such as those in Paranirmitavaśavarta. Performance tantra was taught as a remedy for [desiring] orgasm through smiling at each other, for beings such as those in Nirmāṇarati. Yoga tantra was taught as a remedy for [desiring] orgasm through holding each other, for beings such as those in Tuṣita. Highest yoga tantra was taught as a remedy for [desiring] orgasm through the conjoining of sexual organs, for beings such as those in Trāyastriṃśa and below. From *Tantra of True Union*:

> Even a tantra of the four kinds,
> those of smiling, gazing,
> embrace, and likewise copulation . . .[800]

From the *Hevajra Tantra*:

> Even a tantra of the four [kinds],
> those of smiling, gazing,
> embrace, and likewise copulation . . .[801]

THE FOUR TANTRAS WERE TAUGHT IN ACCORD WITH THE CATEGORIES OF AFFLICTIONS.

[303] From *Perfectly Illuminating Lamp*:

> Action tantra was taught in consideration of those who were the best and the middling in the family of ignorance. Performance tantra was taught to those who were the inferiors in the family of ignorance. Yoga tantra was taught to the inferior and middling in the desire, anger, and ignorance families. Highest yoga tantra was taught to those who were superior in the families of desire, anger, and ignorance. Yoginī tantra was taught to those who were superior to the superior in the desire, anger, and ignorance families.[802]

Other earlier masters have described other ways of categorizing the tantras.

The four tantras were taught in order to teach individuals in the four castes

Action tantra was [taught] to those in the brahman caste, who delighted in cleanliness and purity and aspired to liberation through asceticism and hardship. Performance tantra was [taught] to those in the *vaiśya* caste, who were unable to practice severe asceticism and hardship and would not engage in lowly activities. Yoga tantra was [taught] to those in the *kṣatriya* caste, who could not perform asceticism and enjoyed the pleasures of the senses. Highest yoga tantra was [taught] to those in the śudra caste, who made no distinction between cleanliness and dirt, ate anything, performed lowly tasks, and had few conceptions. Alaṃkakalaśa teaches this in his commentary to the *Explanatory Tantra of the Vajra Garland*.[803] Also, it has been taught that:

> Action corresponds to the purity of the brahmans;
> performance to the *vaiśyas*, which is superior to that;
> yoga to the *kṣatriyas* and their many retinues;
> and primordial liberation is for the *śudras*.[804]

The four tantras as taught to the tīrthikas

Action tantra was taught to tīrthikas who had ignorance: the followers of Brahma who believed in liberation through washing, cleanliness, fasting, fire offerings, and so on. Performance tantra was taught to tīrthikas who had anger: the followers of Viṣṇu who taught violence as Dharma. Highest yoga tantra was taught to tīrthikas who had desire: the followers of Īśvara,[805] who engaged in sexual intercourse and ate the five meats and five nectars. Yoga tantra was taught to tīrthikas who had all cognitions equally, were not of a definite type, and followed all three deities. This is said to be the teaching of such teachers as Subhūtipālita and Sarvagarbha. [304]

The four tantras as taught to the four Buddhist traditions

Action tantra was taught to the Vaibhāṣikas, who believed in the true existence of externals and in an indescribable self. Performance tantra was taught to the Sautrantikas, who believed that appearances were consciousness but believed in the duality of the perceiver and the perceived. Yoga tantra was taught to the Cittamātrins, who believed that externals had no true existence but that there was a real nondual self-knowing. The highest yoga tantra was taught to the Mādhyamikas, who believed that relatively there was the dualistic appearance of a perceiver and the perceived but ultimately it had no reality. This is said to be the teaching of such teachers as Ācārya Nāgārjuna.

iii. The differences among the four tantras

There are very many differences among the four tantras, which can be summarized as follows.

The differences among the four tantras in terms of their practitioners

Action tantra was taught to pupils who aspired to many external activities. Performance tantra was taught to pupils who were both interested in the true nature and attracted to many activities. Yoga tantra was taught to those who knew that many activities cause distraction and who were interested solely in meditation on the true nature. Highest yoga tantra was taught to those who were interested solely in nondual wisdom. This is the teaching given in *Lamp of the Three Ways.*[806]

The differences among the four tantras in terms of their ripening empowerments

Action tantra has water and crown empowerments. Performance tantra has five empowerments: water, crown, vajra, bell, and name. Yoga tantra has, in addition to those empowerments, that of the irreversible master and its ancillaries. Highest yoga tantra has the vase empowerment, which corresponds to all those empowerments and in addition, the secret, the prajñā's knowledge, and the fourth empowerments. This is the teaching given in the *Tilaka of Wisdom.*[807]

The differences among the four tantras in terms of their liberating paths

Action tantra has offerings and so on to a deity in front, and it teaches that śamatha and vipaśyanā are accomplished through the deity's meditation and mantra repetition and through the three dhyānas. Performance tantra teaches the four external and internal recitations as meditation with features, and teaches the samādhi of śamatha and vipaśyanā as featureless meditation. Yoga tantra teaches the three samādhis, the overt visualization of deities, and the subtle visualization of their insignia as the yoga of meditation with features, and teaches the union of śamatha and vipaśyanā as the featureless yoga of meditation. Highest yoga tantra teaches the generation stage with its four branches of the sevā sādhana and so on, and teaches an aspect of the completion stage with its practice of self-blessing and so on.

iv. The etymology of the four tantras

[305] Action (*kriyā*) tantra is so called because it primarily teaches external conduct such as washing and cleanliness. From *Commentary to the Enlightenment of Vairocana*:

> Although the action tantras primarily teach external conduct...[808]

From *Perfectly Illuminating Lamp*:

> A tantra that describes washing, changing clothes three times, fasting, and so on is an action tantra.[809]

Performance (*caryā*) tantra is so called because there is an equal performance of both external activity of body and speech and the internal meditation of the mind. From the *Perfectly Illuminating Lamp*:

> That which is principally concerned with *vratas*, siddhis, miracles, and so on is a performance tantra.[810]

From *Vajrapāṇi's Empowerment Tantra*:

> It is the mandala that has the yoga in which activities and yoga are not separate.[811]

Yoga tantra is so called because it principally teaches meditation on the yoga of internal samādhi. From *Commentary to the Crown Jewel of the Lord of the Three Worlds*:

> *Yoga* means resting the mind in equanimity. Yoga tantra is so called because through the power of yoga and through mantras, the bodhisattva's needs are fulfilled, and therefore there is a relationship and familiarity with mantras, mudrās, mandalas, empowerments, and so on.[812]

From *Radiance of the True Nature*:

> As this tantra is primarily meditation . . .[813]

Highest yoga tantra is so called because it primarily teaches the inseparability of wisdom and method and is the highest of all tantras. From the *Latter Guhyasamāja Tantra*:

> The equality of method and wisdom
> is taught to be *yoga*.[814]

From *Lamp of the Three Ways*:

> Having no restrictions in doing all and performing all is the highest of all tantras: the mahāyoga tantra, which was taught by the Bhagavān.[815]

b. The categories of the highest yoga tantra

In highest yoga tantra, there are three categories: father tantras, mother tantras, and nondual tantras. The father tantras were primarily taught in order to train male pupils. The mother tantras were primarily taught in order to train female pupils.

From the *Vajra Tent*:[816]

> The yoga tantras were perfectly taught
> in order to train males. [306]
> The yoginī tantras were taught
> in order to train women.

By implication, the nondual tantras were taught in order to train men and women equally.

The differences between the subjects of the father, mother, and nondual tantras

The father tantras are said to be those that primarily teach vast methods. The mother tantras are said to be those that primarily teach profound wisdom. From *Summary of the Entry into the Meaning of the Highest Yoga Tantras*:

> Those tantras that primarily teach the true nature of vastness are the *method tantras*. Those tantras that primarily teach profundity are the *wisdom tantras*.[817]

Also, the father tantras are said to be those that primarily teach the nature of the generation stage, and the mother tantras are said to be those that primarily teach the nature of the completion stage. From *Illumination of the Secret Nature*:

> Because of the stages in which generation and completion occur,
> yoga is taught to be the generation,
> and completion is called the yoginī.[818]

Therefore, by implication, the nondual tantras are those that teach both profundity and vastness and teach the nature of both stages.

Differences among the generation stages of the highest yoga tantras

The father tantras teach the five tathāgata family buddhas and their retinues to be primarily male. The mother tantras teach the tathāgatas to be in the form of ḍākiṇīs, and thus the principal deities or their retinues are primarily female.

In the father tantras all activities such as summoning the wisdom deities are performed by male deities while the female deities remain motionless. In the mother tantras goddesses perform those actions while the male deities remain motionless. From Vajragarbha's commentary [to the *Hevajra Tantra*]:

> That in which method is perfectly present—
> the practice of the yoginīs—
> I have named, for the immature,
> the *mahāyoginī tantra*.[819]

> That in which there is the performance of method
> and in which wisdom is also present
> I therefore teach to be the *great tantra of method*,
> and that is the difference between them.[820]

The great commentary to the Kālacakra[821] teaches that in the father tantras there is the generation of the vajra ground or the divine palace from out of the melting of the tier of elements. In the mother tantras there is the generation of the divine palace *upon* the tier of the elements. In the nondual tantra, the tier of elements is first generated, dissolved, generated again and then the divine palace is generated upon it.

In the father tantras, the male and female deities have an equal number of arms and faces. In the mother tantras, the male and female deities have an unequal number of arms and faces. [307] In the nondual tantra, the principal male and female deities have an equal number of arms and faces but the retinue's male and female deities have an unequal number.

In the father tantras, most of the main and retinue deities are sitting. In the mother tantras, most of the deities are standing. In the nondual tantra, the principal deities are standing and the retinue is sitting.

In the father tantras, the gurus[822] are seated upon lions, precious thrones, and insignias; they are primarily adorned with precious jewelry, and their insignias are wheels, jewels, and so on; the wrathful deities stand with the left [leg] stretched out and the peaceful deities are seated with the left [leg] majestically posed. They wear silk, and so on.

In the mother tantras, the [deities] are seated on corpses, skulls, and so on. They are adorned in bone adornments, head garlands, and so on. Their insignias are flaying knives, skull bowls, *khaṭvāṅga* staffs, and so on. [The wrathful deities stand with] the right leg stretched out, and [the peaceful deities are seated with] the right leg majestically posed. They wear human skin, elephant skin, or are naked.

In the father tantras, the mandala has no charnel grounds. In the mother tantras, the mandala has charnel grounds.

The Differences among the Completion Stages of the Highest Yoga Tantras

The father tantras primarily teach self-blessing, the stages of awakening, and so on. The mother tantras teach entering the true nature through union with the mahāmudrā, which is the method of the "perfection of wisdom." From *Illuminating Lamp*:

There are no jewels in this world
other than the great self-blessing.
It is natural, pure luminosity,
like a jewel purified by fire.[823]

From the *Vajra Tent*:

The method of the perfection of wisdom
is here called *yoginī*.
There is entry into the true nature
because of union with the mahāmudrā,
and therefore it is called *yoginī tantra*.[824]

The mother tantras primarily teach the nature of the channels. The father tantras primarily teach the nature of the winds. From *Commentary to the Oral Transmission*:

The ḍākinī tantras are those tantras primarily concerned with the channels (*nāḍīs*), so one can recognize them by that. The tantras primarily concerned with yoga methods are primarily about the nature of the winds (*vāyus*), so one can recognize them by that.[825]

The differences among the highest yoga tantras in purity

The father tantras teach that the pure five aggregates are the tathāgatas. The mother tantras teach that the pure five elements are the five goddesses. From the *Guhyasamāja Tantra*:

In brief, the five aggregates are the conquerors;
they are all the tathāgatas.[826]

From the *Hevajra Tantra*: [308]

Pukkasī is taught to be earth...[827]

It is said in the *Rigi Ārali Tantra*:

Earth, water, fire, and air
are here the four goddesses.[828]

The father tantras teach the pure winds to be the five wisdoms. The mother tantras teach the pure channels to be the goddesses. From the *Guhyasamāja*:

These clear natures of the winds
are the nature of the five wisdoms.[829]

From the *Cakrasaṃvara Tantra*:

In these locations are the ḍākinīs;
they truly reside there because of the beautiful form of the
channels.[830]

The differences explained here are not definite methods for categorizing something as a father or mother tantra. They are taught solely in order to indicate a tendency or predominant feature [of those tantras]. The three categories of father tantra, mother tantra, and nondual tantra are simply categories made in the context of elaborated, provisional meaning. As for the definitive meaning, all highest yoga tantras are nondual tantras. *Yoga* and *nondual* both refer to the inseparability of method and wisdom. This is taught concerning all highest yoga tantras. From the *Primordial Buddha* [*Kālacakra Tantra*]:

Yoga does not exist because of the body of method;
it doesn't exist because of wisdom alone.
The Tathāgata has taught that yoga is
the perfect union of wisdom and method.[831]

From the *Latter Guhyasamāja Tantra*:

Yoga is taught to be
the union of means and wisdom.
That which has no substance is wisdom;
method has the characteristics of substance.[832]

From the *Hevajra Tantra*:

> *He* means great compassion
> and *vajra* is said to be wisdom.
> Listen to the tantra that has the nature
> of method and wisdom and is recited by me.[833]

From the great commentary to the *Kālacakra Tantra*:

> Everything naturally has the nature of wisdom and method, the yoga tantra.[834]

From the great commentary to the *Kālacakra Tantra*:

> Therefore, whatever tantra is said to have the nature of method and wisdom is ultimately not a tantra of wisdom and not a tantra of method either.[835]

III. The special general summary [of the Vajrayāna]

This is in three parts:

A. The causal tantra: the individual as a basis
B. The method tantra: the stages of the path
C. The result tantra: the result of practice

A. The causal tantra: the individual as a basis

This is in two parts:

1. A teaching of the general outline of the causal tantra
2. An explanation of the specific categories of the causal tantra

1. A teaching of the general outline of the causal tantra

[309] To summarize the meaning of every tantra in general, there are three tantras: (1) The unique individual as a foundation is the causal tantra. (2) That individual's practice of the stages of the path is the method tantra. (3) The temporary and ultimate results of that practice are the result tantra. From the *Latter Guhyasamāja Tantra*:

> *Tantras* means "continuums."
> There are three tantras:
> the perfect categories of the basis, of the nature,
> and of the result that cannot be taken away.
>
> The outer aspect of the nature is the cause.
> The basis is said to be method and wisdom.
> Thus, there is the result that cannot be taken away.
> Those three summarize the meaning of tantra.[836]

The causal tantra: the individual as a basis

All beings in the six classes of existence have buddha nature, which is the cause of buddhahood. From a sutra:

> Buddha nature completely pervades all beings.[837]

From a sutra:

> Every one of these beings has the cause of buddhahood.[838]

From the *Hevajra Tantra*:

> All beings are indeed buddhas
> but are obscured by extrinsic impurities.[839]

From the *Sublime Continuum*:

> Because the kāya of complete buddhahood is pervasive,
> because the true nature is indivisible,
> and because of "the family," all [beings]
> always have the essence of buddhahood.[840]

That which is called the *causal buddha nature* is also called the *true nature* (*dharmatā*) and the *truth* (*tattva*).

THE WAY IN WHICH THIS [CAUSAL BUDDHA NATURE] RESIDES WITHIN INDIVIDUALS

There is no good or bad in the natural purity of the essence [of beings], but there is purity and impurity in relation to the extrinsic stains of ignorance. Therefore, beings not on the path have an essence that is impure because of those stains; bodhisattvas on the path have an essence that is partially impure because of those stains and therefore somewhat pure; and tathāgatas have an essence that is completely pure. From the *Sublime Continuum*:

> Impure, impure and pure,
> and completely pure describe,
> in that order, the element of a being,
> a bodhisattva, and a tathāgata.[841]

From *Ornament of the Mahayana Sutras*:

> The true nature is the same
> in everyone and yet is pure.
> Therefore, the nature of the sugatas
> is the essence of all beings.[842]

In terms of families, the family of the buddhas is of two kinds: the primordially naturally present family [310] and the truly accomplished and developed family. From the *Sublime Continuum*:

> Know the family to be of two kinds:
> the primordially naturally present
> and the supreme true acquisition.[843]

"Family," "element," "seed," and "cause" all have the same meaning, and therefore the cause is that all beings have the "family of buddhahood." However, there is a difference in terms of inferior and supreme causes in relation to their distance from buddhahood. In particular, the karma that is created in this world of Jambudvīpa can ripen in the same lifetime, so that it can be a most perfect cause. For this, you must have the complete eight freedoms and ten opportunities. Peerless Gampopa has said:

> Freedoms and opportunities,
> conviction, aspiration, and attraction:

> [The first] two are of the body and [the latter] three are of the mind.
> Those five factors summarize the supreme basis.[844]

The eight freedoms are the avoidance of eight unfavorable states. From the *Abbreviated [Perfection of Wisdom in Verse]*:

> By avoiding the eight unfavorable states, you will always find the freedoms.[845]

The eight freedoms are described in the *Commentary on Difficult Points in "Entering the Conduct of a Bodhisattva"*:

> Hells, pretas, animals,
> barbarians, long-lived devas,
> wrong beliefs, the absence of a buddha,
> and idiocy are the eight unfavorable states.[846]

[From *Explanation of "Entering the Conduct of a Bodhisattva"*]:

> Among the ten opportunities are the five opportunities from oneself:
> being human, being born in the central land, having complete faculties,
> not committing the extreme actions, and having faith.[847]

[From *Explanation of "Entering the Conduct of a Bodhisattva"*]:

> Among the ten opportunities are the five opportunities from others:
> the coming of a buddha, his teaching the Dharma,
> the teachings enduring, the followers of [the teachings],
> and those who have compassion for others.[848]

Also, you must have the three kinds of faith: conviction, aspiration, and attraction. From the *Sutra of the Ten Dharmas*:

> Good qualities will not be born
> in humans who have no faith.
> Just as a green sprout [is not born]
> from a seed that has been burned by fire.[849]

From the *Avataṃsaka Sutra*:

> Those who dwell in existence and have little faith
> cannot know the buddhas and bodhisattvas.[850]

2. An explanation of the specific categories of the causal tantra

[311] The Characteristics Vehicle states that an individual as a basis [for liberation] is one of three types: the Hīnayāna family, the Mahayana family, and the uncertain family.

In the Vajrayāna [individuals] are categorized according to the five afflictions—extrinsic stains that hinder the cause of buddhahood, which is the true nature, the naturally present family. There are also [the categories of] the five wisdoms, which are the result of being purified of those [afflictions]: (1) the Vajra or Akṣobhya family, (2) the Tathāgata or Vairocana family, (3) the Ratna or Ratnasambhava family, (4) the Padma or Amitābha family, (5) and the Karma or Amoghasiddhi family. The [Vajrayāna] teaches that "individuals who are bases" belong to one of these five families and are categorized according to afflictions. If anger is strongest, they are in the Akṣobhya family; if stupidity is strongest they are in the Vairocana family, and so on. From the *Vajra Tent*:

> In order to gather beings
> that have anger, stupidity,
> pride, desire, and miserliness,
> I become many forms in the circle of the vajra bearer.[851]

Categories according to color

Black is the Akṣobhya family, white is the Vairocana family, and so on. From the *Hevajra Tantra*:

> Akṣobhya is the deity
> of a yogin who is black.
> Vairocana is the family deity
> of a yogin who is very white.[852]

CATEGORIES THROUGH SIGNS AND OMENS

Those with the mark of a vajra at the base of their ring finger are of the Akṣobhya family; those who have a wheel are of the Vairocana family; and so on. From the *Hevajra Tantra*:

> Whoever [whether man or woman]
> has a nine-pronged vajra
> at the base of their ring finger
> is of the supreme family of Akṣobhya.
>
> A wheel [means they are of the family] of Vairocana.
> [A lotus means they are of the family of Amitābha.
> A great jewel means Ratnasambhava.
> And a sword means they are of the Karma family.][853]

CATEGORIES ACCORDING TO MINDS

There are said to be five kinds of individuals, such as the utpala. From *Illuminating Lamp*:

> From the countless aspects of minds
> there are said to be five kinds of individuals:
> utpala (*blue lotus*), puṇḍārīka (*white lotus*),
> padma (*red lotus*), candana (*sandalwood*), and ratna (*jewel*).
> The omniscient one taught their natures
> through these different names.[854]

Illuminating Lamp also teaches the differences among these individuals:

> Individuals are called *utpala*
> if they are skilled in remembering
> every [teaching] they have heard
> and can instantly repeat them.
>
> Individuals are called *puṇḍārīka*
> if they have heard many [teachings] that should be received
> but lack the ability to teach them.
> They are like bowls of cotton seeds.

Individuals are called *padma*
if they have faith, compassion, and knowledge
and on hearing [the teaching], it pours without difficulty,
like milk, into their open minds. [312]

Individuals are called *candana*
if they have heard few [teachings] but are proud,
say many things that have no basis,
and should not be taken as a pupil.

Individuals are called *ratna*
if they have pure conduct and are skilled and clever,
have wisdom and single-mindedness,
and after hearing [a teaching] are able to teach it excellently.[855]

The first four of those five should primarily be introduced to the teaching and training of the gradual path. The fifth [kind of individual] is the supreme "individual who is a basis." They should be introduced to practice from the beginning and can enter onto the instantaneous path, because their beings have already been trained. From *Illuminating Lamp*:

These four kinds of individuals—
the *utpala* and likewise the *puṇḍārīka*,
the *padma* and the *candana*—
are individuals who should be given public teachings.

Those who are worthy of the completion stage
and are always adorned by good conduct
are the *ratna* individuals
and are vessels for [private] pupil teaching.[856]

Becoming a worthy vessel through training one's being

From the *Hevajra Tantra*:

Those who have committed the five worst actions—
who delight in killing beings—
and those who have a low birth,
those who are stupid and act violently,

and those who have ugly bodies or missing limbs,
even they will become accomplished through [this] meditation.[857]

THE CERTAINTY OF ACCOMPLISHMENT

From the *Hevajra Tantra*:

One who is habituated to the ten good actions,
has veneration for the guru, has control of the senses,
and is free from pride and anger
will most definitely become accomplished.[858]

B. The method tantra: the stages of the path

This is in two parts:

1. The general stages of the path
2. The stages of the Vajrayāna path

1. The general stages of the path in the method tantra

Individuals who are bases must first correctly depend upon a genuine spiritual friend (*kalyāṇamitra*) and listen to definite Dharma teachings.

First, they must meditate upon how important and difficult is the acquisition of "the freedoms and opportunities" and must aspire to acquire their essence.

The path of the lesser being is to meditate on impermanence and reject attachment to the experiences of this life. Then they should meditate upon the sufferings of the three lower existences, avoid their causes, which are bad actions, and practice good actions, which are the causes of happiness within existence. From *Lamp for the Path to Enlightenment*:

It is taught that the least kind of beings
are those who, through whatever methods,
seek merely the happiness of samsara [313]
for their own benefit.[859]

The path of middling beings is to meditate upon the sufferings of all six kinds of existences in samsara and to meditate on the causes and results of karma, thus rejecting attachment to the happiness of samsara. Then they should meditate upon the qualities of liberation, develop the aspiration to attain liberation, and apply themselves to the necessary methods. From [*Lamp for the Path*]:

> The beings who are called *middling*
> are those who cast the happiness of samsara behind them,
> turn away from bad actions,
> and wish to attain peace for themselves alone.[860]

The path of great beings is to meditate on love and compassion for all beings and to turn away from the wish to attain peace for themselves alone. Then they should follow the training of the pratimokṣa, develop bodhicitta, and train in the practice of the bodhisattva's conduct, such as the six perfections, the ten perfections, and so on, thus proceeding through the five paths and the ten levels. From [*Lamp for the Path*]:

> The beings who are supreme
> are those who, by understanding suffering within themselves,
> develop the complete aspiration to truly end
> all the sufferings of others.[861]

2. The stages of the Vajrayāna path in the method tantra

This is in two parts:

a. The manner of entry into the [Mantra]yāna for inferior minds
b. The teaching on the actual Mantra[yāna]

a. The manner of entry into the Mantrayāna for inferior minds

Individuals who are bases of inferior capability are those who in the beginning become afraid upon hearing the Vajrayāna. They have to [first] train their minds through any of the general graduated paths and then enter into the Mantrayāna by stages. From the *Hevajra Tantra*:

> "How does one train
> unworthy beings difficult to train?"

> The Bhagavān answered,
> "First they must practice *poṣadha*[862] and generosity
> and then the ten topics of training.
> Teach them the Vaibhāṣya[863]
> and also the Sūtrānta[864] in that way.
> Subsequently [teach them] the Yogācāra
> and afterward teach them the Madhyamaka.
> When they have understood the entire way of the mantras,
> then they should commence upon Hevajra."[865]

From the *Root Tantra of Cakrasaṃvara*:

> Beings enter, according to their aspiration,
> the categories of sutra, action,
> performance, yoga, or "the final secret"
> in accord with their preference.[866]

From the [*Lamp of the*] *Compendium of Practices*:

> The perfect Buddha presented
> these methods that are like the steps of a stair,
> so that those who are beginners
> could enter the ultimate truth.[867] [314]

b. The teaching on the actual Mantrayāna of the tantra of method

This is in two parts:

i. A summarized teaching of the lower tantras
ii. A teaching of the categories of the highest yoga tantra path

i. A summarized teaching of the lower tantras

This is in two parts:

A) The stages of the path of the action and performance [tantras]
B) The stages of the path of yoga [tantra]

A) The stages of the path of the action and performance tantras

This is in three parts:

1) Preparing your being
2) The sevā rituals
3) The method for accomplishing siddhis

1) Preparing your being in the action and performance tantras

Keeping vows and commitments after receiving the empowerment

If you have only received the action and performance empowerments and the disciple empowerments from the two higher tantras, it is enough to keep just the preliminary general vows preceded by the refuge vow. There will be no need to keep the special vows of the five families or to keep the four commitments, for they are the special commitments and vows of the ācārya empowerment in the higher tantras. From the *Origin of All Vajras*:

> Do not recite the words "Today, you..." and so on, nor bestow the ācārya empowerment and authorization, to those who are not going to keep the vows.[868]

In general, if someone cannot keep [even] the general vows, then they are not worthy vessels, and so it would be inappropriate to give them the empowerment and authorization. Instead, just grant them entry into the mandala that indicates their deity through the casting of a flower. From [*Vajra*] *Pinnacle*:

> If they are not worthy vessels,
> [merely] bestow on them entry [into the mandala].[869]

From [*Vajra*] *Pinnacle*:

> Only give them entry [into the mandala]
> and do not give them all aspects [of the empowerment].[870]

The actual empowerment

It is taught that the action tantras have the liquid and crown empowerments. From the *Tilaka of Wisdom*:

> The action tantras are renowned to have
> the liquid and crown empowerments.[871]

The action tantra texts clearly describe the liquid empowerment. They identify the crown empowerment as either making a [hand] mudrā and placing that on the head or sealing with the family lord.[872] Some Indian texts appear to include some empowerments from the yoga tantras (as far up as the "irreversible" empowerment) within the action tantra empowerments, [315] but the majority of reliable [sources] do not.

The performance tantras teach, in addition to the liquid and crown empowerments, the vajra, bell, and name empowerments, so that they have five empowerments. From the *Tilaka of Wisdom*:

> The vajra, the bell, and similarly the name
> are perfectly and clearly described in performance tantra.[873]

The *Enlightenment of Vairocana* describes the liquid empowerment only, but the *Vajrapāṇi Empowerment Tantra* teaches [the others]. According to many [texts], both the action and performance empowerments should be preceded by the flower garland empowerment and have the concluding supports of mantra, eye medicine, mirror, and teaching authorization [empowerments]. Some [texts] also teach authorizations for the wheel, spear, and so on, and entry into the special vajra-*vrata* conduct, the bestowal of prophecy, and reassurance.

You might think that these concluding supports are inappropriate, because there is no vajrācārya empowerment in the action and performance tantras. However, even though there is no actual vajrācārya empowerment of irreversibility, they are not anomalies, because these concluding supports are empowerments solely for becoming ācāryas of those particular action and performance tantras alone.

The commitments that have to be kept

The *Compendium of Commitments*[874] says that there are thirty root downfalls in action tantra and fourteen root downfalls in performance tantra.

However, as there is no clear teaching on the former, [the number of downfalls in action tantra] should be the same as in performance tantra. The action tantra *Excellent Accomplishment*[875] contains a great deal of teaching on the vidyāmantra discipline (*vinaya*).

In performance tantra, the [downfalls] are the ten bad actions with the addition of the following four: forsaking the Dharma, abandoning the bodhicitta, being miserly, and harming beings. It is taught to keep also all the proscriptions of the bodhisattva vows. Some state that the [*Vajra*] *Pinnacle* says to keep [vows] as in the yoga tantra, located in the section that begins and ends as follows:

> You should not take life...
> ...do not step across...insignias.[876]

2) The sevā rituals [in the action and performance tantras]

This is in two parts:

a) The sevā rituals in action tantra
b) The sevā rituals in performance tantra

a) The sevā rituals in action tantra

The sevā ritual in action tantra has two [kinds of meditation]:

i) The meditation with repetition and recitation
ii) The meditation without repetition and recitation

i) The meditation with repetition and recitation

First the preliminaries

Commentary on the Latter Dhyāna[877] teaches a practice of the vidyāmantra and so on while practicing cleanliness through ritual washing and so on and creating protection for yourself and your location. [316]

Then, the main practice, the deity yoga

Invite the deity into the basis that is either [the visualization] you have generated or a painted image in front of you. Make offerings, praises, confessions, and so on. Then bind the prāṇa and remain in the samādhi of meditating that you are the deity. From the *Latter Dhyāna*:[878]

In the beginning only, make offerings
to the location of the [representation of the] deity's body.
Then those with wisdom, who reside in yoga,
imagine that the Sugata is before them.
Then there is nondifferentiation through
freedom from the aspects [of the senses], and differentiating is abandoned.

They rest in facing the mind's analysis:
the subtle unwavering clarity.
They rest in that kind of nature
and then meditate with the consciousness of the mantra.

Bind and rest in samādhi.
Tightly bind with *prāṇāyāma* (restraint of the life-breath).[879]

Enlightenment of Vairocana teaches that first you generate yourself as the deity, then you invite the deity to be in front of you, and so on.

Then, in the mantra meditation, there are three [mantra] recitations and repetitions: focusing upon the form of the letters in the heart of the deity in front of you; focusing upon the form of the letters in your own heart; and focusing on the sound of the letters. [From the *Latter Dhyāna*]:

Focus on the sound, the mind, and the basis.
The mantra dwells in the unchanging basis.
Repeat the mantra with no aspect imperfect.
If you become tired, relax within yourself.

Changelessness is endowed with syllables.
A basis comes from the basis, and in that way,
when its own mantra is assigned externally,
think of that as the purity of the mind.

Then bring it in through drawing it inward,
and the mind that binds with prāṇāyāma
is applied to the mantra through the knowledge of the mantra
and performs mental repetition and recitation.[880]

Afterward, dedicate the good karma, pray for forgiveness for your errors, and [request] the deities to depart. Those are called the *yogas of the session's conclusion.*

ii) The meditation without repetition and recitation

Practice the deity yoga. Meditate on the samādhi of śamatha and vipaśyanā through the three meditations of *resting in fire*, *resting in sound*, and *the end of sound*. From [the *Latter Dhyāna*]:

> Resting in the mantra's fire is siddhi,
> resting in sound is remembering the bestowal of yoga,
> and the end of sound is the bestowal of liberation:
> Those are the three true natures.[881]

b) The sevā rituals of performance tantra

There are two yogas in the performance rituals: [317]

[i) The yoga with features
ii) The featureless yoga]

i) The yoga with features

First, there are the preliminaries of protecting yourself, your location, and so on. This is followed by "the first syllable," which is meditation on bodhicitta and emptiness. The "second syllable" is arising from that [meditation] as the sound of the mantra. The "first foundation" is the perfect generation of yourself as the body of the Buddha. The "second foundation" is generating the body of the Buddha in front of you.

The external repetition is establishing the mantra circle upon a moon [disc] in the heart, binding with prāṇāyāma, practicing mental repetition, and so on. From the *Enlightenment of Vairocana*:

> Syllable should be conjoined with syllable.
> Similarly, the basis becomes the basis.
> With tight focus, repeat the mantra
> a hundred thousand times in the mind.
>
> The [first] syllable is bodhicitta;
> the second is called the *sound*.

The [first] basis is establishing your deity,
the location of which is your own body.

Know that the second basis
is the complete Buddha, the supreme two-legged being.
The mantrika imagines that a completely pure
moon disc is located there.

Perfectly arrange in its center
the syllables in their correct order.
Press down with the syllables that are drawn in,[882]
perfectly training in prāṇāyāma.[883]

The internal repetition is taught to be generating yourself as the body of the Buddha, generating the Buddha upon a moon in your heart, establishing the mantra on a moon in his heart, and repeating it.

ii) The featureless [yoga of the performance tantra]

When you have gained the śamatha that is focused upon the body of the deity and so on, then meditate on emptiness. From *Enlightenment of Vairocana*:

That which is called *mental transcendence of the world*
totally avoids reabsorbing and so on.
Becoming one with the deity,
and with a mind that focuses on not being different,
create a state of inseparability.
Do nothing other than that.[884]

Thus, in the lower tantras there is meditation on deity yoga, prāṇa, śamatha, and vipaśyanā, but the terms *yoga with features* and *featureless yoga* are used while the terms *generation stage* and *completion stage* are not used, for these latter two phases are the special path of highest yoga tantra.

3) The method for accomplishing siddhis in the action and performance tantras

When you have become adept in sevā, accomplish the siddhis. From *Excellent Accomplishment*:

The extremely superior karmas (*rites*)
are accomplished through special recitations.
If sevā has previously been practiced,
most karmas will be accomplished.[885]

From the [*Tantra Requested by*] *Subāhu*: [318]

In accordance with the ritual, first perform a hundred thousand repetitions
and then engage in the practice of the mantra.
You will then quickly attain the siddhis,
and through the mantra ritual, you will have no afflictions for a long time.[886]

The best siddhis are becoming a vidyādhara, gaining clairvoyance, gaining knowledge of all treatises, and so on. The medium siddhis are invisibility, *rasāyana*,[887] swift feet, and so on. The least siddhis are accomplishing the peaceful, increasing, controlling, and wrathful rites. It is also taught that there are many other siddhis to be accomplished and a variety of ways to achieve them.

B) Within the lower tantras, the stages of the path of yoga tantra

This is in three parts:

1) Preparing your being
2) The sevā rituals
3) The method for accomplishing siddhis

1) Preparing your being in the yoga tantra

In yoga tantra, in addition to the five vidyā empowerments, there is the irreversible ācārya empowerment. This is said to be composed of six empowerments: the irreversible empowerment, the secret empowerment, the authorization, the prophecy, the reassurance, and the praise. From the *Tilaka of Wisdom*:

The empowerment of irreversibility
is very clearly divided in the yoga tantras.

It consists of six particular empowerments,
which are called the *ācārya empowerments*.[888]

Also from the *Tilaka of Wisdom*:

Create a division into eight empowerments
and bestow them on those who aspire to yoga tantra:
water, crown, vajra,
bell, name, *vrata*,
prophecy, giving refuge,
mantra, mudrā, and wisdom.[889]

Thus, there are taught to be eight, with mantra, mudrā, and wisdom as ancillaries.

Only the disciple empowerment appears in the root [yoga] tantra, *Compendium of Truths*, but the explanatory tantra, *Vajra Pinnacle*, teaches in detail the five vidyā empowerments and the ācārya empowerment with its ancillaries.

After completely receiving the empowerment, the commitments to be kept are the vows of the five families, which are the Tathāgata, Vajra, Ratna, Padma, and Karma families. From [*Vajra*] *Pinnacle*:

Go for refuge in
the Buddha, Dharma, and Sangha,
which will make firm the vows
of the buddha families.[890]

These and subsequent lines describe the root commitments. [319] The branch commitments, such as the vows of avoidance, the vows of reliance, and so on, are described in the section that begins and ends:

You should not take life...
...do not step across... insignias.[891]

Some state that the root commitments are fourteen, beginning with not killing and ending with "do not step over the insignia," in accordance with the [preceding] lines:

> Other than those, the father has taught
> [these] fourteen to be defeats.[892]

2) The sevā rituals [of yoga tantra]

There are two yogas in yoga tantra [the yoga with features and the featureless yoga]. The *yoga with features* is the overt yoga, which is focused upon the deity. Having received just the disciple (*śikṣya*) empowerment, you can meditate using the methods of the four yogas. From *Commentary to the First Part [of Compendium of Truths]*:

> Thus, having taught one's own disciples yoga and subsequent yoga...[893]

The four yogas are described in *Commentary on the Śrī Paramādya Tantra*:

> *Yoga* is generating yourself as having the nature of the deity, by meditating on five aspects of the true nature. *Anuyoga* (subsequent yoga) is the superior aspiration of perfectly imagining the wisdom being (*jñānasattva*) entering you and becoming connate with it. *Sarvayoga* (total yoga) is the meditation on yourself as the essence of everything, both animate and inanimate. *Atiyoga* (extreme yoga) is the one-pointed mind in complete meditation on yoga, anuyoga, and sarvayoga.[894]

The procedure for this ritual

According to *Commentary to the First Part [of Compendium of Truths]*, this is how you meditate in each of the four sessions: First, you ritually cleanse yourself, protect yourself and your location, gather the accumulations, and bind with seals. After those preliminaries, you meditate on selflessness, meditate on your deity, make the wisdom being enter, seal this with the four seals, [receive] the empowerment, make offerings, meditate on the great seal of your own deity, and repeat the mantra of your deity.[895]

Through receiving the ācārya empowerment of the master, there is the meditation on the three samādhis: self, completion, and mahāyoga. From the *Long Sādhana of Vajrasattva*:

> Whoever has received the ācārya empowerment practices the mahāyoga and trains perfectly in all rituals.[896]

From *Commentary to the First Part* [*of Compendium of Truths*]:

> ...the yoga that is the practice of the mandala of the ācāryas and the practice of their own deity is called *mahā* (great).[897] [320]

The procedure for this ritual

The *extensive sevā*, as described in the *Vajrodaya*,[898] has three forms: First meditate upon cleansing, the yoga of the wrathful deities, and the circle of protection. Then you emanate the *basis for accumulation* and make homage to it, offer to it, and so on, and then you bind with the seals. After those preliminaries, you meditate upon yourself [as the deity], completion, and mahāyoga, and meditate on the first yoga, the *supreme victor of the mandala*, and the *supreme victor of activity*.

In the *medium sevā*, you meditate on the meaning of the three mantras up until the mahāyoga by emanating a mandala in the heart and arranging the individual essences [of the deities]. Once they enter the heart mandala, you meditate on the meaning of the three mantras while repeating them.

In the *brief sevā*, you practice—as in the mahāyoga—self and completion, repeating the mantra of each deity a hundred thousand times.

In order to make the mind tractable in the overt yoga of focusing on the deity, meditate on the subtle yoga of focusing on the insignia. From *Apatarava*:

> First, meditate for a while on the samādhi of the subtle vajra in order to gain control over your own mind.[899]

This process of meditation is described in *Compendium of Truths*:

> Place the tongue against the palate
> and contemplate the tip of the nose.
> Through contacting the subtle vajra's bliss,
> the mind will rest in meditation.[900]

Adopting the essential points of the physical posture of meditation, maintain mindfulness of the deity yoga. The movement of the breath brings a five-pronged vajra—the color of the deity and the size of a hair tip or a sesame seed—from the heart to the tip of the nose, where it remains. Focus your mind on it one-pointedly. This is taught to accomplish stability. Buddhaguhya taught that while this is being done, don't exhale or inhale. The cultivation of stability according to Śākyamitra:

> The crazed elephant of the mind behaves badly.
> Tie it to the post of the focus
> by using the rope of mindfulness, and then gradually
> bring it under control with the hook of wisdom.[901]

This example of taming an elephant teaches that to make the mind tractable, you need to employ mindfulness and awareness. When the mind has been stabilized, practice radiation and absorption. From *Compendium of Truths*:

> If there occurs the sign
> of contact with the subtle vajra's bliss,[902]
> that sign should pervade;
> the mind should pervade.
> If the mind pervades as you wish,
> it will pervade even the three realms.[903] [321]

From *Compendium of Truths*:

> Then they are drawn in
> as far as the tip of the nose
> [and rest perfectly in meditation.][904]

Featurelessness according to *Compendium of Truths*:

> Enter into the *a* syllable
> and meditate that all the syllables,
> through meditation, [go] from one's own mouth
> to "the mouth," and siddhi will be attained.[905]

It is explained that the syllable *a* means birthlessness, and therefore all the syllables that are repeated are destroyed, and you can meditate upon selflessness. The meaning of "mouth" is doorway, which here means emptiness as one of the "doorways of liberation." Therefore, this is the meaning of both the deity in front and the mantras. This is primarily a teaching on conceptual wisdom. From *Compendium of Truths*:

> That which is called *truly piercing wisdom*
> is renowned as samādhi.
> Therefore if you meditate on the swift accomplishment
> of the mudrā, it will be swiftly accomplished.[906]

This teaches that *truly piercing wisdom* is the view of birthlessness; it is the knowledge that everything has no nature, so that you rest without any conception of anything.

Vajra Pinnacle teaches in detail the featureless meditations of the Tathāgata family, the Vajra family, and the rest. It primarily teaches the vipaśyanā that is analysis with discriminating wisdom. *Compendium of Truths* teaches both śamatha and vipaśyanā. If you practice in this way, meditate by alternating śamatha and vipaśyanā in relation to such key points as agitation and dullness. From *Adornment of Kosala*:

> When there is a predominance of śamatha, dullness causes distraction. When there is a predominance of vipaśyanā, agitation causes distraction.[907]

3) The method for accomplishing siddhis in yoga tantra

It is taught that when you have become adept in sevā, practice dhyāna, mantra repetition and recitation, homa fire rituals, and so on, so as to accomplish siddhis.

Dhyāna accomplishes all worldly siddhis, such as the discovery of treasures, and the supramundane siddhis, such as becoming a vidyā-mantradhara.

Repetition and recitation accomplishes flying in the sky, being able to take on whatever form one wishes, becoming invisible, and so on, through the siddhi of the deity's form and the commitment mudrās (*samayamudrā*).[908] [322]

The homa fire rituals accomplish the activities, such as peaceful, increasing, powerful, wrathful, and so on.

There are many other greater and lesser siddhis that can be accomplished.

ii. A teaching on the categories of the highest yoga tantra path

This is in two parts:

A) The path of ripening
B) The path of liberation

A) The path of ripening in the highest yoga tantra

This is in three parts:

1) The stages preliminary to the ripening [empowerments]
2) A classification of the rituals of the ripening empowerments
3) Keeping the commitments and vows

1) The stages preliminary to the ripening empowerments

This is in three parts:

a) The reason why there must first be a ripening empowerment
b) The teacher and pupil's examination of each other and the pupil's supplication
c) The way in which the master performs sevā and enters into the rite

a) The reason why there must first be a ripening empowerment

If you have entered the Mantrayāna but have not yet received an empowerment, you should not hear [the teaching] and you should not know the meaning of the tantra or teach it to others. Even if you were to practice mantra, dhyāna, and so on, you would not be able to accomplish them. If you have received empowerment, you are a ready vessel for teaching, receiving, and meditating on the great secret and you have obtained the root of all siddhis. From the *Mahāmudrā Tilaka Tantra*:

> First of all, when at some time
> the empowerments are given to pupils,
> then at that time, they become a ready vessel
> for the teaching of the great secret.
>
> Without empowerment, they will have no siddhis,
> like trying to get [seed] oil by crushing sand.

If someone arrogantly
teaches without an empowerment,
the teacher and pupil, even if they have attained siddhis,
will go to hell as soon as they die.

Therefore, with all your effort, beseech your guru
to bestow an empowerment upon you.[909]

From the *Buddhakapāla Tantra*:

For example, the lute is a combination of all its parts.
If there are no strings, it cannot be played.
In the same way, without an empowerment,
you cannot accomplish mantras and meditation.[910]

From the *Vajra Garland Tantra*:

The empowerment is the main thing.
All siddhis are always present in it.
I will teach its exact meaning.
Therefore, to begin with, listen to me well.

In the beginning, whenever pupils
are given a wise true empowerment,
at that time, they become a worthy vessel
for the yoga of the completion stage.

Even though a practitioner knows the tantra's meaning,
if they do not have a true empowerment,
both the teacher and the pupil
will go to an unendurable great hell.[911] [323]

Obtaining an empowerment brings countless temporary and ultimate benefits. From the *Tantra of All Mandalas*:

All the buddhas will know
when you first receive the empowerment.[912]

And following that:

When the practitioners gain that,
they will accomplish all activities,
they will not be harmed by anything,
and deities will make offerings to them.

When they go round in the cycles of samsara,
they will not fall into the lower existences;
neither will they be born with defective limbs
or be born into poverty or an inferior status.

They will remember their previous lives and have great wealth,
they will have good conduct and a beautiful body,
and they will always be reborn
among devas and humans in the higher existences.

Through the power of that merit
they will irreversibly progress to enlightenment and buddhahood,
and before much time has passed,
they will attain complete, supreme enlightenment.[913]

b) The teacher and pupil's examination of each other and the pupil's supplication

The qualities of the gurus are described in the *Vajra Tent Tantra*:

They are stable and possess the profound Dharma.
They are skilled in all branches of knowledge.
They know the homa fire rituals, the mandalas, and the mantras.
They have reached perfection in consecration and tormas.

They perfectly know the ten principles.
They maintain the conduct of a śrāvaka
and venerate the stages of the Mantrayāna.
People feel joy on seeing their physical forms.

They are skilled in drawing mandalas and have completed the mantra
repetitions.
They have completely overcome the root downfalls.
They have complete application to the mantras and tantras
and thus give bliss to all in the world.[914]

The ten principles are explained in the *Vajra Mandala Tantra*:

These are the ten secret principles:
the rites of both repellings,
the secret, the prajñā's wisdom,
the rituals of uniting and separating,
the torma and the vajra repetition,
the ritual of wrathful practice,
the consecration, and blessing the mandala.

The ten external principles
are mandala, samādhi, mudrā,
the gazes, the posture, the repetition recitation,
the homa fire ritual, the offering, the application of activity,
and these aspects in brief.[915]

If you are unable to find a master who has all the characteristics taught in the tantras, don't accept those who have faults and good qualities in equal measure or those who have mostly faults, but choose one who has mostly good qualities. From the *Ultimate Service*:

In the degenerate age, gurus have a mixture of good qualities and
faults; [324]
there are none completely free of bad actions.
When you have properly examined someone with superior good
qualities,
then, children, rely upon that person.[916]

The characteristics of the pupils are explained in the *Vajra Tent*:

Someone who has attained good conduct,
who has not transgressed the command of the sugatas,
who venerates the guru and has love.[917]

The relationship between the guru and pupil is described in the *Vajra Garland Tantra*:

Just as one files a precious substance,
just as one cuts gold so as to analyze it,
in that same way, even the pupil
should analyze for twelve years.

Thus they should examine
each other mutually at all times.
Otherwise, obstacles will occur,
siddhis will be prevented, and you will receive suffering.[918]

From the *Mahāmudrā Tilaka Tantra*:

In the same way that gold is cut and so on,
like a skilled person with something precious,
like a happy man with a maiden,
that is how to examine the guru.
If you don't do so in that way, there will be faults,
and you will never obtain siddhis.[919]

In that way, the master and pupil examine each other. If each proves suitable, the pupil should then supplicate the master. From the *Vajraḍāka Tantra*:

The pupil should pray
again and again to the guru
so that he will draw again the mandala.[920]

From *Fifty Verses on the Guru*:

On bended knee with palms together,
wishing to hear [teachings] and so on, supplicate three times.[921]

The *Vajradāka Tantra* describes in detail the protection that the guru must give the pupil, starting with:

> Imagine an air mandala, shaped like a bow,[922]
> at the soles of the feet of the pupil...[923]

And ending with:

> ...having generated the form of the deity that is to be practiced,
> arrange the protections.[924]

There are various elaborate and simple mandala rites.

c) The way in which the master performs sevā and enters into the rite

If the master has not previously completed sevā, then he must complete it. From the *Compiled Summary of the Four Seats Tantra Mandalas*:

> The master of the supreme mandala
> first applies himself to sevā.
> Then he examines, with strong self-control,
> that particular mandala.
> If the deity has not been pleased,
> it will cause trouble for you.[925] [325]

From *An Excellent Collection*:

> First, gather the accumulations in sevā practice
> and cause obstacles to completely decline.
> If there has been no sevā, there will be no siddhi.[926]

It is taught that the number [of mantra repetitions] in sevā practice are one hundred thousand for the principal deity or for the one on whom your flower fell, and ten thousand for the retinue. From the *Hevajra Tantra*:

> Repeat a hundred thousand for the lord of the mandala
> and ten thousand for the mandala deities.[927]

According to Abhayākaragupta:

> Repeat a hundred thousand for the principal deity in the mandala
> or otherwise a hundred thousand for your own deity.[928]

Another explanation is from the *Saṃvarodaya Tantra*:

> One repetition in the age of perfection
> is doubled in the second age,
> tripled in the third age,
> and quadrupled in the degenerate age.[929]

From *Commentary to the Buddhakapāla Tantra*:

> During the age of perfection, repeat a hundred thousand times.
> During the second age, repeat two hundred thousand times.
> During the third age, repeat three hundred thousand times.
> During the degenerate age, repeat three million, three hundred thousand times.[930]

Based upon that teaching, the gurus teach four hundred thousand repetitions for the principal deity and forty thousand each for the retinue. It's taught that even though you have previously practiced sevā, you should still practice a certain amount of sevā in order to give the empowerment to a pupil, examine omens such as dreams, and request authorization so that authorization will not be withheld. From the *Four Hundred and Fifty Verses*:

> Repeat for the mandala in accordance with its nature,
> and after gaining the omens, draw it correctly.[931]

According to Abhayākaragupta:

> So that there will be no prohibition from the lords of the mandala who dwell in the mandala, and for authorization through gathering the accumulations, practice the consecration of the mandala and the bringing in of the pupils.[932]

The procedure for the rite of entering the mandala: The entry should take place at a good time, date, position of planets and stars, and so on. From the *Tantra of All Mandalas*:

> If a mind that is truly at peace
> performs the mantra invitation
> at a peaceful time and date,
> the desired siddhis will be attained.[933]

Also from the *Tantra of All Mandalas*:

> Those who are wise will not draw a mandala
> upon a bad date, at an inappropriate time,
> in an inappropriate place, or without the rite.
> If someone does so, they will doubtless die.[934] [326]

There are many teachings on the particulars of months, dates, planets, and stars. [The *Tantra of All Mandalas*] gives these other times:

> When the sun and moon are seized by Rahu[935]
> when great marvelous omens appear,
> and during the month of miracles,
> then carefully draw the mandala.[936]

2) A classification of the rituals of the ripening empowerments of the highest yoga tantra

This is in two parts:

a) The presentation of the mandala of the empowerment
b) The process of giving the empowerment through a colored-sand mandala

a) The presentation of the mandala of the empowerment

Generally, among the highest yoga mandalas, those that are drawn with colored powder or painted on cotton, and so on, are well known. The *Buddhakapāla Tantra* describes a mind mandala:

> In the center of a lotus of wisdom
> is a mandala a million yojanas [wide].
>
> This mandala has three levels, and in the center
> the wise one gives empowerment to the pupil.[937]

[A mandala] "a million yojanas" [wide] cannot be created other than within meditation. Therefore, the tantra teaches a mind mandala.

The *Vajra Garland Tantra* teaches a body mandala:

> The body is transformed into the immeasurable palace
> that is the true residence of all the buddhas...[938]

Among these mandalas, the colored powder and painted mandalas are known as "fabricated mandalas," and the mind mandala too can be included within that category. Beginners are given an empowerment with a fabricated mandala. From the *Vajraḍāka Tantra*:

> Activities such as mandalas and so on,
> performed by the mind of artifice,
> eliminate all external activities
> and therefore are praised for beginners.[939]

Empowerments for beginners that use a powder or painted mandala are well known. If the prerequisites for a painted mandala, and so on, cannot be found, then you may give a mind-mandala empowerment to a beginner. Abhayākara[gupta] has said:

> For that reason, perform [the empowerment] through meditation when you do not have all the prerequisites, when you are unable to make them, when they would not be appropriate, or when you cannot obtain them.[940]

You can also give the mind empowerment to beginners who have become adept in yoga and gained stability of mind. Abhayākara has said:

> Therefore, if beginners have stability of mind, [327] to make them worthy you can use the previously described mentally emanated mandala for consecrations and for empowerments.[941]

You can give the body empowerment to those who are adept in yoga and are certain that the various parts of their body and their channels and elements have been purified into being the mandala's residence and residents. According to Ghaṇṭa:

> That which has a nature of being fabricated
> is taught to be the process of empowerment for a pupil.
> That is not what is practiced by the wise;
> they see the true meaning, which brings liberation.[942]

Also according to Ghaṇṭa:

> Those beings are inseparable from
> the naturally created mandala.[943]

It is taught that a guru who is going to give a body-mandala empowerment definitely has to first give the external empowerments.

Some incorrectly teach that the painted-mandala empowerment is given to those with dull faculties, the mind mandala to those with medium faculties, and the body empowerment to those with sharp faculties, and others [incorrectly] teach that [these empowerments] are given, respectively, to pupils with greater, medium, and lesser [conceptual] elaboration.

b) The process of giving the empowerment through a colored-sand mandala

This is in two parts:

i) A general presentation
ii) A detailed explanation of the categories

i) A general presentation

The ritual for empowerment through a colored powder mandala has three parts:

(A) The ground rite
(B) The preparatory rite
(C) The actual empowerment

From the *Net of Illusions Tantra*:

On the first [evening], take complete possession of the ground.
On the second [evening], remain in the preparation.
Enter [the mandala] in the third evening.[944]

There are many teachings in the tantras and mahāsiddha texts about the order of these rites and their various elaborate and detailed forms, but I will explain them in accordance with the texts of Ārya [Nāgārjuna], his pupils, and Abhayākara.

(A) The ground rite

Nāgārjuna teaches that [the ground rite] has four parts:

Purifying and blessing the ground,
taking full possession of the ground, and protecting it.[945]

These must also be preceded by examining and choosing the time [for the rite].

(B) The preparatory rite

[The preparatory rite] is in four parts:

The ground deity and the mandala deities,
the vases, and the pupils
are present in the preparatory rites.[946]

(C) The actual empowerment

The rites of drawing the diagram
and similarly applying the powder.[947]

Thus, there are two stages in making a mandala—drawing the diagram and applying the powder. In addition, the arrangement of the vases, the adornment of the mandala, and so on are required.

Blessing the mandala,
making specific offerings to it, [328]
the ācārya entering himself and...[948]

That teaches that there is (1) the practice of the mandala, (2) giving offerings and tormas, and (3) entering [the mandala] and obtaining the empowerment. This is preceded by the yoga of visualizing yourself as the deity and visualizing whatever vases there are [as the deity].

> Similarly, there is the entry of the pupils,
> the vase empowerment, the secret empowerment,
> the empowerment of the prajñā's wisdom,
> and, similarly, the fourth [empowerment].[949]

This teaches that the pupils enter the mandala and then the four empowerments are given completely.

> The consecration and the homa fire rituals
> are the perfect ancillaries to the mandala.
> Those are the twenty rites.[950]

This teaches that there are the consecration and homa rite, and that there are twenty rites [in total].

That which is not clear in [Nāgārjuna's] text can be understood in the texts written by Nāgabodhi and Abhayākara.

ii) A detailed explanation of the categories [of empowerment through a colored-sand mandala]

This is in three parts:

(A) The ground rite
(B) The preparatory rites
(C) The actual empowerment

(A) The ground rite

Most tantric texts do not teach ground rites such as examination of the site, but in relation to the location of the activities, the *Vajraḍāka Tantra*[951] and the *Tantra of All Mandalas*[952] teach the examination of the site and so on for the purpose of building a new mandala palace and so forth. In accordance with those tantras, Abhayākara[gupta] taught these [rites] in detail:[953]

Examining the site: Survey the directions, color, qualities, earth, and water.

Acquiring the ground: Acquire the ground from both the evident owner—such as a king or the chief of a land or village—and the nonevident owner: the guardians of the land and the goddess of the earth.

Purifying the ground: Examine the serpent and dig.[954] Make the ground clear and then make a platform with the correct characteristics. Finally, purify [the platform] with substances, mantras, samādhi, and unsurpassable purification [rituals].

Taking possession of the ground: Build the mandala palace and meditate on the mandala. The deities listen [to your supplication] and descend [into it]. The pupils make a supplication, so that the ācārya "raises" the mandala.

Subjugating the māras: Pray to the principal [deity] to be the deity that performs that activity; develop [divine] pride; command obstructers [to leave]; and chase them away with a vajra dance and vajra gaze.

Protecting the ground: Visualize Vajrakīla drawing in and stabbing with a *kīla* stake all obstructers who have not obeyed your command and who intend to cause hindrances. [329] Then you practice the meditation on protection and perform the blessing so that obstructers will subsequently not be able to enter.

It is taught that it is not essential to first examine, dig, clean, and so on, the location of the activity. It is explained that this does not mean the ground rite is completely unnecessary; you should do some kind of ground rite. Therefore, it is good to perform whatever rites you are able to do. Nevertheless, the ground rite is not necessary for the painted, mental, and body mandalas.

(B) The preparatory rites

Most tantra texts teach the three lower preparatory rites. The *Tantra of True Union*, the *Net of Illusion Tantra*, Nāgārjuna and his pupils, and so on also teach the preparatory rite of the deity.

There are differing versions of the sequence, such as the preparatory rites of the deity following the preparatory rite of the vase, or the preparatory rite of the pupils coming after drawing the mandala. However, a good sequence is to perform first the preparatory rite of the ground deity, followed by the preparatory rite of the mandala deities, the preparatory rite of the vases, and then the preparatory rite of the pupils.

It is good to perform the preparatory rite of the ground deity before drawing the "ritual diagram," but Nāgabodhi has taught that you do so afterward.[955]

THE WAY [IN WHICH THE PREPARATORY RITE OF THE GROUND DEITY IS PERFORMED]

Generate the ground deity in the center of the mandala. Then the wisdom deities (*jñānasattvas*) merge into [the ground deity], to whom you give offerings and tormas and make a supplication. Then you receive [the ground deity's] permission and meditate that the deity remains as the essence of the ground.

THE PREPARATORY RITE OF THE MANDALA DEITIES

Many have taught that you don't draw the ritual diagram, but Nāgabodhi's teaching that you should draw one is excellent.

THE WAY THIS IS DONE

You make the ritual diagram by using cords of the appropriate material and length, with the blessing and the rite of the ritual diagram, thereby creating a definite residence for the deities. Apply perfumed spots at the points where the deities are located. Meditate that this is the *samaya* mandala and that the mandala that was previously situated in space enters it. Then there are the empowerments, offerings, praises, and supplication.

THE PREPARATORY RITE OF THE VASE

The vases must be correct in terms of their material, features, number, contents, neck adornment, mouth adornment, and so on.

Generate the commitment deities (*samayasattvas*) in the vase. The wisdom deities (*jñānasattvas*) merge with them and then there are the empowerments, offerings, praises, mantra repetitions, and so on.

Some texts do not have the symbolic vase, the generation of deities within it, and so on, but this is a difference only in relation to how simplified or detailed [the instructions are].

THE PREPARATORY RITE FOR THE PUPILS

The pupils should be ready in terms of their qualities, number, ritual cleansing, mandala, and so on. [330] They should develop the motivation, be given the internal empowerment, make a supplication, and have a firm aspiration for the Mantrayāna, so that they become [the ācārya's] child. They should take vows, and the three places [on their bodies] should be blessed, so as to make their beings ready. They should cast a toothpick so as to examine omens of siddhi. They should take sips of oath water to purify themselves of faults of speech. They should be given *kuśa* grass so that their dreams will be undisturbed.[956] They should be given cords of protection so that obstacles will be pacified. They should be taught the Dharma so as to inspire them. They should be taught how to analyze dreams so that they will understand the signs and omens.

Some [texts] do not mention developing the motivation, receiving the internal empowerment, and so on, but this is only a difference that comes from how summarized or detailed [the teachings are].

It is taught that none of the preparatory rites are used for the painted, mind, or body mandalas except that the preparatory rites for the vases and pupils can be used for them. A good [explanation] is that those two preparatory rites are absolutely necessary for the painted and mind mandalas but are unnecessary for the body mandala.

(C) The actual empowerment

This is in four parts:

(1) The mandala's sequence of rites
(2) Practicing, offering, and entering [into the mandala]
(3) Bringing pupils [into the mandala] and giving them the empowerment
(4) The concluding rites

(1) The mandala's sequence of rites

This is primarily the rite of the colored cords. First, you make the ritual diagram and then bless it by creating the wisdom diagram. The ritual diagram is the one made earlier, though many mahāsiddhas have taught that it is made at this time. The wisdom diagram should be made with cords of the appropriate substance, number, colors, lengths, blessing, arrangement, footsteps, circles, and so on.

The rite of the colored [powders] must be carried out correctly in terms of the colored powder's substance, colors, blessing, method of application, and so on. After that you arrange the vases, adorn the mandala, set out the offerings, and so on.

The painted mandala also has the laying out of the painting and then the rest, while the mind and body mandalas have the arrangement of the vases and then the rest.

(2) Practicing, offering, and entering [into the mandala]

Unless it is a body mandala, perform the mantra repetition while meditating that you become the deity and then dissolve. [331] Afterward, visualize the complete mandala in front of you. If it is a colored-powder [mandala], enter the mandala of the preparatory rite. In every kind of [mandala] the wisdom deities enter, offerings are made to them, they are praised, and so on.

At the conclusion of the mantra repetition for the generation of [the deities in the] vase, offer tormas to the mandala deities and to spirits (*bhuta*). Then, enter into the mandala, receive the empowerment, and make the prayers necessary for bringing your pupils into the mandala.

In the case of a body mandala, meditate that your own body is the mandala in accordance with the sādhana and then practice the vase generation and so on. Then emanate a second identical mandala from your body mandala and enter into that body mandala. These two become inseparable for receiving the empowerment and for bestowing the empowerment on your pupils.

Some say that when you are meditating on yourself as the body mandala, you omit meditating on an external mandala in front, entering into it, and giving empowerments to pupils from it, but that is nonsense.

(3) Bringing pupils [into the mandala] and giving them the empowerment

This is in two parts:

(a) Bringing the pupils into the mandala

(b) Bestowing the empowerment on those who have entered the mandala

(a) Bringing the pupils into the mandala

Generally speaking, the entry into the mandala is the preliminary part of the empowerments. First, the pupils are brought to the outside of the [mandala's] curtain in order to make them worthy to enter the mandala. [The pupils] supplicate, are costumed, generate the deity, and are brought to the eastern door; they take the common and special vows, are questioned concerning their family and aspiration, generate the *yogacitta*,[957] and are instructed to keep this [teaching] secret.

Next, the pupils enter inside the curtain in order for their worthiness to be equal to the deities. The pupils, in order to have the same external worthiness as the deities, physically enter inside the curtain while mentally entering the divine palace through the eastern doorway. Then they develop an aspiration to the deities, circumambulate them, and make prostrations to them.

In order to have the same inner worthiness as the deities, the pupils are instructed to keep the four commitments, for they are the roots of all siddhis. Then the wisdom deities descend into them and become stable within them.

In order to understand the omens concerning which siddhis will be accomplished, their vision of the mandala is examined. The pupils are examined to see if they are ready or not to receive the mandala teachings and empowerment. If they are ready, then they recite "the power of truth" and cast a flower [into the mandala], to see which deity's family they belong to.

There is the empowerment of the flower garland, which establishes a strong interdependence for the pupils to be followers of their family deity. [332] They see the mandala, which makes them joyful, and develop strong diligence for accomplishing the Mantrayāna siddhis. This is done by telling them to look with one side of their half-turned face, and then afterward the mandala is completely revealed to them and they meditate on joy.

(b) Bestowing the empowerment on those who have entered the mandala

This is in three parts:

(i) A description of the empowerments
(ii) The way in which the empowerments are given
(iii) The meaning of the empowerments in relation to the graduated path

(i) A description of the empowerments

There are four highest yoga empowerments. From the *Latter Guhyasamāja Tantra*:

The vase is the first empowerment.
Second is the secret empowerment.
Third is the prajñā's wisdom empowerment.
And then there is the fourth—that is how they are.[958]

From the *Tantra of True Union*:

The empowerment has four aspects:
First is the vase empowerment;
second is the secret empowerment;
third is the prajñā's wisdom;
and there is also the fourth—that is how they are.[959]

From the *Hevajra Tantra*:

The ācārya, the secret, the wisdom,
and the fourth—thus they are.[960]

The vase empowerment is categorized into eleven kinds. With the addition of the three higher empowerments, that makes a total of fourteen empowerments. From the *Garland of Vajras Tantra*:

The first is the principal empowerment.
The second has the name "secret."
The third is complete union.
The meaning of the fourth is sublime.

The principal has eleven divisions.
The twelfth is the secret.
The thirteenth is true union.
The fourteenth is the ultimate.
Each empowerment has its own level.[961]

From the *Mahāmudrā Tilaka Tantra*:

First, there is the ācārya empowerment.
Second, the secret supreme empowerment.

> Third, the prajñā's wisdom empowerment.
> And in that way, like that, there is the fourth.
>
> The ācārya empowerment is divided into eleven.
> The secret empowerment is the twelfth.
> The prajñā's wisdom is the thirteenth.
> And like that, in that same way, there is the fourteenth.[962]

The *Vajra Tent Tantra* gives another description:

> The liquid empowerment is the first;
> the crown [empowerment] is the second;
> through the vajra empowerment there is the third;
> your own lord is the fourth;
> the name empowerment is the fifth;
> the sixth is complete buddhahood;
> the seventh is through the vase empowerment; [333]
> the secret empowerment is the eighth;
> from the wisdom empowerment, there is the ninth;
> through union with the vajra of truth,
> the total vajra-*vrata* conduct is given;
> and the teacher himself gives a prophecy;
> those are the stages of the empowerment ritual.[963]

The manner in which the first empowerment is divided into eleven

The eleven empowerments consist of five disciple empowerments and six ācārya empowerments. The *five disciple empowerments* are: the liquid empowerment, the crown empowerment, the vajra empowerment, the bell empowerment, and the name empowerment. According to Ghaṇṭa, the *six ācārya empowerments* consist of the ācārya as the main empowerment and its [five] ancillaries: the mantra empowerment; the prophecy and the assurance, which are counted as one; the vajra-*vrata*; the conduct-*vrata*; and the authorization.

Others have taught that after the preliminary of the three commitments there are: the ācārya main empowerment, the true nature [empowerment] and its stages, the authorization, the *vrata*, the prophecy, and the assurance. There are a variety of teachings on this. For example, it is taught that there is the ācārya main empowerment and second the mantra empowerment, which are supplemented by four more empowerments—the authorization and the rest.

There is also a teaching that there is the bestowal of the three commitments and the ācārya main empowerment, and to these two are added four more empowerments—the authorization and the rest.

There are many teachings that describe the authorization and the rest of those four empowerments to be ancillaries to the ācārya empowerment, but there is no unanimity in all details. Some teach that they are to be added at the end of the disciple empowerment, while others say they should form the conclusion to the four [main] empowerments.

(ii) The way in which the empowerments are given

This is in four parts:

A' The vase empowerment
B' The secret empowerment
C' The prajñā's wisdom empowerment
D' The fourth empowerment

A' The vase empowerment

This is in two parts:

1' The general disciple empowerments
2' The special ācārya empowerments

1' The general disciple [vase] empowerments

1. The liquid empowerment, which bestows the power to wash away the stains of ignorance
2. The crown empowerment, which bestows the power to have the family lord of that buddha adorn the crown protrusion
3. The vajra empowerment, which bestows the power to develop the wisdom that is inseparable from the true nature
4. The bell or lord empowerment, which bestows the power to realize the source of phenomena, which is the lord as the source of unsurpassable wisdom: the inseparability of emptiness and compassion [334]

5. The name empowerment, which plants the seed of one's name as a future buddha

THE FUNCTION OF THE EMPOWERMENTS

According to Abhayākaragupta:

- The preceding flower garland empowerment makes the pupils recognize their buddha family.
- The liquid empowerment gives them the power to wash away the stains of ignorance that obscure the accomplishment of that buddhahood.
- The crown empowerment gives them the power to have the lord of that buddha family as their crown adornment.
- The vajra empowerment gives them the power to acquire the nondual wisdom of that buddha's mind.
- The bell empowerment gives them the power to teach the eighty-four thousand Dharmas of that buddha.
- Through the name empowerment, that buddha bestows the power of their name at buddhahood.[964]

Most texts teach that these five empowerments bestow the power to eliminate the stains that are the five afflictions, transform the impure five aggregates, manifest the five wisdoms, plant the propensities and seeds for the five tathāgatas, and bestow the power to accomplish the siddhis of the five families. From the *Saṃvarodaya Tantra*:

> The five empowerments are the five tathāgatas.[965]

According to Jinabhadra:

> Those who are empowered in that way
> will without doubt become accomplished.
> Whatever deity they truly practice
> they will be able to accomplish its activity.[966]

These empowerments eliminate the faults—ignorance and the five afflictions—and cause the attainment of the goal—vidyā (knowledge), the five wisdoms. Therefore, they are called *vidyā empowerments*. According to Abhayākaragupta:

The six empowerments, such as garlands and water, are practiced as having the power to remedy ignorance. Therefore, they are called *vidyā empowerments*.[967]

2′ The special ācārya [vase] empowerments

1. The vajra commitment, which is inseparable from the nondual wisdom of the minds of all the buddhas or which causes the realization of it
2. The bell empowerment, which brings one to the realization that all phenomena have no real nature
3. The mudrā commitment, which is for accomplishing the deity's body as inseparable from the mahāmudrā
4. The main ācārya empowerment, which is to gain power over the Dharma kingdom of the three realms [335]
5. The liquid empowerment of Vajrasattva, which washes away the stains that obscure accomplishing the state of Vajrasattva
6. The teaching of the true nature and the stages of the ritual in order to realize that the residence and residents of the mandala are of the nature of the Buddha's Dharma
7. The teaching of the true nature and the stages of the ritual in order to accomplish the activities of an ācārya
8. The bestowal of the mantra in order to plant the seeds of the accomplishment of the four activities and purify the realm of mantra's ultimate accomplishment
9. The bestowal of the eye ointment in order to clear away the obscuring veil of the cataracts of ignorance and develop the clairvoyance of divine sight
10. Showing a mirror in order to inspire the realization that all phenomena are without a real nature, just like reflections in a mirror
11. The bestowal of a bow and arrow in order to defeat the four māras and plant the seed of hitting the dharmadhātu target
12. The bestowal of authorization in order to establish the power of activities and deeds that accomplish the two benefits, such as attaining the siddhis of the rites and teaching the Dharma
13. Bestowing *vrata* in order to train in Mantrayāna conduct, such as never being apart from the bodhicitta that has the nature of the five wisdoms

14. The bestowal of prophesy in order to praise and honor [the pupils] by saying, "Without deviating from the established power of [your] name at buddhahood, [you] will be victorious in the higher existences, both below and above the ground"
15. The giving of reassurance in order to make [the pupils] understand that they have been given, through the stages of the empowerments, the ability to attain buddhahood and that they may rejoice in that

These are mostly as taught by Abhayākara. This is called the *ācārya empowerment* because it gives power over the kingdom of the Dharma. Alternatively, it is called the *empowerment of irreversibility*, because it plants the seed of irreversibility. According to Abhayākara:

> It is the ācārya empowerment because it is the empowerment for the Dharma kingdom of the three realms. It is the empowerment of irreversibility because it resembles the empowerment of those who are irreversible and also because it plants the seed of irreversibility.[968]

The disciple and ācārya empowerments are called *vase empowerments* because they principally involve the activity and rituals of the vase. Alternatively, they are called *vase empowerments* because the [Sanskrit] word [for empowerment is] *abhiṣkata*,[969] [which] means "pouring" and "sprinkling." According to Abhayākara:

> The six categories of liquid, crown, vajra, [336] lord, name, and ācārya form the vase empowerment, because within all of them the tathāgatas and the vidyās, such as Locanā, bestow empowerment with a vase.[970]

From the *Seven Yogas*:

> It is a vase empowerment because it [makes the pupil] an appropriate vessel.
> It is an empowerment because of the pouring and sprinkling.[971]

The mandalas through which the empowerment is bestowed

[The empowerment is] based upon the divine residence and residents in the form of an image, such as those made with colored powders or painted on cotton and so on. Alternatively, it is based upon a body mandala and so on. From the *Seven Yogas*:

> It is attained within a mandala
> that is a painting or a body.[972]

That to which the empowerments are given

[The empowerments] are primarily given to the body. Through purifying the body of its stains, the body is made pure. From the *Seven Yogas*:

> One is purified of killing and so on, in both the past and the future,
> and there will be no harm from them.[973]

[The vase empowerment] gives the special power to accomplish the goal of the nirmāṇakāya of buddhahood, along with its activities, and transforms the body into the vajra body. From the *Seven Yogas*:

> Its own essence
> is the nature of the "body vajra."[974]

B' The secret empowerment

The secret empowerment is given so as to transform the pupil into a field of faith and wisdom.

Transforming [the pupil] into a field of faith

When you taste the nectar of bodhicitta that has come from the guru as the male and female deity in union, the power of the deity causes a special bliss to arise, so that doubts and wrong views concerning the conduct of the Mantrayāna are dispelled. According to Ghaṇṭa:

> [The pupil] being in the lotus performs correctly.
> As melting occurs, he declares to the teacher,

"Oh! This is great bliss!"
Even the pupil defeats concepts.[975]

TRANSFORMING [THE PUPIL] INTO A FIELD OF WISDOM

The secret substance that is the essence of all the buddhas is placed in your mouth and enters the lotus of your heart. This causes you to realize the illusory body symbolized by the twelve examples of illusion. From *Oral Transmission*:

That [person's] field is purified
and all phenomena are realized
to have the twelve meanings, such as mirage.[976]

THE ESSENCE OF THE SECRET EMPOWERMENT

It is the samādhi and bliss that come from the taste of the bodhicitta. From the *Mahāmudrā Tilaka Tantra*:

Enter into enjoyment.
At that time, wisdom will arise within,
just like the orgasm of a female.[977]

This empowerment is given through the bestowal of the secret substance of bodhicitta from the guru and his consort. That is why it is called the *secret empowerment*. According to Ghaṇṭa:

The bodhicitta that is relative
bestows the empowerment that is secret.[978] [337]

According to Abhayākara:

The lord of secrets gives an empowerment through the relative bodhicitta of wisdom and method, and therefore it is the secret empowerment.[979]

THE MANDALA BY WHICH THIS EMPOWERMENT IS GIVEN

[The secret empowerment] is given through the mandala of the relative bodhicitta that has come from the guru and consort, which is the melted essence of all the buddhas. From the *Seven Yogas*:

It is attained in the mandala
of what is called *exceptional bodhicitta.*[980]

THAT TO WHICH THE EMPOWERMENT IS GIVEN

[The secret empowerment] is primarily given to the speech, purifying it of stains and making it pure. From the *Seven Yogas*:

> One is purified of lying and so on, in both the past and the future,
> and there will be no harm from them.[981]

[The secret empowerment] gives the special power to accomplish the goal of the saṃbhogakāya of buddhahood, and it transforms speech into the vajra speech. From the *Seven Yogas*:

> Its own essence
> is the nature of vajra speech.[982]

C′ The prajñā's wisdom empowerment

The prajñā's wisdom empowerment is given in order to attain certainty in the four joys of union, and in innate wisdom in particular, through reliance upon a consort (*mudrā*). This serves as a symbolic example for the innateness of the meaning recognized in the fourth empowerment.

THE WAY IN WHICH THE FOUR JOYS ARISE

The passion and heat of the caṇḍālī [generated] by the pupil and consort in sexual union causes the bodhicitta to melt and descend through the locations [of the cakras]. The *Garland of Vajras Tantra* describes the four joys of the descent:

> The great-bliss (*mahāsukha*) cakra is at the crown,
> and that is taught to be "joy."
> "Supreme joy" is in the enjoyment (*saṃbhoga*) cakra.
> "Beyond joy" resides in the dharma cakra.
> "Innate [joy]" is in the emanation (*nirmāṇa*) cakra.
> These create the experience of joys.[983]

The *Garland of Vajras Tantra* also describes the creation of the four joys through [the bodhicitta's] ascent:

> "Joy" in the nirmāṇacakra,
> "supreme joy" dwelling in the dharmacakra,
> "beyond joy" in the saṃbhoga,
> and the "innate" in the mahāsukha
> are taught to be the stages of reversal.[984]

The devotee visualizes a "wisdom consort," imagines he is the deity in sexual union, and physically performs the breathing exercises that cause the heat from the blazing caṇḍālī to melt the bodhicitta. From *Oral Transmission*:

> [In this way, with a mind free of shame,]
> the devotee, with movement in the shape of a bow,
> makes the wisdom fire blaze at the threefold junction
> so that the element melts, and there are the sixteen aspects— [338]
> which are like the jasmine flower—
> to be expelled through breath application.[985]

Therefore, the essence of the third empowerment comes from the four joys, which is the experience of innate wisdom when the bodhicitta descends into the jewel. From *Oral Transmission*:

> Naturally, there is complete peace,
> which is the peace of the dharmakāya.
> That bliss is present in the jewel
> and causes momentary unconsciousness and wavering.
> That is the great accomplishment.[986]

According to Abhayākara:

> The splendor of union with the prajñā
> perfectly demonstrates the true nature.
> Look at the mind, which has entered into
> the jewel from the vajra posture.[987]

This empowerment is called the prajñā's wisdom empowerment because it gives the enduring power of innate wisdom free from thought, and it is an empowerment that is the marvelous bodhicitta, which comes through dependence upon a prajñā, such as an action seal. Abhayākara has said:

> The prajñā is an external young maiden. Wisdom is a mind free of thought so that there is completely pure and innate joy. That is the prajñā's wisdom empowerment.[988]

THE MANDALA THROUGH WHICH THIS EMPOWERMENT IS GIVEN

[The prajñā's wisdom empowerment is given] through the mandala of the consort's vagina. From the *Seven Yogas*:

> It is attained in the mandala
> that is called the *pure vagina*.[989]

THAT TO WHICH THE EMPOWERMENT IS GIVEN

It is bestowed upon the mind, purifying the mind of its stains and making it pure. From the *Seven Yogas*:

> One is purified of avarice and so on, in both the past and the future,
> and there will be no harm from them.[990]

[The prajñā's wisdom empowerment] gives the special power to accomplish the goal that is the dharmakāya, and it transforms the mind into the vajra mind. From the *Seven Yogas*:

> Its very own essence
> is the nature of the mind's vajra.[991]

D' The fourth empowerment

The innate wisdom from the sexual union of the chosen deities[992] in the third empowerment is analogous [to the actual innate wisdom]. The "word empowerment" is given in order to introduce you to the actual innate wisdom, which is the seven aspects of mahāmudrā. It is written that:

> The prajñā's wisdom is used as a symbol,
> and then the precious word empowerment is given.[993]

The actual innate wisdom is described in the *Hevajra Tantra*:

> This wisdom is extremely subtle.
> It is like the center of vajra space.
> It is immaculate, gives liberation, and is peace.
> You yourself are its father.[994]

From the *Guhyasamāja*:

> As it is devoid of all [material] things, [339]
> and because the aggregates, [sensory] elements, and [sensory] bases
> have the equality of the selflessness of phenomena,
> your own mind is primordially unborn
> and has the nature of emptiness.[995]

The principal point is the unborn nature of the uniform selflessness of phenomena. This is the ultimate truth of the luminosity that is the essence of emptiness. However, this is not identifying plain emptiness without the objects of relative appearances, such as the illusion-like deities, or the bliss of their union. The wisdom of the fourth empowerment is Vajradhara, who is endowed with seven aspects. These seven aspects, according to Vāgīśvarakīrti, are:

> *Saṃbhoga*[*kāya*], union, great bliss, having no nature,
> being completely filled with compassion, being continuous, and being without cessation.[996]

There are these seven aspects: the aspect of complete enjoyment, the aspect of union, the aspect of great bliss, and so on. Therefore, it is nonsense to say that the essence of the fourth empowerment is the bliss of union sealed by emptiness; or to say that it is simply a union of knowing and emptiness free from identifying the bliss of the four joys, and so on; or to state that it is merely the union of the clarity and emptiness of your own mind in a state in which you do not even visualize the mahāmudrā (great seal) of the deity's body.

Therefore, the essence of the fourth empowerment is called the *body of the union of bliss and emptiness*, which is your own body in a saṃbhoga[kāya] form. It is also called the *innateness of the inseparability of bliss and emptiness*. According to Atiśa:

> [Then the glorious Heruka said:] "Noble sirs, your knowledge of the experience attained through sexual union with the consort

should be meditated on as luminosity. It is the complete purification of the three consciousnesses; it is the quintessence of the perfection of wisdom.

"The ultimate truth eternally has the qualities of no body, speech, and mind; being liberated from karma and birth; and having extreme clarity like the moon, the sun, fire, and jewels. That ultimate truth transcends being the object of any other vision. See it with the eyes of wisdom and knowledge!

"Thus, to not see anything as having a nature of its own is to see bliss and luminosity.

"Thus, although luminosity has ultimately no cause or result whatsoever, relatively there is the clarity and completeness of the thirty-seven deities, like reflections in a mirror, arising from just the mind and winds. See them as having colors just as a rainbow does, and see them without conceptual exaggeration, just like a moon on water.

"Whatever arises because of causes and conditions is relative. [340] Thus, the inseparable union of the two truths is the great bodhicitta.[997] That is the fourth empowerment."[998]

The [fourth] empowerment is given simply through words to those who aspire toward profundity and vastness. That is why it is called the *word empowerment*. It is superior to the relative empowerments, and therefore is called the *precious* [*empowerment*]. From the *Tantra of Union*:

> If there is aspiration for the profound and the vast,
> bestow the precious word empowerment.[999]

THE MANDALA THROUGH WHICH THIS EMPOWERMENT IS GIVEN

[The fourth empowerment] is given through the mandala of ultimate bodhicitta. From the *Five Stages*:

> The worthy, excellent pupils receive the instructions
> in which the bodhicitta is called ultimate.[1000]

THAT TO WHICH THIS EMPOWERMENT IS GIVEN

[The fourth empowerment] is given to the body, speech, and mind. It purifies the propensity for stains from [all] three doors and bestows the special power to accomplish the goal that is the *svabhavakāya*, which is the inseparability of the three vajras.[1001]

(iii) The meaning of the [four highest yoga] empowerments in relation to the graduated path.

The principal goal of the highest yoga path is the union body (*kāya*) with its seven aspects. However, in order to accomplish that you must first, through stages, eliminate your ordinary form and train in having the appearance of the deity's body. In order to do that you need to receive the vase empowerment, which washes away the stains of the body and gives you the power of the vajra body. Receiving [the vase empowerment] makes you ready to meditate on the generation stage, which is comprised of the three samādhis and their ancillaries. From *Seven Yogas*:

> You must correctly teach it
> to be the three yogas and their ancillaries.
> Realize the absence of the appearances and existences
> of all [sensory] objects, such as form.[1002]

After that, you must train in [seeing] relative forms as like illusions. In order to do that, you have to receive the secret empowerment, which washes away the stains of speech and gives you the power of vajra speech. Receiving [the secret empowerment] makes you ready to meditate on the wind yogas, such as vajra repetition, and on the completion stage of self-blessing. From *Seven Yogas*:

> Teach the samādhi that is like an illusion
> through the essence of vajra repetition.
> Realize the absence of the appearances and existences
> of the inner phenomena, such as the eyes.[1003]

After that, you must train in luminosity and emptiness. In order to do that, you must receive the prajñā's wisdom empowerment, which washes away the stains of your mind and gives you the power of the vajra mind. Receiving [the prajñā's wisdom empowerment] makes you ready to meditate on the completion stage that is comprised of the ultimate luminosity, devoid of perceiver and perceived. From *Seven Yogas*: [341]

Teach, in stages, the *vrata* rites
in order for the supreme siddhi to be attained.
Realize the absence of all phenomena
that have the nature of perceiver and perceived.[1004]

After that, you must train in the union of the relative illusion-like body with the luminosity of entering the ultimate nature. In order to do that, you have to receive the fourth empowerment, which washes away the propensities for the stains of your three doors and gives you the power of the quintessence of the three kāyas' inseparability. Receiving [the fourth empowerment] makes you ready to meditate on the completion stage of the union of the two truths. It is said:

Through these stages of instruction
on the ultimate, on bodhicitta,
there will be the realization
of the nature of nondual, profound clarity.[1005]

To sum up, you must first receive the empowerments, because they wash away the particular stains that will be hindrances and defects in your meditation on the liberating yogas of the two stages, and they bestow the power to accomplish that particular goal. Therefore, [the empowerments] are the root of the path.

If you periodically create a mandala, receive the empowerments, and meditate on the two stages, that will wash away all the hindrances and defects that would prevent your accomplishment of the goal, and it will increase your abilities.

(4) The concluding rites

Abhayākara has taught that [the concluding rites] consist of the peaceful and increasing rites, which are practiced so that offenses of addition and omission in the practice will be eliminated and the deities will be satisfied.

Make an offering to the mandala, accept the gifts [for giving the empowerment], and offer tormas to the external guardians of the directions. Pay homage to the mandala, dedicate the merit, circumambulate it, and pray for forgiveness [for your errors].

[Request] the wisdom deities to depart, and dissolve the emanated [mandala].

Demolish the powder mandala, pull up the stakes (*kīla*), pour the colored powder into [a body of] water, hold a celebration with a *gaṇacakra*, and so on.

3) Keeping the commitments and vows of the highest yoga

This is in three parts:

a) The categories of the highest yoga commitments and vows
b) The way to keep those commitments and vows
c) The methods for repairing the vows and commitments when they have been broken

a) The categories of the highest yoga commitments and vows

The root vow of the Mantrayāna within these vows is the general vow of training in bodhicitta. Among the vows specific to the Mantrayāna, there are the vows for each of the five families. From the *Vajra Pinnacle*:

> Go for refuge to the Three Jewels:
> the Buddha, the Dharma, and the Sangha...
> and perform the activity of offering as much as you can.[1006] [342]

The general vows of the five families are taught in the section that begins

> Other than those, the father has taught
> [these] fourteen to be "defeats."[1007]

and ends:

> ...do not step across...insignias.[1008]

This teaches the root downfalls, the serious commitments, the commitments of avoidance, the commitment of reliance, and so on.

Some teach that these are the vows of yoga tantra alone, but many mahāsiddhas have taught these in detail within the context of declaring them the vows of the highest yoga [tantra]. Therefore, they are necessary to the highest yoga.

There are two kinds of commitments: root commitments and branch commitments. Ācārya Bhavideva[1009] taught the root commitments in accord with what is taught in the *Kālacakra*, *Vajrapañjikā*, *Kṛṣṇayamāri*, and so on:

> The holder of the vajra has taught that siddhis follow the master.
> Therefore, maligning him is taught to be the first root downfall.
> The second downfall is taught to be transgressing the command of the Sugata.
> The third is to be angry with a vajra sibling and to speak harmfully to him.
> The Conqueror has taught the fourth to be forsaking love for beings.
> The fifth is to lose bodhicitta, which is the root of the Dharma.
> The sixth is criticizing the Dharma of your own tradition or that of others.
> The seventh is telling that which is secret to beings who are not completely ripened.
> The eighth is maligning the aggregates, which are the five buddhas.
> The ninth is having doubts about phenomena, which are pure by nature.
> The tenth is to be always loving toward the malevolent.
> The eleventh is to have concepts concerning phenomena that are beyond words, and so on.
> The twelfth is to disturb the minds of those who have faith.
> The thirteenth is not to keep whatever commitments you encounter.
> The fourteenth is to malign women, who have the nature of wisdom.[1010]

Those are the fourteen [root downfalls]. If you commit these, it will cut through the roots of the path, like cutting through the roots of a tree, so that however much effort you make, you will have no siddhis but will fall into the lower existences. If you keep these commitments, you will have planted the roots of all siddhis. That is why they are called the *root downfalls*.

Nāgārjuna describes eight branch commitments:

> Acquiring a prajñā through force,
> acquiring her nectar through force,
> not keeping the secrets from an unworthy person,
> quarreling within the community,
> teaching a different Dharma to the faithful, [343]

spending seven days among the śrāvakas,
being proud of a false yoga,
and teaching the Dharma to those without faith:
These are taught to be the serious downfalls.[1011]

Some Tibetans add these three to make a total of eleven:

Teaching the nature of the secret without properly practicing union,
Engaging in the mandala activity, without practicing correct sevā, and so on,
Spending time, without purpose, in observing the prohibitions of the two vows.[1012]

If you commit these downfalls, even though the roots of the path are not completely destroyed, there will be temporary obstacles; it's similar to cutting off the branches of a tree. If you keep these vows, there will be a perfection of all temporary and ultimate siddhis. Therefore they are called the *branch downfalls.*

b) The way to keep those commitments and vows

The presentation of the vows and commitments and their demarcation

First, you have to gain certainty through hearing and contemplation. From *Fifty Verses on the Guru*:

Having been made a worthy vessel
through receiving the mantras and so on,
you must then read and keep
the fourteen root downfalls.[1013]

You must eliminate the four causes of the root downfalls—ignorance, many afflictions, inattentiveness, and lack of respect—and you must cherish more than your own life the vows and commitments exactly as they were taught to you. From the *Saṃvarodaya Tantra*:

For those who wish to gain the supreme siddhi at all costs,
even giving up their life will be easy,
even the time of death will be easy.
Always keep the commitments![1014]

From a tantra:

> From this day on, you, my child,
> even at the cost of your life and your bones,
> must never malign the Dharma,
> the bodhicitta, or the Ācārya.[1015]

The harm that comes from not keeping the vows and commitments

Even if you practice [so as to gain] the siddhis, you will fail to accomplish them and you will be reborn in the lower existences. From the *Samāyoga Tantra*:

> Those who have forsaken the vows
> and those who do not know the nature of the secrets,
> even though they practice, they will not accomplish anything.[1016]

From *Endowed with Wisdom*:

> If someone breaks his commitments,
> let alone attaining siddhis,
> it will be difficult even to gain a human rebirth.[1017]

According to Bhavideva:

> Otherwise, those who break the commitments
> will be seized by the māras.
> Then they will experience suffering: [344]
> They will face downward and fall into the hells.[1018]

The benefits of keeping the vows and commitments properly

The best individual will attain the supreme siddhi within his or her lifetime, the medium will accomplish it within seven lifetimes, and the least within sixteen lifetimes. From the *Saṃvarodaya Tantra*:

> Subsequently, be dedicated to practicing
> the commitments exactly as they are in the instructions.
> By continuing to be a worthy vessel,

the stages of meditation on the cakra and so on
and the genuine, perfect instructions
will bring accomplishment, and nothing else will.[1019]

From *Endowed with Wisdom*:

If you stay within the commitments,
even if, through the power of karma, there is no accomplishment in this life,
the siddhi will be attained in another lifetime.[1020]

From *Treasury of Secrets*:

Those who have properly received the empowerments
will receive them in every lifetime,
and within seven lifetimes,
even if they do not meditate, they will attain siddhi.[1021]

From *Five Commitments*:

If you are without downfalls,
you will accomplish all within sixteen lifetimes.[1022]

c) The methods for repairing the vows and commitments when they have been broken

If the four causes of downfalls result in the breaking of commitments and vows, they must be repaired. First, you must confess your transgression. According to Nāgārjuna:

The stages of serious root downfalls
should be learned from the ritual.
If they are broken, you must confess.[1023]

The object for the confession

Confess to the mandala [deities] from the empowerment in which you promised to keep the vows and commitments. From the *Kṛṣṇayamāri Tantra*:

> If someone, through becoming heedless,
> harms their commitment to the guru,
> they should draw a mandala
> and confess their bad actions to the sugatas.[1024]

Alternatively, you can make a confession through the meditation and mantra repetition of Vajrasattva. From *Adornment of the Essence*:

> Visualize Vajrasattva well
> and repeat the hundred syllables
> as in the practice, twenty times each.
> Your downfalls and so on will be blessed
> so that they will not increase.
> That is what the supreme siddhas have taught.
>
> Therefore, practice it at the conclusion of sessions.
> If you recite it a hundred thousand times,
> you will become the embodiment of complete purity.[1025]

In order to repair the commitments and vows, or to take the vows again, enter the mandala and receive the empowerment. From the *Summarized Kālacakra Tantra*:

> Those who have a root downfall should once again enter this mandala in order to purify themselves of it.[1026] [345]

From the commentary to the *Kālacakra Tantra*:

> If root downfalls occur after you have received the seven empowerments, or the vase and secret empowerment, then enter the mandala again in order to purify them.[1027]

Primarily, you need to receive empowerments from the holy gurus. If there is no guru from whom you can receive them, bring yourself into the mandala to receive the empowerments. According to Abhayākara:

> It is taught that if you have broken your commitments, receive the empowerment through the ritual that the guru employed to bring you into [the mandala]. Therefore, take the empowerment in that

way. However, this is only in the case of the holy guru being very far away, or if there would be hazards, such as a dangerous journey, [in order to go to him] and not in any other circumstances.[1028]

B) The path of liberation in the highest yoga tantra

This is in two parts:

1) A general description of the two stages
2) An individual description of each of the two stages

1) A general description of the two stages

This is in five parts:

a) The essence of the two stages
b) An explanation of the names
c) Their definite number
d) Their sequence
e) Their stages of meditation

a) The essence of the two stages

The generation stage is meditation on the mandala residence and residents as clear as a reflection in a mirror. The completion stage is when the elaboration of the generation stage is seen as a dream and you meditate on nonelaboration, which is like space. From the *Hevajra Tantra*:

> The one who keeps *vrata* should meditate on elaboration
> through the yoga of the generation stage,
> and seeing elaboration to be like dreams,
> become, through elaboration, nonelaborate.[1029]

From the great commentary to the *Kālacakra Tantra*:

> That which is free from such thoughts as the *hūṃ* and *phaṭ*,
> which are taught within the generation stage,
> that is the yoga of the completion stage.[1030]

Also, it is taught that the generation stage is the stage of birth within ordinary existence, which is the basis for purification. The completion stage is the stages of death, the successive dissolution of the elements when that ordinary life is completed. From both the *Five Stages* and the *Compendium of Practices*:

> Birth is called *relative truth*
> and the name of death is *ultimate knowledge.*
> The attainment of those two stages,
> through the kindness of the guru, is future buddhahood.[1031]

b) An explanation of the names of the two stages

[346] The name *generation stage* is used because the stages of seat, insignia, seed, and so on parallel the stages in the birth of beings. You imagine the adornments of faces, arms, and so on—the apparent forms the deities have—and therefore their birth is "imaginary." This is primarily the stage of meditating on the clear appearance of the deities, and therefore it is called the *generation stage.*

The name *completion stage* is used because it parallels the stages of dissolution at death. The colors, shapes, and so on of the generation stage dissolve into the *anusvāra* and finally the *nāda.*[1032] It is the stage where the elaborations of the three doors sequentially cease. When that process is completed there is resting in an equanimity that is a state of nonelaboration-like space. According to Śāntipa:

> Through the stages of mantra and features and so on, there is the generation of the deities, which is the practitioner's generation. Whatever is like that is the stage of generation.
>
> Completion is innate. This nature of the practitioner—the innate, the truth, and so on—is called the *nature of truth.* Whatever the yogin meditates on in that way is the completion stage.[1033]

According to Subhagavajra:

> Generation is called "generation" because of the generation of the moon [disc] and so on. The rest [of the term] is "stage."

Completion is called "completion" because it is the wisdom of "the great empty," in which method is complete. Alternatively, it is because the qualities are made complete through its completion. The rest [of the term] is "stage."[1034]

c) The definite number of the two stages

The generation stage and the completion stage are definitively counted as two in the unsurpassable liberating path of the great secret. From the *Hevajra Tantra*:

Having rested in the two stages—
the generation stage
and the completion stage—
there is the Dharma teaching by the vajra holder.[1035]

From the *Latter Guhyasamāja Tantra*:

The buddhas taught the Dharma.
They dwell properly in the two stages:
the stage of generation
and, likewise, the stage of completion.[1036]

The faults to be eliminated are definitely of two kinds: the concepts of attachment to the ordinary and the concepts of attachment to the sublime deities. Therefore, there are two definite remedies for eliminating those faults. From the *Vajra Tent*:

In order to defeat the concepts of ordinariness,
there is the well-known true meditation.
The meditation when resting in the nature
is not meditation and neither is it not meditating.[1037]

Moreover, there are definitely two kinds of results: the general siddhis and the supreme siddhi. [347] Therefore, there are two stages of methods for obtaining those two results. From the *Latter Guhyasamāja Tantra*:

Because of the division into general and supreme,
there are declared to be two kinds of sevā:

the general is the four vajras,
the supreme is the six branches.[1038]

d) The sequence of the two stages

For an ordinary individual who is practicing the Mantrayāna highest yoga path of liberation, first there is the generation stage and then there is meditation on the completion stage. From *Five Stages*:

The complete Buddha taught this method
in the form of the steps of a stairway
to those who dwelled perfectly in the generation stage
and wished to [enter] the completion stages.[1039]

This means that first you meditate on the elaborate yogas and purify ordinary thoughts. When you know the nature of thoughts, meditate on nonelaborate nonthought, through which there is liberation. From Vajragarbha's commentary [to the *Hevajra Tantra*]:

The conceptual rites are taught first,
when you are in bondage to thoughts and propensities.
When the nature of thoughts is known,
there is total engagement in nonthought.[1040]

Nāgārjuna, his pupils, and many others have taught that you first accomplish a stable generation stage and then meditate on the completion stage. This means that those with dull faculties, who have no previous practice, have to make the first stage stable before training in the later stage, just like ascending a stairway.

Mahāsiddha Saroruha, Ajitacandra, and others have taught that you practice the generation stage in the first part of the session and meditate on the completion stage in the latter part of the session. This refers to those who are somewhat adept and have medium faculties, in which case they can alternate training in the two stages, like [the feet when] walking. Some Tibetan lamas have taught that right from the beginning you meditate on both stages simultaneously. This is taught for those with sharp faculties who have become perfectly adept, able to meditate on the union of the two stages, like a bird flapping both wings simultaneously. However, when a gradualist individual trains in the path of liberation they must train first in the generation stage and then the completion stage.

e) The stages of meditation in the two stages

This is in three parts:

i) At first there must be the "imaginary" generation stage.
ii) When a special completion stage has been developed, the simple generation stage becomes unnecessary.
iii) The reason one must meditate on the union of both stages [348]

i) At first there must be the "imaginary" generation stage.

Vajragarbha asked the Bhagavān why one needs to practice the generation stage when it is the completion stage that contains the meaning of innate great bliss. He replied, "The power of your faith in the completion stage has caused you to fall away from the generation stage," and taught that the generation stage is a base upon which the completion stage is based, like a flower and its scent. As is said in the *Hevajra Tantra*:

> [Vajragarbha asked:]
> "This is the yoga of the completion stage (*utpannakrama*).[1041]
> Its bliss is known as great bliss.
> That bliss has no generation meditation (*utpannabhāvana*).
> [So] what is to be gained by generation?"
>
> The Bhagavān answered:
> "This great bodhisattva
> is spoiled by the power of faith.
>
> "In the absence of the body, where would bliss be?
> One would be unable to say 'bliss.'
>
> "Bliss pervades all beings
> in the form of pervaded and pervader.
>
> "Just as a scent dwells in a flower,
> and there is none in the absence of a flower,
> in that same way, in the absence of form and so on,
> bliss would not be obtained."[1042]

Ordinary individuals, who are trapped in the net of thoughts, can't start by training in the stage of completion, which is without thought. Therefore, to begin with, they must meditate upon the stage of generation in order to become purified of thoughts. From Vajragarbha's commentary [to the *Hevajra Tantra*]:

> Seeing the three kinds of beings
> trapped in the net of thoughts,
> he taught particular types and numbers of methods
> that would bring them liberation.
>
> He taught the conceptual rites first
> to those bound by the propensity for thoughts.[1043]

Therefore, you first purify yourself of thoughts in the generation stage and then meditate on the completion stage. For example, in order to purify the land, you first plant buckwheat,[1044] and when the [ground] has been purified, then you plant *salu* rice.[1045] From Vajragarbha's commentary [to the *Hevajra Tantra*]:

> At first, you plant buckwheat
> in order to purify the field.
> Afterward, you plant *salu* rice seeds
> in that purified field: It is like that.[1046]

ii) When a special completion stage has been developed, the simple generation stage becomes unnecessary.

Until you have developed a special, stable realization of the natural, uncontrived completion stage, you must depend on the contrived, imaginary generation stage, so as to be able to develop [the completion stage]. However, when [the completion stage] has been developed, there is no need for deliberate meditation on a contrived yoga such as a mere generation stage that is conceptual and imaginary. [349] For example, you use a boat to cross to the other side of a river, but when you've reached the other side, there's no need for the boat anymore. This is described in the *Vajraḍāka Tantra*:

Practice contrived meditation
and contrived repetition
in order to realize natural yoga.

When you have realized the natural yoga,
which is beyond the external contrived yoga,
don't practice that which is contrived.

For example, you enter a boat
and cross a river in it.
When you reach the other side, you abandon it.
That is what you do with contrived [yogas].[1047]

Therefore, the contrived yogas are advocated as teachings for beginners, but when a special, natural completion stage has been developed, engaging in contrived [yogas] is to be ignorant of the ultimate and will be a cause of afflictions and suffering. From the *Vajraḍāka Tantra*:

Activities, such as mandalas
or anything performed by the contrived mind,
are external activities that are illuminating
and are therefore advocated for beginners.
All those siddhis are located in this life,
not in the true knowledge of the conquerors.[1048]

Also from the *Vajraḍāka*:

The contrived actions of beings
who follow the tantras
bring suffering through their efforts.

Therefore, efforts in the rites of activities
such as mandalas and so on
are external and devoid of liberation,
so those beings create nothing but afflictions.[1049]

iii) The reason one must meditate on the union of both stages

The generation stage without the completion stage, which is just the application of thoughts about deities, can only bring the attainment of worldly siddhis, not the ultimate siddhi. From the great commentary to the *Kālacakra Tantra*:

> Becoming adept in meditation on the mandala circles,
> which are thoughts about form and so on,
> brings accomplishment of worldly siddhis,
> but how could they ever accomplish the desired great siddhi?[1050]

Thus millet and not rice grows from millet seeds. In the same way, nonconceptual results don't come from conceptual seeds. Instead, the continuum of ordinary thoughts is the root of suffering. From Vajragarbha's commentary [to the *Hevajra Tantra*]:

> Rice does not grow
> from millet seeds.
> Conceptual seeds give rise
> to conceptual results.[1051]

From the *Samantabhadra Sādhana*: [350]

> There isn't any suffering in existence
> that is other than the continuum of ordinary thought.[1052]

Therefore, those who are not ready to practice the deep, vast Dharma should first be taught the conceptual generation stage with its mudrās, mandalas, and so on. But it's taught that if their minds have gradually become trained, a teacher who tells them they can achieve buddhahood through meditation on mudrās and mandalas alone is a māra. From Vajragarbha's commentary [to the *Hevajra Tantra*]:

> For those not ready
> for the deep and vast Dharma,
> I have taught that which is attractive,
> such as mudrās, mandalas, and mantras.

> Those future masters
> who teach Buddha Vajrasattva and the like
> through mudrās, mandalas, and mantras
> will be of the family of māras.[1053]

However, you can't attain the supreme siddhi solely through the completion stage without the generation stage, because in order to obtain the result of Vajradhara's union, you have to meditate on the union of the generation and completion stages while you are upon the path. From the *Hevajra Tantra*:

> This is the yoga of the completion stage.
> Its bliss is known as great bliss.
> That bliss has no generation meditation.
> [So] what is to be gained by generation?[1054]

In answer to that question, the Buddha taught that the generation stage is a base upon which the completion stage is based, like a flower and its scent. Moreover, a completion stage without the generation stage will be nothing other than a nonconceptual state without the perception of the appearance aspect of deities, and that cannot bring the attainment of buddhahood. From the *Tantra of Union*:

> Buddhahood does not come from nonthought,
> and it does not come from having thought.[1055]

Therefore, the generation stage is the method of practicing the body of union, while the completion stage is its wisdom. Therefore, they should be meditated on in union. From *Lamp of the Path*:

> Method without wisdom
> and wisdom without method
> are taught to be "bondage."
> Therefore both ways should be rejected.[1056]

However, when a special completion stage has been developed, will the generation stage become unnecessary or contrary? At that time, you won't need to meditate on a purely conceptual generation stage, but you will still need to have the generation stage that is the appearance of an illusion-like circle of deities. From *Five Stages*:

> The application of mantras and mudrās, [351]
> the concepts of mandalas and so on,
> the homa fire ritual, torma offering, and all other [rites]
> should always be seen as illusions.

And so on, until:

> What need is there to say much here?
> The yogins in the Vajrayāna
> should see whatever it is they visualize
> to all be the same as illusions.[1057]

2) An individual description of each of the two stages

This is in three parts:

a) The generation stage
b) The completion stage
c) The conduct that enhances the path

a) The generation stage

This is in two parts:

i) General summaries of the generation stage
ii) The deity sādhanas

i) General summaries of the generation stage

In general, the generation stage is summarized as the three samādhis. From the *Vajra Garland Tantra*:

> There is the *first yoga* and similarly,
> in brief, the *supreme king of the mandala*
> and the *supreme king of activity*, which is the supreme yoga.[1058]

The *first yoga* is the generation of the divine palace (*vimāna*) and so on until [the generation of] the principal deity and his consort. The *supreme king of the mandala* is the subsequent generation of the complete mandala with all [the deities] arranged in their own places. The *supreme king of activity* is the entry of the wisdom deities and all the remaining rites.

THE FOUR SEVĀ SĀDHANAS

From the *Latter Guhyasamāja Tantra*:

> *Sevā* rite is first.
> *Upasevā* is second.
> *Sādhana* is third.
> *Mahāsādhana* is fourth.[1059]

Sevā is comprised of the meditation beginning with emptiness and up to the generation of the divine palace. *Upasevā* starts with the generation of the principal deity and continues up to the blessing of the sense bases (*āyatana*). *Sādhana* is the blessing of the body, speech, and mind and so on. *Mahāsādhana* is the empowerment and so on.

Some teach that *sevā* is the generation of the commitment being (*samaya-sattva*) and that *upasevā* is the blessing of the sense bases.

THE FOUR YOGAS

From the *Black Yamāntaka Tantra*:

> The first meditation is *yoga*.
> The second is *upayoga*.
> The third is *atiyoga*.
> The fourth is *mahāyoga*.[1060]

Yoga is the generation of the divine palace as a residence and continues until the generation of the causal Vajradhara. *Upayoga* is the generation of the resultant Vajradhara. *Atiyoga* is the generation of the complete mandala. [352] *Mahāyoga* is the blessing of body, speech, and mind and the rest of the rites.

THE SIX BRANCHES

In the *Vajra Tent*:

> Complete the location of the buddha
> and then meditate on the five aspects
> that are the nature of truth, the completely good.
> Then practice the sādhana of your special deity
> and, similarly, arrange the mandala,

> and then the offerings, praise, nectar, and so on.
> When you have meditated through these stages,
> that is said to be the six branches of yoga.[1061]

The six branches are explained as follows. The Vairocana branch is the generation of the divine palace, complete with the seats. The Vajrasattva branch is the generation of all the deities and the entry of the wisdom deities. The Akṣobhya branch is the empowerment. The Ratnasambhava branch is tasting the nectar. The Amitābha branch is the offering. The Amoghasiddhi branch is the praise.

ii) The deity sādhanas

This is in three parts:

(A) The individuals who practice the deity sādhanas
(B) The locations for the practice of the deity sādhanas
(C) The methods for practicing the deity sādhanas

(A) The individuals who practice the deity sādhanas

I have already explained how special individuals, who are bases, train themselves through the general and special paths. However, they particularly need to obtain the ripening empowerment and keep the commitments and vows that they took when receiving the empowerment. From the *Samāyoga Tantra*:

> Those who have not entered the mandala,
> those who have forsaken their commitments,
> and those who do not know the secret [teaching]
> will not gain accomplishment even if they practice.[1062]

(B) The locations for practice of the deity sādhanas

Beginners should [meditate] in a solitary and pleasant place, such as in the mountains, but if that is not possible, then they can meditate at night in their own home. From the *Vajra Tent*:

> ... in mountains and valleys of herbs
> adorned with flowers and fruits.[1063]

From the *Hevajra Tantra*:

> At the time of initial practice,
> a place considered beautiful
> is where the mantrin, resting in meditation
> with a one-pointed mind, will become accomplished.[1064]

When you have gained some stability of mind, it is recommended to meditate in places such as charnel grounds. From the *Vajra Tent*:

> The siddhis are bestowed upon those who practice sevā sādhanas
> in charnel grounds, on river banks,
> and in forests, where there are no people or villages.[1065] [353]

(C) The methods for practicing the deity sādhanas

This is in three parts:
(1) The sādhana's preliminaries
(2) The actual generation stage
(3) The intersession yogas

(1) The sādhana's preliminaries

This is in three parts:
(a) Offering tormas to pacify hinderers
(b) Gathering the two accumulations to create favorable factors
(c) Meditating on the circle of protection to prevent adverse factors

(a) Offering tormas to pacify hinderers

In this location, having gathered all the necessary utensils, sit on the required seat facing the required direction in the required sitting posture, and so on. Then begin by making a torma offering to the spirits. From the *Hevajra Tantra*:

> If yogins, for good fortune, make an offering to all spirits with this offering cake . . .[1066]

The *Ocean of Ḍākinīs*, *Illumination of the Particulars*, and the texts of Saroruha also teach that you make a torma offering at the beginning of a sādhana. This is done in order to pacify obstacles from hinderers and deceivers. From the *Hevajra Tantra*:

> Vajrasattva taught the offering cake
> in order to protect the lives of beings
> from hinderers and deceivers.[1067]

(b) Gathering the two accumulations to create favorable factors

The gathering of the accumulations according to the *Vajra Tent*:

> Make offerings to the vajra-holding guru;
> perform the completely pure seven;
> and develop the motivation for enlightenment.[1068]

The field for gathering the accumulations

Light from the seed in your heart invites the guru and the mandala circle to come into space before you. Some teach that the field of accumulation is emanated from the seed's light rays, and some say that the light illuminates the field of accumulation. In [the *Vajra Tent*] itself, the goddesses and so on that are emanated from the seed in the heart make the offerings, recite the refuge, and so on.

The "completely pure seven" are refuge, confession of bad actions, rejoicing, dedication, request, supplication, and reliance on the path. Some [texts] also teach "keeping vows."

At the end, if you earlier invited the field of accumulation deities, they depart. If you emanated them, they are absorbed. If you [simply] visualized them, they cease to be an object [of visualization].

Then there is the meditation on the *four immeasurables*. From the *Hevajra Tantra*:

> First, meditate on love;
> second, meditate on compassion;
> third, meditate on rejoicing;
> and in conclusion, on impartiality.[1069] [354]

From the *Vajra Tent*:

> Refresh your mind
> with the four *brahmavihāras*.[1070]

Then there is the gathering of the accumulation of wisdom. From the *Hevajra Tantra*:

> Then also, [first] the enlightenment of emptiness...[1071]

From the *Vajra Tent*:

> A yoga of birthlessness
> unstained by the conceptualization
> that distinguishes between truth and falsity
> is a perfect description of this birth.[1072]

This teaches meditation on emptiness. According to the teachings, recite the *svabhāva* mantra[1073] or the *śūnyatā* mantra[1074] and meditate on the mantra's meaning. The *svabhāva* mantra's meaning is that all perceived and perceiving phenomena are naturally and completely devoid of a nature of their own. You then meditate on emptiness as this absence of a nature. The *śūnyatā* mantra's meaning is meditation on the nature of the indivisibility of the emptiness of the object and the wisdom of the subject.

You become aware of that [emptiness] through familiarization with certainty in the view of birthless emptiness: All phenomena are primordially without essence, nature, or selfhood and therefore are free from all the elaboration created by conceptual embellishment. Texts by the mahāsiddhas teach that you gain certainty in emptiness through [the process of] "destruction" without practicing familiarization. Some call that the "forceful method of meditation on emptiness" or "meditation through destruction."

Some texts teach that you meditate on emptiness after the world and its inhabitants are dissolved into luminosity. In this teaching, when you have dissolved the appearances of the world and its inhabitants into luminosity, you must maintain mindfulness of both objectlessness and the mantra's meaning of emptiness.

Some others teach that you generate the clear appearances of the pure divine residence and residents and so on, and then meditate that the entire impure world and its inhabitants are the emptiness of nothingness. But that is nonsensical.

Atiśa has explained the purpose for this meditation on emptiness:

> Thus, you repeat the two mantras three times each. This is done so that you can realize emptiness, sustain the mindfulness of emptiness, maintain a stable state, complete the accumulation of wisdom, eliminate the concepts of an ordinary body, speech, and mind, and realize that the entire residence and residents are manifestations of emptiness.[1075]

(c) Meditating on the circle of protection to prevent adverse factors

The general protective circle [355] is a meditation on a floor, walls, roof, and so on made from *vajra* crosses (*viśvavajra*). From the *Hevajra Tantra*:

> First, meditate that a *raṃ* becomes a sun.
> In its center is a *hūṃ* that becomes a vajra cross.
> Meditate that the vajra cross [manifests]
> walls with a fastened roof.[1076]

The special protective circle is a yellow wheel with ten spokes on which there are ten wrathful deities who destroy hinderers. From the *Vajra Tent*:

> The wheel of protection is majestic.
> It blazes like the fire of the end of the eon.
> It spins and is totally immovable...[1077]

Also from the *Vajra Tent*:

> Through the application of ten *hūṃ*,
> sequentially arrange the ten wrathful deities.[1078]

That is also found in the Guhyasamāja.

In most sādhanas, the protective wheel is as taught by Abhayākara: There is a *hūṃ* in the center of the wheel and ten wrathful deities arranged on the spokes. He also taught that if hinderers are causing great harm, they should be drawn in, stabbed with stakes (*kīla*), and so on.

In the Cakrasaṃvara teachings, the general protective circle has wrathful deities arranged upon either an eight-spoke or ten-spoke wheel. The mantra of the four-faced [deity] binds the main and intermediate directions and then manifests the door and corner guardians, who stab with stakes and so on.

Some teach that at this point, the blessing of the sense bases, the entry of the wisdom deities, and the empowerments can be included within the meditation on the wrathful deities, but this is an overelaboration that is not found in most reliable sources.

(2) The actual generation stage

This is in three parts:

(a) The practice of the generation stage
(b) The way the impure basis is purified [in the generation stage]
(c) The different categories of meditation and mantra recitation

(a) The practice of the generation stage

This is in three parts:

(i) The generation of the divine palace as the residence
(ii) The generation of the deities as the residents
(iii) The completing ancillaries

(i) The generation of the divine palace as the residence

From the *Hevajra Tantra*:

> Imagine a "vagina" in the element of space.
> Meditate first upon its center,
> the wheel, in the correct way
> and upon the correct appearance of the deities.
>
> *Wheel* means "earth," *first* means "water,"
> and *in the correct way* means "fire."
> *Of the deities* means "the great wind"
> and *the correct appearance* means "the meditator."[1079]

Therefore, as is taught in most texts, you generate the *dharmodaya*, the tier of successive elements, and so on, as the base for the generation of the divine palace. [356] There are many variations of this, for example: (1) The tier of elements melts and becomes a vajra cross, with the divine palace generated in its center. (2) Without a tier of elements in a *dharmodaya*, you generate the divine palace upon a multicolored lotus and vajra cross. (3) You generate the divine palace and the deities simultaneously in the center of a multicolored lotus and vajra cross upon the tier of elements and Mount Meru.

There are many teachings on the palace itself, such as that it appears from *bhrūṃ*, from a wheel, or from a dissolved Vairocana and so on. From the *Hevajra Tantra*:

> The Teacher spoke thus about the mandala:
> "It is square and brightly blazing.
> It has four doors and has great brilliance.
> It is adorned by hanging tassels and loops.
> Multicolored garlands and yak tails are fastened to it,
> and eight pillars beautify it."[1080]

From the *Latter Definition Tantra*:

> It has four corners and four doors.
> Four porticos adorn it.
> Loops and tassels beautify it.
> It is perfectly adorned by flags and garlands.[1081]

Such details are taught in all the tantras. The Cakrasaṃvara, Hevajra, and other such tantras teach that you meditate on charnel grounds outside the palace. From the *Saṃvarodaya Tantra*:

> In the center of the vajra tent
> is the adornment of eight charnel grounds.[1082]

From the *Vajraḍāka Tantra*:

> Create a circle of light
> outside the double line of colored earth.

> Create the charnel grounds with their trees and so on
> outside of that circle.[1083]

The *Saṃvarodaya Tantra* teaches that the charnel grounds are within the vajra wall, while the *Vajraḍāka Tantra* teaches that they are outside "the circle of light." Therefore, there is no one definitive version.

According to the *Saṃvarodaya Tantra*, the charnel grounds are:

> Caṇḍogra and Gahvara,
> Vajrajvālā and Karaṅkakina,
> Aṭṭahāsa in the Iśāna [direction],
> Lakṣmīvana in the Hutāśana [direction],
> Ghorāndhakāra in the Nirṭi [direction],
> And in the Vāyu direction is Kilikilārava.[1084]

It teaches in detail how in each charnel ground there is a tree, a land guardian (*kśetrapāla*), and so on. You then meditate on the seats and such of the mandala deities inside the divine palace.

(ii) The generation of the deities as the residents

This is in two parts:

- A' A general teaching on the classification of the methods for generating deities [357]
- B' A specific teaching on the methods for generating the deities and their retinues

A' A general teaching on the classification of the methods for generating deities

This is in two parts:

- 1' A method of generation that accords with the four kinds of birth
- 2' The categories of the processes of generation

1' A method of generation that accords with the four kinds of birth

In general, although the process of generating the deity parallels "the four kinds of birth," which are the different ways of being born within samsara's existences, there are many variations in this process.

In a womb birth, the activity or the sounds of the parents' sexual desire invokes the consciousness in the bardo, which enters in between the white and red elements and takes birth. In the same way, [the deities] melt into a sphere that is invoked by song, so that through moon, sun, insignia, and seed, the deity is born. Alternatively, birth first occurs in the womb from the white and red elements and then [the being] comes out from the womb. In the same way, a deity arises from the bodhicitta produced by the union of the male and female deities and emanates from the womb and so on. From the *Latter Definition Tantra*:

> Those who meditate conceive of womb birth
> as occurring through the activity of song.[1085]

From *Commentary to the Saṃvarodaya Tantra*:

> The birth that is a womb birth is an emergence from the melted bodhicitta produced by the motion of the male deity's vajra and the female deity's lotus.[1086]

Egg birth is the sphere formed by the blending of the red and white elements of the parents with a consciousness from the bardo, thus creating an egg-born being. In that way, without an invocatory song to melted [deities], there is the generation of the deity's body from a sphere that is the blending of the moon, sun, insignia, and seed [syllable]. From the *Latter Definition Tantra*:

> Egg birth is without song,
> avoiding both sound and silence.[1087]

From *Commentary to the Saṃvarodaya Tantra*:

> The birth that is birth from an egg is the generation of the complete deity in stages starting from the moon and sun and continuing until the seed [syllable] and insignia.[1088]

Birth from warm moisture is the entry of a consciousness from the bardo into the combination of warmth and moisture, so that there is a birth created by warmth and moisture. In that way, the body of the deity is generated just from a seed syllable upon a moon and so on. From *Commentary to the Saṃvarodaya Tantra*:

> Birth from just the moon and seed is birth from warmth and moisture.[1089]

Spontaneous birth does not rely on any substance whatsoever, yet instantaneously there is a totally complete body. Similarly, without even a seed syllable, the body of the deity is instantaneously generated completely from luminosity. Ghaṇṭa wrote:

> Imagine [the generation] without a seed,
> like beings who are spontaneously born.[1090]

From *Commentary to the Saṃvarodaya Tantra*: [358]

> Instantaneous generation from luminosity, without such things as seed [syllables], is the birth that is spontaneous.[1091]

2'' The categories of the processes of generation

This is in two parts:

- a' Generation through the five enlightenments
- b' Generation through the four procedures and so on

a' Generation through the five enlightenments

Imagine that upon a seat such as a lotus, the vowels transform into a moon [disc] and the consonants into a sun disc. In their middle[1092] is the insignia of the deity adorned by the deity's seed syllable. The seed syllable radiates and absorbs light rays, and the entire [moon, sun, and insignia] transform into the complete body of the deity. From the *Hevajra Tantra*:

> The seed is in the center of
> the vowel moon and the consonant sun.
> That itself has been said to be the deity (*sattva*)
> and is the nature of supreme joy.
>
> The light of its own body emanates,
> filling the mandala of space.

> Gather them back in and draw them into the heart
> and become the embodiment of wrath.[1093]

The way in which these are the five enlightenments (*abhisaṃbodhi*): (1) The moon is enlightenment through mirror-like wisdom. (2) The sun is enlightenment through the wisdom of equality. (3) The seed and insignia are enlightenment through discriminating wisdom. (4) The blending of them all is enlightenment through accomplishing wisdom. (5) The complete body is enlightenment through the dharmadhātu wisdom. It is said in the *Hevajra Tantra*:

> The moon has mirror wisdom; the one with seven steeds[1094] has equality;
> the seeds and insignias of one's own deity are said to be discrimination;
> that they all become one is accomplishment; and the completion is the pure true nature.
> The wise should meditate upon [these] aspects through [these] five described ways.[1095]

Some texts teach that the sun and the moon, or a white moon and a red moon, are the mirror wisdom; those two transformed into one are the equality wisdom; the seed is the discriminating wisdom; the insignia is the accomplishing wisdom; and the complete body is the dharmadhātu wisdom.

It is not definitive that the vowels and consonants generate a sun and moon. In some [texts] the vowels and consonants generate a moon that is white with a red glow.

It is also taught that the vowels become a white moon and the consonants generate a red moon, which is essentially the same meaning as in the generation of a sun and moon.

It is taught that this generation from the sixteen vowels and the forty-two consonants [359] symbolizes the causes of the thirty-two primary and eighty secondary signs [of a great being].

Generally speaking, the moon symbolizes the white element of the father, the sun symbolizes the red element of the mother, and the seed [syllable] symbolizes the bardo consciousness. From the *Saṃvarodaya Tantra*:

The vowels and consonants liquefy
[and the supreme joy is attained.]
[The consciousness] is present in the form of a spot
in between the semen and the blood.[1096]

In the same way, it's taught that the blending of all those [into one] symbolizes conception; and the deity's body becoming complete symbolizes the full development of the fetus and its birth from the womb.

b' Generation through the four procedures (kalpa) and so on

1. Generation through the four vajra aspects: (1) meditation on emptiness; (2) the seed of the deity upon a seat, such as a lotus and sun, and its radiation and absorption of light rays; (3) the generation of the complete body of the deity; and (4) the establishment of the three syllables at the three places [of the body] and so on. From the *Latter Guhyasamāja Tantra*:

First is emptiness and bodhicitta.
Second is absorption into the seed.
Third is the complete image.
Fourth is the placement of the syllables.
Perform the sevā of ordinary practice
through these four vajra aspects.[1097]

From the *Hevajra Tantra*:

First, the enlightenment of emptiness.
Second, absorption into the seed.
Third, the complete form.
Fourth, the placement of the syllables.[1098]

2. Generation through three vajra procedures. These consist of (1) the deity's seed upon a seat such as a lotus and sun, (2) the seed's transformation into an insignia adorned by the seed, and (3) the insignia's transformation into the generation of the complete deity. From the *Hevajra Tantra*:

[The yogi] should meditate on a *raṃ* in his own heart,
which becomes a sun disc.

Upon it is created a *hūṃ*,
which has the nature of method and wisdom.

The *hūṃ* transforms into a vajra
that is black in color and terrifying.
[The yogi] should meditate upon the nature of the *hūṃ*
that is present in the middle of the vajra's central sphere.

[The yogin] should watch the *hūṃ* transform
and meditate upon [being] the embodiment of wrath.[1099]

3. Generation simply from the quintessential syllable, and 4. Instantaneous complete generation. Those are both easy to understand.

It is taught that all these [forms of generation] require the completing ancillaries: the entry of the wisdom deities, the empowerments, the offerings, the praises, and so on.

B' A specific teaching on the methods for generating the deities and their retinues

The process of generation through invocatory song to melted [deities]
According to the *Vajra Tent*:

First, you imagine the deities (*sattvas*).[1100]
Then the circle of ḍākinīs is emanated.
At the entry of the gandharva [360]
contemplate the fluid.[1101]
The intermediate goddesses make an invocation.
The leader of the circle having been invoked,
there are Moha[1102] and the others at the eyes and so on.
The vajras[1103] are arranged in the three places.[1104]

It's taught that you generate the causal Vajradhara and consort. Their union emanates the retinue of deities who are arranged in their [appropriate] places. Then the letter or *nāda* that symbolizes the bardo [consciousness] enters the causal Vajradhara. That creates the condition for the deity and consort to melt into bliss and take the form of a spherical drop (*bindu*). The goddesses in the intermediate directions make an invocation through song, causing the resultant Vajradhara to appear and so on.

The texts of some mahāsiddhas teach that the syllable that symbolizes the bardo enters the causal Vajradhara and then the deity and consort melt into a sphere of bodhicitta that emanates the four goddesses whose invocatory song generates the resultant Vajradhara. That union of deity and consort then emanates their retinue arranged in their specific locations.

Some [texts] teach that you practice in that way as far as the generation of the resultant Vajradhara, but then the union of the male and female deities generates the residence and residents of the mandala in the lotus of the consort. This is progressively emanated outward; [the mandala deities] accomplish their activities and are arranged in their individual locations.

According to some in the Nāgārjuna tradition of Guhyasamāja, during this "supreme king [of the mandala]" stage, the deity and consort's union causes them to gradually dissolve into luminosity. Then the invocatory song of the goddesses causes the "body of unity" to arise. In this context, the invocatory song to the melted [deities] and the manner of their melting has a completely different symbolism and meaning, and therefore their key points are not the same.

Mahāsiddha texts teach a process of *generation without an invocatory song*: You generate the causal Vajradhara; the letter or *nāda* that symbolizes the bardo [consciousness] enters it so that it melts; then you generate the resultant Vajradhara and the union of the deity and consort emanates the retinue [deities], arranged in their individual locations.

Some teach that the causal Vajradhara melts and transforms into moon and sun discs or that the causal Vajradhara melts and merges into a separate moon and sun disc. In the center [of the sun and moon discs] is the insignia of the deity together with the seed syllable, and from them are generated the resultant Vajradhara that then emanates the retinue.

Some teach that there is no actual generation of the causal Vajradhara deities but that the letter or *nāda* that symbolizes the bardo [consciousness] appears in the gap between the conjoined moon and sun discs and then from that is generated the causal Vajradhara, which is the seed [syllable] of the deity. [361] That radiates and absorbs light rays, and then all blend and generate the resultant Vajradhara, which is the deities and their retinue and so on.

There are many different such descriptions, all approaches of individual tantra texts.

The symbolic meaning of the presence or absence of invocatory songs

It is taught that the melting accords with the buddhas doing nothing but resting in the kāya of great bliss (*mahāsukhakāya*) when there are no worthy pupils; the invocatory songs accord with demonstrating the form kāyas and benefiting beings until the time has come to teach pupils. The absence of the melting and the invocatory songs accords with the aspect of [the buddhas] always remaining to benefit beings and never dissolving [their bodies] for even an instant.

The generation of the two Vajradharas

Both causal and resultant Vajradharas can be generated through the five awakenings or through any appropriate [process such as] the three procedures. The causal and resultant Vajradharas have no single definitive form, and therefore can have differing colors, [and numbers of] faces and arms.

The generation of the retinue

They can be generated in various ways, such as by the five awakenings or the three processes, or they can simply be generated from an essence or seed [syllable].

The tier of three deities

This occurs in the majority of practices. The commitment being (*samayasattva*) is the deity that is generated in the practice; it has the same meaning as *sāmayika*.[1105] The wisdom being (*jñānasattva*) is the deity that is visualized in the heart of the commitment being, where it is seated upon a lotus and sun, for instance. It can have different appearances. It may, for example, resemble the commitment being, or it may be a deity that differs in color [and number of] faces and arms, or it may be a seed syllable that transforms into an insignia. The samādhi being (*samādhisattva*) is a seed syllable or insignia that is meditated upon within the heart of the wisdom being. If the wisdom being is itself [being visualized as] an insignia, the samādhi being will be in the form of a seed syllable that adorns it. In some practices only the principal deity of the mandala may have a tier of three deities. In others, all the deities [in the mandala] may have them.

Most texts also teach the blessing of the sense bases and so on. While many [texts] teach that the deities are generated from just the seed syllables, some teach that you meditate on an arrangement of the seed syllables alone without meditating on the deities themselves. [362]

(iii) The completing ancillaries

According to the *Vajra Tent*:

> The wisdom truly enters.
> The empowerment is tasting
> the nectar of the eight vidyās.
> The eight goddesses make offerings.
> The leader of the circle is praised.[1106]

Thus it is taught that you should practice the entry of the wisdom deities, the empowerment, the offerings, and the praises.

The entry of the wisdom being

Light rays from the seed syllable in the heart invite the wisdom mandala's residence and residents, who are identical to your meditation, to come from their natural abodes. The offerings and so on are made. The wisdom-being [mandala] enters the commitment-being mandala.[1107] Imagine with conviction that they have merged to become one.

Some texts teach that the invitation is made through the sound *pheṃ*, or through the sound of the joy of sexual union, and so on. Some texts teach that only the wisdom deities and not their divine palaces are invited. There are many other versions, such as inviting the buddhas and bodhisattvas in the ten directions without their having any definite resemblance to the commitment deities.

The purpose for the entry of wisdom deities

According to the instructions in *Ears of Grain*,[1108] [the entry of wisdom deities is practiced] in order to truly think that all tathāgatas have a single identity, so that you will have conviction in equality.

Atiśa taught that [the entry of wisdom deities is practiced] in order to end thoughts of separation between yourself and the wisdom deities, in order to have the enduring pride of inseparability [from the deities], and in order to receive blessing.[1109]

Some teach that the commitment being is inferior and the wisdom being is superior, and that therefore if you don't make the wisdom being enter, the commitment being will be a mindless image unable to bestow siddhis, but this is nonsense.

The empowerment

This is the meditation where light from the seed syllable in the heart invites the empowerment deities, and because of offerings and supplication, they give empowerment. In the *Hevajra Tantra*, there is an extensive teaching on this, for example:

> [The deity's] own seed, [imagined] in [his] own heart, radiates a ray. Its black light in the form of a hook draws in all the buddhas in the three realms and the eight matrikas make offerings to them.[1110]

The empowerment deities

In most texts the empowerment deities are identical to [the deities in] the meditated mandala during the empowerment.

The empowerment

The majority of texts teach only the "liquid empowerment." Saroruha and Atiśa [both] teach four empowerments. [363] There are gurus who have taught that the vase empowerment alone will suffice for meditation on the generation stage but that all four empowerments are necessary [for meditation] related to the completion stage. However, this is not something definitive.

The purpose of the empowerment

[The empowerment is given] in order to wash away the stains of faults and to enable you to accomplish the goal. From the *Hevajra Tantra*:

> It is poured upon (*sicyate*) [you] and bathes (*snāpyate*) [you];
> That is why it is called an empowerment (*seka*, a "pouring").[1111]

Atiśa taught eight purposes of an empowerment:[1112] (1) to eliminate obstacles, (2) to eliminate obscurations, (3) to eliminate [following] the Hīnayāna, (4) to make someone into a worthy vessel for [mantra] repetition, (5) [to make someone into a worthy vessel for] meditation, (6) to bestow the power to accomplish the activities, such as the peaceful [activity], (7) to fill with the experience of bodhicitta, and (8) to achieve buddhahood in the future.

The application of the seals

There are many different versions, among which the *Hevajra Tantra* teaches one in detail:[1113]

- Nature sealed by nature: For example, Akṣobhya, who is the nature of the mind, is applied as a seal to the nature of consciousness, which is [Akṣobhya,] the deity that is the purity of anger.
- The body sealed by the mind: Akṣobhya, [the deity of] the purity of the mind, seals those of the family of Vairocana, the deity of the purity of the body.
- The mind sealed by the body: The seal of Vairocana, [the deity of] the purity of the body, is applied as a seal to those of the family of Akṣobhya, the deity of the purity of the mind.
- The result sealed by the cause: Amitābha, [who is the deity of] the purity of desire, which is the cause, seals those who are of the family of Amoghasiddhi, the deity of the purity of envy, which is the result.
- The cause sealed by the result: Ratnasambhava, the deity of the purity of miserliness, which is the result, seals those of the family of Amitābha, the deity of the purity of desire, which is the cause.

There are also teachings on a system of mutual sealing between the families and those who belong to the families, between [the deities] who are generated and those who generate them, and between cause and result. From Vajragarbha's [Hevajra] commentary:

> The children are sealed according to their family
> and the children seal the families.
> The father seals the son
> and the son seals the father.
> The result seals the cause
> and the cause seals the result.[1114]

Thus, there are many kinds [of seals], but most texts teach the seals of the family and the family member, which is easier to understand.

THE PURPOSE OF SEALING

[The seal is applied] because you need to meditate without error on the families in order to accomplish the general and special siddhis. From the *Hevajra Tantra*: [364]

> Sealing is marking with a sign.
> The families are identified by marking.
> There will be no siddhis and no siddhas
> from meditation practice on a misidentified family.[1115]

TASTING THE NECTAR AND MAKING OFFERINGS AND PRAISES

Different texts teach different methods, but all teach that these are to be done while knowing that the offerer, the offering, and the recipient are birthless emptiness.

THE PURPOSE OF TASTING THE NECTAR AND MAKING OFFERINGS AND PRAISES

It is taught that these practices are done so that you will know that your entire field of experience, such as the substances of sensory delight, are a display of immaculate bliss and emptiness.

(b) The way the impure basis is purified [in the generation stage]

This is in two parts:

(i) A description of the impure basis
(ii) The purification

(i) A description of the impure basis

This is in three parts:

A' The process of dying
B' The way the bardo manifests
C' The way birth takes place

A' The process of dying

Birth, death, and the bardo are here taught to be the impure basis that the generation stage purifies. This principally refers to a human being who possesses the six elements.[1116]

Death means the dissolution of such aspects as the twenty-five evident aspects: the five aggregates, the four elements, the six faculties, the five sensory objects, and the five wisdoms. There are many signs of their dissolution, but we can simplify the stages of dying into the evident dissolution of the four elements:

- When the earth element of the body merges into water, this causes: (a) the external sign of the body being unable to move and an inability to hold anything; (b) the internal sign of a perception of something like smoke.
- When the water element merges into fire, this causes: (a) the external sign of the body sweating and the saliva in one's mouth drying up; (b) the internal sign of a perception of something like a mirage; and (c) the cessation of the thirty-three kinds of thoughts that arise from aversion.
- When the fire element merges into air, this causes: (a) the external sign of the warmth of the body leaving its extremities; (b) the internal sign of a perception of something like fireflies; and (c) the cessation of the forty kinds of thoughts that arise from attachment.
- When the air element merges into consciousness, this causes: (a) the external sign of the exhalations lengthening and the inhalations becoming imperceptible; (b) the internal sign of a perception of something like lamp flames fluttering in the wind; and (c) the cessation of the seven kinds of thoughts that rise from ignorance.

The subtle process of dissolution consists of the three visions: When consciousness merges into *appearance,* this causes a bright white appearance that is like a cloudless sky filled with moonlight. When *appearance* merges into *increase,* this causes a red appearance that is like a cloudless sky filled with sunlight. When *increase* merges into *attainment,* [365] this causes a black appearance that is like a cloudless sky filled with an all-pervading darkness. Then your mindfulness diminishes until you become completely unconscious. When you recover consciousness, there is the experience of *luminosity.* This is like the clear sky at dawn, free from the factors that stain space: moonlight, sunlight, and darkness.[1117]

B′ The way the bardo manifests

Attainment arises from the *luminosity*; *increase* arises from *attainment*; *appearance* arises from *increase*, each lasting for only an instant. The eighty kinds of thought arise from *appearance*, after which the bardo body, which is a wind-mounted consciousness, is created.

At first, there are the momentary appearances from the propensities of your past life. They become less and less clear until the appearance of the body of your next life arises. This is explained in the great commentary to the Kālacakra: The [bardo] body takes on the form it will have on being reborn; it has all sensory faculties; it can pass through anything except its future birthplace; it is endowed with miraculous physical powers; the body increases through eating smells; it can be seen by other bardo beings of the same class and [by living beings] with divine sight; it moves around in search of smells and its birthplace; it has all kinds of perceptions because of good or bad karma; it has very little stability; the length of its lifetime can be up to seven days but this is not definite, for if it is not reborn, it experiences a "little death," which is like fainting briefly, and then comes back into the bardo for another "lifetime" of seven days. If it does not encounter the accumulation of factors necessary for rebirth, this process can repeat until forty-nine days have passed, and then it will definitely be reborn.

There is no bardo if you are be reborn in the formless realm; instead a "formless aggregation" is created at the very spot where you died. Otherwise, before rebirth in the desire or the form realms, a bardo definitely occurs.

C′ The way birth takes place

When you are reborn, there can be four kinds of births. If it is going to be a *spontaneous rebirth*, you will have a craving for a certain location, and your attachment and aversion cause a "little death," which is like a brief faint, from which you take rebirth. If it is going to be birth through *warm moisture*, your attachment and aversion toward smell and taste will cause you to briefly [366] faint, followed by rebirth. If it is going to be birth from a *womb* or an *egg*, your attachment and aversion on seeing your [future] parents having sex will cause you to briefly faint, followed by rebirth.

The moving winds, which are the nature of the bardo existence, dissolve. A subtle form of [the succession of] appearance, increase, attainment, and luminosity will occur. Rebirth takes place when attainment reappears from luminosity. Then increase arises from attainment; appearance arises from increase; and thoughts arise from appearance.

The special air element that has the power to create a basis for consciousness arises from the air that "rides" upon *appearance*. From that air element arises the fire element. Similarly, from the fire element arises the water element, and from the water element arises the earth element. From those elements, the aggregates and so on are generated.

The *Saṃvarodaya Tantra* in particular teaches the process of birth from a womb:[1118] When in the bardo you see your [future] parents lying with each other, you enter your father through his mouth or through the crown of his head and then exit from his genitals to enter your mother's vagina, where conception takes place in the middle of the semen and blood. Then you develop in the womb.

The semen and blood contain the four elements: earth creates its solidity, water creates its cohesion, fire creates its ripening, and air creates its increase. There is a gradual development through the vitality of the mother's air, blood, and so on.

In the first week, [the embryo] is in the form of a *kalala*.[1119] In the second week it is in the form of an *arbuda*.[1120] In the third week it is in the form of a *peśī*.[1121] In the fourth week it is in the form of a *ghana*.[1122] Then it solidifies, and in the fifth month, while having a form like a fish, it develops limbs. In the seventh month, hair, nails, and so on, develop. In the eighth month, the sensory faculties of the eyes, ears, nose, tongue, body, and mind develop. In the ninth month, the body is completely developed, and in the tenth month it is born from the womb.

(ii) The purification [through the generation stage]

There are specific [purifications] in relation to particular qualities of [an individual who is] an impure basis, but for now, in order to make it easy to understand, [purification] will be explained in a general manner.

The impure basis is someone who, having accumulated karma for rebirth from a womb, dies, becomes a bardo being, enters a womb in the world of humans, is born from the womb when the body is fully developed, and then accomplishes a variety of actions in that lifetime.

The purification consists of the gathering of the accumulations; the meditation on emptiness; the divine palace (within which there is the causal Vajradhara); the *nāda* or syllable that enters [the causal Vajradhara]; [367] [the causal Vajradhara] melting; the invocation through song; the arising as the resultant Vajradhara; and so on.

The way in which these correspond with each other

Gathering the accumulations through the field of accumulation corresponds with the accumulation of karma that is the cause for rebirth.

The meditation on emptiness corresponds with the stages of death.

The tier of elements, the divine palace, and the seats [of the deities] correspond with the environment of the world and the location where the rebirth takes place.

The deity and consort who are the causal Vajradhara corresponds with the mother and father.

The *nāda* or syllable entering [the causal Vajradhara] corresponds with the bardo beings seeing their parents having sex and then entering the father's mouth or head and so on until conception in the womb.

The melting of the deity and consort corresponds with the parents losing consciousness from orgasm.

The invocatory song by the goddesses causing the resultant Vajradhara to arise corresponds with the bardo being entering the semen and blood and then passing through the stages of *kalala*, *arbuda*, and so on, and being made firm by the earth element, cohesive by water, ripe by fire, and increased by air, until there is the complete development of the body.

If there is no melting and invocatory song and there is entry of the *nāda* or syllable, then that corresponds to the [entry of] the bardo being, but if there is no [entry of the *nāda* or syllable], then the seed syllable corresponds to the bardo being while the moon and sun correspond to the father's white element and the mother's red element.

The generation of the deity through the stages of the seed syllable transforming into the insignia and so on corresponds to the body becoming completely developed through such stages as the form of a fish developing limbs. The commitment being corresponds to the temporary body, which is the individual's elements and the evidently created body. The wisdom being corresponds to the energy of the body's winds, channels, and bodhicitta. The samādhi being corresponds to the natural, subtle body composed of only mind and wind.

Blessing the sense bases corresponds to the complete development of such [internal] sense bases as the eyes and so on awakening and cognizing the six [external] sense bases such as form. Blessing the body corresponds to the complete development of the different parts of the individual's body. Blessing the speech corresponds to the complete development of the eight locations of speech and so on. Blessing the mind corresponds to the complete development of the mind directing its mindfulness toward objects.

If there is the emanation of deities as in the "supreme king of the mandala" [stage of the practice], that corresponds to the birth of a male or female individual. [368]

The majority of texts do not clearly teach the correspondence between the completing practices and the impure basis, but the entry of the gurus or wisdom deities corresponds to the engaging consciousnesses waking from the *ālaya*, drawing in externals, and returning to the *ālaya*.

Receiving empowerment corresponds to washing stains from the baby and so on. Sealing corresponds to attaining a status within the family. Offering corresponds to the sensory faculties becoming extremely attached to objects so that craving increases and taste is experienced. Praising corresponds to obtaining all worldly qualities so that others will praise [the individual] for being wise, clear, and so on.

(c) The different categories of meditation and mantra recitation

This is in two parts:

(i) A description of meditation on the mandala
(ii) A description of repetition of the mantra

(i) A description of meditation on the mandala

This is in two parts:

A' Meditation on the mandala
B' Mindfulness of purity

A' Meditation on the mandala

This is in three parts:

1' The categories of "realized" meditation
2' The beginner's maintenance of the visualization
3' The teaching on the complete mastery of the generation stage

1′ The categories of "realized" meditation

Generally speaking, individuals meditating on the generation stage can be classified into four types depending on which stage of the path has developed in an individual.

THE BEGINNER

In the beginning you learn the generation stage, gradually gaining clear images of the obvious deities and sustaining that clarity for brief periods. This is a sequential meditation of all the practices as presented in the sādhanas. According to Dīpaṃkara[bhadra]:

> The beginner rises in the morning
> and repeats [mantras] excellently, as before.[1123]

From *Ears of Grain*:

> In this way alone, the beginner performs all the practices, leaving nothing out.[1124]

THOSE WHO HAVE HAD SOME WISDOM DESCEND [UPON THEM]

In this stage, having been able to visualize the evident deities for brief periods of time, you meditate on the subtle aspects in sequence. This means that after a brief meditation on the evident mandala, you meditate on the sequence of subtleties, such as blessing the sense bases. [According to Dīpaṃkara:]

> Those who have had some descent of wisdom
> bless the eyes, the body, and the rest
> with the *vrata* of mantra conduct
> and between sessions be focused on repeating [the mantra].[1125]

According to the *Commentary to the Three Hundred and Fifty Verses*,[1126] this means that between all sessions you quickly create the mandala, bless the eyes and so on and the body and so on, do the preliminaries of pleasing, offering, [369] praising, and tasting nectar, and then carefully repeat the mantra.

Those who have gained some power of wisdom

In this stage, after quickly creating all the obvious and subtle [aspects of the] mandala, you are able to practice *radiation and absorption*. This means you briefly meditate on the complete mandala and then practice radiation and absorption. [According to Dīpaṃkara:]

> There are those who at all times perfectly
> practice radiation and absorption.
> They gain some of the power of wisdom.
> They correctly use this yoga day and night.[1127]

From *Ears of Grain*:

> Those who have gained the signs that have been taught and have mental stability in the first yoga have some power of wisdom and meditate by briefly emanating the mandala.[1128]

Those who have truly gained the power of wisdom

This is the stage of perfecting the generation stage and meditating on the completion stage. This means that you briefly create the complete mandala and then meditate on a completion-stage practice. [According to Dīpaṃkara:]

> Meditate on attaining the power of true wisdom.
> With the three supreme cakras filled by the particles of the
> element,[1129]
> a body with the nature of a reflection
> will accomplish the activity of benefiting beings.[1130]

From *Ears of Grain*:

> Those who have stability of mind throughout the entire familiarized mandalas have the power of wisdom. They accomplish a vast benefit for beings through radiation and absorption. Realizing the true nature manifests the bodhicitta and eliminates the subtlest of subtle stains.[1131]

2′ *The beginner's maintenance of the visualization*

When you have attained the clear appearance of the mandala residence and residents and have a stability that cannot by harmed by any factor, train in the stable pride of being the deity.

The way [you gain stable pride]

Texts by mahāsiddhas teach that after mastering the generation practices, you meditate on the mandala, and when you become tired, you practice mindfulness of purity, repetition [of the mantras], and so on. In that way, you meditate sequentially on the practices as described in the sādhanas. You meditate by clearly visualizing whatever deity it is as clearly as you can and develop stable pride in each practice by thinking "I am this [deity]."

In this stage you maintain the visualization of the entire mandala with mindfulness and awareness. If other appearances arise, you don't become involved with them but continue to meditate on the visualization, progressively lengthening the duration of the visualization. [370] Maintaining the focus through mindfulness and awareness is like taming an elephant. According to Śākyamitra:

> The crazed elephant of the mind behaves badly.
> Tie it to the post of the focus
> by using the rope of mindfulness, and then gradually
> bring it under control with the hook of wisdom.[1132]

The gurus have taught that if you are unable to visualize the entire mandala, then first visualize a part of the body of the principal deity, such as his main face, and then gradually attain a "clear appearance." Alternatively, look again and again at a painting or statue of the *yidam* deity so that it will appear clearly in your mind, just as when people imagine over and over someone they desire until they appear clearly as if truly present. According to Dharmakīrti:

> When dreaming about thieves, for instance,
> or when overpowered by desire, fear, or misery,
> you see something that has no reality
> as being present in front of you.[1133]

If you meditate first on something in front of you in that way, it will be easier to meditate on yourself as being the same as that. It's like when you perfectly memorize the movements of a dancer so that you can perform the same movements yourself. When you have become very familiar with [an image], it will appear clearly in that way. According to Dharmakīrti:

> Therefore, whatever you become very familiar with,
> whether it be true or false,
> when that familiarization is complete,
> it will become nonconceptually clear in the mind.[1134]

You should also know that throughout every stage of training in the generation stage, the entire appearance of the mandala and all that appears to the mind is just relative appearance with essentially no reality; they are ultimately empty. You must train in [seeing] everything that arises as illusions. From the *Vajra Tent*:

> Just as the moon on the water
> is neither true nor false,
> in the same way, the bodies in
> the mandala circle have an unblemished nature.[1135]

3′ The teaching on the complete mastery of the generation stage

This training in the generation stage enables you to visualize distinctly the shapes, colors, faces, arms, adornments, and so on of the entire, obvious [mandala] residence and residents, and also all the colors, faces, arms, and so on of the subtle *āyatana* deities and the rest. From *Commentary to the Black Yamāntaka*:

> Because of that, you can freely see the vajra bodies and the rest as if they were a fruit in the palm of your hand. This is the attainment of the power of wisdom, and therefore it is practiced at any time between sessions.[1136] [371]

You need to be able to practice naturally, with both the appearance of the mandala circle and the pride of yourself being the deity, for as long as you wish, without the interruption of any other thoughts. From *A Garland of Pearls*:

> Siddhi means the stability of the mind. You attain that when you appear every day in the form of the deity and naturally have the pride of [being the deity].[1137]

To become like this you have to receive the empowerment, keep the commitments and vows correctly, know the key points of maintaining the visualization, and apply great effort with a tractable mind. Then you will attain stability in a short time, such as in six months or a year. From *Thousand-Verse Commentary to the Compendium of Truths*:

> Meditate upon the great vajradhātu mandala every day for as long as you can directly see it. Alternatively, with the three samādhis as a preliminary, meditate for six months or a year.[1138]

Just as fire comes from rubbing kindling sticks together, the mind should continuously meditate so that the elixir of yoga never disappears, and the mind should avoid any activity that would distract the mind, until the desired siddhi has been accomplished. According to Ācārya Śūra:

> Diligently practice meditation
> through continuous yoga.
> Fire will not be produced by friction
> if you repeatedly rest.
> Yoga has the same nature.
> So don't stop until you have the attainment.[1139]

B′ Mindfulness of purity

All the mahāsiddha texts teach that if you tire of meditating on the deity, [practice] mindfulness of purity. According to the *Shining Jewel Tantra*:

> The yogin who cannot meditate
> should be mindful of purity.[1140]

There are many descriptions of methods for mindfulness of purity, among which are the following.

The relative purity of the deity

Visualizations of the deity are pure in being the great qualities of the buddhas. From the *Hevajra Tantra*:

> Because of compassion, the eyes are red.
> The eyes are pure because of the three vajras.
> The body is black because of love.[1141]

The body's aggregates, sensory elements, and so on are pure because they are deities. From the *Guhyasamāja Tantra*:

> The five buddhas are taught to be
> the nature of the five aggregates. [372]
> Locanā and the rest of the four goddesses
> are the nature of earth and so on.[1142]

The body's channel elements and so on are pure as deities. According to Lūyipa:

> The twenty-four ḍākas
> are the elements of the body.[1143]

The adornments are pure as mantras. According to Lūyipa:

> The ḍāka channel mantra and so on
> are the brahman thread and so on.[1144]

The ultimate purity of the true nature

This is the purity of the true nature. Know that all things in samsara and nirvana are naturally pure, birthless emptiness. From the *Hevajra Tantra*:

> The purity of all things
> is indeed declared to be the true nature.[1145]

The purity of self-knowing

In the completion stage, know that everything is the display of connate bliss and emptiness. From the *Hevajra Tantra*:

> That which has the nature of self-knowing is purity.
> There is no liberation through any other purity.
> Because [sensory] objects are essentially pure,
> self-knowing is supreme bliss.[1146]

THE PURPOSE OF MINDFULNESS OF PURITY

The gurus have taught that [mindfulness of purity] is for the purpose of dispelling attachment to the separateness of path and result. Some state that it is for the purpose of dispelling the mind's attachment to reality, but that is incorrect.

(ii) A description of repetition of the mantra

This is in four parts:

A' The nature of the rosary
B' The categories of the levels of mantra repetition
C' The manner of repeating the mantra
D' The benefits and so on of repeating the mantra

A' The nature of the rosary

It's taught that if you become tired in deity-yoga meditation, repeat the mantra. According to Abhayākara:

> Therefore, know these two stages.
> Dwell in true solitude
> and meditate on the circle of deities.
> If you tire of this, repeat their mantras.[1147]

THE ROSARY FOR REPEATING THE MANTRAS

The *Tantra of True Union* teaches specific and general kinds of rosaries and the number of their beads:

> The kinds of rosaries
> specific to peaceful practices
> are crystal, mother of pearl, and pearl,
> those that are naturally white, and so on.

The specific rosaries used by the wise
in increasing practices
are gold, silver, copper,
and lotus-seed rosaries.

[The rosaries] renowned for controlling [practices]
are [made from] all scents, such as saffron,
that are specifically blessed
and rolled into beads.

Rudrākṣa[1148] and soapberry[1149] [seed rosaries]
and, similarly, [rosaries of] human bone [373]
are employed in wrathful practices
and are famed for their use in sorcery.

Bodhi seeds will perform all the practices
of peaceful, increasing, controlling, and sorcery [rites].

There should be fifty [beads] for mantra practice.
Controlling rites require half that number.
The peaceful practices should have a hundred.
Similarly, for increasing practice add an extra eight.
In sorcery there should be sixty.[1150]

[The *Tantra of True Union*] also teaches the rosary thread, how to thread the beads, how to bless the rosary, how to count with them, and so on. The *Vajraḍāka Tantra*'s description of how to count:

Place [the rosary] upon the index finger for peaceful [practice].
Lay it upon the middle finger for increasing.
It is taught to be the ring finger for controlling.
The little finger is used for sorcery.

Use the thumb as a hook
imagining that you draw in the deities.[1151]

B′ The categories of the levels of mantra repetition

Generally speaking, there are three kinds of mantra repetition. From *Ears of Grain*:

> Moving on from this [vajra repetition] alone, I now describe other repetitions. There is *mantra repetition*, which is just reciting the mantra. There is *form repetition*, which is being mindful of the deity yoga alone. There is *yoga repetition*, which is contemplating the true nature alone.[1152]

Ears of Grain also teaches four ways of practicing the mantra repetition.

The samaya repetition

As the breath rises from the seed syllable in the heart, the deities of the mandala are emanated [from the seed syllable] and accomplish the benefit of beings. As the breath enters [the seed syllable, the deities] reenter the seed syllable. When you first recite the mantra of a particular deity, the deities are emanated; when you conclude reciting [the mantra, the deities] are absorbed. This is also taught to be the *radiation-absorption mantra repetition*. Concerning this, according to Dīpaṃkara:

> The wisdom bodies are emanated and you repeat.
> As you recite, the prāṇa causes emanation.
> The mantra forcefully absorbs.[1153]

The palanquin mantra repetition

Imagine that all phenomena are equal. Meditate that a line of mantras enters your mouth and, passing through your vajra, enters the lotus of the consort; passing through her central channel, it exits from her mouth and enters your mouth, and [continues to] circle in this way. This is also taught to be the *litter mantra repetition*.

The fierce mantra repetition

The line of mantras goes from your own mouth into your consort's mouth, exits from her lotus into your vajra, and circles in that way. That is also called the *wrathful repetition*.

These [last two] are described in the *Shining Jewel*:

> Then as the wise repeat the mantra,
> it circles through the mouths of the deity and consort [374]
> like the circle made by a whirled torch,
> its color according to the nature of its activity.[1154]

In the wrathful repetition, the mantra is recited fiercely. From the *Guhyasamāja*:

> When you can hear the syllables of the mantra,
> that is taught to be the wrathful repetition.[1155]

Some teach that *samaya repetition* is repeating the essence and quintessence mantras; *palanquin repetition* is the gentle mantra circle; *fierce repetition* is the harsh mantra circle; and *wrathful repetition* is the repetition of all mantras. However, most mahāsiddha texts teach that any of the first three levels of mantra repetition can be used for the repetition of all mantras.

Some texts teach four repetitions that consist of the first two from above with the addition of *circular repetition* and *vajra repetition*.

Circular repetition is when the mind arranges the mantra, with the letters standing up in a circle, like a circle of lamps, around the seed syllable in the heart, and as you repeat it, it is as if you are writing the letters with your mind.

Vajra repetition is where the repetition conjoins with the inhalation, exhalation, and retention of the breath. The gurus have taught that there are five kinds [of vajra repetition]: (1) *mental repetition*, which is repeating [the mantra] in the mind without reciting the mantra's words; (2) *cessation repetition*, which is a mental repetition [of the mantra] while the breath is stopped; (3) *Vajra repetition*, which is repetition [of the mantra] conjoined with inhalation and exhalation; (4) *whisper repetition*, which is repeating [the mantra] with merely the movement of the lips and tongue; and (5) the *repetition that resembles reciting the Vedas*, which is repeating [the mantra] with syllables that are half their length and in a very secret voice.

C′ The manner of repeating the mantra

Concerning mantras in general, Atiśa has said:

> The bodhicitta that is an inseparability of method and wisdom is the essence of the deity.[1156] It is [called] *essence*, because it invokes that [bodhi]citta. It is [called] *quintessential*, because it strongly invokes [that bodhicitta]. It is [called] *mantra* because it protects (*trai*) from a worldly mind (*manas*). It is [called] *vidyā mantra* because it develops special wisdom through repeated invocation. It is [called] *dhāraṇī mantra* because it develops the memory (*dhāraṇa*) that never forgets the bodhicitta.[1157]

Vajragarbha's commentary [to the *Hevajra Tantra*] teaches that the root mantra is the body [of the deity], the essence [mantra] is the speech, the quintessential [mantra] is the mind, and the seed syllable is wisdom:

> The root mantra is the nature of the body.
> The essence mantra is the nature of the speech.
> The quintessence [mantra] is the mind.
> The mind mantra is called the essence.
> *Wisdom* is the name for the seed [syllable]
> that is taught to be the wisdom mantra.[1158]

The order of the mantra repetitions

[375] It is taught many times in the sādhanas that the mantra repetitions should be done in the order of essence, quintessence, and root mantras. The practice instructions teach that the essence or quintessence mantras are the principal mantra repetition and that the other mantras are repeated to the extent that you have time to do so.

Vajragarbha's commentary [to the *Hevajra Tantra*] teaches that the sequence of mantra repetitions is seed[-syllable mantra], quintessence [mantra], essence [mantra], and root mantra. For it states:

> The seed, the quintessence,
> the essence, and the root mantras
> are taught to be the repetition and meditation of
> wisdom, mind, speech, and body, in that order.[1159]

Some say that as the body is the most evident, it is easier to invoke, while the speech and mind are increasingly subtle, so that you must begin by repeating the root mantra and then proceed to the essence and then the quintessence mantras, but this is nonsense.

The colors and so on of the mantras are taught in relation to categories of activity, but in the beginning, during sevā practice, there is no need to change the color of the deity and mantra. However, some say the mantras should be red in order to bring the deity under your power. According to Subhagavajra:

> The methods of mantra repetition:
> like a whirling torch,
> like a hurled hand-tethered spear,
> like a bunch of feathers,
> like a woven cord,
> like links of a chain—
> which one is to be used should be known from the context.[1160]

The gurus have taught that the appearance of the mantra's syllables and light rays can be like a whirling torch for the peaceful [practices], like a hurled hand-tethered spear for the wrathful [practices], like a bunch of feathers for the increasing [practices], and like a woven cord or a chain of metal links for the controlling [practices].

Many mahāsiddhas have taught that while you repeat the mantra, you imagine that all the principal deity's faces and all of the retinue are also reciting it.

While repeating the mantra also avoid all faults of mantra repetition. From [the *Tantra Requested by*] *Subāhu*:

> Your reciting and repeating should be neither too slow nor too fast,
> neither too loud nor too quiet,
> the words should not have the four vowels or the *anusvāra* omitted,
> and it should not be done while talking or distracted by something else.[1161]

According to Śrīphalavajra:

> "Clearly" means with all four vowels complete, without any omission, neither too long nor too slow, and undistorted by inhalation or exhalation. Clarity does not mean a loud sound made strongly and forcefully.[1162]

D' The benefits and so on of repeating the mantra

Mantra repetition purifies all the afflictions, [376] which are what you wish to eliminate, and brings under your power the entire accumulation of good qualities, which is what you wish to accomplish. From the *Vajra Pinnacle*:

> Why are they called *mantras*?
> It's because the mantras call out to everything,
> defeat the snares of the afflictions,
> and bring all the qualities of buddhahood.[1163]

Mantra repetition also successfully invites the buddhas and accomplishes the supreme and general siddhis. From the *Vajra Tent*:

> In order to make the ḍākinī
> and your own lady come to you,
> make the mantras within their hearing.
>
> It is like when you use your voice
> to call out loudly to certain people
> so that they come to you.
> In the same way, all the tathāgatas will come to you.[1164]

From Vajragarbha's commentary [to the *Hevajra Tantra*]:

> All deities will be accomplished through the mantra.
> Whomever the mantrika practices well
> they will grant the supreme [siddhi].[1165]

Some give various description of signs, numbers, and lengths of times for sevā practices at this point. However, I have already explained sevā's numbers and periods of time in [the teaching on] the preliminaries for accomplishing all activities, the empowerments, becoming an ācārya that can give consecration, and so on.

There are a variety of teachings on the numbers of mantras required for the practices of each activity. However, you need to continue mantra repetition until you have accomplished the siddhis, so therefore there are no definitive numbers for the mantras. From Vajragarbha's commentary [to the *Hevajra Tantra*]:

> Until the siddhis are given,
> diligently make offerings and repeat [the mantra].
> Otherwise, the mantra's siddhi
> will not arise in an inferior practice.[1166]

(3) The intersession yogas

This is in two parts:

(a) Concluding a session with torma offering and prayers of aspiration
(b) Teachings on other yogas

(a) Concluding a session with torma offering and prayers of aspiration

It is taught that a yogin who is dedicated to the generation stage trains in four sessions. According to Jālandhara, the four sessions are:

> The stages of "blessings in four sessions" are these periods of meditation: dawn, noon, afternoon, and night.[1167]

Concluding a session

When ordinary life ends and the stages of death come to a conclusion, there will first be the luminosity of death followed by reappearance in the bardo as a mental body, which is nothing but mind and wind.

Corresponding to that [at the end of a session], the world and its inhabitants, the residence and residents, dissolve into you. Then you dissolve into luminosity and [377] reappear from luminosity as the body of the deity, which is like an illusion. According to Ghaṇṭa:

> The light of the seed [syllable] causes the lord of wisdom,
> the mandala deities, and the multistoried palace
> to appear, become light, and dissolve in stages.[1168]

Making torma offerings

According to the *Latter Definition Tantra*:

> According to the stages of this practice,
> make offerings in the four intersession periods.[1169]

This teaches that you make offerings in the four intersession periods. Abhayākara and many others have taught that you make the offerings to the mandala deities and to spirits such as the direction guardians.

There are differing teachings on this, such as offering tormas to mundane torma guests after they have transformed into the mandala deities or offering the tormas to them without their transforming [into mandala deities].

The purpose [of offering tormas]

[Offering tormas] removes all obstacles and brings the swift accomplishment of all activities. From the *Saṃvarodaya Tantra*:

> If there is no intoxicating offering cake,[1170]
> the activities will not be accomplished quickly.
> That is why the previous buddhas
> have perfectly praised the offering cake.[1171]

From *Yoginī's Activity*:

> Make offerings for the activity you desire
> and in particular offer an offering cake.[1172]

According to Durjayacandra:

> Continually offer an offering cake
> in order to remove all obstacles.[1173]

The prayer of aspiration

Dedicate the good karma from meditation, repetition, and so on to be causes of enlightenment. In that way, they will not be wasted, and you will have planted seeds for temporary and ultimate results. From a sutra:

> When a drop of water has fallen into a great ocean,
> it will not cease to exist for as long as the ocean exists.
> In that same way, good karma that is completely dedicated to
> enlightenment
> will not cease for as long as enlightenment does not cease.[1174]

(b) Teachings on other yogas

The yoga of conduct

Rely upon the continuous mindfulness of visualizing yourself as the deity, and practice a conduct free of any misconduct. From the *Hevajra Tantra*:

> Completely absorbed in the yoga of Nairātmyā
> or otherwise in the yoga of the glorious Heruka,
> one who wishes for siddhi will not remain
> even for an instant in any other thought.[1175]

According to Jñānapāda:

> Throughout all your conduct
> never lose the samādhi of [being] the deity.[1176]

Practicing in that way, every movement of your body and every word you speak will be mudrās and mantras. From *Yoginī's Activity*:

> Remaining on the level of the glorious Heruka, [378]
> the entire range of the movement
> of your limbs and all your words
> will be mudrās and mantras.[1177]

From the *Samantabhadra Sādhana*:

> Continually actualize perfectly resting in meditation.
> The perfect Buddha has taught that
> for those who attain that state of mind,
> all their actions of body, speech, and mind
> will be in the form of mudrās and mantras.[1178]

The yoga of eating

From the *Four Seats Tantra*:

> The yogin who dedicates before
> consuming [even] a little food or drink,

that yogin who performs such conduct
will never fall into debt.[1179]

THE WAY THE DEDICATION [OF FOOD] IS MADE

Bless the drink and food as nectar. Visualize yourself as the deity and consume it as an offering to the deity. According to Jñānapāda:

Those who, even when eating,
have a body that is the mandala of the deities
just as in their meditation
and who bless their food as nectar
will have satisfaction in a state of inseparability through eating.[1180]

Alternatively, you consume [food] as an internal fire offering. According to Ḍombipa:

Then the yogins should imagine
that a *raṃ* syllable in the place of water
transforms into a blazing pit shining with light.
Imagine that within it, a *paṃ* transforms into an eight-petalled lotus
upon which is the mandala of the deity.
Imagine that your mouth is a hearth pit
and perfectly meditate that your two hands are *hūṃs*
that transform into vajra ladles.[1181]

THE YOGA OF SLEEPING

Go to sleep within the luminosity and emptiness of the gradual dissolution of the environment and its inhabitants. Alternatively, go to sleep in the state of innate joy from the bliss of melting, which is inseparable from the emptiness of luminosity. According to Ghaṇṭapa, after the entire world and its inhabitants dissolve into the *hūṃ*:[1182]

Then they dissolve into the *hūṃ* and its sun disc in the heart:
the sun [dissolves] into the *ū*, [which dissolves] into the *ha*'s head,
  [which dissolves] into the crescent,
[which dissolves] into the circle, [which dissolves] into the *nāda*,
which enters into the state of objectlessness.[1183]

According to Jñānapāda:

> Thus, even when sleeping,
> the samādhi of great Vajradhara
> causes desire to follow great desire:
> The fire of wisdom melts the body,
> and all phenomena become and remain mind.[1184]

THE YOGA OF WAKING UP

The invocatory song of the four goddesses causes you to emerge as the body of the deity. According to Jñānapāda:

> Also, even when waking up,
> the invocation by the four immeasurables
> causes you to remember your previous prayers,
> and through illusion-like yoga,
> the samādhis successively awaken.[1185] [379]

Some [texts] teach that you should imagine you are being awakened by the music of the ḍākas and yoginīs and that you arise as the deity.

b) The description of the completion stage

This is in three parts:

i) The categories of the completion stage
ii) A summary of the key points
iii) The stages of meditation

i) The categories of the completion stage

This is in two parts:

(A) The completion stage of the father tantras
(B) The completion stage of the mother tantras

(A) The completion stage of the father tantras

The *Guhyasamāja Root Tantra* teaches a completion stage in six stages:

The body, on being focused upon the mantra,
invokes the speech and the mind,
so that there is the supreme siddhi that is to be accomplished
and the mind has true joy and beauty.[1186]

That is said to be a teaching on the six stages: physical solitude, vocal solitude, mental solitude, the illusory body, luminosity, and union. [Āryadeva's] *Lamp of the Compendium of Practices* also teaches these six stages. Nāgārjuna taught five stages in his *Five Stages*: (1) the stage of *vajra repetition*, or *vocal solitude*; (2) the stage of *focusing on the mind*, or *mental solitude*; (3) the stage of *self-blessing*, or the *illusory body of relative truth*; (4) the stage of *true enlightenment*, or the *luminosity of the ultimate truth*; (5) the stage of *nondual wisdom*, or the *union of the two truths*. It is explained that *physical solitude* is included within the generation stage or in vajra repetition. From the *Five Stages*:

The nature of the winds, in stages, truly enters the nature of the mantra.
Understand the focus of the mantra, and train in the vajra repetitions.
The yogin who remains within the vajra repetitions will attain the focus of the mind.
Remaining in the illusion-like samādhi, train completely in the true extreme.
Arising from the true limit, you will attain nondual wisdom.
Remaining in the samādhi of union, there will be no training in anything else.[1187]

From the *Latter Tantra of the Guhyasamāja*:

Withdrawal and dhyāna,
prāṇa and concentration,
mindfulness and samādhi,
these are called the *six branches of yoga*.[1188]

The branches of withdrawal, dhyāna, prāṇa, concentration, mindfulness, and samādhi are the six branches of the completion stage. *Illuminating Lamp* also explains them in that way. [380] They have the same name as the six branches found in other tantras but differ in terms of their key features. There are various ways of including them into the five stages.

Ācārya [Buddha]jñānapāda primarily taught the completion stage as profound, clear, nondual wisdom. From the *Tilaka of Liberation*:

> Therefore, profound clear enlightenment
> brings liberation through the realization of nonduality.
> Realization is not gained through profundity alone,
> and the same is true concerning clarity.
>
> I have no faith in those who state
> that unimpeded profundity is liberation.
> Therefore, it is the realization of the nondual nature
> that brings certain attainment of the result in this life.[1189]

Profundity is explained to be the mind having entered the true nature, and clarity is the deity's body, the body of mahāmudrā. From *Tilaka of Liberation*:

> It is free from all conceptualization,
> beyond all thoughts and words,
> like space, the source of all stainlessness,
> and is called the "unnamable profundity."
>
> Having the form of mahāmudrā,
> it is like an illusion, a rainbow.
> When we and others train in it,
> it is called "true clarity."[1190]

Nonduality is explained to be the simultaneous, and not alternating, accumulation of profundity and clarity. From *Oral Transmission*:

> Completely devoid of all thought,
> the immeasurable cause of perfection
> appears as mahāmudrā,
> which is the supreme nature of nonduality
> ripening oneself and others with its rays.[1191]

(B) The completion stage of the mother tantras

From *Ocean of Ḍākas*:

> Withdrawal and, similarly,
> dhyāna, prāṇāyāma, concentration,
> mindfulness, and samādhi
> are the six aspects of yoga's features.[1192]

The thousand-verse commentary to Cakrasaṃvara also gives this teaching on six yoga branches. There are also the six yogas of Cakrasaṃvara in the lineage of Ācārya Anupamarakṣita.[1193] From *Ocean of Ḍākas*:

> Their own bodies are the same as an illusion.
> This self-blessing is subtle.
> The vajra repetition has its own characteristics.
> There is "enlightenment," the treasure of the mind.
> Beyond that, there is union.[1194]

Thus, in this teaching of five stages, the five are self-blessing, vajra repetition, "enlightenment" (*abhisambodhi*), focusing on the mind, and union. [381] Mahāsiddha Lūyipa summarizes these into three: (1) meditating on the deity's body being like a rainbow is the process of self-blessing; (2) dissolving [the deity's body] through the meditation of subsequent dissolution is the process of true enlightenment (*abhisambodhi*); and (3) arising as the luminous body is the process of union.

Ghaṇṭa taught the following five levels: the self-blessing stage, the vajra-cross stage, the jewel-filled stage, the Jalandhara stage, and the inconceivable stage. The first four stages make the channels, winds, drops, and mind tractable. The last stage causes luminosity and arising in union. Kambala and Kṛṣṇapa's teaching on the completion stage is in agreement with this.

The *Hevajra Tantra* describes the Hevajra completion stage:

> The caṇḍālī blazes in the navel.[1195]

This teaches caṇḍālī yoga or drop yoga. Many siddhas teach only the caṇḍālī. From the *Vajra Tent*:

> Meditate that the ḍāka, the size of a mustard seed,
> is residing at the tip [of the channel].
> Within that mustard seed are all beings,
> all the animate and inanimate, in the three realms.
> Through meditating in that way
> you will perfectly accomplish self-blessing.[1196]

That teaches the "subtle yoga" or the "process of self-blessing." The Black Samayavajra also teaches this completion stage of the subtle drop.

Mahāsiddha Saroruha teaches the deity's body as the self-blessing of the channel-wind yoga, the subsequent dissolution [of the deity's body] as the process of entering luminosity, and the process of arising from that [luminosity] as the body of union.[1197]

Thus, it is taught in all mother tantra completion stages that the illusion-like world and inhabitants enter and arise from luminosity and accomplish union.

ii) A summary of the key points of the completion stage

The descriptions of the completion stage given in various tantras are for the purpose of accomplishing the "training union," which causes the accomplishment of the goal: the "nontraining union," which is the wisdom body.

The training union is accomplished through the process of the illusion-like deity's body entering into and arising from luminosity. This entry into and arising from [luminosity] must have the completion stages of both relative self-blessing and ultimate luminosity. [382] Those two completion stages are necessary for the accomplishment because they make the channels, winds, and drops tractable.

There are slightly differing ways of practicing these [completion stages]. The father tantras rely first upon the three "solitudes" in order to accomplish the union through the stages of illusory body and luminosity. The mother tantras rely first upon the yoga of channels, winds, and drops in order to accomplish union through the stages of connate bliss and emptiness.

Subdividing these categories results in many different ways of practice, so there is no one definitive form. Nevertheless, all the essential points of the completion stage are contained within these three: the relative completion stage of self-blessing, the ultimate completion stage of mahāmudrā luminosity, and the completion stage of the inseparable union of the two truths.

Therefore, I will teach here a definitive general description of the completion stages in the tantras.

iii) The stages of meditation in the completion stage

This is in three parts:

(A) The completion stage of self-blessing
(B) The completion stage of the luminosity of mahāmudrā
(C) The completion stage of inseparable union

(A) The completion stage of self-blessing

This is in two parts:

(1) The yoga of channels, winds, and drops
(2) The description of the illusory body

(1) The yoga of channels, winds, and drops

This is in two parts:

(a) The common yoga
(b) The caṇḍālī yoga

(a) The common yoga

In general, at the beginning of all completion stages, you need to make the channels, winds, and drops tractable. Father tantra practitioners meditate on: (1) *physical solitude*, which is meditation on the subtle [drop] at the lower door and generating the connate bliss of melting as a result of the winds entering and dissolving into the central channel; (2) *vocal solitude*, which is meditation on the prāṇa of the three drops being at the tips of the three [channels] and generating the four empties[1198] as a result of the dissolving of the winds; and (3) *mental solitude*, which is generating the four special empties as a result of dissolving the winds in the heart through external and internal methods. However, what I explain here will be in conformity with the approach of the mother tantras.

In order to effectively practice and realize the vajra body, your bodhicitta must be in a stable condition. Bringing your winds, which are mobile, under control stabilizes your bodhicitta. In order to do that, you must train in the channels, which are immobile. Therefore, meditate, in the correct sequence, on the channels, winds, and drops.

The channels (nāḍī)

[383] In general, there are seventy-two thousand [channels] in the body: twenty-four thousand for the flow of bodhicitta, twenty-four thousand for the flow of blood, and twenty-four thousand for the movement of wind. They are further subdivided into 3.5 million. From the *Vajra Garland Tantra*:

> I shall explain the nature of
> the permanent flow of the channels:
>
> Twenty-four thousand
> are known as the descent of the bodhicitta.
> They perfectly increase all bliss.
> These are constantly marvelous channels.
>
> Twenty-four thousand
> are known as the descent of the blood.
> They have the nature of the shining sun.
> These are constantly marvelous channels.
>
> Twenty-four thousand
> are known as the movement of the winds.[1199]

From Vajragarbha's commentary [to the *Hevajra Tantra*]:

> They are seventy-two thousand [in number].
> There is the same number of goddesses in the body.
> The number of pores means that
> there are three and a half million,
> which is established from the number of body hairs.[1200]

The main channels are the hundred and twenty channel "petals" that come from the four cakras. The most important among them are the twenty-four [channels] at the twenty-four sites, such as the crown of the head. The most important of all [channels] are the three channels. From the *Saṃvarodaya Tantra*:

> A hundred plus twenty
> are said to be the main channels.
> The places and sites of the channels
> are said to number twenty-four.
> In their center are the three channels,
> which are connected to them and all-pervasive.[1201]

From the *Tantra of True Union*:

> The categories of the four cakras
> results in a hundred plus twenty [channels].[1202]

The three channels and four cakras are not only the principal channels but are also the bases of the four kāyas. From the *Saṃvarodaya Tantra*:

> The *lalanā* is wisdom as form.
> The *rasanā* exists through method.
> In between them resides the *devī*,
> the *aṃ* syllable, Viśvarūpiṇī,[1203]
> the *devī* that has the nature of the four kāyas,
> the one who bestows all the siddhis.[1204]

From the *Vajra Garland Tantra*:

> The supreme palaces of all deities,
> the bases of the dharma, saṃbhoga,
> nirmāṇa, and mahāsukha,
> are also called *the cakras*.[1205]

The winds (vāyu)

From the *Tantra Revealing the Hidden Meaning*:

> The [winds] are taught to be *life-force holding*, *downward expelling*, *upward moving*, [384] *pervading*, and *equally residing*.[1206]

Thus, there are the five root winds: the life-force wind (*prāṇa*), the downward-expelling wind, the upward-moving wind, the pervading wind, and the equalizing or "equal-heat" wind. There are also:

The nāga, the turtle, and the lizard,
Devadatta and Dhanujaya.[1207]

Thus, there are taught to be five branch winds: the nāga wind, the turtle wind, the lizard wind, the Devadatta wind, and the Dhanujaya[1208] wind.

The *Vajra Garland Tantra* teaches 108 winds, among which the most important is the life wind (*prāṇa*) that moves through the nose. From the *Vajra Garland Tantra*:

From the flow of the doorway of the nose,
the movement of life (*prāṇa*) and control (*āyāma*)
is constantly in movement,
and this is taught to be prāṇa.[1209]

From *Five Stages*:

That which is the life of all beings
and which is called *wind* performs all activity.
It is the steed of the consciousness
and has a fivefold and a tenfold nature.[1210]

This [wind] moves 21,600 times each day. In the *Mahāmudrā Tilaka Tantra*:

First, the number of exhalations
and inhalations are twenty-one thousand.
Counting in this way, there are six hundred
that definitely move within a day and night.[1211]

The meditation on wind

In the father tantras you principally practice vajra repetitions, but here you mainly meditate on pressing together the prāṇa and the downward[-expelling wind]. From the *Saṃvoradaya*:

The mind conjoins the wind that moves upward
with [the wind that moves] downward.
Familiarization with that yoga
brings attainment of the eternal state.[1212]

It is important not to be in error concerning the essential points of the four yogas. According to Nāropa:

> Inhalation, filling, squeezing,
> and firing like an arrow are the four aspects.
> If you do not know the four yogas,
> you risk your good qualities becoming faults.[1213]

The benefit of meditating on the winds and the harm of not meditating on them

From the *Vajra Garland Tantra*:

> If the yogins meditate on the winds,
> they will quickly attain the siddhis.[1214]

From the *Saṃvarodaya Tantra*:

> If you do not know the wind yoga,
> or if you know but do not meditate,
> you will be harmed by various sufferings
> and become an insect in samsara.[1215]

The drops (bindu)

In general, the white and red drops descend twenty-four thousand times each. In particular, they are taught to be the descent of bodhicitta through thirty-two channels. From the *Vajra Garland Tantra*:

> Twenty-four times a thousand:
> know these to be the descent of the bodhicitta.[1216]

From the *Hevajra Tantra*: [385]

> There are thirty-two channels. They are the thirty-two that convey bodhicitta.[1217]

As to which element descends through which channel, the *Tantra of True Union* says:

Abhedyā is in Pullīra
and is said to "descend into the teeth and nails."

Sūkṣmarūpinī, which is in Jālandhara,
similarly descends to the head hair and body hair.[1218]

The text continues in that way.

The channels of those drops

The power of the white element is present in the form of *haṃ* at the crown of the head inside the central channel. The power of the red element is present in the form of a "short *a*" at the navel. From the *Tantra of True Union*:

[The lotus that is present in the heart has four petals and a center.]
The channels, which are present within them, have the nature of a lamp flame.
They extend downward, like the flower of a plantain tree.
The ḍāka that is present within has the width of a mustard seed.
The seed that is the indestructible *hūṃ* drips like [melting] snow.
This heart joy of beings is taught to be "Spring."
Nairātmyā, who has the form of Vāḍabāgni,[1219] is called "the drop."
The karmic winds' exhortation causes it to blaze in the navel's mandala.[1220]

This meditation on the yoga of channels, winds, and drops makes the channels, winds, and drops tractable. One will then be able to perfectly dissolve the winds in the central channel and cause the bliss of melting. This definitely requires the ability to make the winds enter the central channel and activate a genuine bliss and heat.

Each of the four cakras have entrances for the wind to enter the central channel, but here I will explain how the wind enters the central channel as the result of mastering the *a-stroke* and the navel cakra.

When the wind correctly enters [the central channel], you pass through the following stages: The sign of earth dissolving appears, which is like clouds or a mirage. The sign of water dissolving appears, which is like smoke. The sign of fire dissolving appears, which is like fireflies. The sign of air dissolving appears, which is like lamp flames. The sign of consciousness dissolving appears, which is like a cloudless sky. From the *Vajra Tent*:

First, there is the appearance of clouds,
second, something like smoke,
third, the appearance of fireflies,
fourth, the burning of lamp flames,
fifth, a continuous radiance
that is like a cloudless sky.[1221]

From *Oral Transmission*:

Through becoming adept in holding,
there is the reversal of earth.

The appearance that is like a mirage
should be known as the first sign.

In the same way, through the reversal of water,
there is an appearance like smoke,
which should be known as the second [sign].

Through the complete reversal of fire,
there is the third [sign], which is like space.

When likewise the air reverses, [386]
there is an appearance like lamp flames,
which should be known as the fourth sign.

Similarly, through the reversal of consciousness
there is the profound clear nonduality
that is like a cloudless sky.
That clarity is the fifth sign.[1222]

(b) The caṇḍālī yoga

The mother tantra tradition teaches that self-blessing, mahāmudrā luminosity, and all inseparable unions are included within the caṇḍālī yoga. Therefore, even though caṇḍālī is not necessarily a part of the completion stage's self-blessing, I will teach it here in this section.

Meditate on the three channels and four cakras and imagine that there is a short *a* at the navel, a *hūṃ* at the heart, an *oṃ* at the throat, and an upside-down *haṃ* at the crown of the head.

The wind yoga causes the caṇḍālī to blaze. The heat causes the *haṃ* to melt. Meditate on the samādhi of bliss and emptiness that this causes. From the *Tantra of True Union*:

> In the navel, the form of an *a* that is known as "the short."
> In the heart, a *hūṃ* is the length of two measures.
> In the throat is the form of an *oṃ* that is extended to three measures.
> At the forehead is this form of *haṃ*, an indestructible sound and quintessence.
> It drips in the form of nectar and is perfectly present day and night.
> It creates sound and the fire creates joy.[1223]

Also from the *Tantra of True Union*:

> [This self-arisen essence
> is known as the dharmakāya.]
> Its wisdom is innate.
> Therefore, the Rupinī that is present
> through the exhortation of the karmic winds
> blazes in the navel mandala.[1224]

It is also taught that there are many syllables in the channel-cakras, such as the seed [syllables] of the five-family buddhas and the four consorts. From the *Hevajra Tantra*:

> The blazing caṇḍālī in the navel
> incinerates the five tathāgatas
> and also incinerates Locanā and the rest.
> When the *haṃ* is burned, the moon flows.[1225]

This meditation, as a result of the wind's correct entry, causes the union of the four joys and four empties to arise. That is the realization of caṇḍālī. According to Tilopa:

> The fire of caṇḍālī in the navel
> increases from being the faintest.

There is a flow of nectar from the *haṃ*, the succession of the four joys, and the four results, such as "correspondence with cause."[1226]

According to Nāropa:

Externally, there is the illusory body of the deity. [387]
Internally, there are the three channels and the four cakras.
Above, there is the form of the syllable *haṃ*.
Below, there is the *a*-stroke—the caṇḍālī.
Above and below are the wheels of wind.
In between, the practice of the vase prāṇāyāma
causes the experience of bliss, emptiness, and clarity.
The name for this is the *caṇḍālī instructions*.[1227]

The four joys according to the *Hevajra Tantra*:

Through *joy* there is some bliss.
Supreme joy is greater than that.
Through *cessation* there will be no passion.
That which remains is *innate joy*.[1228]

THE WAY IN WHICH THE [JOYS] ARISE

The four joys of descending occur as a result of the melted bodhicitta descending through the four cakras, starting with the crown of the head. From the *Vajra Garland Tantra*:

It is taught that *joy* is that which is in
the great bliss cakra at the crown of the head.
Supreme joy is in the saṃbhoga cakra.
Cessation of joy dwells in the dharma cakra.
Innate joy is in the nirmāṇa cakra.
They cause the experience of the joys.[1229]

From the *Tantra of Great Bliss*:

Joy is the descent of semen
from the crown to between the eyebrows and to the throat.

Supreme joy [is the descent] from the throat to the heart.
Then there is cessation of joy.
Manifold pleasure is [the descent] from the navel
until the secret lotus is reached.
For as long as [the semen] is not ejaculated
from the tip of the secret jewel, there is innate joy.[1230]

The four ascending joys arise when the bodhicitta is stabilized and then is drawn backward from the jewel through the four locations, starting with the navel. From the *Vajra Garland*:

Joy is in the nirmāṇa cakra.
Supreme joy resides in the dharma cakra.
Cessation is in the saṃbogha.
Innate [joy] in the great bliss.
Those are taught to be the stages of reversal.[1231]

From among those four joys, the true realization of caṇḍālī is the wisdom of the inseparability of innate joy and luminosity.

There are the two innate [joys]: the symbolic innate [joy], which has a subtle duality of subject and object, and the true innate [joy], which has the nonduality of subject and object.

You have to learn the details [of caṇḍālī] through receiving practice instructions from your guru. From the *Hevajra Tantra*:

Nothing else can describe the innate [joy].
It cannot be found in anything [else].
It is known by yourself through [your own] merit
and through relying upon your time with the guru.[1232]

(2) The description of the illusory body

[388] This is in two parts:

(a) The actual instructions for the illusory body
(b) The instructions for ancillaries to the illusory body

(a) The actual instructions for the illusory body

Meditation on the stage of self-blessing of the illusory body is greatly praised. From the *Ocean of Ḍākas*:

> A yogin who has no self-blessing
> is like a piece of chaff.
> The herds of ordinary beings
> do not know those supreme qualities.
> Therefore, you will attain supreme enlightenment
> if you meditate on this illusion.[1233]

From *Five Stages*:

> Those who have not attained
> the stage of self-blessing
> will merely tire themselves meaninglessly
> with sutras, tantras, and conceptualization.
>
> O lord, who has the nature of all the buddhas!
> Those who have attained the level of self-blessing
> will attain, without any doubt,
> buddhahood within their lifetime.[1234]

Although the illusory body that has to be accomplished is the secret illusory body, first you must meditate on the general illusory body, which is called the *illusion-like samādhi*. From *Five Stages*:

> Afflictions and karma are the body of the path.
> The doer and the result
> are like mirages and dreams.
> They are exactly the same as a gandharva city.
>
> If you do not know this samādhi
> you will focus upon the relative,
> and various kinds of illness will occur.
> They are healed by the medicine of illusion.[1235]

First, you must train in [seeing] the entire outer environment of the world, the beings that inhabit it, and all other objects and appearances as being like illusions. According to Tilopa:

> In all your activity, whether sitting still or moving,
> train in [seeing] the worlds and beings throughout the three realms
> [as being like] the examples of dreams and illusions.[1236]

You have to meditate with certainty using all the examples of illusion, such as reflections in a mirror. From the *Vajradāka Tantra*:

> The one who sees [all] as being the same as
> reflections in a mirror, dreams,
> illusions, a gandharva city, or optical illusions,
> that one is called a *lord*.[1237]

The *impure illusory body* is the meditation on your own and others' bodies as being like reflections, your speech like echoes, and your minds like mirages. From the *Saṃvarodaya Tantra*:

> Beings are seen as [reflections of] the moon on water.
> What is heard is truly perceived as identical to echoes.
> Even the mind should be seen as the same as a desert mirage.[1238]

Thus, the *general illusory body* means that all the phenomena of samsara and nirvana have no nature of their own and yet they appear, because they have the form of illusions.[389] From the *Hevajra Tantra*:

> That is the nature of all things
> and is present as illusory form.[1239]

From the *Vajradāka Tantra*:

> All the beings of the three realms,
> without exception, are like illusions.
> Both stationary and moving beings
> have no existence as perceivable objects.
> The things that are seen and touched
> are all like illusions.[1240]

Thus, the *pure illusory body* is meditation on the residence and residents of the wisdom mandala, which are exemplified by the twelve examples of illusions. That is the special illusory body. From *Five Stages*:

> It is the same as the clear appearance of
> the reflection of an excellent painting of Vajrasattva
> in a spotless mirror.
> It has the best of all aspects, and
> it is a body that one never tires of gazing at—
> an excellent pupil relies upon it.
> This is what is taught to be "self-blessing."
> By its characteristics, which demonstrate illusion,
> this acts as a definitive example,
> [showing that] relative truth is an illusion.[1241]

According to Tilopa:

> The deities are an illusion, [like] reflections in a mirror,
> the same as the clear reflection [in a mirror]
> of an excellent painting of Vajrasattva.
> The one who sees that as an illusory form,
> in accord with the twelve examples of illusion,
> sees the meaning of the illusion yoga.[1242]

Here is the way that this [reflection of Vajrasattva] is the same as the twelve examples of illusions:

1. It is like an illusory person, because although it has no true existence, the limbs, the principal physical parts, and so on are complete.
2. It is like a moon on water, because just one can pervade everywhere.
3. It is like an optical illusion, because it has no material existence.
4. It is like a mirage, because it is unstable with each moment.
5. It is like a dream, because it is created by the mind.
6. It is like an echo, because it arises from causes and conditions.
7. It is like a gandharva city, because there is no certainty to its appearance.
8. It is like clouds or illusions, because one appears as many.
9. It is like a rainbow, because it is [both] vivid and immaterial.
10. It is like lightning, because it is impermanent and swift.
11. It is like water bubbles, because it instantly appears.

12. It is like a reflection in a mirror, because it is an appearance without a nature of its own.

The dissolving of winds into the central channel brings out the three or the four empties. At the culmination of this "attainment" or "luminosity," there instantaneously appears a deity's body formed from wind and mind alone. This is what is called the *secret illusory body*. That is the genuine illusory body. From *Five Stages*: [390]

> Truly possessing the winds,
> the three consciousnesses
> reappear as the body of the yogin.
> That is taught to be the illusory body.[1243]

From the *Summarized Five Stages*:

> The illusory body that has appearance,
> arises from mind and wind alone.[1244]

The gurus have taught that the true illusory body is the deity's body (which is just wind and mind) arising from "the special empty," which is the dissolving of the wind in the heart, while the facsimile of the illusory body is the appearance of the deity (which is again just wind and mind) arising from "the empty," which is merely the wind dissolving wherever it is. This is exemplified by the twelve examples of illusion in the same way as before. According to Nāgārjuna:

> Through reflections in a mirror,
> know the illusory body.
> [Its] colors are like a rainbow,
> and its pervasion is like a moon's [reflection] on water.[1245]

That is a teaching that uses three examples: (1) The instantaneous complete body is like a reflection in a mirror. (2) The clarity and distinctness of the colors are like a rainbow. (3) The complete pervasion by a single thing is like a moon's [reflection] on water.

(b) The instructions for ancillaries to the illusory body

This is in two parts:

(i) The instructions on sleep and dreams
(ii) The instructions on bardo and transference

(i) The instructions on sleep and dreams

From the *Summarized Five Stages*:

> Because of the wind of the caṇḍālī yoga,
> the mind's object of focus becomes great bliss.
> Train in dream and illusion as one.
> Blend the three bardos.
> Transform the afflictions into the path of wisdom.
> Transference is that which gains the swift path.
> And *purapraveśa* is its ancillary.[1246]

Based upon this, gurus have taught dream, bardo, transference, and *purapraveśa* to be the four ancillaries to the illusory body. However, that is not what is meant by this text. It does not seem to be the case that Nāgārjuna and his pupils taught transference and *purapraveśa* as ancillaries to the illusory body. However, Tilopa and Nāropa did teach those four to be ancillaries to the illusory body.

From the *Instruction Through Similes* [on the six Dharmas of Nāropa]:

> The meditation on the illusory body
> has the two [aspects] of training and beyond training.
> The training has two aspects:
> the stage of "true comprehension" and
> "the consecration of oneself."[1247]

That teaching on the illusory body practice itself is followed [in that text] by:

> "The consecration of oneself"
> has these four aspects: transference,
> *purapraveśa*, dreams, and bardo.[1248]

The dream instructions are preceded by the instructions for sleep. [391]

Having mastered the sequence of four empties in falling asleep, luminosity arises as the path. While the yogins are awake, they manifest the four empties of the winds dissolving into the central channel. As a result, when they go to sleep the wind dissolves [into the central channel]. This causes the definite sequence of space filled with moonlight, which is *appearance*, space filled with sunlight, which is *increase*, and space filled with complete darkness, which is *attainment*. When that concludes, there arises *luminosity*, which is like a sky free of the three polluting factors. Recognize it and rest in equanimity.

It is taught that those who are unable to attain this through the power of wind (*vāyu*) may be able to do so through the power of aspiration, but then it will be difficult [for them] to definitively master the sequence of the four empties.

If you can adopt *deep sleep without appearances* as the path, there will be the special luminosity of sleep. When that state of no appearances ceases, and there are both obvious and subtle appearances, that is called the *attenuated luminosity*, which is merely the simple luminosity of sleep and not the actual luminosity of the four empties. According to Nāropa:

> At the border between sleep and dreams
> are two strong factors contrary to dreaming:
> dullness that has the nature of the dharmakāya
> and the experience of unelaborated, empty luminosity.
>
> Subsequently, whatever appears arises as bliss.
> That natural, uncontrived nature
> is given the name the *teaching of luminosity*.[1249]

From *Instructions through Similes*:

> The aggregates and so on enter the subtle element.
> The element enters the subtle mind.
> The mind enters into ignorance and thus goes to sleep.
> Afterward, it is luminosity, which is the nature of wisdom.[1250]

Some say that when those with the samādhi of mental stability sleep, they have the luminosity of deep sleep, and when they are neither awake nor dreaming, that is the attenuated luminosity of the arising of clear appearances.

However, those are not the true luminosity of sleep. The first is explained to be the common simple luminosity and the second is the luminosity of experience.

The actual instructions for dreams

The arising of the various appearances of dreams are adopted as the path. When yogins begin to arise from the luminosity of sleep into dreams, they instantaneously arise as the illusory body, as previously explained. If they are unable to do that, they should become aware that dreams are dreams, train in seeing the appearances of dreams as illusions, train in mastering dreams, [392] become habituated to the path of familiarization, and develop a pure realm to which they will ascend.

From the *First and Second Instructions through Similes*:

> There are five aspects to dreams.
> Know that they are mindfulness,
> knowledge of illusion, training,
> habituation to familiarization, and upward transference.[1251]

Mindfulness of dreams and so on are the methods for training in seeing the body as an illusory body. The main part of the dream practice is to become familiarized with that illusory body. In particular, the central dream practice is training in appearing from the luminosity of sleep as the illusory body of a dream.

The training in realms—in which you create the world where you will achieve buddhahood—is an ancillary.

The purpose of the sleep and dream instructions

They are very effective on the path, because the practices of dissolving into luminosity and arising as an illusory body, whether awake or asleep, are mutually beneficial.

It's taught that if you meditate in sleep and dreams, which is far more subtle than meditation while you are awake, it will enable you to master the arising of the illusory body of the bardo from the luminosity of death. From *Instructions through Similes*:

> Dreams are truly illusions.
> If you do not know them to be illusions
> [and therefore don't know the bardo to be an illusion],[1252]

> you will not be able to prevent rebirth from the bardo
> and so will take birth again and again
> and be a wanderer in the three realms of samsara.[1253]

(ii) The instructions on bardo and transference

The bardo instructions are the adoption of the bardo as the path by those who have trained while both awake and asleep in absorption into luminosity and arising as the illusory body. According to Nāropa:

> You must blend the experience
> of dream with the bardo mind.
> This key point of blending and transference in dream and bardo
> is given the name *bardo instructions*.[1254]

The best individual

They are those who are able to master the bardo. They have attained every realization of the two stages, developed true luminosity, and are close to the attainment of the illusory body. For them the luminosity of death arises as the true luminosity. Otherwise, instead of arising in the bardo, they arise as the training [stage's] union body, and through absorption into and arising from luminosity, they manifest, upon that very basis, the nontraining union. From *Instructions through Similes*:

> Appearances dissolve and thoughts dissolve.
> The evident dissolve and the subtle dissolve.
> After the dissolving, there arises
> the habituated and the natural luminosity.
>
> After that there is both the training
> and the nontraining union body.
> It is taught that the result is attained
> just through becoming the nontraining [union body].[1255] [393]

The medium individual

They have reached the conclusion of the generation stage, gained the experience of the completion stage, and have trained, while both awake and asleep, in arising as an illusory deity-body from the luminosity that was created by the four empties. Such individuals rest in equanimity for as long as they can within the luminosity of death. When the bardo appears, they appear as an illusion-like deity and practice absorption into the analogous luminosity, arising from that as an illusory body. They prevent the [bardo] existence of forty-nine days, complete every level and path, transfer to a pure realm, and so on, and attain supreme accomplishment on that very basis. From *Instructions through Similes*:

> Alternatively, first of all remember
> whatever meditation you previously trained in.
> When you remember it at the right time,
> the first "becoming" will be prevented.
>
> Afterward, if you habituate yourself with the above
> during the period of seven weeks,
> then those forty-nine days will pass
> and "becoming in samsara" will be prevented.
>
> Thus, reside in illusion
> and train in luminosity,
> and you will enter luminosity.[1256]

THE LEAST INDIVIDUAL

They have received the empowerment, kept the commitments, been diligent in the two stages, and have experience in the instructions of illusory body and dreams. Such individuals master the bardo, bring illusory appearances into the path, meditate on the deity, close the doorways to impure rebirths, choose a womb, take rebirth, and before long will gain the supreme accomplishment. From *Instructions through Similes*:

> They have the bodily form from their previous existence.
> They have all their [sense] faculties and are unimpeded.[1257]
> They have the karmic power of miracles.
> They have the divine sight that sees others of the same kind.[1258]
>
> Those bardo beings will see
> the sight of method and wisdom.
>
> They should visualize the gurus,
> remember the secret empowerment,

avoid all jealousy and anger,
and meditate on bliss or nonthought.[1259]

THE INSTRUCTIONS ON TRANSFERENCE

Instructions through Similes teaches that there are three transferences:

The process of the stage of generation,
the true illusory [body], and luminosity.[1260]

The best is transference into luminosity; the medium is transference as the illusory body; and the least is transference in the generation stage. The first two are absorption into the luminosity of death and arising as the illusory body of the bardo, which is here merely given the name "transference."

THE TRANSFERENCE OF THE GENERATION STAGE

From *Instructions through Similes*: [394]

Seal the apertures
with the syllables *kṣuṃ* and so on.
Meditate that your own mind
is the body of the deity, like a rainbow.

Alternatively, you dissolve into a *hūṃ*
and practice, repeatedly, without pause,
that it exits through the Brahma aperture
and goes to Akaniṣṭha.[1261]

According to Nāropa:

Eight doorways are the exits to samsara.
One doorway is the door to mahāmudrā.
Close the eight doors and open the one door.
The arrow of the mind is on the bow of the breath
and is propelled by the bowstring of *hik* and *ka*
in order to hit the *haṃ* in the center of the head
and transcend the nature of consciousness.
That is called the instructions on transference.[1262]

The gurus have taught three transferences: (1) transference through training, (2) transference through a forceful method, and (3) transference through an arrangement of the body.

THE PURPOSE OF TRANSFERENCE

From the *Four Seats Tantra*:

> This path purifies one even of
> killing a brahman every day,
> committing the five limitless bad actions,
> stealing, and committing sexual misconduct.
> so that you will be unstained by bad karma
> and will leave the faults of existence far behind.[1263]

It is taught that the best [individual] will go to the pure realms or paradises and will there complete all the superior paths and attain the supreme [siddhi]. The medium [individual] will be reborn as a basis for the Mantrayāna conduct and after a certain number of lifetimes will attain the supreme [siddhi]. The least [individual] will be reborn in the higher realms, enter the path, and will eventually attain purity.

The instructions on *purapraveśa*, the ancillary to transference, from *Instructions through Similes*:

> There is the *purapraveśa*:
> Visualize your object [for *purapraveśa*] in front of you.
> Focus without distraction on your breath and mind
> so that your awareness becomes clearer.
> Familiarize yourself with that over a long time,
> and then abandon your body,
> acquire a meritorious body,
> and accomplish every benefit for beings.[1264]

According to Nāropa:

> When your own body can no longer be [used] for methods,
> then the suitable body of another becomes your object for a base.
> In between [you and it] are the syllable and the wind (*vāyu*) as a steed.

Through the circle of interdependent wind,
abandon your own body like an empty house
and [enter] the other body as a nirmāṇakāya.
That is called the instructions for *purapraveśa*.[1265]

THE PURPOSE OF PURAPRAVEŚA

It is taught that when you no longer have the ability to accomplish the two benefits with your own body as a base, you should enter the excellent body of another so as to be able to accomplish those benefits.

(B) The completion stage of the luminosity of mahāmudrā

[395] This is in two parts:

(1) The categories of meditation on luminosity
(2) The method of meditation on luminosity

(1) The categories of meditation on luminosity

The tantras contain many praises of innate luminosity. In particular, it is taught that it is the very nature of all Dharma teachings such as mantras and deities. From the *Hevajra Tantra*:

The mantra and deity reside
in the nonelaborate nature.[1266]

Also from the *Hevajra Tantra*:

It is the mantra repetition, the austerities, and the homa fire ritual offerings.
It is the mandala deities and the mandala.[1267]

All sutras and tantras were taught so that [beings] could unite with this realization. From *Five Stages*:

That which is taught
in the various sutras and tantras—
it is all this emptiness;
nothing else is taught.[1268]

If you attain that, you attain irreversibility, and will have the supreme attainment in this lifetime. From *Five Stages*:

> Perfectly attaining true enlightenment,
> you will realize the pure realm.
> In this lifetime of irreversibility,
> you will become omniscient in a buddha realm.[1269]

Generally speaking, luminosity is comprised of three luminosities: those of basis, path, and result.

Basis luminosity is the luminosity of the true nature, the luminosity of sleep, and the luminosity of death. These definitely arise to everyone, whether they meditate on the path or not and whether they recognize them or not.

Path luminosity is comprised of:

- General luminosity: This is the view that realizes phenomena as birthless emptiness.
- Secret luminosity: This is the luminosity of the "fourth empty" resulting from the dissolving of the winds into the central channel, or it is the luminosity that is recognized within the experience of the innate [joy] from among the four joys.

In the latter, there is:

- Analogous luminosity: The innate [joy] or "fourth empty" that [still] has the duality of subject and object.
- The true luminosity: The innate [joy] or "fourth empty" that has no duality of subject and object.
- The ultimate luminosity: The manifestation of the nonconceptual wisdom that realizes the true nature; this wisdom is like a stainless sky and is without even the subtlest duality.
- Result luminosity: The luminosity of the "nontraining union."

Secret luminosity is the luminosity that you have to accomplish but must be preceded by general luminosity. [396] From the [*Latter*] *Definition Tantra*:

> Phenomena, which have the nature of selflessness,
> are as stainless as space.
> Meditate continuously upon vajra emptiness,
> which is as stainless as space.[1270]

From the *Bodhicitta Commentary*:

> Those who do not know emptiness
> are not bases for liberation.
> Those ignorant ones will circle through
> the dungeons of the six classes of existence.[1271]

The practitioners of the mother tantras make the channels, winds, and drops tractable and then meditate on the wisdom of the four joys through dissolving the winds and in particular through innate wisdom. This is taught to be the mahāmudrā luminosity's completion stage. From the *Saṃvarodaya Tantra*:

> The complete enlightenment of great bliss
> is thus the supreme mahāmudrā.[1272]

From the *Accomplishment of the Secret*:

> The innate self-knowing knowledge,
> the mahāmudrā, the supreme good,
> is present in dependence on the ordinary body;
> those with little wisdom do not see it.[1273]

The four joys from dissolving the wind are the four empties. From the *Mahāmudrā Tilaka Tantra*:

> Those joys are taught to be *appearance*
> and the supreme *increase* of appearance.
> The "special joy" is known as *attainment*,
> and the innate [joy] is *luminosity*.[1274]

Therefore, through bringing out the innate [joy], the winds dissolve and luminosity naturally appears. From *Accomplishment of the True Nature*:

> You are liberated from the accumulation of thoughts through the innate winds remaining in their own location. Every kind of satisfaction arises through the power of the nature of emptiness.[1275]

When you bring out the innate [joy], the world and its beings are absorbed, in stages, into luminosity. From *Special Illumination*:

> The caṇḍālī's blazing causes the moon at the crown to melt. It successively fills the cakras so that there are the specific categories of joy and so on, culminating in the innate joy and the elimination of all thoughts. Thus, there comes the time when you do not contemplate the mandala but gradually absorb it into emptiness.[1276]

(2) The method of meditation on luminosity

The noble teachers and their pupils have taught that in order to meditate on luminosity you must have accomplished the illusory body. It is absolutely necessary to have the experience of the winds entering the central channel, remaining in [the central channel], and dissolving into the central channel. Nothing else other than that can bring out the true, secret luminosity.

There are many methods for meditation on luminosity, but all mahāsiddha texts teach the method of entering luminosity by dissolving the world and its inhabitants through either of two meditations. [397] These are described in *Five Stages*:

> The pupil who has received the instructions
> trains in two yogas:
> The stage of total eclipse
> and the stage of subsequent dissolution.[1277]

Thus there are the two dhyānas: *total eclipse* and *subsequent dissolution*.

Total eclipse: Meditate that you are the illusion-like body of the deity as a tier of the three deities. Light from the samādhi being causes the body to gradually dissolve, from top and bottom, into the wisdom being. The [wisdom being] dissolves into the samādhi being. The [samādhi being] dissolves into [that syllable's] circle [, i.e. the *anusvāra*, which dissolves into] the *nāda*. Finally, the *nāda* dissolves into objectless luminosity and you rest unwavering in a state of equanimity.

Subsequent dissolution: Light from the samādhi being illuminates the entire world and its inhabitants. The environment—the world—is transformed into light and dissolves into its inhabitants—beings. They are transformed into light and dissolve into you. Then you [dissolve] as in the total eclipse.

In both [total eclipse and subsequent dissolution] the dissolving into luminosity is the same as when your breath on a mirror gradually disappears from the outer edges inward. From *Five Stages*:

> The total eclipse is taught to be
> [the dissolving of everything] from the head to the feet
> until [the dissolving] reaches the heart
> and the yogin enters the final limit.
>
> In the stage of subsequent dissolution,
> first all the animate and inanimate
> are transformed into luminosity,
> and subsequently you do the same with yourself.
>
> Just as the steam from your breath
> completely dissolves upon a mirror,
> in that way the yogin repeatedly
> enters into the true limit.[1278]

Repeating these two dhyānas is the extremely profound key point for dissolving the winds and bodhicitta into the heart so that the signs of the sequential dissolution of earth, water, fire, air, and consciousness will manifest. From the *Latter Guhyasamāja Tantra*:

> The mind is transformed into the vajra of cessation
> and then there is the possession of signs.
> The vajra of enlightenment has taught that there are
> five aspects to the nature of the signs.
>
> The first is like a mirage.
> The second is like smoke.
> The third is like space.
> The fourth shines like lamp flames.
> The fifth is a continuous radiance,
> which is like a cloudless sky.[1279]

According to Kambala:

> The first [sign] is like the appearance [of a mirage] to a thirsty deer.
> The second sign has the form of smoke. [398]
> The third is like the appearance of fireflies.
> The fourth is a brightness like lamp flames.
> The fifth sign is an unnamable radiance,
> which is like a cloudless sky.
> When you have obtained these signs
> you will have attained the mahāmudrā.[1280]

Then, the four empties appear in sequence: There arises the *appearance* or the "empty," which is like moonlight in a cloudless sky. There is *increase* or the "very empty," which is like sunlight. There is *attainment* or the "great empty," which is like an all-pervading complete darkness. There is *luminosity* or the "all empty," which is like the dawn sky free from the three causes of pollution. From *Five Stages*:

> Night is the aspect of appearance, which is clarity. The spreading of sunlight is the increase of appearance. Darkness is the attainment of appearance. By their own natures, they do not come at one time.
>
> That which is not night, day, nor darkness is completely devoid of a nature of its own. The supreme guru has called it instantaneous enlightenment, and that is the goal of the supreme yogin.[1281]

Dualistic appearances have yet to be purified during analogous luminosity. Therefore, even though the perception of pure space has appeared, it is when true luminosity is attained that [conceptual] elaboration is purified. That is why it is so named. From the *Saṃvarodaya Tantra*:

> When the truth is reached,
> all thought is through no thought.
> When there is thought through no thought,
> then there will be nonconceptuality.[1282]

From *Clear Summary*:

The samādhi that is not generated by methods,
[but] by the dhyāna that knows the nature,
is self-illuminating, and its essence is nonthought.
That is the stage of ultimate luminosity.[1283]

The gurus have explained that *actual luminosity* is when you generate true luminosity, which is the special fourth empty that comes from dissolving the winds into the heart through using outer and inner methods. *Analogous luminosity* is when [you generate] the similitude of luminosity, which is the simple fourth empty that comes from the natural dissolving of the winds.

(C) The completion stage of inseparable union

This is in two parts:

(1) The categories of union
(2) The method of meditation on union

(1) The categories of union

In general, the Mahayana's common union is the union of method—objectless compassion—with wisdom—supreme emptiness. [399] According to Saraha:

Those who dwell in emptiness without compassion
will not gain the supreme path.
Those who meditate only on compassion
will remain in samsara and will not attain liberation.
Those who are able to unite the two
will not remain in either samsara or nirvana.[1284]

The special union in the path of the tantras is the union of method, which is innate bliss, with wisdom, which is the emptiness of luminosity. From the *Saṃvarodaya Tantra*:

The accomplishment of complete enlightenment
is through the union of method and wisdom.
That itself, which is also the unsurpassable
dwelling place of all the buddhas,

> is Vajrasattva's residence within
> the knowledge of inseparability.
> For as long as the causes of enlightenment . . . [1285]

The one taste of the object, which is emptiness, and the subject, which is bliss, is like blending milk and water. This is what is called *union*. From the *Tantra of True Union*:

> The two that are combined
> in the nondual union,
> which is like water mixed with milk,
> are known as wisdom and method.[1286]

According to Ācārya Nāgārjuna:

> The oneness that comes
> through abandoning thoughts of both
> samsara and nirvana
> is the attainment of union.[1287]

[Nāgārjuna] goes on to teach twenty-one such unions. Here, however, *union* will mean the union of the two truths, which is taught by all mahāsiddhas. From *Five Stages*:

> When the relative and the ultimate,
> their individual aspects having been known,
> are truly blended together,
> that is taught to be union.[1288]

Relative truth is the appearance of the illusion-like body in the self-blessing of the body. Ultimate truth is entering into the true nature of the luminosity of the mind. Union is when these become one, without alternating, without one being absent when the other is present. From *Five Stages*:

> Through knowing that, one will know,
> one after another, self-blessing and luminosity.
> The stage of union is solely
> the merger of those two.[1289]

According to Nāgabodhi:

> Profundity is nonthought.
> Vastness is the forms of the buddhas.
> Those two are taught to be the two truths:
> the relative and the ultimate. [400]
> Know them through distinguishing them
> and meditate on the immaculate state
> in which they are blended into one.[1290]

The union of training according to *Five Stages*:

> The great yoga of training
> in residing on the level of union
> becomes meditation on union
> so that even one's conduct is inseparable from it.[1291]

The union beyond training:

> Remaining in the samādhi of union,
> there is no more training in anything.[1292]

The first of those two, the union where you train in familiarization with the path, is the coming and going, the arising and reversing, of the process of the three empties. The second of those two, the union beyond training in the path, does not have the arising and reversal of the process of the three empties.

(2) The method of meditation on union

The world and its inhabitants dissolve in stages, and the illusory body arises from the state of luminosity brought on by the four empties. According to [Atiśa] Dīpaṃkara:

> That mind rests in a luminosity that is devoid of the three consciousnesses...[1293] *Nondual union* is the arising of the illusory body from that state of inconceivable luminosity, and gaining

> retention, [so called] because it is gained through remembering the illusion-like deity's body.[1294]

Through the stages of self-blessing, wind and mind alone arise from luminosity, like a fish leaping out of water. From *Five Stages*:

> The stages of self-blessing,
> which are combined consciousness and wind
> that are light rays that take on various forms,
> will sometimes benefit beings.
>
> Just as a swift fish leaps
> out from clear river water,
> so a network of illusory manifestations
> arises from the clear all-empty.[1295]

This [illusory body] comes from the wisdom of the single luminosity that results from the successive dissolution of the empties and from its accompanying subtle air element that is [the wisdom's] steed. It is taught to be the vajra body—the essence of Vajradhara, which is as inseparable as your shadow and cannot be destroyed by anything. From *Lamp of the Compendium of Practices*:

> Therefore, the host of appearances that have the one basis of emptiness create the appearances of all worlds, just like space creating appearances. They are accompanied by the subtle element, the indestructible quintessence of the vajra body, which is as inseparable as a shadow. [401] It is immutable and immaculate and therefore completely free from all propensity for affliction. It is the attainment of lordship just by wishing for it, like a fish leaping out of water, or like briefly falling asleep and waking up again. It is the form that is the quintessence of a body that embodies supreme joy. Its name is Great Vajradhara.[1296]

Is there any difference between this [illusory body] and the illusory body comprised of wind and mind that arises from and reenters the empty because of the wind dissolving? Yes, there is a vast difference. The arising of the body that is just wind and mind from the empty caused by the wind dissolving is simply the illusory body alone. Resting in equanimity within the luminosity of the dissolution of the illusory body's environment and inhabitants is simply luminosity alone. Therefore, these two alternate with each other.

However, the appearance of the illusory body from the state of luminosity must be the simultaneous union of the mind in the state of luminosity with the appearance of the illusory body. Therefore [*Five Stages* has the previously quoted passages that contain the lines]:

> Are truly blended together...[1297]

And

> The merger of those two.[1298]

The gurus have taught that true union is the arising of an illusory body from the state of true luminosity, while the facsimile of union is the arising of an illusory body from the state of analogous luminosity.

c) The conduct that enhances the path

This is in three parts:

i) The teaching on conduct in relation to stages of time and individuals
ii) A general description of conduct
iii) A description of heruka conduct in particular

i) The teaching on conduct in relation to stages of time and individuals

Generally speaking, the Buddha taught three kinds of conduct: the conduct free from attachment by pupils with inferior aspiration; the conduct of the levels [of enlightenment] (*bhūmi*) and the perfections by pupils with vast aspiration; and the conduct of desire by those with profound aspiration.

The third of those three conducts, Mantrayāna conduct, is comprised of (1) the conduct at the time of the ripening empowerment, which is the conduct that makes the individual a worthy vessel for the path's meditation; (2) the conduct from when you first meditate on the path until you reach the supreme attainment, which is the conduct that generates the ungenerated path; and (3) the conduct that increases every realization within the two stages, which is the conduct of enhancement. [402]

You have to have attained heat in order to perform the conduct of enhancement. From the *Hevajra Tantra*:

> When you have attained a little heat,
> if you wish to perform the conduct
> and if you wish to attain siddhi,
> carry out conduct in the following way.[1299]

The *Hevajra Tantra* describes *heat*:

> The misfortunes of fear, madness,
> suffering, misery, injury, and so on,
> and desire, anger, and great ignorance
> do not afflict the adept.
>
> Perceiving thus the arising
> of beneficial and harmful results...[1300]

Thus, the gurus have taught that: The *lesser heat* is when the mind is not distracted by lesser thoughts, such as fear, suffering, and so on. The *medium heat* is when the mind does not become afflicted by greater thoughts of the three poisons. The *great heat* is accomplishing the activity of destroying or caring for those to be trained. There is nothing wrong with someone like a householder starting their meditation on the path with the conduct of desire.

The *Condensed* [*Sādhana*] teaches what corresponds to the practice of the desire yoga at the first level of meditation:

> Completely reject the five desires,[1301]
> do not be afflicted by asceticism,
> follow the yoga tantra,
> and accomplish enlightenment through bliss.[1302]

Practitioners can accomplish the supreme [siddhi] during their lifetime by dedication to vows, and for that purpose they should train in the conduct that is appropriate to their level. From *Five Stages*:

Even if someone knows the categories of the appearances of
[the true] nature
and relies upon the four principles,
if they do not train in the three aspects,
they will not attain the result.[1303]

From the *Hevajra Tantra*:

The mudrā yogin accomplishes
in the nonaccomplishment of undifferentiated characteristics.[1304]

The levels for the performance of the conducts are:

- The period when generation-stage practitioners have reached the fulfillment of the generation stage and are practicing the great general siddhis
- The period of time when completion-stage practitioners have made their winds and minds tractable and are practicing the main practice of the illusory body
- The period of time when [practitioners] have become familiarized with analogous luminosity and are practicing true luminosity
- The period of time when [practitioners] have accomplished the training union and are practicing the union beyond training

The harm from careless conduct not in conformity with individual levels of accomplishment

From *Heruka Abhisamaya*:

The yoga Dharma that is without yoga
proceeds to the mudrā,
but the way of wisdom without wisdom
will without doubt lead to hell.[1305] [403]

From *Establishing the Truth*:

Those who know that
and depend upon the goddess
will become accomplished, or otherwise
they will fall into the great hell.[1306]

THE BENEFITS FROM CORRECT CONDUCT

From the *Kālacakra Root Tantra*:

> An untouchable, such as a cane worker,
> and those who have committed the five worst actions
> will attain buddhahood within one lifetime
> if they follow the Mantrayāna conduct.[1307]

From the *Hevajra Tantra*:

> The supreme, perfect conduct
> by which the final accomplishment is reached.[1308]

ii) A general description of conduct

The Samāyoga[1309] and Guhyasamāja teach that there are three activities: the elaborate conduct, the unelaborate conduct, and the extremely unelaborate conduct.

THE ELABORATE CONDUCT

In a pleasant location, [there should be] a square, three-storied temple made of bricks, with four doors and porticoes. Place the kitchen—or whatever might cause an obstacle—on the ground floor. In an upper floor, [a group of] yogis and yoginīs, in the same number as the deities in the mandala, should wear masks and take the role of each individual deity, thus forming a mandala. In four daily sessions, they should enhance the yoga through performing a very elaborate conduct, with enjoyment of sensory pleasures, practice of the three samādhis, singing, dancing, communicating through secret signs, and so on.

THE UNELABORATE CONDUCT

This is the same as the elaborate conduct apart from the elaboration of singing, dancing, and so on. In the extensive form [the practitioners] are the same number as the deities of the mandala. The medium form has five action seals, and in the simplified form one relies upon a single seal.

The extremely unelaborated conduct

You continually perform the conduct of relying upon the wisdom mudrā except for when you are eating, drinking, defecating, or urinating.

The purpose of the conducts

These conducts are intended to increase the wisdom of bliss and emptiness and the mind's focus on nothing other than great bliss and the forms of the deities. The conducts will accomplish these goals within six months, three months, or one month. Other texts that teach three conducts such as the elaborate conduct and so on do not differ on these essential points.

The Tantra of True Union teaches four conducts: *avadhūtī* conduct, excellent conduct, *vrata* conduct, [404] and victorious conduct. Some texts teach [only] two categories of conduct: *avadhūtī* conduct and excellent conduct. *Avadhūtī* conduct is also named *shaking-off*[1310] *conduct*, *princely conduct*, and the *secret conduct*. Excellent conduct is also named *victorious conduct*, the *regent's conduct*, and *great Gaṇapati's conduct*.

According to the *Samāyoga Tantra* there are four conducts: the conduct of beginners, the conduct of those with some power of wisdom, the conduct of those with greater power of wisdom, and the conduct of liberation.

In Cakrasaṃvara and the Essence of Accomplishment[1311] teachings, there are four conducts: excellent conduct, secret or hidden conduct, *vrata* conduct, and victorious conduct. These [teachings] mostly correspond with the key points taught in the *Tantra of True Union*, although there are a few differences in terms of the names and nature of the conducts.

The gurus have taught that during the beginner stage, correctly keep the general and special commitments and vows, which are the *excellent conduct*, and whether you are lay or ordained, dedicate yourself to meditation on a path free from transgressions. Follow this conduct until you attain the sign of heat in the meditative equanimity of the completion stage.

During the stage when there is some power of wisdom, do not actually perform the activities of a yogin but, while avoiding all transgressions, secretly engage in the Mantrayāna conduct: practicing with a consort, [consuming] the five meats and the five nectars, and so on. This is called the *secret* or *hidden conduct*. Engage in this conduct until your realization is stable within both meditation and post-meditation.

During the stage when wisdom has greater power, engage with your consort in the Dharma of the yogin, practicing all the Mantrayāna *vratas* in a group. This is the *vidyā-vrata* conduct. Follow this conduct when you have gained stability and continue with it until you attain the supreme power [of wisdom].

When you are liberated from the bondage of existence, you will be able to crush all opposition without hesitation and have power over existence. That is the *victorious conduct*. This conduct is for benefiting other beings who have to be trained.

iii) A description of heruka conduct in particular

This is in three parts:

(A) Secret conduct
(B) *Vrata* conduct
(C) Victorious conduct [405]

(A) The secret conduct

Practitioners who have attained the lesser heat must first, before engaging in *vrata* conduct, perform the secret conduct for a month or so, in order to achieve the key points. From the *Hevajra Tantra*:

> The one who has attained siddhi, who is well established
> through a constant practice of yoga,
> should act for one month in secret...[1312]

[The *Hevajra Tantra* teaches] the particular locations:

> [It is said to be auspicious to meditate]
> at a single tree or in a charnel ground,
> or likewise the lovely dwelling of a matrika
> or otherwise in an unpopulated wilderness.[1313]

[The *Hevajra Tantra* also describes] the mudrā consort with the necessary qualities and the way in which you train:

> Take this vajra maiden, who has a pretty face and large eyes,[1314]
> who has received the empowerment, has compassion,
> who is the color of the dark blue lotus,
> and make her understand the conduct that is to be performed.

> If there is no one from the vajra family,
> perform with someone from the family of your chosen deity
> or otherwise someone from another family.
> Take her who has been made ready
> by the emission of the seed of enlightenment.[1315]

[The *Hevajra Tantra*] describes reliance upon the five meats and five nectars:

> ... and his food should be the five nectars.[1316]

Also [from the *Hevajra Tantra*]:

> ... that which begins *na*, *ga*, and *ha*,[1317]
> that has *śva* after and *śva* in the beginning.[1318]
> Likewise, the five nectars should be consumed
> because they are the cause of accomplishment in Hevajra.[1319]

Gain stability of mind in yoga by practicing in secrecy every mantra activity that defeats the concepts of dualism:

> That conduct, which is said to have a terrifying form,
> was not taught for the purpose of enjoyment
> [but] for examining your own mind
> to see whether it is stable or unstable.[1320]

[The *Hevajra Tantra*] describes the harm of not keeping the mudrā yoga secret:

> If not kept secret, snakes, thieves, kings, and fire will cause suffering.[1321]

(B) Vrata *conduct*

When practitioners who have reached the level of medium heat engage in *vrata* conduct, they pay homage to the guru, offer all their possessions, and even dedicate their body to the benefit of beings. From the *Tantra of True Union*:

I pay homage to the lord of all,
to the glorious vajra master.[1322]

From the *Hevajra Tantra*:

He should make an offering of his body
and afterward commence upon the conduct.[1323]

THE INDEFINITE LOCATION [FOR THE CONDUCT]

From the *Tantra of True Union*:

A crossroads, a mountain,
a single tree, or a charnel ground.[1324]

From the *Tantra of True Union*:

Wandering in other lands,
in mountain caves, and in jungles, [406]
in the great primordial charnel grounds,
or along the shores of a great ocean.[1325]

THE SPECIFIC COMPANIONS [FOR THE CONDUCT]

This should principally be the prophesied consort (*mudrā*), but anyone you are able to attract will suffice. From the *Hevajra Tantra*:

The mantrin obtains an instruction
that the yoginīs give to him:
"Take such and such a consort
and accomplish the benefit of beings, vajra holder!"[1326]

From the *Hevajra Tantra*:

Alternatively, he should attract and choose
a consort through his own power.

[He should take her] from among the devas, the asuras,
the humans, and even from the *yakṣas* and *kiṃnaras*,
[and perform the conduct with firm conviction].[1327]

The body adornments [according to the *Hevajra Tantra*]:

> [The meditator should wear]
> divine earrings on the ears,
> a circlet on the crown of the head,
> a pair of bracelets on the arms,
> a girdle around the waist,
> and similarly anklets on the feet,
> armlets on the upper arms,
> a necklace of bones at the throat,
> a tiger skin for clothing,
> [and his food should be the five nectars.][1328]

From the *Hevajra Tantra*:

> He should make a thief's hairstyle[1329] as a crown
> and there unite with the one who manifests from *hūṃ*.[1330]

[The *Hevajra Tantra*] has many such teachings, for example:

> His loincloth should be multicolored,
> and he should be adorned with the ashes of a cremated corpse.[1331]

The particular armlets, song, dance, food, drink, and so on [according to the *Hevajra Tantra*]:

> Wisdom has the form of the *khaṭvāṅga* staff.
> The form of method is the *ḍamaru* drum.
> And the yogin is the purification of anger.
>
> The song is present as the pure form of the mantra,
> and the dance is known to be the meditation.
> Therefore the yogin should
> always sing and dance.
>
> He should also take the "medicine"
> and constantly drink the fluid.[1332]

The conduct of equanimity, without attachment to any good or bad sensory experiences:

> Consuming whatever food
> and, likewise, drink that is obtained,
> he should not even have attachment
> caused by thoughts of pleasure and displeasure.
>
> The mantrin should not have thoughts
> of what can and cannot be eaten,
> what can and cannot be drunk,
> or what is pleasing and displeasing.[1333]

[The *Hevajra Tantra* teaches] the conduct that is free of the concepts of the afflictions and the eight worldly dharmas:

> Avoiding expressions of craving, stupidity,
> fear, anger, and embarrassment,
> abandon sleep and self
> and perform the conduct without hesitation.[1334]

[The *Hevajra Tantra* also teaches]:

> Do not wash or keep clean
> and do not give up sexual activity.[1335]

[The *Hevajra Tantra* teaches] manifesting the innate truth without practicing the conceptualized yoga:

> Leaving behind homa fire rituals, sacrifice, and asceticism, [407]
> abandoning mantras and meditation,
> free from commitments and vows,
> the excellent yogin performs the conduct.[1336]

[The *Hevajra Tantra* teaches] the conduct that has no fear because of the sharpness of realization:

> Even if a *daitya*[1337] equal to Indra
> should definitely appear before him,
> he should have no fear
> but wander like a lion.[1338]

From the *Tantra of True Union*:

> Completely forsaking all fear:
> the wise meditate in that way.[1339]

However, one does not forsake activity that has the motivation of compassion for beings and respect for the guru. [From the *Tantra of True Union*]:

> For the sake of all beings
> he continually drinks with compassion.[1340]

[Also from the *Tantra of True Union*:]

> The pupil who has attained siddhi,
> the one who has the true appearance of wisdom,
> that siddha pays homage to the guru
> in order to eliminate the cause of Avīci.[1341]

Moreover, there are taught a variety of activities, in a variety of various costumes, such as in the guise of a tīrthika or with the behavior of a lunatic. All of these are for the sake of cutting through the elaboration of dualism, for enhancing the innate truth, for stabilizing the realization of unity, and so on. Know the categories of yoga meditation that accord with the circumstances.

(C) The victorious conduct

When practitioners have attained great heat with great compassion, they practice the victorious activity in order to tame other beings. From the *Tantra of True Union*:

> Resting the mind in enlightenment,
> they engage in the victorious activity.[1342]

From the *Tantra of True Union*:

> Those with great wisdom wander
> in order to take care of beings.[1343]

THE PARTICULAR COMPANIONS

This teaches reliance upon the vidyā girl, as explained before, who may be a deva, an asura, or something else. For example, from the *Tantra of True Union*:

> Because of this, all the meditators
> will declare "complete victory."
> Remaining in this way for a while,
> the yogin who does not destroy the true nature
> should attract and act with
> his chosen vidyā goddess,
> who is extremely beautiful.
> She should be a beautiful lotus, a jewel,
> bringing joy to the vidyādhara,
> the daughter of a deva, or a *yakṣiṇī*...[1344]

THE PARTICULAR QUALITIES

For one's own benefit, there is the complete liberation from all obscurations and the elimination of all thoughts of subject and object. [408] For the benefit of others, there is the ability to bring satisfaction, through the Dharma, through material things, and so on, to all beings obscured by afflictions in the ten directions. From the *Tantra of True Union*:

> [The yogins] also engage in complete victory
> and become completely liberated from all obscurations.
> They completely fulfill the wishes of all
> those residing in the ten directions
> who are obscured by the obscuration of birth.
> Through meditation and elimination, they completely eliminate
> the entire [duality of] subject and object.[1345]

At this time, all that they need is given to them by deities, they are able to eliminate the suffering of old age and sickness, they are liberated from the bad karma and obscurations of the three doors, and they have become a basis for the great nondual union. From the *Tantra of True Union*:

> A plenitude of all that is truly necessary,
> without having to acquire it, is bestowed by deities.
> They are completely free from old age and illness.
> There is no duality, and the three locations have no bad karma.[1346]

THE SPECIFIC ACTIVITIES

This means benefiting beings through caring and destruction—the proper ways of caring for those who have aspiration and the proper ways of destroying those who have no faith, and then instilling faith in them, caring for them, and so on.

C. The result tantra: the result of practice[1347]

This is in three parts:

1. A general teaching on the way siddhis are accomplished
2. A specific explanation of progress through the paths and levels
3. The particular way to accomplish the supreme siddhi

1. A general teaching on the way siddhis are accomplished

The results of meditation on the path of the two stages is taught to be the lesser siddhi of the four activities, the medium [siddhi] of the eight siddhis, and the supreme [siddhi] of buddhahood. From *Illuminating Lamp*:

> I will also teach the purpose:
> It is for the peaceful and other activities
> and similarly for the eight siddhis,
> and the supreme [purpose] is buddhahood.[1348]

It is explained that the first two are the general siddhis and the latter is the supreme siddhi. From the *Latter Guhyasamāja Tantra*:

> The siddhis of invisibility and so on
> are taught to be "ordinary."

> The attainment of buddhahood was taught
> by the Buddha to be the supreme siddhi.[1349]

The general siddhis can be accomplished even in the generation stage. The supreme siddhi must be accomplished through the completion stage. From the *Latter Guhyasamāja Tantra*:

> Because of the categories of ordinary and supreme
> there are said to be the two sevās.
> The general are the four vajras,
> the supreme is through the six branches.[1350] [409]

The *pacifying* activity of the four activities is the pacification of such things as illness, demons, and one's own and others' bad karma and obscurations. The *increasing* [activity] is the increase of life, wisdom prosperity, and so on. The *controlling* [activity] is summoning and bringing under one's power humans, such as kings and ministers, and nonhumans, such as spirits (*bhūtas*). The *wrathful* [activity] is killing, chasing away, dividing, paralyzing, and so on the ranks of the enemies.

THE EIGHT SIDDHIS

From the *Vajra Tent*:

> Eye salve and swift feet,
> sword and subterranean accomplishment,
> pills and traveling through the air,
> invisibility and "extraction of essences" (*rasāyana*).[1351]

The eyes salve: By applying the blessed substance to your eyes, you see such things as treasure under the ground. *Swift feet*: By applying the blessed substance to your feet, you are able to travel many *yojanas* in a short time. *Sword*: By holding the blessed sword, you are able to go in a moment to wherever you wish. *Subterranean*: Your body can travel many *yojanas* underground. *The pills*: By taking a blessed pill each day, you gain the five clairvoyances and the like. *Traveling through the air*: You can miraculously travel through the air and use that as your field of activity and so on. *Invisibility*: By putting the blessed substance onto your forehead, no one will be able to see you. *Rasāyana*: There are the three *rasāyanas*: those of body, life, and possessions.

You become like a sixteen-year-old, live for as long as the sun and moon, and can change iron and such into gold.

In agreement with that, from the *Tantra Requested by the Four Goddesses*:

> Pills and eye-salve siddhis,
> subterranean and sword siddhis,
> flying through the air and invisibility,
> immortality and defeating illness.[1352]

Also from the *Vajra Tent*:

> One who attains and accomplishes
> becoming a vidyādhara cakravartin
> and invokes a sublime female
> will attain the vajra siddhi.[1353]

When this passage talks of becoming a vidyādhara and so on, *vidyādhara* (knowledge-holder) means that through possessing the knowledge (*vidyā*) of the mantra, you become like a sixteen-year-old, whatever possession you wish for appears from space, and you can go to any buddha realm [410] and listen to teachings from a nirmāṇakāya.

The meaning of *cakravartin* is easy to understand.

"Invokes a sublime female" means that having accomplished [invoking] a *yakṣiṇī*, you will be granted any of the eight siddhis.

In order to accomplish these siddhis through the first stage, the generation-stage practitioner who is dedicated to the mantra must practice through mantra repetition, homa fire rituals, substances, *yantra*, and so on. Those who are dedicated to the internal supremacy accomplish them through meditation alone, without depending on substances and so on.

The minor activities, such as peaceful and increasing, are immediately accomplished through a stable deity practice and the complete repetition of the mantras.

The mahāsiddhas dedicated to mantra first correctly follow the general and specific practices, performing the conduct for six months. If there is no accomplishment, they repeat the instruction for the practice for another six months. Doing this two or three times will bring accomplishment. If that doesn't bring accomplishment, then the instruction of wrathful practices will definitely bring accomplishment. From the *Latter Guhyasamāja Tantra*:

Until [practitioners] can see [what has been described],
they should meditate on the two aspects for six months.

They should continually do everything,
fulfilling all their desires.

If after six months
they do not see what has been described,
they should carry out three times the practices
and the vows, just as they have been taught.

If practitioners practice in this way
and yet still do not see,
if their activities have not been accomplished,
they will accomplish them through engaging in wrathful practice.

At that time, the wisdom
will definitely be accomplished.[1354]

It's taught that with dedication to the internal, and without relying upon enhancing rituals, the performance of this conduct for six months will accomplish all siddhis without any impediment. Learn from numerous tantras and commentaries the methods for accomplishing these siddhis. The accomplishment of the supreme siddhi in this life, or in the bardo, or in a future life, according to the level of your capabilities, will be explained further on.

2. *A specific explanation of progress through the paths and levels*

This is in two parts:

a. The categories of the paths and levels
b. The way to progress through the paths and levels

a. *The categories of the paths and levels*

Generally speaking the Perfection Vehicle teaches that there are thirteen levels: the two levels of ordinary beings are the level of the beginner and the level of *activity through aspiration*. Then there are the ten levels of the bodhisattva, such as Perfect Joy and so on. [411] Then there is the level of buddhahood, which is called *complete illumination*.

The principal levels are the [ten] levels of the ten perfections. Their etymology: The first level is named Perfect Joy. The second is Stainless. The third is Shining. The fourth is Blazing. The fifth is Difficult to Master. The sixth is Manifest. The seventh is Gone Far. The eighth is Undisturbed. The ninth is Excellent Intelligence. The tenth is Dharma Clouds. From *Ornament of the Mahayana Sutras*:

> [The first] is called Perfect Joy,[1355]
> because perfect joy arises
> on seeing the nearness of enlightenment
> and the accomplishment of benefit for beings.
>
> [The second] is called Stainless,[1356]
> because it is free from the stains of mistaken effort.
>
> [The third is called] Shining,[1357]
> because it has the great radiance of the Dharma.
>
> [The fourth is called] Blazing,[1358]
> because it has the qualities conducive to enlightenment,
> which are like an incinerating light,
> and therefore, this level incinerates both [obscurations].
>
> [The fifth] is called Difficult to Master,[1359]
> because it is difficult for the wise
> to have the ability to perfectly ripen beings
> while also protecting their own minds.
>
> [The sixth] is called Manifest,[1360]
> because both samsara and nirvana
> are caused to manifest
> through the perfection of wisdom.
>
> [The seventh] is called Gone Far,[1361]
> [because one has gone far] in relation to the one path that has to be traversed.

[The eighth] is definitively called Undisturbed,[1362]
because the two identifications[1363] cannot disturb it.

The [ninth] level is Excellent Intelligence,[1364]
[because of] its excellent, specific, correct knowledge.

[The tenth] is Dharma Clouds,[1365] because, like clouds,
the two[1366] spread through the sky of the Dharma.[1367]

From the Vajrayāna tradition's [*Latter*] *Definition Tantra*:

[There are] Beyond Example, Endowed with Wisdom,
And the thirteenth, which is the Vajra Level.[1368]

Thus, there are taught to be thirteen levels: The ten levels, such as Perfect Joy, and above them the eleventh, named Beyond Example, the twelfth, named Endowed with Wisdom, and the thirteenth, the Vajra Level.

The *Hevajra Tantra* teaches special names for the twelve levels, such as Pīṭha and Upapīṭha:

Pīṭha and Upapīṭha,
Kṣetra and Upakṣetra,
Chandoha and Upachandoha,
Melāpaka and Upamelāpaka,
Pīlava and Upapīlava,
Śmaśāna and Upaśmaśāna:
Those are the twelve.[1369] [412]

The correspondence of the general and special names of the twelve levels

From the *Tantra of True Union*:

Pīṭha is "Perfect Joy."
Similarly, Upapīṭha is "Stainless."
Kṣetra is known as "Shining."
Upakṣetra is "Blazing."
Chandoha is "Manifest."
Upachandoha is "Difficult to Master."

Melāpaka is "Gone Far."
Upamelāpaka is "Undisturbed."
Śmaśāna is "Excellent Intelligence."
Upaśmaśāna is "Dharma Clouds."[1370]

From the [*Latter*] *Definition Tantra*:

Pīlava is "Beyond Example" and similarly
Upapīlava is "Great Wisdom."[1371]

The *Vajra Mandala Adornment Tantra*[1372] teaches twelve levels: (1) the level of complete light, (2) the level of nectar light, (3) the level of space light, (4) the level of vajra light, (5) the level of jewel light, (6) the level of the lotus holder, (7) the level of karma light, (8) the level beyond example, (9) the level without example, (10) the level of the wisdom light, (11) the level of omniscience, and (12) the level of knowing individual natures. Those are the one level of ordinary beings together with the generally known eleven levels.

The presentation of the paths

The Perfection Vehicle teaches five paths:

- The path of accumulation [so named because this] is where one principally gathers the accumulation of good actions.
- The path of engagement, [so named] because of engagement with the realization of the truth.
- The path of seeing, [so named] because of seeing the noble truths.
- The path of meditation, [so named] because of familiarization with meditation on the true nature.
- The path of completion, [so named] because of reaching the state of nirvana.

The paths of accumulation and engagement are provinces of ordinary beings. The paths of seeing and meditation are provinces of the āryas. Those four paths are the training to reach a higher stage and therefore are taught to be *paths of training*. The path of completion is the province of buddhas, and as there is no higher path to train for, it is taught to be the *path of no training*.

The correspondence between the paths and levels

The level of the beginner is the path of accumulation. The level of activity through aspiration is the path of engagement. The first level is the path of seeing. The remaining nine levels are the path of meditation. The level of buddhahood is the path of completion.

b. The way to progress through the paths and levels

The general way in which you follows the levels and paths of mantra

The beginner's level, which is the path of accumulation, is the level where one obtains the ripening empowerment, gains stability of mind through the two liberating stages, and develops every "stained quality." [413]

The level of aspiration, which is the path of engagement, is the level where one attains the indicatory luminosity and the secret illusory body.

The first level, Perfect Joy, which is the path of seeing, is when one manifests true luminosity. The second level, Stainless, up to the twelfth level, Endowed with Wisdom, which are all the path of meditation, is when there is the training in union. The thirteenth level, the Vajra Level, which is the path of completion, is when the nontraining union is manifest.

The particular way of the mother tantra tradition

The beginner's level, which is the path of accumulation, is when mental stability in the two stages is attained, all conditions are transformed into the path, and immaculate experiences arise.

The level of aspiration, which is the path of engagement, is when the wind enters the central channel and there is the manifestation of the analogous innateness, which is the inseparability of bliss and emptiness in the descent of the four joys, and the increase of the excellent qualities of the channels and winds.

The twelfth level is attained when the ascent of the four joys manifests the true innateness. The stabilization of vital energy, from the secret region up to the crown of the head, loosens the thirty-two knots of the central channel, clarifies the channels of the twenty-four sites, purifies away obscurations from the six cakras, and causes the twelve sets of 1,800 karmic winds to cease.

When the vital energy is stabilized in one half of the secret area's cakra, the following channels become clear: the Pullīra (Pūrṇagiri) at the crown of the head, Jālandhara at the crown protrusion, Oḍḍiyāna at the right ear, and

Arbuda at the nape. Also, the four channel knots in the central channel are loosened.

When half of the secret area's cakra is purified of obscuration, this causes one set of 1,800 karmic winds to cease and the attainment of Pīṭha, which is the first level: *Perfect Joy*.

When the vital energy is stabilized in the remaining half of the secret area's cakra, the following channels become clear: Godāvari at the left ear, Rameśvarī at the point between the eyebrows, Devikoṭa at the two eyes, and Mālava at the two shoulders. Also, four channel knots [in the central channel] are loosened.

When the remaining half of the secret area's cakra is purified of obscuration, another set of 1,800 karmic winds cease, and there is attainment of Upapīṭha, which is the second level: *Stainless*.

Similarly, when the vital energy is stabilized in one half of the navel's cakra, the following channels become clear: Kāmarūpa at the two armpits and Oḍra at the two breasts. Also, two channel knots [in the central channel] are loosened, and there is attainment of Kṣetra, which is the third level: *Shining* and so on. [414]

Attaining the first level is the path of seeing and the remaining levels are the path of meditation. The attainment of the thirteenth level, which is the path of completion, is when the subtlest aspects of the channels, winds, and drops are clear and free of obscuration, the ordinary body is purified, and the rainbow wisdom-body is attained.

3. The particular way to accomplish the supreme siddhi

This is in three parts:

a. The presentation of the kāyas of buddhahood
b. The way in which they are manifested
c. Their uninterrupted activity

a. The presentation of the kāyas of buddhahood

This is in two parts:

i. A brief teaching on the categories of the kāyas of buddhahood
ii. The teaching on Vajradhara endowed with the seven aspects

i. A brief teaching on the categories of the kāyas of buddhahood

In general, it is taught that there are four kāyas of buddhahood: the svabhavakāya, the dharmakāya, the saṃbhogakāya, and the nirmāṇakāya. From *Ornament of Realization*:

> There is the correct description of the four aspects:
> the svabhava and the saṃbhoga,
> and similarly also the nirmāṇa,
> together with the activity of the dharmakāya.[1373]

The svabhavakāya is taught to be the perfection of elimination, as it has eliminated the afflictions and so on. From *Ornament of Realization*:

> The Sage's *svabhavakāya*
> is the nature and characteristics
> of all immaculate qualities
> and the complete purity of all training.[1374]

The dharmakāya is presented as perfect realization of the thirty-seven factors for enlightenment and more. From *Ornament of Realization*:

> The factors for enlightenment; the immeasurables;
> and the successive liberations;
> the nine states of concentration; . . .

And so on until:[1375]

> . . . the eighteen distinctive qualities of the Sage alone, explained
> to be eighteen;
> that which is called *omniscience*, and the *dharmakāya*.[1376]

The saṃbhogakāya is presented as the appearance of a body adorned with the primary and secondary signs to pupils in the pure buddha realms. From *Ornament of Realization*:

> Because this embodiment of the thirty-two primary
> and the eighty secondary signs

completely enjoys the Mahayana,
it is called the *saṃbhogakāya* (enjoyment body) of the Sage.[1377]

The nirmāṇakāya is presented as the accomplishment of benefit for beings through a variety of manifestations, which continue for as long as there is existence, to a variety of pure and impure pupils. From *Ornament of Realization*:

That kāya that accomplishes
a variety of benefits for all beings equally,
for as long as there is existence, [415]
is the uninterrupted *nirmāṇakāya* of the Sage.[1378]

These [four] can be summarized as the inseparability of the svabhavakāya and dharmakāya, which is the inseparability of the qualities of elimination and realization. From *Compendium of the Mahayana*:

The svabhavakāya is the dharmakāya of the tathāgatas, because it is thc locus of power over everything.[1379]

They can be summarized into three [kāyas]: the svabhavakāya as the basis and the saṃbhogakāya and nirmāṇakāya as the based. From *Ornament of the Mahayana Sutras*:

Know that the three kāyas
include all the kāyas of the buddhas.[1380]

Also from *Ornament of the Mahayana Sutras*:

The categories of the kāyas of the buddhas:
There is the svabhava, the saṃbhoga,
and the other kāya is the nirmāṇa.
The first is the basis for the other two.[1381]

The characteristics of the three kāyas are also explained [in *Ornament of the Mahayana Sutras*]:

> The svabhavakāya is equal
> and subtle. The saṃbhogakāya
> is said to be related to it
> and enjoying nine pleasures.
> The nirmāṇakāya is said to be
> the uncountable emanations of the Buddha.
> The perfection of the two benefits
> is present in all these aspects.[1382]

The summary

The result of freedom, the perfection of self-benefit, is the ultimate kāya or the true kāya. The result of maturation, the perfection of benefiting others, is the relative kāyas or symbol kāyas. From the *Sublime Continuum*:

> The kāya of ultimate truth and the relative kāyas based upon it
> are the benefits for oneself and the benefits for others.
> They are the results of liberation and maturation
> and have 64 million qualities.[1383]

Also from the *Sublime Continuum*:

> The ultimate kāya
> is the basis of benefit for oneself.
> The indicatory kāya of the rishi
> is the basis of the benefit for others.[1384]
>
> The first kāya has the qualities of liberation,
> such as the powers and so on.
> The second has the qualities of maturation,
> the signs of a great being.[1385]

ii. The teaching on Vajradhara endowed with the seven aspects

The arising of the illusory body from true luminosity is the training union. This becomes the nontraining union, which is Vajradhara endowed with seven aspects. These seven aspects, according to Vāgīśvarakīrti, are:

> Saṃbhoga[kāya], union, great bliss, having no nature,
> being completely filled with compassion, being continuous, and being without cessation: [416]
> The buddhahood that has the seven aspects
> I have stated here is also stated validly by wise ones with complete meditation.[1386]

The saṃbhoga aspect is the kāya created from the inseparability of wind and mind and adorned by the primary and secondary signs.

The aspect of union is to remain in union with the *vidyā* with whom there is intercourse.

The aspect of great bliss is to be filled with immaculate great bliss.

The aspect of having no nature is that things and so on have no existence of their own.

The aspect of being filled with compassion is the complete pervasion of great objectless compassion.

The aspect of being continuous is remaining for as long as space exists.

The aspect of being without cessation is presence throughout all time as the unceasing family.

This [Vajradhara] has the nature of four kāyas, three kāyas, or two kāyas:

The *svabhavakāya*, or noncomposite dharmakāya, is the luminosity of the object, which has the two purities.

The wisdom dharmakāya or *great bliss kāya* is the luminosity of the subject.

However, *dharmakāya* is the name for the luminosity of the nonduality of subject and object. The form kāya based upon that, which is formed from mind and wind alone, is called the *saṃbhogakāya*. These two kāyas are one in essence, only differing in terms of contrasts. Therefore, together they are the *nondual wisdom kāya* or the *union kāya*. As that [kāya] is filled completely with compassion, there arise many emanations, such as the supreme nirmāṇakāya, in order to benefit the infinite beings that are to be trained. These are called the *nirmāṇakāya*.

Some explain that the three kāyas are the seven aspects:

The dharmakāya, which is free of all elaboration, is the aspect of having no nature. The saṃbhogakāya is created in Akaniṣṭha, where the union kāya, adorned by the primary and secondary signs, appears to pure pupils. Those are the three aspects of saṃbhoga, union, and great bliss. The nirmāṇakāya is the uninterrupted accomplishment of benefit for various pupils through various methods. Those are the three aspects of great compassion, continuity, and having no cessation. However, although this explanation exists, it is not the meaning of the seven aspects.

b. The way in which the kāyas of buddhahood manifest

This is in two parts:

i. How to gain the supreme siddhi in this life [417]
ii. How to gain the supreme siddhi in the bardo or in future lives

i. How to gain the supreme siddhi in this life

The supreme individual can attain the supreme [siddhi] in this lifetime. From the *Tantra of True Union*:

> The buddhahood that is achieved
> after tens of millions of incalculable eons
> you will accomplish through sacred bliss
> even within this lifetime.[1387]

The process

It is taught that having concluded all generation and completion stages and attained training union, engaging in conduct will bring attainment of the signs of supreme accomplishment: the eight qualities of lordship. From *Lamp of the Compendium of Practices*:

> Through training in the three kinds of conduct for half a month, or for one month, or for six months, there will appear signs of the attainment of the siddhi of mahāmudrā. These are the signs: subtle forms, lightness of touch, pervasion, true attainment, complete appearance, stability, power, and the fulfillment of a variety of desires.[1388]

If you attain the signs of supreme accomplishment, or see that you are capable of the conduct that is its direct cause, then in one week you will attain accomplishment through that conduct of the direct cause. From the *Vajra Tent*:

> It can be accomplished in one day,
> or in two days through the ritual,
> or three days through the yoga,
> or similarly, in four days.
> The fifth day of yoga
> will accomplish it without a doubt.
>
> Make offerings with flowers and so on.
> Rest in stable meditation.
> Unite with the mudrā.
> Correctly practice the vajra offering.
>
> When the vajra sun has set,
> if you practice this yoga correctly,
> there is no doubt that when the sun rises,
> there will be accomplishment.[1389]

The external enlightenment is at the time of dawn. The inner enlightenment is uniting with the mudrā. At the moment when there is luminosity from the dissolving of the winds, the ordinary body is purified. This will manifest the wisdom body that is the inseparability of the ultimate luminosity from the immaculate body, which is like a rainbow. From the *Vajra Tent*:

> The mahāmudrā siddhi is the great siddhi.
> It is not the province of all siddhis.
> At that time its body is obtained,
> and instantly, there is great bliss.
>
> Instantly, [you have] the retinue,
> the meditation, the mantra,
> and instantly [you are] Buddha Vairocana,
> whose shoulders are embraced by Locanā.[1390]

It's taught that countless marvelous signs appear at the time of the supreme siddhi. From the *Tantra of True Union*: [418]

> When the vidyā is accomplished, there will be this kind of excellence: The earth will shake in six ways because of its joy, pleasure,

> and delight. There will be the sounds of cymbals in the abode of the māras. In all the ten directions there will be shooting stars like the fire at the eon's end. There will be the sound of a great stormy ocean. Meteors will fall everywhere, and there will be a blazing radiance of wisdom like the fire at the end of the eon.[1391]

There will be these and other signs. Countless male and female deities will offer many specific offerings and supplicate you, calling out, "Victory! Victory!" and declaring "Excellent!"

ii. The way to gain the supreme siddhi in the bardo or in future lives

The medium individual achieves the supreme siddhi in the bardo. From *Oral Transmission*:

> Because of some deluded thoughts about self,
> [your] physical body will be left behind.
> You will not attain accomplishment in this life,
> but your mind can accomplish the vajra body,
> and you will gain true accomplishment in the bardo.[1392]

The process

Those who have mastered the generation stage are extremely adept in absorption into luminosity and arising as the illusory body. When they die, the luminosity of death will manifest as the true luminosity. If it doesn't, then the illusory body will appear instead of the bardo, and they will attain the supreme siddhi in that form. From *Oral Transmission*:

> When my mind enters into space,
> there is clarity and joy, a realization that is like space.
> Then, when the form of a child of five years
> who possesses miraculous powers is created,
> there is bliss beyond example and perfect realization.
> When I am propelled from there
> into another life, the emanation form
> will be truly, perfectly realized.[1393]

The least individual attains the supreme siddhi in another lifetime.

Those who have applied themselves to the two stages and have gained experience in the instructions of illusory body and dream take control in the bardo and transform it into the path, preventing impure rebirths and taking birth as a vidyādhara, and attain the supreme siddhi with that as a basis. From *Oral Transmission*:

> If the three kāyas are not accomplished,
> I will become a chief vidyādhara
> and eventually accomplish the mahāmudrā.[1394]

Moreover, those who have received empowerments, kept the commitments, meditated as much as they can on the two stages, and made pure prayers will also gain a special rebirth and before long will attain the supreme siddhi. From the *Vajra Tent*:

> Even if they do not attain enlightenment, [419]
> they will be born again and again
> into a life as a cakravartin
> or otherwise will be born as kings.
> They will truly go to pure realms,
> be born as one of the wise in Sukhāvatī,
> or among the ḍākinīs, or in Tuṣita.[1395]

There is also the previous teaching on the attainment of buddhahood in three, seven, or sixteen lifetimes.

c. The uninterrupted activity of the kāyas of buddhahood

From *Ornament of Realization*:

> Thus, it is said that for as long as there is samsara,
> this activity will be an uninterrupted continuity.[1396]

Thus, it is taught that the activity of buddhas continues for as long as there is samsara. This is because: (1) in the past, at the beginning of the path of training, they developed the bodhicitta for the sake of all beings; (2) they see themselves and all beings as equal in having buddha nature; and (3) their deeds are not completed until there are no more beings. From the *Sublime Continuum*:

> Because of his dedication to liberating others,
> because he sees self and beings as the same,
> and because his task is unending,
> his deeds do not cease while there is samsara.[1397]

THE WAY IN WHICH THERE IS ENGAGEMENT IN ACTIVITY

There is a natural presence [of activity] through five [aspects]: (1) the variety of the natures of those to be trained, (2) the methods for training them, (3) the activity of training, (4) the locations of training, and (5) the time of training. From the *Sublime Continuum*:

> There is always the effortless activity of the Lord
> appearing in the places and times
> that accord with the nature of pupils, the training methods,
> and the actions that will train the nature of the pupils.[1398]

What kind of examples can we give for this? From the *Sublime Continuum*:

> The Tathāgata is like Indra and a drum,
> like clouds, Brahma, the sun,
> and a jewel, like an echo,
> the sky, and the ground.[1399]

The manifestation of the appearance of the body is like Indra: like the image of Indra being reflected on a ground of beryl. The body of the Buddha appears in the perception of those to be trained and benefits beings. From the *Sublime Continuum*:

> Just as the reflection of the body of the Lord of Devas
> appears on a pure ground of beryl,
> in the same way, the reflection of the body of the Lord of Sages
> appears on the pure ground of the minds of beings.[1400] [420]

The speech's perfect instruction is like the great drum of the devas: Just as the sound of the Dharma comes effortlessly from the great drum of the devas, the sound of the Dharma effortlessly comes from the buddhas to worthy beings. [From the *Sublime Continuum*]:

> Just as, among the devas, through the power
> of the previous good deeds of the devas,
> the Dharma drum repeatedly
> exhorts all the carefree devas
> [with the words "impermanence
> suffering, selflessness, and peace,"][1401]
> and without effort, location, mental forms,
> or conceptualization.
>
> In that same way, although the Lord
> is without effort and so on,
> the Buddha's speech pervades
> all beings without exception.[1402]

The love and knowledge of the [Buddha's] mind pervades like clouds: Rain falls effortlessly from the monsoon clouds causing harvests to grow. In the same way, the buddhas, without thought, but through the power of compassion, increase the virtues of beings. [From the *Sublime Continuum*]:

> Just as, during the monsoon, the clouds
> are the cause of a perfect harvest,
> and a mass of water effortlessly
> streams down upon the earth,
>
> in the same way, from the clouds of compassion,
> the rainwater of the Conqueror's Dharma,
> the cause of the harvest of the virtue of beings,
> falls without conceptualization.[1403]

The manifestation of emanations is like Brahma: Brahma, the king of devas, appears in all the paradises effortlessly without leaving his realm. In the same way, the buddhas effortlessly manifest all the emanations to all the worthy ones in the world without leaving the dharmakāya. [From the *Sublime Continuum*]:

> Just as Brahma, without leaving
> the realm of Brahma,
> effortlessly appears
> in all the deva realms,
>
> in that way the Sage,
> without leaving the dharmakāya,
> effortlessly manifests emanations
> to worthy ones in all realms.[1404]

The radiance of wisdom is like the sun: The rays of sunlight, without thought, cause lotuses and so on to blossom. In the same way, the Tathāgata's Dharma, without thought, causes the wisdom of pupils to blossom. [From the *Sublime Continuum*]:

> Just as the sun, without thought,
> by the instantaneous radiation of its light,
> causes lotuses to blossom
> and causes other things to ripen,
>
> in the same way, the sunrays
> of the Tathāgata's Dharma,
> without thought, reach
> the lotuses that are beings to be trained.[1405] [421]

The secret of the mind is like a precious jewel: A precious wish-fulfilling jewel, though it has no thought, fulfills every need and wish for those in its presence. In the same way, although the buddhas have no thought, they are able to accomplish the benefit of beings with various aspirations in accord with their individual capabilities. [From the *Sublime Continuum*]:

> Just as a wish-fulfilling jewel,
> though it has no thought,
> instantly fulfills the individual wishes
> of those who are in its presence,
>
> in the same way, the wish-fulfilling buddhas
> even though they do not think of it,

cause those with differing thoughts
to hear a variety of Dharma teachings.[1406]

The secret of the speech is like an echo: The sound of an echo arises within the cognition of others, as the reflection of a sound, without any thought or creation, and without being located anywhere, internally or externally. The speech of the tathāgatas resounds in that same way. [From the *Sublime Continuum*]:

Just as the sound of an echo,
without thought, without creation,
and without being located internally or externally,
appears to the cognition of others,

in the same way, the Tathāgata's speech,
without thought, without creation,
and without being located internally or externally,
appears to the cognition of others.[1407]

The secret of the body is like space: There are no objects or appearances in space. It transcends being a visual object, and though you can look high and low at it, it has no existence as that visual appearance. In the same way, even though one sees the appearances of the body of a buddha, it has no existence in that way. [From the *Sublime Continuum*]:

However high or low you look
at space, it has no existence like that.
In the same way, even though everyone
can see the Buddha, he is not like that.[1408]

The way in which compassion engages is like the earth: The earth has no thought, but all beings on the earth prosper by relying on the earth. In the same way, although the buddhas have no thought, the power of compassion causes the roots of virtue to increase in beings. [From the *Sublime Continuum*]:

Just as all beings who dwell on the earth
rely on the "holder of wealth,"

which has no thought, and attain
growth, prosperity, and increase,

in that same way, by relying on the earth
of the perfect Buddha, who has no thoughts,
the roots of virtue in beings
all increase, without exception.[1409]

. . .

[422] Intelligence, the king of mountains, danced and churned
the immeasurable ocean of a multitude of tantras,
from which appeared, seated on the sun[1410] of scripture and logic, a beauty:
the jewel of the teaching that radiated light into the ten directions.[1411]

A series of fortunate, new utpalas
with the bright smiles of the anthers of analysis
in the floating palace of the blossomed petals of "freedoms and opportunities"
are using their young wisdoms in a game of competing with each other.

When immaculate logic examines the meaning of texts
and they are explained at length, the wise are enchanted.
However, because those with little intelligence would be frightened
on seeing such a volume and would avoid it, I have given a condensed teaching.

I have written this with a genuine wish to help, thinking it will be beneficial
as a ship that can sail the ocean of tantras,
as a supreme key that opens the treasury of Mantrayāna texts,
and as a mirror for looking at the beautiful face of the profound meaning.

It is difficult to fathom the path of the profound Mantrayāna,
and my intelligence is too weak to study at length,
so if I will be shamed by my misconceptions and doubts,
I ask the deities and all sublime ones to forgive me.

Through the virtue of my efforts in this, may I and all beings
rely on the supreme vehicle throughout all our lifetimes,
increase our understanding of the great secret path,
and quickly attain the state of powerful Vajradhara.

I, named Gampopa Maṅgala,[1412] on the request of Ācārya Nyima Drakpa,[1413] composed this text on all the key points of the path of the supreme vehicle, which is the wide eye of wisdom. I did so in the waxing half of the third moon of a bird year,[1414] at the great seat named glorious Daklha Gampo,[1415] which is a place prophesied by the Conqueror. Through this, may there be excellent goodness for all beings!

Svasti! (May all be well!)

Table of Tibetan Transliteration

Aro Yeshé Jungné	A ro Ye shes 'byung gnas
Barom Kagyü	'Ba' rom Bka' brgyud
Barompa Darma Wangchuk	'Ba' rom pa Dar ma dbang phyug
Bendom Sherap Jungné	Ban ldom Shes rab 'byung gnas
Bharo Chakdum	Bha ro Phyag rdum
Bodong	Bo dong
Bön	Bon
Butön Rinchen Drup	Bu ston Rin chen grub
Chakriwa	Lcags ri ba
Chengawa Tsültrim Bar	Spyan snga ba Tshul khrims 'bar
Chökyi Drakpa	Chos kyi grags pa
Chökyi Gyaltsen	Chos kyi rgyal mtshan
Chökyi Jungné	Chos kyi 'byung gnas
Chökyi Wangchuk	Chos kyi dbang phyug
Chökyi Yungdrung	Chos kyi g.yung drung
Chöying Dorjé	Chos dbyings rdo rje
Daklha Gampo	Dwags lha sgam po
Dakpo Dülzin	Dwags po 'Dul ldzin
Dakpo Kagyü	Dwags po Bka' brgyud
Dakpo Lhajé	Dwags po Lha rje
Dakpo Nigyom	Dwags po Snyi sgom
Dakpo Tashi Namgyal	Dwags po Bkra shis rnam rgyal
Damchö Lingpa	Dam chos gling pa
Dampa Kor	Dam pa Skor
Daö Shönu	Zla 'od gzhon nu
Darma Dodé	Dar ma mdo sde
Darma Wangchuk	Dar ma dbang phyug
Densathil	Gdan sa mthil
Deshin Shekpa	Bde bzhin gshegs pa

Dergé	Sde dge
Döl	Dol
Dönmo Ripa	Don mo ri pa
Dorjé Dzeö	Rdo rje mdzes 'od
Dorjé Gyaltsen	Rdo rje rgyal mtshan
Dorjé Palwa	Rdo rje dpal ba
Drakpa Sengé	Grags pa seng ge
Drakpa Shedrup	Grags pa bshad sgrub
Drigom Repa	'Bri sgom Ras pa
Drigung Kagyü	'Bri gung Bka' brgyud
Drigungpa	'Bri gung pa
Drogön Gyaltsa	'Gro mgon rgyal tsha
Drogön Rechenpa	'Gro mgon ras chen pa
Drogön Tsangpa Gyaré	'Gro mgon Gtsang pa rgya ras
Drokmi Lotsāwa Shākya Yeshé	'Brog mi Lo tsā ba Shākya ye shes
Dromtön	'Brom ston
Dromtön Gyalwai Jungné	'Brom ston Rgyal ba'i 'byung gnas
Drukchen Pema Karpo	'Brug chen Padma dkar po
Drukpa Kagyü	'Brug pa Bka' brgyud
Düsum Khyenpa	Dus gsum mkhyen pa
dzokchen	rdzog chen
Gampopa Sönam Rinchen	Sgam po pa Bsod nams rin chen
Gangri Karma Rinpoche	Gangs ri kar ma rin po che
Garwang Rinpoché	Gar dbang Rin po che
Geluk	Dge lugs
Geshé Ben Gungyal Tsültrim Gyalwa	Dge bshes 'Ban gung rgyal tshul khrims rgyal ba
Golok	Mgo log
Gompa Tsültrim Nyingpo	Sgom pa Tshul khrims Snying po
Gomtsül	Sgom tshul
Gönpawa Wangchuk Gyaltsen	Dgon pa ba Dbang phyug rgyal mtshan
Götsang	Rgod tshang
Götsang Repa	Rgod tshang Ras pa
Götsangpa Gönpo Dorjé	Rgod tshang pa Mgon po rdo rje
Gungthang	Gung thang
Gya Yöndak	Rgya yon bdag
Gyachak Riwa	Rgya lcags ri ba

Gyagom	Rgya sgom
Gyalthangpa Dechen Dorjé	Rgyal thang pa Bde chen rdo rje
Jamgön Kongtrül	'Jam mgon Kong sprul
Jatsön Nyingpo	'Ja' tshon snying po
Jayülpa	Bya yul pa
Jayülwa Shönu Ö	Bya yul ba Gzhon nu 'od
Jikten Sumgön	'Jig rten Gsum mgon
Jonang	Jo nang
Kagyü	Bka' brgyud
Kamtsang Kagyü	Kam tshang Bka' brgyud
Kangyur	Bka' 'gyur
Kargyü	Dkar brgyud
Karma Chakmé	Karma Chags med
Karma Kagyü	Karma Bka' brgyud
Karma Ngelek Tenzin	Karma Nge legs bstan 'dzin
Karma Pakshi	Karma Pa kshi
Karmapa	Karma pa
Karopa	Ka ro pa
Kathok Rikzin Tsewang Norbu	Kaḥ thog rig 'dzin Tshe dbang nor bu
Khachö Wangpo	Mkha spyod dbang po
Khampa Usé	Khams pa Dbu se
Kharchu	Mkhar chu
Khenting Tai Situ	Khan ting Ta'i si tu
Khutön Tsöndrü Yungdrung	Khu ston Brtson 'grus g.yung drung
Khyapgön	Skyabs mgon
Khyungtsangpa	Khyung tshang pa
Könchok Rinchen	Dkon mchog rin chen
Kor Nirūpa	Skor Nirūpa
Künga Gyaltsen	Kun dga' rgyal mtshan
Künga Paljor	Kun dga' dpal 'byor
Kyopa	Skyob pa
Lama Shang	Bla ma Zhang
Lamchen Gyalpo Rinpoche	Lam mkhyen Rgyal po Rin po che
Latö	La stod
Lhari	Lha ri
Lharipa Namkha Ö	Lha ri pa Nam mkha' 'od

Lhajé Nupchung	Lha rje gnubs chung
Lhodrak	Lho brag
Lingré Pema Dorjé (Lingrepa)	Gling ras Padma rdo rje (Gling ras pa)
Lodrö Rinchen	Blo gros rin chen
Lodrö Yangpa	Blo gros yangs pa
Lorepa Darma Wangchuk	Lo ras pa Dar ma dbang phyug
Mal Yerwapa	Mal Yer ba pa
Marpa Chökyi Lodrö	Mar pa Chos kyi blo gros
Marpa Druptop	Mar pa Grub thob
Marpa Kagyü	Smar pa Bka' brgyud
Martsang Kagyü	Smar tshang Bka' brgyud
Masé Tokden Lodrö Rinchen	Rma se rtogs ldan Blo gros rin chen
Mengom Tsültrim Sangpo	Sman sgom Tshul khrims bzang po
Metön Chenpo	Mes ton chen po
Milarepa	Mi la ras pa
Minyak Tokden Lodrö Rinchen	Mi nyag rtogs ldan Blo gros rin chen
Nakpo Sherdé	Nag po Sher dad
Namchö Mingyur Dorjé	Gnam chos Mi 'gyur rdo rje
Namdruk	Gnam 'brug
Naphur	Sna phur
Natsok Rangdröl	Sna tshogs rang grol
Nedo Kagyü	Gnas mdo Bka' brgyud
Nethang Dölma Lhakhang	Mnyes thang sgrol ma lha khang
Neusurpa	Sne'u zur pa
Ngari Tertön Garwang Dorjé	Mnga' ris gter ston Gar dbang rdo rje
Ngok Chökyi Dorjé	Rngog Chos kyi rdo rje
Ngok Dodé	Rngog Mdo sde
Ngok Lekpai Sherap	Rngog Legs pa'i shes rab
Ngoktön	Rngog ston
Ngoktön Chödor	Rngog ston chos rdor
Nüden Dorjé	Nus ldan rdo rje
Nyethang Dölma Lhakhang	Snye thang sgrol ma lha khang
Nyima Drakpa	Nyi ma grags pa
Nyingma	Rnying ma
Nyiphu Gyergom Chenpo	Snyi phu gyer sgom chen po
Nyukrumpa	Snyug rum pa
Paksam Wangpo	Dpag bsam dbang po

Palpung	Dpal spungs
Palri	Dpal ri
Palyül	Dpal yul
Pamthingpa	Pham thing pa
Pangbu Thül	Spang bu thul
Pangshong Lhari	Spang gshong lha ri
Patsap Lotsāwa Nyima Drak	Pa tshab Lo tsā ba Nyi ma grags
Pema Karpo	Pad ma dkar po
Phadampa Sangyé	Pha dam pa Sang rgyas
Phakdru Dorjé Gyalpo	Phag gru rdo rje rgyal po
Phakdru Kagyü	Phag gru Bka' brgyud
Phakmo Drupa	Phag mo gru pa
Phenyül	Phan yul
Ramoché	Ra mo che
Rangjung Dorjé	Rang byung rdo rje
Ratna Lingpa	Ratna gling pa
Rechung Dorjé Drakpa	Ras chung rdo rje grags pa
Rechung Kagyü	Ras chung Bka' brgyud
Rechungpa	Ras chung pa
Rinchen Phüntsok	Rin chen phun tshogs
Rinchen Sangpo	Rin chen bzang po
Rölpai Dorjé	Rol pa'i rdo rje
Sakya Paṇḍita Künga Gyaltsen	Sa skya Paṇḍi ta Kun dga' rgyal mtshan
Sakya	Sa skya
Sangri Repa	Zangs ri ras pa
Sangyé Lingpa	Sangs rgyas gling pa
Sarawa Kalden Yeshé Sengé	Za ra ba Skal ldan Ye shes seng ge
Shamarpa	Zhwa dmar pa
Shang Gom	Zhang sgom
Shang Rinpoché	Zhang Rin po che
Shang Tsalpa Tsöndrü	Zhang Tshal pa bston 'grus
Shangpa Kagyü	Zhang pa Bka' brgyud
Shapdrung Ngawang Namgyal	Zhabs drung Ngag dbang rnam rgyal
Shawa Lingpa	Sha ba gling pa
Shenphen Sangpo	Gzhan phan bzang po
shentong	gzhan stong

Sherap Jungné	Shes rab 'byung gnas
Shong Lotsāwa Lodrö Tenpa	Shong Lo tsā ba Blo gros brtan pa
Shönu Dawai Özer	Gzhon nu zla ba'i 'od zer
Shönu Lha	Gzhon nu lha
Shuksep Kagyü	Shug gseb Bka' brgyud
Shung	Gzhung
Situ Tenpai Nyinjé	Si tu Bstan pa'i nyin byed
Surmang Kagyü	Zur mang Bka' brgyud
Taklung Kagyü	Stag lung Bka' brgyud
Taklung Thangpa	Stag lung thang pa
Tengyur	Bstan 'gyur
Thangpa Tashi Palwa	Thang pa Bkra shis dpal ba
Thrangu Rinpoche	Khra 'gu rin po che
Thupten Chökor Ling	Thub bstan chos skor gling
Tipupa	Ti pu pa
Trophu Kagyü	Khro phu Bka' brgyud
Trungmasé	Drung rma se
Trungpa Rinpoché	Drung pa Rin po che
Tsal	Tshal
Tsalpa Kagyü	Tshal pa Bka' brgyud
Tsang	Gtsang
Tsangnyön Heruka	Gtsang smyon He ru ka
Tsangpa Gyaré	Gtsang pa rgya ras
Tselé Natsok Rangdröl	Rtse le Sna tshogs rang grol
Tsöndrü Drakpa	Brtson 'grus grags pa
Tsongrong	Gtsong rong
Tsurphu	Tshur phu
Tsurtön	Tshur ston
Tsurtön Wangé	Tshur ston dbang nge
Ü	Dbu
Ugyen Trinlé Dorjé	U rgyan Phrin las rdo rje
Wangchuk Dorjé	Dbang phyug rdo rje
Yasang Kagyü	G.ya' bzang Bka' brgyud
Yelpa Kagyü	Yel pa Bka' brgyud
Yelpa Yeshé Tsekpa	Yel pa Ye shes brtsegs pa
Yeshé Dé	Ye shes sde
Yongé Mingyur Dorjé	Yongs dge Mi 'gyur rdo rje
Yudrakpa Tsöndrü Drakpa	G.yu brag pa Brtson 'grus grags pa

Notes

Abbreviations for frequently cited texts are listed in the technical notes on page 28.

1 For a concise description of the political history of the Karma Kagyü, see Jim Rheingans, "Narratives of Reincarnation, Politics of Power, and the Emergence of a Scholar: The Very Early Years of Mikyö Dorje" in *Lives Lived, Lives Imagined: Biography in the Buddhist Traditions* (Boston: Wisdom Publications, 2010), 241–98.

2 Jamgön Kongtrül's autobiography is available in translation: *The Autobiography of Jamgön Kongtrul: A Gem of Many Colors*, trans. Richard Barron (Chökyi Nyima) (Ithaca, NY: Snow Lion Publications, 1994). Also, Kongtrül's instructions on performing the three-year retreats are found in *Jamgon Kongtrul's Retreat Manual*, trans. Ngawang Zangpo (Hugh Leslie Thompson) (Ithaca, NY: Snow Lion Publications, 1994).

3 Bön is both officially classified as, and is also by nature, a Buddhist school, but as its lineage does not derive from Śākyamuni, it has a popular reputation of being non-Buddhist.

4 The word *kagyü* does appear, however, in the Tibetan translation of some Indian texts. For example, in *Secret Sādhana of Lokeśvara* by Siddharājñī (tenth–eleventh centuries) it is stated that the meditator should imagine Amitābha above his head "encircled by the instruction-lineage (*bka' brgyud*) guru-vidyādharas." However, here *kagyü* is being used in its more general sense, meaning the transmission of instructions. It may be a translation of the Sanskrit *vacanaparaṃparā*, or more probably *upadeśaparaṃparā*, although *upadeśa* is usually translated as *man ngag*.

5 *Bka' babs bzhi yi brgyud pa*. Jamgön Kongtrül, *Treasury of Knowledge*, vol. 1, p. 526.

6 The Nedo Kagyü teachings are also an essential part of the Palyül Nyingma school, which arose in eastern Tibet in the seventeenth century based on the terma of Namchö Mingyur Dorjé (1645–67). Penor Rinpoche (1932–2009), the late head of the Nyingma school, was also the Palyül Nyingma throneholder.

7 Though "luminosity" has gained currency in English, "brightness" would be closer to the original Sanskrit. The Tibetan translation *'od gsal* means "bright light," though Tibetan uses the word "clear" for where we would use "bright." This has led to the term being often translated as "clear light."

8 The Tibetan *bar do* normally refers to the intermediate state between death and birth. This is one of the few Tibetan terms that has become a part of the English language.

9 *Purapraveśa* (*grong 'jug*) is the term used for beginning another life by transferring

into another recently deceased adult body and reanimating it. The more common practice of transferring consciousness to a pure realm on death, which is called *saṃkrānti* (Tibetan: *'pho ba*), appears to be strikingly absent from the list, but it is considered as an ancillary of *purapraveśa*.

10 *Ṣaḍdharmopadeśa*, Toh 2330 Tengyur, rgyud, *zhi*, 270a–271a. This was translated into Tibetan by Nāropa and Marpa.

11 W. Y. Evans-Wentz, *Tibetan Yoga and Secret Doctrines* (London: Oxford University Press, 1935), vii.

12 See also Jamgön Kongtrul Lodrö Tayé, *The Treasury of Knowledge, book 8, part 3: The Elements of Tantric Practice* (Ithaca, NY: Snow Lion Publications, 2008), 123–216, and *book 8, part 4: Esoteric Instructions* (2007), 149–208. Also, Glenn H. Mullin, *The Practice of the Six Yogas of Naropa* (Ithaca, NY: Snow Lion Publications, 1997); Lama Thubten Yeshe, *The Bliss of Inner Fire: Heart Practice of the Six Yogas of Naropa* (Boston: Wisdom Publications, 1998); and Garma C. C. Chang, *The Six Yogas of Naropa and Teachings on Mahamudra* (Ithaca, NY: Snow Lion Publications, 1986).

13 This view states that while all phenomena are empty of a nature of their own, the quintessential buddha nature within all beings is not devoid of its own nature and qualities, but it is empty (*stong*) of all other (*gzhan*) samsaric phenomena. Philosophical views that do not make this exception for buddha nature are called *empty of self* (*rang stong*).

14 A back-translation from Tibetan into Sanskrit that has gained common currency is *anuttarayogatantra*, but this has yet to be found in any Sanskrit text.

15 See also Elizabeth English, *Vajrayoginī: Her Visualizations, Rituals, and Forms* (Boston: Wisdom Publications, 2002).

16 For a detailed description of both stages or phases, see Jamgön Kongtrul, *Creation and Completion: Essential Points of Tantric Meditation*, trans. Sarah Harding (Boston: Wisdom Publications, 1996).

17 For further reading on the generation, or creation, phase, see Jamgön Kongtrul Lodrö Tayé, *The Treasury of Knowledge, book 8, part 3*, and *book 8, part 4*. See also Daniel Cozort, *Highest Yoga Tantra* (Ithaca, NY: Snow Lion Publications, 1986).

18 Important Kagyü works on the mahāmudrā already available in translation include two works by the Ninth Karmapa Wangchuk Dorjé: *Ocean of Definitive Meaning*, trans. Elizabeth Callahan (Seattle: Nitartha, 2001), and *The Mahāmudrā: Eliminating the Darkness of Ignorance*, trans. Alexander Berzin (Dharamsala: Library of Tibetan Works and Archives, 1978). There are also two important works by Dakpo Tashi Namgyal: *Mahāmudrā: The Moonlight—Quintessence of Mind and Meditation*, trans. Lobsang Lhalungpa (Boston: Wisdom Publications, 2006), and *Clarifying the Natural State: A Principal Guidance Manual for Mahamudra*, trans. Erik Pema Kunsang (Hong Kong: Rangjung Yeshe Publications, 2001).

19 For an in-depth study of Saraha, see Kurtis R. Schaeffer, *Dreaming the Great Brahmin: Tibetan Traditions of the Buddhist Poet-Saint Saraha* (Oxford: Oxford University Press, 2004).

20 The dates in *The Blue Annals* do not specify the year elements, and in his translation, Roerich chose 1007/10–87, dates that have commonly been repeated. Those dates, however, do not correspond with the biographies of Maitripa's pupils. It

seems clear that he had to have passed away before Vajrapāṇi moved to Nepal in 1066.

21 'Gos Lo tsā ba, *The Blue Annals*, trans. George N. Roerich (Calcutta: Motilal Banarsidass, 1949), 844.

22 *Blue Annals*, 843.

23 *Blue Annals*, 851.

24 Decleer, Hubert, "The Sacred Biography of Bharo 'Maimed Hand,'" in *Buddha Jayanti Souvenir*, ed. R. Shakya and M. Shakya (Lalitpur: 2538th Buddha Jayanti Organising Committee, 1994).

25 Götsang Repa Natsok Rangdröl, *Rje btsun ras chung ba'i rnam thar* (Xining: Mtsho sngon mi rigs dpe skrun khang, 1992), 268.

26 *Blue Annals*, 843.

27 *Blue Annals*, 843.

28 All twenty-six texts, the *Amanasi* (*skor nyer drug*), are preserved within the Tengyur, the Tibetan canon of commentarial literature.

29 *Blue Annals*, 844–47.

30 See also Daniel P. Brown, *Pointing Out the Great Way: The Stages of Meditation in the Mahāmudrā Tradition* (Boston: Wisdom Publications, 2006).

31 A biography of Tilopa and Nāropa attributed to Marpa is evidently of a later date: Mar-pa Chos-kyi bLo-gros, *The Life of the Mahāsiddha Tilopa*, trans. Fabrizio Torricelli and Acharya Sangye T. Naga (Dharamsala: Library of Tibetan Works and Archives, 1995). In English there is the sixteenth-century work by Lhatsün Rinchen Namgyal to be found in *Life and Teaching of Naropa*, trans. Herbert V. Guenther (Boston: Shambhala Publications, 1986).

32 Tsangnyön's works have even attracted stinging criticism from Tibetan historians, such as the Jonang scholar Tāranatha. See Hubert Decleer, "The Melodious Drum Sound All-Pervading," in *Tibetan Studies: Proceedings of the 5th Seminar of the International Association for Tibetan Studies, Narita 1989*, 2 vols., ed. Ihara Shoren and Yamaguchi Zuiho (Tokyo: Naritasan Shinshoji, 1992), vol. 1, p. 27.

33 For example, Kathok Tsewang Norbu lists ten variant dates for Marpa's life that are found in Kagyü histories, which in Western years would be: b. 991, 997–1084, 1000–1081/85/88, 1002–81, 1006–94/96, 1011–96, 1012–93, 1012–97, 1021–1109, 1024–1107. *Clear Brief Correct Account of a Definite Chronology*, Kathok Rikzin Tsewang Norbu's Collected Works, vol. 3, 640.

34 *Blue Annals*, 414–15.

35 Gampopa Sönam Rinchen, *Tai lo dang nāro'i rnam thar*, in *Selected Writings of Sgam po pa: The Gemur Manuscript* (Dolanji, H.P., India: Tibetan Bonpo Monastic Centre, 1974), 19.

36 His life story is primarily known through the nonhistorical but compelling work of Tsangnyön Heruka: *The Life of Marpa the Translator: Seeing All Accomplishes All*, trans. Nalanda Translation Committee (Boston: Shambhala Publications, 1982).

37 Examples of alternative dates: Kathok Tsewang Norbu comes to a conclusion of 1028–1111 in his *Clear Brief Correct Account of Definite Chronology*; it is 1048–1129 in Dorjé Dzeö's *Precious Treasury that Is the Source of All that Is Required*; Gyalthangpa gives 1055–1128 in his *Golden Succession of the Kagyü*; and the anonymous *Biography and Songs of Shepai Dorjé* has 1036–1123.

38 Lhajé Nupchung, *Gshin rje gshed yang zlog me'i spu gri*, in Kongtrül's *Rin chen gter mdzod chen mo*, vol. *tsa* (Paro: Ngodrup and Sherab Drimay, 1966–80), 417–621. See also Dan Martin, "The Early Education of Milarepa," *Journal of the Tibet Society* 2 (1982): 52–76.

39 Gyalthangpa Dechen Dorjé, *Dkar brgyud gser phreng*, 195.

40 There are numerous biographies of Milarepa in Tibetan. The most popular are the two companion works: Tsangnyön Heruka's *Hundred Thousand Songs of Milarepa*, trans. Garma C. C. Chang (Boston: Shambhala Publications, 1989), and his *Life of Milarepa*, trans. Lobsang Lhalungpa (Boston: Shambhala Publications, 1985).

41 Peter Alan Roberts, "The Evolution of the Biography of Milarepa and Rechungpa," in *Lives Lived, Lives Imagined: Biography in the Buddhist Traditions*, ed. Linda Covill et al. (Boston: Wisdom Publications, 2010), 194. See also Roberts, *The Biographies of Rechungpa: The Evolution of a Tibetan Hagiography* (Abingdon, Oxon: Routledge, 2007).

42 Tsangnyön Heruka, *Rje btsun mi la ras pa'i rnam thar rgyas par phye ba mgur 'bum* (Antwerp: Tibetaans Boeddhistisch Meditatiecentrum), 482, translated in *The Hundred Thousand Songs of Milarepa*, 495.

43 *Thar pa rin po che'i rgyan*. This text, already available in several English-language translations as the *Jewel Ornament of Liberation*, will appear in a translation by Ken Holmes in volume 10 of *The Library of Tibetan Classics*, the volume on the stages of the doctrine (*bstan rim*) genre.

44 A composite biography of Gampopa is found in Jampa Mackenzie Stewart, *The Life of Gampopa* (Ithaca, NY: Snow Lion Publications, 1995).

45 Tatsak Tsewang Gyal, *Dharma History from Lhorong* (pp. 177–80), has earth bird to iron ox (1129–81); *Blue Annals* (pp. 463–65) has fire monkey to earth ox (1116–69).

46 *Blue Annals*, 463.

47 Dakpo Tashi Namgyal, *Mahāmudrā: The Moonlight*; and [Drashi Namjhal], *Teachings of Tibetan Yoga: An Introduction to the Spiritual, Mental and Physical Exercises of the Tibetan Religion*, trans. Garma C. C. Chang (Hyde Park, NY: University Books, 1963).

48 Tatsak Tsewang Gyal, *Dharma History from Lhorong*, 222.

49 Tatsak Tsewang Gyal, *Dharma History from Lhorong*, 207–9.

50 Tatsak Tsewang Gyal, *Dharma History from Lhorong*, 181–99; *The Blue Annals*, 711–15.

51 Tatsak Tsewang Gyal, *Dharma History from Lhorong*, 159–64.

52 Also called Marpa (spelled *Smar pa*) Kagyü, not to be confused with Marpa (spelled *Mar pa*) Kagyü, the name for all Kagyü lineages. Gangri Karma Rinpoche, the present Martsang Kagyü lineage holder, is working to reestablish it as an independent school.

53 Tatsak Tsewang Gyal, *Dharma History from Lhorong*, 352.

54 See also Michael M. Broido, "*Abhiprāya* and Implication in Tibetan Linguistics," *Journal of Indian Philosophy* 12.1 (March 1984): 1–33.

55 Tatsak Tsewang Gyal, *Dharma History from Lhorong*, 645–63; *Blue Annals*, 664–70.

56 Michael Aris, *Bhutan: The Early History of a Himalayan Kingdom* (Warminster, England: Aris & Phillips, 1979).

57 *Blue Annals*, 476.

58 A history of the Karmapas is found in Karma Thinley, *The History of the Sixteen Karmapas of Tibet* (Boulder, CO: Prajna Press, 1980).

59 *Phyag chen rgyas pa nges don rgya mtsho* (Sarnath: Vajravidya dpe mdzod khang, 2006).

60 The Jonang continues to exist as a relatively small independent school, with about sixty monasteries in eastern Tibet. Their *shentong*, or "empty of other," view, which the Karma Kagyü continue to champion, propounds the existence of an unchanging enlightenment that, unlike all other phenomena, is empty only in the sense that it is devoid of anything other than itself and its inherent qualities. See Karl Brunnhölzl, *The Center of the Sunlit Sky: Madhyamaka in the Kagyü Tradition* (Ithaca, NY: Snow Lion Publications, 2004).

61 Kham is the southeast region of the Tibetan plateau and the locale of Dergé and Palpung Monastery. A Karma Kagyü collection of songs by great masters of the Kagyü lineage is to be found in Nalanda Translation Committee, trans., *Rain of Wisdom: The Essence of the Ocean of True Meaning* (Boston: Shambhala Publications, 1980).

62 *Tshogs chos mu tig phreng ba*. This appears to be an uncommon type of Tibetan text, a collection of transcribed lectures to be used as the basis for talks. Gampopa's collected works also include pupils' records of talks he gave. These texts existed in manuscript form for centuries, and therefore published versions have a number of variations from which a critical edition needs to be made. The published editions in which this text appear include: *Selected Writings of Sgam po pa Bsod nams rin chen (Dwags po lha rje) with the Biography Written by His Descendant Sgam po pa Bsod nams lhun grub* (Dolanji: Tibetan Bonpo Monastic Center, 1974); *Collected Works (Gsuṅ 'bum) of Sgam po pa Bsod nams rin chen* (Delhi: Shashin, 1976); *A Treasury of Instructions on the Mahāmudrā (Nges don phyag rgya chen po'i khrid mdzod)* (New Delhi: Shamar Rinpoche, 1997); *Khams gsum chos kyi rgyal po mnyam med sgam po pa 'gro mgon bsod nams rin chen mchog gi gsung 'bum yid bzhin nor bu* (Kathmandu: Shri Gautam Buddha Vihara, 2000); *Collected Works (Gsung 'bum) of Sgam po pa Bsod nams rin chen* (Darjeeling, West Bengal: Kagyu Sungrab Nyamso Khang, 1982); and *Collected Works of Gampopa (Bsod nams rin chen gsung 'bum)* (Sde dge, Tibet: Sde dge par khang chen mo, n.d.).

63 An expression that means worlds (appearance) and beings (existence).

64 The four kinds of behavior are lying down, sitting, moving around, and going somewhere.

65 The seven qualities of a higher existence are a good family, a beautiful body, a long life, health, good fortune, wealth, and great wisdom.

66 Indrabhuti, *The Sādhana for the Accomplishment of Wisdom (Jñānasiddhināmasādhana)*, chap. 14, Toh 2219 Tengyur, rgyud, *wi*, 51a2. The text contains twenty-one short chapters. The quotation is not reproduced exactly; the original, which is in four lines not three, reads:

> With no oars,
> your boat will never reach the far shore.
> Though you may realize all qualities,
> with no guru, existence will have no end.

67 *Recitation of Mañjuśrī's Names (Mañjuśrīnāmasaṃgiti)* v. 141 (or chap. 9, v. 23), Toh 360 Kangyur, rgyud, *ka*, 7b5. See also in Narthang Kangyur, rgyud, *ka*, 10a7; Tok

Palace Kangyur, rgyud, *cha*, 9b4; Kathok bka' ma rgyas pa, *nga*, 11a5; and Nyingma Gyübum, *zha*, 173a3. Gampopa's text here reads *skad cig gcig gis rdzogs sangs rgyas/ skad cig gcig gis bye brag byed*. This reverses the order of the lines in the closest scriptural parallel—the second and third lines of verse 141, which is part of a series of descriptions of Mañjuśrī, the bodhisattva of wisdom. The Dergé Kangyur has *skad cig thams cad rnam bsgom pa/ skad cig mngon rdzogs sangs rgyas*, and thus instead of "one instant makes the difference" it reads "The one who has meditated on all instants." In the Narthang and Tok Palace Kangyurs "has meditated" (*rnam bsgom*) is in the present: "meditates" (*rnam sgom pa*). An earlier translation preserved in the Kama and in the Nyingma Gyübum has *skad cig thams cad bye brag phyes/ kad cig gcig gis rdzogs sangs rgyas*, creating "The one who *differentiates* all instants." This is also, incidentally, the version in Alex Wayman's edition in *Chanting the Names of Mañjuśrī* (Delhi: Motilal Banarsidass, 1985). This earlier translation must be the source for the version in the Gampopa text, despite the corruptions and the line out of order. The difference between the new and old translations—"meditates" vs. "differentiates"—derives from the different Tibetan renderings of the Sanskrit *vibhāva* in *sarvakṣanavibhāvakaḥ/ ekakṣanābhisaṃbuddhaḥ*.

68 This is an idiomatic Tibetan expression for when you are very ill and dying. It describes a sick person lying down, head on hand, and unable to eat.

69 Source unidentified.

70 Source unidentified.

71 *Prātimokṣasūtra*, Toh 2 Kangyur, 'dul ba, *ca*, 20b1. Also in *Aphorisms* (*Udānavarga*), 28:1, Toh 326 Kangyur, mdo sde, *sa*, 236a4. Also verse 183 of the *Dhammapada*.

72 *Atyayajñānasūtra*, Toh 122 Kangyur, mdo sde, *tha*, 153a–b. This is not an exact quotation but a paraphrase of the sutra's verses:

> All things are impermanent,
> therefore meditate on the understanding that is free of attachment.
> The mind is the cause for the arising of wisdom;
> do not seek buddhahood elsewhere.

73 Atiśa, *Entering the Two Truths* (*Satyadvayāvatāra*), Toh 3902 Tengyur, dbu ma, *a*, 73a4. Though not exact, the quote is quite close.

74 "Flaming mouths"—pretas for whom any nourishment bursts into flames in their mouths.

75 *Hevajratantra*, book 1, 5:11, Toh 417 Kangyur, rgyud, *nga*, 5a7. The first line of the citation has reversed the order of the line in the tantra: "There is no meditator and no meditation."

76 The Indian siddha Saraha.

77 Source unidentified.

78 The TBRC lists an Aro Yeshé Jungné, who was a teacher of Dorjé Palwa (1284–1365) and of the Third Karmapa Rangjung Dorjé, but evidently the one referred to here is an earlier master.

79 *Snang shar yin*. Because of the intrinsic ambiguity of Tibetan, *snang* can be a noun, "appearance," or a verb; likewise, it can be either plural or singular. Therefore *snang ba* may be "appear," "appearing," "appearance," or "appearances." *Shar* may be "arise," "arises," "arising," or "arisings." *Yin* may mean "is," "are," or "am." This latitude of interpretation is exploited in the commentary.

80 For example, neglecting your children could be misconstrued as nonattachment.

81 Again, this refers to worlds and beings.

82 Source unidentified.

83 This sentence anthropomorphizes karma to indicate karma created in the past, the results that will come in the future, and the results being experienced in the present so that the karma is finished.

84 The three realms (*khams gsum*) encompass the full range of existence within the Buddhist cosmos. They are the *desire realm*, which includes the six types of rebirth from hell beings up to the lower devas, and the *form* and *formless realms*, higher deva realms that are destinations for those highly accomplished in meditative stabilization.

85 It is tempting to think that there is the possibility of scribal corruption here, the words for "end" and "beginning," *thog* and *mtha'* being somewhat similar, particularly in the cursive script, and Gampopa's texts existed solely as written manuscripts for centuries. The usual contemporary teaching on this subject is that generally samsara has no beginning nor end, but for specific individuals, though samsara has no beginning, it does have an end on their attainment of buddhahood. However, the text seems to be quite specific on this point, presumably implying that the individual's beginning is the beginning of buddhahood and the end is the end of samsara.

86 Source unidentified.

87 Here there is certainly a scribal error in the text, as "self" was repeated instead of "other," and this is a well-known generic statement.

88 The *Ratnaguṇasaṃcayagāthā*, which is actually chapter 84, the verse summary, of the *Eighteen-Thousand-Verse Perfection of Wisdom Sutra* (*Aṣṭādaśasāhasrikāprajñā pāramitā*), Toh 10 Kangyur, sher phyin, *ka*, 173b4.

89 The ten Dharma conducts are: (1) writing out the words of the Buddha, (2) making offerings, (3) performing acts of charity, (4) listening to the Dharma, (5) keeping the Dharma, (6) reading the Dharma, (7) teaching the Dharma, (8) reciting the Dharma, (9) contemplating the meaning of the Dharma, and (10) meditating on the meaning of the Dharma.

90 The six classes of beings, from lowest to highest, are the hell beings, pretas, animals, human beings, asuras, and devas.

91 Source unidentified.

92 *Root Verses on the Middle Way*, 24:8, 14b7.

93 Maitreyanātha, *Ornament of Realization* (*Abhisamayālaṃkāra*), 1:19, Toh 3786 Tengyur, shes phyin, *ka*, 2b5.

94 Source unidentified. This verse is incomplete in all editions, ending midsentence.

95 The "essence teachings" usually refers to the mahāmudrā of Saraha. The "four states" may refer to the four resultant states: stream-entrant, once-returner, nonreturner, and arhat.

96 These have not been identified. This may refer to the nine levels of concentration (*samāpatti*). See page 302.

97 Gampopa explains this analogy in his *Perfectly Auspicious Dharma Lecture* (*Tshogs chos bkra shis phun tshogs*): "The first day of the moon is the moon, but it is not able to illuminate, giving us the analogy of the first day of the moon." Gampopa Sönam

Rinchen, *Collected Works (Gsung 'bum) of Sgam po pa Bsod nams rin chen* (Delhi: Khasdub Gyatsho Shashin, 1976), 162 (80b6).

98 The *three vows* are the three levels of ethical commitments: the vows of individual liberation (such as monastic vows or lay precepts), the vows of a bodhisattva, and the vows of a tantric yogi.

99 Source unidentified.

100 Indrabhuti, *The Sādhana for the Accomplishment of Wisdom* (*Jñānasiddhināma-sādhana*), Toh 2219 Tengyur, rgyud, *wi*, 51a2. This is Gampopa's second use of the quotation, which paraphrases the original source. See footnote 66 above.

101 Source unidentified.

102 These lines do not appear in the *Hevajra Tantra*.

103 Source unidentified. This quotation was also used in the fourth lecture above.

104 Source unidentified.

105 These ten bad actions are the ten things to avoid listed among the ten good actions below.

106 Apparently in all editions, "conciliatory words" and "harsh speech," which would have been contiguous in Tibetan, are missing.

107 Source unidentified, but likely from a perfection of wisdom sutra.

108 Source unidentified.

109 Source unidentified.

110 *Recitation of Mañjuśrī's Names* (*Mañjuśrīnāmasaṃgīti*), Toh 360 Kangyur, rgyud, *ka*, 2a2.

111 *Hevajra Tantra*, book 1, 5:11, 6a7. The citation has reversed the line as in the earlier citation of the full verse. See note 75.

112 Saraha, *Treasury of Dohas* (*Dohakoṣagīti*), Toh 2224 Tengyur, rgyud, *wi*, 71b2.

113 This presumably refers to the *King of Meditations Sutra*, which the Buddha taught to Candraprabhakumāra. The Tibetan form of his name is Daö Shönu. This is also one of Gampopa's names, as he was considered to be a rebirth of Candraprabhakumāra.

114 Lhajé, an honorific term for a physician, is another of Gampopa's names, as he had been a physician before becoming a monk.

115 This is one of at least eight collections of Gampopa's talks, in addition to four texts of oral answers to questions. The compilers are usually anonymous, though the pupils of Gampopa who wrote down the talks are usually named. Some of the compilations are clearly stated to be after Gampopa's lifetime.

116 This is clearly not intended to be a comprehensive lineage list as it leaps from the fourth-century Asaṅga through the seventh-century Śāntideva to the eleventh-century Suvarṇadvīpa Dharmakīrti, who lived in Sumatra and was the teacher of Atiśa. Chengawa Tsültrim Bar (1038–1103) was one of Dromtön's three principal pupils. The name of Gyagom is obscure, but it probably refers to Gampopa's principal Kadam teacher Jayülwa Shönu Ö (1075–1138).

117 Lharipa Namkha Ö, a direct pupil of Lama Shang and Shönu Lha's own teacher.

118 This is a reference to Gampopa, also known as Dakpo Lhajé or Dakpo Rinpoché.

119 *Bodhicaryāvatara*, 1:4, 1b5.

120 *Bodhicaryāvatara*, 2:59, 6a6. An alternative numbering calls this verse 58.

121 *Bhadrakarātrisūtra*, Toh 313 Kangyur, mdo sde, *sa*, 162b2. There is some corruption

in the quotation: *sang dag*, instead of *sang tsam*, *kyi* instead of *kyis*, and *bdag cag* instead of *bdag tu*.

122 *Aphorisms* (*Udānavarga*), 1:33, Toh 326 Kangyur, mdo sde, *sa*, 209b2. Shönu Lha either paraphrased this passage or was using a different translation.

123 In the text, it appears as if both verses are from the same sutra. The source of the second verse has not been identified.

124 *Bodhicaryāvatara*, 6:59, 16b7.

125 *Bodhicaryāvatara*, 2:41–42, 5b2.

126 *Uttaratantra*; The quotation is not to be found in this text. It may be intended as a summation rather than a quote of 4:50, 69b5: "There are five pathways of beings in the beginningless birth and death of samsara. Just as ordure has no pleasant smell, the five kinds of beings have no happiness. Their constant suffering is like that in contact with fire, weapons, lye, and so on." However, the quote here is given in a distinct verse form, and therefore it seems more likely an error of attribution.

127 *Bodhicaryāvatara*, 4:20, 8b6.

128 The text had Akśayamati in error for Śantideva.

129 *Bodhicaryāvatara*, 1:4, 1b5.

130 *Sangs rgyas chos dang...* This is presumably the ubiquitous prayer:

> In the Buddha, the Dharma, and the supreme Sangha
> I take refuge until enlightenment;
> through the merit of my deeds such as generosity,
> may I achieve enlightenment for the benefit of beings.

131 The cubit is the ancient universal measurement based upon the length of one forearm, which therefore has no inherent precise measurement, and different cultures established their own definitive mathematical measurements. In Tibetan culture, there is no such equivalence, but the cubit is usually regarded as the length from the elbow to the tip of the closed fist, while in the Indian texts the cubit (*aratni*) was usually from the elbow to the tip of the little finger.

132 In which the eating of food is transformed into an offering practice, particularly a visualized homa fire ritual, where the stomach is the fire and the arms are the ladles.

133 Vajradhara is called the sixth Buddha because he is in addition to the higher tantra system of five buddha families with their principal buddhas: Vairocana, Akṣobhya, Ratnsambhava, Amitābha, and Amoghasiddhi. As the embodiment of the dharmakāya, he is also considered the source from which these five buddhas emanate.

134 The text has "musagarbha," a corrupt form of *asmagarbha*, the Sanskrit for "stone essence," which is then repeated in Tibetan. These are anything of a precious appearance that are found in rivers, as it is believed the action of the water has brought out the essence of the stones.

135 Source unidentified.

136 *Atyayajñānasūtra*, Toh 122 Kangyur, mdo sde, *tha*, 153a.

137 Source unidentified.

138 Source unidentified.

139 Source unidentified.

140 *The Eight-Thousand-Verse Perfection of Wisdom Sutra* (*Aṣṭasāhasrikāprajñāpāramitā*), Toh 12 Kangyur, sher phyin, *ka*, 3a3. The citation in this edition varies slightly from the canonical text version, which begins: "Thus, that mind is not mind..."

141 Source unidentified.

142 *Treasury of Dohas*, 72b4.

143 "Autumn's cloudless sky" refers to the season after the monsoon, when the rains have cleared the air of dust and the clouds have vanished.

144 Source unidentified.

145 Source unidentified.

146 Source unidentified.

147 *Sdom pa rgya mtsho'i rgyud*. This text has not been identified.

148 Source unidentified.

149 *Ye shes gsang ba sgron ma man ngag rin po che'i rgyud*, Rnying ma'i rgyud 'bum, vol. 4 (*nga*), 4a1.

150 Source unidentified.

151 Gampopa (1079–1153), a.k.a. Dakpo Lhajé, considered an emanation of Candraprabhakumāra.

152 The site of Gampopa's monastery, the first Kagyü monastery, founded in 1137, when Gampopa was around fifty-eight years old. The text has the variant form Daklha Gompo (*dwags lha sgom po*).

153 Lama Shang.

154 The two Buddha statues are those said to have been brought to Tibet by two queens of King Songtsen Gampo in the seventh century. That of the Chinese queen is in the Jokhang, Lhasa's principal temple, and that brought by the Nepalese queen is in the Ramoché temple in Lhasa.

155 There is an annotation to the original Tibetan text identifying the lama as Lhariwa Namkha Ö, even though the text reads as if it is Lama Shang himself. "The emanation of Shang" could be interpreted both ways. Namkha Ö, however, was a direct pupil of Lama Shang, of Düsum Khyenpa (who founded the Karma Kagyü), and particularly of Taklung Tangpa (who founded the Taklung Kagyü).

156 *Spang gshong lha ri*, "pasture-basin divine mountain," the location of Lha Shönu's monastery.

157 Sanskrit for Lha Shönu, "young deity."

158 Also known as Shang Rinpoché and Yudrakpa Tsöndrü Drakpa.

159 In praises, the lasso is a common metaphor for the power of the buddhas' blessing and compassion, with which the buddhas can lasso beings and so rescue them from suffering.

160 This refers to elaborate rituals where various images are made, though most commonly these are made from dough. Particular wooden blocks with a series of molds upon them are used to make a wide variety of representations for ritual use.

161 This does not mean heat literally, and is not a reference to caṇḍālī practice, which has heat as a sign of its success, but is an expression for signs that one is progressing on the spiritual path toward enlightenment. It specifically refers to signs of being on the first stage of the path of engagement, the second of the five paths. The analogy is of heat that comes from rubbing sticks together, which is an indication that one is on the way to creating fire.

162 Aconite is a deadly poison, but it was believed that peacocks were not only immune to poison, it is what produced the iridescent colors of their feathers.

163 The *kāya* of seven aspects is described in the Tashi Namgyal text in chapter 11. See page 609.

164 *Sākarajñānavāda* in Sanskrit, this is a subschool of the Mind Only (*Cittamātra*) school. Its name derives from the assertion that the "aspects" (*ākara*, or *rnam pa* in Tibetan) of consciousness are real in that they are an integral part of the perceiving subject.

165 *Nirākārajñānavāda* in Sanskrit, this is another subschool of the Mind Only school. For Non-Aspectarians, the "aspects" of consciousness are unreal; they are mere concepts constructed by the mind and not an integral part of the perceiving subject.

166 The Māyāvāda school (*sgyu ma smra ba*). The division of the classical Indian Middle Way, or Madhyamaka, school into the Proponents of Illusion and the Utterly Nonabiding school appears to have been quite common before Candrakīrti's writings came to dominate the Tibetan tradition around the late twelfth and early thirteenth centuries. Subsequently, the division of Madhyamaka into Svātrantika and Prāsaṅgika became the norm.

167 Apratiṣṭha (*rab tu mi gnas*).

168 From the Sanskrit *sāccha*, miniature clay molds of stupas, deities, etc. The Tibetan spelling and pronunciation varies between *satsa* and *tsatsa*.

169 *Bdud rtsi*, *amṛta*; the Vajrayāna inner offerings: human feces, urine, menstrual blood, flesh, and semen. The text here has an even more oblique synonym that reads literally as: "the half of ten deathless," as the Sanskrit *amṛta* means "without death."

170 Faith, diligence, mindfulness, samādhi, and wisdom.

171 Literally, don't [completely] cover your own head.

172 Milarepa's pupil Rechungpa (1084–1161). After leaving Milarepa he was principally based in the region of Loro, near the present-day border with Arunachal Pradesh, and therefore became known as Loro.

173 These conducts are explained in the Tashi Namgyal text in chapter 11.

174 *Dkar po chig thub*, literally "single powerful": a remedy—in this case the mahāmudrā realization of the nature of reality—that is sufficient in itself for the attainment of enlightenment.

175 An alternate name for the Sūtrayāna or Perfection Vehicle (Parāmitāyāna).

176 *Panasa*; the jackfruit can be eaten when it is unripe.

177 A corruption of the Sanskrit *iti*; can be loosely translated as "thus." It normally follows the conclusion of a title, quotation, and the like.

178 *Dkar brgyud* "white lineage," a reference to the white cotton robes worn by repas. A phonological development from the more common and original Kagyü (*bka' brgyud*), "instruction lineage."

179 *Enlightenment of Vairocana*. Though the passage describing the posture is on 195b, these lines do not appear in the text.

180 *Treasury of Dohas*, 74a3.

181 These noncanonical but well-known lines may have their first appearance in Gampopa, *Ornament of Precious Liberation: Like a Wish-Fulfilling Gem of Sublime Dharma*, 187a1. However, that early version is "Do not contemplate, do not think, do not know,/ do not meditate, do not analyze, but rest naturally."

182 One of the names used for Gampopa, referring to his previous life as the principal interlocutor in the *King of Meditations Sutra*.

183 The source of the quotation has not been identified.

184 Nāgārjuna, *Suhṛllekha*, Toh 4182 Tengyur, spring yig, *nge*, 43a5.

185 Vasubandhu, *Treatise on the Five Aggregates* (*Pañcaskandhaprakaraṇa*), Toh 4059 Tengyur, sems tsam, *shi*, 12b7. The original text begins with *dran pa gang zhe na*: "What is mindfulness?"

186 A four-line prayer that all beings attain to the state of the guru in his aspects as the buddha, the dharmakāya, the saṃbhogakāya, and the nirmāṇakāya.

187 *Treasury of the Ultimate*, 12b5.

188 *Collected Works of Lingchen Repa Pema Dorjé*, vol. 1, 20a6.

189 *Treasury of Dohas*, 23a5.

190 The hide of the elephant is too thick for thorns to have any effect.

191 *Sūtrālaṃkāra*, 15:15, 19a7.

192 Source unidentified. The only well-known master named *Rgyal ba'i dbang po* is Jinendrabuddhi, the teacher of Dignaga. However, this verse does not appear in his works, nor does it seem likely to be authored by him. As an epithet, this is most likely to refer to Künga Paljor, the second Drukchen.

193 *Bodhicaryāvatāra*, 5:41, 11b6.

194 *Kāśyapa Chapter* (*Kāśyapaparivartasūtra*), Toh 87 Kangyur, dkon brtsegs, *cha*, 133b1. The Kangyur version ends: "...and burns up the discriminating thoughts."

195 *Treasury of Dohas*, 73b5.

196 *Treasury of Dohas*, 71b3.

197 *Treasury of Dohas*, 72a3.

198 The lord of yogins is presumably Milarepa, but the source of this quotation is unidentified.

199 Milarepa, but the source of the quotation is unidentified.

200 *Treasury of Dohas*, 71b2.

201 *Treasury of Dohas*, 71b2.

202 The variant Tillipa is used here, and Tailo is used in the version on page 158.

203 This noncanonical song appears in Wangchuk Gyaltsen's *Great Bliss of Stainless Teachings*, vol. 1, 58a1.

204 Pema Karpo already quoted these lines above. See note 181.

205 Specifically, attachment to the experiences of clarity, bliss, and no thought.

206 The royal capital of Zangskar, a Tibetan region in Kashmir, was at the town of Padum.

207 *Mkhar chu byang chub kyi snying po*. Kharchu at Lhodrak. The retreat place of Padmasambhava's mind. Within a day's walk from Marpa's residence in Lhodrak.

208 His name is spelled Telopa throughout this text, which is the most common Tibetan spelling of his name.

209 Maitreyanātha, *Sūtrālaṃkāra*, 14:13, Toh 4020 Tengyur, sems tsam, *phi*, 18a4.

210 Hevajra Tantra, book 2, 2:51, 16a4.

211 Maitreyanātha, *Madhyāntavibhaṅgakārikā*, Toh 4021 Tengyur, sems tsam, *phi*, 1a4.

212 Tailikapāda (Tilopa), *Mahāmudrā Instructions* (*Mahāmudropadeśa*), Toh 2303 Tengyur, rgyud, *zhi*, 243b3.

213 *Treasury of Dohas*, 72b7.

214 *Eight-Thousand-Verse Perfection of Wisdom Sutra* (*Aṣṭasāhasrikāprajñāpāramitā*), chap. 8, Toh 12 Kangyur, sher phyin, *ka*, 111a2.

215 Text unidentified.

216 Wangchuk Gyaltsen, *The Great Bliss of Stainless Teachings: The Biography of Nāropa*, 58a1.

217 Rangjung Dorjé in *The Treatise Differentiating Consciousnesses and Wisdom* ascribes the view of "fate" (*phywa*) to Bön, atoms to the Vaibhāṣika view, unperceivable externals to the Sautrantika view, and the puruṣa (literally "individual") to the view of the non-Buddhist Sāṃkhya.

218 Here commenting on the verses by Tilopa given above.

219 *Treasury of Dohas*, 75b2.

220 *Treasury of Dohas*, 72a5. The second line does not appear in the Tengyur version.

221 Nāropa, *Summary of the View* (*Dṛṣtisaṃkṣipta*), Toh 2304 Tengyur, rgyud, *zhi*, 244b3. No author is named in any edition of the canon. The translator is Marpa Chökyi Lodrö, Nāropa's pupil, but it is also grouped among nine Tilopa texts. However, later on in this work, Rangjung Dorjé attributes this text to Nāropa.

222 *Bodhicaryāvatāra*, 8:4, 23b2.

223 Ten signs of luminosity: smoke, mirage, clouds, fireflies, sun, moon, shining jewels, eclipse, stars, and light rays.

224 The two experiences of clarity are the clarity of the five senses and the clarity of the mind, as described above.

225 The "immediate condition" (*de ma thag pa'i rkyen*, *anantarapratyaya*), as found in Asaṅga's *Compendium of the Abhidharma* (*Abhidharmasamuccaya*), was applied by Rangjung Dorjé, particularly in his text *Distinguishing between Wisdoms and Consciousnesses* as "the immediate mentation" (*de ma thag pa'i yid*), a subdivision of the seventh consciousness, the "afflicted-mentation consciousness" (*nyon yid rnam shes*, *klistamanasvijñāna*).

226 While good and bad karma bring happiness and suffering in the desire realm, the act of meditation can have the karmic result of rebirth in the form and formless realms.

227 The third of the five paths of accumulation, engagement, seeing, meditation, and no-more training.

228 These four meditation states are also the four dhyāna levels of the formless realm.

229 *Satkāyadṛṣṭiḥ* ("the view of the existent body"), the view that the five aggregates are a self. This was freely translated into Tibetan as *'jig tshogs lta ba*, which in English would be "the view of the perishable aggregate or transitory collection."

230 These texts have not been identified.

231 *Mahāmudrā Instructions* (*Mahāmudropadeśa*), Toh 2303 Tengyur, rgyud, *zhi*, 243b5.

232 *Summary of the View* (*Dṛṣtisaṃkṣipta*), Toh 2304 Tengyur, rgyud, *zhi*, 245b1.

233 Source unidentified.

234 *Summary of the View* (*Dṛṣtisaṃkṣipta*), 245b1. It immediately follows and contrasts with the previously quoted verse.

235 These five kinds of adverse factors are unidentified.

236 Gampopa. The text is unidentified.

237 Dechen Teng, Rangjung Dorjé's retreat center above Tsurphu Monastery.

238 The summer of 1324.

239 Lokeśvara, one of the names of bodhisattva Avalokiteśvara.

240 *Rten*. There are three kinds of representations: statues or paintings to represent a buddha's body, Dharma texts to represent his speech, and stupas to represent his mind.

241 Source unidentified.

242 *Display of the Qualities of Mañjuśrī's Buddha Realm* (*Mañjuśrībuddhakṣetraguṇavyūhasūtra*), Toh 59 Kangyur, dkon brtsegs, *ga*, 279a4. The passage describes a Buddha named *Thunder Melody King*, who, in a very distant realm countless eons ago, addressed in verse a cakravartin king named Akaśa as to how he should dedicate his merit. This is the first verse before the Buddha describes how Akaśa's prayers led to his attainment. The last line of the quotation given here is either a paraphrase or a different translation of the passage in the Kangyur, which reads: "That is the result they will attain."

243 The term *jinaputra*, "child of the conquerors," is usually a synonym for bodhisattva.

244 *Madhyabuddha* (*'bring sang rgyas*), a synonym for pratyekabuddha.

245 Candrakīrti, *Madhyamakāvatāra*, Toh 3861 Tengyur, dbu ma, *'a*, 201b1. This is the opening line of the text. The next line goes on to say: "And the buddhas are born from bodhisattvas./ A mind of compassion, the understanding of nondualism,/ and bodhicitta are the causes of the conquerors and their children."

246 *Prajñāpāramitāsañcayagāthā*. The exact quotation does not appear in this text.

247 *Anavataptanāgarājaparipṛcchāsūtra*, Toh 156 Kangyur, mdo sde, *pha*, 208b4. This is the first line of the Buddha's reply to a question from the nāga king Anavatapta. The words "mahāsattva," "It is thus," and "omniscient" were omitted from the quotation but have been inserted here.

248 Candragomin, *Saṃvaraviṃśaka*, Toh 4081 Tengyur, sems tsam, *hi*, 166b–167a. The quote is the last line of the text. The entire sentence reads: "Because of having compassion and love,/ a good mind does no wrong."

249 The story is given in *Skillful Means Sutra* (*Upāyakauśalyasūtra*), Toh 261 Kangyur, mdo sde, *za*, 303b5. The sutra relates that in a previous life the Buddha was a captain on a ship with five hundred merchants when a robber, skilled in weapons and disguised as a merchant, planned to kill all the merchants for their wealth. Sea deities tell the captain in a dream about the robber's plan and that the merchants are all bodhisattvas. They tell him that he must think of a plan to save them and also save the robber from eons in hells. When the ship is stalled for a week through lack of wind, Mahākaruṇika kills the robber with a sword. The merit of this brought Mahākaruṇika rebirth in the higher realms, and he eventually became the Buddha, while the five hundred merchants will be half of the thousand buddhas of this Good Eon. Oral retellings of this story by lamas vary in the details.

250 Geshé Ben Gungyal Tsültrim Gyalwa, an eleventh-century Kadam master, was a pupil of Gönpawa Wangchuk Gyaltsen (1016–82).

251 Phadampa Sangyé (d. 1117) was an Indian master who came to Tibet and is the source of the "pacification" (*zhi byed*) lineage. The Tibetan name means "Father Sacred Buddha," but his actual name was Kamalaśīla. This has led to his being identified with the Kamalaśīla who was in Tibet in the early ninth century and therefore having a miraculously long life that included swapping bodies. However, the previous Kamalaśīla was assassinated in Samyé.

252 Candrakīrti, *Madhyamakāvatāra*, 3:10, Toh 3861 Tengyur, dbu ma, *'a*, 203b1.

253 In other words, the perfection of wisdom sutras. For example, the *Eight-Thousand-Verse Perfection of Wisdom Sutra* (*Aṣṭasāhasrikāprajñāpāramitā*), chap. 11, Toh 12, Kangyur, sher phyin, *ka*, 128b–129a: "Subhuti! The bodhisattva mahāsattvas who do not hear this perfection of wisdom will have no certainty concerning mundane and supramundane phenomena. Subhuti, you must know that this is their māra activity."

254 Candrakīrti, *Madhyamakāvatāra*, 3:10, Toh 3861 Tengyur, dbu ma, *'a*, 202a6. The complete sentence is: "Generosity that is devoid of gift, receiver, and giver/ is the perfection that is supramundane."

255 *Akṣayamatiparipṛcchāsūtra*, Toh 89 Kangyur, dkon brtsegs, *cha*. The quotation is not from this sutra, nor does it appear in the *Sutra Taught by Akṣayamati* (*Akṣayamatinirdeśasūtra*), Toh 175 Kangyur, mdo sde, *ma*. Perhaps Tai Situ was paraphrasing the following passage from the *Vimalakīrti Sutra* (*Vimalakīrtinirdeśasūtra*), which he cites later in the text: Toh 176 Kangyur, mdo sde, *ma*, 201b1: "Method that is not supported by wisdom is bondage. Wisdom that is supported by method is liberation. Liberation that is not supported by method is bondage. Method that is supported by wisdom is liberation."

256 Nāgārjuna, *Praise to the Three Kāyas* (*Kāyatrayastotra*), Toh 1123 Tengyur, bstod tshogs, *ka*, 70b. The quotation here is derived from a different translation than that found in the Tengyur. See also footnote 260.

257 *Abhisamayālaṃkāra*, 8:12, 11b.

258 This emanation appeared in order to teach the gandharva Nanda, who was proud of his lute playing, the gandharvas being musician deities. The emanation continued to play better than King Nanda, even when all of his strings had snapped!

259 *Sūtrālaṃkāra*, chap. 10, 11b2.

260 *Praise to the Three Kāyas* (*Kāyatrayastotra*), Toh 1123 Tengyur, bstod tshogs, *ka*, 70b3. This passage was already quoted above. Almost all of the elements that make up the verse are the same as in the Tengyur version that was quoted previously, but they are in a different translation and order. Some lines cannot be reconciled as alternative translations and may come from an alternative Sanskrit original, for instance, from a quotation within a commentary.

261 Nāgārjuna, *Ratnāvalī*, Toh 4158 Tengyur, spring yig, *ge*, 107b5.

262 *Bodhicaryāvatāra*, 2:62, 6b1. The quote has been translated to match the canonical version, which also agrees with the Sanskrit.

263 *Smṛtyupasthāna*, Toh 287 Kangyur, mdo sde, *ya*. The quotation is not from this sutra, even though this sutra describes many of these states. The quotation appears, without its source being cited, in Prajñākaramati's *Explanation of Difficult Passages in the Bodhicaryāvatāra* (*Bodhicaryāvatārapañjikā*), Toh 3872 Tengyur, dbu ma, *la*, 45a4. The Situ text has *sang rgyas kyis stongs pa*, and Prajñākaramati has *sangs rgyas mi 'byung dang*: "[Those for whom] a buddha has not appeared."

264 The five extreme acts are killing one's father, mother, or an arhat, wounding a buddha, and splitting the sangha.

265 Source unidentified.

266 Source unidentified.

267 *Saṃvarodayatantra*, chap. 12, Toh 373 Kangyur, rgyud, *kha*, 266a1. This appears to be a very corrupt version of the passage in the tantra, which does not mention

the six elements. The passage actually reads: "The humans born in the three continents/ live well with great prosperity/ but, dull of mind, do not make investigations;/ they have no observation and no analysis./ Those born well in Jambudvīpa are called 'those on the level of karma': /the karma from good actions and from bad—/ whether great, middling, or minor—from their previous lives ripen here/ and appear to beings." This appearance of karma is essential for progress on the path, so that enlightenment can only be attained in Jambudvīpa. This passage is in the context of the description of the four kinds of birth: miraculous, from warm moisture, egg, and womb. Although the six elements were not in this passage, they are characteristics of womb birth: the elements of bone, marrow, and procreative fluid from one's father, and flesh, skin, and blood from one's mother.

268 *Avataṃsakasūtra*, chap. 7, Toh 44 Kangyur, phal chen, *ka*, 90b5.

269 *Daśadharmakasūtra*, chap. 9, Toh 53 Kangyur, dkon brtsegs, *kha*, 166a. The verse was slightly corrupt in having *dkar po'i dge ba*, "good virtue" (literally, "virtue that is white") instead of *dkar po'i chos*, "good qualities." It has been corrected for this translation. Dakpo Tashi Namgyal cites this quote correctly in his text below.

270 *Sāgaramatiparipṛcchāsūtra*, Toh 152 Kangyur, mdo sde, *pha*, 40a5. This is a summarized paraphrase of the passage in the sutra, which reads: "For the lazy, enlightenment is very far, completely far. The lazy do not have generosity. The lazy do not have discipline. The lazy do not have patience. The lazy do not have diligence. The lazy do not have meditation. The lazy do not have wisdom. The lazy do not have benefit for themselves. The lazy do not have benefit for others."

271 *Prajñāpāramitāsañcayagathā*, Toh 13 Kangyur, sher phyin, *ka*, 6a5.

272 *Abhidharmakośa*, 5b4. This translation follows the canonical version. There is a slight deviation in the quotation, the third line of which reads: "*And not having that* causes them to wander in this ocean of worldly existence" (*de med pas* instead of *nyon mongs pas*). The sentence is incomplete, with the last line of the verse being: "And that is why the Teacher taught this." It is one of the first verses in *Treasury of the Abhidharma*.

273 Tai Situ had incorrectly attributed this and the following quotations to Asaṅga's *Compendium of the Abhidharma* (*Abhidharmasammucaya*), Toh 4049 Tengyur, sems tsam, *ri*, 48b4.

274 Vasubandhu, *Pañcaskandhaprakaraṇa*, Toh 4059 Tengyur, sems tsam, *shi*, 13a1. Tai Situ attributed this and the following quotations to Asaṅga's *Compendium of the Abhidharma* (*Abhidharmasammucaya*), Toh 4049 Tengyur, sems tsam, *ri*, 48b4. At this point there is a definition of faith, but it reads: "What is faith? It is having true conviction, attraction, and aspiration for that which exists, that which has qualities, and the powers." I have corrected the attribution in the translation.

275 *Pañcaskandhaprakaraṇa*, 13b3. The passage in the *Abhidharmasammucaya*, on 6a1, reads: "What is diligence? It is the mind's enthusiasm for armor, application, nonestablishment, nonreversal, and nonsatisfaction."

276 *Pañcaskandhaprakaraṇa*, 13a1. The quotation differs slightly from its source and seems to have blended in Tai Situ's memory with the definition from the *Abhidharmasammucaya*. It reads, "What is wisdom? It is the complete discernment of it." This is in reference to the preceding sentence that defines samādhi as "What is samādhi? It is the one-pointedness of mind on the examined object." The passage in

the *Abhidharmasammucaya*, on 48b4, reads: "What is wisdom? It is the complete discernment of phenomena that are examined entities."

277 *Aṣṭasāhasrikāprajñāpāramitā*, chap. 22, Toh 12 Kangyur, sher phyin, *ka*, 216a7. The quotation differs somewhat from the passage in the sutra. The Dergé edition begins with *'di la* ("concerning this") instead of *'di ltar* and has "should respect" (*dgu par bya*) instead of "should rely upon" (*bsten par bya*). In the Toh edition, "spiritual friends" is plural not singular.

278 A well-known verse, but its source has not been identified. It is quoted, without attribution, in *Ears of Grain of Realization* (*Abhisamayamañjarī*), Toh 1582 Tengyur, rgyud, *'a*, 43b6, which in the Sanskrit is attributed to Śākyarakṣita and in the Tibetan translation to Śubhākaragupta. There, the last line is translated as "the guru is the cause and condition" (*bla ma nyid ni rgyu rkyen gyur*), where *rgyu rkyen* presumably translates *kāraṇa*. It also appears in the Sanskrit text, not translated into Tibetan, entitled *Guhyasamayasādhanamāla*, which concludes with *evātra kāranam*, literally "the cause here," which is also interpreted as "helper in this life" instead of "cause of all" (possibly from *sarvatra kāranam*). A liturgical variation in Tibetan omits the third line and adds a fourth: "The guru is the Buddha, the guru is the Dharma,/ in the same way, the guru is the Sangha;/ the guru is the creator of all./ I pay homage to the gurus."

279 The quotation does not appear in this text.

280 *Primordial Buddha*, 58a4. This is the last line of a verse that is given in full on the following page.

281 Aśvaghoṣa, *Compilation of the Vajrayāna Root Downfalls* (*Vajrayānamūlāpattisaṃgraha*), Toh, 2478 Tengyur, rgyud, *zi*, 179a7.

282 Indrabhūti, *Jñānasiddhisādhana*, Toh 2219 Tengyur, rgyud, *wi*, 51a2. The Dergé canon edition reads "...a boat will *be unable* to reach the other shore./ Even if you perfectly *realize* all qualities..."

283 *Hevajra Tantra*, book 1, 8:34, 10a2. The Tibetan has *bdag gi*, genitive, in error for instrumental *bdag gis* (*ātmanā*). *Guruparvan*: Though it literally means a phase of time, this is alluding to methods, so that the Tibetan translation, *dus thabs*, is a compound of time and method.

284 *Bodhicaryāvatāra*, 5:102, 14a5.

285 *Primordial Buddha*, 58a3.

286 The list has not been identified. There is a list of three kinds of service: the offering of one's practice, which is the best service; service with one's body and speech, which is the medium service; and material offerings, which is the least.

287 Sudhana studied under a succession of many teachers, culminating in Maitreya, in the *Gaṇḍhavyūhasūtra*, which is the final section of the *Avataṃsaka Sutra*. The story of Sadāprarudita's hardships and dedication in search of the teachings is given in chapter 30 of the *Eight-Thousand-Verse Perfection of Wisdom Sutra* (*Aṣṭasāhasrikāprajñāpāramitā*).

288 *Sublime Continuum*, 5:18, 72b5.

289 Rangjung Dorjé, *Profound Inner Meaning*, 31a1. The entire verse reads: "Knowledge of the Vinaya, Abhidharma, and Sutras as external/ brings the attainment of the śrāvaka and pratyekabuddha result./ Practicing the profound Sutras, Vinaya, and Abhidharma/ causes one to become a bodhisattva."

290 *Hevajrapiṇḍārthaṭīkā*, 3b1. Together with the preceding lines it reads: "Through the wish for liberation within the three vehicles,/ one dwells in the result of a single vehicle./ There is the śrāvaka, pratyekabuddha, and, here,/ the Mahayana as the third [vehicle]./ It is not the Sage's viewpoint that/ there is a fourth or fifth [vehicle] in buddhahood."

291 *Sublime Continuum*, 5:19, 72b5.

292 Dignāga's *Pramāṇasamuccaya*. Text here actually says *Pramāṇasūtra* (*Tshad ma'i mdo*).

293 Literally this would be "to the state of a conqueror (*jina*)."

294 Candrakīrti, *Entering the Middle Way* (*Madhyamakāvatāra*), Toh 3861 Tengyur, dbu ma, *'a*, 204a1.

295 Āryaśūra, *Jātakamālā*, Toh 4150 Tengyur, skyes rabs, *hu*, 122a1.

296 Six ways of expounding the inner tantras, according to: (1) provisional meaning (*drang don*), (2) definitive meaning (*nges don*), (3) implicit (*dgongs pa can*), (4) explicit (*dgongs min*), (5) literal (*sgra ji bzhin pa*), and (6) metaphorical (*sgra ji bzhin ma yin pa*). See also note 650.

297 The four are reliance on meaning rather than words, reliance on the teachings rather than on individuals, reliance on wisdom rather than consciousness, and reliance on the definitive meaning rather than provisional meanings.

298 *Hevajra Tantra*, book 2, 2:41–44, 15b6.

299 The Third Karmapa, Rangjung Dorjé.

300 Karmapa Rangjung Dorjé, *Profound Inner Meaning*, 18a1: "Thus, the channels, winds, and drops/ appear through dependence./ They are a basis and are called the *vajra body*." 25b5: "Thus, the channels, winds, and drops/ appear from the aspect of the mind./ Therefore this collection of essential points/ is superior to all graduated paths."

301 The teachings being referenced here have not been identified.

302 Buddhajñānapāda, *Muktitilaka*, Toh 1859 Tengyur, rgyud, *di*, 47b2.

303 This verse appears in many sources, sometimes in prose, and its implied meaning varies according to context. Its earliest appearance seems to be circa the early second century C.E. in Aśvaghoṣa's *Saundarananda*, which was not translated into Tibetan. The verse also appears in texts such as Nāgārjuna's *Verses on the Essence of Dependent Origination* and in Maitreya's *Sublime Continuum*. In prose the passage appears in Asaṅga's *Bodhisattva Levels*, in Sthiramati's *Commentary on "Distinguishing the Middle Way from the Extremes*," and in Aśvaghoṣa's (a different author than above) *Awakening of Faith in the Mahayana* (*Mahāyānaśraddhotpāda*), which was not translated into Tibetan and is considered to be of Chinese authorship. It also occurs in Buddhaghosa's circa fifth-century commentary on the Dīgha Nikāya, the *Sumaṅgalavilāsinī*, a Pali text not translated into Tibetan.

304 *Abhidharmakośa*, 6:5, 18b7.

305 Nāgārjuna, *Acintyastava*, Toh 1128 Tengyur, bstod tshogs, *ka*, 77b4. The second half of the verse reads: "Therefore you taught the Dharma/ that is free of extremes."

306 The text, a compendium of the teacher Cārvāka's teachings, was entitled *Bṛhaspatisūtra*, but only quotations from it have survived.

307 The Tibetan name *'Jug stobs* probably refers to Jayarāśibhaṭṭa, the only Cārvāka

author whose work has survived in its entirety and who was also likely a contemporary of Dharmakīrti. The phrase in parentheses is a sublinear annotation in the text.

308 *Tattvas*. It is unclear what five principles are meant here. The Sāṃkhya believe that liberation comes through understanding the twenty-four *tattvas*, or principles, that make up *prakṛti*, the matter in which the soul is trapped. Twenty of these are four sets of five: senses, elements, faculties of activity, and sensory perceptions. This may be what is being echoed here.

309 *Dbang phyug pa*. This is also Tibetan for Śaivites, the followers of Śiva. *Dbang phyug* translates Īśvara, which can mean "Lord" or "Supreme Being" and is one of the names of Śiva, but this is referring to the Nyāyavaiśeṣika tradition of philosophy in which the concept of an all-powerful supreme being was of great importance.

310 Kaṇāda (*Gzegs zan*) is the founder of the Vaiśeṣika school. He wrote the *Vaiśeṣikasūtra* around the second century B.C.

311 (*Rkang mig*). Akṣapāda Gautama was the author of the *Nyāyasūtras* (ca. second century B.C.), emphasizing logic, upon which the Nyāya tradition was founded. The Nyāyas believed in liberation through knowledge, particularly through four means of valid cognition (*pramāṇa*). This greatly influenced the development of the pramāṇa tradition within Buddhism. This tradition and the Vaiśeṣika merged to form the Nyāyavaiśeṣika tradition.

312 In the earlier form of both the Vaiśeṣika and Nyāya traditions, all phenomena were classified into six categories (*padārtha*): substance (*dravya*), quality (*guṇa*), activity (*karma*), generality (*sāmānya*), particularity (*viśeṣa*), and relationship (*samavāya*).

313 *Rgyal dpogs pa*. Jayatīrtha seems the most likely candidate as the original for the Tibetan name. He was a fourteenth-century master of great influence in the Dvaita school, which teaches a dualistic distinction between beings and Viṣṇu.

314 *Rgyal ba dam pa*. This is Mahāvīra, the founder of Jainism. He was an older contemporary of the Buddha. Jainism here is referred to by the name "naked ones" (*gcer bu pa*), which appears to refer to only one of the two schools of Jainism: the Digambara, who on the highest level of ordination wear no clothes. In the Śvetāmbara sect, fully ordained monks wear white robes.

315 To what this refers is unclear. It may reflect the Jain teaching of liberation through knowing seven, or alternatively nine, *tattvas*.

316 Given in the Sanskrit form *Rāhmaṇa*. This is presumably referring to Islam. The Kālacakra tradition lists the great Mleccha teachers as: Adam, Noah, Abraham, Moses, Jesus, Mani, Muhammad, and Mahdi. The Islaimi Muslims, a Shia sect formed in 765, had the above names as their list of prophets with the omission of Mani, the founder of Manicheanism. However, there was a Manichean Islamic sect that formed at that time, which may well be the source for this list.

317 Tai Situ reveals that his knowledge of Bön has come through its casual misrepresentation in some Buddhist texts. Bön is a Buddhist school (though with Miwo Shenrap as its Buddha) that is no more eternalist than the Kagyü tradition itself.

318 *Zin shing* is the Chinese term for Taoism. It is also used in Tibetan as the name of one of the eight hexagrams.

319 The term has its origin in Jainism, but it here refers to all the non-Buddhist religious movements native to India.

320 Only the Vaibhāṣikas believed in the reality of atoms. Atomic theory first appeared

in India among the non-Buddhist Vaiśeṣikas; it appears to be completely absent in the sutras of the historical Buddha. The Sautrāntikas rejected these Abhidharma developments and returned to the early sutras as their primary authority. The theory of atoms often plays an important role in the Mahayana sutras.

321 Sthiramati, *Triṃśikābhāṣya*. The quotation does not come from this text.

322 Jñānagarbha, *Commentary on "Distinguishing the Two Truths"* (*Satyadvayavibhaṅga-vṛtti*). Toh 3881 Tengyur, dbu ma, *sa*, 1b3.

323 *Root Verses on the Middle Way*, 24:14, 15a4.

324 The six Madhyamaka texts of Nāgārjuna are: (1) *Root Verses on the Middle Way, Mūlamadhyamakakārikā*, Toh 3824; (2) *Precious Garland, Ratnāvalī*, Toh 4158; (3) *Overcoming Opponenets in Debate, Vigrahavyāvartanī*, Toh 3828; (4) *Seventy Verses on Emptiness, Śūnyatāsaptatikārikā*, Toh 3827; (5) *Extensive Sutra, Vaidalyasūtra*, Toh 3826; and (6) *Sixty Verses on Logic, Yuktiṣaṣṭikākārikā*, Toh 3825.

325 Nāgārjuna, *Fearing Nothing: A Commentary on the Root Middle Way* (*Mūlamadhy amakavṛttyakuto'bhayā*), chap. 24, Toh 3829 Tengyur, dbu ma, *tsa*, 89a1. The Dergé edition reads as if the last sentence is corrupt with *de dag las* instead of *de dag la*; the Narthang Kangyur, *tsa*, 92b2 does not have that error. The Situ texts had *de ni de nyid la gzigs pa nyid yin pas* in error for *de ni de dag la bden pa nyid yin pas* in the last sentence, which would then read "because of seeing that as the true nature (that-ness)."

326 *Fearing Nothing*, chap. 24, 89a4. This sentence is preceded by: "You might think and wish to say, 'As the birthlessness of all phenomena is the ultimate truth, why do we need to have the terminology of two truths?' I answer that thought:..."

327 *Sūtrālaṃkāra*, 19:15, 30a1.

328 Atiśa Dīpaṃkaraśrījñāna, *Bodhipathapradīpa*, v. 43, Toh 3947 Tengyur, dbu ma, *khi*, 240a2.

329 *Vimalakīrtinirdeśasūtra*, chap. 4, Toh 176 Kangyur, mdo sde, *ma*, 201b1.

330 *Sublime Continuum*, 3:1, 65b1. There is a word play here on *artha*, which can be both "benefit" and "truth" in the Sanskrit.

331 *Sublime Continuum*, 1:55–57, 47a3. Unlike the Tibetan and English, the Sanskrit, with its wider vocabulary, uses synonyms for earth (*pṛthivi* and *kṣiti*), water (*ambu* and *jala*), and space (*vyoman* and *ākāśa*) so as to avoid repetition. The Tibetan translate *ayoniśa*, which means "having no genuine source," with the less-specific *tshul min*, which could mean "incorrect" or "inappropriate." Here it has been translated as "improper."

332 *Praise to the Dharmadhātu*, v. 17, 64a7.

333 *Praise to the Dharmadhātu*, v. 22, 64b2.

334 These sixty-four qualities of buddhahood are comprised of: (a) the thirty-two physical features of the saṃbhogakāya body, such as the marks of wheels on the soles of the feet and the *uṣṇīṣa* on the crown of the head; and (b) the thirty-two mental qualities of the dharmakāya, which are comprised of the ten powers, the four fearlessnesses, and the eighteen distinctive characteristics.

335 *Eight-Thousand-Verse Perfection of Wisdom Sutra* (*Aṣṭasāhasrikāparjñāpāramitā*), Toh 12 Kangyur, sher phyin, *ka*, 3a3. The Dergé edition has "that mind...." "That" (*de*) was omitted in the Tai Situ quotation. It actually is referring to the bodhicitta, stating that one should train in it without becoming proud about it, because that

mind is not mind. Though quoted more correctly later on, here a *la-don* particle instead of the emphasizing particle is used, so it could be taken to mean "there is no mind in that mind."

336 *Praise to the Dharmadhātu*, v. 19, 64a1. "In that same way..." refers to the preceding verse, which described the sun being obscured by five factors: clouds, smoke, fog, eclipses, and dust haze.

337 *Guhyasamāja Tantra*, chap. 2, 94b2.

338 *Sublime Continuum*, 1:62, 57b1.

339 An inversion of the author's name: Maitreyanātha, which means one who has Maitreya as his lord. This teacher has six texts attributed to him in the canon. One of these, a commentary on a text by Nāgārjuna, is usually ignored, for it jars with the later identification of this author with Maitreya himself. Asaṅga and Vasubandhu developed his teachings to an even further level.

340 This subject is addressed by Maitreyanātha in his *Ornament of the Mahayana Sutras*.

341 *Mahāmudrā Tilaka*, chap. 28, 89b6.

342 *Bodhicittavivaraṇa*, v. 2, Toh 1800 Tengyur, rgyud, *ngi*, 38b3. "Buddhas" is followed in Tibetan by the genitive particle *kyi*, which is presumably in error for *kyis*. Lindtner says the genitive should be retained, but with "buddhas" still as the agent of the verb (Chr. Lindtner, *Nagarjuniana: Studies in the Writings and Philosophy of Nāgārjuna* [Delhi: Motilal Banarsidass, 1982], 187).

343 *Treasury of Dohas*, 74a3.

344 *Mu bzhi skye 'gog gi rigs pa*. At the time of its cause, the result was not existent, nonexistent, both, nor neither.

345 Indrabhūti, *Jñānasiddhisādhana*, chap. 1, Toh 2219 Tengyur, rgyud, *wi*, 38a4.

346 Advayavajra (Maitripa), *Ten Verses on the True Nature* (*Tattvadaśaka*), Toh 2236 Tengyur, rgyud, *wi*, 113a1.

347 Source unidentified.

348 *Tattvāvatāra*, chap. 3, Toh 3709 Tengyur, rgyud, *tsu*, 12a3.

349 *Praise to the Dharmadhātu*, v. 37, 65a3. In fact, the Tai Situ text had "mind" *sems zhes* in the second line in error for "a being" *sems can*. That version would read "When obscured by the net of afflictions,/ that is what is called *mind*./ When free from the afflictions,/ that is what is called *buddhahood*. That has been replaced by the canonical version here, as it may easily have been a scribal error not in Tai Situ's original text.

350 *Profound Inner Meaning*, 2b4.

351 The Tibetan has translated *vid* as *rig*, but presumably this is meant to be synonymous with *vedana* "sensation," one of the five ever-present mental events.

352 These are the five "ever-present" (*kun tu 'gro ba*) mental events as listed among the fifty-one mental events in the Abhidharma. *Identification* is also found translated as "perception," although in terms of its definition, *identification* seems closer in most instances. It is not conceptual, as *identification* may seem to imply. An example is animals being able to identify different objects. It is also translated as "ideation."

353 Vasubandhu, *Thirty Verses* (*Triṃśikākārikā*), v. 2, Toh 4055 Tengyur, sems tsam, *shi*, 1a3. The quotation in the Tai Situ text is corrupt. For the sake of clarity, I have followed the version in the Dergé canon. This is a contentious passage and has

been the subject of differing opinions as to what the terms intend. The Tibetan translation by Yeshé Dé is problematic. He also translated Sthiramati's commentary, although without modifying his translation of Vasubandhu's verses, which are given within the body of the commentary. Tai Situ also begins his quotation mid-sentence so that the difficult passage could easily be misinterpreted. I have here followed Sthiramati's commentary in the Sanskrit, which clearly breaks up the compound "nonconscious acquisition-location-discernment" to associate the discernment with location and not with acquisition and not treating it as a separate third element.

354 Vasubandhu, *The Thirty Verses* (*Triṃśikākārikā*), v. 2, Toh 4055 Tengyur, sems tsam, *shi*, 1a5. This is in fact continuous from the preceding quotation. The four neutral afflictions are listed in the following line: (1) the view that there is a self, *ātmadṛṣṭi*, (2) the delusion that there is a self, *ātmamoha*, (3) pride in the self, *ātmamāna*, and (4) love of the self, *ātmasneha*.

355 Asaṅga's *Compendium of the Mahayana* (*Mahāyānasaṃgraha*).

356 *Vajra Pinnacle*, chap. 1, 155a3.

357 *Hevajra Tantra*, book 1, 8:39, 10a5. The Tibetan has translated *jagat* as "beings" (*'gro ba*), but it could have been translated as "world," resulting in: "The entire world has arisen from me./ The three realms have arisen from me./ This entire [world] is pervaded by me./ The visible world consists of nothing else."

358 *Stainless Light*, *tha*, 260b7.

359 *Stainless Light*, *tha*, 125a7.

360 Nāgārjuna *Bodhicittavivaraṇa*, v. 69, Toh 1800 Tengyur, rgyud, *ngi*, 41a1. These are the first three lines of verse 69. The last line is, "When freed from propensities, there is happiness."

361 Vasubandhu, *Thirty Verses* (*Triṃśikākārikā*), v. 2, Toh 4055 Tengyur, sems tsam, *shi*, 1a3.

362 *Laṅkāvatārasūtra*, chap. 8, Toh 107 Kangyur, mdo sde, *ca*, 167a5.

363 *Laṅkāvatārasūtra*, chap. 9, 191a6. This translation follows the Dergé version. In Tai Situ's text, the order of the first two lines is reversed, and in the third line "mind" (*sems*) was replaced by "phenomena" (*chos*), and the verb is "agitated" or "in motion" (*g.yo*) instead of "arise" (*'byung*).

364 *Verses on the Essence of Dependent Origination* (*Pratītyasamutpādahṛdayakārikā*), Toh 3836 Tengyur, dbu ma, *tsa*, 146b3. This short text consists of only seven four-line verses. The last line of this verse is: "which revolves over and over again."

365 *Verses on the Essence of Dependent Origination*, 146b3. It is the verse that precedes the previous quotation. The last line of the verse is: "The twelve phenomena are condensed into three."

366 Candrakīrti, *Clear Words: A Commentary on the "Root Middle Way"* (*Mūlamadhya makavṛttiprasannapadā*), Toh 3860 Tengyur, dbu ma, *'a*, 216b3. "Cessation" has the instrumental particle in the Dergé canonical edition, but not in the Tai Situ text.

367 *Vajra Tent*, chap. 6, 44a4.

368 *Vajra Tent*, chap. 14, 56a2.

369 *Gsang ba dur khrod kyi rgyud*. The citation does not appear in this Nyingma tantra.

370 *Daśabhūmikasūtra*, 31st chapter of the *Avataṃsaka Sutra*, Toh 44 Kangyur, phal

chen, *kha*, 220b4. The line in the Dergé canon edition does not have a call to the bodhisattvas but reads: "In this way, these three realms are nothing but mind."

371 *Laṅkāvatārasūtra*, chap. 8, Toh 107 Kangyur, mdo sde, *ca*, 165a6.

372 *Praise to the Dharmadhātu*, vv. 46–47, 65b1.

373 Nāgārjuna, *Bodhicittavivaraṇa*, v. 22, Toh 1200 Tengyur, rgyud, *ngi*, 39b6. The second line of the Tibetan (the first line in translation) is missing; as the second and third lines both begin with *rnam shes*, the scribe must have skipped a line. Also the end of the first line has a genitive *yi* in error for instrumental *yis*. The verb that should have gone with the instrumental—*snang ba* ("appears")—was in the missing line. Alternatively, if the genitive is correct, it could be translated as "All appearances to consciousness, which have the nature of perceiver and percepts, are nothing other than consciousness and have no external existence whatsoever."

374 *Treasury of Dohas*, 72b5.

375 Nāgārjuna, *Bodhicittavivaraṇa*, v. 22, Toh 1200 Tengyur, rgyud, *ngi*, 39b7.

376 *Sūtrālaṃkāra*, 7:8, 6b5.

377 *Ghanavyūhasūtra*, chap. 3, Toh 110 Kangyur, mdo sde, *cha*, 11b5.

378 *Kāśyapa Chapter* (*Kāśyapaparivartasūtra*), Toh 87 Kangyur, dkon brtsegs, *cha*, 139a2.

379 *Eight-Thousand-Verse Perfection of Wisdom Sutra* (*Aṣṭasāhasrikāprajñāpāramitā*), Toh 12 Kangyur, sher phyin, *ka*, 3a3. This verse was also quoted above. See note 335. This time the quote is more accurate, but "that" is still left out, and thus the hint that it is referring back to bodhicitta.

380 *Enlightenment of Vairocana*, 153b2. The portions in brackets are in the canonical version but were omitted in Tai Situ's citation.

381 *Enlightenment of Vairocana*, 154a2.

382 *Laṅkāvatārasūtra*, chap. 8, Toh 107 Kangyur, mdo sde, *ca*, 179b4.

383 *Bodhicaryāvatāra*, 9:9, 39b3.

384 *Praise to the Dharmadhātu*, v. 11, 64a4. There is a play on words, as the word for *element* as in "element of gold" is *dhātu*, the same word as is used for the element of the buddha nature. The word for "distress" is *kleśa*, the same word used for the afflictions of anger, ignorance, desire, and so on.

385 *Praise to the Dharmadhātu*, vv. 16–17, 64a6. Verse 17 has already been quoted once above.

386 *Sūtrālaṃkāra*, 10:77, 12a3. The quotation in the Situ text repeats "sublime" (*dam pa*) in the fourth line instead of "supreme."

387 *Kāśyapa Chapter* (*Kāśyapaparivartasūtra*), Toh 87 Kangyur, dkon brtsegs, *cha*, 132b1. The quotation differs from the source. The quotation as it appears in the Kangyur version of the sutra reads: "It is easy to remain in a view, the size of Mount Meru, on the individual, but a highly arrogant view on emptiness is not like that."

388 *Root Verses on the Middle Way*, 24:11, 15a2.

389 *Caturdārakasamādhisūtra*, Toh 136 Kangyur, mdo sde, *na*, 173b7. There was some deviation from the canonical version, though without substantially affecting the meaning.

390 *Root Verses on the Middle Way*, 13:7, 8a6.

391 Nāgārjuna, *Praise for the One Who Has Transcended the World* (*Lokātītastava*), Toh 1120 Tengyur, bstod tshogs, *ka*, 69b1. The Situ text has *spangs pa lags*, repeating the

word "abandon," thus meaning "you abandoned them," instead of *shin tu smad*, "strongly rebuked," though by ignoring the grammar, this could be taken as meaning "abandoning the attachment to emptiness."

392 *Gaganagañjaparipṛcchāsūtra*, Toh 148 Kangyur, mdo sde, *pa*, 288a7. In the Dergé Kangyur edition, this quotation begins: "Those who are wise in view/ do not believe in (or 'fixate' on) things or nothing."

393 Śāntarakṣita, *Madhyamakālaṃkāra*, Toh 3884 Tengyur, dbu ma, *sa*, 55b2.

394 Jñānagarbha, *Commentary on "Distinguishing the Two Truths"* (*Satyadvayavibhaṅgavṛtti*), Toh 3881 Tengyur, dbu ma, *sa*, 2a2.

395 Jñānagarbha, *Commentary on "Distinguishing the Two Truths"* (*Satyadvayavibhaṅgavṛtti*), Toh 3881 Tengyur, dbu ma, *sa*, 2a3.

396 *Bodhicaryāvatāra*, 9:2, 31a1. Here the Tibetan has translated *tattva* ("truth" or "true nature," which is usually translated as *de nyid*) as *don dam*, the usual word for "ultimate."

397 Maitreyanātha, *Madhyāntavibhāga*, 1:15, Toh 4021 Tengyur, sems tsam, *phi*, 41a2.

398 *Stainless Light*, *tha*, 144b4. The Tai Situ quote has "is completely liberated from" *rnam par 'grol* instead of "completely transcends" *rnam par 'das* as in the original text.

399 *Sutra Requested by the Nāga King Anavatapta* (*Anavataptanāgarājaparipṛccha-sūtra*), Toh 156 Kangyur, mdo sde, *pha*, 230b2. The same sutra was quoted and identified by name above. That the title was not apparently known here and that the translation here differs from the canonical one indicates that the quotation was perhaps derived from the translation of an Indian treatise or a subsequent Tibetan text. The canonical version has been followed here. The quotation as written in Situ's text reads, "Those who know emptiness are not observant," which must be a scribal error of *min* for *yin*, as it follows a passage describing how we must become observant.

400 *Root Verses on the Middle Way*, 24:19, 15a6.

401 *Ghanavyūhasūtra*, chap. 7, Toh 110 Kangyur, mdo sde, *cha*, 37a7.

402 *Ghanavyūhasūtra*, chap. 7, 37b5.

403 *Bodhicaryāvatāra*, 8:26, 24a7. The translation of the last two lines in the second verse of the quotation follows the order of the Sanskrit. The Tibetan moved the cave to first position and lost the plural signifier.

404 Avadhūtipāda, *Presentation of the Six Dharmas of Dhyāna* (*Dhyānaṣaḍdharmavyavasthāna*), Toh 3926 Tengyur, dbu ma, *ki*, 92b7.

405 Avadhūtipāda, *Presentation of the Six Dharmas of Dhyāna* (*Dhyānaṣaḍdharmavyavasthāna*), Toh 3926 Tengyur, dbu ma, *ki*, 93a4.

406 Danaśila, *Commentary on "Presentation of the Six Dharmas of Dhyāna"* (*Dhyānaṣaḍdharmavyavasthānavṛtti*), Toh 3927 Tengyur, dbu ma, *ki*, 93a7. Tai Situ had ascribed the commentary to Avadhūtipa. This has been corrected in the translation.

407 The commentary actually says that she gradually removed them all until one remained, meaning that one should be by oneself in the hermitage. Danaśila, *Commentary on "Presentation of the Six Dharmas of Dhyāna"* (*Dhyānaṣaḍdharmavyavasthānavṛtti*), Toh 3927 Tengyur, dbu ma, *ki*, 94a3–94a5.

408 *Vajra Garland*, chap. 6, 218a4. There is a discrepancy with the Dergé Kangyur concerning the line "keeping the nose within their gaze (*Sna mthong lta ba'i tshad du zhog*)." The Dergé Kangyur version reads, "Place the nose at the level of the tongue (*sna ni lce yi tshad du bzhag*)."

409 This means when the Buddha was under the Bodhi tree at Bodhgaya.

410 Quotation not found in this text.

411 *Guhyasamāja Tantra*, chap. 2, 94a7.

412 *Hevajra Tantra*, book 1, 8:42, 10a6. Sanskrit: *bhāvyate hi jagat sarvaṃ manasā yasmān na bhāvyate*. The Tibetan translates *jagat* as "beings," which would result in the translation "All beings are meditated on/ by not meditating with the intellect." However, the *jagat*'s meaning as "world" appears to be what was intended here, as the following verse describes meditation on the animate and inanimate, including grass and various plants. The meditation is that they all have the same ultimate nature.

413 Indrabhūti, *Innate Accomplishment* (*Sahajasiddhi*), Toh 2260 Tengyur, rgyud, *zhi*, 3b2.

414 Saraha, *Song of an Inexhaustible Treasure of Instruction* (*Dohakoṣopadeśagīti*), Toh 2264 Tengyur, rgyud, *zhi*, 31a1. In the line "there will be no stain from any activity of acquirement and acquisition," the Situ text has *dgos* (necessity) instead of *gos* (stain), so that it would read: "There is no need for any activity of acquirement and acquisition."

415 An annotation to the text states that this is from the *Seven-Hundred-Verse Perfection of Wisdom* (*Saptaśatikāprajñāpāramitā*), Toh 24 Kangyur, sher phyin, *ka*, 148a1–174a2; however, only the first sentence of this quotation appears on 151a1 of this sutra.

416 *Aṣṭasāhasrikāprajñāpāramitā*, chap. 15, Toh 12 Kangyur, sher phyin, *ka*, 167b5. The Situ quotation has "all phenomena" *chos thams cad*. The Dergé edition has *chos gang yang*, "any phenomenon," which is the translation given here.

417 *Samādhirājasūtra*, chap. 2, Toh 127 Kangyur, mdo sde, *da*, 22a2. This translation follows the Kangyur version. The Situ quotation ends *'du shes spros las de mi thar*, repeating "of identification's conceptual elaboration," while the Dergé Kangyur simply has *'du shes las ni de mi thar*.

418 *Sāgaramatiparipṛcchāsūtra*, chap. 2, Toh 152 Kangyur, mdo sde, *pha*, 22a2.

419 Gyalwa Yangönpa, *A Rosary of Wish-Fulfilling Jewels*, vol. 3, 2b7.

420 Gampopa, *Group Teachings Entitled "Perfection of Qualities,"* 21a4.

421 Indrabhūti, *Innate Accomplishment* (*Sahajasiddhi*), Toh 2260 Tengyur, rgyud, *zhi*, 2b2.

422 Saraha, *Doha Treasury of Mahāmudrā Instructions* (*Dohakoṣamahāmudropadeśa*), Toh 2273 Tengyur, rgyud, *zhi*, 123b2.

423 Prajñākaramati, *Bodhicaryāvatārapañjikā*, chap. 9, Toh 3872 Tengyur, dbu ma, *la*, 190b6. The Situ text has *Shes* [*rab*] *'byung* [*gnas*] *sbas pa* (*Prajnākaragupta*) in error for *Shes* [*rab*] *'byung* [*gnas*] *blo gros*. Perhaps this is the author or scribe's error as a result of being more accustomed to writing Abhayākaragupta ('Jigs med 'byung gnas sbas pa), who is frequently referenced, but it has been corrected for this translation. Also the text has *las* "from" instead of *la* "concerning that," however the meaning is clearer in the Sanskrit: *evaṃ niḥsvabhāvataiva sarvabhāvānāṃ nijaṃ pāramārthikaṃ rūpam avatiṣṭhate/ tadeva pradhānapuruṣārthatayā paramārthaḥ utkṛṣṭaṃ prayojanam abhidhīyate// atrāpi nābhiniveṣṭavyam*.

424 This is a reference to Sakya Paṇḍita Künga Gyaltsen (1182–1251) and his followers. Hashang Mahayana was an eighth-century Chinese Chan master from Dunhuang whose teachings were forbidden by royal decree after his debate with Kamalaśīla in Samyé Monastery, although both sides claimed victory.

425 This refers to the changeless nature of each of the skandhas, each sensory perception, and so on.

426 *Primordial Buddha*, 114a4. For ease of reading I have not made the literal translation. "Consonants" was written as "*Ka*, *kha*, etc.," the beginning of the traditional Sanskrit list of consonants, and "vowels" was written as "*a*, etc.," as the list of vowels begins with *a*. The moon was written as "hare-marked" and the sun as the "day maker." This quite obscure passage, though typical of the Kālacakra, actually follows a passage about the retention of the drops—the semen—which is the subject of this passage.

427 The quotation does not appear to be in this text.

428 *Praise to the Dharmadhātu*, v. 43, 65a6. There is an important discrepancy between the quote and the canonical text. The quotation as given in the Situ text reads: "Meditate on the dharmadhātu, which is the nature of all phenomena (*chos rnams kun gyi rang bzhin nyid*)." The double plural appears to indicate a corruption and therefore the canonical version has been followed here: *Chos rnam rang bzhin med pa nyid*.

429 The text has not been identified.

430 *Guruparamparakramopadeśa*, Toh 3716 Tengyur, rgyud, *tsu*, 181a7.

431 *Guruparamparakramopadeśa*, Toh 3716 Tengyur, rgyud, *tsu*, 181b2.

432 *Bhadrakarātrīsūtra*, Toh 313, Kangyur, mdo sde, *sa*, 162b1.

433 *Sāgaramatiparipṛcchāsūtra*, chap. 4, Toh 152 Kangyur, mdo sde, *pha*, 33b6. This follows a passage about "incorrect identification" of impermanence as permanence, suffering as happiness, and so on.

434 Maitreyanātha, *Distinguishing the Middle Way from the Extremes* (*Madhyāntavibhāga*), chap. 1, Toh 4021 Tengyur, sems tsam, *phi*, 40b4. Tai Situ's text had the quotation attributed to Nāgārjuna.

435 Advayavajra, *A Teaching on the Mudrās of the Five Tathāgatas* (*Pañcatathāgatamudrāvivaraṇa*), Toh 2242 Tengyur, rgyud, *wi*, 122a7. The Situ text has "The tip (*rtse mo*) of a lamp flame" in error for "The continuity (*rgyun*) of a lamp flame," plus some grammatical variation.

436 Source unidentified.

437 *Saṃpuṭa*, 258a3. Tai Situ's text attributed this to the *Enlightenment of Vairocana*.

438 *Abhidharmakośa*, 2:33, 5a5.

439 *Gzugs can*; in this device, the example and the meaning are inseparable. There are twenty categories of this device.

440 Nāgārjuna, *Suhṛllekha*, Toh 4182 Tengyur, spring yig, *nge*, 42b6. The last two lines in the canonical edition do not actually mention meditation. They read: "Know that those five obscurations/ are thieves who steal the wealth of virtue."

441 Tai Situ already used this well-known quote above. See note 303.

442 *Bodhicaryāvatāra*, 8:4, 23b2.

443 *Sems gnas pa*; *cittasthita*.

444 *Yid byed*; *manaskāra*.

445 *'Gogs pa'i snyoms 'jug*; *nirodhasamāpatti*.

446 The Tibetan resolved this to be *sama-āpatti* rather than *sam-āpatti*, therefore translating it as *snyoms 'jug*, which would literally be "entry into equanimity."

447 This appears to be an error by Tai Situ, as a detailed search has not found this list anywhere in the *Perfection of Wisdom Sutras*.

448 *Sūtrālaṃkāra*, 15:4, 19a2.

449 *Abhidharmakośa*, 8:7, 24a2.

450 Source unidentified.

451 The quotation does not appear to be in this text.

452 *Mahāmudrā Tilaka*; although there is partial similarity to a passage at 71a5, the quotation does not appear in this text.

453 *Hevajra Tantra*, book 1, 9:3, 10b7.

454 *Summarized Teaching of the Empowerment* (*Śekhoddeśa*), Toh 361 Kangyur, rgyud, *ka*, 17b5.

455 *Abbreviated Perfection of Wisdom in Verse* (*Prajñāpāramitāsañcayagāthā*), Toh 13 Kangyur, sher phyin, *ka*, 8b3. The line "Those who can see in that way see all phenomena" (*Gang gis de ltar mthong ba de yis chos kun mthong*) differs from the canonical edition, which reads: "The Tathāgata taught to see phenomena in that way" (*De ltar chos mthong pa yang de bzhin gshegs pas bstan*).

456 Atiśa Dīpaṃkaraśrījñāna, *Satyadvayāvatāra*, Toh 3902 Tengyur, dbu ma, *a*, 72a6. Tai Situ gives the title as the *Shorter Truth of the Middle Way*.

457 *Enlightenment of Vairocana*, 153b1.

458 *Enlightenment of Vairocana*, 154a1.

459 *Enlightenment of Vairocana*, 154a4.

460 *Ears of Grain*. The quotation does not appear to be in this text.

461 The tradition of practice stemming from Phadampa Sangyé.

462 Phakmo Drupa, *Innate Union*, in Collected Works, vol. *nga* (4), 258.

463 *Sublime Continuum*, 1:147, 61b1. The Tibetan translated the single concept of *vicitra* ("diverse") with the addition of the idea "vast" (*rgya che sna tshogs*), hence Situ's use of both "vast" and "diverse" in the preceding paragraph.

464 *Compendium of the Perfection of Wisdom* (*Prajñāpāramitāsaṃgraha*), Toh 3809 Tengyur, sher phyin, *pha*, 292a2. This passage means that though the perfection of wisdom is the goal, the name is also used for the path to it.

465 The spelling may appear to be incorrect, as the classical Sanskrit form is *amanaskāra*. In a compound, *manas* for mind should not be declined. *Manasi* means "in the mind," literally. Maitripa defends this grammatical from in his *Teaching Amanasikāra* (*Amanasikāroddeśa*, Toh 2249 Tengyur, rgyud, *wi*, 138b5). A great deal of Buddhist literature, including sutras, is not written in Classical Sanskrit but from a merger of Classical Sanskrit with Middle Indic languages that developed separately from ancient, Vedic Sanskrit. Since the work of Edgerton in the twentieth century, this form of Sanskrit has become known as Buddhist Hybrid Sanskrit. Pali is an example of a Middle Indic language, and Pali also has the terms *manasikāra* and *amanasikāra*. In this edition at least, the marker for the long vowel in *kāra* is missing. Most commonly, this term refers to paying attention when teachings are being given. Its opposite, a negative quality, is inattentiveness. Here as a positive quality, however, this has been translated as "nonattention," although according to Maitripa's gloss it should be "attention on [the syllable] *a*."

466 *Mañjuśrīnāmasaṃgiti*, Toh 360 Kangyur, rgyud, *ka*, 2a3. There are variations from the canonical text because the quotation is obtained from a translation of Maitripa's *Teaching Amanasikāra* (139b7), so that the translation inevitably differs, and the Sanskrit may also have differed. The canonical version reads: "The *a* syllable is

the supreme syllable./ It is the sacred, unchanging, great meaning./ It is the great life force and it is birthless./ It is beyond that which is described in words."

467 *Hevajra Tantra*, book 2, 4:44, 21a1. Situ has derived this quote from the translation of Maitripa's *Teaching Amanasikāra* (140a2). In that translation the order of the words has been considerably rearranged, and there could well be some corruption in its transmission. The translation of the quotation as given in the text would read "[She who is] the nature of the first vowel, Dhiti (Intelligence), is named Prajñā (Wisdom). She is Bhagavatī Prajñā. The union of the stage of perfection...." This verse is in fact a part of the description of Nairātmya, Hevajra's consort.

468 *Avikalpapraveśadhāraṇī*, Toh 142 Kangyur, mdo sde, *pa*. Though there are similar phrases throughout this short text, this quotation does not appear. This quotation is given however in Maitripa's *Teaching Amanasikāra* (139b2). However, in our edition of the Situ text, "gained" (*blang*) has been replaced by "eliminated" (*spangs*).

469 *Avikalpapraveśadhāraṇī*, Toh 142 Kangyur, mdo sde, *pa*. This quotation does not appear in the canonical version.

470 *Teaching Amanasikāra* (*Amanasikāroddeśa*), Toh 2249 Tengyur, rgyud, *wi*, 139b5. *Śākapārthiva*, literally "vegetable king," is a compound that was understood to mean *śāka-bhojī-pārthiva*, "vegetable-eating king." The Tibetan translates this as "king of leaves" (*lo ma'i rgyal po*). Here Maitripa is stating that *amanasikāra* is an abbreviation of *akāramanasikāra* (attention on the syllable *a*) and so the syllable *a* at the front is not, as it is normally taken to be, a negation. Despite this explanation, the Tibetan still translates the *a* as a negative here. Maitripa also uses technical Sanskrit grammatical terms and used a word compound as an example, but the Tibetan has none of these specific grammatical features and has thus become inevitably obscure. Unfortunately the Toh edition increases the confusion by having "*I* syllable" in error for "*A* syllable."

471 Maitripa, *Teaching Amanasikāra* (*Amanasikāroddeśa*), Toh 2249 Tengyur, rgyud, *wi*, 40a2.

472 Literally the honorific word for "hand," which by its addition creates the honorific form of "seal."

473 *Instructions from the Successive Guru Lineage* (*Guruparamparakramopadeśa*), Toh 3716 Tengyur, rgyud, *tsu*, 179a2.

474 *Commentary on Difficult Points in [Maitripa's] "Teaching on Empowerment"* (*Sekanirdeśapañjikā*), Toh 2253 Tengyur, rgyud, *wi*, 154a2.

475 Kālacakrapāda, *Padmanipañjikā*, Toh 1350 Tengyur, rgyud, *na*, 83a3.

476 Source unidentified.

477 Source unidentified.

478 *Stainless Light*, *tha*, 108a3.

479 *Ṣaḍaṅgayogopadeśa*, Toh 1372 Tengyur, rgyud, *pa*, 224a5.

480 Source unidentified.

481 Source unidentified.

482 *Tattvadaśakaṭīkā*, Toh 2254 Tengyur, rgyud, *wi*, 175a7. The source of Sahajavajra's citation is unidentified.

483 *Saṃdhinirmocanasūtra*, chap. 5, Toh 106 Kangyur, mdo sde, *ca*, 13b1. This is abridged and therefore not an exact reproduction of the original passage. The original reads: "Matisāra! This is because the bodhisattvas do not see internal, indi-

vidual acquisition, and they do not see an acquiring consciousness, and that is how things truly are. They do not see the ālaya, they do not see the ālaya consciousness, they do not see accumulation, they do not see mind. They do not see eyes, they do not see form, and they do not see visual consciousnesses. They do not see ears, they do not see sound, and they do not see auditory consciousnesses. They do not see noses, they do not see smells, and they do not see olfactory consciousnesses. They do not see bodies, they do not see tangibles, and they do not see tactile consciousnesses. Matisāra! This is because the bodhisattvas do not see their own internal minds, they do not see phenomena, and they do not see mental consciousnesses. This is how things truly are and so bodhisattvas are called 'wise concerning the ultimate.'"

484 *Samādhirājasūtra*. The quotation has not been located in this sutra. There is a play on words in the last stanza, where *dharma* (*chos*) is used to mean both "phenomena" and "qualities."

485 *Sarvapuṇyasamuccayasamādhisūtra*, Toh 134 Kangyur, mdo sde, *na*, 104a2. This is an abridgment of the passage, which reads: "When all phenomena are seen to naturally cease, at that time one sees correctly. When all phenomena are seen to naturally be at peace, and naturally be in a state of equality, one sees correctly. When all phenomena are seen to be completely unborn, one sees correctly. When all phenomena are seen to be completely unborn, to have never arisen, and to eternally and completely be nirvana, and one does not see a seer nor a seen, if one sees through not seeing, completely not seeing, that is called *seeing correctly*."

486 Quotation has not been located in this sutra.

487 Source of quotation unknown.

488 *Illuminating Words and Meaning: An Explanation of "Yoginī's Activity"* (*Yoginīsaṃ caryānibandhapadārthaprakaśa*), Toh 1423 Tengyur, rgyud, *wa*, 144b6. The tantra itself is Toh 375.

489 *Illuminating Words and Meaning*, 144b7.

490 The ten signs were listed in note 223.

491 Source unidentified.

492 *Hevajra Tantra*, book 2, 567, 25b7. This is an answer given to describe the moment when the true nature is seen. This verse is in Apabhraṃśa not Sanskrit. The first line could also be translated as "no middle or extremes," while the Tibetan translation has a temporal interpretation: "no beginning, middle, or end." The last line has been interpreted in the Tibetan translation as "there is no self and no other."

493 *Pratipattisāraśataka*, Toh 2334 Tengyur, rgyud, *zhi*, 282b2.

494 *Mahābherīsūtra*, Toh 222 Kangyur, mdo sde, *dza*. The quotation has not been located in this text.

495 *Samādhirājasūtra*, chap. 25, Toh 127 Kangyur, mdo sde, *da*, 84b4. The quotation omits, perhaps deliberately, the middle section of this quotation "Those who perfectly know form, perfectly know emptiness./ Those who perfectly know that the qualities/ of form are empty in this way/ will be able to overcome and defeat/ many millions of māras./ Those who perfectly know forms,/ they will also know emptiness." The last line in the Kangyur version reads "Will be completely destroyed" (*rab tu brlag*) instead of "destroyed [so that there is nothing left but] dust" (*rdul du brlag*), translated here as "crushed into dust."

496 *Ratnakaraṇḍasūtra*, Toh 117 Kangyur, mdo sde, *ja*, 250a6.

497 *Summarized Teaching of the Empowerment* (*Śekhoddeśa*), Toh 361 Kangyur, rgyud, *ka*, 20a2. This verse comes in the context of a description of form—of the union of substance and nonsubstance, of form and the formless. "Their union" refers to the inseparability of compassion and emptiness, which is mentioned in the preceding verse. The canonical version has been used here as in the present edition of Situ's text, the lines have been corrupted to the point of unintelligibility, with the order of the third and fourth lines reversed. The canonical version: *Mya ngan 'das pa bral ba'i gzugs/ 'khor ba las 'das mi 'gyur ba/ de dag sbyor ba gnyis med mchog/ rtag dang chad les nges par grol//*. The corrupt version: *Mya ngan 'das dang bral ba'i sems/ 'khor ba las 'das mi 'gyur la/ rtag dang chad les nges par grol/ de gnyis sbyor bas gnyis med gzhan/*. Possible translation: "The mind free from nirvāṇa/ is not beyond saṃsāra,/ and there is true liberation from eternalism and nihilism,/ and through their union, a different nonduality."

498 *Root Verses on the Middle Way*, 16:10, 9b1.

499 Source unidentified.

500 *Bodhisattvacaryānirdeśasūtra*, Toh 184 Kangyur, mdo sde, *tsa*, 103b1. The Dergé text has "body" (*lus*) instead of "perishable aggregation" (*'jig tshogs*). See note 229.

501 *Bodhisattvacaryānirdeśasūtra*, 103b3. The Situ version has "do not *correctly* take up the trainings." The Situ quote simplifies one sentence, eliminating an important but perhaps unfamiliar term, *chos gnas pa*, replacing it with *chos nyid*.

502 *Hevajra Tantra*, book 1, 8:49–51, 10b3.

503 The idea of necessity has been added here, which was not in the earlier list where this heading was mentioned on page 240.

504 The source of the quotation has not been identified.

505 Nāgārjuna, *Bodhicittavivaraṇa*, v. 73, Toh 1800 Tengyur, rgyud, *ngi*, 41a3.

506 Nāgārjuna, *Bodhicittavivaraṇa*, v. 73, Toh 1800 Tengyur, rgyud, *ngi*, vv. 86–89, 41b3.

507 *Mkha' 'gro dra ba sdom pa*. Text unidentified. It is not *Ḍākinsaṃbaratantra*, Toh 406, nor is it *Vajrasiddhajālasaṃbaratantra*, Toh 411.

508 The quotation was not found within this text.

509 The quotation was not found within this text.

510 The quotation was not found within this text.

511 *Hevajra Tantra*, book 2, 4:70, 15a6. The text says the quote is from the *Guhyasamāja Tantra*, but it does not appear there. Also *gang phyir* (because) had been misquoted as *gang zhig* (the one that...).

512 Situ gives the nāga's name as Sāgara, but the citation does not occur in the *Sāgaranāgarājaparipṛcchāsūtra* (Toh 153) but instead appears to be a paraphrase of a passage in *The Sutra Requested by the Nāga King Anavatapta* (*Anavataptanāgarājaparipṛcchāsūtra*), Toh 156, Kangyur, mdo sde, *pha* 228b3: "Those two [disrespect for the guru and the arrogance of praising oneself] are the activites of Māra. They are completely rejected by the bodhisattva. There are another two. What are those two? Wisdom devoid of method and method devoid of wisdom are those two. Wisdom devoid of method is like this: One looks not at all beings but ponders noncomposite phenomena instead. Method devoid of wisdom is the four methods of gathering [followers] performed with a dualistic view. Both of those are the activity of Māra. They are completely rejected by the bodhisattva."

513 Atiśa Dīpaṃkaraśrījñāna, *Bodhipathapradīpa*, v. 43, Toh 3947 Tengyur, dbu ma, *khi*, 240a2.
514 *Abhisamayālaṃkāra*, 1:11, 2a5.
515 Source unidentified.
516 Nāgārjuna, *Bodhicittavivaraṇa*, vv. 2–3, Toh 1800 Tengyur, rgyud, *ngi*, 38b3. Situ quoted this already on page 203. Here the quotation had "aggregates" (*phung po*) in error for "self" (*bdag*). See also note 342.
517 Although this section had been listed as the forthcoming third of four parts of the teaching of meditation, Tai Situ does not distinguish it at this point as a separate section.
518 The quotation does not appear in this text, even where there is a reference to vajra body, speech, and mind on 137a7.
519 *Latter Guhyasamāja Tantra*, 151b1. This quotation is in an alternative translation to that in the canon, presumably obtained from the translation of a commentary that included this quotation.
520 The source of the quotation is unidentified as it does not appear to be in this text. This may seem at first to be simply an inaccurate etymology, but the Indian tradition of etymology known as *nirukta* was a discipline in which a variety of meanings were teased from terms and was not confined to grammatical analysis of their components. Grammatically, *man* is the root word for "think." Adding *tṛ*, as with all such roots, creates an agent: in this case the word *mantṛ* means "thinker." The final *r* in both the English and Sanskrit words is not a coincidence, as it is a structure common to Indo-European languages. Augmenting the ending *tra* creates the word for the tool, or means, for the verb, in this case for thinking. Therefore, literally, *mantra* is a tool employed for thought. The sum of the word's components, however, is, as always, greater than its parts.
521 *Ears of Grain*. The quotation does not appear to be in this text.
522 Source unidentified.
523 Source unidentified.
524 Abhyākaragupta, *Munimatālaṃkāra*, Toh 3903 Tengyur, dbu ma, *a*, 229a5.
525 Abhyākaragupta, *Munimatālaṃkāra*, Toh 3903 Tengyur, dbu ma, *a*, 229b6.
526 Dergé: *lus can*; the Situ text has *yul can*, or "subject."
527 *Sūtrālaṃkāra*, 8a2.
528 The "Bzang spyod smon lam" is a commonly recited prayer based upon a passage in the *Avataṃsaka Sutra*, Toh 44 Kangyur, phal chen, *a*, 360a7. The three quotations given here are not from the popular prayer but from the source itself, although the first of these quotations is dissimilar to its source in the sutra.
529 *Avataṃsaka Sutra*, 360a6.
530 *Avataṃsaka Sutra*, 360b7.
531 Only six are listed.
532 Though *sangs* and *rgyas* are derived from the meanings "awakened" and "blossomed," these meanings in Tibetan have become eclipsed by "purified" and "developed."
533 Source unidentified.
534 Jñānākara, *Mantrāvatāra*, Toh 3718 Tengyur, rgyud, *tsu*, 194b1.
535 *Zhi ba'i blo gros kyis dris pa las* could be taken as being a quotation from a text of that name; however, not only does no such sutra appear to exist, Jñānākara's root text and

commentary are in the form of answers to rhetorical questions that he asks himself. The reason for the insertion of the phrase mentioning a Śāntimati is a mystery.

536 Jñānākara, *Mantrāvatāravṛtti*, Toh 3719 Tengyur, rgyud, *tsu*, 197a6. This passage is a prose version of the verses of the root text.

537 *Mahāmudrāsañcamitha* [sic]. Not included in the Tengyur. See bibliography under Tibetan sources. This has become erroneously known as being by Maitripa as the result of a Rumtek reprint in *Treasury of Dohas*, taken from a manuscript in which the author's name was obscured by an ink stain. This text, however, makes no explicit enumeration of four yogas, so it is possible that another text is being referred to.

538 *Sūtrālaṃkāra*, 7:6 (Skt. 6:6), 6b3.

539 *Sūtrālaṃkāra*, 7:7–8, 6b6.

540 The text actually states *śloka*, which would be the entire two-line verse, but only the first line is meant, as this is the last verse in the chapter.

541 *Sūtrālaṃkāra*, chap. 15, 18b7–21a1.

542 First of the six yogas of the Kālacakra tradition. The second yoga, *dhyāna*, is in the following line.

543 Rangjung Dorjé, *Profound Inner Meaning*, 21b6.

544 Source unidentified.

545 Source unidentified.

546 *Tattvadaśakaṭīkā*, Toh 2254 Tengyur, rgyud, *wi*, 166b6.

547 *Densely Arrayed Adornments Sutra* (*Ghanavyūhasūtra*), chap. 7, Toh 110 Kangyur, mdo sde, *cha*, 37a7.

548 This is one of the texts translated in the present volume. This quotation is to be found on page 153. Tai Situ has—presumably inadvertently—changed the original quotation, making it "In the preliminaries, a true guru" and so on. It has been corrected here to match the original text.

549 Minyak Tokden Lodrö Rinchen, or Masé Tokden Lodrö Rinchen (b. 1386), is better known in the west as Trungmasé, the First Garwang Rinpoché, founder of Surmang Monastery and the Surmang Kagyü, and teacher of Künga Gyaltsen, the First Trungpa Rinpoché. Trungmasé was a pupil of the Fifth Karmapa Deshin Shekpa, and he became the holder of the Aural Tantra lineage of the Karma Kagyü, the principal text for which is the *Vajra Verses* mentioned here. Situ Tenpai Nyinjé wrote a short untitled biography of him in his *Supplement to the String of Infinite Moonstone Jewels*, in his Collected Works vol. *da*, 255a2–255b3.

550 Nāropa, *Vajra Verses of the Aural Tantra* (*Karṇatantravajragāthā*). Toh 2338, Tengyur, rgyud, *zhi*.

551 Referred to here as Maitripa.

552 Source unidentified.

553 Source unidentified.

554 Tai Situ attributes this to the *Precious Garland* (*Ratnāvalī*), the title of a well-known Nagarjuna text, but the actual citation is found in Āryadeva, *Four Hundred Verses* (*Catuḥśatakaśāstra*), Toh 3846 Tengyur, dbu ma, *tsha*, 9a7. A slightly different translation than the canonical version is used by Situ.

555 *Bodhisattvacaryānirdeśasūtra*, Toh 184 Kangyur, mdo sde, *tsa*, 103b6.

556 *Mañjuśrīvihārasūtra*, Toh 196 Kangyur, mdo sde, *tsa*, 270a2.

557 Another name for the Karma Kagyü.

558 The three main pupils of Atiśa: Dromtön Gyalwai Jungné, Khutön Tsöndrü Yungdrung, and Ngok Lekpai Sherap.

559 This verse uses the non-Buddhist imagery of an Indian sadhu, cleansing himself in the Ganges and pleasing Brahmā through asceticism.

560 A footnote in the Tibetan text identifies this as referring to Dakpo Nyigom, yet another name for Gampopa. A chariot is also a synonym for a master or lineage that established a certain practice or view.

561 Better known as Palpung Monastery, in the Dergé region of Kham.

562 This is 1733, six years after the founding of Palpung Monastery. He was then thirty-three years old.

563 Sanskrit for "May there be an increase of good fortune and victory!"

564 *Guhyagarbhatantra*, chap. 5, Toh 832 Kangyur, rnying rgyud, *kha*, 115a5.

565 *Treasury of Dohas*, 72b5.

566 The Cittamātra or Yogācāra school taught three natures: *imaginary* (*kun tu btags pa*, *parīkalpita*), which is an object of cognition that is purely conceptual; *dependent* (*gzhan dbang*, *paratantra*), the nonconceptual cognition of dependently arisen phenomena; and *absolute* (*yongs su grub pa*, *parinispanna*), the direct perception of the nature of the mind. The *absolute* is taught to have two aspects: changeless and irreversible. See Jamgön Kongtrul Lodrö Tayé, *Treasury of Knowledge, book 6, part 3: Frameworks of Buddhist Philosophy* (Ithaca, NY: Snow Lion Publications, 2007), 175–94. See also Dan Lusthaus, *Buddhist Phenomenology: A Philosophical Investigation of Yogācāra* (London: Routledge Curzon, 2002), and Fernando Tola and Carmen Dragonetti, *Being as Consciousness: Yogācāra Philosophy of Buddhism* (Delhi: Motilal Banarsidass, 2006).

567 Gyalwa Yangönpa, *The Great Tantra that Teaches Unimpeded Dzogchen*, 15a3.

568 This is in reference to the Yogācāra's doctrine of three natures. See note 566.

569 This is simply the lack of attachment one has to something that one dislikes.

570 *Hevajra Tantra*, book 2, 4:70, 22b3.

571 *Sublime Continuum*, 1:51, 57a2.

572 *Praise to the Dharmadhātu*, v. 37, 65a3.

573 See note 287.

574 *Zhi byed chu klung chen po'i rgyud*. The citation does not appear in this Nyingma tantra.

575 *Treasury of Dohas*, 71b2.

576 Saraha; source unidentified.

577 Lorepa Darma Wangchuk (1187–1250) was the founder of the lower, or eastern, Drukpa tradition. The source of the quotation has not been identified.

578 Source unidentified.

579 Source unidentified.

580 Source unidentified.

581 *Rnam kun mchog ldan*, "having the supreme of all aspects," a term that refers to an inseparability of emptiness and appearance.

582 *Dran rig*, a compound term formed from *dran pa* ("mindfulness" or "recollection") and *rig pa* ("knowledge" or "knowing"). This can also be translated as "recognition" or "wakefulness."

583 *Daśacakrakṣitigarbhasūtra*, Toh 239 Kangyur, mdo sde, *zha*. This quotation has not been found in this sutra, though a similar passage commences on folio 191b1:

"Those who wish to attain liberation solely through the 'qualities of training' [This is a specific phrase that designates twelve aspects of monastic conduct; 'one who resides in the qualities of training' is a synonym for *śrāvaka*, though here a distinction appears to be made between the two] on hearing the Mahayana teaching will fall into the lower realms./ Like giving milk to someone with a phlegm illness,/ it will act as a poison and will not eliminate the illness./ Similarly the unsuitable vessels who follow the Śrāvaka Vehicle,/ if they hear the Mahayana teachings, they will not understand./ The Cārvākas will fall into the lower existences./ Therefore examine their capabilities before you teach.//"

584 Bodhgaya is a modern name. The text actually uses the traditional Buddhist name for Bodhgaya: Vajrāsana, "the vajra seat."

585 *Cakrasaṃvaraguhyācintatantra*, Toh 385 Kangyur, rgyud, *ga*. This quotation has not been found in the tantra of that name. Also, no reference to it has been located in the works of Gampopa.

586 *Gnad kyi zin tig*. The text has not been identified.

587 The source of the quotation has not been identified. It is not among any of Niguma's known works or biographies.

588 *Samādhirājasūtra*, Toh 127 Kangyur, mdo sde, *da*, 100b6. The first verse in the quotation is the last of several pages of verses that all begin "Whatever man holds this supreme samādhi..." The third line was missing in the present edition.

589 *Avataṃsakasūtra*, Toh 44 Kangyur, phal chen, *kha*, 186a5. These are the "five fears of the bodhisattva on the paths of accumulation and engagement. The latter two lines were corrupted in the Tselé Natsok Rangdrol text to "You cannot be harmed, and you will not fall into death and the lower existences." *'Tsho* ("sustenance") had been corrupted to *'tshe* ("harm"). In one edition *med* ("being without") had become *me* ("fire") and one of the fears had been lost. The fear concerning retinue was changed to the more readable "fears within saṃsāra."

590 The perfection of wisdom sutras.

591 The third level is missing from the available editions of the Tselé Natsok Rangdrol text.

592 The three powers of the body (*lus kyi rtsal gsum*) are said to be the ability to press down flesh with a finger, to swim across a great river, and to have powerful lightness, like a bird. There are also three powers of the speech and the mind.

593 A very common phrase, but this text inexplicably has the nonsensical opposite: "liberated in one through knowing all."

594 The three kinds of emanations are those that are emanated—without being born—in order to accomplish a certain deed at a certain time and place; those that are born like ordinary humans; and the supreme emanation, which is a buddha.

595 The concepts of the agent of an action, the action itself (or a secondary agent), and the object of the action.

596 The Tibetan text has the explanatory annotations of "[ordinary] beings" for thickly obscured, "yogins" for partially obscured, and "buddhas" for unobscured.

597 The Tibetan text has explanatory additions, which appear rather forced: "The worldly is the wrong path, the tīrthika is the mistaken path, the śrāvaka and pratyekabuddha are the erroneous path, and the lower tantras the bondage."

598 *Udumbara*. The fig tree never has flowers. It has also in Tibet been taken to refer to a mythical flower that only blossoms when a Cakravartin or Buddha is born.

599 Explanatory additions to the Tibetan edition specify that the first line describes the view, the second line describe the meditation, the third line describes the conduct, and the fourth line describes the result.

600 Literally one that has had warmth and grease removed. A more common but slightly different metaphor involving intractable leather is that of used butter bags, as butter can no longer soften it, exemplifying a mind that has become impervious to the Dharma through unskillful overexposure to it.

601 The anonymous Tibetan annotations state that the first line describes those who are incapable of meditation, the second line describes those who do not believe in meditation, and the third line describes those who do not understand the essential point of meditation.

602 "Descending to the water goddess" means setting over the sea, and the vermilion clouds are the red clouds of sunset.

603 No information is currently available about Mengom Tsültrim Sangpo. Tselé Natso Rangdröl also wrote an eleven-page folio entitled *Answers to Mengom's Questions* (*Sman sgom gyi dris lan gnyis chos zung 'jug gi ngo sprod zhal gdams*) in which he is referred to as "the supreme vidyādhara of Mengom" (1b1) and as "Tsültrim Rinchen, the great meditator of Men" (*sman sgom chen tshul khrims rin chen*) (11b4).

604 That is, the Rangjung Dorjé text earlier in this volume.

605 *Yi ge bzhi pa*. A teaching on: (1) understanding the basis of the *mind*, (2) methods for following the path of *meditation*, (3) cutting through errors in the *view*, (4) transforming [everything] into the path through *conduct*.

606 Tilopa, *Mahāmudrā Instructions* (*Mahāmudropadeśa*), Toh 2303 Tengyur, rgyud, *zhi*. A song by Tilopa to Nāropa delivered on the banks of the Ganges and therefore popularly known as the "Ganges Mahāmudrā."

607 Kamalaśīla, *Mahāmudrātattvānākṣaropadeśa*, Toh 2325 Tengyur, rgyud, *zhi*.

608 Taught by Nāropa to Marpa.

609 Introduced into Tibet by Vajrapāṇi (born 1017), who was a pupil of Maitripa (998–1063).

610 These teachings are said to be based on the *Cakrasaṃvara Tantra of the Inconceivable Secret* (*Cakrasaṃbaraguhyācintatantra*), Toh 385 Kangyur, rgyud, *ga*.

611 Unidentified.

612 The mahāmudrā tradition of the Drigung Kagyü, the five aspects being: (1) bodhicitta, (2) deity meditation, (3) guru devotion, (4) the nonconceptual view, and (5) dedication. The fourth is itself also called *mahāmudrā*, but all five are taught to be aspects of mahāmudra.

613 For example, Tashi Namgyal's contemporary Karma Chakmé's (1613–78) *Wish-Fulfilling Jewel: A Collection of Mahāmudrā Instructions*.

614 *Gnad gyi gzer drug*. A teaching given by Tilopa: "Do not contemplate, do not think, do not know,/ do not meditate, do not analyze, but rest naturally." Similar lines were quoted in the text by Pema Karpo above. See note 181.

615 *Vast Expanse Free from Extremes* is from Sangyé Lingpa's *Unity of the Gurus' Realization*. *Sun's Essence* is from Ratna Lingpa. *Seeing the Naked Intrinsic Nature* is from Ngari Tertön Garwang Dorjé. The other texts have not been identified.

616 A.k.a. Götsangpa Natsok Rangdröl. Here, he distinguishes himself from Götsangpa Gönpo Dorjé, the well-known Drukpa Kagyü master. Götsang means

Vulture Cave. Both Tselé Natsok Rangdröl and Gönpo Dorjé gained their epithets through dwelling at identically named caves, the former in Palri and the latter in the Latö. The early sixteenth-century Götsang Repa, also known as Natsok Rangdröl, has sometimes been confused with both of these Götsangpas.

617 *'Phel ka phyir skyed*; this translation of the obscure phrase *'phel ka* follows an explanation by Thrangu Rinpoche.

618 The original text has a footnote at this location: "With your body in the posture described above, visualize yourself as Vajrayoginī, as previously described. Within your body, in its center, is the very straight, blue central channel. Its upper end reaches the fontanel, which is adorned by a wheel that has vajra-cross spokes. Its lower end is situated on the anthers of the secret lotus. Its width is that of a medium-sized wheat stalk. On the right side is the red *lalanā*; on the left is the white *rasanā*. Both are of the same length as the central channel, and have the width of the slenderest wheat stalk. None of the three touch each other, and they all resemble hollow pillars."

619 The letter *e* as the first part of the word *evam* (which means "thus"—the opening word of the Buddha's sutras and tantras). It is a euphemism for a triangle and also for emptiness. This is originally in reference to the orthographical shape of the letter in the Gupta script.

620 *Vaṃ* is here an euphemism for "circular" and also clarity or bliss. In the Gupta script this letter is circular.

621 "The ocean" means the stomach, and "Mount Meru" means the spine. Therefore this means that the stomach is pulled inward as much as possible.

622 Like the lens of a magnifying glass, a fire crystal creates heat or fire by focusing the rays of the sun onto a single point.

623 "The demon's (*rākṣasa*) mouth" here means the anus.

624 *Canaka* is definitely the Sanskrit for chickpea, but that seems to be too large for this context. The *Great Tibetan-Chinese Dictionary* defines it as a small pea or pulse.

625 There is no numeral in the text to indicate where practice 9 ends and 10 begins.

626 Rangjung Dorjé, *Illuminating the Profound Path of the Six Dharmas of Nāropa*, 538–93.

627 Mikyö Dorjé, *The Six Dharmas of Nāropa*, 773–892.

628 The phrases in parentheses are annotations in the Tibetan text.

629 Specifically emblic myrobalan.

630 Lying down, sitting, moving around, and going somewhere.

631 A white curled hair between the eyebrows that is one of the characteristics of a buddha. See also note 632.

632 The *uṣṇīṣa* is the protuberance on the crown of the head that is one of the primary signs of a great being, and is characteristic of all buddhas and yidam deities. In the meditation, the practitioners are visualizing themselves as the deity and therefore have an *uṣṇīṣa*.

633 The *shabkyu* is the lowest part of the syllable *hūṃ* in Tibetan and Indian orthography; it represents the vowel *u*.

634 *Appearance*, *increase*, and *attainment* are the names of the successive states of mind at the onset of death. They can also occur more subtly when falling asleep, fainting, or at orgasm. For further details on the *three visions* or *three lights*, see Jamgön Kongtrul Lodrö Tayé, *Treasury of Knowledge, book 6, part 4: Systems of Buddhist Tantra* (Ithaca, NY: Snow Lion Publications, 2005), 252–70.

635 The *four empties* are the *empty*, the *very empty*, the *great empty*, and the *all empty*, which are names for the states of mind at the onset of death, sleep, and so on, and they correspond to appearance, increase, attainment, and luminosity, respectively.

636 The *five enlightenments* or *abhisaṃbodhis* in this context are said to arise: (1) from discrimination, (2) from developing bodhicitta, (3) from the vajra of stability, (4) from the vajra nature, (5) and from the equality of all the tathāgatas.

637 Yangchen is one of the names of Mikyö Dorjé, the Eighth Karmapa (1507–54).

638 This longer name for Akṣobhya does occur when he is the central figure of the Guhyasamāja mandala, but that more elaborate form is not what is intended here.

639 The secret, wisdom, and fourth empowerments. The vase empowerment is not one of the highest empowerments.

640 The forceful method is basically the same practice but with extra techniques of posture, breath control, and a supporting staff.

641 *Gzer lnga*: (1) enhancement through illness, (2) death transformed into an aid, (3) obstacles taken as siddhis, (4) spontaneous liberation of thoughts and concepts, and (5) the afflictions adopted as the path.

642 "Someone who does nothing but eat and sleep," derived from the Sanskrit word for eating, *bhukta*, and the Sanskrit word for sleep, *supta*. The *ka* adds the meaning of "one who."

643 The seven aspects of union that are the nature of the saṃbhogakāya: (1) the saṃbhoga aspect, (2) the aspect of union, (3) the aspect of great bliss, (4) the aspect of the absence of a real nature, (5) the aspect of being filled with compassion, (6) the aspect of unbroken continuity, and (7) the aspect of cessationlessness. See also Tashi Namgyal's description on page 609.

644 Wangchuk Dorjé, the Ninth Karmapa (1556–1603).

645 Mikyö Dorjé, the Eighth Karmapa (1507–54).

646 The Sixth Shamarpa (1584–1630).

647 This would be in 1609. Wangchuk Dorjé, the Ninth Karmapa, had passed away six years earlier, at the age of forty-seven. The nineteen-year-old Shamarpa, already recognized as one of the greatest living scholars, had become his successor. He wrote this text at age twenty-five—his "twenty-sixth year," as in Tibet you are aged one in your first year of life and so on. The year after writing this text, the Shamarpa formally recognized the six-year-old Chöying Dorjé, the Tenth Karmapa (1604–74).

648 This is a retreat at Tsurphu, the seat of the Karmapas, which is to the north of Lhasa in Central Tibet.

649 Jikten Sumgön (1143–1217) was a pupil of Phakmo Drupa and the founder of the Drigung Kagyü school, which had varying degrees of secular power until the seventeenth century.

650 The *six alternatives* (*mtha' drug*, *ṣaṭkoti*) is a classification of types of teachings in the tantras set out by Candrakīrti in his *Illuminating Lamp* (*Pradīpoddyotana*). The six are divided into three pairs. The first pair separates those teachings with a provisional truth (*drang don*, *neyārtha*)—those that require interpretation—from those with a definitive truth (*nges don*, *nitārtha*), whose meaning is evident. The next pair distinguishes those teachings not to be taken literally, whose meaning is veiled (*gongs can*), from those without a hidden meaning (*dgongs min*). The third pair distinguishes those teachings that accord with conventional language (*sgra ji bzhin pa*) from those that do not (*sgra ji bzhin pa ma yin pa*). See also note 296.

651 This is explained by Sherap Jungné by examples. The same necklace worn successively by an ordinary citizen, a minister, or a king changes the level of its status even though the necklace itself does not change. The same food eaten by those three enables the individuals to accomplish different goals. Similarly there is not the slightest difference in terms of the vows that are to be kept—they are all simply avoidance of the ten bad actions and practice of the ten good actions. Held by individuals at different levels, however, they enable different levels of results.

652 This is in reference to lifespan, happiness, virtuous minds, and their opposites.

653 Sherab Jungné in his own commentary to the text defines what he means by the human and divine Dharmas. The human Dharmas are what are necessary for humans within this world, while the divine Dharma is that which brings liberation from it. The sixteen human Dharmas are (1–10) avoiding the ten bad actions; (11–15) respecting father, mother, brahmans, monastics, and elders; and (16) accumulating merit through generosity. The specific mention of brahmans appears to give this an Indic origin. During the development of a legal system in the subsequent medieval period, it appears that avoiding the ten bad actions became separated out as the *ten divine Dharmas*, thus eliminating its soteriological perspective, and a new version of the sixteen human Dharmas developed that incorporated practicing the Dharma as one of its rules. This became attributed to the seventh-century king Songtsen Gampo, giving it more prestige, and it became dominant, eclipsing the version found here. In the present-day system the sixteen human dharmas are (1) devoting oneself to the Three Jewels, (2) seeking out and practicing the Dharma, (3) repaying the kindness of one's parents, (4) respecting the learned, (5) honoring elders and those of high status, (6) helping neighbors and the people of one's area, (7) being honest and humble, (8) being on good terms with family and friends, (9) following and having enduring relationships with good people, (10) being moderate in food and wealth, (11) valuing those who have shown past kindness, (12) repaying debts on time, without cheating in terms of measure or weight, (13) harboring jealousy toward no one, (14) shunning bad advice and being one's own person, (15) speaking gently and little, and (16) not being self-obsessed and being able to take on burdens.

654 In this text this means the three superior trainings of wisdom, conduct, and meditation, which bring liberation from samsara. See the preceding note for the later Tibetan reinterpretation and codification.

655 The four factors that create obstacles are: (1) an inability to take the vows (due, for example, to having committed the five worst acts, being born in the northern continent of Kuru, or being an apparition); (2) an inability to keep the vows (due to debt, enslavement, being in the service of the king, or not having permission from one's parents); (3) an inability to obtain special qualities (because one is sick, for example); and (4) being prevented from benefiting others (because of being rejected by one's followers, and so on). Further reading on this subject can be found in Géza Uray, "The Narrative of Legislation and Organization of the *Mkhas-pa'i dga'-ston*: The Origins of the Traditions Concerning Sroṅ-brcan Sgam-po as First Legislator and Organizer of Tibet," *Acta Orientalia Academiae Scientiarum Hungaricae* 26.1 (1972): 11–68; and in Matthew T. Kapstein, *The Tibetan Assimilation of Buddhism: Conversion, Contestation, and Memory* (New York: Oxford University Press, 2000).

656 The forsaking mind and its seeds, and other accompanying factors, are the essence of the vows in the Cittamātra tradition.

657 The Vaibhāṣikas classed vows as imperceptible forms (*rnam par rig byed ma yin pa'i gzugs, avijñaptirūpa*), the eleventh class of forms in the Abhidharma.

658 Avoiding the three negative actions of the body and the four of the speech makes the seven eliminations, and their ancillaries are all other vows regarding the body and speech.

659 The three negative aspects of the mind are the three basic afflictions: aversion, attachment, and ignorance.

660 *Parājika*: breakage of these vows result in expulsion from the monastic order. There are four defeats: killing a human being, stealing an object of significant value, engaging in sexual intercourse, and lying about one's spiritual attainment.

661 Proscribed actions here means those actions proscribed for monks and nuns that are not usually considered innately negative, such as eating after noon, running, and walking on one's heels.

662 The four black deeds are similar to the four *parājika* defeats mentioned in note 660.

663 The two are *selflessness of the individual*, which is the individual person as subject, and *selflessness of phenomena*, all that is perceived by the individual.

664 The hundredfold twelve qualities are: (1) a hundred samādhis in one instant, (2) visions of a hundred buddhas, (3) knowledge of blessings from a hundred buddhas, (4) shaking a hundred worlds, (5) going to a hundred realms, (6) causing a hundred realms to appear, (7) ripening a hundred beings, (8) remaining for a hundred eons, (9) seeing into the past and into the future for a hundred eons, (10) opening a hundred Dharma doors, (11) manifesting a hundred bodies, (12) each body with a retinue of a hundred bodhisattvas. Compare with Tsele Natsok's list of seven qualities on page 321.

665 The six variations are: (1) the gradual appearance of the qualities, (2) the instantaneous appearance of the qualities, (3) the possession of some qualities and not of others, (4) the qualities are possessed, but they are not perceived by others, (5) the qualities appear in the yogin's own experiences, (6) the appearance of the qualities as described in the scriptures.

666 This is because of the sexual meaning of the third empowerment.

667 This is in reference to the Cittamātra or Yogācāra's three levels of perception; see note 566.

668 These three are: samādhi of the true nature (*de bzhin nyid kyi ting nge 'dzin*), samādhi of complete appearance (*kun tu snang ba'i ting nge 'dzin*), and samādhi of cause (*rgyu'i ting nge 'dzin*).

669 The third realm is the formless realm, where beings take birth through the power of meditation.

670 This is in reference to the Cakrasaṃvara teaching of the nirmāṇakāya as the body, speech, and mind of the ḍākas and ḍākinīs residing in twenty-four sites within the world, which are related to twenty-four sites within the body.

671 The Great Middle Way (*mahāmadhyamaka*), the Great Seal (*mahāmudrā*), and the Great Perfection (*mahāsandhi*), i.e., dzokchen.

672 According to Sherap Jungné's own commentary, this means that the Madhyamaka, mahāmudrā, and dzokchen are the methods and not the realization itself. He adds that being attached to them is like looking at stairs instead of going up them, like

looking at a lamp and not what it illuminates, and like looking at a finger pointing at the moon instead of looking at the moon.

673 One who does nothing apart from meditation but eat (*bhukta*), sleep (*supta*), and defecate (*kuṭhara*). A similiar term, *bhusuka*, means one who only eats and sleeps.

674 The three Dharmas are engaging in correct conduct, aware of the slightest fault; practicing with the understanding that one needs the good qualities of buddhahood; and benefiting others through the inspiration of immeasurable compassion.

675 Sherap Jungné explains in his commentary that they are independent because their cause is the buddha's own samādhi.

676 Sherap Jungné explains in his commentary that a buddha's kāyas are the buddha's teachings arising through dependence on three factors: the attainment of the dharmakāya, the previous commitment to bring beings to buddhahood, and the accumulation by pupils of the karma for attaining buddhahood.

677 These twelve are (1) Sutra (teachings in prose, which includes the Vinaya), (2) *geya* (verses that repeat preceding prose), (3) *vyākaraṇa* (prophecies), (4) *gāthā* (verse), (5) *udāna* (unrequested teachings), (6) *nidāna* (introductions that describe the circumstances in which the teachings were given), (7) *avadāna* (stories of beings' previous lives given as parables in the Vinaya), (8) *itivṛttaka* (accounts of the lives of past buddhas and bodhisattvas), (9) *jātaka* (accounts of the Buddha's own previous lifetimes), (10) *vaipulya* (expansion of previous teachings), (11) *adbhūtadharma* (descriptions of the miracles and qualities of buddhas and bodhisattvas), and (12) *upadeśa* (discourses on the Buddha's teaching; synonymous with Abhidharma).

678 These five perfections are the perfect teacher, Dharma, pupils, time, and place; alternatively, they may be the perfect body, the perfect elimination and realization, the perfect retinue, the perfect realm, and the perfect emanation.

679 *Nidāna*. See note 677.

680 "General sutras" here means the Hīnayāna sutras that cover aspects of Vinaya and Abhidharma.

681 Cittamātra teachings such as the *Avataṃsaka* and *Laṅkāvatāra Sutras*.

682 Sherab Jungné does not have a commentary for this point, which is practically identical to point two.

683 Sarvāstivāda (*thams cad yod smra sde pa*), Mahāsaṃghika (*phal chen sde pa*), Sthaviravāda (*gnas brtan sde pa*), and Sammatīya (*mang bskur sde pa*).

684 A term literally meaning "virtuous one" but referring here to someone who accumulates merit through visualizations, in particular making an offering of the body, as in the *gcod* practice.

685 Sherap Jungné's commentary here is on a different statement, describing the vajra samādhi as all-inclusive.

686 This view is expressed by Lama Shang in the *Ultimate Supreme Path of the Mahāmudrā*, which is included in this compilation. See page 95.

687 The four stages are the four empowerments: vase, secret, wisdom, and word, and this refers to be being allowed to engage in sexual intercourse during the third empowerment.

688 Knowing, for example, that the five aggregates are the five buddhas and so on.

689 The union of emptiness and compassion that arises from the four immeasurables: love, compassion, rejoicing, and impartiality.

690 It is essential that the channels and winds be purified because buddhahood is attained through purifying the impure.

691 (1) Inhalation of the breath, (2) filling of the abdomen with the breath, (3) squeezing down on the retained breath, (4) exhalation like firing an arrow.

692 The one mother is Prajñāpāramitā, "Perfection of Wisdom," commonly referred to as the Great Mother.

693 A pupil of Drigungpa.

694 These five aspects, essential to all teachings are: bodhicitta, the *yidam* deity, devotion to the guru, mahāmudrā, and the dedication of merit.

695 Vasubandhu, *Mahāyānasaṃgrahabhāṣya*, Toh 4050 Tengyur, sems tsam, *ri*. The quote has not been found in this text. See note 780.

696 In other words, buddha nature.

697 Nāgārjuna, *Dharmadhātustava*, v. 2, Toh 1118 Tengyur, bstod tshogs, *ka*, 64a7.

698 Chapter 6 of the *Single Viewpoint*.

699 The trainings of pratimokṣa, bodhisattva, and tantra: chapters 3, 4, and 5 of the *Single Viewpoint*.

700 Chapter 1 of the *Single Viewpoint*.

701 Chapter 2 of the *Single Viewpoint*.

702 Chapter 7 of the *Single Viewpoint*.

703 *Sublime Continuum*, 1:10, 1b3.

704 The nine moods derived from classical Indian theater: beauty, heroism, and ugliness of the body; wrath, laughter, and fear of the speech; compassion, desire, and peace of the mind.

705 *Bhadrakalpikasūtra*, Toh 94 Kangyur, mdo sde, *ka*, 338b5–339b2. These time periods are taught in the context of describing when enlightenment will be attained by the sons, ministers, and queens of a cakravartin who renounced his kingdom and in a later life attained buddhahood as Buddha Dīpaṃkara: "The ten thousand princes will not achieve buddhahood for another sixty-five eons after this eon. After that there will come the eon named Greatly Renowned when they attain the enlightenment of complete buddhahood in that single eon. The eighty-four thousand ministers will not achieve buddhahood during the eighty eons that follow the Greatly Renowned Eon. After that there will be the Starry Eon. During that eon, the eighty-four thousand ministers will achieve the enlightenment of complete buddhahood. For three hundred eons after the passing of the Starry Eon, there will be no buddhas. After that there will come the Arrayed Qualities Eon. During that eon, the eighty-four thousand queens will achieve the enlightenment of complete buddhahood."

706 Vasubandhu, *Abhidharmakośa*, 4:110, Toh 4089 Tengyur, mgon pa, *ku*, 15a4.

707 *Vinayavastu*, Toh 1 Kangyur, 'dul ba, *ka*, 245b1. Thus, the Vinaya and Abhidharma do not agree, as this is also a description of the buddhas in the three incalculable eons.

708 *Sutra of Repaying the Kindness of the Buddha Who Was Skilled in Methods* (*Mahopayakauśalyabuddhasūtra*), chap. 4, Toh 353 Kangyur, mdo sde, *aḥ*, 117b4.

709 This is in accord with the sutra. In the available edition of Dakpo Tashi Namgyal's text, *brgya snyed* had been corrupted to *brgyad*, which would mean just "eight eons."

710 *Bhadrakalpikasūtra*, Toh 94 Kangyur, mdo sde, *ka*, 288a4.

711 Flower-Adorned Essence (*Snying po me tog gis brgyan pa*).

712 *White Lotus of the Holy Dharma Sutra* (*Saddharmapuṇḍarīkasūtra*), Toh 113 Kangyur, mdo sde, *ja*, 121a4.

713 *Laṅkāvatārasūtra*, Toh 107 Kangyur, mdo sde, *ca*, 160b1. This quotation is in fact a corruption of the passage in the sutra and has some grammatical anomalies as a result. Only the last two lines are actually derived, though altered, from the sutra. There will be many such cases in this text, as Tibetan authors normally obtained their quotations from other texts instead of the original in the canon. The passage in the actual sutra is as follows:

> When you realize this nature of the world,
> you will reach the end of impure realms.
> Because the "immature" are stupid,
> they see origination and destruction.
> Those who have wisdom
> do not see origination and destruction.
> That is the divine palace of Akaniṣṭha.
> Having eliminated all bad actions,
> they have continuous nonconceptuality.
> They have abandoned mind and mental origination.
> They have attained power and clairvoyance.
> They attain the power of samādhi
> and will attain buddhahood there as complete buddhas.
> Their emanations attain buddhahood here.
> The emanations of the buddhas will number countless millions.

714 Also known as Vajrāsana and currently Bodhgaya.

715 *Sublime Continuum*, 2:53–56, 64b3.

716 Reconstructed from *Me tog kun tu ston pa*.

717 *Tattvasaṃgraha*, Toh 479 Kangyur, rgyud, *nya*, 1b1–142a7.

718 *Adornment of Kosala* (*Kosalālaṃkāratattvasaṃgrahaṭīkā*), Toh 2503 Tengyur, rgyud, *yi* 1a–*ri* 202a5.

719 *An Explanation of Difficult Points in the Guhyasamāja* (*Guhyasamājapañjikā*), Toh 1917 Tengyur, rgyud, *bi*, 14a3.

720 *Vajraśekharatantra*, Toh 480 Kangyur, rgyud, *nya*, 195a4.

721 *Vajramaṇḍalālaṃkāratantra*, Toh 490 Kangyur, rgyud, *tha*, 29a5.

722 Mañjuśrī Yaśas, *Paramādibuddhoddhṛtaśrīkālacakratantra*, Toh 1346 Tengyur, rgyud, *tha*, 100a5.

723 Puṇḍarīka, *Vimalaprabhā*, Toh 1347 Tengyur, rgyud, *tha*, 125a5.

724 "Lord of the World" (*'Jig rten dbang phyug*), another name for Avalokiteśvara and also one of Śiva's names.

725 Candrakīrti, *Pradīpoddyotanaṭīkā*, chap. 1, Toh 1785 Tengyur, rgyud, *ha*, 9b1.

726 *Rigi-āralitantra*, chap. 5, Toh 427 Kangyur, rgyud, *nga*, 179b6.

727 Present-day Kushinagar in Bihar, India.

728 A mountain range in western India extending from Mahāraśtra to Karnataka. It was believed to be the abode of superhuman beings, in particular the vidyādharas, and these beings and this locality were well known within general Indian literature.

729 Present-day Rajgir in Bihar; the ancient capital of Magadha during the Buddha's lifetime.

730 *Candragarbhaparipṛcchāsūtra*, Toh 356 Kangyur, mdo sde, *a*, 216b6.

731 *Karuṇāpuṇḍarīkasūtra*, Toh 111 Kangyur, mdo sde, *cha*, 56a–128b.

732 Meaning "adorned with an interior that is a ground of flowers."

733 The third month (*nag pa*, *citrā*).

734 Nowadays known as Amaravati stupa because of the change in the name of the area. It was still an active site in the late fourteenth century. However, the stupa, the largest in India, subsequently fell into ruins and was used as a source for building materials. Its ruins were identified by the British in the late eighteenth century, and a large section of the stupa has been preserved in the Amaravati Gallery in the British Museum in London.

735 Shambhala is a circular kingdom, and the area outside the very center is divided into the eight directions. Each of these is divided into twelve areas, making ninety-six principalities, each having its own ruler called a *satrap*.

736 Alaṃkakalaśa, *Profound Meaning: A Commentary on the Vajra Garland Tantra* (*Vajramālātantraṭīkāgāmbhīrārthadīpikā*), Toh 1795 Tengyur, rguyd, *gi*.

737 Bhavyakīrti, *Pradīpoddyotanābhisaṃdhiṭīkā*, Toh 1793 Tengyur, rgyud, *ki*, 2b3.

738 *Explanation of Difficult Points in the Glorious Guhyasamāja* (*Guhyasamājapañjikā*), Toh 1917 Tengyur, rgyud, *bi*, 4a3.

739 *Gzhan 'phrul dbang byed*, the paradise named "Control Over the Emanations of Others," the highest paradise in "the desire realm" and the abode of Māra.

740 "Ignorance vajra," indicating the deity's ability to destroy ignorance. The other deities present are similarly named in relation to other afflictions.

741 One of the names of Śiva.

742 "Lord of Secrets" is an alternative name for Vajrapāṇi.

743 Written as *Magata*. This kingdom south of the Ganges in modern-day Bihar had its capital at the site of present day Rajgir. Its kings were important patrons of the Buddha. King Aśoka was a later king of this dynasty, when the capital had moved north to the southern bank of the Ganges at Pāṭaliputra, the site of modern-day Patna.

744 *Tantrarājaśrīlaghusaṃvara*, Toh 368; Kangyur, rgyud, *ka*, 213b1–246b7. The Tibetan tradition has made the debatable choice of choosing this particular tantra as the "root tantra" among the various Cakrasaṃvara tantras even though it is explicitly presented as a summary. Far from being a root tantra, it appears to be an appendix. There is little information on the deity or its practice. Most of its fifty-one tiny chapters deal with codes of communication between practitioners and a host of magic rituals that use the Cakrasaṃvara mantra for all kinds of remarkable ends, such as creating zombies, changing people into elephants, causing abortions, and transforming one's own body into that of a woman (it is assumed the reader is male) in the space of eleven days. Almost the entirety of this Cakrasaṃvara tantra is irrelevant to contemporary Cakrasaṃvara teachers and practitioners, who are usually unfamiliar with it. The Nepalese Cakrasaṃvara tradition, while it considers the *Abhidhānottara* to be the root tantra, considers the *Saṃvarodaya Tantra* as the most important.

745 *Latter Definition Tantra* (*Abhidhānottaratantra*), Toh 369 Kangyur, rgyud, *ka*. The

Nepalese tradition has appeared to settle upon this tantra as the "root tantra." As David Gray records in his introduction to his translation of the *Cakrasaṃvara Tantra*, the classification of Cakrasaṃvara tantras into root and explanatory tantras is somewhat arbitrary. Butön Rinchen Drup (1290–1364), the compiler of the first comprehensive canon, listed one root and nine explanatory Cakrasaṃvara tantras. However, the ninth, the *Tantra of True Union* (*Saṃpuṭa Tantra*), which is quoted many times in this volume, is an "explanatory tantra" for both the Cakrasaṃvara and Hevajra tantras.

746 This may refer to the sacred mountain Śrīparvata in south east India, the dwelling place of Nāgārjuna and other masters, which is near Dhānyakaṭaka.

747 Alaṃkakalaśa, *Profound Meaning: A Commentary on the Vajra Garland Tantra* (*Vajramālātantraṭīkāgaṃbhīrārthadīpikā*), Toh 1795 Tengyur, rgyud, *gi*. The reference to subjugating the māras at dawn in Bodhgaya is on 2b. This is followed by a list of the major tantras being taught in various realms and locations, concluding with the teaching of the *Hevajra Tantra*, described on 4a2: "Afterward, in this world, in Magadha in order to subjugate the four māras, he taught the greater teaching of the *Hevajra Tantra*, the shorter tantra, and the explanatory tantra." However, this was later than the subjugation of māras that took place at his enlightenment.

748 *Hevajra Tantra*, 1b–30a.

749 *Ḍākinīvajrapañjarātantra*, Toh 419 Kangyur, rgyud, *nga*, 30a–65b.

750 Lit. "central land"; refers here to areas of northern India where the historical Buddha lived and taught, but can also mean any land where a full expression of the Dharma has taken root.

751 Indrabodhi, *Commentary to the Compiled Cakrasaṃvara Tantra* (*Cakrasaṃvaratantrasaṃvarasamuccayavṛtti*), chap. 36, Toh 1413 Tengyur, rgyud, *tsa*, 4b4.

752 *Ḍākārṇavatantra*, Toh 372 Kangyur, rgyud, *kha*, 264a4.

753 The text itself appears to be in error as it reads "after the passing of the seven Kalki Dharmarājas." However the seven Dharmarājas directly precede the founding of the Kalki dynasty founded by Mañjuśrīkīrti. As this is an egregious error, which may have been the result of scribal corruption, it has been corrected, by moving the position of the word Kalki.

754 *Mañjuśrīmūlatantra*, chap. 36, Toh 543 Kangyur, rgud, *na*, 325a6.

755 *Mahābalasūtra*, Toh 947 Kangyur, gzungs dus, *waṃ*, 40a4.

756 Buddhajñānapada, *Mukhāgama*, Toh 1853 Tengyur, rgyud, *di*, 15b3.

757 *Ḍākārṇavatantra*, chap. 6, Toh 372 Kangyur, rgyud, *kha*, 156b7.

758 *White Lotus Sutra*, 20a6; the quotation is paraphrased.

759 *White Lotus Sutra*, 84b6.

760 *Laṅkāvatārasūtra*, Toh 107 Kangyur, mdo sde, *ca*, 175a6. This is a paraphrase.

761 *White Lotus Sutra*, 84b6.

762 Asaṅga, *Mahāyānasaṃgraha*, Toh 4048 Tengyur, sems tsam, *ri*, 2b6

763 *Mdo sde gdams ngag 'bogs pa'i rgyal po*. The text is unidentified.

764 Jñānaśrī, *Koṭidvayāpoha*, Toh 3714 Tengyur, rgyud, *cu*, 115b2.

765 Tripiṭakamāla, *Nayatrayapradīpa*, Toh 3707 Tengyur, rgyud, *tsu*, 16b3.

766 *Lamp of the Three Ways*, 16b3.

767 *Lamp of the Three Ways*, 17b6.

768 *Lamp of the Three Ways*, 22a1.

769 Source unidentified.

770 Jñānaśrī, *Koṭidvayāpoha*, Toh 3714 Tengyur, rgyud, *tsu*.

771 *Stainless Light*, Realm chapter, 17b3.

772 *Guhyasamājatantra*, chap. 13, Toh 442 Kangyur, rgyud, *ca*, 117a6.

773 Jñānākara, *Mantrāvatāra*, Toh 3718, Tengyur, rgyud, *tsu*, 195a7. This translation follows the Tengyur. The four-line quotation given in the text is very corrupt, with a number of lines missing. A translation would read: "Even with the cause, if some conditions/ like a great medicinal tree/ are incomplete, in three lifetimes,/ emptiness is perfectly seen and there is timeless liberation."

774 *Gsang ba'i mdzod*. The text itself does not appear to be extant, but this quotation appears in Saraha's *Buddhakapālatantra* commentary, *Endowed with Wisdom* (*Jñānavatī*), chap. 3, Toh 1652 Tengyur, rgyud, *ra*, 144b6.

775 *Vajra Pinnacle*, 206a4.

776 Padmākara, *Samayapañca*, Toh 1224 Tengyur, rgyud, *nya*, 28b2.

777 *Abhidharmakośa*, 8:39, 25a3.

778 *Lha'i bus zhus pa'i mdo*. This text has not been identified. It is probably no longer extant while quotations from it survive in other texts.

779 *Sublime Continuum*, 4:18, 72b5.

780 Source unidentified. Drakpa Shedrup (1675–1748), in his commentary on the first chapter of the *Abhisamāyālaṃkāra*, identifies this quotation as coming from *Rational System of Exposition*, presumably meaning Vasubandhu's *Vyākhyāyukti*, but these lines do not appear there. The first three lines are also cited in the *Single Viewpoint* text in chapter 10 of this volume; see note 695. There the second and third lines have switched, and instead of "eliminating suffering" (*sdug bsngal spong*) it has "compassionate" (*snying rjer ldan*). The author there identified the source as Vasubandhu's *Commentary on "A Compendium of the Mahayana,"* although these lines have not been found in that text either.

781 *Sublime Continuum*, 5:19, 72b5.

782 *Sublime Continuum*, 1:10–11, 55a5.

783 *Sūtrālaṃkāra*, chap. 12, 13a5.

784 *Subāhuparipṛcchātantra*, Toh 805 Kangyur, rgyud, *wa*, 118b2. This has been translated according to the version in the Dergé canon, where it reads *gsang sngags mdo sde'i tshul du ngas bshad do/*. However the Tashi Namgyal text has a different and clearly corrupt ending: *...tshul du bshad kyi nyon/*, where the *kyi* may be in error for *kyis*. This would then mean "Listen! For [I] will teach..."

785 *Tattvasaṃgraha*, 48a3.

786 Source unidentified.

787 *Subāhuparipṛcchatantra*, Toh 805 Kangyur, rgyud, *wa*, 136a4.

788 Source unidentified.

789 Source unidentified.

790 *Hevajra Tantra*, book 2, 3:54, 19a1. The Kangyur version ends in the instrumental *kyis*, while Tashi Namgyal has *te*. Indian commentaries and Dakpo Tashi Namgyal's Hevajra commentary (which cites the line accurately) explain that "the four" refers to the action, performance, yoga, and yogānuttara (highest yoga) tantras, which are traditionally associated with the four stages of courtship given in the following lines of the verse.

791 Śraddhākaravarman, *Yogānuttaratantrārthāvatārasaṃgraha*, Toh 3713 Tengyur, rgyud, *tsu*, 105b5.

792 *Perfect Lamp*, 2b4.

793 *Vajrajñānasamuccayatantra*, Toh 447 Kangyur, rgyud, *ca*, 284b7.

794 *Tantraśrīlaghusaṃvara*, chap. 51, Toh 368 Kangyur, rgyud, *ka*, 246b3. Sanskrit: *sūtraṃ kriyābhicaryāṇāṃ yogaguhyāntabhedataḥ*. Surviving Sanskrit editions end with: ...*yogaguhyaṃ tu bhedataḥ*. Tashi Namgyal follows a Tibetan commentarial tradition that is dubious in its interpretation of this final verse of the tantra by making more classifications from it than its Indian commentarial antecedents did. Also, the passage as given in this text does not correspond with the version in the Dergé Kangyur. Tashi Namgyal appears to have derived the quotation from the translation of Vīravajra's commentary. He repeats this quotation further on in the text (see page 447), but does not in that instance use this same version. See note 866. The translation here follows the more cogent Dergé Kangyur version. A simpler translation would be: "The categories of sutra, of action and of performance,/ And the final secret of yoga." The surviving Sanskrit version would drop the word "final."

795 *Vajra Tent*, 54b5.

796 Atiśa, *Bodhimārgapradīpapañjikā*, Toh 3948 Tengyur, dbu ma, *khi*, 287a4.

797 *Vajra Mandala*, 51b3.

798 Abhayākaragupta, *Vajra Garland of Mandala Rituals* (*Vajrāvalimaṇḍalasādhana*), Toh 3140 Tengyur, rgyud, *phu*, 1a4. The second line of this quotation is actually the conclusion of the opening supplication of the text.

799 *Vajra Tent*, chap. 13, 54b6.

800 *Saṃpuṭatantra*, chap. 7, Toh 381 Kangyur, rgyud, *ga*, 118a6. Tashi Namgyal's text has the corruption of additional syllables in the third line (first line in English), reading "...as the four tantras in the manner of worms" (*srin bu'i tshul rgyud bzhir gnas*). Tashi Namgyal has also added "holding hands" (*lag bcangs*), which normally comes between gazing and intercourse but in the canonical version this was already expressed by "embrace," though this can also be a euphemism for sexual intercourse.

801 *Hevajra Tantra*, book 2, 3:54, 19a1. In the Dergé Tengyur, this verse is identical to the preceding one from the *Saṃpuṭa*; however, because of the corruption in the Tibetan of Dakpo Tashi Namgyal's text (see the preceding note), they appeared to be different. Both passages address the subject of symbolic language. The last line of the verse is: "...has not spoken of the symbolic language." Book 2 of the *Hevajra Tantra* has the appearance of repeating much from chapter 7 of the *Saṃpuṭa*.

802 *Perfect Lamp*, 3a1.

803 Alaṃkakalaśa, *Profound Meaning: A Commentary on the Vajra Garland Tantra.* (*Vajramālātantraṭīkāgaṃbhīrārthadīpikā*), Toh 1795 Tengyur, rgyud, *gi*.

804 Source unidentified.

805 Īśvara (*dbang phyug*), another name of Śiva.

806 *Lamp of the Three Ways*, 21b4.

807 *Jñānatilakatantra*, Toh 422 Kangyur, rgyud, *nga*, 96b–136b.

808 Buddhaguhya, *Mahāvairocanābhisaṃbodhitantraṭīkā*, Toh 2663 Tengyur, rgyud, *nyu*, 65b4. The entire sentence reads: "Although the action tantras primarily teach external conduct, it is not devoid of internal conduct."

809 *Perfect Lamp*, 2b6.

810 *Perfect Lamp*, 2b6.

811 *Vajrapāṇyabhiṣekatantra*, chap. 4, Toh 496 Kangyur, rgyud, *da*, 91b1.

812 Muditākoṣa, *Trailokyavijayavṛtti*, Toh 2509 Tengyur, rgyud, *ri*, 216b1.

813 Reference seems to be to Sahaśrī Lokanātha's *Tattvāloka*, but the phrase does not appear in this text.

814 [*Guhyasamāja*] *Uttaratantra*, Toh 443 Kangyur, rgyud, *ca*, 150a1.

815 *Lamp of the Three Ways*, 21b7.

816 *Vajra Tent*, 54b5.

817 Śraddhākaravarman, *Yogānuttaratantrārthāvatārasaṃgraha*, Toh 3713 Tengyur, rgyud, *tsu*, 106b7.

818 Kṛṣṇapa, *Guhyatattvaprakāśa*, Toh 1450 Tengyur, rgyud, *wa*, 349b5.

819 The Dergé Kangyur text has "relative yoginī tantra."

820 Vajragarbha, *Hevajrapiṇḍārthaṭīkā*, Toh 1180 Tengyur, rgyud, *ka*, 9b5. The second verse in particular differs from the Dergé canonical version, which reads: "That in which method causes transition (*'pho byed*)/ and in which wisdom is truly present,/ [I] teach to be a "method tantra"/ That is how they are in relative terms/ and that is what the difference between them is."

821 *Stainless Light*, *tha*, 107b1–*da* 297a7.

822 The term *gurus* here refers to the deities, which are in essence the guru in divine form.

823 *Illuminating Lamp*, chap. 1, 11b7.

824 *Vajra Tent*, 54b3. There are significant differences from the canonical version, which itself may be corrupt, but reads: "The method of the perfection of wisdom/ is named *yoginī*./ From union with the mahāmudrā,/ there is the vajra tent of the yoginī/ that depends upon the true nature, and therefore/ it is called *yoginī tantra*."

825 Vitapāda, *Mukkhāgamavṛtti*, Toh 1866 Tengyur, rgyud, *di*, 108a6.

826 *Guhyasamāja Tantra*, chap. 17, 142b6.

827 *Hevajra Tantra*, book 2, chap. 4, 22b1. Sanskrit: *Pṛthivī pukkasī khyatā*. Vajragarbha is here repeating this phrase, which has also occured in book 1, 9:17. However, Tashi Namgyal appears to be misrepresenting the *Hevajra Tantra* to fit into his scheme. The *Hevajra Tantra* does not teach the five goddesses to be the five elements. The five goddesses in the inner circle are in fact said to be the five aggregates (book 1, 9:9 and 10) and also the five afflictions (vv. 18 and 19). Pukkasī is one of the ten yoginīs in the outer circle of the maṇḍala, where there is one yoginī in each of the ten directions. Six of these are the six sensory objects, and the remaining four (the yoginīs of the intermediate directions—northeast and so on) of which Pukkasī is the first in this particular list, are the four elements and not the five elements that Tashi Namgyal states are being described, for space is not enumerated. Nevertheless, Tashi Namgyal correctly describes this system in his own commentary to the *Hevajra Tantra*.

828 *Rigyāralitantra*, chap. 1, Toh 427 Kangyur, rgyud, *nga*, 176b3.

829 This quotation is not from the root tantra but from the explanatory tantra, *Vajra Garland*, 223a2.

830 Source unidentified. The quotation is not found in the *Cakrasaṃvara Tantra*.

831 The quotation was not found in this text.

832 *Latter Guhyasamāja Tantra*, 150a1.

833 *Hevajra Tantra*, book 1, 1:7, 2a3.

834 The citation is not found in the text, but it appears to be derived from a passage that

explains the term "without a family" in *Stainless Light*, 120a5: "Here 'family' is the aspect of wisdom and the aspect of method, and these aspects are discarded. Therefore, that 'tantra without family,' which is without a family, has the nature of wisdom and method, and is a yoga tantra, was taught by the Buddha to be nondual."

835 *Stainless Light*, 187a7.

836 *Latter Guhyasamāja Tantra*, 150a2.

837 Source unidentified.

838 Source unidentified, unless it is a corruption of a line in *King of Meditations Sutra* (*Samādhirājasūtra*), chap. 10, Toh 127 Kangyur, mdo sde, *da*, 22b7. If so, then the main distortion is that *'gyur* ("will become") has been changed into *rgyu* ("cause"). The line comes in this passage: "Just as Dīpaṃkara gave you a prophecy,/ in that way I also will give an evident prophecy./ The world will hear the prophecy I give here./ They will develop a vast and supreme motivation,/ and all these beings will become buddhas."

839 *Hevajra Tantra*, book 2, 4:71, 22a3.

840 *Sublime Continuum*, 1:2, 56a2. The second line is missing in our edition of the Tashi Namgyal text. The word "beings" (*lus can*) was added in the Tibetan translation of the Sanskrit.

841 *Sublime Continuum*, 1:46, 56b6. The Tibetan translation of the Sanskrit leaves out the reference to "element" (*dhātu*), which could also be translated as "realm" here. The Sanskrit specifies it is singular.

842 *Sūtrālaṃkāra*, 10:37, 10a5.

843 *Sublime Continuum*, 1:51, 61b3.

844 *Ornament of Precious Liberation: Like a Wish-Fulfilling Gem of Sublime Dharma*, 10a6.

845 *Prajñāpāramitāsañcayagāthā*, 6:2, Toh 13 Kangyur, sher phyin, *ka*,19b2.

846 Prajñākaramati, *Bodhisattvacaryāvatārapañjikā*, chap. 1, Toh 3872 Tengyur, dbu ma, *la*, 45b4. Tashi Namgyal had attributed the quote incorrectly to the *Applications of Mindfulness Sutra*.

847 Kṛṣṇapa, *Bodhisattvacaryāvatāravivṛttipañjikā*, Toh 3873 Tengyur, dbu ma, *la*, 291b2.

848 Kṛṣṇapa, *Bodhisattvacaryāvatāravivṛttipañjikā*, Toh 3873 Tengyur, dbu ma, *la*, 291b3.

849 *Daśadharmakasūtra*, chap. 9, Toh 53 Kangyur, dkon brtsegs, *kha*, 166a3.

850 *Avataṃsakasūtra*, chap. 7, Toh 44 Kangyur, phal chen, *ka*, 90b5.

851 *Vajra Tent*, chap. 13, 31a1. The quotation is either corrupt or more likely derived from an alternative translation. The canonical passage reads: "In order to gather beings/ that have anger, stupidity,/ pride, desire, and miserliness,/ I have many vajra forms within my [mandala] circle." The passage is referring to the various deity manifestations that are specifically for beings with anger, stupidity, and so on.

852 *Hevajra Tantra*, book 2, 11:5, 29a7. The Tibetan adds "great/very" to the "black," and omits the word "family."

853 *Hevajra Tantra*, book 2, 11:3–4, 29a6. The beginning and end of the source quotation has been added here for greater clarity.

854 *Illuminating Lamp*, chap. 1, 3a7.

855 *Illuminating Lamp*, 3a7.

856 *Illuminating Lamp*, 3b3.

857 *Hevajra Tantra*, book 2, 2:13, 14b5.

858 *Hevajra Tantra*, book 2, chap. 2, 14b6. The Tibetan translates the Sanskrit *tāvat* in its alternative meaning of "meanwhile," while here it has been translated as "most."

859 *Lamp for the Path*, v. 3, 238b1.

860 *Lamp for the Path*, v. 4, 238b2.

861 *Lamp for the Path*, v. 5, 238b2.

862 Tib. *bsnyen gnas*; a special day of observance, during the twenty-four-hour time of which a lay person keeps the eight vows: avoiding killing, stealing, sex, lying, intoxicants, high seats, and the trio of adornments, singing, and dancing.

863 This is the doctrine of the Vaibhaṣika school, known for their extensive Abhidharma teachings and their great commentarial compendium, the *Mahāvibhāṣa*. It is the first in the tantra's list of the four major Sutrayāna schools of Indian Buddhism according to Tibetan doxography.

864 The doctrine of the Sautrāntikas, which had the distinguishing feature of emphasizing the primacy of the sutra teachings as opposed to that of the Abhidharma.

865 *Hevajra Tantra*, book 2, 8:9–11, 27a6. This question is asked by Nairātmyā, who is Hevajra's consort.

866 *Tantrarājaśrīlaghusaṃvara*, chap. 51, Toh 368 Kangyur, rgyud, *ka*, 246b3. This is one interpretation of this problematic verse, which concludes the tantra. See note 794. The quotation ends with *sbyin*, which appears, from comparison with the Dergé Kangyur version and the Sanskrit, to be a corruption of *bzhin*. The quote also has *gsang mtha'i dbye ba las* instead of the Kangyur's *gsang mtha'i dbye ba nyid*.

867 Āryadeva, *Caryāmelāpakapradīpa*, chap. 1, Toh 1803 Tengyur, rgyud, *ngi*, 60b5. This itself is an unattributed quotation from Kambala's *Ālokamāta*. See Christian Wedemyer, *Āryadeva's Lamp* (New York: American Institute of Buddhist Studies, 2008), p.149n49. *Bzhag* was used to translate *nirmitta* and has been translated here as "presented," though in keeping with the Sanskrit it would be better translated as "created."

868 Ānandagarbha, *Sarvavajrodaya*, Toh 2516 Tengyur, rgyud, *ka*, 44a3.

869 *Vajra Pinnacle*, chap. 2, 184b1.

870 *Vajra Pinnacle*, chap. 2, 184b3.

871 *Jñānatilakatantra*, chap. 3, Toh 422 Kangyur, rgyud, *nga*, 100b5.

872 The *family lord* is usually the principal buddha of one of the five families. Yidam deities are often visualized as having such a family lord above their heads.

873 *Jñānatilakatantra*, 100b5.

874 Atiśa Dīpaṃkaraśrījñāna, *Compendium of All Commitments* (*Sarvasamayasaṃgraha*), Toh 3725 Tengyur, rgyud, *tshu*, 45a4.

875 *Excellent Accomplishment Tantra* (*Susiddhikaratantra*), Toh 807 Tengyur, rgyud, *wa*.

876 *Vajra Pinnacle*, chap. 2, 183b4–7. The entire passage reads: "You should not take life./ Do not take what has not been given./ Do not practice sexual misconduct./ Do not speak lies./ Totally forsake alcohol,/ which is the root of ruin./ Follow holy beings./ Respect and honor the yogins./ Guard as well as you can/ the three actions of the body,/ the three actions of the speech,/ and the three actions of the mind./ Do not aspire to the Hīnayāna./ Do not ignore the welfare of beings./ Also do not forsake those in samsara./ Never have attachment to nirvana./ You should not

malign/ the secret devas and asuras/ and should not step across [their] symbols,/ mounts, weapons, and insignias./ Those are taught to be the commitments."

877 Buddhaguhya, *Dhyānottarapaṭalaṭīkā*, Toh 2670 Tengyur, rgyud, *thu*, 7b4.

878 *Dhyānottarapaṭalakrama*, Toh 808 Kangyur, rgyud, *wa*, 224a1.

879 That is, these are particular breath-control practices, the *prāṇa* being the most important of the internal winds, or *vāyus*.

880 *Dhyānottarapaṭalakrama*, 224a3. This continues on directly from where the preceding quotation concluded.

881 *Dhyānottarapaṭalakrama*, 224a6.

882 Hodge points out that this is an obscure description of visualizing a mantra being breathed into one's body from the heart of the Buddha in front and then being breathed back there again. See *Mahā-Vairocana-Abhisaṃbodhi Tantra* (London: Routledge Curzon, 2003), 550.

883 *Enlightenment of Vairocana*, 180a7. The next lines after this quotation define *life-force* (*prāṇa*) to be *vāyu*, the "winds" in the body, and *restraint* (*āyāma*) to be *smṛti* (mindfulness). The combination of these two words forms the term *prāṇāyāma*.

884 *Enlightenment of Vairocana*, 191a2.

885 *Susiddhikaratantra*, Toh 807 Kangyur, rgyud, *wa*, 192a2.

886 *Subāhuparipṛcchātantra*, chap. 11, Toh 805 Kangyur, rgyud, *wa*, 138a2.

887 *Rasāyana* ("extraction of essences") refers to alchemical power to do such things as extend life, regain youth, or change iron to gold.

888 *Jñānatilakatantra*, chap. 3, Toh 422 Kangyur, rgyud, *nga*. This is not a quotation from this tantra but is a brief description in verse from an unidentified source. The related passage in the tantra is on 100b3 onward, classifying the empowerments into four and more empowerments, though the number six is not mentioned.

889 *Jñānatilakatantra*, 100b5.

890 *Vajra Pinnacle*, chap. 2, 183a7.

891 *Vajra Pinnacle*, 183b4–7. This passage was cited above; see note 876.

892 *Vajra Pinnacle*, 183b3. This sentence follows a description of the specific commitments of the five Buddha families. A "defeat," or *pārājika*, is a transgression of a monastic vow that results in expulsion form the sangha, and the Sanskrit term literally means "expulsion." Here, however, the term is used to indicate actions that result in the loss of one's vows.

893 Ānandagarbha, *Illuminating the Truth: A Commentary on the Tantra Entitled "Compendium of Truths of All Tahāgatas: Understanding the Mahayana"* (*Sarvatathāgatatattvasaṃgrahamahāyānābhisamayanāmatantravyākhyātattvālokakarī*), Toh 2510 Tengyur, rgyud *li*, 151b3. The text is usually referred to by its two halves: "Commentary to the First Part" (*stod 'grel*) and "Commentary to the Second Part" (*smad 'grel*).

894 Ānandagarbha, *Śrīparamādivivaraṇa*, Toh 2511 Tengyur, rgyud, *si*. The quotation does not appear in this text.

895 Ānandagarbha, *Illuminating the Truth* (*Tattvālokakarī*), Toh 2510 Tengyur, rgyud, *li*, 147a6.

896 There are two yoga tantra sādhanas of Vajrasattava composed by Ānandagarbha, a longer and a shorter (Toh 2518 and 3340). However, the citation is not found in either.

897 Ānandagarbha, *Illuminating the Truth* (*Tattvālokakarī*), Toh 2510 Tengyur, rgyud, *li*, 151b4. This is the continuation of the sentence unfinished in the previous citation from *Illuminating the Truth*.

898 Ānandagarbha, *Sarvavajrodaya*, Toh 2516 Tengyur, rgyud, *ku*.

899 The source is unidentified.

900 *Tattvasaṃgraha*, 41a6. See note 902.

901 Śākyamitra, *Adornment of Kosala: An Extensive Commentary on "Compendium of Truths"* (*Kosalālaṃkāratattvasaṃgrahaṭīkā*), Toh 2503 Tengyur, rgyud, *yi*, 154b4.

902 *Rdo rje phra mo*, *sūkṣmavajra*. This chapter of *Compendium of Truths* describes the subtle vajras that symbolize the subtle wisdom. The visualizations are elaborate and with many mantras. The vajras, which are Vajrapāṇi transformed into that shape and blessed, are sometimes in the heart and sometimes at the tip of the nose, and they pervade all beings, transforming them.

903 *Tattvasaṃgraha*, 41a6.

904 The quotation has been corrupted in Tashi Namgyal's text, with a line missing. The quotation continues directly from the preceding one, which itself follows on from the quotation given on page 457.

905 *Tattvasaṃgraha*, 134b3. In the Kangyur version instead of "...siddhi will be attained" it says "...merit will be attained."

906 *Tattvasaṃgraha*, 134b4.

907 Śākyamitra, *Kosalālaṃkāra*, Toh 2503 Tengyur, rgyud, *yi*, 3b6.

908 *Samayamudrās* are the hand gestures, usually referred to simply as *mudrās*.

909 *Mahāmudrātilakatantra*, chap. 2, Toh 420 Kangyur, rgyud, *nga*, 66b4.

910 *Buddhakapālatantra*, chap. 3; Toh 424 Kangyur, rgyud, *nga*, 150a1.

911 *Vajra Garland*, chap. 2, 212a2.

912 *Sarvamaṇḍalatantra*, Toh 806 Kangyur, rgyud, *wa*, 166b3.

913 *Sarvamaṇḍala*, 166b3.

914 *Vajra Tent*, chap. 4, 48b6.

915 *Vajra Mandala*. The quotation does not appear in this text.

916 Puṇḍarīka, *Paramārthasevā*, Toh 1348 Tengyur, rgyud, *na*, 4b2.

917 *Vajra Tent*. This quotation does not appear in the text; the closest is at chap. 8, 49a3: "The pupil who understands that/ has perfect service to the guru,/ keeps to the instruction of the guru,/ and attains extensive siddhis."

918 *Vajra Garland*, chap. 2, 212a6.

919 *Mahāmudrā Tilaka*, chap. 2, 66b6.

920 *Vajraḍākatantra*, chap. 46, Toh 370 Kangyur, rgyud, *kha*, 97a6.

921 Aśvagoṣa, *Gurupañcāśikā*, v. 38, Toh 3721 Tengyur, rgyud, *tsu*, 11b1.

922 This means with one curved and one straight side, like a bow and its string.

923 *Vajraḍāka*, chap. 46, 97a7.

924 *Vajraḍāka*, 97b2. The "protections" are made up primarily of a surrounding tent made of vajras around which is a mountain of fire.

925 Āryadeva, *Catuḥpīṭhatantramaṇḍalasamuccaya*, chap. 3, Toh 1613 Tengyur, rgyud, *ya*, 114b3.

926 Durjayacandra, *Suparigrahamaṇḍalasādhana*, Toh 1240 Tengyur, rgyud, *nya*, 130b1. The quotation does not correspond to the present canonical version, which has one line less: "Practice the sevā first./ Without sevā, there is no accomplishment."

927 *Hevajra Tantra*, book 1, 10:23, 12b1.

928 *Vajrāvali*, 6a7.

929 *Saṃvarodaya*, chap. 12, 280a5.

930 Saraha, *Buddhakapālatantrapañjikājñānavatī*, chap. 1, Toh 1652 Tengyur, rgyud, *ra*, 107b11.

931 Dīpaṃkarabhadra, *Rites for the Guhyasamāja Mandala* (*Guhyasamājamaṇḍalavidhi*), Toh 1865 Tengyur, rgyud, *di*, 74b5.

932 *Vajrāvali*, 6b4.

933 *Sarvamaṇḍala*, 143b4.

934 *Sarvamaṇḍala*, 143a1.

935 Rahu is the deity that was believed to cause an eclipse by temporarily swallowing the sun or moon.

936 *Sarvamaṇḍala*, 143a6.

937 *Buddhakapāla Tantra*, chap. 5, Toh 424 Kangyur, rgyud, *nga*, 156b6. The quotation is corrupt; it has lost some lines. In the canonical version the passage reads: "In the center of a lotus of wisdom,/ in a maṇḍala a million yojanas [wide],/ is the body that is the nature of the pure three levels/ and that protects from the terrors of samsara./ Residing in the center of that maṇḍala,/ the wise one gives empowerments to the excellent pupil."

938 *Vajra Garland*, chap. 1, 211b3. The second line here is not found in the tantra, which reads: "The body has the nature of an immeasurable palace/ that, just like its nature/..."

939 Quotation not found in this tantra.

940 *Vajrāvali*, 88b2.

941 *Vajrāvali*, 88b3.

942 Vajraghaṇṭa, *Brief Cakrasaṃvara Empowerment* (*Cakrasaṃvaraṣekaprakriyopadeśa*), Toh 1431 Tengyur, rgyud, *wa*, 219b5. The first line is particularly corrupt in the text, to the point of meaninglessness: *mcos ma bzhis kyi ngo bo dang/* instead of *mcos ma nyid kyi mgo bo gang/*.

943 *Brief Cakrasaṃvara Empowerment*, 219b6.

944 *Māyājālatantra*, chap. 2, Toh 466 Kangyur, rgyud, *ja*. There is a similarity between the first line and a line on 96b6. However, the quotation is not from this text. The source of the quotation has not been identified.

945 *Mandala Rites of Guhyasamāja* (*Guhyasamājamaṇḍalavidhi*), Toh 1798 Tengyur, rgyud, *ngi*, 16a1.

946 *Mandala Rites of Guhyasamāja*, 16a2.

947 *Mandala Rites of Guhyasamāja*, 16a2.

948 *Mandala Rites of Guhyasamāja*, 16a2.

949 *Mandala Rites of Guhyasamāja*, 16a2.

950 *Mandala Rites of Guhyasamāja*, 16a2. The twenty rites: four ground rites, four preparatory rites, two for creating the mandala, three ācārya rites, five pupil rites, and two ancillaries.

951 *Vajraḍāka*, 1b1–125a7.

952 *Sarvamaṇḍala*, 141a1–167b7.

953 *Vajrāvali*, 2a5–7b2.

954 This means deducing, through astrology and geomancy, the location of the nāga

living in the ground of that area, so that one avoids digging in the place where he will be present at that time.

955 Nāgabodhi, *The Guhyasamāja Mandala Rite* (*Guhyasamājamaṇḍalaviṃśatividhi*), Toh 1810 Tengyur, rgyud, *ngi*, 131a7.

956 *Kuśa* grass is particularly sacred in India. The Buddha attained enlightenment on a seat of kuśa grass. In India the recipient of an empowerment would ideally sleep on a mattress and pillow of this grass. In Tibet, a more common grass is used as a substitute, and each pupil receives two stalks, to be used to represent a mattress and a pillow.

957 *Yogacitta*, "aspiration for union," is the higher tantra equivalent of *bodhicitta*, "aspiration for enlightenment."

958 *Latter Guhyasamāja Tantra*, 153a4.

959 *Saṃpuṭa*, chap. 2, 84b5.

960 *Hevajra Tantra*, book 2, 3:10, 17a2.

961 *Vajra Garland*, chap. 2, 212b3.

962 *Mahāmudrā Tilaka*, chap. 2, 67a4.

963 *Vajra Tent*, chap. 15, 64b1. The text in the Dergé canon says that the total vajra *vrata* is "declared" or "described" (*brjod*) instead of "given" (*sbyin*).

964 *Vajrāvali*, 83a4.

965 *Saṃvarodaya*, 18:26, 287b3. Sanskrit: *pañcatathāgatātmakaṃ sekaṃ*. Ths appears to be a corruption of the line "The empowerment that is the nature of the five tathāgatas," though this empowerment is composed of the five empowerments.

966 *Method for Practicing the Cakrasaṃvara Mandala* (*Cakrasaṃvaramaṇḍalavidhi*), Toh 1477 Tengyur, rgyud, *zha*. This is not a quotation from this text but rather an abbreviated paraphrase of a passage that begins on 110b5. The corresponding passage in Jinabhadra's *Cakrasaṃvaramaṇḍalavidhi* is: "For the entry into the *iṣṭadevatā* (chosen deity)/ that one truly wishes for,/ practice to the extent that you are able/ with mental visualization, whether/ best, medium, or lesser./ There will be indubitable renown for oneself and others/ in the accomplishment of the siddhis/ of minor and other actions./ That is the vajrācārya empowerment."

967 *Vajrāvali*, 76b2.

968 *Vajrāvali*, 83b7.

969 The Sanskrit for empowerment is in fact *abhiṣeka*.

970 *Vajrāvali*, 84b3.

971 Vitapāda, *Yogasaptacaturabhiṣekhaprakaraṇa*, Toh 1875 Tengyur, rgyud, *pi*, 70a7. The meaning of the sentence is somewhat obscured in Tibetan and English, as the Sanskrit word for "empowerment" (*abhiṣeka*) has the meaning of sprinkling. See also Tashi Namgyal's etymology for "empowerment" just above on the same page.

972 *Seven Yogas*, 70a5.

973 *Seven Yogas*, 70a5.

974 *Seven Yogas*, 70a5.

975 *Brief Cakrasaṃvara Empowerment*, 222a1.

976 *Oral Transmission*, 5a6.

977 *Mahāmudrā Tilaka*, chap. 2, 67b2.

978 *A Brief Cakrasaṃvara Empowerment*, 221b7.

979 *Vajrāvali*, 78b6.

980 *Seven Yogas*, 70b1.
981 *Seven Yogas*, 70b2.
982 *Seven Yogas*, 70b1.
983 *Vajra Garland*, chap. 20, 231b4.
984 *Vajra Garland*, chap. 20, 231b3.
985 *Oral Transmission*, 6b4. In spite of Tashi Namgyal giving this as an example of generating heat through *visualizing* sexual union, this passage in the tantra itself follows directly upon the description of actual sexual intercourse, hence the reference to freedom from shame at the beginning of the sentence, which is omitted in Tashi Namgyal's quotation. Also, the Dergé Kangyur canon version has "offered" (*phul*) instead of "expelled" (*'phul*).
986 *Oral Transmission*, 6b4. The Dergé Kangyur version has "all phenomena" (*chos kun*) instead of "dharmakāya" (*chos sku*).
987 *Vajrāvali*, 79a6.
988 *Vajrāvali*, 84a4.
989 *Seven Yogas*, chap. 1, 70b4.
990 *Seven Yogas*, chap. 1, 70b5.
991 *Seven Yogas*, chap. 1, 70b5.
992 The Tibetan here has *'dod lha*, literally "desired deity," which is itself a literal translation of the Sanskrit *iṣṭadeva* rather then the usual *yi dam gyi lha*, literally "commitment deity," which is normally rendered into English simply as "*yidam* deity." It is translated here as "chosen diety" in that this is the deity you desire or choose to practice, to whom you make your commitment.
993 Source unidentified.
994 *Hevajra Tantra*, book 2, 11:5, 29b7.
995 *Guhyasamāja Tantra*, chap. 2, 34b2.
996 *Seven Aspects* (*Saptāṅga*), Toh 1888 Tengyur, rgyud, *pi*, 190a5.
997 *Great bodhicitta* is the union of both the relative and the ultimate bodhicitta.
998 Atiśa, *Analysis of Realizing [the Bhagavān]* (*Abhisamayavibhaṅga*), Toh 1490 Tengyur, rgyud, *zha*, 197b2. In the opening address, the Dergé Kangyur has "your *wisdom* (*shes rab*) of the experience" instead of "your *knowledge* (*shes pa*) of the experience."
999 *Saṃpuṭa*, chap. 2, 85a7.
1000 This quotation does not appear in this text.
1001 The vajra body, speech, and mind of buddhahood.
1002 *Seven Yogas*, chap. 1, 70a6. The quotation does not match the passage in the text.
1003 *Seven Yogas*, chap. 1, 70b2.
1004 *Seven Yogas*, chap. 1, 70b6. In the first line, the Dergé Kangyur has "Teach *at that time*" (*de la* presumably translating *tatra*) instead of "Teach *in stages* (*rim par*)."
1005 Source unidentified.
1006 *Vajra Pinnacle*, chap. 2, 183a7. The quotation only gives the beginning and end of the passage, omitting twenty lines of verse that describe commitments.
1007 *Vajra Pinnacle*, 183b3. "Other than that" refers to a preceding description of the commitments of the five Buddha families. On defeats (*pārājika*), see note 660 above.

1008 The entire passage reads: "You should not take life./ Do not take what has not been given./ Do not practice sexual misconduct./ Do not speak lies./ Totally forsake alcohol,/ which is the root of ruin./ Follow holy beings./ Respect and honor the yogins./ Guard as well as you can/ the three actions of the body,/ the three actions of the speech,/ and the three actions of the mind./ Do not aspire to the Hīnayāna./ Do not ignore the welfare of beings./ Also, do not forsake those in samsara./ Never have attachment to nirvana./ You should not malign/ the secret devas and asuras/ and should not step across [their] symbols,/ mounts, weapons, and insignias./ Those are taught to be the commitments."

1009 Bhavideva (*Bha pi lha*) is one of Aśvaghoṣa's alternate names.

1010 Aśvaghoṣa, *A Compilation of the Vajrayāna Root Downfalls* (*Vajrayānamūlāpatti-saṃgraha*) Toh, 2478 Tengyur, rgyud, *zi*, 179a7.

1011 *Gross Downfalls of the Vajrayāna* (*Vajrayānasthūlāpatti*), Toh 2482 Tengyur, rgyud, *zi*, 180b1.

1012 Anonymous, *Branch Commitments* (*Aṅgasamaya*), Toh 2483 Tengyur, rgyud, *zi*, 180b4.

1013 Aśvaghoṣa, *Gurupañcāśikā*, v. 49, Toh 3721 Tengyur, rgyud, *tsu*, 11b7.

1014 *Saṃvarodaya*, chap. 27, 302a7.

1015 *Enlightenment of Vairocana*, 174a6.

1016 The quotation has not been found in this source.

1017 Saraha, *Buddhakapālatantrapañjikājñānavatī*, chap. 13, Toh 1652 Tengyur, rgyud, *ra*, 144b6. Tashi Namgyal had attributed this quote to Saroruhavajra, *Treasury of Secrets*, *Guhyakoṣaśāstra*.

1018 Aśvaghoṣa, *Compilation of the Vajrayāna Root Downfalls* (*Vajrayānamūlāpatti-saṃgraha*), Toh, 2478 Tengyur, rgyud, *zi*, 179b3. Bhavideva is another name that Aśvaghoṣa is known by. He is also known as Maticitra, Mātṛceṭa, and Pitṛceṭa, and is considered identical with Āryaśūra.

1019 *Saṃvarodaya*, 18:36–37, 288a2. This citation is a different translation than that found in the Kangyur version, though it does not differ in meaning.

1020 Saraha, *Jñānavatī*, chap. 13, Toh 1652 Tengyur, rgyud, *ra*, 144b6. Tashi Namgyal had attributed this quote and the next to Saroruhavajra's *Treasury of Secrets*.

1021 Saraha, *Jñānavatī*, chap. 13, Toh 1652 Tengyur, rgyud, *ra*, 144b6.

1022 Padmākara, *Samayapañca*, Toh 1224 Tengyur, rgyud, *nya*, 28b2.

1023 Nāgārjuna, *Gross Downfalls of the Vajrayāna* (*Vajrayānasthūlāpatti*), Toh 2482 Tengyur, rgyud, *zi*, 180b2.

1024 Ratnākaraśānti, *Lamp for Seeing the Path: A Detailed Commentary on the Kṛṣṇayamāri King of Tantras* (*Kṛṣṇayamāritantrarājāprekṣaṇapathapradīpanāmaṭīkā*), Toh 1919 Tengyur, rgyud, *bi*, 256a2.

1025 Mañjuśrīkīrti, *Adornment of the Essence of the General Rites of All Secrets* (*Sarvaguhyavidhigarbhālaṃkāra*), Toh 2490 Tengyur, rgyud, *zi*, 238a6.

1026 *Primordial Buddha*, 68a1.

1027 *Stainless Light*, *tha*, 153b4.

1028 *Vajrāvali*, 85b5.

1029 *Hevajra Tantra*, book 2, 2:28, 15a7. The Tibetan has *rnal 'byor gyi* in error for *rnal 'byor gyis*.

1030 The source of the quotation has not been identified.

1031 *Five Stages*, 52b7. *Compendium of Practices*, 106b3.

1032 The description here is of the dissolution of a seed syllable, where the syllable first dissolves into the *anusvāra*, the circle above the letter, which originally was a nasalization of the vowel, but later and in Tibet is pronounced "m" or "ng." This then dissolves into the *nāda*, which literally means "the sound" but is represented as a flickering line that extends from the *anusvāra*.

1033 The source of the quotation has not been identified.

1034 *Stages of the Mahayana Path* (*Mahāyānapathakrama*), Toh 3717 Tengyur, rgyud, *tsi*, 193a3.

1035 *Hevajra Tantra*, book 1, 8:23, 9b4.

1036 *Latter Guhyasamāja Tantra*, 152a2. The quotation does not exactly correspond to the version in the canon.

1037 *Vajra Tent*, chap. 14, 59a3. The quotation is not the same as in the canon.

1038 *Latter Guhyasamāja Tantra*, 154a4. The quotation does not exactly correspond to the version in the canon, in particular in the last half, where the canon reads "the four vajras are the general,/ the wisdom nectar is the supreme."

1039 *Five Stages*, chap. 1, 45a6.

1040 *Hevajrapiṇḍārthaṭīkā*, 58a4.

1041 The Sanskrit is added in parentheses here because in the *Hevajra Tantra* the terms for the generation and completion stages—*utpannabhāvana* and *utpannakrama*—differ from those now generally known in the West, namely *utpattikrama* and *sampannakrama*.

1042 *Hevajra Tantra*, book 2, 2:33–35, 29b7.

1043 *Hevajrapiṇḍārthaṭīkā*, 58a4.

1044 *Kotapa*. Buckwheat is a short-season crop that does well on low-fertility or acidic soils. In agriculture, it is grown primarily to add nutrients and organic matter to the soil, which is the meaning intended here.

1045 *Salu* is wild rice, which is also planted in a semi-domesticated variety that is considered the highest quality rice.

1046 *Hevajrapiṇḍārthaṭīkā*, 3b7.

1047 *Vajraḍāka*, 124b6. The passage in Tashi Namgyal's text is corrupt with a line missing. The quotation here follows the version in the Dergé canon.

1048 *Vajraḍāka*, 124b7.

1049 *Vajraḍāka*, 125a1.

1050 *Stainless Light*, *da*, 110b3.

1051 *Hevajrapiṇḍārthaṭīkā*, 24a5.

1052 Buddhajñānapāda, *Samantabhadra Sādhana* (*Samantabhadranāmasādhana*), Toh 1855 Tengyur, rgyud, *di*, 35b6.

1053 *Hevajrapiṇḍārthaṭīkā*, 4a2. Dergé Kangyur has Vajrasattva "himself" (*nyid*) instead of Vajrasattva "and the like" (*sogs*).

1054 *Hevajra Tantra*, book 1, 2:33–35, 15b2. This question from bodhisattva Vajragarbha has just been quoted as the beginning of a longer extract on page 502.

1055 The quotation does not appear in this text.

1056 *Lamp for the Path*, v. 44, 240a3.

1057 *Five Stages*, chap. 3, 52a2.

1058 *Vajra Garland*, 272a1.

1059 *Latter Guhyasamāja Tantra*, 154a3.

1060 The source of the quotation has not been identified.

1061 *Vajra Tent*, chap. 7, 44b1. The first verse appears to be from an alternative translation from the Dergé Kangyur, where it reads: "Meditation on the five branches/ and the completely good nature/ ...and practicing your own special deity" *rnam pa lnga po bsgom pa dang/ kun tu bzang po'i rang bzhin dang/ rang gi lhag pa'i lhar bsgrub dang/*. Tashi Namgyal's text has: *rnam pa lnga po bsgom byas te/ kun tu bzang po gdan pa'i dngos/ rang lhag lha yi sgrub thabs bya/*.

1062 *Samāyogaḍākinījālasaṃvaratantra*, Toh 366 Kangyur, rgyud, *ka*, 153a2.

1063 *Vajra Tent*, chap. 12, 53b4.

1064 *Hevajra Tantra*, book 2, 2:3, 14a7. *Bsngags pa* is the Tibetan translation for *mantrin* in this verse, but Dakpo Tashi Namgyal in his comment on this verse has understandably misunderstood it to mean "praise" or "recommendation." However, I have translated the quotation in accordance with its original meaning as it does not conflict with the commentary.

1065 *Vajra Tent*, chap. 4, 35b7.

1066 *Hevajra Tantra*, book 2, 4:94, 23a2. Sanskrit: *anena balinā yadi sarvabhūtān pūjāṃ prakurvanti śubhāya yoginaḥ/*. The Tibetan has this as an independent sentence, meaning that if the offering is made there will be good fortune for the yogin. However, the result of the offering is actually described in the next line: "they will always have happiness."

1067 *Hevajra Tantra*, book 2, 4:92, 22b7.

1068 *Vajra Tent*, chap. 4, 38b6.

1069 *Hevajra Tantra*, book 1, 3:1, 4b6.

1070 *Vajra Tent*, chap. 12, 53b6.

1071 *Hevajra Tantra*, book 1, 3:2, 4b7.

1072 *Vajra Tent*, chap. 12, 53b6.

1073 *Oṃ svabhāva śuddhāḥ sarva-dharmāḥ svabhāva-śuddho 'haṃ* (*Oṃ*. All phenomena have a pure nature, I have a pure nature).

1074 *Oṃ śūnyatā-jñāna-vajra-svabhāva-atmako 'haṃ* (*Oṃ*. My identity is the vajra nature of emptiness wisdom).

1075 *Analysis of Realization*, 189b1.

1076 *Hevajra Tantra*, book 1, 3:2, 4b7. The Tibetan translation actually drops the reference "In its center..." (*tasmin nābhau*).

1077 *Vajra Tent*, chap. 4, 57a3. The final line of the verse is "and it is five hundred *yojanas* wide."

1078 *Vajra Tent*, 53b7.

1079 *Hevajra Tantra*, book 1, 8:1–2, 8b6. The word used for fire literally means "consumer of offerings" (*hutāśana*).

1080 *Hevajra Tantra*, book 1, 10:19–20, 12a6. The line "multicolored garlands and yak tails are fastened to it" (*srakcitracāmarair yuktaṃ*) was translated into Tibetan as "possessing garlands and so on and yak tails."

1081 *Abhidhānottaratantra*, chap. 4, Toh 369 Kangyur, rgyud, *ka*, 256b4.

1082 *Saṃvarodaya*, 17:36, 286a5.

1083 *Vajraḍāka*, chap. 46, 99b1.

1084 *Saṃvarodaya*, 17:36–37, 286a5. Caṇḍogra (*gtum dra*, fierce wrath) is in the east.

Gahvara (*tshang tshing*, wild thicket) is in the north. Vajrajvālā (*rdo rje 'bar ba*, blazing thunderbolts), a variation of Jvālākula, is in the west. Karaṅkakina (*keng rus can*, inhabited by skeletons) is in the south (or west). Aṭṭahāsa (*mi bzad gzhad*, unendurable laughter) is in Indra (*dbang ldan*), i.e., northeast. Lakṣmīvara (*bkra shis mchog*, perfect good fortune) is a variation on the usual Lakṣmīvana (*bkra shis tshal*, grove of good fortune) and is in Agni (*byin za*), which is the southeast. Ghorāndhakāra (*mun pa drag po*, fierce darkness) is in Nirṭi (*bden bral*), which is the southwest. Kilikilārava (*kī li ki la'i sgra*, the sounds of *kilikila*) is in Vāyu (*rlung lha*, deity of air), which is the northwest.

1085 *Abhidhānottaratantra*. The source of the quotation has not been identified.

1086 Ratnarakṣita, *Saṃvarodayatantrapañjikā*, Toh 1420 Tengyur, rgyud, *wa*, 11a4.

1087 *Abhidhānottaratantra*, chap. 4, Toh 369 Kangyur, rgyud, *ka*, 270b3. The canon version has *sgra nyams* while the quote has the more accessible *sgra min*.

1088 *Saṃvarodayapañjikā*, 11a4.

1089 *Saṃvarodayapañjikā*, 11a4.

1090 Vajraghaṇṭa, *Sādhana of Innate Saṃvara* (*Sahajasaṃvarasādhana*), Toh 1436 Tengyur, rgyud, *wa*, 233a6.

1091 *Saṃvarodayapañjikā*, 11a5.

1092 Dakpo Tashi Namgyal has "in between them" (*bar du*), which appears to be a misunderstanding of the ambiguous Tibetan translation of a passage in the *Hevajra Tantra*. The Tibetan merely has *nang du son gyur pa*, which literally means "gone inside." This itself is an over-literal translation of the Sanskrit *madhyagataṃ bhavet*, which just means "present in the middle." The Sanskrit commentaries clearly state that the syllable is on top of the discs.

1093 *Hevajra Tantra*, book 1, chap. 3, 5a5. The Tibetan has *mtshungs*, which is meaningless here.

1094 The "one with seven steeds" is the sun, whose chariot is pulled by seven horses that represent the seven days of the week.

1095 *Hevajra Tantra*, book 1, 8:6–7, 9a2. The English translation of this passage attempts to reflect the original Sanskrit rather than the Tibetan translation. The fourth wisdom *anuṣṭhāna*, which can mean "performance of activity," was translated into Tibetan as *nan tan*, which means "application." This is more commonly translated as *bya grub*: "the accomplishment of activity." The fifth wisdom is *dharmatā*, "the true nature," which is normally translated into Tibetan as *chos nyid*, but here it has been translated as *chos dbyings*, which is the usual translation for *dharmadhātu* and is also the usual name for this wisdom.

1096 *Saṃvarodaya*, 2:36–37, 266a7. A line was missing from the Tibetan: [*paramānanda saṃprāptam*] *ālikāli dravīkṛtam// śukraśoṇitayor madhye bindurūpeṇa tiṣṭhati/*.

1097 *Latter Guhyasamāja Tantra*, chap. 18, 154b4.

1098 *Hevajra Tantra*, book 1, 3:2, 4b7.

1099 *Hevajra Tantra*, book 1, 3:5–7, 5a1.

1100 The commitment being (*samayasattva*), wisdom being (*jñānasattva*), and samādhi being (*samādhisattva*): When there is this triad, it means the deity, the deity in its heart, and the insignia or seed syllable in that deity's heart.

1101 This is the sphere of liquid bodhicitta that the deities have melted into.

1102 The deity Mohavajra (Ignorance Vajra) is at the eyes. The deities that are the vajra or pure forms of the other afflictions are arranged at the other sense faculties.

1103 "Vajras" here refers to the syllables *oṃ*, *āḥ*, and *hūṃ*, representing the buddha body, speech, and mind, arranged at the forehead or crown, at the throat, and at the heart.

1104 *Vajra Tent*, chap. 4, 38b7. The quotation as given by Dakpo Tashi Namgyal differs from the version in the Dergé Kangyur and appears to be from a different translation and is perhaps also corrupted. For the sake of clarity, the Dergé version has been followed here: *Dang po skyes bu bsam de nas/ mkha' 'gro ma yi 'khor lo spro/ dri za mnyam par zhugs pa ni/ khu bar rjes su dran par bya/ mtshams kyi lha mos bskul bar bya// 'khor lo'i 'dren pa bskul nas ni/ mig la sogs pa ti mug sogs/ rdo rje ni gnas gsum dgod.* Tashi Namgyal's version is: *Dang por skyes bu bsam de nas/ rnal 'byor ma yi 'khor lo spro/ dri za rab tu zhugs pa ni/ lhung ste zhu ba rjes su dran/ mtshams kyi lha mo rnams kyis bskul// 'khor lo'i 'dren pa bskul nas ni/ mig la sogs la ti mug sogs/ rdo rje gsum po gnas su dgod.*

1105 The Tibetan translation of *commitment being* (*samayasattva*) is *dam tshig sems dpa'* and for *sāmayika* it is the shorter *dam tshig pa*. See the glossary for discussion of this term.

1106 *Vajra Tent*, chap. 4, 39b1. Dergé Kangyur version: *ye shes rnam par gzhug pa dang/ dbang ni rig ma brgyad rnams kyi/ yang ni dud rtsi myang ba dang/ lha mo brgyad kyis mchod pa nyid/ 'khor lo'i 'dren pa bstod pa'o//*. Tashi Namgyal version: *ye shes dngos por rab bcug la/ rig ma brgyad rnams kyis dbang bskur/ dud rtsi yang ni myang bya zhig/ lha mo brgyad rnams kyis mchod nyid// 'khor lo'i 'dren pa la bstod pa'o.*

1107 The visualized mandala created by the practitioner's mind, which the actual deity mandala will merge with.

1108 Abhayākaragupta, *Ears of Grain of Practice Instructions: An Extensive Commentary on the Tantra of True Union* (*Saṃpuṭatantraṭīkāmnāyamañjarī*), Toh 1198 Tengyur, rgyud, *cha*.

1109 *Analysis of Realization*, 194b1.

1110 *Hevajra Tantra*, book 1, 4:1, 5b5. The first "own" (*sva-*) is omitted in the Tibetan translation. The verb "imagined" with a concluding particle that ends the sentence (*bsam mo*) is added in the Tibetan translation. This translation follows the Sanskrit in making this line into one sentence. The Tibetan is not specific as to whether the light ray is singular or plural, but in the Sanskrit it is singular.

1111 *Hevajra Tantra*, book 2, 3:12, 17a3. Sanskrit: *sicyate snāpyate 'neneti sekas tenābhidhīyate/*. The two verbs are actually in the passive form. It would literally be "[you] are poured upon and bathed by it." *Seka* is etymologically related to *sicyate*, as both are from the root *sic*. In the Tibetan translation, which translates *seka* as *dbang* (power), the meaning of the sentence is lost.

1112 *Analysis of Realization*, 194b6.

1113 *Hevajra Tantra*, especially book 2, 4:81–90, 22b1–7.

1114 *Hevajrapiṇḍārthaṭīkā*, 38a7.

1115 *Hevajra Tantra*, book 2, 4:17, 20a2. Sanskrit: *mudraṇaṃ liṅgaṇāṅkaṃ ca aṅkena lakṣyate kulam/ vyastakulaṃ bhāvanāyogān na siddhir nāpi sādhakaḥ//*. The Tibetan translated *mudraṇaṃ liṅgaṇāṅkaṃ* as simple nouns *phyag rgya rtags dang mtshan ma*, rather than verbal nouns. The Tibetan used the optative *mtshon par bya* to translate *lakṣyate* rather than the passive form. In Tibetan, there is no passive form, but syntactically it has a passive structure for all its transitive verbs anyway. The Tibetan simplified the sentence presumably to avoid repeating *aṅka*. The

Tibetan has *sgrub pa* for *siddha*, which could be taken to mean "accomplishment," but the Sanskrit has *sādhakaḥ*, which is a synonym for *siddha*.

1116 The six elements (*khams*, *dhātu*) are space, air, fire, water, earth, and wisdom.

1117 See note 634 in reference to appearance, increase, and attainment.

1118 *Saṃvarodaya Tantra*, 266a5.

1119 *Kalala* is the technical name for the embryo in the first week. It is derived from *kalana*, meaning a "spot." In Tibetan it was translated as *nur nur po*, which can mean either an oval or oblong or liquidity.

1120 *Arbuda* (*mer mer po*), the shape of the fetus in the second half of the first month. The word can also mean a swelling or a tumor.

1121 *Peśī* is "egg" and also a piece of meat (*ltar ltar po*). Other texts have *nar nar po*.

1122 *Ghana* means a solid lump, while the Tibetan *gor gor po* is a viscid mass or lump.

1123 Dīpaṃkarabhadra, *Rites for the Guhyasamāja Mandala* (*Guhyasamājamaṇḍalavidhi*), Toh 1865 Tengyur, rgyud, *di*, 74b2.

1124 *Ears of Grain*, 103b7.

1125 Dīpaṃkarabhadra, *Rites for the Guhyasamāja Mandala* (*Guhyasamājamaṇḍalavidhi*), Toh 1865 Tengyur, rgyud, *di*, 74b2. The Tashi Namgyal text has *bsgribs* (obscured) in error for *bsgrims* (to be concentrated on, focused on).

1126 Ratnākaraśanti, *Guhyasamājamaṇḍalaviddhiṭikā*, Toh 1871 Tengyur, rgyud, *ni*. This teaching does not appear within the text.

1127 Dīpaṃkarabhadra, *Rites for the Guhyasamāja Mandala* (*Guhyasamājamaṇḍalavidhi*), Toh 1865 Tengyur, rgyud, *di*, 74b3.

1128 *Ears of Grain*, chap. 12, 140b4.

1129 This is referring to the cakras becoming filled by *bindus*, concentrated essences of enlightenment, "element" here referring to the buddha nature.

1130 Dīpaṃkarabhadra, *Rites for the Guhyasamāja Mandala* (*Guhyasamājamaṇḍalavidhi*), Toh 1865 Tengyur, rgyud, *di*, 74b3.

1131 *Ears of Grain*, chap. 12, 140b4.

1132 *Adornment of Kosala* (*Kosalālaṃkāra*), Toh 2503 Tengyur, rgyud, *yi*, 154b4.

1133 Dharmakīrti, *Commentary on Valid Cognition* (*Pramāṇavārttika*), v. 282, Toh 4210 Tengyur, tshad ma, *ce*, 129a5.

1134 Dharmakīrti, *Commentary on Valid Cognition* (*Pramāṇavārttika*), v. 285, 129a6.

1135 *Vajra Tent*, chap. 5, 59b1. The Tibetan in the text reads somewhat peculiarly, and the translation is from the version found in the Kangyur: *Ji ltar chu nang zla ba de/ bden min rdzun pa min pa ltar/ de ltar dkyil 'khor 'khor lo yi/ lus kyi rang bzhin rnyog pa med/*. In Tashi Namgyal's text it read: *Dper na chu nang zla ba ni/ grogs dag bden min rdzun pa'ang min/ de ltar dkyil 'khor 'khor lo 'dir/ dag cing gsal ba'i rang bzhin no/* "For example, the companionship/ of the moon in water is neither true nor false./ In that same way, the circle of this maṇḍala/ has a pure and clear nature."

1136 Ratnākaraśānti, *Lamp for Seeing the Path* (*Prekṣaṇapathapradīpa*), Toh 1919 Tengyur, rgyud, *bi*, 160a7.

1137 Ratnākaraśānti, *String of Pearls: Commentary on the Difficult Parts of the Hevajra Tantra* (*Hevajrapañjikāmuktikāvali*), Toh 1189 Tengyur, rgyud, *ga*, 273b1.

1138 Ānandagarbha, *Illuminating the Truth* (*Tattvālokakarī*), Toh 2510 Tengyur, rgyud, *li*, 148a6. The text was previously referred to as *Commentary on the First Part* [*of Compendium of Truths*]. See note 893.

1139 Āryaśūra, *Summarized Perfections* (*Pāramitāsamāsa*), "Dhyāna" chapter, Toh 3944 Tengyur, dbu ma, *khi*, 229a3.

1140 Prajñendraruci, *Shining Jewel Sādhana* (*Ratnajvālanāmasādhana*). The quotation does not appear in this text.

1141 *Hevajra Tantra*, book 2, 9:11, 27b6. Sanskrit: *Kṛpayā locane rakte kṛṣṇāṅgo maitrīcittataḥ*/. The Tibetan has a genitive *snying rje'i* in error for the instrumental *snying rjes*, so that instead of the eyes being red because of compassion, it reads "the compassionate eyes are red." The line "The eyes are pure because of the three vajras" (*rdo rje gsum gyis dag pa'i spyan*) does not exist in the Sanskrit edition or the Dergé Kangyur edition and there is no room for it metrically, so therefore it is an unwarranted insertion. *Aṅga* was translated into Tibetan as "limbs," although *aṅga* can also mean body. The sentence reads in full as "the limbs [are] black *in* the mind of love," in which the Tibetan particle *la* must be in error for the ablative *las*.

1142 The quotation does not appear in the *Guhyasamāja Root Tantra*, although the subject of the correspondences occurs on 142b5.

1143 Lūyipa, *Realizing the Bhagavān* (*Bhagavadabhisamaya*), Toh 1427 Tengyur, rgyud, *wa*, 192a4.

1144 Lūyipa, *Realizing the Bhagavān* (*Bhagavadabhisamaya*), Toh 1427 Tengyur, rgyud, *wa*, 192a3.

1145 *Hevajra Tantra*, book 1, 9:3, 10b6.

1146 *Hevajra Tantra*, book 1, 9:3, 10b7.

1147 *Vajrāvali*, 6a7.

1148 Tibetan has a corrupt *ru rag sha*. These are the seeds of the *Elaecorpus* bead tree.

1149 *Lung thang*. In Pasang Yonten Arya's *Dictionary of Tibetan Materia Medica* (p. 257), *lung thang mig* and *lung tong* are synonymous and refer to the soapberry tree. The yellow berries contain a hard black seed, which are used to make soap, as they contain saporin. However, other sacred trees may be intended here.

1150 *Saṃpuṭa*, chap. 8, 145b1.

1151 *Vajraḍāka*, chap. 45, 97a1.

1152 *Ears of Grain*, chap. 12, 138b6.

1153 Dīpaṃkarabhadra, *Guhyasamājamaṇḍalavidhi*, Toh 1865 Tengyur, rgyud, *di*, 73b3.

1154 *Ratnajvalatantra*, Toh 396, Kangyur, rgyud, *ga*. The quotation does not appear in this text.

1155 *Guhyasamāja Tantra*, chap. 13, 112b6.

1156 The Dergé Tengyur version begins quite differently: "*Oṃ śrī vajra*, etc., here invokes the essence and is therefore 'the essence [mantra],' which is the bodhicitta that is the inseparability of compassion and wisdom, and of method and wisdom. It the *essence* [mantra] because it invokes that citta."

1157 *Analysis of Realization*, 198b4.

1158 *Hevajrapiṇḍārthaṭīkā*, 24b5. The citation appears to be from an alternative translation than that in the canon, which would yield a slightly different English translation: "The root mantra becomes the body./ The essence [mantra] is the powerful speech./ Similarly, the quintessence [mantra]/ is said to be the mantra of the mind./ That which is taught to be 'the seed of wisdom'/ should be called the wisdom mantra."

1159 *Hevajrapiṇḍārthaṭīkā*, 24b6. The citation uses a different translation than that in the canon. The Tashi Namgyal version perhaps has *las* in error for an original *la*, but there is no equivalent particle in the canonical version, which also does not have the verb *bshad*, meaning "teach," so that it reads: "You should repeat and meditate on/ the seed and the quintessence,/ the essence, and the root mantra/ as, respectively, wisdom, mind, speech, and body."

1160 *Stages of the Mahāyana Path* (*Mahāyānapathakrama*), Toh 3717 Tengyur, rgyud, *tsu*. However, this quotation does not appear in the text.

1161 *Subāhuparipṛcchātantra*, chap. 5, Toh 805 Kangyur, rgyud, *wa*, 126b2.

1162 Śrīphalavajra, *Commentary to the Samantabhadra Sādhana* (*Samantabhadrasādhanavṛtti*), Toh 1867 Tengyur, rgyud, *di*. The quotation does not appear in this text.

1163 *Vajra Pinnacle*, 144a6.

1164 This quotation does not come from the *Vajra Tent Tantra*.

1165 *Hevajrapiṇḍārthaṭīkā*. The quotation does not appear in the text. A passage on 24b5 is closest, but it seems too different to be an alternate Tibetan translation: "Having invoked with a mantra,/ the deity will accomplish all actions./ Therefore, the wise/ should repeat and meditate on the name and body."

1166 *Hevajrapiṇḍārthaṭīkā*, 24b6. The canonical version is slightly different: "Until there are siddhis,/ diligently make offerings and repeat [the mantra]./ Otherwise, there will be no mantra's siddhi/ through an imperfect practice."

1167 Jālandhara, *Vajra Lamp: A Pure Brief Explanation of the Hevajra Sādhana* (*Hevajrasādhanavajrapradīpaṭippaṇīśuddha*), Toh 1237 Tengyur, rgyud, *nya*, 91b2.

1168 Vajraghaṇṭa, *Cakrasaṃvara Sādhana*, Toh 1437 Tengyur, rgyud, *wa*, 236b6.

1169 *Abhidhānottaratantra*, chap. 9, Toh 369 Kangyur, rgyud, *ka*, 272a2.

1170 In the Indian texts, the word for the ritual offering is *bali*, which was a simple edible offering, often a flat circular cake or bread, an essential part of religious life in India. *Tormas* are the sculptured barley-flour offerings of pre-Buddhist Tibetan culture and are an extensive field of study in their own right. However *torma* was used to translate *bali* and replaced them as ritual offerings.

1171 *Saṃvarodaya*, chap. 11, 279b4.

1172 *Yoginīsaṃcaryā*, Toh 375 Kangyur, rgyud, *ga*. The quotation does not appear in this text.

1173 *Hevajra Torma Rite* (*Hevajrabalividhi*), Toh 1287 Tengyur, rgyud, *ta*. The quotation does not appear in the text, and the passage most similar to the quotation (beginning 141a7) is too different to have been due to a mere scribal error: "If you ask, 'What is the purpose of the offering cake?' it is said in the text: To pacify obstacles,/ to situate deities,/ and to repair broken samaya,/ apply yourself as much as you can to the activity of offering cake." The text referred to would be one from the Hevajra corpus.

1174 *Sutra Taught by Akṣayamati* (*Akṣayamatinirdeśasūtra*), Toh 175 Tengyur, mdo sde, *ma*, 107a1. The citation is the verse form of a prose passage in the sutra, the last line of which may be corrupt and should read "...will not cease until there is enlightenment." "It is like this: for example, a drop of water that falls into a vast ocean will never cease to exist nor come to an end until it is burned by the fire at the end of the eon. In that same way, good karma that is completely dedicated to enightenment will never cease to exist nor come to an end until there is the essence of enlightenment." The source for the verse is unkown.

1175 *Hevajra Tantra*, book 2, 2:2, 14a7.

1176 Source unidentified.

1177 *Yoginīsaṃcaryā*, Toh 375 Kangyur, rgyud, *ga*. The citation does not appear in this text.

1178 Buddhajñānapāda, *Samantabhadra Sādhana*, Toh 1856 Tengyur, rgyud 'grel, *di*, 35a7.

1179 *Caturpīṭhatantra*, Toh 428 Kangyur, rgyud, *nga*. The quotation could not be located in this text.

1180 The source of this citation from Buddhajñānapāda could not be identified.

1181 Ḍombipa, *Gaṇacakravidhi*, Toh 1231 Tengyur, rgyud, *nya*, 43b6. The Tashi Namgyal text has a genitive in error for the instrumental so that it would read "Then imagine that a *raṃ* syllable in the yogin's place of water..." The Dergé is slightly corrupt. It has "yoginīs" (*rnal 'byor ma*) in error for "yogins" (*rnal 'byor pa*), and for "pit" it has *khong* in error for *khung*. The Narthang Kangyur (rgyud, *zha*, 45b7) does not have the errors in the Dergé edition.

1182 This line, coming after the author's name, appears in Tibetan to be a part of the quotation, but it is a summary of the passage leading up to the actual citation, where the main deity has dissolved into the deity and consort in his heart.

1183 Vajraghaṇṭa, *Cakrasaṃvara Sādhana*, Toh 1437 Tengyur, rgyud, *wa*, 237a3.

1184 Source of this citation from Buddhajñānapāda remains unidentified.

1185 Source of this citation from Buddhajñānapāda remains unidentified.

1186 *Guhyasamāja Tantra*, 98b6. The citation uses a different translation than that in the canon and may also be corrupt. Therefore it has been replaced by the canonical version. The citation reads: "The body that has realization through that mantra/ invokes the mind of speech,/so that there is perfectly supreme siddhi that is to be accomplished/and the mind becomes blissful and pleased."

1187 *Five Stages*, chap. 1, 45a7.

1188 *Latter Guhyasamāja Tantra*, 154a6.

1189 Buddhajñānapāda, *Muktitilaka*, Toh 1859 Tengyur, rgyud, *di*, 47a2. One of the lines in the Tashi Namgyal text is particularly corrupt. In Dergé, this verse reads: *de zhin thal byung zab mo ni/ grol 'dod de la nga mi dad/ de bas gnyis med rang bzhin du/ rtogs pas tshe 'dir 'bras thob nges/*. The edition of Tashi Namgyal's text has: *de bzhin thal byung zab mpo yis/ grol 'dod de la bdag ma dang/ de bas gnyis med rang bzhin du/ rtogs pas tshe 'dir 'bras thob 'das/*.

1190 *Muktitilaka*, 47b2.

1191 *Oral Transmission*, 3a6.

1192 *Ḍākārṇavatantra*, chap. 8, Toh 372 Kangyur, rgyud, *kha*, 159a5.

1193 *Six Yogas* (*Ṣaḍaṅgayoga*), Toh 1367 Tengyur, rgyud *pa*.

1194 *Ḍākārṇavatantra*, chap. 8, Toh 372 Kangyur, rgyud, *kha*, 159a7.

1195 *Hevajra Tantra*, book 1, 1:32, 3a4. Sanskrit: *caṇḍālī jalita nābhau/*. The Tibetan adds an instrumental particle.

1196 *Vajra Tent*, chap. 4, 57a5.

1197 *Lotus Endowed: A Commentary on Difficult Points in the Hevajra Tantra* (*Hevajratantrapañjikāpadminī*), Toh 1181 Tengyur, rgyud, *ka*.
1198 See note 635.
1199 *Vajra Garland*, 242a2.
1200 *Hevajrapiṇḍārthaṭīkā*, 18b4.
1201 *Saṃvarodaya*, 7:2–3, 272b1. The citation is presumably from a different translation than that of the Kangyur text. The passage is preceded by these lines: "Then I will explain in order/ the cakras of the channels./ The channels that follow the body/ are seventy-two thousand. The channels and proximate channels/ are dependent on the sites."
1202 *Saṃpuṭa*, chap. 2, 78b5.
1203 "She of manifold forms."
1204 *Saṃvarodaya*, 7:21, 173a3. Only the first two lines are from the tantra. The source of the rest from "the *devī* is located in between" is from an unknown source. The tantra itself continues with "the *avadhūtī*, located in between, eliminates [the duality] of perceiver and perceived./ The *lalanā* is the saṃbhogakāya, the *rasanā* the nirmāṇakāya,/ and the *avadhūtī* is the dharmakāya; thus they are the three kāyas//.
1205 *Vajra Garland*, 239a3.
1206 *Sandhivyākaraṇatantra*, chap. 1, Toh 444 Kangyur, rgyud, *ca*, 158b7.
1207 *Sandhivyākaraṇatantra*, chap. 1, Toh 444 Kangyur, rgyud, *ca*, 158b7.
1208 *Dhanujaya*, "victory through the bow," is a synonym for *asura*.
1209 The quotation does not appear in the text, though this subject is covered at *Vajra Garland*, 222b4.
1210 *Five Stages*, chap. 1, 15a7.
1211 *Mahāmudrātilaka*. The quotation does not appear in this source.
1212 *Saṃvarodaya*, chap. 5, 271b5.
1213 Nāropa, *Latter Instructions through Similes* (*Ājñottaropamā*), Toh 2332 Tengyur, rgyud, *zhi*, 273b2.
1214 The quotation does not appear in the text, though this subject is covered at *Vajra Garland*, 226a7.
1215 *Saṃvarodaya*, chap. 5, 271b6.
1216 *Vajra Garland*, 242a2. The quotation does not accurately reproduce the passage in the text, primarily because the middle line of verse has been omitted. The passage in the text reads: "Twenty-four times a thousand/ are the channels, which are always marvelous./ Know these to be the descent of the bodhicitta." Therefore, unlike the version of the text that Tashi Namgyal gives us, 24,000 is the number of the channels, which is made more explicit in the succeeding lines, which state that the movement of the wind and the flow of the blood each pass through 24,000 channels, making a total of 72,000.
1217 *Hevajra Tantra*, book 1, 1:14, 2b1. Sanskrit: *dvātriṃśad bodhicittāvahā*. The word for "channels," *nāḍyaḥ* (*nāḍīs*), occurs in the preceding question to the Buddha and is only implied in this answer. Or this Sanskrit edition may have lost the phrase "there are thirty-two channels."
1218 *Saṃpuṭa*, chap. 6, 112b7. The Tibetan for the entire passage differs markedly from the extant Sanskrit version, as in these lines: *pullīramalaye śirasi nakhadantavahā*

sthitā/ jālandharaśikhāsthāne keśaromasamāvahā// "In Pullīramalaya, in the head, there is that which flows down into the nails and teeth./ In the site of Jalandhara, the crown of the head, there is that which flows down to the head hair and body hair." In the Tashi Namgyal text, *Pullira* is simplified as *pu li ra*. It is the middle-Indic version of the Sanskrit *Pūrṇagiri*. The entire list of the names for these thirty-two channels is given earlier in the *Saṃpuṭa* on 78b5, beginning with Abhedyā and Sūkṣmarūpinī.

1219 *Rgod ma'i me*: a mythical mountain of fire believed to exist within the southern ocean and to be shaped like a mare's head.

1220 *Saṃpuṭa*, chap. 6, 112a6. The first lines, which were not in the Tashi Namgyal text, have been added here from the source in order to make the translation intelligible.

1221 *Vajra Tent*, chap. 4, 39a2.

1222 *Oral Transmission*, 9b1.

1223 *Saṃpuṭa*, chap. 6, 112b2. Drokmi Lotsāwa Shākya Yeshé translated the version preserved in the Kangyur and is quoted from here. Drokmi presumably translated the word *mātrā* as *ma mo*, "a mother goddess," normally written as *mātṛkā*. The description of the *oṃ* at the throat even left a Sanskrit word untranslated. However, in Vīravajra's commentary on the tantra, the word Drokmi translated as *ma mo* is translated as *tshad*, which means a unit of measurement. This is explained by Vīravajra to refer to the duration of the wind at each point as it ascends, the unit of measurement being an eye blink. Here, for clarity, it is the translation of the tantra as found in this commentary that has been used here. Vīravajra, *Jewel Rosary*, chap. 6, part 2, Toh 1199 Tengyur, rgyud, *ja*, 64b3.

1224 *Saṃpuṭa*, chap. 6, 117b7. The first lines have been added from the source for this translation for the sake of clarity.

1225 *Hevajra Tantra*, book 1, 1:32, 3a4. Sanskrit: *caṇḍālī jvalitā nābhau/ dahati pañcatathāgatān/ dahati ca lacanādhīḥ/ dagdhe haṃ sravate śaśī/*. The Farrow Menon Sanskrit edition seems erroneous in assuming *ahaṃ* (because of *sandhi*, their edition has *'ham*), and this is also contradicted by the Sanskrit commentary. The "burned" appears to be a locative absolute, but without the *haṃ* being declined, which the Tibetan has translated as a causal instrumental, grammatically equating *haṃ* and "moon" (which do refer to the same thing) as the agent of "flowing," which has been translated as "dripping." Also, the Tibetan has translated *moon* literally as "having a hare" in reference to the markings on the moon.

1226 *Instructions on the Six Yogas* (*Ṣaḍdharmopadeśa*), Toh 2330 Tengyur, rgyud, *zhi*, 270b1.

1227 Tsangnyön Heruka, *Meaningful to See: A Biography of Marpa Lotsāwa* (Sarnath: Lobsang Tsultim, 1970), 114. The quote as given in the Tashi Namgyal text had a line missing and some variation in the penultimate lines. It read "Above and below, the wheels of air turn./ In between, is the experience of bliss, emptiness, and clarity."

1228 *Hevajra Tantra*, book 1, 8:30, 9b7. Sanskrit: *ānandena sukhaṃ kiñcit paramānandaṃ tato'dhikam/ virāmena virāgaḥ syāt sahajānandaṃ śeṣataḥ/*. The Tibetan has probably a corruption of genitive instead of instrumental for *ānandena*. *Virāmena* was translated into Tibetan as nominative instead of the original instrumental and awkwardly (for subsequent English translation) as *dga' bral*, literally "free of joy," or "joyless." *Virāgaḥ* was translated into Tibetan as "joy without attachment" (*dga' chags bral*).

1229 *Vajra Garland*, 231b4.

1230 Source unidentified.

1231 *Vajra Garland*, chap. 20, 231b3.

1232 *Hevajra Tantra*, book 1, 8:34, 10a2. Sanskrit: *nānyena kathyate sahajaṃ na kasminn api labhyate/ ātmanā jñāyate puṇyād guruparvopasevayā*. The Tibetan has *bdag gi*, genitive, in error for the instrumental *bdag gis* in translating *ātmanā* "by yourself." Although *guruparvan* literally means a period of time, there is an allusion to methods, so that the Tibetan translation is a compound of time and method: *dus thabs*.

1233 *Ḍākārṇavatantra*, chap. 1, Toh 372 Kangyur, rgyud, *kha*, 139b3.

1234 *Five Stages*, chap. 3, 52a7.

1235 *Five Stages*, chap. 3, 53b2. The quotation differs somewhat from the Dergé Tengyur. The first line in the Tengyur edition reads "Afflictions and karma are the *karmic body*," instead of "body of the path" (*las can lus* instead of *lam gyi lus*). The second verse in the Dergé Tengyur edition reads: "If you do not know this kind of samādhi,/ you will focus upon things,/ and various kinds of desire will arise./ They will be healed by the medicine of illusion," in which there is "desire" instead of "illness."

1236 *Instructions on the Six Yogas* (*Ṣaḍdharmopadeśa*), Toh 2330 Tengyur, rgyud, *zhi*, 270b2.

1237 *Vajraḍāka*, chap. 1, 4b2.

1238 *Saṃvarodaya*, 33:24, 310b1. Sanskrit: *dṛśyate ca jagaj jalendutadvat/ śṛṇute ca pratidhvānailasaṃvṛttaiḥ/ paśyate ca marumarīcisaṃcitāḥ*. From the Sanskrit these lines could be translated as "All beings are viewed as like the moon on water; they are heard as being identical with echoes; they are seen as an assembly of desert mirages." The Tibetan translation of the last word as "mind" appears erroneous.

1239 *Hevajra Tantra*, book 1, 10:10, 12b2. "That" refers to "knowledge" (*jñāna*) in an earlier verse.

1240 *Vajraḍāka*, chap. 1, 126a1. The quotation does not appear as it is in the source.

1241 *Five Stages*, 52b7.

1242 *Instructions on the Six Yogas* (*Ṣaḍdharmopadeśa*), Toh 2330 Tengyur, rgyud, *zhi*, 270b2.

1243 *Five Stages*, chap. 3, 52b4.

1244 Nāropa, *Pañcakramasaṃgrahaprakāśa*, Toh 2333 Tengyur, rgyud, *zhi*, 277a2.

1245 *Five Stages*, chap. 3, 52b7.

1246 Nāropa, *Pañcakramasaṃgrahaprakāśa*, Toh 2333 Tengyur, rgyud, *zhi*, 277b7.

1247 Nāropa, *Truly Valid Instructions: Teachings of the Ḍākinīs* (*Ājñāsaṃyakpramāṇa ḍākinyupadeśa*), Toh 2331 Tengyur, rgyud, *zhi*, 271a6. This short text retains the original Sanskrit title (though corrupted into *Āhapramāṇa*...). It is followed by another short text by Nāropa, Toh 2332, the title of which is simply given as *Latter Instructions through Similes*. The instructions are given in both texts, and it appears that both texts are referred to by the title *Instructions through Similes*.

1248 *Truly Valid Instructions*, 271b1.

1249 Nāropa, *Latter Instructions through Similes* (*Ājñottaropamā*), Toh 2332 Tengyur, rgyud, *zhi*. This quotation appears in neither this nor the companion text by Nāropa; however, the instructions on dreams begin at 224a5 and on luminosity at 224b1.

1250 This quote appears in neither text by Nāropa.

1251 *Truly Valid Instructions*, 272a1.

1252 This line was missing in Tashi Namgyal's text.

1253 Nāropa, *Truly Valid Instructions*, 272a3.

1254 Nāropa, *Latter Instructions through Similes* (*Ājñottaropamā*), Toh 2332 Tengyur, rgyud, *zhi*; these lines do not appear in this text, though the subject of blending dream with illusory body for training in the bardo appears on 275a2.

1255 *Truly Valid Instructions*, 272b7.

1256 *Truly Valid Instructions*, 273a2. The passage is very corrupted with a line missing. This is a translation from the canonical edition.

1257 This line is not present in the Dergé edition.

1258 This line is not present in the Dergé edition.

1259 *Truly Valid Instructions*, 273a1. This passage leads directly into the preceding quotation, which begins "Alternatively..."

1260 *Truly Valid Instructions*, 271b2.

1261 *Truly Valid Instructions*, 271b2.

1262 Nāropa, *Vajra Song of the Six Dharmas*, 25. The Tashi Namgyal text differs from the Tengyur version in several places. The second line would read "One doorway is the *path* to mahāmudra." The fifth line would omit "and *ka*," as the Tibetan is *hig gi* instead of *hig ka'i*. The major difference is lines six and seven, which appear as only one line: "The consciousness is fired through the Brahma path."

1263 *Caturpīṭhatantra*, chap. 3, Toh 428 Kangyur, rgyud, *nga*, 226b1. The quote is slightly corrupt in the line about stealing, so that it could mean stealing a statue. There are other slight discrepancies such as "even" following the list of actions instead of a concluding plural. This is the exact form in which the same passage occurs in the *Vajraḍāka Tantra* (Toh 370 Kangyur, rgyud, *kha*, 80a7), which could therefore be said to be the actual source for this quote, and it has been translated accordingly.

1264 *Truly Valid Instructions*, 271b7.

1265 Nāropa, *Vajra Song of the Six Dharmas*, 26.

1266 *Hevajra Tantra*, book 1, 5:11, 6a7.

1267 *Hevajra Tantra*, book 1, 10:41, 13a4.

1268 *Five Stages*, chap. 2, 50b6.

1269 *Five Stages*, chap. 2, 51a2. The quotation differs from the canonical version. The Dergé Tengyur reads: "Perfectly attaining true enlightenment,/ you will go to the pure realm./ As you will not fall back from the buddha realm,/ there [will be] the omniscience of that very life."

1270 *Abhidhānottaratantra*, chap. 69, Toh 369 Kangyur, rgyud, *ka*, 369b7.

1271 Nāgārjuna, *Bodhicittavivaraṇa*, v. 72, Toh 1800 Tengyur, rgyud, *ngi*, 41a3.

1272 *Saṃvarodaya* 3:16, 267b3. The quotation is phrased differently in the Kangyur but with the same meaning. Sanskrit: *mahāsukhābhisaṃbodhir mahāmudrā parā tathā*/.

1273 Padmavajra, *Accomplishment of the Glorious Secret* (*Śrīguhyasiddhi*), chap. 3, Toh 2217 Tengyur, rgyud, *wi*, 10a7. In the Dergé edition the first two two lines read: "The divine substance which is one's own family,/ the supremely pure mahāmudrā" *rang gi rigs pa'i lha rdzas de/ phyag rgya chen po mchog tu dag/*, as opposed to Tashi Namgyal's *rang gis rig pa'i lhan skyes de/ phyag rgya chen po mchog tu dge/*.

1274 *Mahāmudrā Tilaka*. The quote does not appear in the text.

1275 Sahajayoginī Cintā, *Tattvasiddhi*, Toh 2222 Tengyur, rgyud, *wi*, 65b6.

1276 Tathāgatavajra, *Special Illumination: A Commentary on the Explanation of Lūyipa's Sādhana Visualization* (*Lūyipādābhisamayavṛttiṭīkāviśeṣadyota*), Toh 1510 Tengyur, rgyud, *zha*, 299a3.

1277 *Five Stages*, chap. 4, 55a1.

1278 *Five Stages*, chap. 4, 55a1.

1279 [*Guhyasamāja*] *Uttaratantra*, 154b3.

1280 Kambala, *Top-Knot Jewel* (*Ratnacūḍāmaṇi*), Toh 1443 Tengyur, rgyud, *wa*, 251a2.

1281 *Five Stages*, chap. 4, 54b1.

1282 *Saṃvarodaya*, 33:10, 309b7. The version in the Dergé canon differs somewhat: "Just as when contact is made with that true nature,/ there is no thought by any thought./ When the mind is without thought,/ at that time there is the inconceivable." *Ji ltar de nyid la reg nas/ bsam pa kun gyis bsam du med/ gang tshe bsam du med sems pa/ de tshe bsam gyis mi khyab gyur/*. Compare that to the Tashi Namgyal version: *Gang gi tshe na de nyid rig/ bsam pa thams cad bsam du med/ gang du bsam du med sems pa/ de ni bsam gyis mi khyab gyur/*. *Rig* is evidently a scribal corruption as the Sanskrit is *spṛśyate*.

1283 Nāropa, *Clear Summary of the Five Stages* (*Pañcakramasaṃgrahaprakaśa*), Toh 2333 Tengyur, rgyud, *zhi*, 277b3.

1284 *Treasury of Dohas*, 71b1.

1285 *Saṃvarodaya*, 33:19–20, 310a5. There is a textual problem here. The Tashi Namgyal text has *rgyur* (*hetavaḥ*) "as causes" corrupted to *'gyur* "will be," and therefore has ended the quotation at that point: "For that long there will be enlightenment." The Tibetan in the canonical version continues: "For as long as there is the binding of bliss as the cause of complete enlightenment, for that long the practitioner (*sgrub po*) will experience them, until the perfection of supreme bliss (*bde mchog*)..." However, the original Tibetan translation appears to have been based on a Sanskrit edition that read *kṛtasambodhi* "perfect enlightenment" instead of the *krīḍāsambhūti* "origin of play" that appears in all eight editions examined by Shinichi Tsuda. *Sambhara* can also mean "accumulations," as in the "accumulations of merit and wisdom," and also "necessary factors, prerequisites." In Sanskrit therefore this sentence could read "While there are accumulations of bliss, the causes that are produced by play, for that long the yogin experiences them and completes the accumulations." *Yāvantaḥ sukhasambhārāḥ krīḍāsambhūtihetavaḥ/ tavanto 'nu-bhavann eva yogī sambhārapūrakaḥ//*.

1286 The quotation does not appear in this text.

1287 *Five Stages*, chap. 4, 55b3.

1288 *Five Stages*, 56a1.

1289 The quotation does not appear in *Five Stages*.

1290 *Guhyasamāja Mandala Rite* (*Guhyasamājamaṇḍalaviṃśatividhi*), Toh 1810 Tengyur, rgyud, *ngi*, 136a4.

1291 The quotation does not appear in *Five Stages*.

1292 *Five Stages*, chap. 3, 56b3.

1293 *Analysis of Realization*, 200a7. The sentence continues: "...the essence of the perfection of wisdom, without body, speech, or mind, liberated from karma and birth, and very bright, like the moon, the sun, fire, and jewels. It has the quality of always being bright." The passage continues until the next part of the citation given here, which begins at 200b2.

1294 Atiśa, *Analysis of "Realizing [the Bhagavān],"* 200b2. This part of the citation appears to be a summary of this part of the text. In the canon the passage reads: "Now in order to teach the union that is nondual mahāmudrā [the sādhana says,] 'Contemplating that inconceivability...' and so on, in which *inconceivability* means luminosity. From within that state of luminosity, one gains the memory of the previous illusion-like deity-body, which is called *retention* (*gzungs*, *dhāraṇā*). To gain *retention* means to arise as the illusory-like body."

1295 *Five Stages*, 4:30–31, 55a3. The Dergé Tengyur edition has "those light rays that have form" (*gzugs bcas 'od zer*) while the Tashi Namgyal quotation is corrupted to the more obscure (*rang bzhin bcas 'od*) "lights that have that nature." The quotation had replaced the *'gyur* in the Dergé edition with *bshad*, which results in a translation that reads "It was taught that just as fish..." The Sanskrit however makes it clear that the Dergé edition is correct.

1296 *Compendium of Practices*, 91b2.

1297 *Five Stages*, 56a2. The quotation is on page 583.

1298 The quotation is on page 583, although it does not appear in *Five Stages*.

1299 *Hevajra Tantra*, book 1, 6:7, 7a2.

1300 *Hevajra Tantra*, book 2, 2:11, 14b4. The verse ends "...how could those yogins be in Raurava [hell] for even one instant?" The Tibetan translation omits "and so on" at the conclusion of the list of misfortunes.

1301 The desires for pleasurable objects of the five senses.

1302 Nāgārjuna, *Piṇḍīkṛtasādhana*, Toh 1796 Tengyur, rgyud, *ngi*, 1a4.

1303 *Five Stages*, chap. 2, 51a5. This follows the canonical version. The Tashi Namgyal version leaves out "if" and also ends the sentence "...will not *quickly* attain the result."

1304 *Hevajra Tantra*, book 1, 10:18, 12a6. The Tibetan translation reads "accomplishment" instead of "nonaccomplishment" (by reading *lakṣaṇāsiddhau* as *lakṣaṇasiddhau*).

1305 Source unidentified.

1306 Śāntarakṣita, *Establishing the Truth: An Explanatory Text* (*Tattvasiddhi-nāma-prakaraṇa*), Toh 3708 Tengyur, rgyud, *tsu*, 27b5.

1307 *Stainless Light*, *tha*, 117b3.

1308 *Hevajra Tantra*, book 1, 6:1, 6b6.

1309 *Samāyogaḍākinījālasaṃvaratantra*, Toh 366 Kangyur, rgyud, *ka*.

1310 *Kun 'dar*; this is an alternative translation of *avadhūtī* into Tibetan, this name having the implication of purification.

1311 The Essence of Accomplishment (*Grub snying*) is a name for the dohas of Saraha, specifically the trilogy known popularly as the King's Dohas (*Song of Conduct Doha Treasury*, *Dohakoṣanāmacaryāgīti*, Toh 2263), the Queen's Dohas (*Song of an Inexhaustible Treasure of Instruction*, *Dohakoṣopadeśagīti*, Toh 2264), and the People's Dohas (*Treasury of Dohas*, *Dohakoṣagīti*, Toh 2224).

1312 *Hevajra Tantra*, book 2, 2:15, 14b7. The verse ends "...as long as a *mudrā* (i.e., a consort) has not been found."

1313 *Hevajra Tantra*, book 1, 6:5, 7a1. Sanskrit: *ekavṛkṣe śmaśāne vā bhāvanā kathyate śubhā/ mātṛgṛhe tathā ramye 'thavā vijane prāntare*. The Tibetan translation of *vijane prāntare* in this edition is an almost meaningless *dben pa 'am bas mtha' ru*. The Tibetan translation translated *ramye* as "in the night" instead of as the adjective "lovely," even though *ramyā* is a feminine noun and would have a different locative.

1314 The two qualities of a pretty face and large eyes are also in *Hevajra Tantra*, book 2, 2:17. The passages at 4:39 and 8:2–5 also describe the consort.

1315 *Hevajra Tantra*, book 1, 6:8–9, 7a2.

1316 *Hevajra Tantra*, book 1, 6:3, 6b7. The Tibetan has the literal translation "half-ten" for five and "deathless" for *amṛta*. The first half of this verse reads "His clothing should be a tiger skin."

1317 The Sanskrit reads "*na* etc.," "*ga* etc.," and "*ha* etc.," and this refers to *naramāṃsa* (*human flesh*), *gomāṃsa* (*ox flesh*), and *hastimāṃsa* (*elephant flesh*).

1318 The Sanskrit is literally "final *śva*," as the *śva* comes after the initial *a* in *aśvamāṃsa* (*horse flesh*). "The śva that is first" refers to *śvamāṃsa* (*dog flesh*).

1319 *Hevajra Tantra*, book 1, 11:8, 13b1.

1320 *Hevajra Tantra*, book 2, 2:21, 15a3.

1321 *Hevajra Tantra*, book 2, 3:66, 19a7. However the quotation does not appear in the text. This is where the quotation should have come from: "Then, through calamities and thieves,/ through possession, disease, and poisons,/ he will die if he does not speak in the symbolic language,/ even if he is enlightened." *Ity upadravacaurais ca grahajvaraviṣādibhiḥ/ mṛyate 'sau yadi buddho 'pi sandhyābhāṣān na bhāṣayet*. The Tibetan Kangyur version differs slightly: "through violence and thieves,/ through demons, disease, and poison." *'tshe ma dang ni rkun ma dang/ gdon dang rims dang dug gis kyang/*.

1322 *Saṃpuṭa*, 106b3.

1323 *Hevajra Tantra*, book 1, 6:19, 7b1.

1324 *Saṃpuṭa*, 108a6.

1325 *Saṃpuṭa*, 108b4.

1326 *Hevajra Tantra*, book 2, 2:16, 14b7.

1327 *Hevajra Tantra*, book 2, 2:19–20, 15b2. The subsequent line, omitted in the quotation, is added here to help make a cogent English translation.

1328 *Hevajra Tantra*, book 1, 6:2–3, 6b6.

1329 From the commentary: "'thief's hairstyle' means that the hair is coiled on top of the head."

1330 *Hevajra Tantra*, book 1, 6:5, 7a6.

1331 *Hevajra Tantra*, book 2, 3:49, 18b5. The Tibetan *ro bsregs thal ba*, "ashes of a cremated corpse." The available Sanskrit edition has *mṛcaya*, "earth or clay," which is how Farrow translates it.

1332 *Hevajra Tantra*, book 1, 6:12–14, 7a5. Here "medicine" means *catuhsama*, a mixture of four substances: sandalwood, agallochum, saffron, and musk; "fluid" means semen.

1333 Though this would seem to be from the *Hevajra Tantra*, book 2, 3:41–42, 18b1, it differs enough to be either from a different source that is based upon the *Hevajra Tantra* or itself a corruption. The equivalent passage in the *Hevajra Tantra* reads:

"Do not reject whatever food and drink is obtained, whether pleasant or unpleasant." *khānaṃ pānaṃ yathāprāptaṃ gamyāgamyaṃ na varjayet/*. The Dergé edition agrees with the Sanskrit.

1334 *Hevajra Tantra*, book 1, 6:18, 7b1. For "expressions" here the Tibetan translates *ākara* as *'bras bu*, literally "result." For the third line, the Dergé text has *bdag nyid kyis*, which would make the phrase mean "oneself abandons sleep," and Tashi Namgyal's text has *bdag nyid kyi*, which would make the phrase mean "abandon the sleep of self." However in the Sanskrit both "sleep" and "self" are in the accusative.

1335 *Hevajra Tantra*, book 2, 3:42, 18b1. Sanskrit: *snānaṃ śaucaṃ na kurvīta grāmyadharmaṃ na varjayet//*. "The dharma of the town or village" (*grāmyadharma*) is a specific term for sexual activity. However, while in the Sanskrit the admonition is *not* to abandon (*na varjayet*) sexuality, the Tibetan in both the Dergé canon and the Tashi Namgyal text has corrupted the negative *ma* to the intensifier *rab*, thus meaning "give up entirely," which makes no sense in the context of the *Hevajra Tantra*.

1336 *Hevajra Tantra*, book 1, 6:24, 7b3. The *su* in *suyogavan* was not translated into Tibetan. Here in this English it has been rendered as "excellent."

1337 The Tibetan translated *daitya* the same as *asura*, though they are not identical terms. The *daitya* do, however, belong to the class of Indian "demons" who, like the asuras, are enemies of the devas. These particular ones are said to have been born from a goddess named Dīta who wished revenge against Indra.

1338 *Hevajra Tantra*, book 1, 6:54, 7b4.

1339 *Saṃpuṭa*, 108b4. The quotation is not accurate. In the Dergé canon the passage from which this quotation derives reads: "[Wandering in other lands,/ in mountain caves, and in jungles,/ in the great primordial charnel grounds,/] dwelling there, *the wise meditate./ Completely forsaking all fear,/ in that way*, the yogin/ engages in "complete victory."

1340 *Saṃpuṭa*, 109a5.

1341 Source unknown. It is not found in the *Saṃpuṭa Tantra*.

1342 *Saṃpuṭa*, 106b7.

1343 *Saṃpuṭa*, 108a7.

1344 *Saṃpuṭa*, 108b6.

1345 *Saṃpuṭa*, 108b5.

1346 *Saṃpuṭa*, 109a1.

1347 This heading was first mentioned on page 438.

1348 *Illuminating Lamp*, chap. 1, 2b2.

1349 [*Guhyasamāja*] *Uttaratantra*, 154a2.

1350 [*Guhyasamāja*] *Uttaratantra*, 154a4.

1351 *Vajra Tent*, chap. 4, 37a7.

1352 *Caturdevīparipṛccha*, chap. 4, Toh 446 Kangyur, rgyud, *ca*, 280a7.

1353 *Vajra Tent*, chap. 4, 37b1.

1354 [*Guhyasamāja*] *Uttaratantra*, 155a2. The Tashi Namgyal text has a variant translation but also a scribal corruption in the line that reads "when the activity has not been accomplished" (*gang tshe bya ba ma grub na*). His version reads "if they have still not attained enlightenment" (*gal te byang chub ma grub na*).

1355 *Pramuditā*. *Rab tu dga' ba*.

1356 *Vimalā. Dri ma med pa.*
1357 *Prabhākarī. 'Od byed pa.*
1358 *Arciṣmatī. 'Od 'phro ba.*
1359 *Sudurjayā. Sbyang dka' ba.*
1360 *Abhimukhī. Mngon du gyur ba.*
1361 *Dūraṅgamā. Ring du song ba.*
1362 *Acalā. Mi g.yo ba.*
1363 Unshaken by identification either with or without concepts.
1364 *Sādhumatī. Legs pa'i blo gros.*
1365 *Dharmameghā. Chos kyi sprin.*
1366 The two are samādhi and dhāraṇī.
1367 *Sūtrālaṃkāra*, 21:33, 37b3.
1368 *Abhidhānottaratantra*, Toh 369 Kangyur, rgyud, *ka*. The quotation does not appear in this text.
1369 *Hevajra Tantra*, book 1, 7:10, 8a3.
1370 *Saṃpuṭa*, chap. 5, 103a7.
1371 *Abhidhānottaratantra*. The quotation does not appear in this text.
1372 *Vajra Mandala*, 26a1. The Tibetan has translated *maṇḍala* in the title as *snying po*, "essence."
1373 *Abhisamayālaṃkāra*, 1:18, 2b4.
1374 *Abhisamayālaṃkāra*, 8:1, 11a7.
1375 The lines that Tashi Namgyal omits are: "...the ten categories of totality;/ the supports for overpowering/ divided into eight kinds;/ passionlessness; the specific knowledge/ of aspiration, wisdom, and clairvoyance;/ the four called *complete aspects*; the ten powers;/ the ten strengths; the four fearlessnesses; the three that are unguarded; the three applications of memory;/ the state of being without confusion,/ complete transcendence of the tendencies, great compassion for beings..."
1376 *Abhisamayālaṃkāra*, 8:2, 11b1, and skips to 11b3.
1377 *Abhisamayālaṃkāra*, 8:12, 11b7.
1378 *Abhisamayālaṃkāra*, 8:33, 12b6.
1379 Asaṅga, *Mahāyānasaṃgraha*, Toh 4048 Tengyur, sems tsam, *ri*, 37a4. The Tibetan adds the word "phenomena" to make "power over all phenomena." The text then goes on to list the power over various phenomena through the six perfections.
1380 *Sūtrālaṃkāra*, 10:65, 11b3. That *buddha* is in the plural is evident in the Sanskrit.
1381 *Sūtrālaṃkāra*, 10:60, 11a7. Literally the passage reads: There is the svābhāvika, the sāṃbhogya, and the other kāya is the nirmāṇika.
1382 *Sūtrālaṃkāra*, 10:62, 11b1. The Dergé Tengyur has *Rang bzhin sku ni mnyam pa dang*, but Tashi Namgyal has *rang bzhin sku ni ngo bo nyid*. The Sanskrit confirms that the Tengyur version is correct.
1383 *Sublime Continuum*, 3:1, 65b1. There is a word play on *artha* which can be both "benefit" and "truth" in the Sanskrit.
1384 The Sanskrit for this verse does not use *kāya* but two synonyms for body: *śarīra* for the ultimate "body" and *vapu* for that of the *rishi*, or sage, though all are translated as *sku* in Tibetan. *Rishi* is in the singular in Sanskrit but in plural in the Tibetan. Also, the Sanskrit uses the same word (*saṃpatti*) for benefit for oneself and for oth-

ers, while the Tibetan uses two less-common synonyms (*'byor ba* and *phun tshogs*), roughly equivalent to "wealth" and "prosperity."

1385 *Sublime Continuum*, 3:2, 65b2.

1386 Vagīśvarakīrti, *Seven Aspects* (*Saptāṅga*), Toh 1888 Tengyur, rgyud, *pi*, 190a5. The first two lines of this quotation were previously given in the section on the fourth empowerment. This verse is from the introduction to the text, where Vagīśvarakīrti describes the text he is about to write. He says these verses are a quotation but does not specify the source. The third and fourth lines differ from the canonical edition of the text and also appear to be corrupt. The Dergé Tengyur edition reads: "The meaning of the seven aspects that are to be accomplished,/ which I state here, are also validly praised by the wise with complete meditation." *Yan lag bdun ldan don dang ldan pa bsgrub bya 'dir/ bdag 'dod tshad mas yongs bsgom blo can gyis kyang bsngags/*. Tashi Namgyal's version: *Yan lag bdun dang ldan pa'i sangs rgyas 'di nyid ni/ bdag 'dod tshad mas yongs dgos blo can rnams kyang 'dod*. In this instance I have taken the reading of *bsgom* instead of *dgos*, assuming the latter to be a corruption rather than an alternate translation or version. The content of the rest of the text, with its subject matter of "complete meditation," supports this.

1387 *Saṃpuṭa*, chap. 4, 80a5. Sanskrit: *buddhatvam nānyair yat prāptaṃ kalpāsaṃkhyeyakoṭibhir yāvat/ asminnapi janmani tvam prāpnoti satsukhenaiva//*. The Tibetan translation reads "that is not achieved by another [way, even] after..."

1388 *Compendium of Practices*, 105a7. The quotation that appears in Āryadeva's text is from an unknown source, but it appears in other later works. See Wedemeyer, *Āryadeva's Lamp*, p. 326n53. The original is in verse (p. 493) and has been translated as such by Chag Lotsāwa, in Wedemeyer, p. 652n56.

1389 The quotation does not appear in this text.

1390 *Vajra Tent*, chap. 15, 63b7.

1391 *Saṃpuṭa*, chap. 10, 156b3.

1392 *Oral Transmission*, 15b5. The quotation differs from the canonical version: "Because of your conduct of eating/ and some deluded thoughts about self,/ in this lifetime of yours/ your physical body will be left behind/ and will not be truly transformed,/ but your consciousness is indestructible/ and will perfectly accomplish the mahāmudrā." There is no mention of accomplishment in the bardo.

1393 *Oral Transmission*, 15a5.

1394 *Oral Transmission*, 15b1.

1395 *Vajra Tent*, chap. 8, 49b4. The term used for king is *Bhūmipāla, sa skyong*. Literally "Guardian of the land." The Tashi Namgyal text repeats the verb "to go" (*'gro*) instead of the Kangyur text's "born" (*skye*).

1396 *Abhisamayālaṃkāra*, 8:34, 12b7.

1397 *Sublime Continuum*, 4:12, 67b6.

1398 *Sublime Continuum*, 4:1, 67a6.

1399 *Sublime Continuum*, 4:13, 67b7. The name that appears in the verse is Śakra (*rga byin*), which is more common in Tibetan than Indra (*dbang po*), but as Indra is likely to be familiar to the reader, I have taken the liberty of using this name here.

1400 *Sublime Continuum*, 4:29, 68b2. The Lord of Devas is Indra. The term used here for deities is *suras* not *devas*. This was a word created as an antonym for *asura* ("demigod"), where the *a* was taken to mean a negative and thus understood as "anti-god."

In fact *asura* (cf. *ahura* in ancient Iranian) was originally a synonym for *deva*. The Lord of Sages is Śākyamuni.

1401 These two lines were missing from the quotation.

1402 *Sublime Continuum*, 4:31–33, 68b4.

1403 *Sublime Continuum*, 4:42–43, 69a5. The quotation has "for the benefit of beings" (*'gro ba'i don du*) instead of "of the virtue of beings" (*'gro ba'i dge ba'i*).

1404 *Sublime Continuum*, 4:53–54, 69b7.

1405 *Sublime Continuum*, 4:59–60, 70a5.

1406 *Sublime Continuum*, 4:69, 70b3.

1407 *Sublime Continuum*, 4:71–72, 70b5.

1408 *Sublime Continuum*, 4:74, 70b7.

1409 *Sublime Continuum*, 4:75–76; 70b7. Tashi Namgyal's text omits the second line in the first verse.

1410 The word for "sun" used here is actually "seven steeds," as the sun's chariot is drawn by the seven horses that are the seven days of the week.

1411 This is in reference to the Indian myth of the devas churning the primeval ocean with Mount Meru using the nāga king as a rope, thus extracting the nectar of immortality (*soma*) from the ocean.

1412 The twelfth-century Gampopa's other name was Dakpo Lhajé, and the Tibetan for *maṅgalaṃ* is "Tashi," this combination forming the name of the author: Dakpo Tashi.

1413 There are a number of authors by this name but none identified for the time period of Dakpo Tashi Namgyal, so for the present he remains unidentified.

1414 This year may have been 1537, when he was twenty-five; 1549, when he was thirty-seven; 1561, when he was forty-nine; 1573, when he was sixty-one; or 1585, when he was seventy-three.

1415 The monastery founded by Gampopa of which Tashi Namgyal was abbot.

Glossary

Abhayākara/Abhayākaragupta (*'Jig med 'byung gnas sbas pa*, d. 1125). A Bengali who became the leading Buddhist scholar and author of his time, teaching at the monasteries of Vikramaśīla, Vajrāsana, and Odantapuri. He systematized the tantric teachings, thus greatly influencing their future in Tibet. He helped to translate numerous works into Tibetan, and thirty-six of his own works are included in the Tibetan Tengyur.

Abhidharma (*mngon pa'i chos*). The "further Dharma." This set of teachings attempts to give an analytic overview of the foundation and worldview of Buddhism. It is primarily concerned with the constituents of mental activity and their relationship to the process of attaining enlightenment but it also includes descriptions of cosmology and the constituents of the external world. In Tibet, the texts of Vasubandhu and Asaṅga form the basis for the study of Abhidharma.

ācārya (*slob dpon*). This is a traditional Indian title denoting a person of authority because of superior knowledge, spiritual training, or position. In the Buddhist context, it is most often used for a scholar of great renown. Within the context of the tantric empowerment, it refers to the one giving the empowerment.

action seal (*las kyi phyag rgya, karmamudrā*). This is a euphemism for a consort in sexual practices, also called a *vidyā* (*rig ma*, lit. "knowledge [lady]") and a *prajñā* (*shes rab*, lit. "wisdom"). All these terms are naturally feminine nouns so that they can be both abstract terms and signify actual females.

age of perfection (*rdzogs ldan, satyayuga*). The age of goodness and the first of four ages in which humans become progressively more degenerate and their lives progressively shorter. We live in the fourth and most degenerate age.

aggregates (*phung po, skandha*). A systematic breakdown of an individual into five psychophysical "heaps": form, sensations, identifications, mental actions, and consciousnesses.

Akaniṣṭha (*'og min*). Literally, "highest." This is the highest paradise in the form realm and thus the highest physical residence in samsara. It became further elevated in the yoga tantras as the abode of Vairocana and the source of the yoga tantras. In the highest yoga tantras it is the abode of the ultimate Buddha Vajradhara and is entirely outside samsara.

Alakāvatī (*cang lo can*). Literally, "realm of willow trees." On the summit of Mount Meru, it is the realm of Vajrapāṇi.

ālaya (*kun gzhi*) and **ālaya consciousness** (*kun gzhi rnam shes*, *ālayavijñāna*). Literally *ālaya* means a dwelling or abode, as in Himālaya, the "abode of snows." It is translated into Tibetan as *kun gzhi*, which means "basis of everything." However, it primarily relates to the separate mind or continuum of an individual and not a shared universal foundation. The concept existed in early Buddhism as an explanation of why an individual does not cease to exist when consciousness stops and was termed *bhavanga* in the Theravāda tradition. The *ālaya* later became an explanation, particularly in the Cittamātra tradition, for where karmic seeds are stored and was considered the source of an individual's mentally produced experiences. It is usually synonymous with the *ālaya* consciousness, which is the neutral basis for samsara and which ceases upon liberation.

amanasikāra (*yid la mi byed pa*). Literally "nonattention." In early Buddhism, this term signified the negative state of inattentiveness. Maitripa, through reinterpreting the Sanskrit negative marker "a" as the primordial letter *A*, taught that this was a positive quality and really meant attention on the true nature. However, in the context of mahāmudrā, even if the "a" is interpreted as a negative marker, it can mean nonattention or nonengagement as a positive quality.

Amitāyus (*tshe dpag med*). The buddha of long life. Amitāyus is the saṃbhogakāya form of Amitābha and is commonly propitiated in long-life rituals.

Ānanda (*Kun dga' bo*). The Buddha's cousin, who became his attendant for the last twenty years of his life and eventually succeeded to the position of the head of the Buddhist tradition as its second patriarch, after the death of Mahākāśyapa.

anusvāra (*klad skor*). The circle or dot above the letter that nasalizes the vowel. Represented in diacritics as *ṃ*, it is nowadays pronounced as *m* or *ng*.

arhat (*dgra bcom pa*). A "worthy one," who has attained nirvana, or liberation from all the afflictions. The Tibetan translation, which technically should have been rendered *'os pa*, instead reads it as a combination of *ari*, "enemy," and *han*, "kill," producing a literal meaning of "enemy destroyer." *Arihan* was the term used in the Jain tradition that was founded just before Buddhism. Though earlier traditions used the title *arhant* for the Buddha and his enlightened disciples, in the Mahayana tradition it came to mean those who were enlightened only through the non-Mahayana traditions. The *Lotus Sutra*, which coined the term *Mahayana*, declared that arhants would be awakened from their nirvanic bliss by the Buddha after a period of time in order to continue on the Mahayana path of freeing all beings.

ārya (*'phags pa*). "Noble one." This term is applied to those who have reached the path of seeing on whichever vehicle they follow. In terms of the Mahayana path it is synonymous with bodhisattvas.

Āryadeva (*'phags pa lha*). A pupil of the Madhyamaka philosopher Nāgārjuna (second century C.E.), he is the author of such Madhyamaka texts as *Four Hundred Verses*. A later Vajrayāna master of this name who is the author of texts quoted within this volume has been conflated with this earlier Āryadeva.

a-stroke (*a shad*). Refered to by many Western practitioners as *ashay*, a single stroke that resembles the vertical stroke used in Tibetan calligraphy to mark the end of a verse or as the equivalent of a comma or period. The representation of the letter A by a single vertical line is a practice used in the Vartula script. Here it is used to repesent the caṇḍālī flame at the navel, which is a thin vertical that narrows to a point at its apex.

asuras (*lha ma yin*). The enemies of the devas, they are prominent in Indian literature and mythology, in which context they are often translated as "demons." In Tibet asuras are of little cultural importance, only appearing in the classification of the six classes of beings. When the classes of beings are enumerated as five, they are omitted.

avadhūtī (*dbu ma*). *See* central channel

aural tantras (*snyan rgyud, karṇatantra*). Or literally, "ear tantras." This is often misspelled *snyan brgyud* and therefore confused with "oral lineage." It is the specific name for the teachings received by Tilopa from a ḍākinī whose body had vanished so that he received the instructions as words emanating from the syllable *hūṃ*. Therefore these teachings are also known as the *Dharma of the bodiless ḍākinī*.

Avalokiteśvara (*spyan ras gzigs*). The bodhisattva of compassion.

Avīci (*mnar med*). The worst and physically lowest of the hells, where beings remain longer and suffer greater than any other hell.

āyatana (*skye mched*). The Tibetan literally means "arise and increase," while the Sanskrit means "base" or "source." The term is used variously but most commonly for the six organs of perception—which includes the mental faculty—and their perceived objects. It may also refer to the various states of perception in the formless realms.

bardo (*bar do, anantarabhava*). An intermediate state of being that primarily refers to the period between death and rebirth but can also in certain specific contexts be applied more widely.

Bhagavān (*bcom ldan 'das*). An epithet for the Buddha.

bindu (*thig le*). Generally *bindu* means a spot or a dot, as in a leopard or snake's spots, and it is also commonly used for the decorative dot between a woman's eyebrows, which has been anglicized as *bindi*. It can also mean a circle, a zero in mathematics, the *anusvāra* in calligraphy, the colored spots representing deities in a mandala, or a sphere or circle of light, a globule, or a drop. In the context of tantric physiognomy, it refers to an essence, whether the essence of a purity or an impurity, and can occur in various forms, liquid and solid. For example, the white upside-down *haṃ* syllable in the crown of the head is solid white and in the shape of that letter. As a result of sexual excitement, or certain practices, it begins to melt, and drops fall from it down the channel that leads to the penis. These drops are also *bindus*. The subsequent ejaculate is also a *bindu*, and it is in certain contexts a synonym for semen. In those cases it can be translated as "vital essence." Though it is most often rendered as "drop" in this volume, a *bindu* is only technically a liquid "drop" in the context of the semen falling through the central channel; most visualizations involving a *bindu* in the central channel are of a tiny ball of light.

bodhicitta (*byang chub sems*). Most commonly, in a Mahayana context, this refers to the aspiration to become enlightened so that one may free all beings from samsara. This *relative bodhicitta* is sometimes contrasted with *ultimate bodhicitta*, the mind of a buddha, which is free of all misconceptions. Within the higher tantras *bodhicitta* can also be a euphemism for semen.

bodhisattva (*byang chub sems dpa'*). The term can technically be applied to anyone who has taken the bodhisattva vow to attain buddhahood in order to benefit beings, but it usually refers to the deity-like beings who have reached the bodhisattva levels (*bhūmis*).

Brahmā (*tshangs pa*). Before the rise of Śaivism and Vaiśnavism eclipsed them, Brahmā and Indra were the two principal deities in Indian religion, and are therefore featured in the life story of the Buddha, asking him to teach, for instance, after he attained enlightenment.

brahmavihāra. Literally "the dwelling place of Brahmā," this is a pre-Buddhist meditation on love, compassion, rejoicing, and impartiality or equanimity; the contemplation and generation of them were said to lead to rebirth in the realm of Brahmā. This was also taught by the historical Buddha who emphasized that as a general teaching they did not lead to liberation. In Tibetan Buddhism they are more commonly known as the *four immeasurables* and are considered a basis for the development of bodhicitta. Drigungpa, in tune with his presentation of the Buddha's teachings as being unitary, with no anomalies, denies the mundane identity of the immeasurables and states that they are the essence of buddhahood.

Cakrasaṃvara (*'khor lo sdom pa* and *'khor lo bde mchog*). The principal deity in the Kagyü tradition, who appears to have originated in the late eighth century in India. It is explicitly a transmutation of Śiva.

cakravartin (*'khor los sgyur ba'i rgyal po*). An exalted sovereign with universal dominion. The name means "roller of a wheel." In the earliest sutras, cakravartins were mythical kings. On becoming king, they set a magical wheel rolling and wherever it went became their lands; for some it would roll throughout the world.

caṇḍālī (*gtum mo*). The principal practice of the six Dharmas of Nāropa, sometimes rendered as "inner heat" based on the physiological results of the practice. See extended discussion of this term in the introduction.

Candrakīrti (*zla ba grags pa*). A seventh-century Indian author whose Madhyamaka works became seminal to the Tibetan Buddhist tradition. There is also a later Candrakīrti from the end of the first millennium who was an author of Vajrayāna texts. The Tibetan tradition conflates the two, as it regularly does for teachers with the same name, thus enhancing the prestige of texts by the later author.

Cārvāka (*rgyang 'phen pa*). Members of a no longer extant school of thought, with portions of its texts surviving only in attacks upon it by its opponents. It denied that a god or karma created the world or that there is a life after death.

central channel (*dbu ma, avadhūtī*). The main passageway for the winds within the body's subtle physiology, which is manipulated in tantric practice. It runs parallel to the spine.

channel (*rtsa, nāḍī*). The word *nāḍī* can mean any tube or pipe as well as the physical veins and arteries of the body, but in this work it generally refers to the network of subtle channels, analogous to the nervous system, through which flow the winds that are mentally manipulated as part of tantric practice. Although earlier commentaries emphasized that the channels were simply visualizations without a physical existence, later Tibetan tradition attempted to conjoin these with the medical tradition, with inconclusive results.

Characteristics Vehicle (*mthan nyid theg pa, lakṣaṇayāna*). This can refer to the three Piṭikas of all Buddhist traditions though it is sometimes used to refer to the Mahayana alone. It is synonymous with the sutra tradition, or Causal Vehicle, in contradistinction to the tantra, or Vajrayāna.

Cittamātra (*sems tsam*). This school—also known as Yogācāra because of its emphasis on meditation practice—propounded the view that all phenomena are merely manifestations of the mind, which alone is ultimately real. The school grew out of the teachings of Asaṅga and Vasubandhu in the fourth century, and Candragomin was a principal exponent in the seventh century. While Buddhism was often polarized between the views of Cittamātra and Madhyamaka during this period, a kind of synthesis had taken place by the eighth century in the teachings of Śāntarakṣita and his student Kamalaśīla, who were both instrumental in transmitting Buddhism to Tibet.

commitment being (*dam tshig sems dpa', samayasattva*). In deity meditation, the deity imagined by oneself is named the *commitment being*, though rather than "commitment," the meaning of *samaya* (*dam tshig*) here is more likely "symbol," as the deity one imagines is the symbol of the actual deity.

concentrations (*samāpatti*). Literally "attainments," the term *samāpatti* has become synonymous with *samādhi*.

conqueror (*rgyal ba; jina*). The most common term used to refer to the buddhas in Tibetan, though the Sanskrit *jina* is in the West most commonly associated with Jainism. Its etymology refers to being victorious over one's own ignorance and defects, but unlike the English "conqueror" it is solely used for someone who has attained spiritual liberation. *Son of the conquerors* (*rgyal sras, jinaputra*) is a less-frequent and patriarchal synonym for *bodhisattva*. While some Mahāyana masters, such as Asaṅga, did not believe enlightenment was possible in a female body, other Mahayana texts, such as the *Vimalakīrti Sutra*, explicitly countered that view.

crown protrusion (*gtsug tor, uṣṇīṣa*). One of the thirty primary physical marks of a great being that a buddha possesses.

ḍāka (*dpa' bo / mkha' 'gro*). In earlier literature this was a terrifying being of the night that fed on human flesh and haunted the charnel grounds, but nowadays ḍākas are protectors of the Vajrayāna teachings, though they are often eclipsed in this role by their female counterparts, the ḍākinīs.

ḍākinī (*mkha' 'gro ma*). As with the ḍākas, earlier Indian and Buddhist literature represent ḍākinīs as malevolent devourers of humans. This aspect still survives as the class of ḍākinīs known as *flesh eaters*. In the antinomian higher tantras, these creatures became guardians of secret teachings. *Wisdom ḍākinīs* (*jñānaḍākinī*) are those who have attained buddhahood and manifest in the form of a ḍākinī in order to benefit beings. Similarly women who are enlightened, especially if they are not ordained, are known as ḍākinīs, including the mothers and consorts of lamas. The term has thus come to have a wide application, with numerous exegeses as to their symbolism.

degenerate age (*rtsod pa'i dus, kaliyuga*). Our present age, the fourth of four ages, when the teachings of the Buddha have degenerated, realizations have become difficult to attain, and lifespans have become relatively short.

dependent origination (*rten cing 'brel 'byung, pratītyasamutpāda*). The teaching that nothing exists independently. It is often systematized in a teaching on twelve interdependent links, whereby all of samsara comes about in dependence on the first link, ignorance.

Dergé. This kingdom in the east of the Tibetan plateau, in the region of Kham, had independence or at least autonomy for a considerable period. The Dergé monarchy were patrons of Buddhism and funded the Eighth Tai Situ, his building of Palpung Monastery within Dergé, and his edition of the canon, known as the Dergé Kangyur and Tengyur.

devas (*lha*). A general term for any god or deity, but is particularly associated with the gods in Indian mythology who possessed the *amrita*, or nectar of immortality, that the asuras kept trying to steal, without success. By extension it refers to any being who has been reborn in a samsaric paradise.

desire realm (*'dod khams*). This realm includes all existences from the lowest hell to Māra's paradise. One can only be reborn in higher realms through the power of meditation.

Dharma (*chos*). In Buddhist texts, this most often refers to the teachings of the Buddha, which are exalted for their power to liberate from suffering. In Sanskrit this is the general term for "truth" or "religion," but it has many meanings. For instance, it can refer to all phenomena that exist, and also, more specifically, the phenomena that are perceived within the mind alone and not by the senses. In English it tends to refer specifically to Buddhism.

Dharma wheel (*chos kyi 'khor lo, dharmacakra*). This is a metaphor derived from cakravartin, the universal sovereign who had a magic wheel. The early sutras often pair or compare cakravartin kings and buddhas. Thus, the Buddha has his own wheel, but of Dharma instead of secular power. In the Mahayana, there are said to be three "turnings," or more accurately "rollings," of the wheel of Dharma. See the following notes and *cakravartin* above.

Dharma wheel of the four truths (*bden pa bzhi'i chos 'khor*). This refers to the "first turning of the Dharma wheel" and includes all the sutras and Vinaya of the earliest Buddhist schools. The teaching of the four truths, which is the teaching the Buddha gave to his first five pupils in Sarnath, is considered representative of these teachings.

Dharma wheel of the nonexistence of characteristics (*mtshan nyid med pa'i chos 'khor*). This is the "second turning of the Dharma wheel" and includes such Mahayana sutras as the perfection of wisdom sutras, and the earlier sutras on emptiness that feature the bodhisattva Mañjuśrī prominently. Though the subjects are varied, including such sutras as those on Amitābha and his pure realm, this group of sutras is seen as emphasizing emptiness as represented by the Madhyamaka texts of Nāgārjuna.

Dharma wheel of perfect examination (*legs par 'byed pa'i chos 'khor*). This is the "third turning of the Dharma wheel" and includes such sutras as those that emphasize that all phenomena are manifestations of the mind and that all beings possess a buddha nature. These sutras, though numerous and varied, tend to be represented by Asaṅga—who revealed some of these sutras from visions of bodhisattva Maitreya—and by the Yogacāra tradition.

dharmadhātu (*chos kyi dbyings*). This term can mean the entire expanse of phenomena, but also the "essential element" of phenomena, which is emptiness, or an indivisible union of emptiness and fundamental clarity.

dharmakāya (*chos sku*). The "truth body" of a buddha, in contradistinction to a buddha's corporeal form body (*rūpakāya*). *Dharmakāya* originally referred to the teachings themselves, which remained as the Buddha's presence or body even after his form body was gone. As the term evolved, it came to be a synonym for ultimate reality, or emptiness, and the realization of these in the mind of a buddha.

dharmodaya (*chos 'byung*). The "source of phenomena." This is depicted as the tantric symbol of a triangle, which also represents the female genitalia. A more elaborate form is the crossed triangles forming a six-pointed star, representing an aerial view of an inverted pyramid containing the deity, which is upon a triangular base.

dhātu (*khams*). "Element," which can refer to buddha nature, the quintessential nature of the mind, and also to the elements of sensory perception of which there are eighteen: the six consciousnesses (the five sensory consciousnesses and the mental); the six sensory organs, including the faculty of the mind; and the six objects of perception, including mental phenomena.

dhyāna (*bsam gtan*). Synonymous with *samādhi* and *śamatha*, it means "placed" and "fixed" and is etymologically a form of the *dhi* in *samādhi*. The closest translation would be "concentration," for it means the mind fixed upon a point without deviation, but in a less technical context could simply be called meditation, as in the perfection of meditation (*dhyānapāramitā*). In Buddha's time the attainment of various levels of dhyāna was the goal of many of his contemporaries and was a path that he tried. The night before his enlightenment at dawn, he is said to have gone through these levels of dhyāna and then beyond them.

doha (*do ha*). An Apabhraṃśa word meaning "couplet," specifically rhyming couplets with a set meter, a form much favored by tantric authors such as Saraha in around the end of the first millennium.

drop (*thig le*). *See* bindu; tilaka

eight charnel grounds (*dur khrod brgyad*). These are areas in the mandala of such higher tantra deities as Cakrasaṃvara. They are situated around the deity's palace in the four main and the four intermediate directions. In India, charnel grounds were where bodies were brought to be cremated or left to be devoured by animals. They were believed to be both terrifyingly haunted places and propitious places for the practice of the higher tantras.

eight worldly concerns (*'jig rten chos brgyad*). Concern with various kinds of pleasure and displeasure, specifically gain and loss, pleasure and pain, praise and blame, fame and obscurity.

eighteen schools (*nyan thos sde pa bco brgyad*). This is a traditional, convenient enumeration of the various schools of Buddhism prior to the advent of the Mahayana. However the lists for these schools vary considerably, so the number eighteen is unlikely to be exact. They all developed from the initial schism within Buddhism into the Mahāsaṅgika and the more conservative Sthaviravadins. Subsequent schools were often the result of localized development among the widely dispersed sanghas. The Mahayana was a development from *within* these varied schools.

elaboration (*spros pa*, *prapañca*). The tendency of thoughts to multiply in discursive wandering. The Sanskrit word can mean expansion, diffusion, or diversification, and also covers prolixity, creation, and deceit. "Conceptual" is sometimes added to the English to better communicate the meaning.

embellishment (*sgro btags*). Concepts of reification, which conceive something to be other than what it is, such as the assumption of permanence.

emptiness (*stong pa nyid*, *śūnyatā*). The abstract noun from the adjective *empty* (*śūnya*). This concept developed in Mahayana Buddhism to denote the absence of any real nature to phenomena; it is the central philosophical tenet of the Madhyamaka presentation of reality.

factors for enlightenment (*byang chub phyogs kyi chos, bodhipakṣakadharma*). These are thirty-seven aids to enlightenment for śrāvakas, pratyekabuddhas, and bodhisattvas: (1–4) the *four mindfulnesses*, which are of body, sensations, mind, and phenomena; (5–8) the *four eliminations*, which are eliminating the bad that has been created, not creating the bad that has not been created, creating good that has not been created, and increasing what good has been created; (9–12) the *four bases of miracles*, which are aspiration, diligence, contemplation, and analysis; (13–17) the *five powers*, which are faith, diligence, mindfulness, meditation, and wisdom; (18–22) the *five strengths*, which are also faith, diligence, mindfulness, meditation, and wisdom; (23–29) the *seven branches of awakening*, which are mindfulness, wisdom, diligence, joy, being well trained, meditation, and equanimity; and (30–37) the *eight branches of the noble path*, which are right view, thought, speech, effort, livelihood, mindfulness, meditation, and action.

father tantra (*pha rgyud*). The earliest of the higher tantras, principally Guhyasamāja and Yamāntaka. They received this name retrospectively to differentiate them from the later yoginī or mother tantras, in which the role of female deities was more pronounced.

five excellent disciples (*'khor lnga sde bzang po, pañcabhadrapariṣadyā*). The Buddha's first five pupils. They are said to have been his followers while he practiced asceticism but abandoned him when he rejected that path. After his enlightenment, they became his followers once more. They feature in stories of previous lives of the Buddha but do not play a prominent role after this initial year of his teaching.

form realm (*gzugs khams, rūpadhātu*). Seventeen paradises into which beings are born through the power of meditation.

formless realm (*gzugs med khams, arūpadhātu*). Four existences that are states of meditation that a being who dies in one of those four states is born into.

four continents (*gling bzhi*). The four regions surrounding Mount Meru in Abhidharma cosmology that together comprise the inhabited universe. The southern continent, Jambudvīpa, originally referred only to India but came to mean the entire known human world. The other continents or worlds, separated from ours by areas of darkness, are said to be inhabited by distinct races of beings.

four empties (*stong pa bzhi*). Literally, these are empty (*stong pa*), very empty (*shing tu stong pa*), great empty (*stong pa chen po*), and everything empty (*thams cad stong pa*). These are alternative names for appearance, attainment, increase, and luminosity, the visions that arise during the process of death.

four immeasurables (*tshad ma bzhi*). Immeasurable love, compassion, rejoicing and impartiality. *See* brahmavihāra

four stages of the path of engagement (*sbyor lam bzhi*, *catuprayogamārga*). One proceeds through the four stages of the path of engagement as one comes closer to the path of insight, which is also the first stage of the bodhisattvas. The first path of engagement stage is *heat* (*drod*). It is said to be like the heat created when sticks are rubbed together, which presages the appearance of the fire. In the same way, there is here, through mental stability and realization, the omen of the coming "fire" of the wisdom on the path of seeing. The second stage is *summit* (*rtse mo*), when one's good karma or virtue becomes perfected. The third stage is *patience* (*bzod pa*), when one becomes unafraid of one's realization of emptiness. The final and culminative stage is *supreme qualities* (*chos mchog*), when one has attained the highest qualities possible prior to becoming an ārya.

four truths (*'phags pa'i bden pa bzhi*, *catvāri āryasatya*). More fully known as the four truths of the noble ones. These are: the truth of suffering, the truth of the origin of suffering, the truth of cessation of suffering, and the truth of the path to that cessation.

freedoms and opportunities (*dal 'byor*). This refers to the "precious human existence," which is free from eight states that prevent being able to practice the Dharma: being born in hell, as a preta, as an animal, as a long-living deva, in a time when a Buddha has not come, as a "savage" (i.e., in a land without the Dharma), having wrong views, and having impaired faculties. The opportunities are five from oneself: being human, in a land with the Dharma, having all one's faculties, not having done the worst karmic deeds, and having faith. The second five are from others: a Buddha has come, he has taught, the teachings remain, the teachings has followers, and there is a teacher that guides us.

gaṇacakra (*tshogs kyi 'khor lo*). "Circular gathering" is the original meaning, and in India a *gaṇacakra* was held in charnel grounds, with the consumption of the five meats and five nectars. In Tibet, general food and drink are blessed, and the participants, visualized as deities, consume them.

gandharva (*dri za*). Most commonly it means a race of celestial musicians. Literally, however, it means "smell eater," and it is found as the term for the consciousness in between death and birth: the consciousness that enters the womb. The consciousness during that period is said to gain its sustenance from smells.

gandhola (*ghan do ri*). Derived from *gandha* "incense," it means a shrine building that is used primarily for offerings rather than assemblies, such as the Mahābodhi temple in Bodhgaya.

garuda (*khyung*, *garuḍa*). Mythical supreme bird; the enemy of serpents, with a divine semi-human form.

gongpo (*'gong po*). A class of demons who can influence people into doing wrong or becoming obsessed with wealth, power, and so on.

great king (*rgyal chen, mahārāja*). Generally refers to the deities that are kings of the four directions. Their paradises are at the foot of Mount Meru so that each king looks out over one of the four directions.

Guhyapati (*gsang ba'i bdag po*). "Lord of Secrets" is a common alternative name for the deity and bodhisattva Vajrapāṇī (see glossary entry), who is said to have been the compiler of the tantras.

Guhyasamāja (*gsang ba 'dus pa*). Literally, "Secret Assembly"; one of the higher tantric deity practices, and probably the earliest. In later classification it became one of the father tantras.

heruka (*khrag mthung*). The generic name used for Cakrasaṃvara and other higher tantra deities. Like the ḍākinīs, herukas were originally terrifying supernatural creatures of the night, in this case specifically vampires, in that they drank human blood. The name is linguistically of South Indian, not Sanskrit, origin, and the term was translated independently into Chinese and Tibetan as "blood drinker." However, along with the ḍākinī, in the antinomian world of tantra they became embodiments of enlightenment.

Hevajra tantra (*kye rdo rje'i rgyud / brtags gnyis*). There are two separate texts that collectively are called the *Hevajra Tantra*, and as with other tantras, such as the Cakrasaṃvara, the chapters appear to have accumulated over time as a compilation of discrete texts and manuals. The bulk of the tantra is a description of a form of tantric living and practices as were followed in India, much of which is not directly relevant to Tibetan Buddhism.

highest yoga tantra (*bla na med pa'i rgyud, yogānuttaratantra*). One of the terms used for such tantras as Guhyasamāja and Cakrasaṃvara as they began to become prevalent from the eighth century onward. This is in relation to yoga tantras, indicating that they are an advance upon them. These tantras are the pinnacle of the fourfold classification of tantras commonly taught in Tibet, and they also comprise the central diet of most Tibetan Buddhist yogins who do sādhana practice.

Hīnayāna (*theg dman*). The "lesser way," a term that appeared in conjunction with the Mahayana ("great way"). Though *yāna* is more properly "a way," it was translated into Tibetan as *theg pa* meaning "vehicle." Both terms originate in the *Lotus Sutra*, where carriages or vehicles are used as an analogy for the ways, and the Hīnayāna is said to be "lesser" in terms of its goal of individual liberation as opposed to the Mahayana aspiration to emancipate all beings from suffering. The Hīnayāna encompasses both the śrāvaka and pratyekabuddha vehicles.

homa fire ritual (*sbyin bsregs*). The fire offering was a central feature in the traditions based on the Vedas and Brahmanas and had no place in early Buddhism. Well-known pracitioners of homa threw away their implements in a gesture of renunciation on becoming disciples of the Buddha. However in the tantra, the offering to Agni, the deity of fire, is a prelude to offering to the *yidam* deities, and different shapes of hearth, offerings, color of costumes, and so on will bring the accomplishment that is either peaceful, increasing, controlling, or wrathful.

Indra (*dbang po*). Though more commonly referred to in Tibetan as Śatakratu (*brgya byin*), which refers to the hundred Vedic sacrifices he made that gave him the merit to become the king of the devas. In Vedic literature he is the supreme lord of the devas, living on Meru and wielding a thunderbolt. Later, the personification of the universal force Brahman as Brahmā, in a higher paradise above Indra, relegated Indra to second place. During the historical Buddha's time, which was before the rise of Śiva and Viṣṇu, these two deities were the principal deities. In Buddhist cosmology, a number of paradises above Mount Meru came to be envisaged, making Indra even less significant.

Indrabodhi. This is synonymous with Indrabhūti, but it does not refer to only one person. In the Guhyasamāja tradition he is the King of Oddiyāna, who first received these teachings. There was also an Indrabhūti who studied under Tilopa. Another Indrabhūti was the King of Zahor, which is variously identified as the eastern region of present-day Bihar and with the Kangra valley in Northwest India.

innate union (*lhan cig skye sbyor*; *sahajayoga*). Sometimes rendered as "coemergent" or "connate" union, *innate union* means to become united with the natural state that is innate in the mind, or connate with everything that arises within it.

Jambudvīpa (*'dzam bu kling*). The southern continent of the four continents of Buddhist cosmology that surround Mount Meru. The "land of the rose-apple tree" originally designated India alone, but later, in the Indocentric Buddhist cosmology that developed, it came to mean our world.

Kālacakra (*dus kyi 'khor lo*). Literally, "wheel of time," Kālacakra is the latest and the most complex of the Buddhist tantras. It appeared in India sometime around the tenth century. Sometimes, instead of being classed with Cakrasaṃvara and Hevajra as a yoginī or mother tantra, it is given a class of its own: nondual tantra. It is comprehensive in including the other higher tantra deities, and covering also such mundane matters as astrology and military tactics.

Kālaratri (*dus mtshan*). The "night of [the end of] time." One of the fearsome forms of Durga, consort of Śiva, otherwise known as Bhairava. Cakrasaṃvara, who conquered Śiva and took on his form, is portrayed as crushing both Bhairava and Kālaratri underfoot.

Kangyur (*Bka' 'gyur*). A compilation of translations into Tibetan of teachings attributed to the Buddha. There are a number of editions, varying in terms of the quantity and the quality of certain texts, which include Dergé, Narthang, Peking, Lhasa, Coné, Ugra, Phudrak, and Stog Palace.

karma (*las*; honorific *phrin las*). Although it is assigned the root form *kṛ*, "to do," and is cognate with the English "create," it does not mean *activity* or *action* in the general sense of the term as it is also the word used for "ritual." Thus it means an action that has an effect other than the visible present one, so that as well as magical rites, it means any action that has an effect upon one's next life.

kāya (*sku*). A "body" of a buddha that manifests his or her enlightened qualities. Earlier Buddhist texts speak only of two kāyas, a form body (*rūpakāya*) and a formless *dharmakāya*, or "truth body." Later, the form body was divided into two to produce the well-known classification the three kāyas of a buddha: saṃbhogakāya, nirmāṇakāya, and dharmakāya. One also finds additional divisions to produce lists of four or five kāyas.

khaṭvāṅga. A trident held by wrathful meditational deities such as Vajrayoginī.

kīla (*phur bu*). A stake with three sharp edges for destroying the three principal poisons. Associated particularly with Vajrakīla, kīlas were used in ancient Indian rituals as pegs in the ground around a ritual site.

kiṃnara (*mi'am ci*). A classes of nonhuman beings usually portrayed as having animal heads, such as of a horse, and being master musicians.

knowing (*rig pa, vidyā*). Vidyā is the general name for knowledge, as in branches of knowledge and the mind's cognition in general, but gains deeper meaning by context, especially the nonconceptual knowing nature of the mind.

kṣatriya (*rgyal rigs*). One of the four classes of India. This upper class is roughly equivalent to the nobility, providing secular rulers and warriors. According to Buddhist mythology buddhas appear in the dominant class of its time; thus Śakyamuni was a kṣatriya while the previous and next buddhas are brahmans.

Kuru (*sgra mi snyan*). One of the four continents (see entry). The Tibetan translation means "unpleasant sound," referring to a myth that all the beings in Kuru live for a fixed age of a hundred years, at the end of which they hear the "unpleasant sound" of a voice announcing their imminent death.

level (*sa, bhūmi*). The graduated levels of enlightenment that a bodhisattva passes through to attain buddhahood, most often enumerated as ten. They usually refer to the different levels of an enlightened bodhisattva, but they can also include the level of buddhahood and two levels that correspond to the paths of accumulation and engagement.

luminosity (*'od gsal, Prabhāsvara*). The Tibetan means "clear light," whereas the Sanskrit may more correctly be translated as "brightness." Luminosity is too soft a word, but it has gained common usage to describe this vivid aspect of the nature of the mind in contradistinction to its emptiness.

Madhyamaka (*dbu ma*). "Middle Way." Here it does not mean the middle way between asceticism and hedonism as propounded in early Buddhism but the middle way between existence and nonexistence, particularly as advanced in the philosophical tradition descending from Nāgārjuna. Schools of Tibetan Buddhism differ on the exact interpretation of the Madhyamaka view, but the Kagyü school takes literally the teaching that all phenomena are neither existent nor nonexistent.

Mādhyamika (*dbu ma pa*). A follower of the Madhyamaka.

Mahayana (*theg chen, mahāyāna*). The "Great Way" or the "Great Vehicle," a term that is first propagated by the *Lotus Sutra* to demonstrate the superiority of itself but later used retrospectively on various earlier sutras. The Sanskrit word predominantly means "way," but the Tibetan translation has favored the meaning "vehicle." In India, the Mahayana was not a discrete school of Buddhism but was comprised of a wide variety of teachings that appeared *within* the existing traditions. The Mahayana is characterized primarily by altruistic aspiration and vast activities of its bodhisattva ideal, but it came to be associated particularly with the Cittamātra and Madhyamaka philosophical schools.

Maitreya (*byams pa*). The bodhisattva in Tuṣita paradise who will be the next Buddha in a time when the human lifespan has increased to twenty thousand years.

Maitreyanātha (*byams pa mgon po*). The five texts attributed to him are held in great reverence and are precursors to the philosophy developed and propounded by Asaṅga and Vasubandhu and their Cittamātra tradition.

mandala (*dkyil 'khor*; *maṇḍala*). This may refer to any circle or circular arrangement, but in Buddhism it most frequently refers to an arrangement of deities, with a central deity in the center and including the palace they are situated within and around. Three dimensional representations of these are made, but more familiar is a two-dimensional diagram, that uses certain established procedures for representing three dimensions. These diagrams are intended as aids for the visualization of the deities and palaces and are not themselves the objects of meditation, apart from when they serve as the locus for the deity in empowerments.

Mañjuśrī (*'jam dpal*) also known as Mañjugoṣa (*'jam dbyangs*). The bodhisattva of wisdom, and in the early tantras the head of one of the three buddha families.

Mañjuśrīkīrti. Son of the seventh Dharma king of Shambhala, he was an emanation of Mañjuśrī.

Mantrayāna (*gsang sngags theg pa*). The "way of mantra"; a synonym for tantra, the esoteric vehicle of Mahayana Buddhism.

Māra (*bdud*). The Sanskrit literally means "death." In the early sutras Māra is a deity that continually tries to stop the Buddha's enlightenment and the spread of his teachings. Māra has also been portrayed as the personification of obstacles to enlightenment, as in the list of *four māras*: the māra of the body, the māra of the defilements, the māra of death, and the divine māra (the distraction of pleasures). The Tibetan translation of *māra* (*bdud*) is also the name for a class of Tibetan local deities that can function as protectors.

matrikas (*ma mo*, *mātṛkā*). Most commonly a reference to a class of female deities. A group of eight matrikas were in particular worshiped in north India and also make their appearance in Buddhist tantra, though such a popular tradition never existed in Tibet. Although important in the Indian tantric traditions, in Tibet they have lost much of their distinctiveness and are barely distinguishable from ḍākinīs. Nevertheless, appeasing angered matrikas, and requesting their forgiveness and protection, is a regular part of protection rituals.

meditation and post-meditation (*mnyam bzhags* and *rjes thob*; *samāhita* and *pṛṣthalabdha*). *Samāhita* is actually the past participle of the verb *samādha* from which comes the noun *samādhi* and is likewise a general name for a state of meditation. *Pṛṣthalabdha* or *rjes thob* is literally "post-accomplishment" but rendered here as post-meditation. The "accomplishment" refers to the accomplishment of meditation and so refers to the period when, having obtained those qualities, they are put to use in daily life by teaching and benefiting beings. In Tibet, the word was also interpreted to mean the accomplishment of realization while not in a meditation session.

mother tantras (*ma rgyud*). With the development of higher yoga tantras, classifications arose to distinguish newer tantras from their predecessors. The stress on the female deities in such tantras as Cakrasaṃvara resulted in their being termed yoginī tantras. A later classification, which has become dominant in the Tibetan tradition, names this group mother tantras to contrast with Guhyasamāja and Yamāntaka, which are classed as father tantras. The mother tantras are traditionally said to stress wisdom while the father tantras stress method.

Mount Meru (*rib bo mchog rab*). This mountain is the center of the flat disc of the world according to classical Buddhist cosmology.

nāda (*nā da*). Literally, "sound," it is pure sound as an expression of ultimate truth or emptiness and is also symbolized by the attenuated flickering line rising from the *anusvāra*.

nāga (*klu*). Literally "cobra." The worship of the cobra as divine was an important part of Indian culture and remains particularly strong in southern India. They are considered to have a divine form and to live in an underground world, and as they appear everywhere during monsoons (in fact because their nests flood and they are driven up into such places as human habitations), they were considered to control the rains. Also skin illnesses, which can resemble snakeskin, were considered to be caused by the cobra, and therefore in Tibet nāgas are considered responsible for illnesses such as leprosy. In China nāgas were identified with dragons, while Tibet identified them as river deities (*klu*) whose homes are under the ground where springs are located. Nevertheless the cobra element remains as part of their identities, and they are still called "hood endowed," referring to the cobra's flattened neck or hood.

Nāgārjuna (*klu sgrub*). Usually, this refers to the first Madhyamaka philosopher, who lived around the second century before the Mahayana arose as a distinct identity, but there are other authors of the same name, paricularly a tenth-century author of tantric works. The Tibetan tradition assumes all Nāgārjunas to be one author.

nirmāṇakāya (*sprul pa'i sku*). One of the two form bodies (*rūpakāya*) of a buddha. The "emanation body" is the form of a buddha that appears in this world, perceivable by other beings, in contradistinction to the *saṃbhogakāya*, which can only be seen by enlightened beings. Together these are classed as the "form body" of a buddha. The idea of nirmāṇakāya was also extended to emanations that are not obviously a buddha: seemingly ordinary beings, animals, and even matter, such as bridges, boats, food, or whatever would assist beings. The Tibetan term has also become institutionalized to mean anyone who is recognized as the rebirth of a lama.

Nirmāṇarati. "The enjoyment of emanations." The fifth of the six paradises within the realm of desire, according to the Abhidharma.

nirvana (*mya ngan las 'das pa*; *nirvāṇa*). Nirvana comes from the term "to blow out," as in extinguishing a candle, and therefore means "extinguishment" or even "extinction" in the sense of ending the succession of lifetimes and their cause. The Tibetan interpretative translation means "transcending samsara."

objectlessness (*mi dmigs pa*, *dmigs pa med pa*; *anupalabdhi* or *anupalambha*). Literally "nonperception." This is also translated as "nonreferentiality." It is in effect a synonym for emptiness.

Oḍḍiyāna (*O rgyan*). This land where the tantras were promulgated and preserved—which is also called the land of ḍākinīs—has a quasi-mythical status in relation to the Tibetan tradition. It has, however, been identified as the ancient Buddhist kingdom of Udyana in the Swat Valley of northwest Pakistan, though there is no evidence for the practice of higher tantras there. More recent research has brought attention to the region of Orissa (renamed Odisha in November 2010) on the eastern coast of India, which has had a number of variant names but was known as Oḍḍiyāna up to at least the fourteenth century. It was a center for the practice of the higher tantras and was the region where many Buddhist tantras, such as Kalācakra, originated. Lake Chilika, the second largest lagoon in the world, matches the legend of Oḍḍiyāna's lake.

paṇḍita. A title given to an individual recognized for his or her learning. It has entered the English language as pundit, which is the Hindi form.

Paranirmitavaśavarta (*gzhan 'phrul dbang byed*). The paradise ruled by Māra at the apex of the desire realm. The name of the paradise, which means "control over the emanations of others," reveals its superiority over the paradise below, where beings can create miraculous manifestations but not control those of others.

Perfection Vehicle (*phar phyin theg pa, pāramitāyāna*). "The yāna of the [six] perfections" is an alternative name for the Mahayana's sutra tradition.

perfections (*parāmita, pha rol tu phyin pa*). *See* six perfections

performance tantra (*spyod rgyud, caryā*). These are texts and practices based upon the *Mahāvairocana Sutra*, popularly known as the *Mahāvairocana Tantra*. This is important for the Chinese and Japanese tantric traditions. In contemporary Tibetan Buddhism, performance tantra is primarily represented by the practice of Sarvavid Vairocana but is considered inferior in praxis and view to the higher tantras.

piśāca (*sha za*). A class of demons, dating back to the Vedas, whose name is derived either from their yellow color (*pīta*) or their appetite for flesh (*piśa*). The Tibetan translates according to the latter meaning, rendering the term as "flesh eaters," although there is no direct correlation in Tibet's own culture.

pramāṇa (*tshad ma*). "Validity": the study of logic and epistemology, or "valid cognition."

prajñā's wisdom (*shes rab ye shes*). Although *prajñā* is usually translated as wisdom, and *jnāna* is synonymous with it, *prajñā-jñāna* in the context of an empowerment is a reference to the consort, who is referred to as *prajñā*. This is the third empowerment, in which one gains wisdom through union with the consort.

prāṇa (*srog rlung*). This can mean simply "breath," but it never means "air" in general as *vāyu* can mean. It is associated with the principle of life and so was translated into Tibetan as "life air." This has been used as a back translation for *rlung* in general, though technically it is specifically one of the five principal winds.

prāṇāyāma (*srog rtsol*). "Restraining or controlling the breath." This refers to specific breathing practices, primarily involving breath retention. The Tibetan is literally "life effort," referring to the deliberate control of the "life" breath.

pratyekabuddha (*rang rgyal*). In early Buddhism, in contrast to those who were "disciples" (*śrāvaka*), these individuals attained buddhahood not with a teacher but through contemplation of the remains of humans in charnel grounds and so on. In the Mahayana tradition in India there was disagreement as to whether their attainment equaled that of the Buddha. In present-day Tibetan Buddhism, the differing views continue, with the Kagyü, for example, declaring that their realization is less than that of a buddha, while Gelukpas state that while the realization is the same, they lack the compassionate activity for others.

preta (*yi dwags*). One of the six classes of existence, these beings suffer from continuous hunger and thirst. The Sanskrit literally means "departed" and is inspired by the *pitṛ*, or ancestral spirits of India, who, without descendants to make the regular traditional offerings to them, are tormented by hunger and thirst.

primary and secondary signs. These are the signs, or marks, of a great being. There are thirty-two primary and eighty secondary features. The Buddha is said to have had all these features, such as the mark of wheels on the soles of his feet. There were also 216 birthmarks that were considered as "auspicious signs." In the Vajrayāna, they are said to be possessed by all the deities.

propensity (*bag chags, vāsana*). The Sanskrit term is derived from a scent or smell left behind and therefore has the meaning of a trace or impression. The Tibetan has an emphasis on habitual action, or even the apparently instinctive, such as the first actions of a newborn animal. It can also have the meaning of a seed, a latent tendency to act in a certain way, or even, in the Mind Only school, that which causes one's apparently external experiences, as these are said to arise entirely from one's own mind.

purapraveśa (*grong 'jug*). Literally "entering a town," it was also known as *parakāyapravesha* (*gzhan gyi lus la 'jug pa*), "entering another's body." This was a practice designed so that one could transfer one's consciousness into another vacated body, either temporarily or for a lifetime within that body.

quintessence. *See* bindu; tilaka

rākśasa (*srin po*). A class of demons in Indian culture, and though there are various types of them, the most known are the ferocious man-eating kind.

rishi (*drang srong, ṛṣi*). This well-known Indian title originally referred to someone who had received a revelation from the deities of a divine scripture. The term later became one of general respect to a religious master, including the Buddha. The Tibetan translation is "straight," meaning an unwavering mind.

Rudra (*ru dra*). The name first appears in Indian literature in the Vedas as the deity of the jungles, outside civilization. He became a principal deity much later and eventually, under the name of Śiva, one of the most important deities in India today. The tantric deity Cakrasaṃvara is said to destroy Rudra/Śiva, but then adopts his body, sacred sites, and so on. In Tibet, Rudra is most often used as the symbol of powerful, self-fixated, deviant mind.

sādhana (*sgrub thabs*). The term may denote "accomplishment" or the "method of accomplishment," which is the way it is translated into Tibetan. It can refer to any method of practice, usually of a deity, and by association it can mean the liturgical text used in the practice of meditation on a deity that describes the visualizations, mantras, offerings, prayers, and meditations to be performed.

sage (*thub pa*; *muni*). Synonym for buddha. In contrast with rishis, who had received their knowledge through divine revelation, *munis* and buddhas understood deeper meanings within the Vedic rituals from their own understanding. While *buddha* has the meaning "awakened," *muni* has more of the meaning of "inspired." The Tibetan translation literally means "able one."

Śākyamuni (*shā kya thub pa*). The Buddha, the "sage of the Śākyas." As the Buddha was from the Śākya clan and had gained enlightenment through his own contemplation, he became known as the muni of Śākya, or Śākyamuni.

samādhi (*ting nge 'dzin*). This could literally be translated as "concentration," meaning when the mind is completely focused. It therefore refers to a state of meditation free from distraction.

samādhi being (*ting 'dzin sems dpa', samādhisattva*). In deity meditation, the *samādhi being* is the insignia and/or syllable in the deity's heart, symbolizing its essence, as opposed to the form, and is so named because that is what the mind concentrates upon during the practice.

samayasattva (*dam tshig sems dpa'*). *See* commitment being

saṃbhogakāya (*long spyod rdzogs pa'i sku*). A later subdivision of the form body of a buddha, which in earlier Buddhism meant solely the physical presence of the Buddha in this world. As Mahayana and later tantric literature were derived primarily from visions, these immaterial manifestations became an additional subdivision of the form body. As these beings were free of any of the failings of a human body, such as the sickness, aging, and death that afflicted the buddha's form body, they were known as "bodies of complete enjoyment" [of the qualities of buddhahood]. This was then an essential category for establishing the canonical nature of these later teachings.

Sarma (*gsar ma*). Literally "new," this contrasts with the "old" or Nyingma (*rnying ma*) tradition, which has its origins in the first introduction of Buddhism to Tibet in the seventh and particularly eighth centuries. The Sarma traditions are based on teachings that were brought to Tibet from the eleventh century onward, beginning with the translations of Lotsāwa Rinchen Sangpo.

Sautrantika (*mdo sde pa*). The "followers of the sutras," an Indian Buddhist tradition that rejected the canonical status of the Abhidharma. This tradition, like the Vaibhāṣikas, was within the Sarvastivāda school and continued developing through the first millennium.

scriptural baskets (*sde snod, piṭaka*). The separate collections of the Buddha's teachings, originally Sutra, Vinaya, and Mātṛka. The latter evolved into the Abhidharma, although the Tibetan tradition, following the Sautrāntika view on the noncanonical status of the Abhidharma texts, does not have an Abhidharma section in the Kangyur.

self-knowing (*rang rig, svasaṃvedyā*). This can sometimes mean just one's own personal knowledge or perception. It is also particularly used, as in the Mind Only tradition, for consciousness perceiving itself.

sense bases. *See* āyatanas

sevā (*bsnyen pa*). This term is difficult to translate due to its multiple meanings, which include "worship," "attendance," "service," and even "approach," a literal rendering of the Tibetan. It primarily refers to the practice of reciting a great number of mantras in conjunction with meditation on a specific deity. This is understood as both a process of familiarization to bring one's mind closer to the deity and thus to the nature of one's own mind and, in a dualistic sense, a propitiation of the deity. In the more dualistic approach of the lower tantras, this propitiation of the deity ultimately results in the deity's appearance to the devotee to grant a boon or siddhi.

Siddhārtha (*don yod grub pa*). The Buddha's personal name. It means literally "goal accomplished."

six existences (*rigs drug*). The six types of existence in samsara are rebirth as a hell being, preta, animal, human, asura, or deva.

six perfections (*phar phyin drug, saṭpāramitā*). The six central practices of a bodhisattva on the Mahayana path: the perfections of generosity, good conduct, patience, diligence, meditation, and wisdom. The Tibetan for *pāramitā* literally means "gone to the other shore" (*pha rol tu phyin pa*).

śrāvaka (*nyan thos*). "Disciple." The word is derived from the verb "to study" and also "to hear," and the Tibetan translation is "one who listens and hears." This general term was used in contrast with those who attained enlightenment without a teacher, the pratyekabuddha, with whom the śrāvaka exemplifies the Hīnayāna. In early Buddhism the path of the śrāvaka was the direct path to liberation, while a bodhisattva, committed to becoming a buddha and not just free of samsara, had to accumulate merit for many eons.

Śrāvaka Vehicle (*nyan thos theg pa, śrāvakayāna*). "The way of the disciples," a term that is often used as a synonym for the Hīnayāna in contrast with the Bodhisattva Vehicle of the Mahayana.

ten strengths. A buddha has the following ten strengths: (1) the knowledge of what is appropriate and inappropriate, (2) the knowledge of the results of karma, (3) the knowledge of the variety of aspirations, (4) the knowledge of various natures, (5) the knowledge of various capabilities, (6) the knowledge of all paths, (7) the knowledge of the different kinds of meditation, (8) the knowledge of previous lives, (9) the knowledge of deaths and rebirths, (10) the knowledge of the cessation of impurity.

Tengyur (*bstan 'gyur*). The Tibetan canon of translations of commentaries on the Buddha's teachings. It also includes some non-Buddhist works of literature on subjects outside the scope of Buddhist practice, such as astrology, medicine, grammar, and prosody.

terma (*gter ma*). From the word for "treasure," *gter*, termas are discovered teachings, either practices concealed in the mind during a previous life or texts, artifacts, and substances discovered in physical form.

three poisons (*dug gsum*). An expression apparently Tibetan in origin, it is synonymous with the three afflictions of ignorance, attachment, and aversion.

three realms (*khams gsum, traidhātu*). The desire realm, form realm, and formless realm. The desire realm includes all the six existences including some of the devas, such as those in the Tuṣita and Trāyastriṃśa paradises. The form-realm devas are more subtle in their forms and longer lived, and find their abode in the paradise of Akaniṣṭha. Beings in the formless realm have no bodies and rest for thousands of eons in blissful samādhi.

tilaka (*thig le*). The Tibetan uses the term *thig le* for both *tilaka* and *bindu*, both of which can mean mark, spot, dot, or circle. Both terms were and still are used in India to denote a forehead mark, and in English are called *tilak* and *bindi*. The *tilaka* in particular is a traditional Indian mark worn on the forehead by religious devotees and is associated with enlightenment, but in Tibet its application normally occurs only in the context of some higher tantra empowerments. *Bindu* has a wider meaning than *tilaka*, but they both have the connotation of an essential point, a quintessence, and may be rendered here also as "drop." See the *bindu* entry for additional meanings.

tīrthikas (*mu stegs pa*). The Tibetan has taken the etymology inventively to mean "those who ascend on the margin" and uses it to refer to non-Buddhists, but those in the Indian tradition only. The phrase in its original form refers solely to the Jains.

torma (*gtor ma, bali*). *Torma* is Tibetan for a ritual offering cake usually made of barley flour and butter and often elaborately designed and subject to detailed explanations. The Indian precedent, the *bali*, was simply a baked circle of bread, and so the uses of the word *torma* in English translations of the canon are somewhat anachronistic. However, they can be taken in a general sense to mean a ritual food offering.

Trāyastriṃśa. "Thirty-three" paradise. Situated upon the summit of Meru, it is the realm of Indra. The name "thirty-three" alludes to the number of deities living in that paradise.

treatise (*bstan bco*; *śāstra*). A general term for any work by a Buddhist author, in contrast to the sutras and tantras attributed to the Buddha himself.

triple aspects of conceptualization (*'khor gsum*; *trimaṇḍala*). The concepts of one who does an action, the action itself, and the object of the action. See p. 178.

Tuṣita (*dga' ldan*). Originally only vaguely described as a "pleasant" paradise, it became in early Buddhist cosmology a specific paradise high above Mount Meru. In the development of the Maitreya myth, it became his residence while he waits for the time of his descent into this world as the next Buddha.

twenty-four sites (*gnas nyi shu tsa bzhi, pīṭha*). Originally a part of Śaivite lore. These are the sacred places where various parts of Sati's body fell as Śiva carried it through the sky. With the defeat and adoption of Śiva's body by Heruka, thus creating Cakrasaṃvara, he inherited all these sacred places, which play an important role in the Cakrasaṃvara literature and are also correlated with sites within the human body's network of channels and winds.

two accumulations (*tshogs gnyis*). The dualistic accumulation of merit and the nondual "accumulation" of wisdom.

two obscurations (*sgrib gnyis*). The obscuration formed by the defilements and the obscuration of knowledge, the last being named according to what is obscured rather than by the cause of obscuration: the subtlest level of ignorance.

utpala. Transliterated into Tibetan as there was no equivalent Tibetan word, in India it has been used for a variety of flowers, but in Tibet it is usually taken to refer to the blue lotus (*Nymphaea caerulea*).

vacana (*gsungs*). "Speech." *Buddhavacana*, the "word of the Buddha," is the term for the texts represented in the Kangyur. Although all these teachings are not represented as being taught by him directly, they nevertheless express his viewpoint.

Vāḍabāgni. A mythical mountain of fire believed to exist within the southern ocean.

Vaibhāṣika (*bye brag tu smra ba*). Followers of a tradition based on a text commonly referred to as the *Vibhāsa*, which was a compilation of Abhidharma teachings.

vaiśya. The third of the four classes of Indian society; this is the merchant class and was the most important strata of society as a source for followers of Buddhism and Jainism.

vajra (*rdo rje*). The word *vajra* refers to the "thunderbolt," the indestructible and irresistible weapon that first appears in Indian literature in the hand of the Vedic deity Indra. In Tibetan Buddhism, *vajra* is most often used as a modifier to indicate something related to the tantric path, as it symbolizes the swiftness and power of that path and the indestructibility of its animating reality, the dharmakāya.

vajra body (*rdo rje'i sku, vajrakāya*). The physical body of a buddha.

Vajraḍākinī. *See* Vajravārāhī

Vajradhara (*rdo rje 'chang*). The enlightened saṃbhogakāya identity in which the Buddha is said to have taught the tantras. In the Kagyü tradition he is also the personification of the dharmakāya, and the source from which the saṃbhogakāya deities manifest.

Vajrapāṇi (*phyag na rdo rje*). Vajrapāṇi is a wrathful deity that first appears in Buddhist literature as a bodyguard of the Buddha. With the rise of the Mantrayāna, he is promoted to the level of bodhisattva, and his presence in the audience of the Buddha's teachings is an indication that the sutra or tantra contains mantras.

Vajravārāhī (*rdo rje phag mo*). Vajravārāhī, also known as Vajrayoginī, rises to prominence within the Cakrasaṃvara literature. There she is both that deity's consort and features as the central deity in a number of practices. Instead of having a sow's head, as in the goddess Vārāhī, she is sometimes depicted with a sow emerging from the top of her head, its grunt destroying ignorance. She is also the principal deity within the Karma Kagyü tradition.

Vajrayāna (*rdo rje theg pa*). The "Vajra Vehicle" is the path of tantra, and is synonomous with the Mantrayāna.

Vārāṇasī. The oldest city of northeast India on the Gangetic plain, once the capital of its own small kingdom and known by various names. It was a religious center even during the time of the Buddha.

vidyā (*rig pa*). The term *vidyā* can be interpreted as knowledge, a magical spell or mantra, or even as a consort (in which case it is translated into Tibetan as *rig ma*). *See also* knowing.

vidyādhara (*rig 'dzin*). *Vidyādhara*, or "knowledge holder," became in Tibetan an honorific address for a tantric master.

Vinaya (*'dul ba*). The section of the Buddhist canon containing the rules governing the monastic communities and the extensive narrative literature that surrounds that code of conduct. The Tibetan collection of texts under this rubric contain all the sutras of early Buddhism, which in earlier collections form the sutra collection.

Viṣṇu (*khyab 'jug*). One of the central gods in the Hindu pantheon today. He had not yet risen to an important status during the Buddha's lifetime and only developed his own significant following in the early years of the common era.

vrata (*brtul zhugs*). The Sanskrit *vrata* simply means a "vow," but it is commonly used in Hinduism and Jainism to refer to the practice of fasting. The Tibetan means "entering into subjugation" and could be translated as "discipline," but the term is associated most often with extraordinary behavior that is the very opposite of what we think of as discipline. In that context, it is defined as subjugating *ordinary* conduct and entering into *extraordinary* conduct. This may entail living in a charnel ground, for instance, or engaging in various kinds of unpredictable behavior.

wind (*rlung, vāyu*). The word *vāyu* can mean air or wind, or even the god of the air. In the context of the higher tantras it can simultaneously mean the external element of air, the breath, and the winds or energies that flow through the body that cause digestion, defecation, and so on. These grosser winds can be transformed into wisdom winds thorugh completion-stage practices.

wisdom being (*ye shes sems dpa'; jñānasattva*). In deity meditation, the wisdom being is the actual deity itself, which is imagined to blend with the visualized deity in order to inspire the confidence that one actually is the deity.

yakṣa (*gnod sbyin*). Feminine: *yakṣī* or *yakṣiṇī*. A class of supernatural beings, often represented as the attendants of the god of wealth, but the term is also applied to spirits. Though generally portrayed as benevolent, the Tibetan translation means "harm giver," as they are also capable of causing harm.

Yamāntaka (*gshin rje gshed*). "Slayer of Death." This tantra has been retrospectively classed, along with the Guhyasāmaja, as a father tantra. More than in other tantras, there is an emphasis on the power and efficacy of sorcery practices in Yamāntaka literature. Also known as Vajrabhairava, he is considered the wrathful from of Mañjuśrī.

yidam deity (*yi dam*). The Tibetan meaning is "commitment" but refers more accurately to the deity to which one has a commitment. The Sanskrit equivalent, *iṣṭadeva* or *iṣṭadevatā*, means "desired deity," emphasizing one's attraction to or choice of a deity.

yoga (*rnal 'byor*). Cognate with the English *yoke*, it has the meaning of "union." The Tibetan translated it as "united" (*'byor*) with the natural state (*rnal*). It is also glossed as the active form *sbyor ba*, which conveys such meanings as "application," "practice," and "endeavor."

yoga tantras (*rnal 'byor rgyud*). This is the third of the four classes of tantras following the action (*kriyā*) and performance (*caryā*) tantras. *Compendium of Truths*, the principal yoga tantra, presented itself as a method for liberation, unlike the earlier practices that used ritual and mantra for worldly goals.

Yogācāra (*rnal sbyor spyod pa*). This is synonymous with Cittamātra, the tradition based on the teachings of Maitryanātha, Asaṅga, and Vasubandhu, with an emphasis on all phenomena as being a mental experience. It remains a strong influence on the Kagyü tradition. *See also* Cittamātra

yoginī (*rnal 'byor ma*). Though a term for a female practitioner, particularly a practitioner of the higer tantras, it is also applied for the nonhuman tantric females in a manner synonymous with ḍākinī.

yojana. The longest unit of distance in classical India. The lack of a uniform standard for the smaller units means that there is no precise equivalent, especially as its theoretical length tended to increase over time. Therefore it can be between four and ten miles.

Bibliography

Works Cited in the Texts

Kangyur and Nyingma Gyübum (Canonical Scriptures)

Abbreviated Perfection of Wisdom in Verse. *Prajñāpāramitāsañcayagāthā*. *She rab kyi pha rol tu phyin pa sdud pa tshigs su bcad pa*. Toh 13, sher phyin *ka*. 1b1–19b7.

Aphorisms. *Udānavarga*. *Ched du brjod pa'i tshoms*. Toh 326, mdo sde *sa*. 209b–253a7.

Applications of Mindfulness. *Smṛtyupasthāna*. *Dam chos dran pa nye bzhag*. Toh 287, mdo sde *ya* 82a1–*sha* 229b7.

Avataṃsaka Sutra. *Avataṃsakasūtra*. *Sangs rgyas phal po che zhes bya ba shin tu rgyas pa chen po'i mdo*. Toh 44, phal chen *ka*. 1b1–363a6. Translated from the Chinese in Cleary 1984.

Bringing Out the Hidden Meaning Sutra. *Saṃdhinirmocanasūtra*. *Dgongs pa nges par 'grel pa*. Toh 106, mdo sde *ca*. 1b1–55b7.

Buddhakapāla Tantra. *Buddhakapālatantra*. *Sangs rgyas thod pa zhes bya ba'i rnal 'byor ma'i rgyud*. Toh 424, rgyud *nga*. 143a1–167a5.

Cakrasaṃvara Tantra of the Inconceivable Secret. *Cakrasaṃvaraguhyācintyatantra*. *'Khor lo sdom pa gsang ba bsam gyis mi khyab pa'i rgyud kyi rgyal po*. Toh 385, rgyud *ga*. 196a1–199a1.

Casket of Jewels Sutra. *Ratnakaraṇḍasūtra*. *Dkon mchog gi za ma tog yi mdo*. Toh 117, mdo sde *ja*. 248a1–290a7.

Compendium of All Vajra Wisdom Tantra. *Vajrajñānasamuccayatantra*. *Ye shes rdo rje kun las btus pa zhes bya ba'i rgyud*. Toh 447, rgyud *ca*. 282a1–286a6.

Compendium of Truths (*of All Tathāgathas Sutra*). *Tattvasaṃgraha* (*Sarvatath āgatatattvasaṃgrahasūtra*). *De bzhin gshegs pa thams cad kyi de kho na nyid bsdus pa'i mdo*. Toh 479, rgyud *nya*. 1b1–142a7. For the Sanskrit see *Digital Sanskrit Buddhist Canon*.

Dhārāṇi of Entering Nonthought. *Avikalpapraveśadhāraṇī*. *Rnam par mi rtog par 'jug pa'i gzungs*. Toh 142, mdo sde *pa*. 1b1–6b1.

Densely Arrayed Adornments Sutra. *Ghanavyūhasūtra*. *Rgyan stug po bkod pa'i mdo*. Toh 110, mdo sde *cha*. 1b1–55b7.

Display of the Qualities of Mañjuśrī's Buddha Realm. Mañjuśrībuddhakṣetraguṇavyūhasūtra. 'Jam dpal gyi sangs rgyas kyi zhing gi yon tan bkod pa'i mdo. Toh 59, dkon brtsegs *ga.* 248b1–297a3. Chapter 15 of *Ratnakūṭa Sutra* collection.

Eight-Thousand-Verse Perfection of Wisdom Sutra. Aṣṭasāhasrikāprajñāpāramitā. Shes rab pha rol tu phyin pa brgyad stong pa. Toh 12, sher phyin *ka.* 1b1–286a6. For the Sanskrit see *Digital Sanskrit Buddhist Canon.*

Eighteen-Thousand-Verse Perfection of Wisdom Sutra. Aṣṭādaśasāhasrikāprajñāpāramitā. Toh 10, sher phyin *ka* 1b1–*ga* 206a7.

Enlightenment of Vairocana. Mahāvairocanābhisambodhi. Rnam par snang mdzad chen po mngon par rdzogs par byang chub pa rnam par sprul pa byin gyis rlob pa shin tu rgyas pa mdo sde'i dbang po'i rgyal po. Toh 494, rgyud *tha.* 151b2–260a7. Translated in Hodge 2003.

Entry into Laṅka Sutra. Laṅkāvatārasūtra. Lang kar gshegs pa'i mdo. Toh 107, mdo sde *ca.* 56a1–191b7.

Excellent Accomplishment Tantra. Susiddhikaratantra. Legs par grub par byed pa'i rgyud chen po las sgrub pa'i thabs rim par phye ba. Toh 807, rgyud *wa.* 168a1–222b7.

Four Seats Tantra. Caturpīṭhatantra. Rnal 'byor ma'i rgyud kyi rgyal po chen po dpal gdan bzhi pa. Toh 428, rgyud *nga.* 181a1–231b5.

Great Drum Sutra. Mahābherīsūtra. Rnga bo che chen po'i le'u. Toh 222, mdo sde *dza.* 84b5–126b7.

Great Power Sutra. Mahābalasūtra. Stobs po che. Toh 947, gzungs 'dus *waṃ.* 30b5–41a7.

Guhyasamāja Root Tantra. Guhyasamājatantra. De bzhin gshegs pa thams cad kyi sku gsung thugs kyi gsang chen gsang ba 'dus pa. Toh 442, rgyud *ca.* 90a1–148b6.

Heart Sutra. Bhagavatīprajñāpāramitāhṛdaya. Bcom ldan 'das ma shes rab kyi pha rol tu phyin pa'i snying po. Toh 531, rgyud *na.* 94b1–95b3. For the Sanskrit see *Digital Sanskrit Buddhist Canon,* tantra section.

Hevajra Tantra. Hevajratantra. Kye'i rdo rje zhes bya ba rgyud kyi rgyal po. Toh 417, rgyud *nga.* 1b1–13b5.

Kāśyapa Chapter. Kāśyapaparivartasūtra. 'Od srungs gis zhus pa lung bstan pa mdo; Toh 87, dkon brtsegs *cha.* 119b1–151b7. Chapter 43 of the *Ratnakuṭa Sutra* collection.

King of Meditations Sutra. Samādhirājasūtra. Ting nge 'dzin rgyal po'i mdo. Toh 127, mdo sde *da.* 1b1–170b7.

Latter Definition Tantra. Abhidhānottaratantra. Mngon par brjod pa'i rgyud bla ma. Toh 369, rgyud *ka.* 247a1–370a7.

Latter Guhyasamāja Tantra. [*Guhyasamāja*] *Uttaratantra. Rgyud phyi ma.* Toh 443, rgyud *ca.* 90a1–157b7.

Lotus of Compassion Sutra. Karuṇāpuṇḍarīkasūtra. Snying rje chen po'i pad ma dkar po. Toh 111, mdo sde *cha.* 56a1–128b7.

Lotus Sutra. See *White Lotus of the Holy Dharma Sutra*

Mahāmudrā Tilaka Tantra. Mahāmudrātilakatantra. Phyag rgya chen po'i thig le zhes bya ba rnal 'byor ma chen mo'i rgyud kyi rgyal po. Toh 420, rgyud *nga*. 66a1–90b7.

Mañjuśrī Root Tantra. Mañjuśrīmūlatantra. 'Jam dpal gyi rtsa ba'i rgyud. Toh 543, rgyud *na*. 105a1–351a6.

Net of Illusions Tantra. Māyājālatantra. Rgyud kyi rgyal po chen po sgyu 'phrul dra ba. Toh 466, rgyud *ja*. 94b1–134a7.

Ocean of Ḍākas Tantra. Ḍākārṇavatantra. Mkha' 'gro rgya mtsho rnal 'byor ma'i rgyud kyi rgyal po chen po. Toh 372, rgyud *kha*. 137a1–264b7.

Prātimokṣasūtra. So sor thar ba'i mdo. Toh 2, 'dul ba *ca*. 1b1–20b7.

Primordial Buddha Kālacakra Tantra. Paramādibuddhoddhṛtaśrīkālacakratant ra. Mchog gi dang po'i sangs rgyas las phyung ba rgyud kyi rgyal po dpal dus kyi 'khor lo. Toh 362, rgyud *ka*. 22b1–128b7. Also in the Tengyur below. See Henning 2007; Wallace 2001, 2005, and 2009.

Purification of the Lower Existences. Sarvadurgatipariśodhanatantra. De bzhin gshegs pa dgra bcom pa yang dag par rdzogs pa'i sangs rgyas ngan song thams cad yongs su sbyong ba gzi brjid kyi rgyal po'i brtag pa. Toh 483, rgyud *ta*. 58b1–96a3.

Recitation of Mañjuśrī's Names. Mañjuśrīnāmasaṃgiti. 'Jam dpal ye shes sems dpa'i don dam pa'i mtshan yang dag par brjod pa. Toh 360, rgyud *ka*. 1b1–13b7. Narthang: rgyud *ka* 1–18b6. Edition and translation in Wayman 1985.

Rigi Ārali Tantra. Rigyāralitantra. Ri gi ā ra li'i rgyud kyi rgyal po. Toh 427, rgyud *nga*. 176a2–180b7.

Root Kālacakra Tantra. Not extant. Quotations from this are derived from its commentary *Stainless Light* (*Vimalaprabhā*). See entry below under Puṇḍarīka.

Root Tantra of Cakrasaṃvara (*Brief Cakrasaṃvara Tantra*). *Tantrarājaśrīlaghusaṃvara. Rgyud gyi rgyal po dpal bde mchog nung ngu*. Toh 368, rgyud *ka*. 213b1–246b7. Translation can be found in Gray 2007.

Samāyoga Tantra. Samāyogaḍākinījālasaṃvaratantra. Sangs rgyas thams cad dang mnyam par sbyor ba mkha' 'gro ma sgyu ma bde ba'i mchog ces bya ba'i rgyud phyi ma. Toh 366, rgyud *ka*. 151b1–193a6.

Saṃvarodaya Tantra. Saṃvarodayatantra. Bde mchog 'byung ba. Toh 373, rgyud *kha*. 265a1–311a6. Translation of select chapters can be found in Tsuda 1974.

Secret Charnel Ground Tantra. Guhyaśmāśanalalatatantra. De bzhin gshegs pa thams cad kyi sku dang gsung dang thugs kyi gsang ba dur khrod khu byug rol pa'i rgyud. In *Rnying ma'i rgyud 'bum*, vol. 15, pp. 213–321. Thimbu, Bhutan: Dingo Khyentse Rimpoche, 1975.

Secret Essence Tantra. Guhyagarbhatantra. Gsang ba'i snying po de kho na nyid rnam par nges pa. Toh 832, rnying rgyud *kha*. 110b1–132a7.

*Secret Lamp of Wisdom Tantra. Jñānaguhyadīparatnopadeśatantra Ye shes gsang *ba sgron ma man ngag rin po che'i rgyud*. In *Rnying ma'i rgyud 'bum*, vol. 4, pp. 2–24. Thimbu, Bhutan: Dingo Khyentse Rimpoche, 1975.

Seven-Hundred-Verse Perfection of Wisdom. *Saptaśatikāprajñāpāramitāsūtra*. *Shes rab kyi pha rol tu phyin pa bdun brgya pa*. Toh 24, sher phyin *ka*. 148a1–174a2.

Shining Jewel Tantra. *Ratnajvalatantra*. *Rin chen 'bar ba'i rgyud kyi rgyal po*. Toh 396, rgyud *ga*. 224b4–227b2.

Skillful Means Sutra. *Upāyakauśalyasūtra*. *Thabs mkhas pa*. Toh 261, mdo sde *za*. 283b2–310a7. Translated in Tatz 1994.

Stainless Light (by Puṇḍarīka). *Vimalaprabhākālacakratantraṭīkā*. *Bsdus pai rgyud kyi rgyal po dus kyi 'khor lo'i 'grel bshad*. Toh 845, dus 'khor 'grel bshad *śrī*. 1a–355b. Citation references are to the Tengyur volume below under Puṇḍarīka.

Summarized Teaching of the Empowerment. *Śekhoddeśa*. *Dbang mdor bstan pa*. Toh 361, rgyud *ka*. 14a1–21a6.

Sutra of the Excellent Night. *Bhadrakarātrisūtra*. *Mtshan mo bzang po*. Toh 313, mdo sde *sa*. 161b1–163b5.

Sutra of the Good Eon. *Bhadrakalpikasūtra*. *Bskal pa bzang po*. Toh 94, mdo sde *ka*. 1b1–340a5.

Sutra of Mañjuśrī's Dwelling. *Mañjuśrīvihārasūtra*. *'Jam dpal gnas pa*. Toh 196, mdo sde *tsa*. 266b1–271b2.

Sutra of Repaying the Kindness of the Buddha Who Was Skilled in Methods. *Mahopayakauśalyabuddhasūtra*. *Thabs mkhas pa chen po sangs rgyas drin lan bsab pa'i mdo*. Toh 353, mdo sde *aḥ*. 86a2–198b7.

Sutra Requested by Akṣayamati. *Akṣayamatiparipṛcchāsūtra*. *Blo gros mi zad pa*. Toh 89, dkon brtsegs *cha*. 175b2–182b6. Chapter 45 of the *Ratnakūṭa Sutra* collection.

Sutra Requested by Candragarbha. *Candragarbhaparipṛcchāsūtra*. *Zla ba snying pos zhus pa'i mdo*. Toh 356, mdo sde *aḥ*. 216a5–220b5.

Sutra Requested by Gaganagañja. *Gaganagañjaparipṛcchāsūtra*. *Nam mkha' mdzod kyis zhus pa'i mdo*. Toh 148, mdo sde *pa*. 243a1–330a7.

Sutra Requested by Kāśyapa. See *Kāśyapa Chapter*

Sutra Requested by the Nāga King Anavatapta. *Anavataptanagarājaparipṛcchāsūtra*. *Klu'i rgyal po ma dros pas zhus pa*. Toh 156, mdo sde *pha*. 206a1–253b7.

Sutra Requested by the Nāga King Sāgara. *Sāgaranāgarājaparipṛcchāsūtra*. *Klu'i rgyal po rgya mtshos zhus pa*. Toh 153, mdo sde *pha*. 116a1–198a3.

Sutra Requested by Sāgaramati. *Sāgaramatiparipṛcchasūtra*. *Blo gros rgya mtshos zhus pa*. Toh 152, mdo sde *pha*. 1b1–115b7.

Sutra of the Samādhi that Accumulates All Merit. *Sarvapuṇyasamuccayasamādhisūtra*. *Bsod nams thams cad bsdus pa'i ting nge 'dzin*. Toh 134, mdo sde *na*. 70b2–121b7.

Sutra of Samādhi for Four Youths. Caturdārakasamādhisūtra. Khye'u bzhi'i ting nge 'dzin. Toh 136, mdo sde *na.* 144b2–179a4.

Sutra Taught by Akṣayamati. Akṣayamatinirdeśasūtra. Toh 175, mdo sde *ma.* 79a–174b.

Sutra Teaching Bodhisattva Conduct. Bodhisattvacaryānirdeśasūtra. Byang chub sems dpa'i spyod pa bstan pa. Toh 184, mdo sde *tsa.* 96b6–105b7. Narthang: mdo sde *ba,* 153a4–167a2.

Sutra of the Ten Dharmas. Daśadharmakasūtra. Chos bcu pa. Toh 53, dkon brtsegs *kha.* 164a5–184b7. Chapter 8 of the *Ratnakūṭa Sūtra* collection.

Sutra of the Ten Levels. Daśabhūmikasūtra. Sa bcu pa'i mdo. Toh 44, phal chen *kha.* 166a5–283a7. Chapter 31 of the four-volume *Avataṃsaka Sutra* collection. Translation from the Chinese in Cleary 1984.

Tantra of All Mandalas. Sarvamaṇḍalatantra. Dkyil 'khor thams cad kyi spyi'i cho ga gsang ba'i rgyud. Toh 806, rgyud *wa.* 141a1–167b7.

Tantra of the Great River of Pacification. A li ka li gsang ba bsam gyi myi khyab pa chu klung chen po'i rgyud. In *Zhi byed snga bar phyi gsum gyi skor,* vol. *ka,* 6–109. Thimphu, Bhutan: Druk Sherik Parkhang, 1979.

Tantra Requested by the Four Goddesses. Caturdevīparipṛcchā. Lha mo bzhis yongs su zhus pa. Toh 446, rgyud *ca.* 277b3–281b7.

Tantra Requested by Subāhu. Subāhuparipṛcchātantra. Dpung bzang gis skus pa. Toh 805, rgyud *wa.* 118a1–140b7.

Tantra Revealing the Hidden Meaning. Sandhivyākaraṇatantra. Dgongs pa lun bstan pa. Toh 444, rgyud *ca.* 158a1–207b7.

Tantra of True Union. Saṃpuṭatantra. Yang dag par sbyor ba. Toh 381, rgyud *ga.* 73b1–158b7.

Ten Wheels of Kṣitagarbha Sutra. Daśacakrakṣitigarbhasūtra. Chen po las sa'i snying po'i 'khor lo bcu pa. Toh 239, mdo sde *zha.* 100a1–241b4.

Tilaka of Wisdom. Jñānatilakatantra. Ye shes thig le rnal 'byor ma'i rgyud kyi rgyal po chen po mchog tu rmad du byung ba. Toh 422, rgyud *nga.* 96b6–136b4.

Vajraḍāka Tantra. Vajraḍākatantra. Rdo rje mkha' 'gro'i rgyud. Toh 370, rgyud *kha.* 1b1–125a7.

Vajra Garland Explanatory Tantra. Vajramālābhidhānatantra. Bshad rgyud rdo rje phreng ba. Toh 445, rgyud *ca.* 208a1–277b3.

Vajra Mandala Adornment Tantra. Vajramaṇḍalālaṃkāratantra. Rdo rje snying po rgyan. Toh 490, rgyud *tha.* 1b1–82a7.

Vajra Pinnacle Tantra. Vajraśekharatantra. Gsang ba rnal 'byor chen po'i rgyud rdo rje rtse mo. Toh 480, rgyud *nya.* 142b1–274a5.

Vajra Tent Tantra. Ḍākinīvajrapañjarātantra. Mkha' 'gro ma rdo rje gur zhes bya ba'i rgyud kyi rgyal po chen po'i brtag pa. Toh 419, rgyud *nga.* 30a4–65b7.

Vajrapāṇi's Empowerment Tantra. Vajrapāṇyabhiṣekatantra. Lag na rdo rje dbang bskur ba'i rgyud chen po. Toh 496, rgyud *da.* 1b1–156b7.

Vimalakīrti Sutra. *Vimalakīrtinirdeśasūtra*. *Dri ma med par grags pas bstan pa*. Toh 176, mdo sde *ma*. 175a1–239b7.

Vinayavastu. *'Dul ba gzhi*. Toh 1, 'dul ba *ka–nga*. 1b1–302a5.

White Lotus [of the Holy Dharma] Sutra. *Saddharmapuṇḍarīkasūtra*. *Dam pa'i chos pad ma dkar po*. Toh 113, mdo sde *ja*. 1b1–180b7.

Wisdom upon Passing Away Sutra. *Atyayajñānasūtra*. *'Da' ka ye shes*. Toh 122 mdo sde *tha*. 153a1–153b1.

Yoginī's Activity. *Yoginīsaṃcaryā*. *Rnal 'byor ma'i kun tu spyod pa*. Toh 375, gyud *ga*. 34a1–44b5.

Tengyur (Canonical Treatises)

Abhayākaragupta. *Adornment of the Muni's View*. *Munimatālaṃkāra*. *Thub pa'i dgongs pa'i rgyan*. Toh 3903, dbu ma *a*. 73b1–293a7.

———. *Ears of Grain of Practice Instructions: An Extensive Commentary on the Tantra of True Union*. *Saṃpuṭatantraṭīkāmnāyamañjarī*. *Yang dag par sbyor ba'i rgyud gyi rgyal po'i rgya cher 'grel pa man ngag gi snye ma zhes bya ba*. Toh 1198, rgyud *cha*. 1–316a7.

———. *Vajra Garland of Mandala Rituals*. *Vajrāvalimaṇḍalasādhana*. *Dkyil 'khor gyi cho ga rdo rje phreng ba*. Toh 3140, rgyud *phu*. 1a1–94b4.

Advayavajra (Maitripa). *A Teaching on the Mudrās of the Five Tathāgatas*. *Tathāgatapañcamudrāvivaraṇa*. *De bzhin gshegs pa lnga'i phyag rgya rnam par bshad pa*. Toh 2242, rgyud *wi*. 120b3–122b3.

———. *Ten Verses on the True Nature*. *Tattvadaśaka*. *De kho na nyid bcu pa*. Toh 2236, rgyud *wi*. 112b7–113a6. Translated in Brunnhölzl 2007: 140–41.

Alaṃkakalaśa. *Profound Meaning: A Commentary on the Vajra Garland Tantra*. *Vajramālātantraṭīkāgaṃbhīrārthadīpikā*. *Rnal 'byor chen po'i rgyud dpal rdo rje phreng ba'i rgya cher 'grel pa zab mo'i don gyi 'grel pa*. Toh 1795, rgyud *gi*. 1–220a7.

Ānandagarbha. *Commentary on the Śrī Paramādya Tantra*. *Śrīparamādivivaraṇa*. *Dpal mchog dang po'i 'grel pa*. Toh 2511, rgyud *si*. 1a1–49b2.

———. *Explanation of Difficult Points in the Guhyasamāja*. *Śrīguhyasamājapañjikā*. *Dpal gsang ba 'dus pa'i dka' 'grel*. Toh 1917, rgyud *bi*. 1–81a7.

———. *Illuminating the Truth: A Commentary on the Tantra Entitled "Compendium of Truths of All Tahāgatas: Understanding the Mahayana."* *Sarvatathāgatatattvasaṃgrahamahāyānābhisamayanāmatantravyākhyātattvālokakarī*. *De bzhin gshegs pa thams cad kyi de kho na nyid bsdud pa theg pa chen po mngon par rtogs pa zhes bya ba'i rgyud kyi bshad pa de kho na nyid snang bar byed pa*. Toh 2510, rgyud *li* 1a1–*shi* 317a7.

———. *Sādhana Method of Vajrasattva*. *Vajrasattvasādhanopāyikā*. *Rdo rje sems dpa'i sgrub pa'i thabs*. Toh 2518, rgyud *ku*. 62a5–67a3.

———. *Sādhana Method Named "The Generation of Vajrasattva."* *Vajrasattvodayanāmasādhanopāyikā*. *Rdo rje sems dpa' 'byung ba zhes bya ba'i sgrub thabs*. Toh 3340, rgyud *shi*. 57b8–71a3.

———. *Origin of All Vajras. Sarvavajrodaya. Rdo rje dbyings kyi dkyil 'khor chen po'i cho ga rdo rje thams cad 'byung ba.* Toh 2516, rgyud *ku* 1a1–*lu* 50a4.

Anonymous. *Branch Commitments. Aṅgasamaya. Yan lag dam tshig.* Toh 2483, rgyud, *zi.* 180b4.

———. *Creating the Happiness of All Beings: The Manjuvajra Mandala Ritual. Mañjuvajrodayamaṇḍalavidhisarvasattvahitāvahā. 'Jam pa'i rdo rje 'byung ba'i dkyil 'khor gyi cho ga sems can thams cad kyi bde ba bskyed pa.* Toh 2590, rgyud *ngu.* 225a5–274a7.

Anupamarakṣita. *Six Yogas. Ṣaḍaṅgayoga. Sbyor ba yan lag drug.* Toh 1367, rgyud *pa.* 198b5–207a3.

Āryadeva. *Compiled Summary of the Four Seats Tantra Mandalas. Catuḥpīṭhatantramaṇḍalasamuccaya. Rgyud kyi rgyal po dpal gdan bzhi pa zhes bya ba'i dkyil 'khor gyi cho ga snying po mdor bsags pa.* Toh 1613, rgyud *ya.* 113a4–138a1.

———. *Four Hundred Verses. Catuḥśatakaśāstra. Bstan bcos bzhi brgya pa zhes bya ba'i tshig le'ur byas pa.* Toh 3846, dbu ma *tsha.* 1a1–18a7. Translation by Ruth Sonam in Aryadeva 2008.

———. *Hundred Verses on the Essence of Understanding. Pratipattisāraśataka. Go bar byed pa snying po brgya pa.* Toh 2334, rgyud *zhi.* 278b1–283a2.

———. *Lamp of the Compendium of Practices. Caryāmelāpakapradīpa. Spyod pa bsdus pa'i sgron me.* Toh 1803, rgyud *ngi.* 57a2–106b7. Translation in Wedemeyer 2008.

Āryaśūra. *Jātakamālā. Skyes pa'i rabs kyi rgyud.* Toh 4150, skyes rabs *hu.* 1b1–135a7. Translated fom Sanskrit by J. S. Speyer in 1895, available with Sanskrit in Āryaśūra 2007, which was revised in comparison with the Tibetan in Āryaśūra 1983. Also translated from the Sanskrit by Peter Khoroche in Āryaśūra 1989 and by Justin Meiland in Āryaśūra 2009.

———. *Summarized Perfections. Pāramitāsamāsa. Pha rol tu phyin pa bsdus pa.* Toh 3944, dbu ma *khi.* 217b1–235a5.

Asaṅga. *Bodhisattva Levels. Bodhisattvabhūmi. Rnal 'byor spyod pa'i sa las byang chub sems dpa'i sa.* Toh 4037, sems tsam *wi.* 1a1–213a7. Part of chapter 1 has been translated in Roth 1975–76, chapter 4 has been translated in Willis 1979, and chapter 10 has been translated in Tatz 1986. Summary and extracts in Bendall 1905, 1906, and 1911.

———. *Compendium of the Abhidharma. Abhidharmasammucaya. Chos mngon pa kun las btus pa.* Toh 4049, sems tsam *ri.* 44b1–120a7. Translation in Asaṅga 2001.

———. *Compendium of the Mahayana. Mahāyānasaṃgraha. Theg pa chen po bsdus pa.* Toh 4048, sems tsam *ri.* 217b5–223b2.

Aśvaghoṣa. *Compilation of the Vajrayāna Root Downfalls. Vajrayānamūlāpattisaṃgraha. Rdo rje theg pa rtsa ba'i ltung ba bsdus pa.* Toh 2478, rgyud *zi.* 179a6–179b5.

———. *Fifty Verses on the Guru. Gurupañcāśikā. Bla ma lnga bcu pa.* Toh 3721, rgyud *tshu.* 10a2–12a2. For the Sanskrit see *Digital Sanskrit Buddhist Canon.*

Atiśa Dīpaṃkaraśrījñāna. *Analysis of "Realizing [the Bhagavān]." Abhisamaya-vibhaṅga. Mngon par rtogs pa rnam par 'byed pa.* Toh 1490, rgyud *zha.* 186a1–202b3.

———. *Compendium of All Commitments. Sarvasamayasaṃgraha. Dam tshig thams cad bsdus pa.* Toh 3725, rgyud *tshu.* 44a1–49b1.

———. *Entering the Two Truths. Satyadvayāvātara. Bden pa gnyis la 'jug pa.* Toh 3902, dbu ma *a.* 72a3–73a7.

———. *Lamp for the Path to Enlightenment. Bodhipathapradīpa. Byang chub lam gyi sgron ma.* Toh 3948, dbu ma *khi.* 241a–293a. Translation in Rinchen 1997. For the Sanskrit see *Digital Sanskrit Buddhist Canon.*

Avadhūtipāda. *Presentation of the Six Dharmas of Dhyāna. Dhyānaṣaḍdharma-vyavasthāna. Bsam gtan gyi chos drug rnam par bzhag pa.* Toh 3926, dbu ma *ki.* 92b7–93a5.

Bhavyakīrti. *Perfectly Illuminating Lamp. Pradīpodyotanābhisaṃdhiṭikā. Sgron ma gsal bar byed pa'i dgongs pa rab gsal zhes bya ba bshad pa'i ṭīkā.* Toh 1793, rgyud *ki.* 1a1–292a7.

Buddhaguhya. *Commentary to the Enlightenment of Vairocana Tantra. Mahā-vairocanābhisaṃbodhitantraṭīkā. Rnam par snang mdzad mngon par byang chub pa'i rgyud chen po'i 'grel bshad.* Toh 2663, rgyud *nyu.* 65ba3–260b7. Translated in Hodge 2003.

———. *Commentary on the Latter Dhyāna. Dhyānottarapaṭalaṭīkā. Bsam gtan phyi ma rim par phye ba rgya cher bshad pa.* Toh 2670, rgyud *thu.* 1a1–38a3.

Buddhajñānapāda. *Tilaka of Liberation. Muktitilaka. Grol ba'i thig le.* Toh 1859, rgyud *di.* 47a1–52a7.

———. *Oral Transmission Entitled "Meditation on the True Nature of the Two Stages." Dvikramatattvabhāvanānāmamukhāgama. Rim pa gnyis pa'i de kho na nyid bsgom pa zhes bya ba'i zhal gyi lung.* Toh 1853, rgyud *di.* 1a1–17b2.

———. *Samantabhadra Sādhana. Kun tu bzang po zhes bya ba'i sgrub pa'i thabs.* Toh 1855, rgyud *di.* 28b6–36a4.

Candragomin. *Twenty Vows. Saṃvaraviṃśaka. Sdom pa nyi shu pa.* Toh 4081, sems tsam *hi.* 166b1–167a5. Translated in Tatz 2001.

Candrakīrti. *Clear Words: A Commentary on the "Root Middle Way." Mūla-madhyamakavṛttiprasannapadā. Dbu ma rtsa ba'i 'grel pa tshig gsal ba.* Toh 3860, dbu ma *'a.* 1a1–200a7.

———. *Entering the Middle Way. Madhyamakāvatāra. Dbu ma la 'jug pa.* Toh 3861, dbu ma *'a.* 201b1–219a7. Translation in Huntington 1989.

———. *Illuminating Lamp. Pradīpodyotanaṭīkā. Sgron ma gsal bar byed pa zhes bya ba'i rgya cher bshad pa.* Toh 1785, rgyud *ha.* 1–201b2.

Danaśila. *Commentary on "Presentation of the Six Dharmas of Dhyāna." Dhyāna-*

ṣaḍdharmavyavasthānavṛtti. Bsam gtan gyi chos drug rnam par gzhag pa'i 'grel pa. Toh 3927, dbu ma *ki.* 93a5–94b3.

Dharmakīrti. *Commentary on Valid Cognition. Pramāṇavārttika. Tshad ma rnam 'grel gyi tshig le'ur byas pa.* Toh 4210, tshad ma *ce.* 94b1–151a7. The fourth chapter is translated in Tillemans 2000.

Dignāga. *Compendium of Valid Cognition. Pramāṇasamuccaya. Tshad ma kun las btus pa zhes bya ba'i rab tu byed pa.* Toh 4203, tshad ma *ce.* 1b1–13a7.

———. *Compendium of the Perfection of Wisdom. Prajñāpāramitāsaṃgraha. Shes rab kyi pha rol tu phyin ma bsdus pa'i tshig le'ur byas pa.* Toh 3809, sher phyin *pha.* 292b4–294b7.

Dīpaṃkarabhadra. *Rites for the Guhyasamāja Mandala. Guhyasamāja-maṇḍalavidhi. Gsang ba 'dus pa'i dkyil 'khor gyi cho ga.* Toh 1865, rgyud *di.* 69a4–87a3.

Ḍombipa. *Gaṇacakra Rite. Gaṇacakravidhi. Tshogs kyi 'khor lo'i cho ga.* Toh 1231, rgyud *nya.* 43a1–45a4.

Durjayacandra. *An Excellent Collection of the Sādhanas of the Mandala Rituals. Suparigrahamaṇḍalasādhana. Dkyil 'khor gyi cho ga'i sgrub thabs bzang po yongs su gzung ba.* Toh 1240, rgyud *nya.* 130a3–154a7.

———. *Hevajra Torma Rite. Hevajrabalividhi. Kye rdo rje'i gtor ma'i cho ga.* Toh 1287, rgyud *ta.* 141a6–143b1.

Indrabhūti. *Innate Accomplishment. Sahajasiddhi. Lhan cig skyes grub.* Toh 2260 Tengyur, rgyud, *zhi.* 1a1–4a3.

———. *Sādhana for the Accomplishment of Wisdom. Jñānasiddhisādhana. Ye shes grub pa zhes bya ba'i sgrub pa'i thabs.* Toh 2219, rgyud *wi.* 36b7–60b6.

Indrabodhi. *Commentary to the Compiled Cakrasaṃvara Tantra. Cakrasaṃvara-tantrasaṃvarasamuccayavṛtti. 'Khor lo sdom pa'i rgyud kyi rgyal po bde mchog bsdus pa zhes bya ba'i rnam par bshad pa.* Toh 1413, rgyud *tsa.* 1a1–119b7.

Jālandhara. *Vajra Lamp: A Pure Brief Explanation of the Hevajra Sādhana. Hevajrasādhanavajrapradīpaṭippaṇīśuddha. Kye rdo rje'i sgrub thabs kyi mdor bshad pa dag pa rdo rje sgron ma.* Toh 1237, rgyud *nya.* 73a2–96a1.

Jinabhadra. *Method for Practicing the Cakrasaṃvara Mandala. Cakrasaṃvara-maṇḍalavidhi. Bde mchog gi dkyil 'khor bya ba'i thabs.* Toh 1477, rgyud *zha.* 80b7–116b1.

Jñānagarbha. *Commentary on "Distinguishing the Two Truths." Satyadvaya-vibhaṅgavṛtti. Bden pa gnyis rnam par 'byed pa'i tshig le'ur byas pa.* Toh 3881, dbu ma *sa.* 1b1–3b2. Translated in Eckel 1986.

Jñānākara. *Commentary to "Entering the Mantrayāna." Mantrāvatāravṛtti. Gsang sngags la 'jug pa'i 'grel pa.* Toh 3719, rgyud *tsu.* 196b1–208a7.

———. *Entering the Mantrayāna. Mantrāvatāra. Gsang sngags la 'jug pa.* Toh 3718, rgyud *tsu.* 194a4–196b1.

Jñānakīrti. *Entering the Truth. Tattvāvatāra. De kho na nyid la 'jug pa zhes bya ba bde bar gshegs pa'i bka' ma lus pa mdor bsdus te bshad pa'i rab tu byed pa.*

Toh 3709, rgyud *tsu*. 39a2–76a4. Extracts translated in Brunnhölzl 2007: 135–36.

Jñānaśrī. *Elimination of the Two Extremes*. *Koṭidvayāpoha*. *Rdo rje theg pa'i mtha' gnyis sel ba*. Toh 3714, rgyud *tsu*. 115a7–120a2.

Kālacakrapāda. *Instructions on the Six Yogas*. *Ṣaḍaṅgayogopadeśa*. *Sbyor ba yan lag drug gi man ngag*. Toh 1372, rgyud *pa*. 224a4–226b4.

———. *Lotus Endowed: A Commentary on Difficult Points*. *Padmanipañjikā*. *Padma can zhes bya ba'i dka' 'grel*. Toh 1350, rgyud *na*. 72b5–220a7.

Kamalaśīla. *Letterless Mahāmudrā*. *Mahāmudrātattvānākṣaropadeśa*. *De kho na nyid phyag rgya chen po yi ge med pa'i man ngag*. Toh 2325, rgyud *zhi*. 266b2–267b2.

Kambala. *Top-Knot Jewel*. *Ratnacūḍāmaṇi*. *Bde mchog gi sgrub thabs rin po che gtsug gi nor bu*. Toh 1443, rgyud *wa*. 251a7–272b3.

Kṛṣṇapa. *Explanation of "Entering the Conduct of a Bodhisattva." Bodhisattvacaryāvatāravivṛttipañjikā*. *Byang chub sems dpa'i spyod pa la 'jug pa'i rnam par bshad pa'i dka' 'grel*. Toh 3873, dbu ma *la*. 288b1–349a7.

———. *Illumination of the Secret Nature*. *Guhyatattvaprakāśa*. *Gsang ba'i de kho na nyid rab tu gsal ba*. Toh 1450, rgyud *wa*. 349a–355b7.

Lūyipa. *Realizing the Bhagavān*. *Bhagavadabhisamaya*. *Bcom ldan 'das mngon par rtogs pa*. Toh 1427, rgyud *wa*. 186b3–193a1.

Maitreyanātha. *Distinguishing the Middle Way from the Extremes*. *Madhyāntavibhāga*. *Dbus dang mtha' rnam par 'byed pa*. Toh 4021, sems tsam *phi*. 40b1–45a6.

———. (*Mahayana Treatise on the*) *Sublime Continuum*. *Mahāyānottaratantraśāstra*. *Theg pa chen po rgyud bla ma'i bstan bcos*. Toh 4024, sems tsam *phi*. 54b1–73a7. Also known as *Ratnagotravibhāga*. Translation by Rosemary Fuchs in Maitreya 1999; by E. Obermiller with Sanskrit text edited by E. H. Johnston in Prasad 1991; by Ken and Katia Holmes in Thrangu 1994; and translated from the Sanskrit and Chinese in Takasaki 1966. See also Mathes 2008.

———. *Ornament of the Mahayana Sutras*. *Mahāyanasūtrālaṃkāra*. *Mdo sde rgyan*. Toh 4020, sems tsam *phi*. 1a1–39a4. For the Sanskrit see *Digital Sanskrit Buddhist Canon*. Translated from Sanskrit, Tibetan, and Chinese in Thurman et al. 2004.

———. *Ornament of Realization*. *Abhisamayālaṃkāra*. *Shes rab kyi pha rol tu phyin pa'i man ngag gi bstan bcos mngon par rtogs pa'i rgyan zhes bya ba'i tshig le'ur byas pa*. Toh 3786, shes phyin *ka*. 1a1–13a7. For the original Sanskrit, see *Digital Sanskrit Buddhist Canon*. Translated in Conze 1954. Also see Obermiller 1933.

Maitripa. *Teaching Amanasikāra*. *Amanasikāroddeśa*. *Yid la mi byed pa ston pa*. Toh 2249, rgyud *wi*. 138b4–140a5.

Mañjuśrīkīrti. *Adornment of the Essence of the General Rites of All Secrets*.

Sarvaguhyavidhigarbhālaṃkāra. Gsang ba thams cad kyi spyi'i cho ga'i snying po rgyan. Toh 2490, rgyud *zi*. 232b2–243b3.

Mañjuśrī Yaśas. *Primordial Buddha Kālacakra Tantra. Paramādibuddhoddhṛtaśrī-kālacakratantra. Mchog gi dang po'i sangs rgyas las phyung ba rgyud kyi rgyal po dpal dus kyi 'khor lo*. Toh 1346, rgyud *tha*. 101a1–107a7. Also in the Kangyur above. See Henning 2007; Wallace 2001, 2005, and 2009.

Muditākoṣa. *Commentary to the Crown Jewel of the Lord of the Three Worlds Trailokyavijayanāmavṛtti. 'Jig rten gsum las rnam par rgyal ba zhes bya ba'i 'grel pa*. Toh 2509, rgyud *ri*. 216a5–283a7.

Nāgabodhi. *Guhyasamāja Mandala Rite. Guhyasamājamaṇḍalaviṃśatividhi. Gsang ba 'dus pa'i dkyil 'khor gyi cho ga nyi shu pa*. Toh 1810, rgyud *ngi*. 131a5–145b3.

Nāgārjuna. *Commentary on Bodhicitta. Bodhicittavivarṇa. Byang chub sems kyi 'grel pa*. Toh 1800, rgyud *ngi*. 41a1–42b5. Translated in Lindtner 1982 and 1986.

———. *Condensed Sādhana. Piṇḍīkṛtasādhana. Sgrub pa'i thabs mdor byas pa*. Toh 1796, rgyud *ngi*. 1–11a2.

———. *Fearing Nothing: A Commentary on the "Root Middle Way." Mūlamadhyamakavṛttyakuto'bhayā. Dbu ma rtsa bai 'grel pa ga las 'jigs med*. Toh 3829, dbu ma *tsa*. 29b1–99a7.

———. *Five Stages. Pañcakrama. Rim pa lnga pa*. Toh 1802, rgyud *ngi*. 45a5–57a1. For the Sanskrit see *Digital Sanskrit Buddhist Canon*.

———. *Gross Downfalls of the Vajrayāna. Vajrayānasthūlāpatti. Rdo rje theg pa'i sbom pa'i ltung ba*. Toh 2482, rgyud *zi*. 180a7–180b3.

———. *Letter to a Friend. Suhṛllekha. Bshes pa'i sprin yig*. Toh 4182, spring yig *nge*. 40b4–46b3. For the Sanskrit see *Digital Sanskrit Buddhist Canon*. Translated by Padmakara Translation Group in Nagarjuna 2005.

———. *Mandala Rites of Guhyasamāja. Guhyasamājamaṇḍalavidhi. Gsang ba 'dus pa'i dkyil 'khor gyi cho ga*. Toh 1798, rgyud, *ngi*. 15b1–35a7.

———. *Praise to the Dharmadhātu. Dharmadhātustava. Chos kyi dbyings su bstod pa*. Toh 1118, bstod tshogs *ka*. 63b5–67b3.

———. *Praise to the Inconceivable. Acintyastava. Bsam gyis mi khyab par bstod pa*. Toh 1128, bstod tshogs *ka*. 76b7–79a2. Translated in Lindtner 1986.

———. *Praise for the One Who Has Transcended the World. Lokātītastava. 'Jig rten las 'das par bstod pa*. Toh 1120, bstod tshogs *ka*. 68b4–69b4. Translated in Lindtner 1986.

———. *Praise to the Three Kāyas. Kāyatrayastotra. Sku gsum la bstod pa*. Toh 1123, bstod tshogs *ka*. 70b3–71a2. Translated primarily from the Sanskrit in Brunnhölzl 2007: 18–19.

———. *Root Verses on the Middle Way. Mūlamadhyamakakārika. Dbu ma rtsa ba'i tshig le'ur byas pa shes rab ces bya ba*. Toh 3824, dbu ma *tsa*. 1a1–19a6. Translated by J. L. Garfield in Nāgārjuna 1995.

———. *Precious Garland. Ratnāvalī. Rgyal po la gtam bya ba rin po che'i phreng ba*. Toh 4158, spring yig *ge*. 107a1–126a4. Translated by Jeffrey Hopkins in Nagarjuna 1997.

———. *Verses on the Essence of Dependent Origination. Pratītyasamutpādahṛdayakārikā. Rten cing 'brel bar snying po'i tshig le'ur byas pa*. Toh 3836, dbu ma *tsa*. 146b2–146b7.

Nāropa. *Clear Summary of the Five Stages. Pañcakramasaṃgrahaprakāśa. Rim pa lnga bsdus pa gsal ba*. Toh 2333, rgyud *zhi*. 267a7–278a7.

———. *Latter Instructions through Similes. Ājñottaropamā. Bka' dpe phyi ma*. Toh 2332, rgyud *zhi*. 273a4–276a7.

———. *Summary of the View. Dṛṣtisaṃkṣipta. Lta ba mdor bsdus pa*. Toh 2304, rgyud *zhi*. 244a5–245b3.

———. *Truly Valid Instructions: Teachings of the Ḍākinīs. Ājñāsaṃyakpramāṇaḍākinyupadeśa. Bka' yang dag pa'i tshad ma zhes bya ba mkha' 'gro ma'i man ngag*. Toh 2331, rgyud *zhi*. 271a3–273a3.

———. *Vajra Verses of the Aural Tantra. Karṇatantravajragāthā. Snyan rgyud rdo rje'i tshig rkang*. Toh 2338, rgyud *zhi*. 302b6–304b4.

Padmākara. *Five Commitments. Samayapañca. Dam tshig lnga pa*. Toh 1224, rgyud *nya*. 26b7–28b6.

Padmavajra. *Accomplishment of the Glorious Secret. Śrīguhyasiddhi. Rgyud ma lus pa'i don nges par skul bar byed pa*. Toh 2217, rgyud *wi*. 1a1–28b4.

Prajñākaramati. *Commentary on Difficult Points in "Entering the Conduct of a Bodhisattva." Bodhicaryāvatārapañjikā. Byang chub kyi spyod pa la 'jug pa'i dka' 'grel*. Toh 3872, dbu ma *la*. 41b1–288a7.

(Puṇḍarīka/Avalokiteśvara). *Stainless Light: A Commentary on the Kālacakra Tantra. Vimalaprabhākālacakratantraṭīkā. Bsdus pa'i rgyud kyi rgyal po dus kyi 'khor lo'i 'grol bshad rtsa ba'i rgyud kyi rjes su 'jug pa stong phrag bcu gnyis pa dri ma med pa'i 'od*. Toh 1347, rgyud *tha*. 107b1–*da* 297a7. Also in the Kangyur; see above.

———. *Ultimate Approach. Paramārthasevā. Don dam pa'i bsnyen pa*. Toh 1348, rgyud *na*. 1–20a3.

Prajñendraruci. *Shining Jewel Sādhana. Ratnajvālanāmasādhana. Rin chen 'bar ba zhes bya ba'i sgrub pa'i thabs*. Toh 1251, rgyud *nya*. 214a3–241b2.

Rāmapāla. *Commentary on Difficult Points in [Maitripa's] "Teaching on Empowerment." Sekanirdeśapañjikā. Dbang bskur ba nges par bstan pa*. Toh 2253, rgyud *wi*. 143a5–160b7.

Ratnākaraśānti, *Extensive Commentary on Rites of the Guhyasamāja Mandala. Guhyasamājamaṇḍalaviddhiṭīkā. Gsang ba 'dus pa'i dkyil 'khor gyi cho ga'i 'grel pa*. Toh 1871, rgyud *ni*. 59a–130a.

———. *Lamp for Seeing the Path: A Detailed Commentary on the Kṛṣṇayamāri King of Tantras. Kṛṣṇayamāritantrarājāprekṣaṇapathapradīpanāmaṭīkā. Gshin rje gshed nag po'i rgyud kyi rgyal po mngon par mthong ba lam gyi sgron ma zhes bya ba'i rgya cher bshad pa*. Toh 1920, rgyud *bi*. 173a1–258b2.

———. *String of Pearls: Commentary on the Difficult Parts of the Hevajra Tantra. Hevajrapañjikāmuktikāvali. Dgyes pa'i rdo rje'i dka' 'grel mu tig phreng ba.* Toh 1189, rgyud *ga*, 221a1–297a7.

Ratnarakṣita. *Commentary to the Saṃvarodaya Tantra. Saṃvarodayatantra-pañjikā. Dpal sdom pa 'byung ba'i rgyud gyi rgyal po chen po'i dka' grel padma can zhes bya ba.* Toh 1420, rgyud *wa*. 1–101b3.

———. *The Stages of Innate Union. Sahajayogakrama. Lhan cig skyes pa'i rnal 'byor gyi rim pa.* Toh 1246, rgyud *nya*. 194b6–196a3.

Sahajavajra. *Commentary on "Ten Verses on the True Nature." Tattvadaśakaṭīkā. De kho na nyid bcu pa'i rgya cher 'grel pa.* Toh 2254, rgyud *wi*. 160b7–177a7. Translated in Brunnhölzl 2007: 141–201.

Sahajayoginī Cintā. *Accomplishment of the True Nature. Tattvasiddhi. Dngos po gsal ba'i rjes su 'gro ba'i de kho na nyid grub pa.* Toh 2222, rgyud *wi*. 63a5–68b5.

Śākyamitra. *Adornment of Kosala: An Extensive Commentary on "Compendium of Truths." Kosalālaṃkāratattvasaṃgrahaṭīkā. De kho na nyid bsdus pa'i rgya cher bshad pa kosala'i rgyan.* Toh 2503, rgyud *yi* 1a1–*ri* 202a5.

———. *Lamp of the Compendium of Conduct: An Extensive Commentary. Caryāsamuccayapradīpaṭīkā. Spyod pa bsdus pa'i sgron ma zhes bya ba'i rgya cher bshad pa.* Toh 1834, rgyud *ci*. 237b1–280b2.

Śāntarakṣita. *Ornament of the Middle Way. Madhyamakālaṃkāra. Dbu ma rgyan gyi tshig le'ur byas pa.* Toh 3884, dbu ma *sa*. 53a1–56b3. Translated in Śantarakṣita 2005 (by the Padmakara Translation Group), in Doctor 2004, and in Blumenthal 2004.

———. *Establishing the Truth: An Explanatory Text. Tattvasiddhināmaprakaraṇa. De kho na nyid grub pa zhes bya ba'i rab tu byed pa.* Toh 3708, rgyud *tsu*. 26b1–39a2.

Śāntideva. *Entering the Conduct of a Bodhisattva. Bodhicaryāvatāra. Byang chub sems dpa'i spyod pa la 'jug pa.* Toh 3871, dbu ma *la*. 1a1–40a7. For the Sanskrit see *Digital Sanskrit Buddhist Canon*. Translated by Stephen Batchelor (1979), Padmakara Translation Group (1997), Alan and Vesna Wallace (1997), and Kate Crosby and Andrew Skilton (1995).

Saraha. *Doha Treasury of Mahāmudrā Instructions. Dohakoṣamahāmudropadeśa. Do ha mdzod ces bya ba phyag rgya chen po'i man ngag.* Toh 2273, rgyud *zhi*. 122a3–124a7.

———. *Endowed with Wisdom: A Commentary on Difficult Points in the Buddhakapāla Tantra. Buddhakapālatantrapañjikājñānavatī. Sangs rgyas thod pa'i rgyud kyi dka' 'grel ye shes ldan pa.* Toh 1652, rgyud *ra*. 104b1–150a2.

———. *Song of an Inexhaustible Treasure of Instruction. Dohakoṣopadeśagīti. Mi zad pa'i gter mdzod man ngag gi glu.* Toh 2264, rgyud *zhi*. 28b6–33b4.

———. *Treasury of Dohas. Dohakoṣagīti. Do ha mdzod kyi glu.* Toh 2224, rgyud *wi*. 70b5–77a3. See Guenther 1993 and Schaeffer 2004.

———. *Song of Conduct Doha Treasury. Dohakoṣanāmacaryāgīti. Do ha mdzod ces bya ba spyod pa'i glu.* Toh 2263, rgyud *zhi.* 26b6–28b6.

Saroruhavajra. *Treasury of Secrets. Guhyakoṣaśāstra. Sngags kyi bstan bcos gsang ba'i mdzod ces bya ba.* Not in the Toh Tengyur, but in Peking 4688, rgyud *phu.* 136b2–142a7. Narthang: rgyud *phu,* 135a3–140b2.

Sāroruha. *Lotus Endowed: A Commentary on Difficult Points in the Hevajra Tantra. Hevajratantrapañjikāpadminī. Kye'i rdo rje'i rgyud kyi dka' 'grel padma can.* Toh 1181, rgyud *ka.* 126b1–173a7.

Siddharājñī. *Secret Sādhana of Lokeśvara. Lokeśvaraguhyasādhana.* 'Jig rten dbang phyug gsang ba'i sgrub thabs. Toh 2140, rgyud *tshi.* 205a–210a.

Śraddhākaravarman. *Summary of the Entry into the Meaning of the Highest Yoga Tantras. Yogānuttaratantrārthāvatārasaṃgraha. Rnal 'byor bla na med pa'i rgyud kyi don la 'jug pa bsdus pa.* Toh 3713, rgyud *tsu.* 105b1–115a7.

Śrīphalavajra. *Commentary to the Samantabhadra Sādhana. Samantabhadrasādhanavṛtti. Kun tu bzang po'i sgrub pa'i thabs kyi 'grel ba.* Toh 1867, rgyud *di.* 139b3–187b4.

Sthiramati. *Commentary on "Distinguishing the Middle Way from the Extremes." Madhyāntavibhāgaṭīkā. Dbus dang mtha' rnam par 'byed pa'i 'grel bshad.* Toh 4032, sems tsam *bi.* 189b2–318a7.

Subhagavajra. *Stages of the Mahayana Path. Mahāyānapathakrama. Theg pa chen po'i lam gyi rim pa.* Toh 3717, rgyud *tsu.* 183a6–194a4.

Śubhākaragupta. *Ears of Grain of Realization. Abhisamayamañjarī. Mngon par rtogs pa'i snye ma.* Toh 1582, rgyud *'a.* 25b1–44a3.

Tailikapāda (Tilopa). *Mahāmudrā Instructions. Mahāmudropadeśa. Phyag rgya chen po'i man ngag.* Toh 2303, rgyud *zhi.* 242b7–244a5.

Tathāgatavajra. *Special Illumination: A Commentary on the Explanation of Lūyipa's Sādhana Visualization. Lūyipādābhisamayavṛttiṭīkāviśeṣadyota. Lū yi pa'i mngon par rtogs pa'i 'grel pa'i ṭi kā khyad par gsal byed.* Toh 1510, rgyud *zha.* 285a4–308b2.

Tilopa (Tailopa). *Instructions on the Six Yogas. Ṣaḍdharmopadeśa. Chos drug gi man ngag.* Toh 2330, rgyud *zhi.* 270a7–271a3. Translated in Mullin 1997.

Tripiṭakamāla. *Lamp of the Three Ways. Nayatrayapradīpa. Tshul gsum gyi sgron ma.* Toh 3707, rgyud *tsu.* 6b6–26b1.

Vagīśvarakīrti. *Seven Aspects. Saptāṅga. Yan lag bdun pa.* Toh 1888, rgyud *pi.* 190a3–203a3.

Vajragarbha. *Extensive Commentary on the Condensed Meaning of the Hevajra. Hevajrapiṇḍārthaṭīkā. Kye'i rdo rje bsdus pa'i don gyi rgya cher 'grel pa.* Toh 1180, rgyud *ka.* 1–126a7.

Vajraghaṇṭa. *Brief Cakrasaṃvara Empowerment. Cakrasaṃvaraṣekaprakriyopadeśa. 'Khor lo sdom pa'i dbang gi bya ba mdor bsdus pa.* Toh 1431, rgyud *'grel, wa.* 219b3–222b5.

———. *Cakrasaṃvara Sādhana. Bcom ldan 'das 'khor lo'i bde mchog sgrub pa'i thabs rin po che yid bzhin gyi nor bu.* Toh 1437, rgyud *wa.* 233b5–237b2.

———. *Sādhana of Innate Saṃvara. Sahajasaṃvarasādhana. Bde mchog lhan cig skyes pa'i sgrub thabs.* Toh 1436, rgyud *wa.* 233a4–233b5.

Vajrapāṇi. *Instructions from the Successive Guru Lineage. Guruparamparakramopadeśa. Bla ma brgyud pa'i rim pa'i man ngag.* Toh 3716, rgyud *tsu.* 164b2–183a5.

Vasubandhu. *Commentary on "Compendium of the Mahayana." Mahāyānasaṃgrahabhāṣya. Theg pa chen po bsdus pa'i 'grel pa.* Toh 4050, sems tsam *ri.* 121b1–190a7.

———. *Rational System of Exposition. Vyākhyāyukti. Rnam par bshad pa'i rigs pa.* Toh 4061, sems tsam *shi.* 29a2–134b2

———. *Thirty Verses. Triṃśikākārikā. Sum cu pa'i tshig le'ur byas pa.* Toh 4055, sems tsam *shi.* 1a1–3a3. Translated in Anacker 1984.

———. *Treasury of the Abhidharma. Abhidharmakośa. Chos mngon pa'i mdzod.* Toh 4089, mngon pa *ku.* 1a1–25a7. For the Sanskrit see *Digital Sanskrit Buddhist Canon.* French translation by La Vallée Poussin in Vasubandhu 1923. The French translated to English by Leo Pruden in Vasubandhu 1988–90.

———. *Treatise on the Five Aggregates. Pañcaskandhaprakaraṇa,* Toh 4059 Tengyur, sems tsam, *shi.* 11b4–17a7. Translated in Anacker 1984 and in Engle 2009.

Vīravajra. *Illuminating Words and Meaning: An Explanation of "Yoginī's Activity." Yoginīsaṃcaryanibandhapadārthaprakaśa. Rnal 'byor ma kun spyod ma'i bshad thsig don rab tu gsal ba.* Toh 1423, rgyud *wa.* 139a3–153a3.

———. *Jewel Rosary: An Extensive Commentary on the Tantra of True Union, the Great Secret and Foundation of All Tantras. Sarvatantrasya nidānamahāguhyaśrīsampuṭatantraṭīkā-ratnamāla. Rgyud thams cad kyi gleng gzhi dang gsang chen dpal kun tu kha sbyor zhes bya ba'i rgyud kyi rgyal po'i rgya cher bshad pa rin chen phreng ba.* Toh 1199, rgyud ja. 1–111a2.

Vitapāda, a.k.a. Vaidyapāda. *Commentary to the Oral Transmission. Mukhāgamavṛtti. Mdzes pa'i me tog ces bya ba rim pa gnyis pa'i de kho na nyid bsgom pa zhal gyi lung gi 'grel pa.* Toh 1866, rgyud *di.* 87a3–139b3.

———. *Seven Yogas: A Treatise on the Four Empowerments. Yogasaptanāmacaturabhiṣekhaprakaraṇa. Sbyor ba bdun pa zhes bya ba dbang bzhi'i rab to byed pa.* Toh 1875, rgyud *pi.* 69b6–75b4.

Tibetan Works

Anonymous. *Biography and Songs of Shepai Dorjé. Dpal bzhad pa'i rdo rje'i rnam thar mgur chings dang bcas pa,* in three editions: (1) "Life of the Buddhist saint Mila-repa." Untitled manuscript no. Ms Tibet.a.11(r). Oriental Reading Room, Bodleian Library, Oxford. (2) *The Profound Life of Noble Mila.*

Rje bstun mid la ras pa'i rnam thar zab mo. Handwritten manuscript, folio 36.280 (IIB R-16). Newark Museum Tibetan Collection, Newark. (3) Published with incorrect attribution to Rangjung Dorjé in *The Dark Treasury: The Songs of Mila Shepa Dorje, Compiled by Rangjung Dorje. Mi la bzhad pa rdo rje'i gsung mgur mdzod nag ma zhes pa karma pa rang byung rdo rjes phyogs gcig tu bkod pa*. In *The Collected Works of the Third Karmapa Rangjung Dorje* (*Karma pa rang byung rdo rje'i gsung 'bum*), vol 3. Zi ling: Mtshur phu mkhan po lo yag bkra shis, 2006.

Gampopa Sönam Rinchen (Sgam po pa Bsod rnams rin chen). *Group Teachings Entitled "Perfection of Qualities." Tshogs chos yon tan phun tshogs*. In *Khams gsum chos kyi rgyal po dpal mnyam med sgam po pa 'gro mgon bsod nams rin chen mchog gi gsung 'bum yid bzhin nor bu* (*Dwags po'i bka' 'bum*), vol. *ka*, 505–75. Kathmandu: Khenpo S. Tenzin and Lama T. Namgyal, 2000.

———. *Treasury of the Ultimate: Introduction to the Essence. Snying po'i ngo sprod don dam gter mdzod*. In *Collected Works of Sgam po pa Bsod rnams rin chen*, vol. *ga*, section *ra*. Kathmandu: Khenpo S. Tenzin and Lama T. Namgyal, 2000.

———. *Ornament of Precious Liberation: Like a Wish-Fulfilling Gem of Sublime Dharma. Dam chos yid bzhin nor bu thar pa rin po che'i rgyan*. In *Rtsib ri spar ma*, vol. 1, pp. 33–479. Darjeeling: Kagyu Sungrab Nyamso Khang, 1975–85.

———. *Tai lo dang nāro'i rnam thar*. In *Selected Writings of Sgam po pa Bsod nams rin chen (Dwags po lha rje), with the Biography Written by His Descendant Bsod nams lhun grub*. Dolanji, H.P., India: Tibetan Bonpo Monastic Center, 1974.

Gyalwa Yangönpa (Rgyal ba yang dgon pa). *The Great Tantra that Teaches Unimpeded Dzogchen. Rdzogs pa chen po zang thal du bstan pa'i rgyud chen mo*. In *Teachings on the Unimpeded Realization of Dzogchen* (*Rdzogs pa chen po dgongs pa zang thal gyi chos skor*), vol. 3. Delhi: Tashigang, 1979.

———. *A Rosary of Wish-Fulfilling Jewels. Bka' 'bum yid bzhin nor bu'i phreng ba*. Delhi: Tashigang, 1979.

Lingchen Repa Pema Dorjé (Gling chen ras pa Pad ma rdo rje). *Collected Works of Lingchen Repa Pema Dorjé. Gling chen ras pa padma rdo rje'i gsung 'bum*. India: Khams pa sgar gsung rab nyams gdo khang, 1985.

Mikyö Dorjé (Mi bskyod rdo rje). *The Six Dharmas of Nāropa. Nāro chos drug*. In *Collected Works (Gsung 'bum) of Karmapa Mikyö Dorjé*, vol. 23, pp. 773–892. Lhasa: 2004.

Nāropa. *Mahāmudrā in Brief. Mahāmudrāsañcamitha* [sic]. *Phyag rgya chen po tshig bsdus pa*. Not included in the Tengyur. The Sanskrit may be a corruption of *Mahāmudrāsaṃcita*. It has elsewhere been erroneously attributed to Maitripa. Included in *Eight Doha Treasures. Do ha mdzod brgyad ces bya ba phyag rgya chen po'i man ngag gsar bar ston pa'i gzhung*. Darjeeling: Kargyu sungrab nyamso khang, 1978–85.

———. *Vajra Song of the Six Dharmas. Chos drug dril ba rdo rje'i mgur.* Not included in the Tengyur. Included in *Anthology of Kagyü Masters (Sgrub brgyud gong ma kyis zhal gdams phyogs sgrigs nor bu'i bang mdzod)*. Delhi: Byang A ri mnyam med 'bri gung bka' brgyud chos sde, 2001.

Ngari Tertön Garwang Dorjé. *Mahāmudrā: Seeing the Naked Intrinsic Nature. Phyag chen gnyug ma gcer mthong.* Delhi: Lama Dawa, 1983.

Phakmo Drupa (Phag mo gru pa). *Innate Union. Lhan cig skyes sbyor.* In *The Collected Works of Phag-mo dru-pa (Dus gsum sangs rgyas thams cad kyi thugs rje'i rnam rol dpal ldan phag gru rdo rje rgyal po mchog gi gsung 'bum rin po che)*, vol. *nga* (4 of 9), pp. 256–82. Kathmandu: Khenpo Shedrub Tenzin and Lama Thinley Namgyal, 2003.

Rangjung Dorjé (Rang byung rdo rje). *Illuminating the Profound Path of the Six Dharmas of Nāropa. Zab lam nā ro chos drug gi gsal byed spyi chings khrid yig dang bcas pa (Gser zhung ma).* In *Collected Works of Karmapa Rangjung Dorjé (Karma pa rang byung rdo rje'i gsung 'bum)*, vol. 9, pp. 538–93. Zi ling: Mtshur phu mkhan po lo yag bkra shis, 2006.

———. *Profound Inner Meaning. Zab mo nang gi don.* Sikkim: Rumtek Monastery blockprint, n.d.

Ratna Lingpa. *Mahamudrā: The Sun's Essence. Phyag rgya chen po nyi ma'i snying po.* Bylakuppe, Karnataka, India: Pema Norbu Rinpoche, 1984.

Sangyé Lingpa. *Unity of the Gurus' Realization. Bla ma dgongs 'dus.* 13 vols. Gangtok: Sonam Topgay Kazi, 1972.

Tatsak Tsewang Gyal (Rta tshag Tshe dbang rgyal). *The Dharma History from Lhorong (The Marvelous, Rare, Special Text Known by the Name of the Place Where It Was Written: An Excellent Description of the History of the Dharma, Known as "The Dharma History from Lhorong" or "The Dharma History from Tatsak"). Lho rong chos 'byung (Dam pa'i chos kyi byung ba'i legs bshad lho rong chos 'byung gnam rta tshag chos 'byung zhes rtsom pa'i yul ming du chags pa'i ngo mtshar zhing dkon pa'i dpe khyed par can).* Mtsho sngon (Quinghai): Bod ljongs bod yig dpe rnying dpe skrun khang, 1994.

Tsangnyön Heruka (Gtsang smyon Heruka / Khrag 'thung rgyal po). *Meaningful to See: A Biography of Marpa Lotsāwa. Sgra bsgyur mar pa lo tsa'i rnam par thar pa mthong ba don yod.* Sarnath: Lobsang Tsultim, 1970.

———. *The Hundred Thousand Songs of Milarepa. Rje btsun mi la ras pa'i rnam thar rgyas par phye ba mgur 'bum.* Antwerp: Tibetaans Boeddhistisch Meditatiecentrum, n.d.

Wangchuk Gyaltsen (Dbang phyug rgyal mtshan). *Great Bliss of Stainless Teachings: A Biography of Nāropa. Nā ro pa'i rnam thar dri med legs bshad bde chen.* Palampur, H.P., India: Sungrab nyamso gyunphel parkhang, 1972–76.

Translator's Bibliography

Anacker, Stefan. *Seven Works of Vasubandhu, the Buddhist Psychological Doctor*. Religions of Asia Series. Delhi: Motilal Banarsidass, 1984.

Aris, Michael. *Bhutan: The Early History of a Himalayan Kingdom*. Warminster, England: Aris and Phillips, 1979.

Āryadeva. *Aryadeva's Four Hundred Stanzas on the Middle Way*. Trans. Ruth Sonam. Ithaca, NY: Snow Lion Publications, 2008.

Āryaśūra. *Garland of the Buddha's Past Lives*. Trans. Justin Meiland. 2 vols. New York: Clay Sanskrit Library, 2009.

———. *The Jātakamālā of Aryasūra*. Trans J. S. Speyer. New Delhi: Akshaya Prakashan, 2007.

———. *Jātakamālā: The Marvelous Companion*. Berkeley, CA: Dharma Publishing, 1983.

———. *Once the Buddha Was a Monkey: Ārya Śūra's Jātakamāla*. Chicago: University of Chicago Press, 1989.

Asaṅga. *Abhidharma Samuccaya: The Compendium of the Higher Teaching (Philosophy)*. Trans. into French by Walpola Rahula; into English from French by Sara Boin-Webb. Fremont, CA: Asian Humanities Press, 2001.

Aśvaghoṣa. *The Awakening of Faith in the Mahayana* (*Mahāyānaśraddhotpāda*). New York: Columbia Unversity Press, 1967.

Bendall, Cecil, and Louis de la Vallée Poussin. "*Bodhisattva-bhūmi*: A Textbook of the Yogācāra School. An English Summary with Notes and Illustrative Extracts from other Buddhistic Works." *Le Muséon*, n.s., 6 (1905): 38–52; 7 (1906): 213–30; and "*Bodhisattva-bhūmi*: Sommaire et notes." *Le Muséon*, n.s., 12 (1911): 155–91.

Blumenthal, James. *The Ornament of the Middle Way: A Study of of the Madhyamaka Thought of Śāntarakṣita*. Ithaca, NY: Snow Lion Publications, 2004.

Broido, Michael M. "*Abhiprāya* and Implication in Tibetan Linguistics." *Journal of Indian Philosophy* 12.1 (March 1984): 1–33.

Brown, Daniel P. *Pointing Out the Great Way: The Stages of Meditation in the Mahamudra Tradition*. Boston: Wisdom Publications, 2006.

Brunnhölzl, Karl. *The Center of the Sunlit Sky: Madhyamaka in the Kagyü Tradition*. Ithaca, NY: Snow Lion Publications, 2004.

———. *Straight from the Heart: Buddhist Pith Instructions*. Ithaca, NY: Snow Lion Publications, 2007.

Cleary, Thomas. *The Flower Ornament Scripture: A Translation of the Avatamsaka Sutra*. Boston: Shambhala Publications, 1984.

Conze, Edward. *Abhisamayālaṅkāra*. Serie Orientale Roma 6. Roma: Istituto Italiano per il Medio ed Estremo Oriente, 1954.

Cozort, Daniel. *Highest Yoga Tantra*. Ithaca, NY: Snow Lion Publications, 1986.

Dalai Lama, Dzong-ka-ba, and Jeffrey Hopkins. *Yoga Tantra: Paths to Magical Feats*. Ithaca, NY: Snow Lion Publications, 2005.

Dakpo Tashi Namgyal. *Clarifying the Natural State: A Principal Guidance Manual for Mahamudra*. Trans. Erik Pema Kunsang. Hong Kong: Rangjung Yeshe Publications, 2001.

———. *Mahamudra—The Moonlight: Quintessence of Mind and Meditation*. Trans. Lobsang Lhalungpa. Boston: Wisdom Publications, 2006.

———. [Drashi Namjhal]. *Teachings of Tibetan Yoga: An Introduction to the Spiritual, Mental and Physical Exercises of the Tibetan Religion*. Trans. Garma C. C. Chang. Hyde Park, NY: University Books, 1963.

Davidson, Ronald M. *Indian Esoteric Buddhism: A Social History of the Tantric Movement*. New York: Columbia University Press, 2002

Decleer, Hubert. "The Melodious Drum Sound All-Pervading: Sacred Biography of Rwa Lotsāwa." In *Tibetan Studies: Proceedings of the 5th Seminar of the International Association for Tibetan Studies, Narita 1989*, pp. 13–28. Nara City: Naritasan Shinshoji, 1992.

———. "The Sacred Biography of Bharo 'Maimed Hand.'" In *Buddha Jayanti Souvenir*. Ed. R. Shakya and M. Shakya. Lalitpur: 2538th Buddha Jayanti Organising Committee, 1994.

Digital Sanskrit Buddhist Canon. http://www.uwest.edu/sanskritcanon/dp/.

Doctor, Thomas H. *Speech of Delight: Mipham's Commentary on Śāntarakṣita's Ornament of the Middle Way*. Ithaca, NY: Snow Lion Publications, 2004.

Dorjé Dzeö (Rdo rje mdzes 'od). *The Precious Treasury that Is the Source of All that Is Required: Great Kagyü Biographies. Bka' brgyud kyi rnam thar chen mo rin po che'i gter mdzod dgos 'dod 'byung gnas*. Kangra, H.P., India: Tzondu Senghe, 1985.

Eckel, Malcolm David. *Jñānagarbha's Commentary on the Distinction Between the Two Truths: An Eighth-Century Handbook of Madhyamaka Philosophy*. Albany: State University of New York Press, 1986.

Engle, Artemus B. *The Inner Science of Buddhist Practice: Vasubandhu's Summary of the Five Heaps with Commentary by Sthiramati*. The Tsadra Foundation Series. Ithaca, NY: Snow Lion Publications, 2009.

English, Elizabeth. *Vajrayoginī: Her Visualizations, Rituals, and Forms*. Boston: Wisdom Publications, 2002.

Evans-Wentz, W. Y., ed. *Tibetan Yoga and Secret Doctrines*. London: Oxford University Press, 1935.

Gampopa [sGam.po.pa]. *The Jewel Ornament of Liberation*. Trans. Herbert V. Guenther. Boston: Shambhala Publications, 1986.

———. *The Jewel Ornament of Liberation: The Wish-Fulfilling Gem of the Noble Teachings*. Trans. Khenpo Konchog Gyaltsen Rinpoche. Ithaca, NY: Snow Lion Publications, 1998.

Giebel, Rolf, trans. *Two Esoteric Sutras: The Adamantine Pinnacle Sutra [and] The Susiddhikara Sutra*. Berkeley: Numata Center, 2001.

Giebel, Rolf, trans. *The Vairocanābhisambodhi Sutra*. Berkeley: Numata Center, 2006.

Gö Lotsāwa Shönu Pal ('Gos lo tsā ba Gzhon nu dpal). *The Blue Annals. Deb ther sngon po*. New Delhi: International Academy of Indian Culture, 1974.

———. *The Blue Annals*. Trans. George N. Roerich. Calcutta: Motilal Banarsidass, 1949.

Götsang Repa Natsok Rangdröl (Rgod tshang ras pa Sna tshogs rang grol). *The Life of Lord Rechungpa: A Mirror that Clearly Reveals the Path to Wisdom and Liberation. Rje btsun ras chung pa'i rnam thar rnam mkhyen thar lam gsal bar ston pa'i me long ye shes kyi snang ba*. Qinghai: Mtsho sngon mi rigs dpe skrun khang, 1992.

Gray, David B., trans. *The Cakrasaṃvara Tantra*. New York: American Institute of Buddhist Studies, 2007.

Guenther, Herbert. *Ecstatic Spontaneity: Saraha's Three Cycles of Dohā*. Nanzan Studies in Asian Religions. Fremont, CA: Asian Humanities Press, 1993.

Gyalthangpa Dechen Dorjé (Gyal thang pa [Rgya ldang pa] Bde chen rdo rje). *Golden Succession of the Kagyü. Dkar brgyud gser phreng*. Tashijong, Palampur, H.P., India: Sungrab Nyamso Gyunphel Parkhang, 1973.

Gyaltsen, Khenpo Könchog, trans. *The Great Kagyu Masters: The Golden Lineage Treasury*. Ithaca, NY: Snow Lion Publications, 1990. Translation of Dorjé Dzeö 1985.

Henning, Edward. *Kālacakra and the Tibetan Calendar*. Treasury of the Buddhist Sciences. New York: Columbia University, 2007.

Hodge, Stephen, trans. *Mahā-Vairocana-Abhisaṃbodhi Tantra with Buddhaguhya's Commentary*. London: Routledge Curzon, 2003.

Huntington, Jr., C. W., with Geshe Namgyal Wangchen. *The Emptiness of Emptiness: An Introduction to Early Indian Mādhyamika*. Honolulu: University of Hawaii, 1989.

Jamgön Kongtrul Lodrö Thayé ('Jam mgon kong sprul blo gros mtha' yas). *Autobiography of Jamgön Kongtrul: A Gem of Many Colors*. Trans. Richard Barron (Chökyi Nyima). Ithaca, NY: Snow Lion Publications, 1994.

———. *Creation and Completion: Essential Points of Tantric Meditation*. Trans. Sarah Harding. Boston: Wisdom Publications, 1996.

———. *Jamgon Kongtrul's Retreat Manual*. Trans. Ngawang Zangpo (Hugh Leslie Thompson). Ithaca, NY: Snow Lion Publications, 1994.

———. *Treasury of Knowledge. Shes bya kun khyab* (*Theg pa'i sgo kun las btus pa gsung rab rin po che'i mdzod bslab pa gsum legs par ston pa'i bstan bcos shes bya kun khyab*), 3 vols. Xining: Mi rigs Dpe skrun khang, 1982.

———. *Treasury of Knowledge, book 6, part 3: Frameworks of Buddhist Philosophy: A Systematic Presentation of the Cause-Based Philosophical Vehicles*.

Trans. Elizabeth M. Callahan. Ithaca, NY: Snow Lion Publications, 2007.

———. *Treasury of Knowledge, book 6, part 4: Systems of Buddhist Tantra: The Indestructible Way of Secret Mantra.* Trans. Elio Guarisco and Ingrid McLeod. Ithaca, NY: Snow Lion Publications, 2005.

———. *Treasury of Knowledge, book 8, part 3: The Elements of Tantric Practice: A General Exposition of the Process of Meditation in the Indestructible Way of Secret Mantra.* Trans. Elio Guarisco and Ingrid McLeod. Ithaca, NY: Snow Lion Publications, 2008.

———. *Treasury of Knowledge, book 8, part 4: Esoteric Instructions: A Detailed Presentation of the Process of Meditation in Vajrayāna.* Trans. Sarah Harding. Ithaca, NY: Snow Lion Publications, 2007.

———. *Treasury of Precious Termas. Rin chen gter mdzod chen mo.* Paro: Ngodrup and Sherab Drimay, 1966–80.

Kathok Tsewang Norbu. *Clear Brief Correct Account of Definite Chronology: Seeds of the Biographies of Some Holy Beings, such as Marpa, Milarepa, and Gampopa. Mar mi dwags po jo bo rje yab sras sogs dam pa 'ga' zhig gi rnam thar sa bon dus kyi nges pa brjod pa dag ldan nyung gsal.* In *Kathok Rikzin Tsewang Norbu's Collected Works. Kaḥ thog rig 'dzin tshe dbang nor bu'i bka' 'bum*, vol. 3, pp. 640–54. Beijing: Krung go'i bod rig pa dpe skrun khang, 2006.

Kapstein, Matthew T. *The Tibetan Assimilation of Buddhism: Conversion, Contestation, and Memory.* New York: Oxford University Press, 2000.

Karmapa Wangchuk Dorjé (Karma pa Dbang phyug rdo rje). *Mahāmudrā: The Ocean of Definitive Meaning. Phyag chen rgyas pa nges don rgya mtsho.* Sarnath: Vajravidya dpe mdzod khang, 2006.

———. *Mahāmudrā: The Ocean of Definitive Meaning.* Trans. Elizabeth Callahan. Seattle: Nitartha, 2001.

———. *The Mahāmudrā: Eliminating the Darkness of Ignorance.* Trans. Alexander Berzin. Dharamsala: Library of Tibetan Works and Archives, 1978.

[Lhatsün Rinchen Namgyal]. *Life and Teaching of Naropa.* Trans. Herbert V. Guenther. Boston: Shambhala Publications, 1986.

Lindtner, Christian. *Nagarjuniana: Studies in the Writings and Philosophy of Nāgārjuna.* Delhi: Motilal Banarsidass, 1982.

———. *Master of Wisdom: Six Texts by Nāgārjuna.* Berkeley: Dharma Publishing, 1986.

Lusthaus, Dan. *Buddhist Phenomenology: A Philosophical Investigation of Yogācāra.* London: Routledge Curzon, 2002.

Maitreya, Arya. *Buddha Nature: The Mahayana Uttaratantra Shastra with Commentary.* Trans. Rosemary Fuchs. Ithaca, NY: Snow Lion Publications, 1999.

Marpa Chökyi Lodrö [Mar-pa Chos-kyi bLo-gros]. *The Life of the Mahāsiddha Tilopa.* Trans. Fabrizio Torricelli and Acharya Sangye T. Naga. Dharamsala: Library of Tibetan Works and Archives, 1995.

Martin, Dan. "The Early Education of Milarepa." *Journal of the Tibet Society* 2 (1982): 52–76.

Mathes, Klaus-Dieter. *A Direct Path to the Buddha Within: Gö Lotsāwa's Mahāmudrā Interpretation of the Ratnagotravibhāga*. Boston: Wisdom Publications, 2008.

Mullin, Glenn H. *The Practice of the Six Yogas of Naropa*. Ithaca, NY: Snow Lion Publications, 1997.

Nāgārjuna. *The Fundamental Wisdom of the Middle Way*. Trans. Jay L. Garfield. Oxford: Oxford University Press, 1995.

———. *In Praise of Dharmadhātu*. Trans. Karl Brunnhölzl. Ithaca, NY: Snow Lion Publications, 2007.

———. *Nagarjuna's Letter to a Friend*. Trans. Padmakara Translation Group. Ithaca, NY: Snow Lion Publications, 2005.

———. *Nāgārjuna's Precious Garland*. Analyzed, translated, and edited by Jeffrey Hopkins. Ithaca, NY: Snow Lion Publications, 1997.

Nalanda Translation Committee, trans. *Rain of Wisdom: The Essence of the Ocean of True Meaning*. Boston: Shambhala Publications, 1980.

Obermiller, Eugene. *Analysis of the Abhisamayālaṃkāra*. Calcutta Oriental Series 27. London: Luzac & Co., 1933.

Prasad, H.S., ed. *Uttaratantra of Maitreya*. Sanskrit text. ed. E. H. Johnston, trans. E. Obermiller. Delhi: Sri Satguru Publications, 1991.

Rheingans, Jim. "Narratives of Reincarnation, Politics of Power, and the Emergence of a Scholar: The Very Early Years of Mikyö Dorje." In *Lives Lived, Lives Imagined: Biography in the Buddhist Traditions*, ed. Linda Covill et al., pp. 241–98. Boston: Wisdom Publications, 2010.

Rinchen, Geshe Sonam. *Atisha's Lamp for the Path to Enlightenment*. Trans. Ruth Sonam. Ithaca, NY: Snow Lion Publications, 1997.

Roberts, Peter Alan. *The Biographies of Rechungpa: The Evolution of a Tibetan Hagiography*. Abingdon, Oxon: Routledge, 2007.

———. "The Evolution of the Biography of Milarepa and Rechungpa." In *Lives Lived, Lives Imagined: Biography in the Buddhist Traditions*, ed. Linda Covill et al., pp. 181–203. Boston: Wisdom Publications, 2010.

Roth, Gustav. "Observations on the First Chapter of Asaṅga's *Bodhisattvabhūmi*." *Indologica Taurinesia* 3–4 (1975–76): 403–12.

Śāntarakṣita. *The Adornment of the Middle Way: Shantarakshita's* Madhyamakalankara *with Commentary by Jamgön Mipham*. Trans. Padmakara Translation Group. Boston: Shambhala Publications, 2005.

Śāntideva. *Bodhicaryāvatāra*. Trans. Kate Crosby and Andrew Skilton. Oxford: Oxford University Press, 1995.

———. *A Guide to the Bodhisattva Way of Life*. Trans. Alan and Vesna Wallace. Ithaca, NY: Snow Lion Publications, 1997.

——— [Shantideva]. *A Guide to the Bodhisattva's Way of Life*. Trans. Stephen Batchelor. Dharmasala: Library of Tibetan Works and Archives, 1979.

——— [Shantideva]. *The Way of the Bodhisattva*. Trans. Padmakara Translation Group. Boston: Shambhala Publications, 1997.

Schaeffer, Kurtis R. *Dreaming the Great Brahmin: Tibetan Traditions of the Buddhist Poet-Saint Saraha*. Oxford: Oxford University Press, 2004.

Shamar Khachö Wangpo (Zhwa dmar Mkha' spyod dbang po). *Clouds of Blessings. Byin rlabs kyi sprin phung*. In *Collected Writings of the Second Zhvad mar Mkha' spyod dbang po (Mkha' spyod dbang po gsung 'bum)*, vol. 1, pp. 188–317. Gangtok, Sikkim: Gonpo Tseten, 1978.

Siklós, Bulcsu, trans. *The Vajrabhairava Tantras*. Tring: The Institute of Buddhist Studies, 1996.

Situ Tenpai Nyinjé, a.k.a. Situ Chökyi Jungné (Si tu Bstan pa'i nyin byed, Chos kyi 'byung gnas). *A Supplement to "A String of Infinite Moonstone Jewels: Biographies of the Precious Karma Kamtsang Lineage." Karma kaṃ tshang brgyud pa rin po che'i rnam thar rab 'byams nor bu'i chu shel gyi phreng ba'i kha skong*. In Chos kyi 'byung gnas, *Gsung 'bum*, vol. *da*. Kangra, H.P., India: Palpung Sungrab Nyamso Khang, 1990.

Skorupski, Tadeusz, trans. *Kriyāsaṃgraha: Compendium of Buddhist Rituals*. Tring: The Institute of Buddhist Studies, 2002.

Stewart, Jampa Mackenzie. *The Life of Gampopa*. Ithaca, NY: Snow Lion Publications, 1995.

Takasaki, Jikido. *A Study on the Ratnagotravibhāga (Uttaratantra) Being a Treatise on the Tathāgatagarbha Theory of Mahāyāna Buddhism*. Rome Oriental Series 33. Rome: Istituto Italiano per il Medio ed Estremo Oriente, 1966.

Tatz, Mark, trans. *Asanga's Chapter on Ethics with the Commentary of Tsong-Kha-Pa: The Basic Path to Awakening, the Complete Bodhisattva*. Lewiston, NY: The Edwin Mellen Press, 1986.

———. *Difficult Beginnings: Three Works on the Bodhisattva Path [by] Candragomin*. Boston: Shambhala Publications, 2001.

———. *The Skill in Means (Upāyakauśalya) Sūtra*. Delhi: Motilal Banarsidass, 1994.

Thinley, Karma. *The History of the Sixteen Karmapas of Tibet*. Boulder, CO: Prajna Press, 1980.

Thrangu Rinpoche. *Uttaratantra: A Treatise on Buddha-Essence*. Bibliotheca Indo-Buddhica Series 131. Delhi: Satguru Publications, 1994.

Thurman Robert et al., trans. *The Universal Vehicle Discourse Literature (Mahāyānasūtrālaṃkāra) by Maitryanātha/Āryāsaṅga, Together with Its Commentary by Vasubandhu*. New York: American Institute of Buddhist Studies, 2004.

Tillemans, Tom J. F. *Dharmakīrti's Pramāṇavārtika: An Annotated Translation of the Fourth Chapter (parārthānumana)*. Vienna: Österreichischen Akademie der Wissenschaften, 2000.

Tola, Fernando, and Carmen Dragonetti. *Being as Consciousness: Yogācāra Philosophy of Buddhism*. Delhi: Motilal Banarsidass, 2006.

[Tsangnyön Heruka]. *The Hundred Thousand Songs of Milarepa*. Trans. Garma C. C. Chang. Boston: Shambhala Publications, 1989.

———. *The Life of Marpa the Translator: Seeing All Accomplishes All*. Trans. Nalanda Translation Committee. Boston: Shambhala Publications, 1982.

———. *The Life of Milarepa*. Trans. Lobsang Lhalungpa. Boston: Shambhala Publications, 1985.

Tsele Natsok Rangdrol. *Lamp of Mahamudra*. Trans. Erik Pema Kunsang. Kathmandu: Rangjung Yeshe, 1988.

Tsuda, Shiniichi. *The Samvarodaya-Tantra: Selected Chapters*. Tokyo: Hokuseido Press, 1974.

Uray, Géza. "The Narrative of Legislation and Organization of the *Mkhas-pa'i dga'-ston*: The Origins of the Traditions concerning Sroṅ-brcan Sgam-po as First Legislator and Organizer of Tibet." *Acta Orientalia Academiae Scientiarum Hungaricae* 26.1 (1972): 11–68.

Vasubandhu. *L'Abhidarmakośa. Traduit et annoté par Louis de la Vallée Poussin*. Paris: Paul Geuthner, 1923. Available to read online at Internet Archive: www.archive.org/details/labhidharmakosat01vasuuoft.

———. *Abhidharmakośabhāṣyam*, 4 vols. Trans. from French by Leo Pruden. Berkeley: Asian Humanities Press, 1988–90.

Wallace, Vesna A. *The Inner Kālacakratantra: A Buddhist Tantric View of the Individual*. Oxford: Oxford University Press, 2001.

———. *The Kālacakratantra: The Chapter on the Individual Together with the Vimalaprabhā*. Treasury of the Buddhist Sciences. New York: Columbia University Press, 2005.

———. *The Kālacakratantra: The Chapter on the Sādhana Together with the Vimalaprabhā*. Treasury of the Buddhist Sciences. New York: Columbia University Press, 2009.

Wayman, Alex. *Chanting the Names of Mañjuśrī: The Mañjuśrī-nāma-saṃgīti, Sanskrit and Tiebtan Texts*. Delhi: Motilal Banarsidass, 1985.

Wedemeyer, Christian. *Āryadeva's Lamp that Integrates the Practices (Caryāmelapakapradīpa): The Gradual Path of Vajrayāna Buddhism according to the Esoteric Community Noble Tradition*. New York: American Institute of Buddhist Studies, 2008.

Willis, Janice Dean. *On Knowing Reality: The Tattvārtha Chapter of Asaṅga's Bodhisattvabhūmi*. New York: Columbia University Press, 1979.

Yeshe, Lama Thubten. *The Bliss of Inner Fire: Heart Practice of the Six Yogas of Naropa*. Boston: Wisdom Publications, 1998.

Index

A

Abbreviated Perfection of Wisdom in Verse, 177, 184, 247–48, n246, n455

Abhayākaragupta, 12, 137, 273, 425, 491, 513, 547, n185, n423, n520. See also *Adornment of [the Muni's] View*; *Ears of Grain of Practice Instructions*; *Vajra Garland of Mandala Rituals*

Abhidharma, 189, 201, 374, 391, 409, 410, 425, n289, n320, n352, n657, n677, n680, n707, n863, n864. *See also* scriptural baskets; *Treasury of Abhidharma*

ācārya empowerment, 448–49. 454–56, 477–79, 481–82

Accomplishment of the True Nature (Sahajayoginī Cintā), 578

Accomplishment of the Secret (Padmavajra), 578, n1273

Accomplishment of Wisdom. See *Sādhana for the Accomplishment of Wisdom*

action tantra. *See* four tantras: action

Adornment of Kosala: An Extensive Commentary on "Compendium of Truths" (Śākyamitra), 459, 535

Ornament of Precious Liberation (Gampopa Sönam Rinchen), 18

Adornment of the Essence of the General Rites of All Secrets (Mañjuśrīkīrtī), 497

Adornment of [the Muni's] View (Abhayākaragupta), 276

Adornment of the Vajra Mandala Tantra, 428

Advayavajra, 285, n551. *See also* Maitripa; *Teaching on the Mudrās of the Five Tathāgatas*; *Ten Verses on the True Nature*

afflicted mentation (afflicted mind), 163, 165, 211, 212, 213, 292, n225

afflictions (Skt. *kleśa*), 69, 90, 130, 251, 328, 381, n384, n659, n1235
- absence of, 150, 207, 245–46, 318, 454, 595
- arising of realization and wisdom, 102, 103, 124
- and bliss, 161, 298
- and buddhahood, 207, 265, 293, 385, 408, 597, 607, n349
- and dependent origination, 214–16
- as empty, 39, 146, 420
- errors, obstacles, downfalls, 184, 188, 380, 494, 504
- liberation from, 89, 189, 420
- and mandala deities, 43–44, n740, n1102
- manifest and latent, 165–66
- Mantrayāna path and, 260, 321, 324, 370, 384, 401, 429, 565, n740, n827, n1102
- meditational stability and, 107
- neutral, n354
- pervaded by mind, 87
- purification of, 44–45, 156, 158, 160, 164, 201, 375, 423, 545, 569
- remedy for, 58, 391
- and śamatha, 242, 300, 302
- source of, 88, 163, 165, 200, 212, 291
- *See also* dependent origination; five afflictions

Askṣobhya, 357, 360–62, 442, 443, 509, 526, n133, n638
ālaya, 33, 163, 165–66, 171, 208, 283, 291–93
  abode of karmic seeds, 201, 212, 213, 398
  bodhisattva path, 258, 394, n483
  dependent origination, 213, 215, 228, 292
  and emanation of deities, 532
  and mentation, 211–13, 215, 241, n363
  as naturally pure mind, 213, 229, 291, 314–15
  purification and transformation, 208, 313, 320
  samsara and nirvana, 293
  See also dependent origination
Amitābha, 6, 357, 360–61, 442, 443, 509, 526, n4, n133
Amoghasiddhi, 357, 442, 509, 526, n133
Analysis of "Realizing [the Bhagavan]" (Atiśa), 513, 524, 525, 542–43, 584, n998, n1293, n1294
Apatarava, 457, n899
appearance, increase, and attainment, 213, 364, 528, 529, n634, n635. *See also* four empties
"appearances, arising, are," 40–41, 43
Applications of Mindfulness Sutra, 182, 441n846, n263
Aro Yeshé Jungné, 40, n78
Aspectarian doctrine, 105, n164
Asu, 12
Atiśa Dīpaṃkaraśrījñāna, 5, 11, 14, 35–36, 63, 287, 288, 524, 525, n70, n116, n558. See also *Analysis of "Realizing [the Bhavagan]"*; *Entering the Two Truths*; *Lamp for the Path to Enlightenment*
avadhūti. *See* channels, central
Avalokiteśvara, 5, 132, n239, n724
Avataṃsaka Sutra, 183, 218, 277, 278, 319, 442, n287, n370, n528, n589, n681
awareness, 8, 77, 156, 166, 243, 254, 352
  and clarity, 300, 575
  mindfulness and, 143, 164, 305, 458, 535
  See also four yogas; śamatha; vipaśyanā

B

bardo, 8, 362–67, 517, 519, 527–30, 546, 569, 571–74, n1252, n1254, n1392
  beginners' attainment, 121–22, 283
  causal Vajradhara, 521–22, 531
  supreme siddhi, 601, 611, 613–14
  See also rebirth; six Dharmas of Nāropa
Bhaiṣajya, 6
Bhavideva (Aśvaghoṣa), 493, 495, n1009, n1018
bhūmi. *See* levels
Binding Net of the Ḍākinīs, 270, n507
bindu, 7, 340, 360, 521, 534n1129, 559. *See also* channels, winds, and drops; drops
birthless nature, 41, 42. *See also* birthlessness
birthlessness, 44, 61, 76, 110, 147, 197, 458–59
  fault of, 39–40
  See also birthless nature
Black Yamāntaka Tantra, 508, n1060
bliss, clarity, and nonthought, 41, 101, 121–22, 151n205, 161–62, 262–63, 279, 299, 302, 309–310, 371, 563n1227
Blue Annals (Gö Lotsāwa), 11, 12, 13, 15, 18, 19, 23, n20, n45
bodhicitta, 31–203 *passim*, 221, 249–85 *passim*, 307, 312–450 *passim*, *452, 481–614 *passim*
  aspiration and engagement, 127
  physiological (semen), 8, 192, 336–83 *passim*, 483–87, 517–31 *passim*, 555–64 *passim*
  relative and ultimate, 31–32, 33, 489, 491
bodhisattva, 16, 49, 177, 185, 216, 221, 249, 268, 275, 280, 380–81, 440,

n243, n253, n289, n512, n589, n699
vow of conduct, 187, 380, 450, n98
body mandala empowerment, 468–69, 472, 474, 475, 483
Brief Cakrasaṃvara. Empowerment (Vajraghaṇṭa), 469, 483–84, 484, 546, n942
Bringing Out the Hidden Meaning Sutra, 258–59, n483
Buddha Dīpaṃkara, 403, 404, 405, n707
Buddha (Siddhartha Gautama), 2, 3, 16, 36, 189–90, 266, 287, 399, 402–17. *See also* Śākyamuni
buddha (Tib. *sangs rgyas*), 278
buddha nature, causal, 439, 440
Buddhakapāla Tantra, 6, 461, 467–68, n937

C
cakras, 8, 370, 383, 534, 605, n1201
four joys, 485, 563
instructions for caṇḍālī practice, 343, 344, 345, 561, 562, 579
number and arrangement of, 339, 343, 556, 557, 560
Cakrasaṃvara, 2, 6, 285, 333, 355, 413
Cakrasaṃvara Tantra of the Inconceivable Secret, 307–8, 331, 437, n585, n610
caṇḍālī (Tib. *gtum mo*), 7–8, 50–51, 337–47, 553, 561–64. *See also* six Dharmas of Nāropa
Candrakīrti, 190, 217, 287. See also *Entering the Middle Way*; *Illuminating Lamp*
Candraprabhakumāra, 61, 81, 137, n113, n151, n182. *See also* Gampopa
Cāryapa, 5
Casket of Jewels Sutra, 265
central channel (Skt. *avadhūti*), 7–8, 136, 339, 541, 555, n618
dissolving winds into, 560, 568, 570, 577, 579, 605–6
empowerments, 336, 337
training in, 340–46, 359–60, 367–68, 371
See also channels, winds, and drops
channels, winds, and drops, 38, 192, 281, 292, 394, n644
completion stage, 554, 555–56, 560, 578, 606
See also central channel; drops; *lalanā*; *rasanā*; winds
Characteristics Vehicle, 50, 375, 376, 391, 442
chö (Tib. *gcod*). *See* severance practices
Chökyi Drakpa, 21
Chökyi Yungdrung, 19
Cittamātra, 375, 381, 391, n164, n566, n656, n667, n681
classes of individuals, 93–96, 307, 533–34
gradualist, 93, 94, 95, 101–6, 108, 284, 296, 307, 323, 375, 501
immediate, 96, 284, 296
indeterminate (nonsequential), 93, 101, 106, 307
See also five wisdoms
Clear Summary of the Five Stages (Nāropa), 581–82
Commentary on Bodhicitta (Nāgārjuna), 203, 214, 218, 219, 249, 271–72, 578, n342, n360, n373, n516
Commentary on Difficult Points in "Entering the Conduct of a Bodhisattva" (Prajñākaramati), 236, 441, n423, n846
Commentary on "Ten Verses on the True Nature" (Sahajavajra), 257, 283
Commentary on the Compendium of the Mahayana (Vasubandhu), 397, n695
Commentary on the Latter Dhyāna (Buddhaguhya), 450–51, 452
Commentary on the Śrī Paramādya Tantra (Ānandagarbha), 456, n894
Commentary on the Thirty Verses (Sthiramati), 195, n321
Commentary to the Black Yamāntaka (Ratnākaraśānti), 536, n1136
Commentary to the Enlightenment of

Vairocana (Buddhaguhya), 432, n808
Commentary to the First Part [of Compendium of Truths] (Ānandagarbha), 456, 457, n893, n897
Commentary to the Oral Transmission (Vitapāda), 436
Commentary to the Saṃvarodaya Tantra (Ratnarakṣita), 517, 517–18, 518
commitment being (Skt. *samayasattva*), 72, 356–57, 360–61, 508, 523, 524–25, 531, n1100, n1105
commitments. See *samaya*
Compendium of All Vajra Wisdom Tantra, 427
Compendium of Truths, 407, 411, 425, 455, 456, 457, 458, 459, n893, n900, n902, n904, n905
Compiled Summary of the Four Seats Tantra Mandalas (Āryadeva), 465
completion stage
  definition of, 7, 54–55, 58, 206, 208, 285, 498–99
  of father tantras, 550–52, 554, 555, 558
  of inseparable union of two truths, 554, 555, 582
  of luminosity of mahāmudra, 555, 576, 578
  of mother tantras, 434, 550, 553–54, 578
  self-blessing, 254, 432, 490, 554, 555, 583, 585
  six branches of, 551
  See also sādhanas; two stages
Condensed Sādhana (Nāgārjuna), 587
conduct
  of a *bhusuka/bhusuku*, 370, 387, n642, n673
  classifications of, 323, 324, n173
  heruka, 586, 591
  mantra conduct, 273, 533, n519
  special conduct of wisdom, 387
  ten Dharma conducts, 47, n89
  three conducts, 323, 370, 586, 589–90
  two conducts, 50, 51, 52, 109, 117, 272, 386, 590, n808
  See also four conducts; three trainings
consort practice, 8, 18. *See also* empowerment: prajñā's wisdom

D

Daklha Gampo, 17, 81, 620, n152, n1415
Dakpo Kagyü, 4, 17, 18–19, 65, 202, 265, 307. *See also* Kagyü
Dakpo Lhajé, 4, 17, 81, 257, 285–86, n118, n151, n1412. *See also* Gampopa
Dakpo Tashi Namgyal, 4, 5, 8, 15, 18, 20, 24, n18, n269, n709, n790, n801, n1064, n1092, n1104, n1413
Dalai Lama V Ngawang Losang Gyatso, 1, 25
Dampa Kor Nirūpa, 11
Darma Wangchuk (Barompa), 19
deity sādhana. *See* sādhana
Densely Arrayed Adornments Sutra, 214, 220, 229
dependent origination, 120–21, 184, 192, 196, 197, 209, 215, 228–29, 312, 327, 377, 392. *See also* afflictions: dependent origination; ālaya: dependent origination
Dhāraṇi of Entering Nonthought, 253, n468
dharmatā, 98, 439, n1095. *See also* buddha nature, causal; ultimate truth
dhyānas, 116, 165, 242–43, 281, 300, 302–3, 407, 431, 579–80. *See also* samādhi
discriminating wisdom, 144, 165, 208, 209, 229, 459, 519
Distinguishing the Middle Way from the Extremes (Maitreyanātha), 157, 227, 239n434, n397
Dīpaṃkara. *See* Atiśa Dīpaṃkaraśrījñāna; Buddha Dīpaṃkara; *Rites for the Guhyasamāja Mandala*
doha, 9–10, 12–13, n1311
Doha Treasury of Mahāmudrā Instructions (Saraha), 236

Ḍombipa, 266, 288, n499. See also *Gaṇacakra Rite*
dreams and illusions, 49, 59, 148–49, 292
appearances as, 35, 42, 46, 348
six perfections as, 56
See also three yogas: substance yoga
dream yoga, 8, 353–58, 569–72. *See* also six Dharmas of Nāropa
Drigung Kagyü, 4, 6, 16, 21–22, n612, n649
Drigung Nüden Dorjé, 6
Drigungpa, 21–22, 389, 395, 397, n693. *See also* Jikten Sumgön
Drokmi Lotsāwa, 15, n1223
Dromtön, 11, 14, 63, n558
drops (Skt. *bindu*), 7, 336, 350, 555–56, 559, n426
See also channels, winds, and drops; red element; white element
Drukpa Kagyü, 4, 6, 12, 23, n616
dzokchen, 18, 38, 41, 43, 51, 77, 172, 250, 251, 301, n671, n672

E
Ears of Grain Practice Instructions (Abhayākaragupta), 250, 270, 273, 524, 533, 534, 541, n278, n460, n509, n521
eight failings, 303–5
eight freedoms, 182, 440–41
Eight-Thousand-Verse Perfection of Wisdom, 77, 158, 178, 185, 201, 221, 234, n140, n277, n287, n335, n379, n416
Elimination of the Two Extremes (Jñānaśrī), 419, 421
empowerment deities, 525
Endowed with Wisdom (Saraha), 495, 496, n1017, n1020
Enlightenment of Vairocana, 135, 221, 237, 249, 449, 451, 452–53, 495, n179, n380, n427, n437, n882, n883
Entering the Conduct of a Bodhisattva (Śāntideva), 68, 70, 182, 222, 231, n262, n403
Entering the Mantrayāna (Jñānākara), 279, 422, n536, n773
Entering the Middle Way (Candrakīrti), 176, 178, 190, n245
Entering the Truth (Jñānakīrti), 206
Entering the Two Truths (Atiśa), 37, 248, n73, n456
Entry into Laṅka Sutra, 214, 215, 218, 222, 418, n363
Establishing the Truth (Śāntarakṣita), 588
Excellent Accomplishment Tantra, 450, 453–54
Excellent Collection of the Sādhanas of the Mandala Rituals (Durjaya-candra), 465, n926
Explanation of "Entering the Conduct of a Bodhisattva" (Kṛṣṇapa), 441
Explanatory Tantra of the Vajra Garland. See *Profound Meaning: A Commentary on the Vajra Garland Tantra*
Extensive Commentary on the Condensed Meaning of the Hevajra (Vajragarbha), 189, 434–35, 501–6 *passim*, 543–46 *passim*, 556, n290, n819, n820, n1053, n1159, n1165, n1166

F
father tantras, 370, 433–38. *See also* completion stage: father tantras; highest yoga tantra
fault of appearances, 39
Fearing Nothing: A Commentary on the Root Middle Way (Nāgārjuna), 196–97, n325, n326
Fifty Verses on the Guru (Aśvaghoṣa), 464, 494
"firing like an arrow," 339, 340, 341, 559
five afflictions, 442, 480, n827. *See also* afflictions
Five Commitments (Padmākara), 422–23, 496
five Dharmas of dhyāna, 136, 233
five enlightenments (Skt.

abhisaṃbodhi), 359, 413, 518, 519, n636
five meats and five nectars, 109, 430, 590, 592, 594, n169, n1316
five poisons, 44, 282
five powers, 109, 318, n170. *See also* samādhi
five sights, 274, 276, 308
Five Stages, (Nāgārjuna), 489, 499–507 *passim*, 551–88 *passim*, n1000, n1235, n1269, n1289, n1291, n1295, n1298
five wisdoms, 113, 278, 282, 437, 442, 480, 481, 528, n829. *See also* classes of individuals
four conducts
  avadhūti conduct, 590, 591
  excellent conduct, 272, 323–24, 590
  victorious conduct, 118, 323, 591, 596
  vrata conduct, 281, 387, 449, 455, 478, 498, 590, 591, 592
  See also conduct
four empowerments, 203, 282, 317, 393, 471, 479, 525, n687
four empties, 359, 555, 562, 568, 570, 572, 578, 581, 584, n635. *See also* appearance, increase, and attainment
Four Hundred and Fifty Verses. See *Rites for the Guhyasamāja Mandala*
Four Hundred Verses (Āryadeva), 286, n554
four karmas, 16
four tantras, 95, 374, 393, 426–34, n790, n800, n808
  action (Skt. *kriyā*), 411, 427–32, 449–50, n799, n809
  performance (Skt. *caryā*), 411, 427–32, 448–50, 452–53
  yoga, 407, 411, 427–32, 449, 450, 454–56, 459, 492, 587, n834, n896
  See also highest yoga tantra
fourth empowerment, 128, 301, 336, 431, 487–91
four truths, 50, 374, 409, 410
four yogas, 60, 112, 151, 279, 281–82, 306–28 *passim*, 456, 508, 559, n537. *See also* awareness; nonelaboration; nonmeditation; one-pointed yoga; one taste; śamatha
four yogas of the power of breath, 394, n691

G

Gampopa Sönam Rinchen, 287, 288. *See also* Candraprabhakumāra; Dakpo Lhajé
  Kagyü lineage, 1, 4, 14, 16, 19, 20, 23–24, 63
  life, 13, 17–18, n62, n560, n1412, n1413, n1415
Gaṇacakra Rite (Ḍombipa), 549, n1181
Garland of Pearls (Ratnākaraśānti), 536–37
generation stage, 6–7, 128, 499, 501–3, 507, 533
  conclusion of, 546–50
  empowerment, 525–26
  gathering of the two accumulations, 511–13
  generation of deity residents, 516–25
  generation of divine palace, 514–16
  mantra repetition, 539–46
  meditation on the mandala, 532–39
  protection circle, 513–14
  purification, 527–32
  seals, 526–27
  torma offerings, 510–11
  See also sādhanas; two stages
Geshé Ben, 177, n250
Gomtsül, 18, 19, 23, 24, 62
Great Commentary. See *Stainless Light*
Great Drum Sutra, 264, n494
Great Perfection. *See* dzokchen
Great Power Sutra, 416
Great Tantra that Teaches Unimpeded Dzogchen (Gyalwa Yangönpa), 291
Guhyasamāja Root Tantra, 202, 233, 270, 272–73, 421–22, 433, 436, 538
guru yoga. *See* preliminary practices

H

Heruka Abhisamaya, 588, n1305
Hevajra Tantra, 38, 58, 186, 214,

234–35, 253, 263, 270, 414, 427–47 *passim*, 498–595 *passim*
Hevajra Torma Rite (Durjayacandra), 547, n1173
highest yoga tantra, 6, 393, 427–28, 432–37, 453, n14, n790
commitments and vows, 492
empowerments, 95, 285, 333, 431, 460, 467, 476, 490
on Buddha's life, 407, 411–14
path of liberation, 498, 501
to whom taught, 7, 17, 428, 429, 430, 431
See also completion stage; father tantras; generation stage; mother tantras; nondual tantras
Hīnayāna, 105, 378, 442, 525, n680, n876, n1008
differences from other vehicles, 375, 382, 421, 424
life and teachings of buddhas, 403, 409, 410
śrāvakas and pratyekabuddhas, 49, 59, 418
hundred-syllable mantra. *See* Vajrasattva mantra
Hundred Verses on the Essence of Understanding (Āryadeva), 263

I

Illuminating Lamp (Candrakīrti), 408, 435–36, 443, 443–44, 444, 551, 598, n650
Illuminating Words and Meaning: An Explanation of "Yoginī's Activity" (Vīravajra), 261, 547, 548, n1172, n1177
Illumination of the Secret Nature (Kṛṣṇapa), 434
Illusion doctrine, 105, n166
illusory body, in six Dharmas of Nāropa, 8, 347–53, 354–69 *passim*, 484, 563–69. *See also* completion stage; six Dharmas of Nāropa
innate union (Skt. *sahajayoga*), 135, 168, 252, 257, 284, 285
Innate Accomplishment (Indrabhūti), 234, 236
Innate Union (Phakmo Drupa), 251–52
Instructions from the Successive Guru Lineage (Vajrapāni), 237–38, 254
Instructions on the Six Dharmas (Tilopa), 5, n10
Instructions on the Six Yogas (Kālacakrapāda), 256, 562–63, 566, 5567
Instructions through Similes (Nāropa). See *Truly Valid Instructions*

J

Jambudvīpa, 37, 179, 183, 410, 413, 414, 417, 440, n267
Jamgön Kongtrül, 2, 4, 15, 16, 20, n2
Jātakamālā (Āryaśūra), 190
Jatsön Nyingpo, 5
Jikten Sumgön, 4, 21, n649. *See also* Drigungpa
Jñānadākinī Niguma, 315, n587
Jonang, 3, 5, 25, n32, n60

K

Kadam, 5, 11, 14–15, 17–18, 63, 285–86, n116, n250, n552, n553
Kagyü, 1–7, 12, 14–15, 17, 18, n6. *See also* Dakpo Kagyü; *individual subsect names*
Kālacakra Root Tantra, 227, 247, 255, 265, 416, 497, 589, n398, n476. See also *Summarized Kālacakra Tantra; Primordial Buddha Kālacakra Tantra; Stainless Light*
Kambala, 5, 553, n867. See also *Top-Knot Jewel*
Kangyur and Tengyur, 25
Karma Kagyü (Karma Kamtsang), 1, 4–6, 19, 23–25, 287, 371, n6, n60, n61, n549, n557
Karmapa I Düsum Khyenpa, 1, 23–24, n155
Karmapa II Karma Pakshi, 24
Karmapa III Rangjung Dorjé, 24, 168, n236. See also *Profound Inner Meaning*

Karmapa IV Rölpai Dorjé, 24
Karmapa V Deshin Shekpa, 24–25, n549
Karmapa VII Chödrak Gyatso, 192, n301
Karmapa IX Wangchuk Dorjé, 24–25, 372, n18, n644, n647
Karmapa X Chöying Dorjé, 25, n647
Kāśyapa Sutra, 145, 221, 223, n387
King of Meditations Sutra (*Samādhirājasūtra*), 235, 259, 260, 265, 316, n113, n182, n417, n484, n486, n495, n588
knowledge, 282, 336, 431
Könchok Rinchen, 21
Kṛṣṇayamāri Tantra. See *Lamp for Seeing the Path: A Detailed Commentary on the Kṛṣṇayamāri King of Tantras*
Künga Paljor, 23, 145n192

L

lalanā, 8, 339–40, 557, n618, n1204. *See also* channels, winds, and drops
Lama Shang (Tsöndru Drakpa), 13, 16, 19–20, 21, 23, 24, 81, n117, n155. *See also* Shang Gom
Lamp for Seeing the Path: A Detailed Commentary on the Kṛṣṇayamāri King of Tantras (Ratnākaraśānti), 496–97, n1024
Lamp for the Path to Enlightenment (Atiśa), 271, 428, 445, 446, 632n70
Lamp of the Compendium of Practices (Āryadeva), 447, 499, 551, 585, 611, n867
Lamp of the Three Ways (Tripiṭakamāla), 419, 419–20, 420, 420–21, 431, 433
Latter Definition Tantra, 413, 515, 517, 546, 577, 603, 604, n745, n1085, n1087, n1368, n1371
Latter Dhyāna, 451, 452, n880
Latter Guhyasamāja Tantra, 273, 433–39 *passim*, 476–77, 500–501, 508, 520, 551, 580, 598–601 *passim*, n519, n1036, n1038, n1354
Letter to a Friend (Nāgārjuna), 241, n440
Lharipa Namkha Ö, 20, 65, 81, n117, n155
Lharjé Nupchung, 16
Lingré Pema Dorjé (Lingrepa), 12, 23
Long Sādhana of Vajrasattva, 456–57, n896
looking at the mind, 58, 80, 171, 248. *See also* vipaśyanā
Lorepa Darma Wangchuk, 298, n577
Lotus Endowed: A Commentary on Difficult Points (Kālacakrapāda), 254–55
Lotus Endowed: A Commentary on Difficult Points in the Hevajra Tantra (Sāroruha), 554
luminosity, in six Dharmas of Nāropa, 8, 358–62, 362–68 *passim*, 570. *See also* completion stage; six Dharmas of Nāropa

M

Madhyamaka, 196, 204, 206, 249, 250–51, 260, 374–75, 386, 447, n60, n166, n324, n672
Mahākaruṇika, 177, n249
mahāmāyā (illusory manifestations), 408
Mahāmāyā, Queen, 408
Mahāmāyā Tantra, 6
Mahāmudrā Tantra, 50, n94
Mahāmudrā: The Moonlight (Dakpo Tashi Namgyal), 19, 24, n18, n47
Mahāmudrā Tilaka Tantra, 203, 246–47, 460–61, 464, 477–78, 484, 558, 578, n452, n1211, n1274
Mahayana Treatise on the Sublime Continuum (Maitreyanātha), 69–70, 189–202 *passim*, 252, 293, 398–406 *passim*, 423–40 *passim*, 609–19 *passim*, n126, n330, n331, n463, n840, n841, n1383, n1384, n1399, n1400, n1403, n1409
Maitripa, 9, 11, 12, 13, 15, 63, 285, 287, n20, n36
mandala offering. *See* generation stage:

meditation on the mandala; preliminary practices: mandala offering
mantra repetition, 7, 431, 541–46, 576
instructions on practice, 72, 422, 459, 465, 475, 497, 541, 543–45, 600
suitable students, 420, 525
See also generation stage: mantra repetition; preliminary practices: Vajrasattva mantra
Mandala Rites of Guhyasamāja (Nāgārjuna), 470, 471
māras, 91, 92, 214, 329, 408, 506, 613
Buddha's subjugation of, 411–12, 414, n747
instructions for overcoming, 61, 163, 186, 187, 252, 472, 481, 495, n280, n495
Marpa Chökyi Lodrö, 3–4, 6, 11, 14–15, 16, 63, 287, n33, n36
meditation and post-meditation, 51, 111, 116, 121, 258, 306
four yogas, 312, 314, 315
path, 113–15, 296, 306, 307, 320, 348, 590
union of, 104, 116, 279, 312, 314, 315
mentation (Skt. *manas*), 163, 165, 211–17, 237, n225
Milarepa, 1, 4, 12, 14, 15–18, 19, 63, 284, n37
mind vajra, 211, 223, 273
mother tantras, 2, 3, 6, 370, 416, 433–38. *See also* completion stage: mother tantras; highest yoga tantra

N

nādīs. *See* channels
Nāgārjuna, 5, 10–11, 287, 413n746. *See also titles of his works*
nāgas, 108, 131, 413, 414–15
Nakpo Sherdé, 12
Nālandā, 13, 14
Namchö Mingyur Dorjé, 5, n6
Nāropa, 3–4, 11, 13–14, 15, 34, 63, 133, 153, 287, 288, n31, n606. See also *Clear Summary of the Five Stages*; six Dharmas of Nāropa; *Summary of the View*; *Truly Valid Instructions*; *Vajra Verses of the Aural Tantra*
Net of Illusions Tantra, 469–70, n944
Ngoktön, 15
nine vehicles, 50
nine yogas, 50, n96
Non-Aspectarian doctrine, 105, n165
nonattachment, 38, 41–42, 87, 91, 292, n80, n569
nonattention (Skt. *amanasikāra*), 55, 105, 113, 253–54, n465, n469
nonduality, 14, 42, 113, 125–26
realization of, 110, 116, 117, 118–19, 120. *See also* nondual wisdom; vipaśyanā
nondual tantras, 411, 433, 434, 435, 437
nondual union, 105, 254, 335, 583, 584, 598
nondual wisdom, 71, 103, 206, 387, 431, 480, 481, 610
instructions for practice, 256
realization of, 105, 117
stages, 551, 552
See also nonduality; three trainings
nonelaboration, 53, 60, 62, 91, 112, 146–48, 279–80, 306, 314–15
empowerments, 282, 294
levels and training, 62, 311–12, 318, 319–20, 498–99
postmeditation, 114
samādhi, 308
See also four yogas
nonmeditation, 78, 123, 280, 285, 308–9
definition, 53, 62, 113–15, 313, 314–15
empowerments, 282
levels and training, 62, 96, 115, 124, 150, 279–80, 314, 320–21
śamatha, 296
See also four yogas
Nyingma, 1, 3, 5, 14, 18, 21, 23, 25, 50, n6

O

objectlessness, 32, 35, 53, 157, 239, 368, 512, 549

Ocean of Dākas Tantra, 416, 417, 553, 565
Ocean of Definitive Meaning (Wangchuk Dorjé), 24
Oḍḍiyāna, 13, 357, 412, 414, 415, 416, 605
one-pointed yoga, 127, 137–44, 306, 308, 309–10, 311
  definition, 60, 280, 317
  empowerments, 282
  obstacles, 241
  path, 62, 111–12, 137, 156, 227, 233, 258, 279, 314–15, 317–18
  postmeditation, 114, 314
  samādhi, 53
  See also four yogas
one taste, 248, 252, 282, 308, 336, 368, 369
  definition, 53, 112–13, 279, 312, 314–15, 583
  levels, 318, 320, 371
  path and training, 61–62, 123, 149, 150, 163, 243, 262, 270, 280, 312–14
  post-meditation, 115, 314
  samādhi, 258, 308
  See also four yogas
  Oral Transmission (Buddhajñānapāda), 416–17, 484, 486, 552, 561, 613, 614, n756, n985, n986
Origin of All Vajras (Ānandagarbha), 448
Ornament of Realization (Maitreyanātha), 179, 271, 607, 607–8, 608, 614, n1375
Ornament of the Mahayana Sutras (Maitreyanātha), 144, 156–57, 180, 198, 220, 223, 242–43, 277, 280, 425, 440, 602–9 *passim*, n386, n1380, n1381, n1382

P

Padmasambhava, 5
Paksam Wangpo, 23
Palpung Monastery, 2, 25, n61, 288n561
path of accumulation, 187, 203, 258, 276, 280–81, 316–17, 370, 392, 604, 605
path of engagement, 280–81, 309, 317–18, 370–71, 604, 605, n161. *See also* signs of heat
path of meditation, 123, 128, 164, 280–81, 318–19, 321, 331n605, 604, 605, 606
path of no [more] training, 281, 321, 604
path of seeing, 123, 128, 164, 203, 280–81, 318–19, 371, 381, 604, 605, 606, n227
Pema Karpo, 4, 23
perfection of wisdom, 77, 127, 158, 207, 234, 252, 259, 270, 291, 435, n416
Perfection of Wisdom Sutra. See *Eight-Thousand-Verse Perfection of Wisdom Sutra*
Perfection Vehicle, 46–47, 123n175, 187, 258
  compared to Mantrayāna, 257, 283, 376, 418, 418–21
  paths and levels, 279, 280, 317–18, 318, 375, 601, 604
Perfectly Illuminating Lamp (Bhavyakīrti), 427, 428, 429, 432
performance tantra. *See* four tantras: performance
Phakdru Kagyü, 20–21
Phakmo Drupa (Dorjé Gyaltsen), 20, 21, 23, 251, n649. See also *Innate Union*
phowa. *See* six Dharmas of Nāropa; transference of consciousness
piṭakas. *See* scriptural baskets
postmeditation. *See* meditation and postmeditation
Praise to the Dharmadhātu (Nāgārjuna), 201, 207, 218, 222–23, 237, 398, n336, n349, n384, n385, n428
Praise to the Inconceivable (Nāgārjuna), 194, n305
prajñā's wisdom empowerment, 485–87
pratimokṣa vows, 119, 379
pratyekabuddhas, 54, 121, 176, 244, 392

errors and obstacles, 49, 59, 166, 271, 300, 387
levels, 320, 382
Pratyekabuddha Vehicle, 417, 418
Prayer for Excellent Conduct, 277, n528
Precious Garland (Nāgārjuna), 181–82, 286n554, n324
preliminary practices, 20, 73, 135, 333–34, 337
guru yoga, 74–75, 135, 155, 204, 206, 294, 307, 334
mandala offering, 20, 73–74, 79, 317
precious human birth, 20, 65–66, 70, 94
refuge, 73, 94, 118, 135, 167, 317, 333, 375
Vajrasattva mantra, 70–72, 317, 333–34
See also mantra repetition
Primordial Buddha Kālacakra Tantra, 186, 187, 236–37, 437, 497, n280, n426, n831, n1026. See also *Kālacakra Tantra*
Profound Inner Meaning (Rangjung Dorjé), 189, 192, 211, 281, n289, n300. *See also* Karmapa III Rangjung Dorjé
Profound Meaning: A Commentary on the Vajra Garland Tantra (Alaṃkakalaśa), 430, n747
purapraveśa, 5, 9, 11, 569, 575–76, n9. *See also* transference of consciousness

R
Radiance of the True Nature (Sahaśri), 433, n813
Rāmapālā, 12
rasanā, 8, 339–40, 557, n618, n1204. *See also* channels, winds, and drops
rebirth, 48, 275, 370, 529, 530, 531, 572
bardo, 8–9, 362, 365–66, 529
classes of individuals, 573, 614
desire, form, and formless realms, 162, 302, n84, n226
good and bad, 8–9, 38, 57, 68, 231, 302, 304, 495
See also bardo; tulku tradition
Rechungpa, 6, 12, 17, 18, 23, 118, n172
Recitation of [Mañjuśrī's] Names, 253, n466
Record of Key Points, 308–9, n586
red element, 519, 531, 560. *See also* drops
refuge. *See* preliminary practices: refuge
relative truth, 47, 159, 195–96, 214, 312, 551, 583. *See also* two truths
Rigi Ārali Tantra, 408, 436–37
Rinchen Phüntsok, 6
Rites for the Guhyasamāja Mandala (Dīpaṃkarabhadra), 466, 533, 534, 541, n1125
Root Tantra of Cakrasaṃvara, 413, 427, 447, n744, n794, n866
Root Verses on the Middle Way (Nāgārjuna), 48, 196, 223, 224, 228, 265, n324

S
Sādhana for the Accomplishment of Wisdom (Indrabhūti), 34, 53, 205, n66, n100
sādhanas, 373, 507, 508, 509, 510, 513, 533, 535, 543. *See also* completion stage; father tantras; generation stage; mother tantras
Śākyamuni, 67, 86, 123, 384, 389
life, 403, 404–5, 407, 408, 413–14
lineage, 63, 81
See also Buddha
Sakya Paṇḍita, 21
samādhi, 51, 53, 75, 109, 155, 164, 249, 463, n276, n1235
bliss, clarity, nonthought, 90, 120, 203, 240, 241, 260
in Buddha's life, 407, 411, 412–13, n675, n713
deity yoga, 450, 451, 452, 457, 459, 472, 548
dhyānas, 243, 302, 303
illusion-like, 551, 565
levels and paths, 307–8, 316, 317, 318, 319, 381, 386, 603n1366
in Mantrayāna, 205, 383, 419, 432, 484, 490, 562, 582, n685

obstacles and errors, 156, 166, 242, 305
one taste, 258
sleep, 550, 570
three faultless samādhis, 384, n668
of union, 551, 584
yogas, 310, 553
See also dhyānas; śamatha: five powers; four formless samādhis; three trainings
samādhi being (Skt. *samādhisattva*), 368, 523, 531, 579, n1100
Samantabhadra Sādhana (Buddhajñānapāda), 505, 548
śamatha, 24, 95, 153, 171, 240–41, 285, 297–98, 452
essential points for the body, 232–33, 457. *See also* seven Dharmas of Vairocana
essential points for the mind, 233–39
four formless samādhis, 242, 244
four tantras, 431–32, 453
four yogas, 279, 309
instructions for practice, 141, 143, 144, 155–58, 168, 459
nine methods of stabilizing mind, 242, 244
obstacles and errors, 151, 162, 166, 241–42, 299–304
path of, 262, 264, 290, 296–97, 386
six clairvoyances, 243–44, 274, 275, 276
union with vipaśyanā, 160, 203, 239, 242, 250, 258, 260–62, 299–301, 309–10
See also awareness; dhyānas; four yogas; samādhi
samaya, 273, 336–37, 473, 541, 542, n1173
Samāyoga Tantra, 495, 509, 590, n1016
Saṃvarodaya Tantra, 183, 245–46, 466–96 *passim*, 515–83 *passim*, n267, n451, n744, n965, n1019, n1201, n1204, n1238, n1272, n1282, n1285
Śāntideva, 63, n116, n128. See also *Entering the Conduct of the Bodhisattvas*
Śāntipa, 308, 426, 499
Saraha, 9–11, 12, 40n76, 285, 287, 422n774, n95, n1311. See also *Doha Treasury of Mahāmudrā Instructions*; *Song of an Inexhaustible Treasure of Instruction*; *Treasury of Dohas*
scriptural baskets (Skt. *piṭakas*), 50, 83, 189, 373, 374, 391, 393, 409, 425–26. *See also* Abhidharma; Vinaya
Secret Charnel Ground Tantra, 218, n369
secret empowerment, 336, 365, 431, 483–85
Secret Essence Tantra, 290
Secret Lamp of Wisdom Tantra, 79
Sequence on the Four Mudrās (Vīravajra), 237, n429
sevā, 256, 393, 432, 448–66, 494, 500–01, 508, 510, 520, 544, 545, n926
seven aspects of union, 325–27, 371, n643
seven Dharmas of Vairocana, 136, 233, 348. *See also* essential points for the body
seven factors of enlightenment, 318
Seven Yogas (Vitapāda), 482, 483, 484–85, 485, 487, 490, 490–91, n971, n1002, n1004
severance practices, 5, 301
Shang Gom, 81, n153. *See also* Lama Shang
Shapdrung Ngawang Namgyal, 23
Shamarpa I Drakpa Sengé, 24
Shamarpa II Khachö Wangpo, 24
Shamarpa VI Chökyi Wangchuk, 5, 25, 372, n646, n647
Sherap Jungné, 4, 21–22
Shining Jewel Tantra, 537, n1140
Shönu Lha, 20
signs of heat, 91, 123, 124, 128, 131, 151, 263, 323, n161. *See also* path of engagement
six consciousnesses, 110, 157, 158–60,

163–65, 211, 213, 299–300, 301, 313
six Dharmas of Nāropa, 2, 5, 7–9, 25, 333, 569. *See also* bardo; caṇḍālī; dream yoga; illusory body; luminosity; transference of consciousness
six perfections, 47, 127, 198, 375, n1379
  instructions for practice, 32, 56
  motivation, 46, 177
  path, 94, 394, 419, 446
  See also dreams and illusions
six yogas of Nāropa. *See* six Dharmas of Nāropa
Song of an Inexhaustible Treasure of Instruction (Saraha), 234, n414
sorcery, 15, 16, 22, 23, 385, 540
Special Illumination: A Commentary on the Explanation of Lūyipa's Sādhana Visualization (Tathāgatavajra), 579
śrāvaka, 59, 121. 176, 244, 381, 392, 394, n709
  conduct, 378, 387
  levels, 320, 382
  obstacles and errors, 49, 164, 166, 271, 299, 376, 418, 494
  teachings by, 190, 424
Śrāvaka Vehicle, 417, 418, n583
Stages of the Mahayana Path (Subhagavajra), 499–500, 544, n1160
Stainless Light (Puṇḍarīka), 214, 408, 421, 435, 438, 497, 498, 505, n834, n1030. See also *Kālacakra Root Tantra*
Sublime Continuum. See *Mahayana Treatise on the Sublime Continuum*
Sukhasiddhī, 5
Summarized Five Stages (Nāropa), 568, 569
Summarized Kālacakra Tantra (Mañjuśrīkīrti Kalki), 416, 497, n1026. See also *Kālacakra Tantra*
Summary of the Entry into the Meaning of the Highest Yoga Tantras (Śraddhākaravarman), 427, 434
Summary of the View (Nāropa), 160, 167, n221, n234
Surapāla, 13
Sutra of Samādhi for Four Youths, 224, n389
Sutra of the Complete Gathering of Qualities, 47, n88
Sutra of the Excellent Night, 66, 238, n121
Sutra of the King of the Teaching of Instructions, 419, n763
Sutra of the Samādhi that Accumulates All Merit, 259, n485
Sutra of the Ten Dharmas, 183, 441, n269
Sutra of the Ten Levels, 218, n370
Sutra Requested by Akṣayamati, 178, 547, n255, n1174
Sutra Requested by Devaputra, 423, n778
Sutra Requested by Gaganagañja, 225, n392
Sutra Requested by Kāśyapa, 145, 221, 223, n387
Sutra Requested by Sāgaramati, 184, 235, 238, n270, n433
Sutra Requested by the Naga King Anavatapta, 177, 228, 270–71, n247, n399, n512
Sutra Teaching Bodhisattva Conduct, 266, 266–67, 286, n500, n501
svabhavakāya, 178, 180, 207–8, 278, 490, 607, 608, 609, 610

T
Tai Situ I Chökyi Gyaltsen, 25
Tai Situ VIII Tenpai Nyinjé (Chökyi Jungné), 2, 25
Tai Situ IX, 2
Taklung Thangpa, 21, n155
Taklung Kagyü, 21
Tantra of All Mandalas, 461, 467, 471
Tantra of Great Bliss, 563–64, n1230
Tantra of the Great River of Pacification, 294, n574
Tantra of the Ocean of Vows, 78, n147
Tantra of the Unimpeded View. See *Great Tantra that Teaches Unimpeded Dzogchen*
Tantra of True Union, 240, 429, 472,

477, 539–40, 557, 559–60, 562, 583–613 *passim*, n437, n745, n800, n1218, n1220, n1223, n1224, n1286, n1339, n1387
Tantra of Vairocana's Enlightenment, 221, n380
Tantra Requested by Subāhu, 425, 426, 454, 544, n784
Tantra Requested by the Four Goddesses, 600
Tantra Revealing the Hidden Meaning, 557
tantras, 83, 191, 214, 223, 250, 255, 414–17, 424, 426–28, 438–39, 504, 515, 554, 576, 582, 619, n650, n747, n1411. *See also* father tantras; four tantras; mother tantras; nondual tantras; three tantras
Teaching Amanasikāra (Maitripa), 253–54, n466, n467, n468, n470
Teaching on the Mudrās of the Five Tathāgatas (Advayavajra), 239, n435
ten opportunities, 182–83, 440, 441
Ten Verses on the True Nature (Advayavajra), 206, n346
Ten Wheels of Kṣitigarbha Sutra, 305, n583
terma, 5–6, 16, 22, 331, 385, n6
Thirty Verses (Vasubandhu), 212, n353, n354
Thousand-Verse Commentary to the Compendium of Truths (Ānandagarbha), 537, n1138
three freedoms from faults, 39
Three Jewels, 40, 46, 94, 118, 127, 184, 363, 368, 399–400, 492, n653
three tantras, 426–27, 438–39
  causal, 438–45
  method, 434, 445–46, 438, n820. *See also* path
  result, 438–39, 598
three trainings, 188, 378, 394, 399, 418, 425, n699. *See also* conduct; nondual wisdom; samādhi
three turnings of the wheel of Dharma, 374
three vehicles, 50, 188, 376, 394, 417, n290, n758
three vows, 51, 397, 398, n98
three wisdoms, 188, 193, 250
three yogas, 54–55, 55, 490, n1002
  mantra yoga, 54–55
  phenomena yoga, 41–42, 54–55
  substance yoga, 54–55. *See also* dreams and illusions
Tilaka of Liberation (Buddhajñānapāda), 192–93, 552, n1189
Tilaka of Wisdom, 431, 449, 454–55, n888
Tilopa, 3, 4–5, 9, 13, 34, 63, 133, 153, 158, 287, 288, n31, n606
Tipupa, 12
Togan Temur, 24
transference of consciousness, 5, 8–9, 122, 366–69, 394–95, n9. *See also* six Dharmas of Nāropa
Treasury of Dohas (Saraha), 59, 77, 136–59 *passim*, 203–4, 219, 290, 295, 582, n220, n537, n1284, n1311
Treasury of Instructions (Jamgön Kongtrül), 4, 20, n62
Treasury of Precious Termas (Jamgön Kongtrül), 16
Treasury of Secrets (Saroruhavajra), 422, 495n1017, 496, n744, n1020
Treasury of the Abhidharma (Vasubandhu), 184, 193, 241, 243, 404, 423, n272
Treatise on the Five Aggregates (Vasubandhu), 137, 184, 185, n185, n273, n274, n275, n276
Truly Valid Instructions: Teachings of the Dākinīs (Nāropa), 569, 571–75 *passim*, n1247, n1252, n1256, n1259
Tsalpa Kagyü, 4, 19–20
Tsangnyön Heruka, 14, 15, 16, 17–18, n32, n36, n40, n1227
Tsangpa Gyaré, 6, 23
Tselé Natsok Rangdröl, 25, 319n589, 322n591, n616
Tsurphu Monastery, 2, 24, n639, n648

tulku tradition, 21, 24. *See also* rebirth
tumo (*gtum mo*). *See* caṇḍālī; six Dharmas of Nāropa
two extremes, 166, 199, 225
  embellishment and denigration, 197, 199
  eternalism and nihilism, 170, 194–95, 327
  existence and nonexistence, 220–25
  existence and peace, 198–99
  identity and nonidentity, 225–27
two stages, 203–5, 491, 498–502, 572, 573, 587, 598, 605, 614. *See also* completion stage; generation stage
two truths, 48, 50, 170, 194–97, 265, 282, 387, 491, n326, n545
  Dharma of realization, 425
  union of, 489, 491, 551, 554, 583–84
  See also relative truth; ultimate truth

U
Ultimate Service (Puṇḍarīka), 463
ultimate truth, 47, 159, 194–97, 199, 325, 363, 447, 488, 489, 551, 583, 609, n325, n326, n330, n1383. *See also* dharmatā; two truths
Uttaratantra. See *Mahayana Treatise on the Sublime Continuum*
Utterly Nonabiding doctrine, 105, n166

V
Vāgīśvarakīrti, 488, 609–10, n1386
Vairocana, 356, 360–61, 408, 411, 612
  buddha families, 442, 443, 509, 515, 526, n133
  seven Dharmas, 136, 233, 348, 357, n179
Vairocanarakṣita, 12–13
vajra body, 62, 67, 192, 336, 383, 384, 483, 490, 555, 585, 613, n300, n1001
Vajraḍāka Tantra, 464–71 *passim*, 503–16 *passim*, 540, 566, n939, n1047, n1240, n1263
Vajra Garland Explanatory Tantra, 232–33, 414, 437n829, 461–507 *passim*, 539, 556–64 *passim*, n408, n747, n938, n961, n983, n984, n1209, n1214, n1216
Vajra Garland of Mandala Rituals (Abhayākaragupta), 428, 466–98 *passim*, 539, n798
Vajra Lamp: A Brief Explanation of the Hevajra Tantra (Jālandhara), 546
vajra hell (Skt. Avīci), 269, 305, 385, 596, n1341
Vajrakīlaya, 5
Vajra Mandala Adornment Tantra, 407, 428, 463, 604, n915, n1372
Vajrapāṇi, 11, 12, 331n609, 410, 412, 413, 414, 415, n20, n742, n902
Vajrapāṇi's Empowerment Tantra, 432
Vajra Pinnacle Tantra, 213, 233, 270, 407–22 *passim*, 448–59 *passim*, 492, 545, n409, n508, n876, n892, n1006, n1007
Vajrasattva mantra, 20, 71–72, 333
Vajra Tent Tantra, 217, 414, 428–42 *passim*, 462–64 *passim*, 478, 500–61 *passim*, 599–614 *passim*, n824, n851, n917, n963, n1037, n1061, n1077, n1104, n1106, n1135, n1164, n1389, n1395
Vajravārāhī, 2, 6, 416, *See also* Vajrayoginī
Vajra Verses of the Aural Tantra, (Nāropa), 285, n549
Vajrayoginī, 413. *See also* Vajravārāhī
vase breath, 140, 341, 358, 359
vase empowerment, 336, 431, 479–83
Vasubandhu, 287, n339. See also *Thirty Verses*; *Treasury of the Abhidharma*; *Treatise on the Five Aggregates*
Vijñaptivāda, 230
Vinaya, 155, 186, 189, 251, 374, 385, 391, 392, 425, n289, n677, n680, n707
  essential points of Vinaya pratimokṣa, 378–80
  compilation of, 409, 410
  vehicles, 378, 394
  See also scriptural baskets
vipaśyanā, 24, 95, 244–54
  analytic meditation, 146, 258, 298–99

four tantras, 431–32, 453
four yogas, 137, 144, 279
generation and completion stage, 285
great bliss, 245, 262–63
instructions for practice, 153, 158, 160, 168, 203, 239–40, 290, 296, 452, 459
looking at the mind, 242, 248
nonthought, 262–63, 299
obstacles and errors, 151, 162, 166, 301–4
self-knowing knowledge, 160, 245, 259, 262, 299
union with śamatha, 242, 258–61, 262–67, 299–301, 310
See also awareness; bliss, clarity, and nonthought; looking at the mind

Viśvarūpiṇī, 557, n1203

vrata conduct. See four conducts: *vrata* conduct

W

water-torma offering, 36, 38

white element, 345, 346, 519, 531, 560. *See also* drops

White Lotus of the Holy Dharma Sutra, 405, 417, 418, n758

white panacea, 120, 126, 252, n174

winds (Skt. *vāyu*), 38, 136, 171, 364, 384, 394, 531, 551, n300
completion stage of mother tantras, 553–60, 562, 568, 570, 577–80, 582, 588, 605–6, 612
father tantras, 436, 437
instructions for practice, 51, 120, 140, 339–40, 345, 358
life-force (Skt. prāna), n879, n883
obstacles, 323
path of engagement, 281, 371
purification, 337, 394, n690
root and branch, 292, 336, 557–58
secret empowerment, 95, 336
six Dharmas of Nāropa, 350, 489, 529
vajra body, 192, 383
See also channels, winds, and drops

wisdom being (Skt. *jñānasattva*), 71, 356–57, 361, 368, 456, 523–25, 531, 579, n1100

wisdom body, 281, 325, 407, 554, 606, 612

Wisdom upon Passing Away Sutra, 36, 75–76, n72

Y

yantra (Tib *'khrul khor*), 9, 342–43, 600

yidam, 6–7, 46, 61, 206, 333, n632, n694, n872, n992
instructions on six Dharmas of Nāropa, 350, 356–57, 358, 359–60, 365, 368–69, 395
instructions on visualization, 71, 535

yoga. *See* four yogas; nine yogas; three yogas

yoga tantra. *See* four tantras: yoga

yogacitta, 476, n957

Yoginī's Activity, 547, 548, n1172, n1177

yoginī tantras. *See* mother tantras

Yongé Mingyur Dorjé, 5

Yong Le, 24–25

About the Contributors

PETER ALAN ROBERTS was born in Wales and lives in Hollywood, California. He obtained a B.A. in Sanskrit and Pali and a Ph.D. in Tibetan Studies (on the biographies of Rechungpa) from Oxford University (Harris-Manchester College). For more than thirty years he has been working as an interpreter for lamas and as a translator of Tibetan texts. He specializes in the literature of the Kagyü and Nyingma traditions with a focus on tantric practices.

GESHE THUPTEN JINPA was trained as a monk at the Shartse College of Ganden Monastic University, South India, where he received the Geshe Lharam degree. Jinpa also holds a B.A. honors in philosophy and a Ph.D. in religious studies, both from Cambridge University, England. Jinpa has been the principal English-language translator for His Holiness the Dalai Lama for over two decades and has translated and edited numerous books by the Dalai Lama. His own works include *Songs of Spiritual Experience* (coauthored) and *Self, Reality and Reason in Tibetan Philosophy*. He is currently the president of the Institute of Tibetan Classics and lives in Montreal with his wife and two daughters.

The Institute of Tibetan Classics

The Institute of Tibetan Classics is a nonprofit, charitable educational organization based in Montreal, Canada. It is dedicated to two primary objectives: (1) to preserve and promote the study and deep appreciation of Tibet's rich intellectual, spiritual, and artistic heritage, especially among the Tibetan-speaking communities worldwide; and (2) to make the classical Tibetan knowledge and literature a truly global heritage, its spiritual and intellectual resources open to all.

To learn more about the Institute of Tibetan Classics and its various projects, please visit www.tibetanclassics.org or write to this address:

Institute of Tibetan Classics
304 Aberdare Road
Montreal (Quebec) H3P3K3
Canada

The Library of Tibetan Classics

"This new series edited by Thupten Jinpa and published by Wisdom Publications is a landmark in the study of Tibetan culture in general and Tibetan Buddhism in particular. Each volume contains a lucid introduction and outstanding translations that, while aimed at the general public, will benefit those in the field of Tibetan Studies immensely as well."

—Leonard van der Kuijp, Harvard University

"This is an invaluable set of translations by highly competent scholar-practitioners. The series spans the breadth of the history of Tibetan religion, providing entry to a vast culture of spiritual cultivation."

—Jeffrey Hopkins, University of Virginia

"Erudite in all respects, this series is at the same time accessible and engagingly translated. As such, it belongs in all college and university libraries as well as in good public libraries. *The Library of Tibetan Classics* is on its way to becoming a truly extraordinary spiritual and literary accomplishment."

—Janice D. Willis, Wesleyan University

Following is a list of the thirty-two proposed volumes in *The Library of Tibetan Classics*. Some volumes are translations of single texts, while others are compilations of multiple texts, and each volume will be roughly the same length. Except for those volumes already published, the renderings of titles below are tentative and liable to change. The Institute of Tibetan Classics has contracted numerous established translators in its efforts, and work is progressing on all the volumes concurrently.

1. *Mind Training: The Great Collection*, compiled by Shönu Gyalchok and Könchok Gyaltsen (fifteenth century). NOW AVAILABLE
2. *The Book of Kadam: The Core Texts*, attributed to Atiśa and Dromtönpa (eleventh century). NOW AVAILABLE
3. *The Great Chariot: A Treatise on the Great Perfection*, Longchen Rapjampa (1308–63)
4. *Taking the Result As the Path: Core Teachings of the Sakya Lamdré Tradition*, Jamyang Khyentsé Wangchuk (1524–68) et al. NOW AVAILABLE
5. *Mahāmudrā and Related Instructions: Core Teachings of the Kagyü Schools*. NOW AVAILABLE
6. *Stages of the Path and the Ear-Whispered Instructions: Core Teachings of the Geluk School*
7. *Ocean of Definitive Meaning: A Teaching for the Mountain Hermit*, Dölpopa Sherap Gyaltsen (1292–1361)
8. *Miscellaneous Tibetan Buddhist Lineages: The Core Teachings*, Jamgön Kongtrül (1813–90)
9. *Sutra, Tantra, and the Mind Cycle: Core Teachings of the Bön School*
10. *Stages of the Buddha's Teachings: Three Key Texts*. FORTHCOMING SOON
11. *The Bodhisattva's Altruistic Ideal: Selected Key Texts*
12. *The Ethics of the Three Codes*
13. *Sādhanas: Vajrayana Buddhist Meditation Manuals*
14. *Ornament of Stainless Light: An Exposition of the Kālacakra Tantra*, Khedrup Norsang Gyatso (1423–1513). NOW AVAILABLE
15. *Lamp Thoroughly Illuminating the Five Stages of Completion*, Tsongkhapa (1357–1419)
16. *Studies in the Perfection of Wisdom*
17. *Treatises on Buddha Nature*
18. *Differentiations of the Profound View: Interpretations of Emptiness in Tibet*
19. *Elucidation of the Intent: A Thorough Exposition of "Entering the Middle Way,"* Tsongkhapa (1357–1419)
20. *Tibetan Buddhist Epistemology I: The Sakya School*
21. *Tibetan Buddhist Epistemology II: The Geluk School*
22. *Tibetan Buddhist Psychology and Phenomenology: Selected Texts*
23. *Ornament of Higher Knowledge: A Exposition of Vasubandhu's "Treasury of Higher Knowledge,"* Chim Jampalyang (thirteenth century)
24. *A Beautiful Adornment of Mount Meru: Presentation of Classical Indian Philosophies*, Changkya Rölpai Dorjé (1717–86)

25. *The Crystal Mirror of Philosophical Systems: A Tibetan Study of Asian Religious Thought*, Thuken Losang Chökyi Nyima (1737–1802). NOW AVAILABLE
26. *Gateway for Being Learned and Realized: Selected Texts*
27. *The Well-Uttered Insights: Advice on Everyday Wisdom, Civility, and Basic Human Values*
28. *A Mirror of Beryl: A Historical Introduction to Tibetan Medicine*, Desi Sangyé Gyatso (1653–1705). NOW AVAILABLE
29. *Selected Texts on Tibetan Astronomy and Astrology*
30. *Art and Literature: An Anthology*
31. *Tales from the Tibetan Operas*
32. *Selected Historical Works*

To receive a brochure describing all the volumes or to stay informed about *The Library of Tibetan Classics*, please write:

Wisdom Publications
Attn: Library of Tibetan Classics
199 Elm Street
Somerville, MA 02144 USA

or send a request by email to:
info@wisdompubs.org.

The complete catalog containing descriptions of each volume can also be found online at www.wisdompubs.org, where you can sign up for an email newsletter dedicated to *Library of Tibetan Classics* news.

Become a Benefactor of the Library of Tibetan Classics

The Library of Tibetan Classics' scope, importance, and commitment to quality make it a tremendous financial undertaking. Please consider becoming a benefactor. Donations of any amount are welcome and invaluable to the development of the series. Contributors of US$2,000 or more will receive a copy of each volume as it becomes available and will have their names listed in all subsequent volumes. Simply send a check made out to Wisdom Publications or contact us with your credit card information.

Library of Tibetan Classics Fund
Wisdom Publications
199 Elm Street
Somerville MA 02144
USA
617-776-7416 ext. 21

Wisdom is a 501(c)3 nonprofit corporation, and all contributions are tax-deductible to the extent allowed by law.

To keep up to date on the status of the *Library of Tibetan Classics*, visit wisdompubs.org. Sign up for the email news list for the *Library of Tibetan Classics* while you are there.

About Wisdom Publications

Wisdom Publications is dedicated to making available authentic Buddhist works for the benefit of all. We publish translations of Buddhist sacred texts, commentaries and teachings of past and contemporary Buddhist masters, and original works by the world's leading Buddhist scholars. We publish our titles with the appreciation of Buddhism as a living philosophy and with the special commitment to preserve and transmit important works from all the major Buddhist traditions.

Wisdom Publications
199 Elm Street
Somerville, Massachusetts 02144 USA
Telephone: 617-776-7416
Fax: 617-776-7841
Email: info@wisdompubs.org
www.wisdompubs.org

Wisdom is a nonprofit, charitable 501(c)(3) organization affiliated with the Foundation for the Preservation of the Mahayana Tradition (FPMT).

Mind Training

The Great Collection

Translated and edited by Thupten Jinpa

720 pages, cloth, ISBN 0-86171-440-7, $49.95

"The practice of mind training (*lojong*) is based on the essential Mahayana teachings of impermanence, compassion, and the exchange of self for other that the eleventh-century master Atiśa brought to Tibet from India. The *lojong* teachings are a source of inspiration and guidance shared by masters of all Tibetan traditions. This makes Thupten Jinpa's translation of *Mind Training: The Great Collection* a natural choice for publication as part of the *Library of Tibetan Classics* series. For the first time, this early collection of the instructions of the great Kadampa masters has been translated in its entirety. The clarity and raw power of these thousand-year-old teachings are astonishingly fresh, whether studied as a complete anthology or opened at random for inspiring verses on the heart of Buddhist practice."

—*Buddhadharma: The Practitioner's Quarterly*

"In an era when Buddhist meditation is largely equated with simply calming the mind and developing mindfulness, this compendium of methods for training the mind gives a glimpse of the tremendous richness and depth of the Buddhist tradition. With the current rise of positive psychology, in which researchers are seeking a fresh vision of genuine happiness and well-being, this volume can break new ground in bridging the ancient wisdom of Buddhism with cutting-edge psychology."

—B. Alan Wallace, author of *The Attention Revolution*

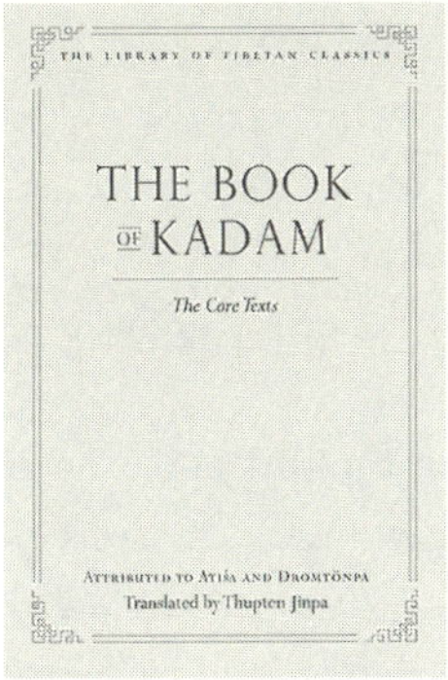

The Book of Kadam

The Core Texts

Atiśa Dīpaṃkara and Dromtönpa

Translated by Thupten Jinpa

752 pages, cloth, ISBN 0-86171-441-5, $59.95

The Kadam school, which emerged from the teachings of the Indian master Atiśa (982–1054) and his principal student, Dromtönpa (1005–64), is revered for its unique practical application of the bodhisattva's altruistic ideal in day-to-day life. Although the Kadam school no longer exists as an autonomous lineage within Tibetan Buddhism, its teachings have become fully incorporated into the teachings of all four major schools of Tibetan Buddhism, especially the Geluk school. One of the most well-known sets of spiritual teachings stemming from Atiśa and Dromtönpa is a special collection of oral transmissions enshrined in the *Book of Kadam*, sometimes referred to as the "Kadam emanation scripture." The central text in this volume is the twenty-three-chapter dialogue between Atiśa and Dromtönpa that is woven around Atiśa's *Bodhisattva's Jewel Garland*. Also included are selected stories of Dromtönpa's past lives, an explanation of the Kadampa *heart-drop* practice by Khenchen Nyima Gyaltsen, a short text by the Second Dalai Lama, and the well-known *Sayings of the Kadam Masters* compiled in the twelfth century. The *Book of Kadam* is undisputedly one of the great works of Tibetan Buddhism.

Taking the Result as the Path

Core Teachings of the Sakya Lamdré Tradition
Translated and edited by Cyrus Stearns
Foreword by His Holiness Sakya Trizin
784 pages, cloth, ISBN 0-86171-443-1, $59.95

"The Sakya school of Tibetan Buddhism has been the most conservative in maintaining the secrecy of its lineage's special practices. *Taking the Result as the Path* represents a major breakthrough by bringing these teachings to light with the full blessings of the Sakya masters. In nearly seven hundred pages of translation, the indefatigable Cyrus Stearns presents an anthology of essential texts on Lamdré. This collection will be an invaluable resource for practitioners of the Lamdré system."

—*Buddhadharma: The Practitioner's Quarterly*

"No one is better suited than Cyrus Stearns to offer the first major translation of Lamdré teachings to the world. He has studied intimately with the most revered leaders of the Sakya tradition for decades. Beyond this, Stearns possesses a quality that sets him apart from most translators today—he is a poet. Few have transmuted the verse or the prose, the earthy imagery or the celestial style of Tibetan Buddhist teachings, with comparable eloquence and inspiration; few are endowed with the capacity to inspire students of Tibetan Buddhism through force of the sheer beauty of the translated word. The Sakya tradition will henceforth be known to English audiences in all its splendor thanks to this new translation."

—Kurtis R. Schaeffer, *University of Virginia*

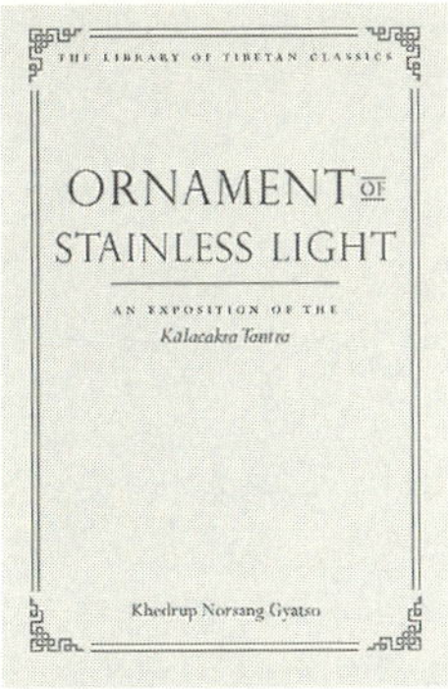

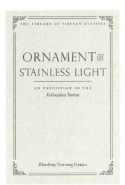

Ornament of Stainless Light

An Exposition of the Kālacakra Tantra
Khedrup Norsang Gyatso
Translated by Gavin Kilty
736 pages, cloth, ISBN 0-86171-452-0, $49.95

"A radiant gem drawn from the vast ocean of Tibetan literature on the Kālacakra tantra. It provides a clear, comprehensive summary of the basic structure and essential features of this important system of mysticism. Also, Khedrup Norsang Gyatso's interpretations of controversial issues in the Kālacakra contribute to our understanding of the evolution of Tibetan theories of mysticism. Gavin Kilty's faithful translation makes this work easily accessible—it is a fitting inaugural volume for the *Library of Tibetan Classics*."

—John Newman, MacArthur Professor of Asian Religions, New College of Florida

"When the Dalai Lama performed the Kālacakra initiation for a crowd of 20,000 at Madison Square Garden in 1991, a page was turned in the history of tantra. It was perhaps because of the popularity of this event and the success of others like it that when he was asked to select a text for the inaugural volume of the important new *Library of Tibetan Classics* series, the Dalai Lama chose a commentary on the Kālacakra tantra. The inaugural volume, *Ornament of Stainless Light*, is an important resource for anyone who has attended or will attend one of the many public performances of the Kālacakra initiation around the world."

—Buddhadharma: The Practitioner's Quarterly

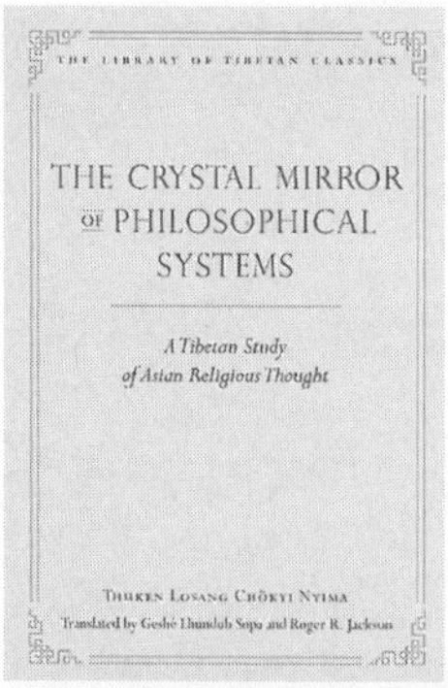

The Crystal Mirror of Philosophical Systems

A Tibetan Study of Asian Religious Thought
Thuken Losang Chökyi Nyima
Translated by Geshé Lhundub Sopa et al.
Edited by Roger Jackson
696 pages, cloth, ISBN 0-86171-464-4, $59.95

The Crystal Mirror of Philosophical Systems by Thuken Losang Chökyi Nyima (1737–1802) is arguably the widest-ranging account of religious philosophies ever written in pre-modern Tibet. Like most Tibetan texts on philosophical systems, this work covers the major schools of India, both Buddhist and non-Buddhist, but then goes on to discuss in detail the entire range of Tibetan traditions as well, with separate chapters on the Nyingma, Kadam, Kagyü, Shijé, Sakya, Jonang, Geluk, and Bön schools. Not resting there, Thuken goes on to describe the major traditions of China—Confucian, Daoist, and the multiple varieties of Buddhist—as well as those of Mongolia, Khotan, and even Shambhala. *The Crystal Mirror of Philosophical Systems* is unusual, too, in its concern not just to describe and analyze doctrines, but to trace the historical development of the various traditions.

"This impressive translation of a fascinating and vitally important book shows how sophisticated, eighteenth-century Tibetan Buddhists could come to terms with diverse world religious traditions."

—Guy Newland, Central Michigan University,
author of *Introduction to Emptiness*

"Thuken's *Crystal Mirror of Philosophical Systems* is a unique work, seeking to document the full range of philosophical traditions known in Tibet, including Indian, Chinese, and, above all, indigenous Tibetan traditions. This translation is precise and a pleasure to read."

—Matthew T. Kapstein, École Pratique des Hautes Études and the University of Chicago, editor of *Buddhism Between Tibet and China*

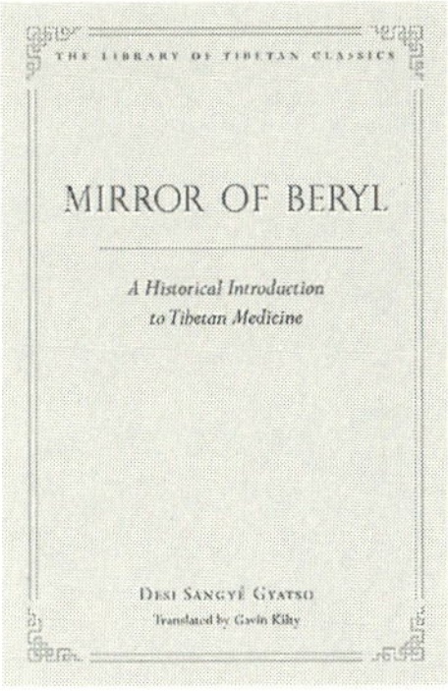

Mirror of Beryl

A Historical Introduction to Tibetan Medicine
Desi Sangyé Gyatso
Translated by Gavin Kilty
696 pages, cloth, ISBN 0-86171-467-9, $59.95

In the present historical introduction, Desi Sangyé Gyatso (1653–1705) traces the sources of influence on Tibetan medicine to classical India, China, Central Asia, and beyond, providing life stories, extensive references to earlier Tibetan works on medicine, and fascinating details about the Tibetan approach to healing. He also provides a commentary on the pratimokṣa, bodhisattva, and tantric Buddhist vows.

"Desi Sangyé Gyatso, the author of the *Mirror of Beryl*, was the most powerful man in Central Tibet and had access to the very best library resources. His 1703 work is a tour de force, built as much on what earlier Tibetan scholars had written on the subject as on his immediate knowledge of the field. Gavin Kilty's translation is as elegant and accurate as his earlier work and is a testimony to his fine understanding of the original Tibetan text. This is a truly wonderful book, one that I and others will no doubt consult with pleasure time and again for years to come."

—Leonard W. J. van der Kuijp,
Professor of Tibetan and Himalayan Studies, Harvard University